Enduring Controversies in Military History

ENDURING CONTROVERSIES IN MILITARY HISTORY

Critical Analyses and Context

Volume 2

Spencer C. Tucker, Editor

An Imprint of ABC-CLIO, LLC
Santa Barbara, California • Denver, Colorado

Library of Congress Cataloging-in-Publication Data

Names: Tucker, Spencer, 1937– author.
Title: Enduring controversies in military history : critical analyses and context / Spencer C. Tucker, editor.
Description: Santa Barbara, California : ABC-CLIO [2017] | Includes bibliographical references and index.
Identifiers: LCCN 2016047936 (print) | LCCN 2016052968 (ebook) | ISBN 9781440841194 (set : alk. paper) | ISBN 9781440848131 (volume 1 : alk. paper) | ISBN 9781440848148 (volume 2 : alk. paper) | ISBN 9781440841200 (ebook)
Subjects: LCSH: Military history. | Military policy.
Classification: LCC D25 .T828 2017 (print) | LCC D25 (ebook) | DDC 355.009—dc23
LC record available at https://lccn.loc.gov/2016047936

ISBN: 978-1-4408-4119-4 (set)
978-1-4408-4813-1 (vol. 1)
978-1-4408-4814-8 (vol. 2)
978-1-4408-4120-0 (ebook)

21 20 19 18 17 1 2 3 4 5

This book is also available as an eBook.

ABC-CLIO
An Imprint of ABC-CLIO, LLC

ABC-CLIO, LLC
130 Cremona Drive, P.O. Box 1911
Santa Barbara, California 93116-1911
www.abc-clio.com

This book is printed on acid-free paper ♾

Manufactured in the United States of America

For Jinwung Kim, professor of history and distinguished scholar
of Korean history at Kyungpook National University,
Republic of Korea

Contents

INTRODUCTION

Historians interpret events differently. All of us approach subjects from different points of view based on our own life experiences, training, knowledge, and biases, whether these are recognized or not. Obviously the passage of time provides a clearer perspective as to the importance and impact of a particular event, while new evidence in the form of memoirs and documents—often appearing decades or even generations after the event itself—allows for fresh assessment of it.

After consulting with other scholars and historians, I have assembled a collection of essays treating 64 topics in the long history of world conflict that have been the subject of different interpretations. The essays selected range in time from ancient history to the contemporary world: from the Peloponnesian War to whether women in the U.S. military should be allowed to serve in combat units.

The topics are arranged in loose chronological fashion, grouped in seven major eras: ancient Greece and Rome (500 BCE–500 CE), 5 topics; the Middle Ages (500–1500), 6 topics; the emergence of modern Europe and the Americas (1500–1825), 10 topics; the rise of imperialism and nationalism (1825–1914), 11 topics; the world at war (1914–1945), 12 topics; the Cold War (1945–1991), 12 topics; and the new millennium (1991–present), 8 topics. Each topic has a brief introduction and a background essay.

Some of the background essays are relatively short; others, such as that on the Vietnam War, are necessarily longer because the essays themselves make reference to events without necessarily explaining what they were. Following the background essay, each topic has between two and five position essays. An expansive list of books for further reading on the subject closes out each topic.

Some topics lent themselves to different approaches. Among these are the topics that address the key factors behind the fall of the Roman Empire and the primary causes of World War I. Here the authors address the one central issue that they believe was paramount.

Other topics lent themselves to pro and con approaches. Examples of this include whether it would have been better from a military standpoint for Britain and

France to have gone to war with Germany in October 1938 at the time of the Munich Conference rather than in September 1939, when war was thrust upon them with the German invasion of Poland; whether U.S. president Harry S. Truman was justified in relieving General Douglas MacArthur from his commands of U.S. forces in the Pacific and the United Nations Command during the Korean War; and whether the United States was justified in dropping atomic bombs on Japan.

The reader will find much of interest here. Thus, in the discussion of the use of the atomic bombs against Japan, one author notes that aircraft flying from U.S. Navy and Royal Navy carriers had largely severed interisland traffic and that Japan's land transportation net had also been badly disrupted. Massive firebomb raids by B-29 Superfortress bombers had largely burned out the major Japanese major cities, and the Japanese people were on a starvation diet.

But would these circumstances have been sufficient to bring surrender? Japan had assembled large numbers of suicide craft and kamikaze aircraft with which to contest any American landing attempt, and a number of its military leaders were determined that Japanese honor could be met only by a fight to the last. There is also controversy within a controversy regarding estimates of probable American casualties in an invasion of the Japanese home islands. Certainly, given Japanese resistance at places such as Iwo Jima and Okinawa, casualties would have been heavy.

In these circumstance Emperor Hirohito, himself a controversial figure for his role in the war, found his voice, for the atomic bombs gave him the excuse to take into his own hands the difficult decision to surrender. But fanatics among the generals were determined that his remarks not be heard by the Japanese people. A military putsch that included an attempt to assassinate the emperor was averted only by the narrowest of margins.

Were there not also other factors at play in the employment of the atomic bombs? It is certainly worth pointing out the savage nature of the fighting in the Pacific theater with no holds barred and war to the knife hilt. Was the atomic bomb simply an additional degree in the already existing horror? The bomb's high cost and lengthy development and its availability probably furthered the inevitability of its use. Certainly, President Truman remarked afterward that he had no qualms about the decision, but others in authority who knew of the bomb opposed its use. Were geopolitical factors at play? The American capacity for strategic bombing had been strikingly demonstrated in the Pacific theater, and now the atomic bomb was added to the equation. Thus, to what extent was employing the bomb an opening salvo of the Cold War, designed as a signature warning to the leadership of the Soviet Union? All of these factors were at play to some degree. They and other matters are all discussed in the essays on this topic. Here, as with the other topics, it will be up to the reader to decide.

In my editing of entries I have made stylistic and formatting changes. I have, however, taken special care not to interfere with the authors' points of view.

Assisting me in the topic selection were military historians Dr. Timothy C. Dowling; Dr. Jerry Morelock, Colonel, U.S. Army Rtd; and Dr. David T. Zabecki, Major General, U.S. Army Rtd. I am especially grateful to my associate of long standing with ABC-CLIO projects, Dr. Paul G. Pierpaoli Jr. He wrote a large number of the topic introductions as well as some of the essays.

Hopefully students and academics and others with a general interest in military history will find this work informative in its factual content but also useful in understanding how historians approach topics and inform others about the rich fabric that is our shared history.

Spencer C. Tucker

PART V (Continued)

THE WORLD AT WAR (1914–1945)

36. Did the 1919 Paris Peace Settlement and Specifically the Treaty of Versailles with Germany Make World War II Inevitable?

Lasting from January 18, 1919, until January 21, 1920, the Paris Peace Conference marked the official end of World War I. Although delegates from all Allied nations were in attendance, the Big Four—U.S. president Woodrow Wilson, British prime minister David Lloyd George, French prime minister Georges Clemenceau, and Italian prime minister Vittorio Orlando—dominated the yearlong conference. They drew the boundaries of postwar Europe, set war reparations payments for the Central Powers, and agreed to create an international security organization that would later become the League of Nations, the precursor of the modern-day United Nations. They also granted France control over Alsace-Lorraine, a region in modern-day northeastern France that had been previously controlled by Germany, demilitarized Germany's Rhineland, and assigned Germany and its allies total responsibility for damage caused to the Allies and associated powers between August 1914 and November 1918. Not surprisingly, historians continue to discuss the lasting impact of the Paris peace settlement and the Treaty of Versailles. To what extent the various treaties signed in Paris in 1919 influenced the emergence of World War II remains a hotly debated subject.

Dr. Carole Fink, in the first perspective essay, asserts that the Paris Peace Conference and the Treaty of Versailles were inherently controversial. She points out that Paris was not a good locale for the talks, that there were too many differences among the victorious Allies, and that the various disarmament clauses were too one-sided. Furthermore, the leaders in Paris failed to consider the enormity of new ideologies such as Bolshevism, their own weaknesses, and Germany's potential strength in the postwar era. Invariably, these problems help set the stage for World War II. In the second essay, Dr. Priscilla M. Roberts argues that the Paris proceedings had created exaggerated initial expectations, which were systematically undone by a well-organized effort to discredit the Paris peace settlement and the Treaty of Versailles. Wilsonian rhetoric and ideals quickly fell victim to French and British demands for a punitive peace and were further undone by adverse political events in the United States. Furthermore, the settlement was forced upon the Germans, who did an excellent job of dismantling it during the 1920s and 1930s. Finally, Dr. Spencer C. Tucker asserts that it was the Allied powers' inability and disinclination to enforce the Paris peace settlement, rather than the treaties themselves, that brought about the next world war. He argues that France was in too weak a position and Britain and the United States too disengaged from world affairs to ensure that Germany met the settlement's demands. Instead, they relied on Germany to monitor itself, which proved unworkable.

Background Essay

On January 18, 1919, representatives of the victorious powers in World War I assembled in Paris to draft peace settlements with the vanquished. Russia did not take part. Civil war was then raging there, and efforts to cobble together a united delegation failed. Although the delegations of five countries (Britain, France, the United States, Italy, and Japan) played important roles, the conference was dominated by the Big Three of Britain, France, and the United States. U.S. president Woodrow Wilson and British prime minister David Lloyd George stood together on most issues, meaning that French premier Georges Clemenceau was the odd man out.

On April 28, the conferees approved creation of the League of Nations. Wilson's cherished project, it emerged as a voluntary membership. Economic sanctions were its strongest enforcement weapon.

The peace treaties, all named for Paris suburbs, were as follows: the Treaty of Versailles with Germany (June 28, 1919), the Treaty of Saint-Germain with Austria (July 20, 1919), the Treaty of Neuilly with Bulgaria (November 27, 1919), the Treaty of Trianon with Hungary (March 21, 1920), and the Treaty of Sèvres with the Ottoman Empire (August 10, 1920), superceded by the Treaty of Lausanne (July 24, 1923).

The most important of these treaties was that with Germany. France sought to detach the entire Rhineland from Germany and make it independent with a permanent Allied occupation force. Britain and the United States opposed this and, to break the impasse, offered France a guarantee to come to its support should it ever be attacked by Germany. Clemenceau was forced to yield. The Treaty of Versailles restored Alsace and Lorraine to France and gave Belgium the small border enclaves of Moresnet, Eupen, and Malmédy. In recompense for the deliberate destruction of French coal mines by the withdrawing Germans, France received the coal production of the Saar region of Germany for 15 years. The Saar itself would be under League of Nations administration, with its inhabitants free to determine their future at the end of that period.

The so called Council of Four: (from left) British prime minister David Lloyd George, Italian prime minister Vittorio Orlando, French premier Georges Clemenceau, and U.S. president Woodrow Wilson at the Paris Peace Conference in France, May 27, 1919. (Library of Congress)

Plebiscites would decide the future of northern and southern Schleswig. Germany was to cede most of Posen and West Prussia to the new state of Poland, with a plebiscite to be held in districts of Upper Silesia. Gdansk (Danzig) would be a free city under the League of Nations but within the Polish customs union to provide that state with a major seaport. Germany also ceded Klaipėda (Memel, now part of Lithuania), and all the German colonies were made mandates under League of Nations supervision.

The Rhineland and a belt east of the Rhine 30 kilometers (18 miles) deep would be permanently demilitarized. The Allies were allowed to occupy the Rhineland for up to 15 years, with Germany to bear the costs. The German Army was restricted to 100,000 officers and men and was denied all military aircraft, heavy artillery, and tanks. Its navy was limited to six pre-Dreadnought battleships in capital ships and was not permitted submarines.

In the highly controversial Article 231, Germany accepted responsibility for having caused the war, establishing the legal basis for reparations. Germany was to pay for all civilian damages in the war. (The bill, presented in May 1921, was $33 billion.) In the meantime, Germany was to pay $5 billion. Germany was also to hand over much of its merchant ships and fishing fleet. It was also to build 200,000 tons of shipping for the Allies annually for a period of five years. While the other major signatories approved the Treaty of Versailles, the U.S. Senate never ratified it.

The treaties with the other defeated powers imposed restrictions on their military establishments and demanded reparations. That with Austria confirmed the breakup of the former Dual Monarchy. Hungary, Czechoslovakia, Yugoslavia, and Poland all became independent states. Austria was forced to cede from its own territory Eastern Galicia to Poland as well as the Trentino, Trieste, and Istria to Italy. Italy also secured the South Tirol (Tyrol). Shorn of its raw materials and food-producing areas, Austria was hard-hit economically. Many of its citizens favored union with Germany (Anschluss), which was, however, expressly forbidden.

Hungary lost almost three-quarters of its pre–World War I territory and two-thirds of its people. Czechoslovakia gained Slovakia, Austria secured western Hungary, and Yugoslavia took Croatia and Slovenia and part of the Banat of Temesvar. Romania received the remainder of the Banat and Transylvania, with its large Magyar population, along with part of the Hungarian plain.

Bulgaria was forced to yield territory to the new Yugoslavia and to cede Western Thrace to Greece and thus port facilities on the Aegean Sea. Bulgaria gained minor territory at the expense of the Ottoman Empire.

The Ottoman Empire renounced all claims to non-Turkish territory. The Kingdom of the Hejaz in Southwest Asia became independent. France secured a mandate over a new state of Syria (to include Lebanon), while Britain gained one over Mesopotamia (the future Iraq, to include Mosul) and Palestine. Smyrna (present-day Izmir) in eastern Anatolia and the hinterland was to be administered by Greece for five years, after which a plebiscite would decide its future, while Italy gained the Dodecanese Islands and Rhodes, with Greece receiving the remaining Turkish islands in the Aegean as well as Thrace. Armenia became independent. The treaty also established an autonomous Kurdistan. The straits were internationalized, and territory adjacent to them was demilitarized.

Turkish nationalists such as General Mustafa Kemal were outraged, and they set out to drive the Greeks from Anatolia. Turkish military success led to the new negotiated Treaty of Lausanne in 1923. Although the new Republic of Turkey gave up all claim to the non-Turkish areas, it recovered much of Eastern Thrace as well as Imbros and Tenedos. The remainder of the Aegean Islands went to Greece. Italy retained the Dodecanese Islands. Greece retained Cyprus. There was no autonomy for Kurdistan and no independent Armenia. The straits were to be demilitarized and open in times of peace to ships of all nations.

Spencer C. Tucker

Perspective Essay 1. The Controversial Treaty of Versailles

No peace arrangement in history has stirred up as much controversy as the treaty signed in the Hall of Mirrors of the Palace of Versailles on June 28, 1919. From Eastern Europe to Africa and from the Middle East to East Asia, the Treaty of Versailles left its mark on the entire world, and its authors have long been praised or castigated for their handiwork.

The treaty had ideological as well as military roots. After three years of intense fighting, a war-weary Europe was wracked by scarcity, mutiny, and revolution. In November 1917, the new Bolshevik government in Russia published the Allies' secret wartime agreements and called for a "peace without victory." In response, U.S. president Woodrow Wilson on January 8, 1918, outlined his version of a just peace based on self-determination and a new international order. However, on the military front things were less clear. In March 1918, the German Reich achieved a spectacular victory in the East and launched a major offensive in the West. The Allies, anticipating a long struggle, were entirely unprepared for the collapse of the Central Powers in the late summer of 1918. The protracted armistice negotiations between October 4 and November 11, 1918, revealed that Berlin's expectations of a soft "Wilsonian" peace might well be frustrated by the differing U.S., British, and French versions of how the Great War would end.

The choice of Paris as a conference site had far-reaching consequences. Close to the trenches and battlefields and flooded by diplomats, advisers, the press, and assorted pressure groups, the French capital was a less than ideal locale for calm deliberations. Wilson's presence—unprecedented for a U.S. president—dominated the proceedings, and the absence of the Germans, Bolsheviks, and neutrals had their effect. After paying lip service to an open gathering, the Big Three—the United States, the United Kingdom, and France—assumed control of the peacemaking.

The Allied differences soon became apparent. While Wilson assigned precedence to creating the League of Nations to prevent future wars, David Lloyd George sought to expand Britain's empire and revive Europe's balance of power, and Georges Clemenceau hoped to build firm barriers against a still strong, unrepentant Germany and the Soviet menace. During the next five months while the three politicians worked out the specifics, their public grew impatient. Moreover, Eastern Europe was threatened by hunger, disease, communism, and interstate warfare, and the colonial world erupted with violence. When the Germans were finally invited to see the treaty terms, their protests produced a few last-minute concessions, but the final text, signed under the threat of renewed hostilities, was a patched-together document containing notable inconsistencies, mixing Wilsonian principles and punitive clauses and leaving important colonial questions (notably China and the Middle East) unanswered.

The Treaty of Versailles's territorial provisions left Germany largely intact, with only minor territorial losses and a porous barrier of small bickering neighbors in the East. Nonetheless, the egregious denials of self-determination—the detachment of the Saar, Danzig, and Memel; the prohibition against Anschluss with German Austria; and the creation of 6 million German minorities in the new states of Eastern Europe as well as the seizure of Germany's overseas possessions—all became ammunition for the critics' charges of Allied hypocrisy. Reparations—which when finally established in 1921 were far less than Germany had imposed on France in 1871 and Russia in 1918—nevertheless became entangled in inflammatory debates over war guilt and the danger of world economic chaos.

The treaty's disarmament clauses, applied one-sidedly against Germany, ushered in a decade and a half of futile international negotiations to fulfill Wilson's promise of universal disarmament, and the economic penalties imposed on Germany belied the pledge to remove all economic barriers. Versailles's clauses on war criminals raised German ire but were in the end only weakly enforced by German civilian courts. The League of Nations, from which Germany and Soviet Russia were initially excluded (and the United States refused to join), became neither the robust collective security institution its supporters had envisaged nor an effective vehicle for peaceful treaty revision.

Once the treaty was signed, disgruntled British delegate John Maynard Keynes fired the opening salvo on the dire economic consequences of the peace. American conservatives chided Wilson for curtailing U.S. sovereignty and liberals for betraying his ideals. The small nations complained that their claims had been ignored, Italy and Japan resented their second-class treatment at Versailles, and colonial peoples protested their cavalier redistribution by the Allies.

Germans vehemently opposed the treaty. Although the treaty left the Reich essentially intact, more populous than France, and still in command of substantial resources, it had also imposed humiliating clauses and excluded it from the new international system—which was unlikely to be accepted by German leaders or by a public that refused to accept the reality or the consequences of defeat.

Could the peacemakers have done a better job? Using Versailles as a negative example, the victors after World War II eschewed a comprehensive peace settlement. Only in October 1990, 40 years after Germany had been defeated and occupied, did that war finally end.

But the statesmen at Paris, following historical precedents, sought to set Europe and the world in a new and more peaceful direction as soon as possible. The Treaty of Versailles liberated Belgium, France, Eastern Europe, and Russia from German domination. The treaty also gave birth to the League of Nations, the International Labor Office, and the Permanent Court of International Justice as well as organizations to quell drug and white slave traffic, aid refugees, and promote intellectual cooperation, and it also created arrangements to protect Europe's minorities and the populations of newly mandated territories.

The authors of the Treaty of Versailles failed to take account of the war's devastation, the ideological forces it had unleashed, their own weakness, and Germany's potential strength. Born at an exceptional moment when Russia had been vanquished and the United States had tipped the balance in European affairs, the Treaty of Versailles was an old-fashioned victors' settlement clothed in democratic garb that Germany, once it regained its full strength, was determined to challenge and that its former opponents, more disunited than ever, were unable to resist.

Carole Fink

Perspective Essay 2. Exaggerated Expectations

From virtually the moment that it was created, the Treaty of Versailles, signed in June 1919 between Germany and the Allied Powers—most notably the United Kingdom, France, the United States, Italy, and Japan—who had for more than four years fought World War I, received bad press. The treaty was the culmination of six months of tense bargaining at the Paris Peace Conference, negotiations not so much between Germany and its former opponents as among the various Allied powers themselves. Contemporary disappointment with the Treaty of Versailles owed much to the high expectations aroused during the war itself that the subsequent peace settlement would inaugurate a new era in international relations.

In April 1917, the United States joined those other nations already at war with Germany. Thereafter in a series of eloquent speeches, most notably his January 1918 "Fourteen Points" address, U.S. president Woodrow Wilson sought to appeal to progressives in all the warring powers, including Germany, by committing his own country and the Allied states to a program of liberal war aims envisaging the establishment of a new international order. The United States fought, Wilson stated, to "make the world safe for democracy." Among the objectives he publicly proclaimed were a nonpunitive peace settlement, whose terms would preclude both annexations of territory by victorious powers from the defeated and the imposition of indemnities by the winners on the losers; an end to secret diplomacy and the negotiation of undisclosed agreements among great powers; a territorial settlement based on respect for the principles of nationalism and popular consent; and the creation of a new international organization that would arbitrate future disputes among nations, thereby preventing conflicts from escalating into outright war.

Wilson's rhetoric was carefully crafted to stimulate support for Allied war aims not just among liberal forces within the United States and the Allied powers but also in those countries with which they were at war. He was particularly conscious of the imperative to counter the attraction of the Bolshevik communist regime, headed by Vladimir Lenin, that took power in Russia—originally one of the Allies—in November 1917 on a program of making peace with Germany, Russia's prime wartime enemy. Lenin, who led the world's first-ever communist government, was as hostile to the Allied powers as to Germany. Wilson and Allied leaders sought to neutralize the appeal of Lenin's calls for immediate peace and the overthrow by the workers of all capitalist governments.

Wilson headed a state that joined the war only reluctantly. Like many Americans, he thought his own country somewhat aloof from and superior to the aristocratic and imperialist European nations, considering them politically and morally suspect. When negotiating armistice terms in the autumn of 1918, German leaders insisted on dealing primarily with Wilson in the hope of pledging the Allied nations to impose a lenient peace. When Wilson arrived in London and Paris in late December 1918, he received a hero's welcome, applauded by cheering crowds as the statesman who would dramatically remake the world in his preferred American-style image.

Popular enthusiasm, however, proved transitory. The Versailles peace settlement, negotiated primarily among the leaders of the major powers in the coalition opposing Germany, soon demonstrated the limits of Wilson's influence. Bolshevik Russia concluded a separate highly disadvantageous peace with Germany in early 1918 and by 1919 was immersed in a bitter civil war in which Allied forces often assisted the anti-Bolshevik White armies. No Russian representatives attended the peace conference. France, the country on whose soil the bulk of fighting on the wartime Western Front had taken place, suffered heavy manpower losses during the war and was determined to prevent any German resurgence. British prime minister David Lloyd George won reelection in late 1918 by promising to squeeze the Germans "until the pips squeak." In the mid-term 1918 U.S. elections, Wilson's own Democratic Party lost control of Congress to the predominantly anti-German and conservative Republicans. The president's leverage for negotiating a liberal peace settlement was limited.

The treaty as ultimately negotiated deprived Germany of its colonies, which became mandates under the new League of Nations, territories usually administered by one or another of the victorious Allies; severely restricted German military and naval forces; left the strategically vital Rhineland and economically valuable Saar region under Allied control for many years; consigned substantial areas in East Prussia to the newly reconstituted Polish state; and held Germany guilty for beginning the war and responsible for paying reparations to the Allied powers (though not the United States) for human and material losses they had suffered during the conflict. Initially both Germany and Russia were excluded from the League of Nations, the international organization the treaty established, with its objective being to mediate future disputes among nations. German officials were summoned to Versailles in May 1919 and given no real alternative to accepting the treaty.

When the peace terms were announced, many liberals who had once supported Wilson—including such leading members of the U.S. peace conference delegation as future Republican president Herbert Hoover—were deeply disillusioned. Hoover blamed the treaty's shortcomings on European statesmen. Others, including the prominent journalist Walter Lippmann, turned bitterly against Wilson, publicly repudiating the peace settlement on the grounds that the president had betrayed his principles. The most prominent such critic was John Maynard Keynes, a young British economist and treasury adviser and economist at the conference whose best-selling book *The Economic Consequences of the Peace,* published shortly afterward, portrayed the peace settlement as economically unviable, imposing impossibly onerous financial burdens on Germany while disrupting European trade patterns by carving out numerous small and often mutually hostile nations from the former Habsburg, Ottoman, and Russian Empires. Keynes's influential book, embellished with sparkling vitriolic pen portraits of leading statesmen at the conference, almost immediately became the classic indictment of the Versailles peace, its reverberations still resounding decades later. German politicians of every party quickly made such complaints their own, and opposition to the Versailles settlement as unfair and unworkable almost immediately became German political orthodoxy. Other critics condemned the treaty as a Carthaginian peace designed to breed future wars, a devil's bargain that ultimately precipitated World War II.

One can, however, make a strong case that the Treaty of Versailles was the victim of exaggerated initial expectations followed by a determined, well-orchestrated campaign by its opponents to discredit it. Many subsequent historians, among them Margaret MacMillan in her vivid history of the Paris Peace Conference, Zara Steiner of Cambridge University, and Yale-based Patrick O. Cohrs, have questioned the validity of the more severe criticisms of its conditions. Moreover, by the standards of previous peace treaties, the terms that Germany received in 1919 were by no means especially harsh, particularly not when compared to those that German leaders had forced on defeated France in 1871 and intended to impose on other European powers had they won the war.

The reparations bill eventually assessed on Germany was, historians often argue, moderate and manageable. Unfortunately, payments were to be made over several decades—a perpetual humiliating reminder of past defeats that proved to be a constant political irritant. Steiner suggests that during the 1920s, German officials demonstrated remarkable diplomatic skill in discrediting and dismantling much of the Versailles settlement, regaining international acceptance from Britain and the United States at the expense of vulnerable France's position. Cohrs further argues that by the later 1920s, Anglo-American policies on reparations and the 1925 Treaties of Locarno had brought genuine if still precarious stabilization to Europe, equilibrium that collapsed in the 1930s due not primarily to shortcomings in the 1919 peace settlement but instead to the overwhelming international economic crisis of 1929–1933 that brought an extremist Nazi regime to power in Germany. From this perspective, the failure of statesmen of the 1930s to deal effectively with the challenges confronting them, not the treaty's intrinsic weaknesses, was the fundamental factor in the eventual collapse of the Versailles peace settlement.

Priscilla M. Roberts

Perspective Essay 3. Failure to Enforce the Paris Peace Settlement

There was much debate about the Paris peace settlement of 1919. Critics on the Right claimed that World War II would not have occurred had the French been allowed to write the settlement, while those on the Left maintained that the Treaty of Versailles was too harsh to conciliate the Germans. The reality is that the settlement was a compromise and did not significantly diminish German power. Despite its territorial losses, in 1919 Germany was still the most powerful state in Europe,

Britain, France, and the United States failed to cooperate on enforcement of the settlement. It was this fact rather than the treaty's severity or lack thereof, that made possible the renewal of world war by Germany. Given this, there is little reason to believe that the victors would have done any better with a harsher or more lenient settlement.

The Allied solidarity of 1918 disappeared before the ink was dry on the treaties. Many Americans now believed that their participation in the war had been a mistake, and the United States withdrew into isolation. Britain disengaged from the European continent. This left France alone among the great powers to enforce the settlement. Yet France was weaker in terms of population and economic strength than Germany. In effect, it was thus left up to the Germans themselves to decide whether they would abide by the treaty provisions, and this was a blueprint for disaster.

Right from the beginning the Germans violated the treaty's provisions and got away with it. The General Staff remained, although under another name and clandestinely. Germany maintained equipment that was to have been destroyed and arranged with other states to develop new weapons and train military personnel.

The German government also deliberately adopted obstructionist policies, and in 1923 it halted major reparations payments. French premier Raymond Poincaré, believing that if the Germans were allowed to break even part of the settlement the rest would soon unravel, sent French troops into the Ruhr. Chancellor Wilhelm Cuno's government adopted a policy of passive resistance, urging the workers not to work and promising to pay their salaries, hoping thereby to secure sufficient time for the United States and Britain to force France to quit the Ruhr. Although pressure from them was forthcoming, Poincaré held firm, and the result was catastrophic inflation in Germany. The ensuing financial chaos wiped out the middle class, many of whom now lost faith in democracy. This coupled with the worldwide economic depression in the early 1930s brought Adolf Hitler to power.

Seemingly Poincaré had won, for Germany now agreed to pay reparations under a scaled-down schedule, and French troops were withdrawn from the Ruhr. But the high cost of the occupation for French taxpayers and the opposition of Britain and the United States brought the Left to power in France in 1924. It reversed Poincaré's go-it-alone approach. Indeed, the occupation of the Ruhr was France's last independent military action in Europe between the wars. From this point forward, France followed the British lead regarding Germany.

By the 1930s, the national boundaries were still basically those agreed to in 1919. Italy, Germany, and Japan were not satisfied with this situation, however. These revisionist powers would risk war to bring change. The status quo powers of France, Great Britain, and the United States saw no benefit in changing conditions, but they were also unwilling to risk war to defend the 1919 settlement. From the Japanese invasion of Manchuria in 1931 to the outbreak of war in Europe in 1939, force was used by those who wanted to upset the status quo but not by those who sought to maintain it. The West seemed paralyzed. This was partly in consequence of the heavy human cost of World War I, but it was also the result of the Great Depression and racist attitudes (as in Ethiopia and China).

The chain of events that culminated in the September 1939 German invasion of Poland began in Asia in 1931, when Japan seized Manchuria. The international community, although it condemned Japan's actions in the League of Nations, did nothing to reverse this. Manchuria was larger than France and Germany combined, but its acquisition merely whetted the appetites of the Japanese nationalists, and Japanese forces soon moved against China proper. Had the great powers been able to agree on a policy and act militarily, Japan would have been forced to withdraw. Such a war would have been far cheaper than fighting a world war later, but the world economic depression apparently precluded such sacrifice. Financial pressure, in accordance with Article 16 of the League of Nations Covenant, might also have compelled Japanese withdrawal, but even this was beyond Western resolve. The failure to enforce collective security was a fateful blunder.

Germany was next to take advantage. Hitler, who came to power in January 1933 by entirely legal means, was determined to reverse the verdict of World War I and realize the territorial expansion sought by German leaders in that conflict. He regularly precipitated crises, playing on Western hopes and fears and taking advantage of the narrow nationalist approach of most Western leaders. In 1933 he withdrew Germany from both the League of Nations and the ongoing international disarmament conference meeting in Geneva. In July 1934 Austrian Nazis, acting with the tacit support of Berlin, attempted to seize power in Austria to achieve Anschluss (union with Germany). This effort failed, however, largely because Italian dictator Benito Mussolini pledged to defend Austrian independence, and Germany was then still largely disarmed.

Paris, London, and Rome protested but did nothing to compel Berlin to observe its treaty obligations. In fact, Britain now took the first step in the appeasement of Germany. Despite having promised its ally France that it would not undertake any action regarding Germany without consultation with Paris, in June 1935 London signed a naval agreement with Berlin that condoned the latter's violation of the Treaty of Versailles. It permitted the Reich to build a surface navy up to 35 percent that of Britain in size—in effect, a navy larger than those of either France or Italy. It also allowed Germany 45 percent of the Royal Navy in submarines, specifically prohibited Germany by the Treaty of Versailles. It was, of course, another postdated German check.

In October 1935, believing with some justification that he had Western support, Mussolini invaded Ethiopia (Abyssinia), and in May 1936 Italian forces entered Addis Ababa. Again the League of Nations stopped short of meaningful sanctions. Those on oil would have brought the Italian war machine to a halt. British and French condemnation of Italy's actions, however, helped drive Mussolini to the side of Hitler.

The seminal event on the road to World War II occurred when Hitler remilitarized the Rhineland. On March 7, 1936, he sent some 22,000 troops, armed with little more than small arms, into the Rhineland in defiance of the Treaty of Versailles but also of the Locarno Pacts of 1925, which Germany had voluntarily negotiated. The French government did nothing. The French grossly overestimated the forces in the operation and believed Hitler's false claims about his military. In a vain cover for its own inaction, Paris appealed to Britain for support, but London made it clear that Britain would not fight for the Rhineland, which was, after all, German territory. Had the French acted, even alone, their forces would have rolled over the Germans, and this probably would have been the end of Hitler. Acquisition of the Rhineland provided Germany a buffer for its industrial heart of the Ruhr and a springboard for invading France and Belgium.

Almost immediately after the German remilitarization of the Rhineland, another international crisis erupted—civil war in Spain—beginning in July 1936. Under British pressure and fearful of a widened war, the Western democracies rejected aid to the legitimately elected Spanish republican government. The fascist states of Germany and Italy fully supported the fascist or nationalist side, making possible its victory in 1939. The intervention also cemented an alliance between Germany and Italy.

In 1937 full-scale fighting broke out between Japanese and Chinese troops, bringing the Second Sino-Japanese War of 1937–1945. Japan never declared war against China, however, which enabled it to avoid U.S. neutrality legislation and purchase raw materials and oil. But this also allowed Washington to send aid to China.

In the West by 1938 the situation was such as to encourage Hitler to embark on his own territorial expansion. Mussolini was now linked with Hitler, France was undergoing ministerial instability, and in Britain appeasement was at full ebb. Austria was Hitler's first step. The Reich absorbed German-speaking Austria in March 1938, and the West did nothing. Anschluss greatly strengthened Germany in Central Europe, bringing that country into direct contact with Italy, Yugoslavia, and Hungary. Czechoslovakia was almost isolated and clearly Hitler's next target.

Hitler had added 6 million Germans in Austria to the Reich, but another 3.5 million lived in Czechoslovakia. Hitler demanded that the Sudetenland, where most lived, be surrendered to Germany in its entirety. Czechoslovakia, which had a well-trained 400,000-man army and a military alliance with France, rejected Berlin's demands. Hitler threatened war, and Britain and France again gave way. At the Munich Conference in September 1939, British prime minister Neville Chamberlain gave Hitler virtually everything he demanded. At the time it seemed to many not too high a price to pay for peace.

In retrospect, it would have been better for the West to have fought Germany rather than capitulating at Munich. The lineup against Germany might have included the Soviet Union and Poland, but even discounting these, the German Army would have been forced to fight against France and Britain as well as Czechoslovakia. Despite Hitler's claims to the contrary, Germany was not ready for war in September 1938.

Then in March 1939, Hitler absorbed the Czech portion of the rump state—Bohemia and Moravia. He also secured sufficient equipment to arm 20 divisions. Any increase in armaments that Britain and France achieved by March 1939 was more than counterbalanced by these German gains.

Hitler's seizure of the rest of Czechoslovakia clearly demonstrated that his demands were not limited to Germans. His repudiation of the formal pledges given at Munich at last convinced the British that they could no longer trust him. Indeed, in the worst possible circumstances, with Czechoslovakia lost and the Soviet Union now distrustful of the Western powers, Britain changed its East European policy and agreed to do what the French had sought in the 1920s. Britain and France extended a series of guarantees to the smaller states now threatened by Germany, especially Germany's next target: Poland. Mussolini, however, took advantage of the situation to send Italian troops into Albania in April 1939.

The Western powers began to make belated military preparations for the inevitable, and they worked to secure a pact with the Soviet Union. Yet their guarantee to Poland gave the Soviet Union protection on its western frontier, virtually the most it could have secured in any negotiations.

Hitler now put pressure on Poland for the return of the Polish Corridor, and thanks to a nonaggression pact with the Soviet Union on August 23, 1939 (its secret provisions provided for a sharing of Poland and the Baltic states and for the Soviets to furnish immense stores of raw materials to Germany), Hitler ordered the German invasion of Poland. He did not expect the British and French to act. In any case, he said, Germany must accept the risks and act with "reckless resolution."

It was miscalculation and lack of will by the leaders of the Western democracies that had made possible World War II. Pursuit of narrow nationalism and isolationism at the expense of a wider world community and the failure to enforce international treaties, rather than the shortcomings of the Paris peace settlement of 1919, brought about World War II.

Spencer C. Tucker

Further Reading

Albrecht-Carrie, René. *A Diplomatic History of Europe since the Congress of Vienna.* New York: Harper and Row, 1958.

Andelman, David A. *A Shattered Peace: Versailles 1919 and the Price We Pay Today.* Hoboken, NJ: Wiley, 2008.

Bailey, Thomas A. *Wilson and the Peacemakers: Combining Woodrow Wilson and the Lost Peace and Woodrow Wilson and the Great Betrayal.* New York: Macmillan, 1947.

Birdsall, Paul. *Versailles, Twenty Years After.* New York: Reynal and Hitchcock, 1941.

Boemeke, Manfred F., Gerald D. Feldman, and Elisabeth Glaser, eds. *The Treaty of Versailles: A Reassessment after 75 Years.* New York: Cambridge University Press, 1998.

Cohrs, Patrick O. *The Unfinished Peace after World War I: America, Britain and the Stabilisation of Europe, 1919–1932.* New York: Cambridge University Press, 2006.

Ferguson, Niall. *The Pity of War: Explaining World War One.* New York: Basic Books, 1999.

Fromkin, David. *A Peace to End All Peace: The Fall of the Ottoman Empire and the Creation of the Modern Middle East.* New York: Macmillan 1989.

Hoover, Herbert. *The Ordeal of Woodrow Wilson.* New York: McGraw-Hill, 1958.

Keylor, William R., ed. *The Legacy of the Great War: Peacemaking, 1919.* Boston: Houghton Mifflin, 1998.

Keynes, John Maynard. *The Economic Consequences of the Peace.* London: Macmillan, 1919.

Knock, Thomas J. *To End All Wars: Woodrow Wilson and the Quest for a New World Order.* New York: Oxford University Press, 1995.

Lederer, Ivo J., ed. *The Versailles Settlement: Was It Foredoomed to Failure?* Boston: D. C. Heath, 1960.

Lentin, Antony. *Guilt at Versailles: Lloyd George and the Pre-History of Appeasement.* London: Methuen, 1985.

Lentin, Antony. *Lloyd George and the Lost Peace: From Versailles to Hitler, 1919–1940.* New York: Palgrave Macmillan, 2001.

MacMillan, Margaret. *Paris 1919: Six Months That Changed the World.* New York: Random House, 2002.

Marks, Sally. *The Illusion of Peace: International Relations in Europe, 1918–1933.* 2nd ed. New York: Palgrave Macmillan, 2003.

Mayer, Arno J. *Politics and Diplomacy of Peacemaking: Containment and Counter-Revolution at Versailles, 1918–1919.* New York: Knopf, 1967.

Nicolson, Harold. *Peacemaking, 1919: Being Reminiscences of the Paris Peace Conference.* Boston: Houghton Mifflin, 1933.

Paxton, Robert O. *Europe in the Twentieth Century.* New York: Harcourt Brace Jovanovich, 1975.

Schwabe, Klaus. *Woodrow Wilson, Revolutionary Germany, and Peacemaking, 1918–1919: Missionary Diplomacy and the Realities of Power.* Chapel Hill: University of North Carolina Press, 1985.

Sharp, Alan. *The Versailles Settlement: Peacemaking after the First World War, 1919–1923.* 2nd ed. New York: Palgrave Macmillan, 2008.

Steiner, Zara S. *The Lights That Failed: European International History, 1919–1933.* New York: Oxford University Press, 2005.

Walworth, Arthur. *Wilson and His Peacemakers: American Diplomacy at the Paris Peace Conference, 1919.* London: Norton, 1986.

Watson, David Robin. *Georges Clemenceau: A Political Biography.* New York: David McKay, 1976.

37. Would the Republicans Have Won the Spanish Civil War If There Had Been No Foreign Intervention?

The Spanish Civil War (1936–1939), a bloody rebellion against the newly elected Spanish Republic by Nationalist forces led by Francisco Franco, was shaped by the intervention of various foreign powers. The Nationalists were supported by Nazi Germany and fascist Italy, while the Republicans were backed by the Soviet Union and volunteer fighters from across Europe and the Americas. For the Italians and Germans, intervention in the Spanish conflagration was undertaken for a variety of reasons, some of them ideological, some of them strategic. Certainly they hoped to empower Franco, who harbored at least quasi-fascist beliefs and who would later go on to establish a potent totalitarian dictatorship, but they also saw the war as a way in which to test new military tactics and technology, which would be put to use during World War II. They also believed that a Spanish government under Franco's control would not stand in the way of their ambitious military and territorial aspirations. Ultimately the Spanish Republicans and their allies went down to defeat. Although the war's exact death toll has never been accurately determined, the most careful estimates indicate that about 600,000 Spaniards were killed on both sides. At least half a million more lived on as refugees in bleak camps on the French side of the Pyrenees. The question of whether the Republicans could have held their own against the Nationalists without foreign intervention continues to be debated by historians.

In the first perspective essay, Dr. Wayne H. Bowen argues that the Spanish Republic could not have defeated Nationalist rebels even if there had been no outside interference. Bowen further asserts that deep political divisions within the Spanish Republican government virtually ensured a Nationalist victory. In contrast, in the second perspective essay Dr. Spencer C. Tucker maintains that the armed forces of the Spanish Republic could have indeed defeated the Nationalist side in the Spanish Civil War had there not been intervention by foreign powers. He argues that the levels of personnel and war matériel contributed by Nationalist allies tipped the balance against the Spanish Republicans. Finally, Dr. Francisco J. Romero Salvadó analyzes how the Republicans could have won the civil war except for foreign intervention. Like Tucker, Salvadó concludes that foreign intervention on the side of the Nationalists doomed the Spanish Republic. Furthermore, the lack of will on the part of Republican allies all but ensured their defeat.

Background Essay

There was a saying that "Europe stops at the Pyrenees," for in the early 1930s Spain was a poverty-stricken country, lagging behind the rest of Western Europe in social and economic reforms. Most of the land and natural wealth were controlled by fewer than 5,000 powerful families in a population of some 20 million. The Catholic Church played a powerful role in the country but was part of the establishment, opposed to meaningful reform.

With social unrest rampant, Spanish king Alfonso XIII in 1923 called on Antonio Primo de Rivera to establish an authoritarian corporate state. But harsh repression could not remove the social and economic problems, and the worldwide economic depression of the early 1930s struck Spain hard. Widespread strikes led to violence, and in April 1931 after local elections went overwhelming against the Crown, Alfonso XIII was forced into unlamented exile.

Spain thus became a republic, and there were high hopes that this would begin a new era for the country. The Republicans pushed through reforms to benefit the workers and the peasants and also moved to curtail the special privileges of the church and the wealthy. Then in 1933 when the centrists and the Right won a majority in the Cortes, they curtailed the reforms and restored the special establishment privileges. They also jailed some 30,000 leftists. The army was also swept clean of those unsympathetic with the political Right, known as the Nationalists.

On February 16, 1936, national elections were again held. The parties on the Left (republicans, socialists, syndicalists, and communists) had combined in a Popular Front and turned out of power the coalition of conservative republicans, clericals, and monarchists. Manuel Azaña formed a cabinet that immediately undertook a social reform program to include redistribution of land, the development of nonparochial schools, and legislation designed to curtail church influence. In May, Azaña was elected president of the republic.

As expected, the political Right defied the mandate. Government awareness that the Nationalists were planning a coup d'état caused the latter to launch their effort prematurely. The rebellion began on July 18, 1936, in a revolt of army regiments in Spanish Morocco. It was led by Generals José y Sacanell Sanjurjo, Emilio Mola Vidal, Juan Yagüe, and Francisco Franco. They were determined to prevent the Republicans from destroying the character and traditions of their ancestral Spain.

Spain now fell into civil war. The Nationalists, also known as the Fascists, had the bulk of the army, the Catholic Church, the die-hard monarchists, and the conservative old-line families who controlled the majority of the wealth of Spain. They also had the Spanish Foreign Legion and the powerful paramilitary groups of the Carlists and the Falange. The government side, known as the Republicans, or Loyalists, could count on the navy, which was solidly Republican, and also had the bulk of the air force, the peasants and workers, and the most industrialized part of Spain, the Madrid-Valencia-Barcelona triangle. The loyalties of the middle class were fairly evenly divided.

One would have assumed that the legitimately elected Republican government could have secured military assistance in the form of weaponry from the Western democracies. This was not the case. While the French government was willing, the British government was not, and France was forced to halt arms shipments to the Republican side when the British threatened that if the civil war in Spain morphed into a wider European war, Britain might not honor its pledge to aid France against Germany. This threat was sufficient to secure French capitulation. The United States proclaimed its neutrality. But "neutrality," as it turned out, benefited the Fascists.

Although Mexico provided some military assistance to the Republican side, the only substantial aid came from the Soviet Union, and this was paid for by Spanish gold reserves. It also did not equal the assistance provided by the Fascist states to the Nationalists. In 1936 the republic was not, as the Fascists claimed, communist.

Supporters of the Spanish Republic preparing to defend positions in the capital city of Madrid in 1936 during the Spanish Civil War. (Universal History Archive/UIG via Getty Images)

Indeed, in the first elections to the Cortes in 1931, none of the 473 elected deputies were declared communists, and in the 1936 elections there were only 145 communist deputies. The Republican majority in the Cortes was made up of liberals and socialists from a wide range of political parties who were basically no more liberal than the New Dealers of President Franklin Roosevelt in the United States or the Labor Party of Ramsay MacDonald in Great Britain. However, in the long years of warfare, Soviet military assistance eventually led to the subversion of the republic, and the communists took charge. This need not have been the case.

The British government clung to a noninterventionist policy, and London even secured a pledge from the 27 national governments, including all the great powers, to a nonintervention treaty. But Germany and Italy completely ignored this and continued to send substantial aid to the Fascists, while the Soviet Union continued aid to the republic. In the end, Soviet assistance to the republic was insufficient against that provided by the Fascist powers to the Nationalist side, which came to enjoy considerable superiority in both airpower and artillery and in March 1939 claimed victory.

The toll of the fighting has never been accurately determined. Some 600,000 Spaniards died in the war, and afterward another 100,000 were executed by the victorious Nationalists. Half a million more Spaniards became refugees in wretched camps on the French side of the Pyrenees.

Spain was left with deep wounds that many decades later still had not healed. The West did not come off well in Spain, and its failure to stand up for democracy encouraged other demands by the dictators elsewhere. Perhaps the most important effect internationally of the civil war in Spain was to bring Germany and Italy together in what came to be known as the Rome-Berlin Axis.

Spencer C. Tucker

Perspective Essay 1. No Assistance, Same Result

The Spanish Republic could not have defeated Nationalist rebels regardless of outside interference. Had there been no foreign assistance to either side and had the Spanish Republicans been forced to fight the Spanish Nationalists alone, the civil war would have ended in much the same way with victory for the rebels, led by General Francisco Franco.

The government of the Spanish Republic was simply too politically divided, militarily inept, and focused on internal revolution to defeat the right-wing insurgency that began on July 17, 1936. The Nationalist rebellion clearly benefited from assistance from Nazi Germany, fascist Italy, and authoritarian Portugal, but Soviet assistance to the Spanish Republic, especially in the form of political advice and guidance on internal affairs, was far more essential to maintaining the coalition of Republican forces from collapsing into an exclusively left-on-left civil war within the broader Spanish Civil War.

When the Spanish Civil War began in July 1936, launched as an attempted coup by conservative, monarchist, and anti-Republican military officers throughout the peninsula and the colonies, the armed forces, as a single entity controlled from Madrid, fragmented. While much of the air force and navy remained loyal to the Republic, the vast majority of army officers and the best units of the army, including all forces in Spanish Morocco, the Canary Islands, and other territories, went over to the rebels. While the initial uprising on July 17–18 was small, initiated by perhaps 1,000 conspirators, it gained momentum quickly.

The military rebellion failed in the major cities of Madrid and Barcelona as well as in the separatist regions of Catalonia and the Basque Country. It succeeded, however, in Seville, along the Portuguese border, and in much of the rural and conservative central and northern countryside. While this uprising was therefore unsuccessful in winning a quick triumph over the Spanish Republic, even in this initial failure the Nationalists established the conditions for their eventual victory, while the Republicans fatally crippled their own long-term prospects for survival. In those areas of Spain where the rebels failed, their efforts were stopped not by organized military units that remained loyal to the Republicans, since there were few that did, but instead by spontaneously formed workers' militias.

These enthusiastic but untrained socialist, communist, and anarchist forces preserved the Republic during the summer of 1936, but at the same time they prevented the organization of a real Spanish Republic military establishment. Along with their military activities, these militias began a social revolution that rejected traditional hierarchy. The Catholic Church, business leaders, and landowners were viewed with suspicion, and many suffered summary execution in areas controlled by the Republican side.

More critically in terms of the actual conflict, military officers, regardless of their actual sympathies, were seen as inherently disloyal to the Republic and, if not immediately executed, were stripped of their rank and privileges. Even those who had pro-Republican credentials were viewed as class enemies. Republican militias executed more than 1,000 military officers, and the Spanish Republic purged another 2,000–3,000 from the services. Fewer than half of the 6,000–7,000 officers initially in Republican zones were allowed to remain in uniform, and even then they were typically not permitted to hold major commands.

Faced with these difficult conditions, the relatively small numbers of officers who initially supported the Republic were not able to lend their talents to military operations. In many cases, they defected to the Nationalist cause. The few pro-Republican officers and security officials initially trapped in the Nationalist zone most often opted to remain where they were. Discomfort at the politics of the Franco regime was far more bearable than nearly certain incarceration, and perhaps execution, at the hands of anarchists and others on the other side.

Many historians have pointed to foreign intervention from Adolf Hitler's Germany and Benito Mussolini's Italy as having been indispensable to the Nationalist side. The initial event that is argued to have been most critical was the airlift of the Army of Africa—the colonial Spanish force in Morocco that included the most effective army units and enthusiastically joined the rebellion—to the mainland. From July to October 1936, German and Italian air units transported this army across the straits to join Nationalist units in southern Spain.

Although this airlift enabled the Nationalists to move the Army of Africa—the strongest force in the prewar Spanish Army—into battle more rapidly, the rebels would still have been able to bring this force to the peninsula by other means. The Spanish Navy did not go over in its entirety to the rebels—it was divided between the two camps. However, the Nationalists did control the two most powerful navy cruisers along with the majority of combat-worthy vessels. While ferrying the Army of Africa in ships would have been more dangerous than an airlift, the rebels had the resources to make it happen. Most of the Spanish Air Force remained loyal to the republic, but the outdated aircraft controlled by Madrid would not have posed an obstacle to a sea operation of this kind.

Once the Army of Africa reached Spain from Morocco, the Nationalists had a significant operational and strategic advantage over the Republicans. With perhaps 40,000 Spanish and Moroccan soldiers, the Army of Africa had a unified command, significant experience in maneuver warfare, the highest concentration of combat veterans in the Spanish military, and, with the associated Spanish Legion, the best-led, best-equipped, and best-motivated soldiers in the Spanish Civil War.

During the Spanish Civil War, Germany and Italy provided consistent and effective military aid to the Nationalists. The Soviet Union was less reliable a patron for the Republicans. The Soviet Union did not send its best weapons to the Spanish Civil War, reserving those for its own military forces. Even more, it overcharged for the mostly outdated military equipment it did send—tanks, aircraft, artillery, and small arms. Germany dispatched the Condor Legion, a combined unit providing air support, communications, training, and other military assistance, and Italy sent 50,000 infantry, organized in the Corps of Volunteer Troops (Corpo Truppe Volontarie). The Soviet Union sent fewer personnel, perhaps only 2,000, including advisers and actual combatants. In the end, these foreign forces provided additional weapons and belligerents but did not turn the tide of battle in either direction.

Another component of foreign assistance to the Spanish Republic was the approximately 40,000 men and women of the International Brigades, volunteer units from much of Europe, the United States, and elsewhere. Recruited, organized, and led through the efforts of the Communist International (Comintern) and socialist parties, these forces included such prominent figures as George Orwell, Ernest Hemingway, and future West German chancellor Willy Brandt. While these foreign soldiers did provide a morale boost to the Spanish Republicans, their presence was never strategically decisive. Foreign volunteers, including from Ireland, Romania, and the United Kingdom, also served on the Nationalist side but in relatively small numbers, perhaps as few as 3,000, and with even less military significance than that of the opposing International Brigades.

There was an international debate early in the conflict, with an attempt to prevent foreign intervention. These efforts, in and out of the League of Nations, resulted in the British-led Non-Intervention Agreement of August–September 1936. It was intended to isolate Spain from foreign states, allowing Spaniards to fight or negotiate their own end to the war. Although Germany, Italy, and the Soviet Union all violated this agreement, there was rough parity, considering all foreign assistance. This made internal resources even more telling in regard to the eventual outcome.

Units that were more strategically significant were the domestic militias that rallied to the Nationalists. Unlike on the Republican side, where these movements formed spontaneously from trade unions, leftist political parties, or even working-class neighborhoods, many of the monarchist militias that supported the Nationalists had an organizational history that predated the Spanish Civil War, with long-term existence, structure, commanders, and training. For example, the militias of the Carlist movement—ultra-Catholic monarchists who supported a rival dynasty to that of the Alfonsine Bourbons who had reigned for much of the 19th century—lent immediate support to the military rebellion. Especially strong in the province of Navarre, they had units throughout northern and northwestern Spain, which aided in the seizure of much of this territory early in the conflict. Known as Requetés, their distinctive red berets marked their affiliation with the Carlist movement, sometimes known as Traditionalists, responsible for three civil wars against the central Spanish government in the 19th century. In 1936, however, the Carlists aligned with the same Alfonsine Bourbons they had previously fought, providing indispensable forces for the Nationalist rebellion. The Spanish Falange, an indigenous semifascist party, also joined the Nationalist side, seeing its militia grow quickly to more than 100,000 volunteers. Most of these units were commanded by current or former military officers, who provided the professional leadership that Republican militias, often led by democratically elected workers, typically lacked.

Franco was an experienced commander who provided the overall strategic and political leadership that kept his Nationalist coalition nominally unified. He had served with distinction as an officer in Morocco, as head of Spain's infantry academy, and at the cabinet level as minister of war in the early 1930s, when he had organized a successful military campaign against an uprising by leftist coal miners. Unlike his counterparts on the Republican side, Franco had experienced warfare at all levels and understood the necessity for a single commander in wartime.

The Republican zone witnessed open and often violent conflicts between the various factions. The Nationalists, however, kept their significant ideological differences in check, focusing instead on their collective war effort. In April 1937 Franco forcibly merged all political parties in the rebel areas, whether monarchist, fascist, conservative republican, or representing other factions, into a single authoritarian movement, the Falange Española Tradicionalista y de las JONS, with himself at its head. Although an unwieldy amalgam of rival parties, it did impose unity. While the semifascist, authoritarian, Catholic, and vaguely monarchist ideology of this movement satisfied none of the formerly independent parties, Franco convinced these groups to support this cobbled-together nominal party through the war and beyond.

The Nationalists also benefited from the loyalty of the vast majority of the pre-civil war professional officers, the men most prepared to lead soldiers in battle, plan the logistics that fuel modern warfare, and ensure stability in newly occupied areas. Unlike in the Republican zone, where prewar military service was viewed with strong suspicion, the Nationalists welcomed officers willing to serve in the rebellion. Indeed, officers were considered among the elite under the Franco regime.

The rebels certainly benefited from the initial geographic alignment and the corresponding resources. Much of rural Spain, with its agricultural production, either rallied to the Nationalist uprising or was soon conquered by Franco's forces. Hunger was never a major concern for the Nationalists, with an effective system of rationing ensuring distribution to the few urban areas they controlled. Within a year the Nationalists had consolidated control over all of western Spain, including the entire border with Portugal, a supportive right-wing dictatorship. In the Republican zone, however, major cities such as Madrid and Barcelona consistently ran short of food, a situation that worsened throughout the war. The prewar market systems for providing food collapsed as parties on the Republican side dismantled the capitalist economy. Hunger, shortages, and seizures of agricultural goods by Republican governments characterized the ongoing food crisis, which even reached the front lines, weakening the ability of the Republic to fight effectively.

While foreign assistance was more valuable to the Nationalist cause, had the Spanish Civil War been fought entirely by Spaniards, the outcome would have been the same: victory by the military rebels and their conservative allies against the Spanish Republic. The Spanish Republic lacked the core of military officers, geographic advantages, preexisting militia units, and unity of effort that characterized the Nationalist war effort under Franco.

Wayne H. Bowen

Perspective Essay 2. German Military Assistance Was Key

The armed forces of the Spanish Republic could have defeated the Nationalist side in the Spanish Civil War if there had not been intervention by foreign powers. Certainly, the Republican side would have had a better chance at winning without foreign intervention.

The military lineup at the start of the rebellion slightly favored the government side. The rebel Nationalists, also known as the Fascists, had some two-thirds of the army (about 40,000 of 60,000 men) and, thanks to purges when the Right was in power, also had some 90 percent of the officers. The 24,000-man Army of Africa was solidly Nationalist, but a substantial number of these would have to remain in Morocco to maintain Spanish control there. The Nationalists also enjoyed the support of the Spanish Foreign Legion and the powerful paramilitary forces of the Carlists (some 14,000 men) and the Falange (50,000). The Nationalists could also count on some two-thirds of the Civil Guard, or about 22,000 men. They also had the church, the die-hard monarchists, and the conservative old-line families who commanded the wealth of the country.

The government side, known as the Republicans and the Loyalists, could count on the navy, which was solidly Republican. The Nationalists possessed only 1 old battleship, 1 cruiser, 1 destroyer, and several gunboats and coastal sloops. The Republican fleet included 1 battleship, 3 cruisers, 15 destroyers, and 10 submarines. The Republican Navy was, however, poorly organized and decidedly short of officers. The Republicans also had almost all the Spanish Air Force aircraft and more than half its personnel. Perhaps more important, the Republicans had the support of the peasants and workers and also the most industrialized part of Spain, the Madrid-Valencia-Barcelona triangle. (The loyalties of the middle class were fairly evenly divided.) The Republicans also had the great advantage of controlling the nation's gold reserves. The Republican side was short of arms, but the gold could be used to purchase these.

The Nationalist advantage in troop numbers was also offset to a considerable degree by the fact that the best of these—the Army of Africa and the Spanish Foreign Legion—were in Africa and would have to be gotten to Spain. A number of senior army officers also refused to join the insurrection. Early on the Republicans easily won control of the major cities of Spain, after which the Nationalists found themselves with only about 53 percent of the army (30,000 on the mainland and 24,000 in North Africa) and only a third each of the air force and navy. Well aware of the problems facing the Nationalists, as early as July 16 Nationalist general Francisco Franco, who became leader of the revolt, solicited foreign assistance.

German and Italian aid came early on. On July 26, with the war only a week old, the Nationalists approached German chancellor Adolf Hitler about purchasing 10 Ju-52 trimotor transports to ferry Franco's troops from Morocco to Spain. This was critical to Nationalist hopes, since the Republican-dominated navy effectively blocked transportation of Nationalist troops by sea. Hitler immediately agreed to loan such aircraft with full German aircrews and fighter aircraft protection. Beginning on July 29 the Germans flew 20,000 crack Spanish and Moroccan troops to Nationalist-controlled Seville in southern Spain, where an air head was established. This may have been the decisive event of the war, certainly in the early going.

In November 1936 the Germans formed the Kondor (Condor) Legion. It numbered some 6,000 men and more than 100 aircraft, but as many as 19,000 men and 300–400 planes served in Spain over the course of the war. The Condor Legion consisted of aviation and aviation support units drawn from the regular German military. Germany sent its best aircraft, including the superb Messerschmitt Bf-109 fighter and the Heinkel He-111 bomber. It also field-tested new aircraft, such as the Junkers Ju-87 Stuka dive-bomber. The Republicans had nothing that could match these. Spain also proved immensely useful for the Germans as a training ground for new theories of air-ground cooperation, which was so devastatingly effective early in

World War II. German air support was decisive in the outcome of the civil war. Also, the Condor Legion's 88mm flak guns, sent to provide air defense, eventually became the backbone of Nationalist artillery batteries as highly mobile field artillery.

Mussolini wanted Italy to be involved. Somewhat deterred by his military advisers who feared a general European war for which Italy was unprepared, he at first provided only equipment and technicians. Later he dispatched significant numbers of army troops. This Italian intervention was both larger and less effective than that of Germany. Some 40,000 Italian soldiers went to Spain along with several hundred aircraft, many of them bombers.

The attitude of the Soviet Union toward the Spanish Civil War was somewhat curious. Soviet leader Joseph Stalin believed that an all-out victory by either side was undesirable. A Republican victory would produce a left-wing Spanish government that in all likelihood would not acquiesce to Kremlin control. Even a wholly Stalinized Spain would mean only a weak ally at the other extremity of Europe, and it would antagonize his allies, Britain and France. Success by Franco would serve to weaken France and help free Hitler to concentrate on aggression in Eastern Europe. Stalin thus decided to help the Republican side, not to win but rather not to lose. It would buy him time to rearm the Soviet Union. Stalin also thought that the Spanish Civil War might ultimately involve Germany, Italy, France, and Britain in a general European war that would leave the Soviet Union the dominant power on the continent.

Soviet aid throughout the civil war was sharply limited and subject to restrictions. No Soviet military units were sent to Spain, only military equipment (small arms, planes, tanks, and artillery), a few thousand advisers, and some pilots. This was in sharp contrast to the actual fighting units sent there by Germany and Italy.

The military balance depended on the attitude of the Western democracies of Britain, France, and the United States. With the majority of French public opinion favoring the Republican side in the war, Premier Léon Blum promised to supply the Spanish Republican government with 20 bombers and small quantities of machine guns, artillery pieces, and rifles as well as bombs and ammunition. In Britain, however, appeasement was at full tide. Prime Minister Stanley Baldwin (followed in 1937 by Neville Chamberlain) insisted on nonintervention and embargoing military supplies to either side. Chamberlain warned Blum that if France aided the Republican side in Spain and the civil war morphed into a general European conflict in which Germany invaded France, Britain might not honor its treaty to support France. In short, London opposed any policy that might lead to a general European conflict. The British Conservative Party, then in power, also feared that the communists might control a victorious Spanish Republican government, which seemed to many of them a greater danger than a Fascist victory.

Britain's position caused France to reverse its stance. Besides, the 1936 elections in France were bitterly contested, and there was also concern that the ideological struggle in Spain would spill across the Pyrenees into France. But the overriding consideration was that France desperately needed British support against Germany.

Britain took the lead in drafting a nonintervention agreement. The Western democracies believed that it would give the Republican side in the war a good chance to win if the major powers agreed to it. Ultimately 27 nations, including all the great powers, signed the agreement. Yet men and supplies continued to reach the Fascist side from Germany and Italy. It was only relatively late that significant military aid reached the Republican side from the Soviet Union.

The United States was still in the grip of isolationism, and the Catholic Church was immensely successful in trumpeting the republic as "godless" and magnifying excesses against the church in Spain. Washington enforced the embargo, although strangely large quantities of American oil reached Franco's war machine. Mexico was the only Western country to help the Loyalist side. It sent 18,000 rifles.

Volunteers from other countries did fight for both the Republican and Fascist sides in the war. The vast majority of these were on the Republican side. Some 40,000 men came from 54 nations, and 8,000 died in Spain.

In the end the communists took control of the Republican government, simply because the Soviets were the only ones supplying the Republicans with military assistance. The Republicans staked all on an offensive in July 1938 along the Ebro River, committing 100,000 of 400,000 men in their army. The offensive was halted by Fascist airpower and artillery, the military difference throughout the civil war. The failure of this summer offensive spelled the beginning of the end for the Republic. At the end the Republican side was fighting with virtually no equipment, with old and rusty guns, and with crude homemade bombs.

If the Spanish Civil War had been left to the Spaniards themselves, the Republicans would have had the edge. Outside aid in the form of airpower and artillery was the difference.

Spencer C. Tucker

Perspective Essay 3. Foreign Intervention Denied Republican Victory

The Republicans could have won the civil war except for foreign intervention. After losing the general elections in February 1936, the national bloc of fascists, monarchists, conservatives, and Catholics abandoned the constitutional road to power (via the ballot box) and sought to destroy a left-wing and progressive republic through a coup d'état. They assumed that their uprising would meet with prompt success. They counted on the advantage of a surprise strike so as to eliminate those senior officers reluctant to break their oath of loyalty to the government. They could also rely on the mobilization of thousands of civilians, members of the different right-wing parties.

After the military rebellion began in the Moroccan Protectorate in the evening of July 17, 1936, it spread to mainland Spain in the following days. Although General Francisco Franco's propaganda suggested that divine providence guided the fulfillment of his crusade, there are sound foundations to speculate that without foreign intervention, the rebellion would have petered out.

After a week of bloody clashes, the military sedition had largely failed. With the exception of a few cities in the south and in Oviedo (Asturias), the Canary Islands, and the Balearics (with the exception of Menorca), the rebels, or Nationalists, controlled only the traditionally conservative areas of Galicia, Old Castilla, and Navarra. In contrast, a combination of the swift response of the unions and the loyalty of the greater part of the state police, security forces, and senior army officers meant that nearly two-thirds of the country remained in the hands of the republic. Furthermore, the Spanish Air Force (albeit quite small) and the country's huge gold reserves remained in the hands of the government. The Army of Africa, containing the fierce Foreign Legion and the Regulares (indigenous Moorish troops commanded by Spanish officers), Spain's most battle-hardened professional military force, led by Franco, was paralyzed by the problem of transport across the Strait of Gibraltar after sailors stayed loyal to the republic, overpowered their officers, and retained control of the fleet. The rebellion's days appeared numbered.

Lacking significant modern weaponry and any important arms industry, both sides rapidly looked abroad to obtain vital military supplies. Consequently, the response of the European great powers essentially determined the course and outcome of the war.

The first hints of foreign reaction favored the republic, which was the legally established government of Spain and a member of the League of Nations and most international forums. Both Italy, exhausted after its weary Abyssinian experience, and Germany, whose expansionist plans lay in Central Europe, turned down the Nationalists' initial pleas for aid. At the same time, neighboring France, ruled by a similar left-wing coalition, the Front Populaire under the socialist Léon Blum, appeared ready to help its Spanish counterparts and deliver weapons. However, the international reaction soon changed dramatically.

On July 25, the French government reversed its initial stance. Crucial sectors of the economic and diplomatic establishment, the armed forces, and the Catholic Church sympathized with the Spanish rebels. Faced domestically with similar political polarization as Spain, there were fears that direct involvement in that conflict could induce "patriotic France" to emulate its Spanish counterparts. Simultaneously, the Blum cabinet was under huge pressure from Britain, France's vital ally, to avoid arming the republic. Class, upbringing, and vast financial interests in Spain led the British ruling elites to loathe the left-wing republic. Moreover, both Stanley Baldwin's existing administration and, from May 1937, that of Neville Chamberlain were committed to appeasing the fascist dictatorships.

Tragically for the republic, both Adolf Hitler and Benito Mussolini undertook decisive action. On July 25, Hitler made the fateful decision to provide military aid. Two days later, Mussolini also committed himself to the Spanish adventure. They both believed that the reward for what they first assumed would be a secretive and small-scale operation could be huge: a vital ally in a strategically key area.

Fascist aid together with French paralysis altered dramatically what otherwise would have merely been the repression of ill-armed and isolated pockets of resistance. From early August 1936 German and Italian aircraft performed the first major airlift in history, transforming a botched coup into the inexorable and bloody advance northward of the Army of Africa's crack troops. In October as they reached the gates of Madrid, the republic seemed on the verge of defeat. However, the timely intervention of the Soviet Union resulted in prolonging the conflict.

On September 14, the Kremlin abandoned its initial cautious approach. It could not countenance the emergence of another right-wing dictatorship in Europe that, moreover, would seal the encirclement of its potential ally, France. Furthermore, Moscow regarded the successful defense of a Popular Front administration as the bridgehead toward a future understanding with the Allies founded on the common fear of Nazi expansionism. Simultaneously, the Communist International took advantage of the resounding international appeal of a besieged republic, resisting a military insurrection backed by Italy and Germany, to organize the recruitment of volunteers to fight in Spain: the International Brigades. Communist parties were instructed to organize the enrollment and transport of individuals. Their success, attracting volunteers from 54 countries from around the world, was unique in modern European warfare.

The first deliveries of Soviet weapons and the psychological boost provided by the formation of the first International Brigades proved decisive. In November 1936 against all expectations, General Franco's troops were held at the gates of Madrid. Short of manpower and now facing a better-equipped enemy, Nationalist hopes for a swift capture of the capital and the conclusion of the war vanished. In fact, the stalemate in Madrid was a very serious blow for them. With their elite troops bogged down and badly crippled by casualties, the insurgents even contemplated defeat.

The potentially fatal setback for the Nationalists at Madrid was gradually undone by the internationalization of the conflict. As the significant increase in foreign armament and manpower flowing into Spain transformed hitherto relatively small-scale armed clashes into major battles, the flawed implementation of a nonintervention agreement (NIA) sealed the republic's tragic fate.

Despite ideological and strategic reasons and even glaring evidence of Italian assistance to the Nationalists, the French Popular Front's only response in August 1936 was an appeal to the other European powers to subscribe to a NIA in Spain. This policy was regarded by the French government as the best available solution to withstand massive internal and external pressures and keep the administration afloat. At that stage, the French prime minister believed that an effective arms embargo would help the Spanish government. In fact, it embodied France's retreat before British pressure and revealed in full its weakness.

Twenty-seven European nations, including all the major powers, agreed to abide by the NIA. It became a smoke screen behind which, to a greater or lesser extent, Germany, Italy, and the Soviet Union intervened in Spain. The NIC perpetrated one of the most outrageous diplomatic farces ever seen in Europe. Indeed, a committee intended to supervise an arms embargo consistently turned a blind eye to flagrant breaches of the agreement. The Soviet ambassador, Ivan Maisky, called the NIC the ideal Japanese wife: a woman who sees nothing, hears nothing, and says nothing.

In 1937, the initially disorganized Republican forces had become an efficient Popular Army capable of mounting well-planned offensives that again and again surprised the enemy. However, small gains on the battlefields followed by bloody stalemates and painful losses revealed that the sheer material superiority of the Nationalists, courtesy of the NIA, prevailed over the Republicans' courage and even tactical planning. Indeed, the crippling embargo tilted the balance in favor of the insurgents. While General Franco obtained on credit crucial oil deliveries from the main Anglo-American companies and weapons from the dictatorships, the Spanish government had to send its gold reserves abroad to the Soviet Union to finance the war effort.

Eventually as the Mediterranean route became too dangerous, Russian weapons had to be dispatched to French Atlantic ports and then smuggled into Spain across the border. This led to permanent shortages of necessary supplies and overpriced and often obsolete equipment. In terms of manpower, the disparity was also colossal. Some 35,000 genuine volunteers, who had to be armed and trained, joined the International Brigades. Additionally, around 2,100 military personnel came from Russia. In contrast, nearly 80,000 Italians (the Corpo di Truppe Volontarie), 19,000 Germans (the Condor Legion), and 70,000 African mercenaries fought in the Nationalist ranks.

The NIA's inefficiency was the consequence of being an instrument of British diplomacy whose objectives were not those portrayed by official propaganda—that is, the prevention of foreign participation in the war. It was created to ensure the confinement of the Spanish conflict. However, it also formalized the legal anomaly that a democratically elected government was on a par with a military coup, restrained the French from rushing to help its embattled sister Popular Front, eliminated a potential confrontation with the fascist powers, and provided the perfect facade to conceal hostility toward the republic, maintaining a semblance of neutrality for domestic public opinion.

Indeed, in the spring of 1938 it appeared to British statesmen that it was France's reckless behavior, allowing the entry of military equipment to Spain across its border, and not the presence of Italo-German divisions that flouted the NIA's principles. British diplomacy therefore yielded a great success when, after the collapse of the French Popular Front, a new administration, led by Edouard Daladier, closed the border, the only safe channel of arms for the beleaguered republic.

In 1938, the worsening of the international situation offered the republic some glimmer of hope. On March 12, 1938, Germany annexed Austria (the Anschluss) and made plans for the next prize, the Sudetenland (Czechoslovakia). On July 25, the Republican Army launched an ambitious offensive. Its troops crossed the Ebro River, taking the Nationalists by surprise, and established a bridgehead 40 kilometers into enemy territory. The Battle of the Ebro became the longest and bloodiest of the entire war. However, the fate of the conflict was ultimately decided in the European chancelleries.

As it seemed that war was about to break out in Europe, Republican optimism contrasted with Nationalist gloom. On September 27, Franco reassured the Allies of his neutrality in the event of a continental conflict. However, they could not ignore the vast amount of Italo-German weapons and troops in Spain. Nationalist headquarters feared that as soon as hostilities began on the continent, the republic would declare war on Germany and link its fortune to that of the Western democracies. The insurgents would then find themselves geographically isolated from their friends and starved of military supplies, if not at war with the Allies. As it turned out, the international situation could not have evolved more favorably for Franco. Despite the gravity of the crisis, appeasement prevailed, and the Czechs were browbeaten into surrendering the territory the Germans wanted.

On November 16, 1938, the Battle of the Ebro ended. It had taken the Nationalists almost four months to regain the territory lost in July. Despite their material inferiority, the Republicans had not been routed, but morale had plummeted. Hopes of reversing the unfairness embodied by the NIA had been shattered in Munich. While the republic could not replace its massive material losses, the Nationalists, promptly rearmed by Germany, launched a decisive offensive into Catalonia that concluded in February 1939. At that stage, the government still held 30 percent of Spanish territory. However, the republic did not fight until the bitter end but instead imploded when some leading political and military figures revolted in a vain attempt to negotiate a conditional end to the conflict. Clashes between rival Republican forces ruined the possibility of further resistance. The war officially concluded on April 1.

Nationalist propaganda during and after the conflict succeeded in rewriting history. The military coup was described as a glorious crusade, and its leader, General Franco, was hailed as "Caudillo Invicto" (Undefeated Chieftain). In fact, based on material evidence, Franco was no new Napoleon. It had taken Franco 33 months of steadfast struggle to succeed. Without thousands of African mercenaries, constant and massive Italo-German aid, and the NIA's farce, the republic would have won the war.

Francisco J. Romero Salvadó

Further Reading

Alpert, Michael. *A New International History of the Spanish Civil War.* Basingstoke, UK: Palgrave Macmillan, 2004.

Alpert, Michael. *The Republican Army in the Spanish Civil War, 1936–1939.* New York: Cambridge University Press, 2013.

Anderson, James M. *The Spanish Civil War: A History and Reference Guide.* London: Greenwood/ABC-CLIO, 2003.

Beevor, Antony. *The Battle for Spain: The Spanish Civil War, 1936–1939.* London: Weidenfeld and Nicolson, 2006.

Bolloten, Burnett. *The Spanish Revolution: The Left and the Struggle for Power during the Civil War.* Chapel Hill: University of North Carolina Press, 1979.

Bowen, Wayne H., and José Alvarez, eds. *A Military History of Modern Spain.* Westport, CT: Praeger Security International, 2007.

Brenan, Gerald. *The Spanish Labyrinth: An Account of the Social and Political Background of the Civil War.* Cambridge: Cambridge University Press, 1993.

Broué, Pierre, and Émile Témime. *The Revolution and the Civil War in Spain.* Cambridge, MA: MIT Press, 1972.

Buchanan, Tom. *Britain and the Spanish Civil War.* Cambridge: Cambridge University Press, 1997.

Carr, Raymond. *The Spanish Tragedy: The Civil War in Perspective.* London: Phoenix, 2000.

Casanova, Julián. *The Spanish Republic and Civil War.* Cambridge: Cambridge University Press, 2010.

Ealham, Chris, and Michael Richards. *The Splintering of Spain.* New York: Cambridge University Press, 2005.

Esenwein, George R. *The Spanish Civil War: A Modern Tragedy.* New York: Taylor and Francis, 2005.

Graham, Helen. *The Spanish Civil War: A Very Short Introduction.* New York: Oxford University Press, 2005.

Graham, Helen. *The Spanish Republic at War, 1936–1939*. New York: Cambridge University Press, 2002.

Habeck, Mary, Ronald Radosh, and Grigory Sevostianov, eds. *Spain Betrayed: The Soviet Union in the Spanish Civil War*. New Haven, CT: Yale University Press, 2001.

Howson, Gerald. *Arms for Spain: The Untold Story of the Spanish Civil War*. London: John Murray, 1998.

Jackson, Gabriel. *The Cruel Years: The Story of the Spanish Civil War*. New York: John Day, 1974.

Jackson, Gabriel. *The Spanish Republic and the Civil War, 1931–1939*. Princeton, NJ: Princeton University Press, 1965.

Keene, Judith. *Fighting for Franco: International Volunteers in Nationalist Spain during the Spanish Civil War, 1936–1939*. London: Leicester University Press, 2001.

Kowalsky, Daniel. *Stalin and the Spanish Civil War*. New York: Columbia University Press, 2008.

Matthews, Herbert L. *Half of Spain Died: A Reappraisal of the Spanish Civil War*. New York: Scribner, 1973.

Orwell, George. *Homage to Catalonia*. New York: Harcourt, Brace, 1952.

Othen, Christopher. *Franco's International Brigades: Foreign Volunteers and Fascist Dictators in the Spanish Civil War*. London: Reportage, 2008.

Payne, Stanley G. *The Spanish Civil War, the Soviet Union, and Communism*. New Haven, CT: Yale University Press, 2004.

Preston, Paul. *The Coming of the Spanish Civil War*. London: Macmillan, 1973.

Preston, Paul. *The Spanish Civil War: Reaction, Revolution, and Revenge*. New York: Norton, 2006.

Proctor, Raymond L. *Hitler's Luftwaffe in the Spanish Civil War*. Westport, CT: Greenwood, 1983.

Puzzo, Dante Anthony. *Spain and the Great Powers, 1936–1941*. New York: Columbia University Press, 1962.

Radosh, Ronald, Mary Habeck, and Grigory Sevostianov. *Spain Betrayed: the Soviet Union in the Spanish Civil War*. New Haven, CT: Yale University Press, 2001.

Seidman, Michael. *The Victorious Counter-Revolution: The Nationalist Effort in the Spanish Civil War*. Madison: University of Wisconsin Press, 2011.

Taylor, F. Jay. *The United States and the Spanish Civil War, 1936–1939*. New York: Bookman Associates, 1971.

Thomas, Hugh. *The Spanish Civil War: Revised Edition*. New York: Modern Library, 2001.

Toynbee, Philip, ed. *The Distant Drum: Reflections on the Spanish Civil War*. New York: David McKay, 1976.

Westwell, Ian. *Condor Legion: The Wehrmacht's Training Ground*. London: Ian Allan, 2004.

38. Would France and Great Britain Have Been Better Served to Go to War with Germany in 1938?

Historians tend to focus on the September 1938 Munich Agreement, which ceded Czechoslovakia's Sudetenland to Germany, as a great turning point that made World War II virtually inevitable. France and Britain's appeasement of Germany at Munich and the abandonment of their Czech allies only emboldened Adolf Hitler to undertake even more aggressive steps to control vast regions of Europe. Yet there had been clear signs that hinted at Hitler's true intentions as early as 1935 when he began to rearm, a move forbidden by the 1919 Treaty of Versailles. In 1936 Hitler remilitarized the Rhineland, again ignoring previous diplomatic agreements. Neither France nor Britain took any meaningful steps to oppose these moves. Meanwhile, Hitler's rearmament program was accelerating rapidly, while France and Britain took a far more casual approach to military preparedness. In March 1939 when Hitler took control of the rest of Czechoslovakia, against his promises made the year before, it was too late to save the Czechs and largely too late to stop Hitler from triggering a world war.

In the first perspective essay, Marcos A. Vigil asserts that France and Britain were justified in eschewing war in 1938 because it was not possible for them to defeat Germany decisively. The horrors of World War were still fresh in the minds of their citizens, who supported appeasement. He also points out that Britain did not see Czechoslovakia as a vital interest while arguing that France's government was highly unstable. Furthermore, neither country's armed forces were prepared for war in 1938. The second essay, by Dr. Paul J. Springer, makes similar arguments. Neither nation was prepared for war; each needed time to revitalize and augment its armed forces. Furthermore, war in 1938 would have meant handing Germany a one-front war and would have invited an early German invasion of Western Europe, which would have proven disastrous. In the third essay, Dr. Spencer C. Tucker asserts that France and Britain would have indeed been better off waging war with Germany in 1938 because Germany would not have prevailed at that time. The Czechs were already girding for war and in fact had a potent and modern military establishment by 1938. Germany would not have been able to count on Italy or Japan for support, leaving it to fight a war on its own. Tucker also points out that Germany was not prepared for a major war in 1938 and argues that France and Britain repeatedly exaggerated German military strength.

Background Essay

In the Locarno Pacts of October 1925, Germany voluntarily guaranteed its western borders and agreed not to use force to change its existing eastern borders. The pacts also recognized the right of France, which had mutual assistance treaties with both Poland and Czechoslovakia, to go to war to defend these countries. The British government, however, eschewed any guarantees regarding Eastern Europe and maintained that position until 1939.

In October 1933, new German chancellor Adolf Hitler withdrew Germany from the League of Nations and the Geneva Disarmament Conference. In response, in June 1934 the Soviet Union, Poland, and Romania mutually guaranteed their existing frontiers. In July, abetted by Hitler, the Nazis in Austria attempted to seize power there and achieve union with Germany (Anschluss), expressly forbidden by the 1919 peace settlement. Italian dictator Benito Mussolini threatened force against Germany, then largely unarmed, and Hitler backed down.

In January 1935 France and Italy signed a pact to cooperate regarding Central Europe and reaffirming the territorial integrity of Austria. Italy secretly promised to aid France with its air force in the event Germany should try to remilitarize the Rhineland, while France would provide troops to aid Italy should the Germans threaten Austria.

In March Hitler announced that Germany would rearm, increasing its army to more than 500,000 men (the Treaty of Versailles of 1919 limited it to 100,000). The French, British, and Italian governments protested but took no action. In May 1935, however, France and the Soviet Union signed a five-year mutual assistance pact, although they never concluded a military convention to coordinate an actual response to German aggression. That same month the Soviet Union and Czechoslovakia signed a similar pact, but the Soviet Union was not obligated to armed assistance unless France first fulfilled its commitments to Czechoslovakia, pledged in 1924.

Britain took the first step in the appeasement of Germany. In June 1935, without consulting its ally France, Britain signed a naval agreement with Germany that violated the Treaty of Versailles. London agreed to Germany building a surface navy of up to 35 percent the tonnage of the Royal Navy, thus permitting Germany a navy larger than those of either France or Italy. Britain also allowed Germany 45 percent of the Royal Navy in submarines, which had been prohibited. That October Mussolini sent troops into Ethiopia (Abyssinia), conquering it the next spring. The League of Nations condemned Italy but rejected meaningful sanctions.

Noting the general European diplomatic disarray and taking advantage of a bitterly fought French national election, on March 7, 1936, Hitler sent 22,000 lightly armed troops into the Rhineland. Remilitarization of this German territory violated the Treaty of Versailles and the Locarno Pacts. Incredibly, France had no contingency plan, and its intelligence services grossly exaggerated the size and strength of the German forces. Paris appealed to London, but the British made clear that they would not fight for the Rhineland. Had the French acted alone, their forces would have rolled over the Germans, probably bringing down Hitler.

During 1936–1939, civil war raged in Spain. German "volunteers" undoubtedly made possible the Nationalist victory over the Republicans. French plans to aid the Republicans were stymied by a British warning that if this resulted in a general European war, Britain would not honor its pledge to defend France against Germany. Only the Soviet Union, among major powers, assisted the Republicans.

The Spanish Civil War brought together Germany and Italy, which also intervened on the Nationalist side. On October 25, 1936, they formed the Rome-Berlin Axis. Then in March 1938 with Italy's blessing, Hitler sent troops into Austria and added it to Germany.

Czechoslovakia was the next target. Its was largely at German mercy, and Bohemia-Moravia now protruded into the Reich. Some 3.5 million Germans lived in Czechoslovakia and had long complained about discrimination. Czechoslovakia, however, was a democracy; it had an alliance with France and a well-trained and well-armed military. Hitler now pushed the demands of the German minority into outright union with Germany.

In May 1938 during key Czechoslovakian elections, Germany threatened an invasion. Confident in French support, Czechoslovakia mobilized. France and the Soviet Union stated their willingness to go to war, and Hitler backed down. The crisis unnerved Western leaders, however; they now pondered whether Czechoslovakia, formed only in 1919, was worth war. By mid-September Hitler was again threatening invasion. Should that occur, France would have to decide whether to honor its pledge to defend Czechoslovakia. If it did so, this would bring on a general European war.

In this critical situation British prime minister Neville Chamberlain flew to Germany to meet with Hitler. Hitler informed him that the Sudeten Germans must be permitted to unite with Germany and that he would risk war to accomplish this. The British and French then decided to force self-determination on Prague.

The British and French decision to desert Czechoslovakia resulted from many factors. Both countries dreaded another general war, including the threat of air attacks against London and Paris. Britain had begun to rebuild the Royal Air Force only in 1937, and the Germans duped the French as to their actual air strength. The Western Allies also discounted Soviet assistance; its military was still recovering from Soviet leader Joseph Stalin's purges. In France and especially in Britain, there were those who hoped to encourage Hitler to move against Russia so that communism and fascism might destroy one another.

Chamberlain desperately wanted to avoid war. A businessman before entering politics, he believed in the sanctity of contracts and, despite evidence to the contrary, could not accept that the leader of Germany was a blackmailer and a liar. But the West had in 1919 championed "self-determination of peoples," and by this Germany had a right to all it had hitherto demanded. The transfer of the Sudetenland to the Reich did not seem too high a price for a satisfied Germany and a peaceful Europe. Finally, there were Hitler's statements that once his demands upon Czechoslovakia had been satisfied, he would have no further territorial ambitions in Europe.

Under heavy British and French pressure, on September 21, 1938, Czechoslovakia accepted the Anglo-French proposals. Hitler then upped the ante, demanding immediate occupation with everything left in place. This brought the most serious international crisis in Europe since 1918. Prague said that Hitler's demands were unacceptable, as they would not allow Czechoslovakia time to organize its new defenses. London and Paris agreed and decided not to pressure Prague. A general European war appeared inevitable.

Hitler then reluctantly agreed to a conference at Munich, and Chamberlain, French premier Edouard Daladier, and Mussolini traveled there to meet with Hitler on September 29. The Soviets were not invited, and Czechoslovakia was not officially represented. The agreement of September 30 gave Hitler everything he

The September 1938 Munich Conference. Left to right: British prime minister Neville Chamberlain, French premier Edouard Daladier, German chancellor Adolf Hitler, Italian premier Benito Mussolini, and Italian foreign minister Count Galeazzo Ciano. (Photo12/UIG via Getty Images)

demanded, and on October 1 German troops marched across the frontier. Poland and Hungary also demanded and received Czechoslovakian territory that contained their national minorities. The Munich Agreement effectively ended the French security system, its guarantees apparently worthless. Stalin saw in Munich an effort by the Western powers to encourage Germany to move east.

In March 1939, his pledges to the contrary, Hitler forced Bohemia and Moravia to become German protectorates, while Slovakia and Ruthenia became independent. These actions, however, proved that Hitler's demands were not limited to Germans.

British leaders were at last convinced that they could not trust Hitler. With Poland being Germany's next target, Britain and France extended to Poland a formal guarantee to defend it against a German attack. Too late, Britain reversed its East European policy and agreed to do what the French had sought in the 1920s.

Britain and France now sought an alliance with the Soviet Union. Instead, on August 23, 1939, Stalin signed a nonaggression pact with Germany, making it possible for Hitler to invade Poland on September 1. Britain and France declared war two days later, beginning World War II.

Spencer C. Tucker

Perspective Essay 1. Allied Resolve Was Lacking in 1938

When considering the political and military realities of 1938, the decision to delay conflict was well founded because of the lack of public support in Britain and France for war and because it was not possible for those countries to have achieved a decisive victory.

In March 1938, Germany annexed Austria into the Third Reich. Soon thereafter, German leader Adolf Hitler made territorial demands on Czechoslovakia in regard to the Sudetenland, where approximately 3 million people of German origin lived. Hitler demanded that the German areas in Czechoslovakia be united with their homeland. The Czechoslovakian government initially rejected Hitler's demands and relied on military alliances that the Czechs had forged with France and Russia to bolster their defense. However, with Hitler threatening war, the leaders of Great Britain and France agreed in the Munich Conference to surrender those portions of Czech territory that were mainly inhabited by ethnic Germans. Czechoslovakia was not a signatory to the agreement.

Setting aside the advantages of hindsight, there are several political and military realities of 1938 that we should consider to explain why delaying conflict with

Germany was necessary. The first was that after the vast bloodbath of the "war to end all wars," the British and French people opposed involvement in another major conflict while the carnage of World War I was still fresh (Britain and France together had suffered nearly 8 million dead or wounded). There was widespread public support for the policy of appeasement as indicated by a poll taken after the Munich Agreement, which determined that 57 percent of the respondents were satisfied with British prime minister Neville Chamberlain's leadership, while only 33 percent were dissatisfied (10 percent had no opinion).

At the time many, including Chamberlain, believed that Hitler was a leader who could be reasoned with. Chamberlain's actions thus far were seen by many people as efforts to unify ethnic Germans in one nation. It was thought that many people in Austria and in the Sudetenland wanted to be a part of the German nation and that they should have the right of self-determination. It was difficult to justify war over areas where many people actually wanted to be a part of Germany. Hence, the defense of Czechoslovakia was not seen as a vital national interest of Britain. A decision by the governments of Britain and France to go to war over Czechoslovakia would likely have ended up in a vote of no confidence and the dissolution of those governments. The French government was particularly unstable (between 1930 and 1940 there were no less than 24 different French governments). Barring any drastic change in the situation (such as a German invasion of Poland), it was not politically feasible for the governments of Britain and France to go to war in September 1938.

Second, the armed forces of Britain and France were not ready for a major conflict. For example, the Royal Air Force had only five squadrons of modern fighters (about 100 Hawker Hurricanes, the mainstay of the Battle of Britain), and deliveries of the vaunted Spitfire had just begun. It is likely that these aircraft would have been restricted to home defense, while older, less capable fighters were forward deployed to France. Many of these older aircraft were biplanes with fixed undercarriages, poor firepower, and a relatively slow speed.

There was great concern in Britain about the ability of German aircraft to attack British cities. The early warning radar network, so crucial in the Battle of Britain, was not yet fully developed. The destruction of the Spanish town of Guernica by the German Air Force during the Spanish Civil War had produced dire predictions about the losses Britain might suffer in an air war. The British Air Staff was predicting civilian casualties from air attacks on London of upwards of 20,000 in the first day and 150,000 in the first week.

As for the British Army, it was primarily employed in policing the British Empire and would need to be greatly expanded for war (conscription had not yet been introduced). In 1938, Britain would only have been able to dispatch 2 divisions to France. In contrast, by May 1940 the British had 10 divisions in France.

Regarding the French, they maintained a defensive strategy sparing of manpower and based on World War I positional warfare. Their Maginot Line was the prime example of this. Although the French had a large army, it was a short-service conscript force that by necessity was in constant training and was not offensively oriented.

The French Air Force was large, but in September 1938 some 80 percent of its 1,350 aircraft were considered obsolete. Due to the poor condition of their forces and their reliance on a defensive strategy, there was little Britain or France could have done to stop a German invasion of Czechoslovakia.

Supporting the conclusion of a lack of Allied offensive action is the so-called Phony War, or Sitzkrieg, of September 1939, when the French and British militaries largely remained in place while the German armed forces overran Poland. Given this, it is likely that with a year less to prepare for war Britain and France would have put forth little offensive action on the Western Front in support of the Czechs. At most, the French would have tied down a few German divisions on the border with France while the British deployed what meager forces they had across the English Channel. And with the poor state of the U.S. armed forces and with U.S. isolationist policies, little help could be expected from America.

Germany's armed forces were perceived to be the most modern and powerful in Europe. Germany had been rearming since 1933 and was turning out modern combat aircraft and refitting its army with new tanks. The German propaganda machine benefited from the performance of the German Air Force contingent, known as the Condor Legion, in the Spanish Civil War. Visitors to Germany such as American aviator Charles Lindbergh were given tours of major aircraft manufacturers and shown their latest aircraft. After his second visit to Germany, Lindbergh concluded that the Luftwaffe was "ten times superior to that of Russia, France, and Great Britain." Lindberg was convinced that given the strength of Germany's air force, it could not be defeated by the Western democracies. His opinion carried great weight. Similarly, French Air Force chief of staff General Joseph Vuillemin received a similar tour of German Air Force facilities and aircraft just prior to the Munich Conference and concluded that the French Air Force would be swept from the skies by the Luftwaffe in only two weeks. With such testimonials, it is easy to understand why the British and French leaders wanted more time to modernize their forces.

Hindsight is 20-20. The decision of British and French leaders to delay war was based on sound reasoning at the time. Their choice to avoid war in 1938 was based on the known weakness of their armed forces versus the perceived strength of that of the Germans as well as the strong antiwar sentiment of their populations. There was a lack of will among the people and a lack of capability in the Allied militaries of 1938, and Hitler was still perceived to be a leader who could be reasoned with. In such a situation, any attempt to go to war in 1938 would have been political suicide for the governments of Britain and France, and they would have gained nothing. Not until the German takeover of all of Czechoslovakia in March 1939 and the invasion of Poland on September 1 of that year would the people of France and Britain finally realize the danger that Hitler posed to Europe and only then acquiesce to yet another major war on the continent and beyond.

Marcos A. Vigil

Perspective Essay 2. Britain and France Were Not Prepared for War in 1938

World War II was by far the deadliest and most destructive conflict in human history. As such, the decisions of virtually every leader have been subjected to analysis and second-guessing whether they involved strategic effects or tactical maneuvers. One of the most persistent counterfactual arguments has been the idea that Adolf Hitler and Nazi Germany could have been stopped from triggering a global conflict. This would require that the Western powers refuse to engage in appeasement and instead stand up to the German dictator, including the use of force, to stop his ambitions. This argument offers a panacea to historical apologists who ardently believe that a firm denial of German demands in 1938 would have saved tens of millions of lives. Unfortunately, it ignores the political, diplomatic, and military realities of that pivotal year, preferring to embrace the myth of an illusory missed opportunity that never existed.

By 1938 Hitler had served ample notice of his territorial ambitions, beginning with the publication of his autobiographical account *Mein Kampf* (My Struggle) in 1925, which essentially laid out his entire vision for the short-term future of Germany. On October 19, 1933, he withdrew Germany from the League of Nations, and in 1936 he ordered German troops to remilitarize the Rhineland. Both actions triggered protests in international forums but no direct action to halt the aggressive moves. Likewise, the Western powers did next to nothing as German forces intervened in the Spanish Civil War, beginning in 1936. In 1938 Hitler seized control of Austria, which was then united with Germany. Still, the international community did nothing. Politically, Hitler had managed to significantly improve his military position without firing a shot, and he was nowhere near the limits of his territorial goals.

Despite their victory in World War I, Britain and France hardly emerged from that conflict as proud conquerors. Rather, they acted more like lucky survivors and took major steps to ensure that no repeat conflict would occur. For the British this included naval limitations treaties, curtailing their most significant military advantage, to prevent a renewed naval arms race. The British also constructed a chain of air defense radar installations to provide advanced warning of an airborne attack that might otherwise completely bypass the Royal Navy. While useful, these stations remained inherently defensive, further underscoring the British unwillingness to engage in another ruinous fight on the continent. For the French, preparedness in the interwar period entailed a defensive mind-set that triggered the construction of an enormous chain of massive fortifications, the Maginot Line, along the German frontier. The French assumed that these positions would prevent any German attack into Alsace and Lorraine. These fortifications offered little in the way of power projection capabilities, and the rest of the French military budget shrank to account for their construction. Both the British and the French had built up their defenses in the pursuit of security but in return could do little to influence a war in Central or Eastern Europe.

German planners certainly understood the reasons for German defeat in World War I, and they had no intention of repeating the same mistakes. The most important consideration for the German military was to avoid a two-front war of attrition. To prevent a repeat reoccurrence, Hitler sought first to secure the German flanks and then to ensure through diplomacy that Germany would not fight on multiple fronts. Germany also secured agreements with the Soviet Union to allow it facilities for the testing of military equipment in direct contravention of the Treaty of Versailles. To the south, Germany secured its flank by an alliance with Italy in 1936.

In the summer of 1938 Hitler sought to solve the problem created by the geography of Czechoslovakia, which seemed like a dagger pointed at the heart of Germany. The nation was created from the remnants of the Austrian Empire in the aftermath of World War I and included a significant number of ethnic Germans concentrated along the border with Germany. Hitler used alleged mistreatment of these German citizens of Czechoslovakia to demand the cession of the so-called Sudetenland. This provoked the greatest international crisis since World War I, as the British and French threatened to intervene to guarantee Czech territorial integrity.

Although Czechoslovakia possessed a well-trained army and strong border fortifications, any unilateral conflict with Germany would certainly lead to defeat. There was simply no possibility of the Czechs winning such a conflict, and neither the British nor the French possessed the capability to save them. They thus turned to diplomacy in the hopes of negotiating a solution that would forestall a conflict. After tense talks in Munich between Hitler, British prime minister Neville Chamberlain, French prime minister Edouard Daladier, and Italian prime minister Benito Mussolini, Hitler emerged with all he wanted. Although Chamberlain's announcement that there would be "peace in our time" proved woefully incorrect, there was nothing the Western allies could have done to save Czechoslovakia in 1938.

The Munich Agreement served as a major wake-up call for the British and French governments. Both increased their military budgets and enhanced training, construction of military equipment, and the development of modern military doctrine and operational plans. Even with such advanced warning, however, they still proved incapable of saving Poland from a German invasion in September 1939. Eight months later German forces overran France in six weeks, in the process driving the 400,000-member British Expeditionary Force from the continent in complete disarray.

Had Britain and France declared war on Germany in 1938, they would have faced a well-prepared enemy that had rearmed itself and planned for a one-front war. Such an action would have tipped their hand to no advantage and likely provoked an earlier German invasion of the West, almost certainly with the same results. Had Germany turned west in 1938, the Soviets no doubt would have remained aloof, leaving the British and French to be defeated in detail by a far better prepared and more determined and more numerous foe.

Paul J. Springer

Perspective Essay 3. The Year 1938 Was a Missed Opportunity

Britain and France would have been far better served to have gone to war in September 1938 than a year later. The Munich Conference of September 30, 1938, represented not only a failure of Allied resolve but also a failure of Allied military intelligence. Fortified by their own reluctance to fight for Czechoslovakia, the leaders of both countries believed estimates by their intelligence services that Germany would have an easy time of conquering Czechoslovakia and that war should therefore be postponed. There was simply no way that Germany could have prevailed in a world war commencing in 1938, but Adolf Hitler wanted war and fully intended to invade Czechoslovakia if the West did not give him what he wanted.

Well aware of the danger not only from Germany but also other potentially hostile neighbors, Czechoslovakia had embraced preparedness. It had a well-trained 400,000-man army, the important Skoda munitions complex at Pilsen, and strong fortifications along the western border facing Germany, although those facing Austria, now part of Germany, were only in progress. Unfortunately for the Czechs, these areas were in the Sudetenland, the area where the minority German population being wooed by Hitler was concentrated. Hitler talked of arming the Sudeten Germans, but what impact this might have had in actual war with Germany is impossible to assess.

Germany entered into the Czechoslovakian venture alone, its actions uncoordinated with its Italian and Japanese allies. Italy certainly could not be counted on. Italian leader Benito Mussolini rejected going to war even in September 1939 and cast his lot with Hitler only in June 1940, with British forces driven from the continent and France on the brink of surrender. Japan delayed joining World War II until December 1941. Nor were German actions coordinated with the would-be Czechoslovakia rivals Hungary and Poland.

Germany was far from ready for war in 1938. Its latest military venture, the "invasion" of Austria in March, revealed major problems. The French and British simply exaggerated German strength. The French intelligence service, the Deuxième Bureaux, estimated that Germany had 90 active divisions when in fact it had just 48 divisions, with only three 3 panzer and 4 motorized infantry divisions. These new types of divisions that would wreak such havoc in the blitzkrieg operations against Poland a year later and France in 1940 were still in formation. The army was short of equipment and lacked training. Support services were weak and depended largely on reservists. The so-called West Wall ordered by Hitler, to be built along the frontier with France following the May 1938 crisis, was also far from ready.

In late September 1938, the German Air Force possessed 3,037 first-line aircraft, including transports, but had almost no reserve. Half of the German planes were earmarked for use in Czechoslovakia, leaving the rest too thinly stretched to counter any serious offensive by the French air force (1,454 first-line aircraft with 730 in reserve) and Royal Air Force (1,606 first-line aircraft with 412 in reserve). Czechoslovakia also added another 1,600 aircraft. Other problems for the Luftwaffe were poor serviceability and a shortage of bombs.

The French were the particular target of German deception. In August 1938, chief of staff of the French Air Force General Joseph Vuillemin received a tour of Luftwaffe facilities. Planes were flown from one field to another ahead of his arrival to give the illusion of greater numbers. He was also shown the sleek new He-100, never placed in production, and was told that two assembly lines were already producing it, with a third about to open. In fact, Germany was producing aircraft at the rate of only 300 a month. Vuillemin provided the French government with a gloomy assessment, predicting that "should war break out as you expect late in September, there won't be a single French plane left within a fortnight." The Germans knew about their success through their wiretaps of the French embassy. Certainly both the British and French political leaders feared destruction of their capitals by the much-touted Luftwaffe.

The German Navy was completely inadequate and relatively far weaker than it would be in September 1939. Hitler had informed its commander, Admiral Erich Raeder, not to expect war before 1944, and Raeder was busy building a balanced fleet, which was totally inadequate for world war. Germany was especially deficient in submarines, with just 36, and only 12 of these were suitable for Atlantic operations.

There was also considerable resistance to Hitler's plan for war from within Germany. During the May and September crises there was a noticeable lack of support from among the German public. A military parade down the Wilhelmstrasse in Berlin on September 27 had been greeted with sullen indifference. The German generals knew the true state of their nation's readiness, and many were convinced that Hitler was leading the nation to destruction.

Greatly alarmed at the direction of events, during August and early September 1938 several German emissaries traveled to London with messages from the opposition, including head of the Abwehr (German military intelligence) Admiral Wilhelm Canaris and chief of the General Staff General Ludwig Beck. They warned London of Hitler's intentions and urged a strong British stand. Beck even pledged, prior to his resignation in mid-August, that if Britain would agree to fight for Czechoslovakia, he would stage a putsch to unseat Hitler. Nothing came of these warnings, as London was firmly committed to appeasement.

The Allies were far stronger and better placed than Germany. British troops would have had to be assembled and transported to the continent, but the French had 65 active divisions and 35 in reserve. Only 8 German divisions were in the west facing France, and 3 divisions were on the Polish frontier because the Germans did not trust Polish intentions. This left 37 divisions for the invasion of Czechoslovakia, but these would encounter approximately 30 Czechoslovakian divisions, not counting reserves.

Thus, the French and Czechoslovaks would have an advantage of two to one in ground strength, and given time this would only grow with the addition of the British Army. France had more tanks than Germany, and these were generally better armored and more heavily gunned. France also had many more artillery pieces than Germany.

An additional factor was the German economy, which was badly strained by Hitler's massive rearmament program, the construction of the West Wall, and the mobilization of hundreds of thousands of men for the army. Germany was also deficient in stocks of key raw materials, especially petroleum and rubber. Germany possessed petroleum reserves sufficient for only four months of war. A British naval blockade would have been especially damaging, unlike September 1939 when Germany could count on the Soviet Union.

This discussion largely discounts British strength, apart from the Royal Air Force, as the British rearmament program had begun only the year before. Although Germany had twice as many long-range bombers as Britain and France combined (1,580 to 824), there was rough parity in fighter aircraft (1,000 versus 962 for Britain and France combined), and Royal Air Force pilots were better trained.

In addition to the Czechoslovakian, French, and British militaries, there was also the pledge of Soviet involvement. Soviet leader Joseph Stalin understood Hitler's oft-stated determination to secure lebensraum (living space) "in the East." Although no military convention had been concluded to go with the 1935 pact, the Soviet Union was obligated to go to war if Germany attacked and France honored its pledge to defend Czechoslovakia. Indeed, in the May 1938 crisis the Soviet Union had stated its willingness to go to war. Undoubtedly, this was a factor in Hitler backing down. Western leaders, however, foolishly discounted the Soviet Union, the military of which was still reeling from Stalin's costly purges that had consumed the vast bulk of its leadership.

Poland might also have come in on the Allied side. Polish foreign minister Jósef Beck informed the British that his government might modify its policy and would, in any case, never side with Germany. Poland had a mutual assistance treaty with

France, and Poland's leaders certainly knew that they would be the next country to fall victim to Hitler's demands. There were already German rumblings about the Polish Corridor and the return of Gdansk (Danzig) and the alleged mistreatment by the Poles of their German minority. But even without the Soviet Union and Poland, the three nations of Britain, France, and Czechoslovakia were far stronger militarily than was Germany.

Later those responsible for the Munich debacle advanced the argument that it bought a year for the Western democracies to rearm. British prime minister Winston Churchill dismissed this. While he noted in *The Gathering Storm* that British fighter squadrons equipped with modern aircraft rose from only 5 in September 1938 to 26 by July 1939, he also stated that "The year's breathing space said to be 'gained' by Munich left Britain and France in a much worse position compared to Hitler's Germany than they had been at the Munich crisis."

Indeed, it was the German military that benefited most from the Munich Agreement and its aftermath in March 1939, when Hitler took the Czech regions of Bohemia and Moravia and 35 highly trained and well-equipped Czech divisions disappeared from the anti-Germany order of battle. Hitler also eliminated what he had referred to as "that damned airfield," while the output of the Skoda arms complex now supplied the Reich's legions. The Wehrmacht absorbed 1,582 aircraft, 2,000 artillery pieces, and sufficient equipment to arm 20 divisions. The Germans secured nearly a third of the tanks they deployed against France and the Low Countries in May 1940. Indeed, between August 1938 and September 1939 Skoda produced nearly as many arms as all British arms factories combined. Any increase in armaments that Britain and France had achieved was thus more than counterbalanced by German gains in Czechoslovakia. The Western giveaway at Munich also meant the effective end of resistance to Hitler in Germany. The German generals were staggered by what had transpired, and the opposition to Hitler simply evaporated.

Although this is impossible to predict with certainty, it seems reasonable to conclude based on what we know of Czechoslovakian military plans, coupled with difficult terrain and Czech defenses, that these would have prevented a quick German victory. Generally poor weather in October would also have limited the Luftwaffe, the pilots of which lacked instrument training. The Czech Air Force had already been dispersed on the German mobilization to secondary fields, preventing the destruction of a large part of it on the ground, as would occur in Poland and the Soviet Union at the start of the German invasions.

If Hitler had indeed invaded Czechoslovakia, the German generals might have overthrown him. If this had not happened and Britain and France had chosen not to fight, Germany would have conquered Czechoslovakia but not with the speed or low cost that Hitler envisioned. It probably would have taken a month or two and the price would have been costly, involving destruction of the Czechoslovakian military stocks and also greatly diminishing those of the invader. Taking

Czechoslovakia would certainly not have alleviated Germany's situation as far as raw materials was concerned, forcing it either to turn next to Romania (for petroleum), probably bringing in the Soviet Union, or toward the Low Countries and France, but a campaign here would have been very different than that of 1940.

By every indicator, Britain and France would have been far better served militarily to have fought Germany in September 1938 rather than a year later. War in 1938 would have certainly brought a German defeat and in far shorter and much less bloody fashion than in 1939–1945.

Spencer C. Tucker

Further Reading

Boyce, Robert, ed. *French Foreign and Defense Policy, 1918–1940: The Decline and Fall of a Great Power.* New York: Routledge, 1998.

Buckley, John. *Air Power in the Age of Total War.* Bloomington: Indiana University Press, 1999.

Churchill, Winston. *The Gathering Storm.* Boston: Houghton Mifflin, 1948.

Cooper, Matthew. *The German Army, 1933–1945.* Chelsea, MI: Scarborough House, 1990.

Deutsch, Harold C. *The Conspiracy against Hitler in the Twilight War.* Minneapolis: University of Minnesota Press, 1968.

Dutton, David. *Neville Chamberlain.* London: Arnold, 2001.

Eubank, Keith. *Munich.* Norman: University of Oklahoma Press, 1963.

Faber, David. *Munich, 1938: Appeasement and World War II.* New York: Simon and Schuster, 2009.

Goldstein, Rick, and Igor Lukes, eds. *The Munich Crisis, 1938: Prelude to World War II.* New York: Frank Cass, 2005.

Gole, Henry G. *Exposing the Third Reich: Colonel Truman Smith in Hitler's Germany.* Lexington: University Press of Kentucky, 2013.

Hucker, Daniel. *Public Opinion and the End of Appeasement in Britain and France.* Cornwall, UK: TJ International, 2011.

Irving, David. *Göring: A Biography.* New York: William Morrow, 1989.

Irving, David. *The War Path: Hitler's Germany, 1933–1939.* New York: Viking, 1978.

Killen, John. *A History of the Luftwaffe.* Garden City, NY: Doubleday, 1968.

Lorell, Mark A. "The Politics of Economic Debate: Anglo-American Perceptions of Germany's Preparedness for War, 1937–1939." PhD dissertation, University of Washington, 1977.

Murray, Williamson. *The Change in the European Balance of Power, 1938–1939: The Road to Ruin.* Princeton, NJ: Princeton University Press, 1984.

Murray, Williamson. "The War of 1938: Chamberlain Fails to Sway Hitler." In *What If?*, Vol. 2, *Eminent Historians Imagine What Might Have Been,* edited by Robert Cowley, 655–680. New York: Berkley Books, 2001.

Neville, Peter. *Hitler and Appeasement: The British Attempt to Prevent the Second World War.* London: Hambledon Continuum, 2006.

Noguères, Henri. *Munich, "Peace for our Time."* Translated by Patrick O'Brian. New York: McGraw-Hill, 1965.

Rich, Norman. *Hitler's War Aims: Ideology, the Nazi State, and the Course of Expansion.* New York: Norton, 1973.

Shirer, William L. *Berlin Diary.* New York: Knopf, 1941.

Shirer, William L. *The Rise and Fall of the Third Reich: A History of Nazi Germany.* New York: Simon and Schuster, 1960.

Smetana, Vit. *In the Shadow of Munich: British Policy towards Czechoslovakia from 1938 to 1942.* Prague: Charles University in Prague, 2008.

Smith, Gene. *The Dark Summer: An Intimate History of the Events That led to World War II.* New York: Macmillan, 1987.

Taylor, Telford. *Munich: The Price of Peace.* Garden City, NY: Doubleday, 1979.

Thompson, Lawrence. *The Greatest Treason: The Untold Story of Munich.* New York: William Morrow, 1968.

Wark, Wesley K. *The Ultimate Enemy: British Intelligence and Nazi Germany, 1933–1939.* Ithaca, NY: Cornell University Press, 1985.

Watt, Donald Cameron. *How War Came: The Immediate Origins of the Second World War, 1938–1939.* New York: Pantheon Books, 1989.

Weinberg, Gerhard L. *Germany, Hitler, and World War Two: Essays in Modern German and World History.* Cambridge: Cambridge University Press, 1995.

Weinberg, Gerhard L. *A World at Arms: A Global History of World War II.* New York: Cambridge University Press, 1994.

Whaley, Barton. *Covert German Rearmament, 1919–1939: Deception and Misrepresentation.* Frederick, MD: University Publications of America, 1984.

39. What Were the Key Factors That Led to the Japanese Decision to Attack Pearl Harbor?

A defining moment of World War II, Japan's December 7, 1941, bombing of Pearl Harbor served as the primary and immediate catalyst for U.S. entry into the conflict, which had been raging officially since September 1939. After the United States declared war on Japan on December 8, on December 11 Germany and Italy, both allies of Japan, declared war on the United States. The Americans then declared war on Germany and Italy later that same day, ensuring American involvement in both the Pacific and European theaters. By December 1941 Japan had been at war with China for quite some time, and U.S.-Japanese relations were at a nadir. With the major European powers already engaged in conflict in Europe, Japan, stung by America's recent oil embargo, decided to take advantage of the situation and further expand its Asiatic hegemony. From the perspective of the American public, the Pearl Harbor attack seemed irrational and impossible to comprehend. Nevertheless, both the Japanese government and its population understood the attack in terms they considered logical and necessary. Those terms, however, continue to be debated by historians to this very day.

Dr. Jessica Chapman, in the first perspective essay, asserts that Japan's propaganda machine in many ways had prepared the Japanese public for the assault on the United States and the continued war against China by creating an image of Japanese racial and moral superiority in the face of a decadent West and an inferior Asian mainland. As a consequence, the Japanese public's initial reaction to the Pearl Harbor bombing was one of gratification rather than shock and surprise. Dr. Eric Han argues that the Pearl Harbor assault stemmed from Japan's desire to continue its path of imperial ascendancy and to continue the Sino-Japanese War that had begun in 1937. This effort would allow the nation to assert its authority across Asia, all in an attempt to stem Western imperial influence. The attack on Pearl Harbor, then, became a symbol of Japan's desire to end U.S. power in the Pacific and increase Japanese authority over China (and Asia at large). Dr. Barbara A. Gannon maintains that the Japanese attack on Pearl Harbor was the direct result of two separate and distinct decisions: the Japanese decision that an attack on the United States was essential to national security and the decision of Japanese naval officers that their wartime operational strategy must include a surprise attack on the U.S. Pacific fleet in Hawaii. She concludes that although Japanese strategy had relied on the United States accepting the Japanese Pacific empire as a fait accompli, an operational strategy that was premised on a surprise attack on U.S. soil made such acquiescence impossible because the attack prompted the United States to settle for nothing less than the destruction of the Japanese Empire.

Background Essay

The December 7, 1941, Japanese attack on the U.S. Pacific Fleet base at Pearl Harbor in the Hawaiian Islands brought the United States into World War II and to warfare between forces of the United States, Britain, and the Netherlands with Japan in the Pacific Ocean area. Japan was already at war with China.

By early 1941, tensions between Japan and the United States had reached the breaking point. Japan's invasion of China beginning in 1937 and its occupation of French Indochina in 1940 and 1941 had led President Franklin D. Roosevelt to embargo scrap metal and oil and to freeze Japanese assets in the United States. The Japanese particularly resented the embargo on oil, which their government characterized as "an unfriendly act." Japan had no oil of its own and had limited stockpiles. Without oil, the Japanese would have to withdraw from China.

With the British, French, and Dutch locked in war with Germany in Europe, an army-dominated government in Tokyo sought to take advantage of the weakness of these countries in Asia to push its own plans to secure hegemony and resources. Japan was determined to seize this opportunity, even if that meant war with the United States. U.S. president Franklin D. Roosevelt's administration misread Tokyo's resolve, however. The administration believed that it could force Japan to back down. As it turned out, it was a case of an unstoppable force and an immovable object.

Both sides visualized the same scenario for a war in the Pacific. The Japanese would seize U.S. and European possessions in the Far East, forcing the U.S. Navy to fight its way across the Pacific to relieve them. Somewhere in the Far East, a great naval battle would occur to decide Pacific hegemony.

In March 1940, commander of the Combined Fleet Admiral Yamamoto Isoroku scrapped the original Japanese war plan—which called for using submarines and cruisers and destroyers with the Long Lance torpedo and savaging the U.S. battle fleet as it worked its way west—in favor of a preemptive strike against the U.S. fleet, which in May 1940 Roosevelt had shifted from San Diego to Pearl Harbor on the island of Oahu in an effort to deter Japan. Yamamoto believed that such a preemptive strike, destroying the U.S. carriers and battleships, would buy time for Japan to establish its defensive ring. Yamamoto also misread American psychology in believing that such an attack might demoralize the American people and force Washington to negotiate a settlement that would give Japan hegemony in the western Pacific.

With both sides edging toward war, U.S. Pacific Fleet commander Admiral Husband E. Kimmel and U.S. Army lieutenant general Walter C. Short made their dispositions for the defense of Oahu. Both men requested additional resources from Washington, but the United States was only then rearming, and what little assistance was available was spread between Hawaii and the U.S. possession of the Philippines.

The Japanese meanwhile trained extensively for the Pearl Harbor strike. They also fitted their torpedoes with wooden fins so they could be dropped from torpedo-bombers in the shallow waters of Pearl Harbor, and they planned to use large bombs from high-flying level-flight aircraft as well as from dive-bombers. No deck armor would be able to withstand these.

Following the expiration of its secret self-imposed deadline for securing an agreement with the United States, Tokyo ordered the attack to proceed. On November 16, 1941, Japanese submarines departed for Pearl Harbor, and 10 days later the First Air Fleet, commanded by Vice Admiral Nagumo Chūichi, sortied. This attack force was centered on six aircraft carriers with 423 aircraft, 360 of which were to participate in the attack. Accompanying the carriers were 2 battleships, 2 heavy cruisers, 2 light cruisers, 11 destroyers, 35 submarines, and 9 oilers.

Surprise was essential if the attack was to be successful. The Japanese maintained radio silence, and Washington knew only that the fleet had sailed. A war warning had been issued to military commanders in the Pacific, but there was considerable complacency, as few American leaders thought the Japanese would dare attack Pearl Harbor.

Nagumo planned to approach from the northwest, move in as close as possible before launching his aircraft, and then recover them farther out, forcing any U.S. air reaction force to fly two long legs. Nagumo ordered the planes to launch beginning at 6:00 a.m. at a point about 275 miles north of Pearl Harbor.

The attack took the Americans by surprise, and only a few aircraft were able to get airborne and contest the Japanese. In only some 140 minutes, the Japanese sent to the

Aftermath of the Japanese attack on Pearl Harbor, December 7, 1941. The battleship *West Virginia* is in the background. (Library of Congress)

bottom four of the eight battleships of the U.S. Pacific Fleet. The *Arizona* and *Oklahoma* were both a total loss. Four other battleships were damaged and out of service. One minecraft and three auxiliaries were also sunk but subsequently raised and returned to service. Eight other ships, including three cruisers and three destroyers, were also damaged. A total of 188 U.S. army and naval aircraft were destroyed, and 159 were damaged. The attack killed 2,403 Americans, including 68 civilians, and there were 1,178 military and civilian wounded. The attack cost the Japanese only 29 aircraft that failed to regain the carriers and were lost to all causes. An additional 111 planes were damaged, of which 20 were later written off. Only 64 personnel were killed, and 1 was captured.

The chief drawbacks in the attack from the Japanese point of view were that the three U.S. Pacific Fleet carriers were absent at the time of the attack. All of the battleships, with the exception of the *Arizona* and *Oklahoma,* were also repaired and returned to service, and the aircraft losses were soon replaced.

The Japanese also failed to hit the oil tank storage areas, without which the fleet could not remain at Pearl. Nor had they targeted the dockyard repair facilities. Nagumo had won a smashing victory but was unwilling to risk his ships to remain longer in the area for a second strike. The task force recovered its aircraft and departed.

Yamamoto's preemptive strike was a brilliant tactical success. The Japanese could now carry out their plans in the South Pacific without fear of significant U.S. naval intervention. However, the Pearl Harbor attack, coming as it did without formal declaration of war, outraged the American people and united them solidly behind war with Japan. The fighting in the Pacific theater of World War II was long and costly, but Japan was defeated.

Spencer C. Tucker and T. Jason Soderstrum

Perspective Essay 1. Japan Determined to Dominate Asia

In the 1850s encroachments by the great powers compelled Japan to open its doors to the world, and when it responded by modernizing, militarizing, and entering the imperial race the Western powers came back with what Japanese leaders perceived to be an array of racially motivated snubs, slights, and double standards. At the same time, under the pretext of Pan-Asian kinship and resistance to Western imperialism, the Japanese sought domination over other Asians, whom they regarded as racially inferior. The result was a uniquely racist, xenophobic ideology that paved the way for Japan's imperial expansion, beginning with China in 1894.

The wars that followed would bring Tokyo increasingly into conflict and competition for resources with the Western powers until it became clear in 1941 that the Japanese Army would either have to withdraw from territory it occupied in China and Indochina or go to war with the United States. By that time, Japanese militarists had seized control of government and had rallied public support behind Japan's imperialist policies by claiming that the empire was essential to Japanese prosperity, security, and even national survival. They capitalized on effective propaganda that depicted Japan as the divinely sanctioned leader of Asia's fight against imperialism, in the process building popular support for the decision to attack Pearl Harbor on December 7, 1941.

Japan's unique response to Western imperialism spared it from being carved up into spheres of influence and exploited, as had occurred in China. The arrival of Commodore Matthew Perry and the Convention of Konagawa (Japan-U.S. Treaty of Amity and Friendship) in 1854 forced Japan to end its policy of seclusion and open itself to foreign trade. This immediately provoked a racist, xenophobic movement known as "expel the barbarians and revere the emperor." The Boshin War of 1868–1869 ended the ruling Tokugawa shogunate and restored political power to the imperial court. The new Japanese leaders worked to strengthen the central government with an eye toward modernizing the country so that it could withstand foreign inroads. During the ensuing Meiji era Japanese leaders emphasized military and economic development, for which it turned to the Western industrialized nations for guidance.

Japan became Westernized economically, politically, and even to a degree culturally, despite widespread scorn for the Western powers, and emerged from the process as Asia's first industrialized nation. To fuel its industrial capitalist economy, Japan was forced to compete with the other great imperial powers for resources and territory. Beginning in 1894, Japan began to establish an empire that, thanks to wars with both China (1894–1895) and Russia (1904–1905), included Taiwan (then known as Formosa), Korea, Manchuria, and parts of northern China.

At the same time, however, the United States and major European powers refused to regard Japan as an equal deserving of great power rights and privileges. In 1905 when U.S. president Theodore Roosevelt helped broker an end to the Russo-Japanese War, however, he spoke of a "Monroe Doctrine for Japan" in which Japan would carve out a sphere of influence in Asia and prevent further encroachments into the region by European powers. For Japanese policy makers and intellectuals, this was Japan's hope—that the Europeans and the Americans would recognize it as a great power possessing "special interests." There was a double standard in U.S. diplomacy, however. The most glaring inconsistency was Washington's demand for an "open door" to conduct trade in China while insisting on a "closed door" in the Western Hemisphere.

Beginning in 1931, Japanese militarists exploited long-standing grievances with the Western powers—particularly with the United States, which set its sights ever more on East Asian markets—to cast its bellicose actions in China as part of a "holy war" to liberate Asian peoples from Western imperial domination. That year saw a new level of Japanese military aggression in mainland Asia. Japanese Army lieutenant colonel Ishiwara Kanji came up with a scheme whereby the Japanese Army might take all of Manchuria. From the outset Ishiwara envisioned a great struggle between the white and yellow races that would pit Japan against the United States.

On September 18, 1931, Ishiwara arranged to have a bomb blow up a section of tracks of the Japanese-controlled Southern Manchuria Railway. Blaming this on Chinese soldiers, Ishiwara ordered Japanese troops to seize a nearby Chinese military barracks, while Japanese Kwantung Army units seized control of Manchurian population centers. He did all this without informing new Kwantung Army commander General Honjō Shigeru or the Japanese Army General Staff in Tokyo. Presented with a fait accompli, the Japanese government went along with what became a Japanese military takeover of Manchuria. As foreign criticism of Japanese aggression mounted, the Japanese public—inspired by the press, radio, and the entertainment industry—and the Imperial Military Reservists Association celebrated the army's actions and scorned both China and the Western powers.

Within six months, Japan had established the puppet state of Manchukuo. This occurred just one week after U.S. secretary of state Henry Stimson proclaimed what became known as the Stimson Doctrine: that the United States would not recognize any government created as a result of Japanese actions in Manchuria. In March 1933, Japan withdrew from the League of Nations when the international body responded to Chinese entreaties by refusing to recognize the Japanese conquest and proclamation of the independent state of Manchukuo. Japanese propagandists insisted that the resulting diplomatic isolation was just another instance of Japan's victimization at the hands of the Western powers.

Many civilian Japanese officials were shocked by the military's actions in Manchuria, but they went along with the imperialists' expansionist ambitions. Foreign Minister Shidehara Kijuro, who generally favored good relations with China and the West, was forced to defend the fait accompli in Manchuria. And Emperor Hirohito was advised by his staff not to challenge the military so as to avoid provoking a rebellion within the military that could threaten peace and order at home. Prime Minister Wakatsuji Reijorō panicked but was unable to place any check on military affairs. He soon resigned, but his successor, Inukai Tsuyoshi, also proved unable to prevent the rogue Japanese military from continuing its aggression in China.

After Inukai was assassinated in 1932, only 4 of 14 prime ministers between 1932 and 1945 were civilians. In early 1936, a small faction of militarists within the Japanese Army even attempted a coup to oust leftists from government entirely. The rebels were easily defeated but not before the militarists dealt an additional blow to the role of civilians in the government by demanding that new cabinet appointments be approved by army and navy ministers.

Propaganda emphasizing the importance of Manchuria to the Japanese economy helped to legitimize military activity and facilitated the right-wing military seizure of power within the government that was essentially complete by 1937. By then, the Ministry of Education was deeply involved with efforts to prepare the populace to mobilize for what promised to be a protracted war. In May 1937 the ministry published and distributed to schools 300,000 copies of *Kokutai no hongi* (The Fundamentals of the National Polity), which stressed the superiority of the Japanese people and government over other nations. Eventually, 2 million copies were in circulation.

Meanwhile, Japanese incursions into China proper went forward. In the China Incident of July 7, 1937, the Japanese Army used the brief disappearance of one of its soldiers near the Marco Polo Bridge as an excuse to initiate violent attacks on Chinese troops throughout northern China. The march to the capital city of Nanjing (then Nanking) began in November, when additional Japanese troops landed in the Bay of Hangzhou. The Nanjing Massacre in December was a horrific orgy of rape and murder, directed mainly at civilians. It is almost certain, however, that this action had not been ordered by Tokyo, which was still concerned about international opinion. Although China received an outpouring of international sympathy, the United States remained officially neutral largely so that it could continue trading with both nations.

The jingoistic Japanese press explained the Nanjing Massacre to the Japanese public in the same terms that it had used for years to defend Japanese expansion: Japan was fighting a holy war in the name of the emperor, which justified any action no matter how brutal. Moreover, propagandists reminded people of the inherent racial inferiority of the Chinese people. Some, including Emperor Hirohito, were privately uneasy with these explanations and felt that the events at Nanking undermined Japan's claims that it was fighting on behalf of Asian fraternity and independence from the Western powers. But the overwhelming public message put forth by the government and the press was that the army's actions were justified. Certainly this line encountered little resistance from a public that by this time not only accepted but often participated actively in advancing the militarists' propaganda.

The China Incident had provoked infighting within the army between expansionists and nonexpansionists. The latter feared that becoming further embroiled in China would divert resources needed to defend against the Soviet Army to the north. During the summer of 1938, Japanese provocation of Soviet troops massed along the Manchurian border brought major fighting along the triborder area of Korea, Manchukuo, and the Soviet Union. More Japanese troops perished than did Soviet troops, but little territory changed hands. The emperor ordered the army to stop the war, but the generals disregarded his orders and carried on. The Japanese Army abandoned its plans to attack northward, however, thenceforth orienting its activities to the south.

In 1940, Japan's political parties that had already been largely silenced by dominant militarist figures were officially disbanded and replaced in an effort to secure even greater support for the war in China. The Imperial Rule Assistance Association that emerged in their stead was intended to make people from all levels of society follow in lockstep behind the militarist government. The association controlled who ran for election, imposed emperor worship on all institutions beginning with schools, and launched propaganda campaigns to encourage self-sacrifice and denial as Japanese virtues necessary to endure and prevail in the impending war with the West.

In July 1940, U.S. president Franklin Roosevelt signed the Export Control Act. It authorized the president to prohibit the export of essential defense materials, and under this act on July 31 the United States restricted exports of aviation motor fuels and lubricants and iron and scrap steel. Japan signaled its refusal to succumb to U.S. pressure on September 27, 1940, by signing a Tripartite Pact with Germany and Italy, which established the Rome-Berlin-Tokyo Axis (the Axis powers of World War II). That same month, Japanese troops took advantage of the defeat of France by Germany to occupy northern French Indochina to close off that route for military assistance to China. In retaliation, Roosevelt embargoed effective October 16 "all exports of scrap iron and steel to destinations other than Britain and the nations of the Western Hemisphere." As Japan had no oil of its own and limited reserves, this threatened Japan's ability to maintain its military presence in China. Japan thus faced the options of withdrawing from China or carrying out an aggressive move to secure oil in Southeast Asia. The former was out of the question, as the military insisted that Japan's national survival depended on its control of China.

Then in July 1941 Japanese troops occupied southern Indochina. In response, the United States froze all Japanese economic assets. Japanese propaganda held this up as yet another instance of efforts by the Western powers to strangle and destroy Japan without cause.

According to some scholars, Japan's leaders had already made up their minds to wage war against the United States by the time they occupied Indochina, if not sooner. Others blame the United States, especially Secretary of State Cordell Hull, for the failure of diplomacy. In this view, a more flexible U.S. approach to negotiations in the fall of 1941 might have postponed hostilities or even prevented them entirely. Hull did not attempt serious negotiations with Tokyo until 1941, at which point he pursued an all-or-nothing strategy to pressure Japan to withdraw from both Southeast Asia and mainland China. After a brief period of diplomatic deadlock, Japanese leaders perceived the November 26, 1941, Hull Note, which insisted on a total Japanese withdrawal from both China and Indochina as an ultimatum tantamount to a declaration of war by the United States. Japanese warships had already set sail on the mission, but by December 1 Tokyo cemented its decision to take its chances and launch a surprise attack on Pearl Harbor in hopes of gaining a desperately needed upper hand against the United States. Largely thanks to years of effective propaganda, the people of Japan welcomed the attack as a heroic blow against the exploitative Western imperialist powers and were prepared to make the necessary sacrifices that a "holy war" would demand.

Jessica M. Chapman

Perspective Essay 2. The Logic of a Japanese "Holy War"

Although the Japanese decision to attack the U.S. Pacific Fleet at Pearl Harbor has at times been ridiculed as "strategic imbecility," it nonetheless demonstrated a certain logic. In the summer of 1941, the United States had imposed crippling economic sanctions to check Japan's military expansion in Asia. Japan in turn sought to eliminate the interference of a rival power in the Pacific. The main historical factors that led to this situation, however, lie with Japan's revolutionary diplomacy and imperialist expansion during the previous decade. The December 7, 1941, attack was a gambit to sustain the ongoing Sino-Japanese War (1937–1945) that had already caused several million deaths. The war in China, proclaimed by Japanese authorities as a holy war (*seisen*) to rid Asia of Western imperialism, furnished both strategic necessity and moral justification for the Pearl Harbor attack.

Japanese leaders understood that the attack was a dangerous gamble. Japan's military received precise reports on the commanding U.S. lead in various war-related indicators, such as an advantage of 24 to 1 in steel production and 8 to 1 in aircraft production. Moreover, total war would demand tremendous sacrifice from the populace. Japan in the 1930s was a democracy with universal male suffrage and political parties with real influence. What moral justifications could generate the popular support to expand the war so drastically? The answer to this question lies in the objectives and justifications for the ongoing Sino-Japanese War. Japanese planners believed that Japan's security required the maintenance of colonial possessions on the mainland and espoused a Pan-Asianist ideology that argued for Japanese leadership in a grand Asian struggle against Western domination.

In that sense the Pacific war was an amplification of the war in China, which reveals the United States and its allies as rival colonial powers in the Pacific and the Japanese population as active participants in war and imperialism. The United States and Japan emerged as imperialist powers in tandem; the United States seized the Philippines and Hawaii between 1895 and 1905, while Japan annexed Taiwan and Korea from 1895 to 1910. The two countries were, however, late entrants to the colonial game. Other European powers had already established numerous colonies.

The British controlled India, Malaya, Burma, and Hong Kong; the French controlled Indochina; and the Dutch controlled the East Indies. Moreover, since the Opium Wars (1839–1842 and 1856–1860) these same powers had forced China to accept a semicolonial status, slicing from its territory an array of concessions and treaty ports where their nationals lived above Chinese law.

Western imperial domination in Asia played a paramount role in Japan's diplomatic calculus. From the 19th century through the 1920s, Japan's civilian leadership preferred to maintain its empire in cooperation with the Western powers. They joined a series of international conventions to mitigate imperialist rivalries, stabilize colonial possessions, and constrain further expansion. This multilateralist diplomatic course was defined by participation in the League of Nations, treaties governing naval armaments (the Washington Naval Treaty of 1922), the open-door policy in China and respect for its territorial integrity (the Nine-Power Treaty of 1922), and renunciation of warfare to settle international disputes (the Kellogg-Briand Pact of 1928).

Ten years prior to Pearl Harbor, however, the Japanese Army began directly challenging this multilateralist status quo. In September 1931, a Japanese force tasked with protecting Japanese-owned railways in Manchuria—today China's northeastern provinces—launched an invasion to seize that territory from Chinese warlord Zhang Xueliang. This attack was not authorized by the civilian leadership in Tokyo, but the government accepted army explanations that Chinese sabotage to the railway made a military response unavoidable. In the spring of 1932, the army established the puppet state of Manchukuo to rule Manchuria. This act contravened the Nine-Power Treaty, and in 1933 Japan withdrew from the League of Nations after the body condemned the invasion.

Nevertheless, the Japanese takeover of Manchuria was popular among the Japanese public. Populist politics in fact empowered the state to reject multilateralism and pursue further imperialist expansion. Since the institution of a new election law in 1925, all adult Japanese males had the right to vote in elections for the lower house of the Japanese Diet.

The electorate's growing discontent with the weakness of cooperative diplomacy in defending Japanese interests brought hawkish politicians to power. The December 1931 election installed Prime Minister Inukai Tsuyoshi, whose cabinet was much more accommodating of military action than the preceding Wakatsuki cabinet. In addition, Japan's army and navy knew that public opinion gave them greater latitude to act and to castigate uncooperative politicians and bureaucrats.

Several strands of argument informed the public mood, including the perceived need for Japan to secure colonial possessions for its survival. At the start of the 1930s, Japanese government agencies promoted the notion that Manchuria was Japan's lifeline (*seimeisen*)—a defensive bulwark against Soviet and Chinese threats and a market and source of raw materials in a world spiraling into Great Depression protectionism. The public and mass media in turn championed arguments that Japan's self-preservation was at stake. An influential faction of the Japanese public thus felt that Japan's position in Manchuria had to be defended to the death.

These convictions also drew from the racial ideology of Pan-Asianism, which justified a Pan-Asian struggle against Western imperialism. These ideas emerged from the polemics of late 19th-century adventurers, patriots, idealists, and populists in Japan who contended that Japan and its Asian neighbors enjoyed a natural solidarity. For its earliest advocates, it was an idealist vision of uniting Asian civilization that contested the Japanese state's pragmatic agenda to join the Western powers and remake itself in their image.

Pan-Asianism acquired an instrumental, realist edge as Japan gained power and influence. In the first two decades of the 20th century, earlier formulations of equality among Asians and common struggles against outside forces gave way to a self-serving attitude that Asia would be better off colonized by fellow Asians. In that regard, the ideology became applicable to realpolitik, and Japanese leaders deployed it to justify extending power over Asia at the expense of the Western powers. Populist support for Japan's position in Manchuria would thus lure Japan into further military campaigns against China.

A fragile peace between China and Japan collapsed in July 1937 when Chinese and Japanese troops clashed at the Marco Polo Bridge west of Beijing. Fighting quickly spread down China's eastern coast, sparking total war between the two countries. Japan's civilian leaders may not have desired to wage war in China at this time, but they joined with their military chiefs in calling for a strong show of force. When Japanese troops captured the Chinese capital of Nanjing (then Nanking), mass rallies at home deliriously celebrated the victory.

Despite the Japanese military's systematic brutality toward the Chinese, Japanese propagandists insisted it was a *seisen* to rid East Asia of Western influence. The government built concrete plans from these invocations of Asian solidarity. In a speech on November 3, 1938, Prime Minister Konoe Fumimaro declared that Japan would help construct "a new order for ensuring permanent stability in East Asia" by linking Japan, Manchukuo, and China. Using the idea of a common Asian civilization, he pushed for a political alliance and the creation of a self-sufficient economic sphere. The United States condemned this scheme as a further violation of the open-door policy in China.

Japanese hopes for a quick victory faded, however, as the war in China devolved into a stalemate. Konoe underestimated the depth of Chinese nationalism and anti-Japanese sentiment and incorrectly believed that the Chinese harbored as much antagonism toward Anglo-American imperialism as that of the Japanese. Nevertheless, Konoe and other Japanese leaders persisted in plans to establish Asian self-sufficiency. Diplomats and military men concurred that retreat from China was unacceptable; on the contrary, they believed that Japan would have to expand its territorial control in order to crush resistance in China and secure its position there.

The Japanese Navy in particular clamored for establishing bases in Southeast Asia in order to tap the oil reserves of the Dutch East Indies. This southern advance would also help cut off foreign support to China. In July 1940, the Japanese foreign ministry coerced Great Britain to close the Burma road to Chongqing (Chungking), the new capital of the Republic of China. On September 23, 1940, Japanese forces entered the northern part of French Indochina to cut off another route used by the United States, Britain, and France to send supplies to the Chinese military. Finally, on January 31, 1941, the Japanese cabinet resolved to militarily conquer Indochina and inaugurate the Greater East Asia Co-Prosperity Sphere, an expansive zone of Asian cooperation and self-sufficiency.

These maneuvers widened the conflict and menaced the U.S.-controlled Philippines, the Dutch East Indies, and British-held Malaya and Burma. Japan's commitment to winning the war in China now directly threatened other colonial powers in the region. When the Japanese Army forced its way into southern Indochina at the end of July 1941, the United States swiftly froze all Japanese business assets in protest and imposed an oil embargo. These acts became a stranglehold on Japanese military action. In late August, Admiral Yamamoto Isoroku proposed a surprise attack to cripple the U.S. Pacific Fleet in Hawaii and allow Japanese forces to seize the U.S. and European colonies of the Philippines, Malaya, Burma, the Dutch East Indies, British Borneo, Guam, and Hong Kong. A lightning conquest of these territories would, he believed, provide the resources for the army to finally subjugate China while forcing Britain and the United States to accept the fait accompli of Japanese dominance in Asia.

Japan's leadership did not immediately act on Yamamoto's plan, but the oil embargo locked them into a strict timetable. On September 6, a conference involving the emperor, military chiefs, and cabinet members determined that if negotiations with the United States did not restore trade in strategic materials and provide promises not to interfere with the war in China, Japan would be forced to go to war. Chief of the Naval General Staff Nagano Osami claimed in October 1941 that the Japanese Navy was consuming 400 tons of oil an hour and that Japan would exhaust its stocks within two years even without war with the United States. He also believed that Japan's military power had already peaked in comparison to that of the United States. Japan's advantages were shrinking over time; strategic common sense demanded a decision on an attack as soon as possible.

The Japanese Army's determination to maintain a long-term troop presence in China, however, doomed negotiations with the United States. The replacement of Prime Minister Konoe with Tojo Hideki on October 18 brought no breakthrough. The last U.S. response to Japanese proposals was the so-called Hull Note of November 26 in which U.S. secretary of state Cordell Hull called upon Japan to "withdraw all military, naval, air and police forces from China and from Indochina." This, of course, the Japanese Army steadfastly refused to do. On December 1, the emperor endorsed Yamamoto's plan for a preemptive strike on the U.S. Pacific Fleet.

The December 7, 1941, Japanese attack on the U.S. Pacific Fleet at Pearl Harbor was no mere continuation of the war in China but rather its culmination. Japan's revolt against cooperative diplomacy was now complete. Japanese leaders had precipitated a crisis from which they could not or would not back down. They continued to pursue the same goals they had sought in Manchuria and in the Sino-Japanese War: securing territory and natural resources and calling for a Pan-Asian struggle against Western influence. The need for economic security contained in the Manchurian "lifeline" argument evolved into the pursuit of a new order and ultimately the creation of the Greater East Asia Co-Prosperity Sphere. Tojo's commitment to the war in China, even in the face of an economic blockade, would prevent any compromise to avert conflict with the United States. Finally, the moral legitimacy of the Pearl Harbor attack depended on the rhetoric of Pan-Asianism, since the attack would rectify the glaring contradiction in Japan's professed war aims. By 1941, Japan's holy war to liberate Asia had already killed millions of fellow Asians. Only after December 7 would Japan finally wage war against its avowed foe, Anglo-American imperialism.

Eric Han

Perspective Essay 3. A Disastrous Military Decision

The attack on Pearl Harbor was a Japanese military disaster, caused by two separate Japanese decisions: that an attack on the United States was essential to Japan's national security and that success in the war dictated a surprise attack on the U.S. Pacific Fleet based at Pearl Harbor in the Hawaiian Islands. Assessed separately, these decisions may have had some merit, but examined together, they proved to be disastrous. On one hand, Japanese officials calculated that any war with the United States would succeed because a war-weary U.S. nation would negotiate a settlement and accept Japanese hegemony in the Pacific. On the other hand, Japanese naval officers planned and executed a surprise attack on Hawaii, a U.S. territory, and because of this infamous act, the United States would settle for nothing less than the destruction of the Japanese Empire.

To understand Japan's decision to go to war with the United States, one must study events of the 19th century. The strategic imperative of the Japanese nation in the first half of the 20th century was to expand the Japanese Empire. This was difficult, because Japan had come late to the colonial race; the British, French, and Dutch had been colonizing the Pacific region for centuries. Asia's largest nation, China, was not a colony, but all the major imperial powers interfered in its internal affairs, dividing this ancient nation into spheres of influence. In fact, Japan was the only large truly independent nation in the Pacific in the first half of the century.

Japan had retained its independence because it Westernized during the Mejia Restoration in the second half of the 19th century and modernized its military and naval forces. In the 1904–1905 Russo-Japanese War, the Japanese won their first military struggle against a Western power. In the aftermath of the victory, Japan occupied and later annexed the Korean Peninsula. Finally, after a relatively quiet period, which included a brief flirtation with democracy, Japan made expansion the centerpiece of its national strategy. The Japanese invasion of Manchuria in 1931 signaled the emergence of a new empire in the Pacific but one that would last for only 14 years.

The United States came late to the race for empire. It was only at the very beginning of the 20th century that the United States began to colonize the Pacific region in earnest. The U.S. victory in the 1898 Spanish-American War brought the Philippines and other areas in the Pacific under the U.S. flag. Hawaii also became a U.S. territory. At the same time, foreign interests in China came under attack by Chinese Nationalists in the Boxer Rebellion (1899–1901), centered in Beijing (then known as Peking). The United States joined a number of other nations on a punitive expedition against the rebels. Despite this intervention and heavy indemnities placed by the foreign governments on the Chinese for their role, Washington advocated an open-door policy in China. Thus, when Japan took control of Manchuria in 1931, the United States protested this action. Indeed, the United States became the principal opponent of Japanese imperial expansion in the Pacific.

Manchuria was only the start. The next decade saw a series of crises that pitted the United States against Japan. The Japanese Army undertook an invasion of China proper in 1937. After its capture of Nanjing (then Nanking) that December, the Japanese Army went on a rampage. The ensuing Nanjing Massacre saw the slaughter of at least 50,000 Chinese, most of them civilians.

As the fighting in China continued, Japan came more under military role. Although an outright military coup failed, the military nonetheless came to dominate the civilian government in the 1930s, and in 1941 Japanese minister of the army General Tojo Hideki became prime minister.

At the same time, another world war had erupted in Europe in September 1939. By 1941 Germany had conquered not only Poland, Norway, and the Low Countries but also France, and that June Germany invaded the Soviet Union. Japan took advantage of French weakness to occupy French Indochina. At almost the same time, the Japanese signed the Tripartite Treaty with Germany and Italy, firmly aligning these three states. Though concerned about Japanese expansion, the United States had few apparent military options; most Americans rejected actions that might bring their participation in yet another world war.

Despite strong isolationist sentiment, the United States attempted to contain Japanese expansion. President Franklin Roosevelt and his administration instituted a number of economic measures in an effort to constrain Japan. Initially, the United States denied the Japanese access to such critical resources as scrap metal. Eventually, the United States embargoed oil. Japan had no oil of its own and relied on the United States for most of its energy imports, and this action cut to the very heart of the Japanese economy and, more important, Japan's military and naval power.

While Japan and the United States entered into negotiations, neither side was prepared to give way on key issues. The U.S. government demanded that Japan withdraw from both Indochina and China. The Japanese government refused. Ultimately, the Japanese decided to attack the United States in the belief that it threatened the centerpiece of Japan's national strategy, the expansion of a Japanese Empire.

The decision to attack the United States was directly tied to the failure of diplomacy with the United States; however, there was no necessary connection between the two. Diplomacy could have failed, and the Japanese could have avoided attacking the United States. Instead, they might have focused solely on their movement into Southeast Asia that targeted the oil reserves in the Dutch West Indies (modern-day Indonesia). Since Germany occupied the Dutch homeland of the Netherlands, this area was vulnerable to invasion. While Great Britain had large military resources in this area, it was then engaged in a life-or-death struggle with Germany, and this might limit Britain's military response to a Japanese incursion. Given British military weakness, a preemptive attack on its possessions may have made some sense. Less clear is the reason Japan attacked the United States. U.S. Pacific possessions did not contain oil, so invading those areas would not address Japan's fuel shortages. Moreover, the United States was neither occupied by nor fighting Germany. Japanese leaders must have assumed, then, that the United States would give its full attention to a Pacific war. It may have been an understanding of the power of the United States and the limitations of other Western powers that prompted the Japanese to plan a knockout blow against the U.S. Pacific Fleet.

The Japanese decided to attack the United States because of their perceptions of its strength as a Pacific power and its weakness at home. Assuming that Americans would merely accept Japanese hegemony in the Pacific region seems puzzling unless one understands that the Japanese believed in their inherent ethnic superiority, particularly in martial affairs. Many Japanese regarded the United States as a "mongrel nation" unable to bear the cost in blood and treasure that a protracted war spanning the vast Pacific could bring. In contrast, die-hard Nationalists considered the Japanese racially superior and of warrior stock capable of defeating the Americans. Similarly, American racism affected U.S. government policy before the Pearl

Harbor attack. Officials consistently underestimated Japanese military power and Japanese determination to mount a preemptive attack against the U.S. Pacific Fleet. Racism on both sides was key in understanding the Pearl Harbor attack and the conflagration that followed.

In assessing the decision for war, one must understand the racial attitudes that led the Japanese to underestimate U.S. staying power. Less obvious but more pertinent, the Japanese overestimated the willingness of the United States to oppose Japan should Japanese forces attack the overseas possessions of other nations. It was not staying power the United States lacked but rather starting power. Until the Japanese struck at Pearl Harbor, isolationist sentiment was strong in the United States. Germany had attacked and defeated Poland, Norway, the Low Countries, and France and in June 1941 had invaded the Soviet Union. Britain was fighting for its very survival. Yet the United States remained on the sidelines, unwilling to go to war. It was thus easy for the Japanese to conclude that if the United States was unwilling to fight for Europe, it would not do so for European colonies in Asia. The first Japanese stumble on the road to Pearl Harbor was their assumption that the United States would not have opposed Japanese aggression.

The second Japanese stumble was, by any standards, much more egregious: the decision to execute a preemptive strike on U.S. territory. While detailed operational planning did not begin until after the Imperial Conference in September, as early as February 1941 Vice Admiral Yamamoto Isoroku, commander of the Japanese Combined Fleet, articulated his guidance on initial operations against the United States. "In the event of outbreak of war with the United States, there would be little prospect of our operations succeeding unless, at the very outset, we can deal a crushing blow to the main force of the American fleet in Hawaiian waters." Based on this guidance, his operational planner, Commander Genda Minoru, determined that the attack must be "a perfect surprise." While Yamamoto wanted a surprise attack on the U.S. Pacific Fleet, he assumed that war would be declared just prior to the attack. Yamamoto had lived in the United States and understood the consequences of a preemptive strike without this notification; however, as it worked out the message was delayed in delivery, and this added to the intense anger of Americans regarding the attack and their determination to secure revenge in the destruction of the Japanese Empire.

While the origin of the decision for war may be clear, the reason that Japanese Navy leaders decided to attack in this manner is less obvious. While all military and naval commanders value the element of surprise in operations, it may have been the experience of the Russo-Japanese War that most influenced Japanese naval officers. This war had also begun with a surprise attack on the Russian fleet at Port Arthur, in this case three hours before Japan declared war. After World War II, a former Japanese naval officer reflected on the decision to attack Pearl Harbor and ascribed it to the prewar navy's obsession with the "one big battle," based on the

Battle of Tsushima Straits, the greatest Japanese victory of the Russo-Japanese War. "The idea of the Battle of Tsushima prepossessed us," he said, "this fatal 'One Decisive Battle' Idea."

While the Japanese Navy might be blamed for its myopic obsession with decades-old victories, it is usually the responsibility of civilian authority to assess operational plans against national strategy. If the Imperial Council calculated that a successful end to any war with the United States required the United States to cede much of the Pacific to the Japanese, then these officials needed to assess the navy's operational plans based on this calculation. The operational strategy that the Japanese Navy chose meant that their national strategy, which relied on U.S. willingness to accept Japanese hegemony, failed at about 7:56 a.m. on December 7, 1941, when the Japanese launched their attack on Pearl Harbor.

Barbara A. Gannon

Further Reading

Auer, James E. ed. *From Marco Polo Bridge to Pearl Harbor: Who Was Responsible?* Tokyo: Yomiuri shimbun, 2006.

Buruma, Ian. *Inventing Japan, 1853–1964.* New York: Modern Library, 2004.

Clausen, Henry C. *Pearl Harbor: Final Judgment.* New York: Crown, 1992.

Dower, John W. *Cultures of War: Pearl Harbor/Hiroshima/9-11/Iraq.* New York: Norton, 2010.

Goldstein, Donald M., and Katherine V. Dillon. *The Pearl Harbor Papers: Inside the Japanese Plans.* Dulles, VA: Brassey's, 1993.

Iriye, Akira. *China and Japan in the Global Setting.* Cambridge, MA: Harvard University Press, 1992.

Iriye, Akira. *The Origins of the Second World War in Asia and the Pacific.* Harlow, UK: Longman, 1987.

Jansen, Marius B. *The Japanese and Sun Yat-sen.* Stanford, CA: Stanford University Press, 1970.

Jansen, Marius B. *The Making of Modern Japan.* Cambridge, MA: Belknap, 2000.

Kershaw, Ian. *Fateful Choices: Ten Decisions That Changed the World, 1940–1941.* New York: Penguin, 2007.

Masao, Maruyama. "Thought and Behavior Patterns of Japan's Wartime Leaders." In *Thought and Behavior in Modern Japanese Politics,* 84–134. New York: Oxford University Press, 1969.

Miller, Edward S. *Bankrupting the Enemy: The U.S. Financial Siege of Japan before Pearl Harbor.* Annapolis, MD: Naval Institute Press, 2007.

Mueller, John. "Pearl Harbor: Military Inconvenience, Political Disaster." *International Security* 16(3) (Winter, 1991–1992), 175–180.

Prange, Gordon W., with Donald M. Goldstein and Katherine V. Dillon. *At Dawn We Slept: The Untold Story of Pearl Harbor.* New York: Harper and Row, 1975.

Record, Jeffrey. *Japan's Decision for War in 1941: Some Enduring Lessons.* Carlisle, PA: U.S. Army War College, Strategic Studies Institute, 2009.

Russell, Henry Dozier. *Pearl Harbor Story.* Macon, GA: Mercer University Press, 2001.

Saaler, Sven. "Pan-Asianism in Modern Japanese History: Overcoming the Nation, Creating a Region, Forging an Empire." In *Pan-Asianism in Modern Japanese History: Colonialism, Regionalism, and Borders,* edited by Sven Saaler and Victor J. Koschmann, 1–18. London: Routledge, 2007.

Saito, Hirosi. "A Japanese View of the Manchurian Situation." *Annals of the American Academy of Political and Social Science* 165 (January 1933): 159–166.

Satterfield, Archie. *The Day the War Began.* New York: Praeger, 1992.

Toland, John. *Infamy: Pearl Harbor and Its Aftermath.* Garden City, NY: Doubleday, 1982.

Weintraub, Stanley. *Long Day's Journey into War: December 7, 1941.* New York: Dutton, 1991.

Willmott, H. P. *Pearl Harbor.* London: Cassell, 2001.

Young, Louise. *Japan's Total Empire: Manchuria and the Culture of Wartime Imperialism.* Berkeley: University of California Press, 1998.

40. Did the Requirement for Unconditional Surrender Help or Hinder the Allied Effort in World War II?

From January 14 to 24, 1943, U.S. president Franklin D. Roosevelt, British prime minister Winston L. S. Churchill, and the Combined Chiefs of Staff met at a hotel complex in Casablanca, Morocco (then a French protectorate), to discuss Allied wartime strategy following Operation TORCH*, the code name for the Anglo-American invasion of French North Africa that took place in November 1942. Although invited, Soviet leader Joseph Stalin declined to attend due to the dire military situation in the Soviet Union. At the time, German and Soviet troops were locked in a brutal battle at Stalingrad. On February 12, 1943, almost three weeks after the conference ended, President Roosevelt announced to the world that the Allies would accept only unconditional surrender from the Axis powers of Germany, Japan, and Italy. A negotiated settlement or an armistice, such as the one that ended World War I, would not be an option. Although unconditional surrender became an Allied assumption after February 1943, historians continue* *to debate the wisdom of the Allies' decision to make this a requirement for ending the conflict as well as the overall effect it had on the subsequent Axis war effort.*

In the first perspective essay, Dr. David M. Keithly asserts that the insistence on unconditional victory was an impediment to Allied victory. Initially Churchill was not at ease with Roosevelt's decision, believing that it might stiffen Axis resolve. Keithly adds that the demand became a potent Axis propaganda tool, but he also points out that unconditional surrender helped reassure the Soviets, thereby keeping them in the war and demonstrating to them that there would be no peace that did not include the Soviet Union. Similarly, Dr. Michaela Hoenicke Moore argues that unconditional surrender hindered the Allies' psychological warfare efforts during the conflict and made it appear to civilians living in Axis nations that the Allies intended to utterly destroy their countries and "enslave" them by postwar occupation. Roosevelt, however, was determined to avoid the mistakes made in World War I, after which a series of negotiated peace settlements helped set the stage for World War II. Finally, Adam Lehman asserts that unconditional surrender aided more than hindered the Allied war effort. Roosevelt viewed the demand as a potentially powerful propaganda ploy that would bolster the morale of war-weary citizens in the Western democracies. He also saw it as the basis upon which a newly shaped postwar world might be built. On the other hand, Lehman acknowledges that unconditional surrender ended up having unforeseen negative consequences at war's end, most notably the creation of a massive power vacuum in Central and Eastern Europe. This invited Soviet occupation and domination of many of those areas, which in turn helped ignite the Cold War.

Background Essay

Unconditional surrender means total surrender without conditions or terms. During January 14–24, 1943, British prime minister Winston Churchill and American president Franklin D. Roosevelt met at Casablanca, Morocco, a gathering also attended by the Free French leader Charles de Gaulle and French general Henri Giraud, who represented the Vichy government. Soviet leader Joseph Stalin was invited but declined, pleading his country's critical wartime situation.

At Casablanca on January 24, 1943, Roosevelt summarily announced that "The elimination of German, Japanese, and Italian war power means the unconditional surrender by Germany, Italy, and Japan." Caught off guard by the announcement, Churchill nonetheless supported the president. In his Guildhall Speech of June 30, 1943, Churchill declared that unconditional surrender meant "that [the Axis] willpower to resist must be completely broken, and that they must yield themselves absolutely to our justice and mercy."

Japanese signatories arrive aboard the U.S. Navy battleship *Missouri* in Tokyo Bay for the official surrender ceremonies ending World War II in the Pacific, September 2, 1945. (National Archives)

The term "unconditional surrender" was identified in U.S. history with Union brigadier General Ulysses S. Grant in 1862 during the American Civil War when he demanded the surrender without terms of Fort Donelson, Tennessee. The demand for unconditional surrender had not been U.S. policy in conflicts with other nations prior to World War II. In this conflict it sprang from the widespread belief in Germany after World War I that the German armed forces had not been defeated on the battlefield but instead had been "stabbed in the back" by the civilian government. This myth greatly assisted the rise to power of Adolf Hitler. To obviate another such legend, Roosevelt demanded unconditional surrender, which would make it clear to all that the Axis powers had been defeated militarily. Unconditional surrender would also allow the victors to dictate peace terms that might destroy the racist, aggressive philosophies extant in the Axis states. In addition, the policy reassured Stalin and Nationalist Chinese leader Jiang Jieshi (Chiang Kai-shek) that the United States and Great Britain were committed to the war effort and to the complete defeat of the Axis nations.

Under unconditional surrender, there would be no negotiations with members of the Axis. There would also be no "recognition" or "vacuum" rule, meaning that enemy leaders would not be able to act or exercise political authority. The victorious alliance would install a military government to exercise governmental functions.

In one sense, this declaration played into the hands of the Axis leadership. German minister of propaganda Joseph Goebbels told the German people, "Enjoy the war; the peace will be awful." Some also charged that the declaration prolonged the war because it precluded negotiations with the German Resistance.

Douglas B. Warner

Perspective Essay 1. A Hindrance to Allied Victory

On January 16, 1943, at the close of the Casablanca Conference, U.S. president Franklin D. Roosevelt informed the press that peace would be achieved only with the total elimination of German and Japanese military power, which would necessitate the unconditional surrender of Germany, Italy, and Japan. Roosevelt was thinking of the end of World War I when an armistice concluded hostilities, allowing German leaders to say that their nation had not been defeated militarily. The British—and Prime Minister Winston L. S. Churchill in particular—did not appear comfortable with Roosevelt's remarks, although Churchill immediately announced his support publicly. He later said that he would not have used those words. He remained convinced that such an absolute and categorical expression of policy would stiffen Axis resolve. Certainly, the Allied demand for unconditional surrender became a handy propaganda instrument for the Axis powers.

Some have argued that the insistence on unconditional surrender actually prolonged the war. British military historian B. H. Liddell Hart, for example, asserted that the demand for unconditional surrender strengthened German resolve and was skillfully exploited by Joseph Goebbels's Propaganda Ministry, especially when it could be coupled with alleged scenarios such as the Morgenthau Plan to convert postwar Germany into a primarily agricultural and pastoral country. According to Liddell Hart, implacable German resistance in the last two years of the war was in part the consequence of the unconditional surrender policy.

Albert Speer, Germany's minister of armaments, lent credence to the argument that demands for unconditional surrender hardened German resistance. He suggested that Adolf Hitler entertained no illusions about the seriousness of the Allied position on Germany's surrender and that the führer realized that the Nazis had burned all their diplomatic bridges. Speer repeatedly told his cohorts that there was no turning back. This implies that the resistance to Hitler might otherwise have overthrown his regime, but it is doubtful that many Germans would have been attracted to this course by Allied assurances of moderation. British historian Hugh R. Trevor-Roper dismissed the controversy as "much ado about nothing." Terms could only be made with holders of power or alternative power brokers. Some German military leaders might have been ready to bargain with the Allies, but conditions that included abolition of the German military would probably not have been acceptable to them. In fact, German military opposition to Hitler failed, and the German democratic opposition was badly fragmented and often a will-o'-the-wisp. To be sure, Allied leaders were in concurrence on the point that the war would have to end with Axis surrender. U.S. historian Gerhard Weinberg noted that the difference between surrender and unconditional surrender was merely a matter of nuance.

The demand for unconditional surrender had another advantage for the Western leaders. Both the British and U.S. governments sought to assure the Soviet Union that they were in the conflict for the duration and hence would not consider an arrangement with the Germans at Moscow's expense. In emphasizing the diplomatic aspects of the unconditional surrender policy, U.S. political scientist Vojtech Mastny suggested that the latter was in part intended to reassure the Kremlin. Joseph Stalin displayed substantial skepticism, in public at least, about the British and American determination to remain in the war and assumed that given the chance they would negotiate with Germany behind his back. After all, he himself had approached the Germans on several occasions about a deal. Until the winter of 1943, Stalin portrayed the war as an exclusively Russian-German conflict that, by implication, could be settled in a mutually advantageous manner between two belligerents.

David M. Keithly

Perspective Essay 2. An Obstacle to Allied Psychological Warfare

At the end of the U.S.-British conference concerning wartime strategy held at Casablanca, Morocco, during January 14–23, 1943, U.S. president Franklin D. Roosevelt, with British prime minister Winston Churchill at his side, announced that the defeat of the Axis powers would require unconditional surrender. This proclamation was the one war aim pertaining to Nazi Germany that the Allies publicly announced during World War II. It was immediately criticized by some in the American media as likely to stiffen the German resolve to fight and thus prolong the war and increase American casualties.

Indeed, "unconditional surrender" proved to be an encumbrance to psychological warfare. In subsequent explanations, British and American leaders stated that this policy did not mean the enslavement of the German people. Roosevelt clarified that "unconditional surrender" did not mean the destruction of the enemy population, but he emphasized that it did aim at the destruction of Nazism, fascism, and militarism. Despite negative media reaction to the announcement of the demand for unconditional surrender, there was little disagreement among political and military officials regarding its validity and purpose.

Roosevelt, who had been assistant secretary of the navy during World War I, had regarded the armistice with Germany ending that war to be a mistake that had given rise to the "stab-in-the back legend" of a German Army undefeated in the field. In U.S. wartime planning, the term "unconditional surrender" had been discussed approvingly from the time the United States entered World War II in December 1941. Soon thereafter Roosevelt announced that compromise could not end the conflict, thus also ruling out any substantive contacts and negotiations with the German resistance to Adolf Hitler. Domestically, the president intended his announcement to quell a public outcry, especially among the liberal media and intellectuals, regarding the negotiated deal struck in November 1942 with Vichy France admiral Jean Louis Darlan to quell resistance to the Allied troops after their landing in North Africa (Operation TORCH). Similarly, the Soviet ally had to be reassured that Britain and the United States were determined not to enter into separate deals with parts of the German leadership.

In addition to public apprehension over the demand for unconditional surrender, sections of the U.S. government, such as the emigrant-staffed Research and Analysis Branch of the Office of Strategic Services, pointed to the troublesome effects of the unconditional surrender policy from a psychological warfare point of view, especially when compared with the Soviets' alternative strategy of holding out a prospect of democratic self-rule, as embodied in the Free Germany Committee.

Michaela Hoenicke Moore

Perspective Essay 3. An Assist to Allied Victory

At the news conference following the Allied Conference in Casablanca, Morocco, in January 1943, U.S. president Franklin Delano Roosevelt related how in February 1862 during the American Civil War, Brigadier General Ulysses S. Grant had insisted on unconditional surrender from the Confederate forces at Fort Donelson, Tennessee. In a play on his initials, Grant came thereafter to be known in the North as "Unconditional Surrender Grant." Roosevelt then announced that the Allies would insist on "unconditional surrender" from the Axis powers.

Roosevelt said at the time that the elimination of German, Japanese, and Italian war power meant their unconditional surrender in order to secure "future world peace." He was criticized at the time and has been since for this demand, with many regarding it as an impediment to an earlier peace and having thus unnecessarily prolonged the war. Instead of encouraging dissent against Hitler, unconditional surrender carried the dangerous potential of even more German support for continuing the war effort because there was no perceived alternative. Opponents to Roosevelt's unconditional surrender policy argue that it led to the eventual destruction of the German military, created a political power vacuum in Eastern Europe, and left the Soviet Union in position to dominate this area throughout the second half of the 20th century.

Despite the criticism, Roosevelt's commitment to unconditional surrender actually did more to aid the Allied victory than hinder it. Roosevelt's comments were not casual but instead were a calculated political maneuver, deliberately announced at Casablanca to aid the Allied war effort by bolstering morale. First, Roosevelt's declaration served to reassure Soviet leader Joseph Stalin (absent at Casablanca) that the Allies were unwaveringly commited to defeating Nazi Germany and that there would be no armistice or separate peace with their common enemy, Germany. Second, it helped forestall any attempt by Stalin to abandon his allies and negotiate a separate peace with Germany, should the besieged Stalingrad fall and the German war machine emerge victorious in eastern Russia in 1943. While the tide of the war was beginning to shift, anything short of a united front against the Axis powers could have represented disaster for the Allies.

Although the policy of unconditional surrender did harden the resolve of some of the Axis combatants, it did not turn every German or Japanese citizen against the Allies. Hoping to end the war, highly placed members of the German military and political establishment continued their efforts to try to eliminate Adolf Hitler. There were a number of plots to assassinate Hitler even after Roosevelt's declaration at Casablanca.

Privately, Roosevelt realized that unconditional surrender was at best idealistic war propaganda, but he was willing to come as close as possible to meeting that goal. In Italy after the overthrow of Benito Mussolini, Roosevelt was willing to see negotiations with any representative of the Italian government as long as they were not identified as members of the previous fascist regime. On May 23, 1944, just a few weeks before the D-day invasion, Roosevelt considered retracting the unconditional surrender policy for Germany if the National Socialist government was overthrown by its own people. Although this was rejected by both British prime minister Winston Churchill and Secretary-General Stalin, it does show that Roosevelt was not intractable regarding changes in the Allied policy or strategy if it meant saving American lives.

As a pragmatic politician, Roosevelt knew that any post-Hitler German government would demand a negotiated settlement in order to end the war. With Hitler as the scapegoat, members of the German high command could hope to be immune from any war crimes trials that might occur after the war. This would also serve to frustrate Roosevelt's efforts to remodel the German nation and purge any future Nazi threat. If a post-Hitler German government sued for peace, Roosevelt and Churchill would have been hard-pressed to convince their nations to continue the war effort. Similar arguments can be made regarding the governments of both fascist Italy and imperial Japan. Roosevelt's goal was not only to win the war but also to not lose the peace, as had been the case with the Allied-imposed peace settlement following World War I at Paris in 1919.

Roosevelt died in April 1945. His successor as president, Harry S. Truman, continued to support the Allied policy of unconditional surrender. Hoping to convince the Japanese imperial government to surrender after the fall of Nazi Germany in May 1945, Truman delivered a statement emphasizing that "unconditional surrender" did not mean extermination or enslavement of the Japanese people but instead meant an opportunity to avoid ultimate destruction. Truman further promised an escalation of U.S. military actions that would decimate the Japanese military, devastate Japanese industrial war production, and ruin the Japanese economy. The Japanese willingness to "fight to last man" became an untenable ideology, especially in the face of atomic warfare. After the employment of the atomic bomb on the Japanese cities of Hiroshima and Nagasaki in August 1945 and with the personal intervention of Hirohito, the Japanese chose unconditional surrender that nonetheless allowed retention of the emperor, as opposed to annihilation.

In the end, unconditional surrender aided more than hindered the Allied war effort. The policy created a firm ideological resolve leading to the successful conclusion of Allied military operations. Despite oppositions and doubts, the demand for unconditional surrender allowed the Allies to avoid a negotiated peace and established the opportunity to reshape the geopolitical voids left in the wake of the Axis powers.

Adam Lehman

Further Reading

Archer, Christon I., John R. Ferris, Holger H. Herwig, and Timothy H. E. Travers. *World History of Warfare.* Lincoln: University of Nebraska Press, 2002.

Armstrong, Anne. *Unconditional Surrender.* New Brunswick, NJ: Rutgers University Press, 1961.

Berthon, Simon. *Allies at War: The Bitter Rivalry among Churchill, Roosevelt, and de Gaulle.* New York: Carroll and Graf, 2001.

Beschloss, Michael R. *The Conquerors: Roosevelt, Truman and the Destruction of Hitler's Germany, 1941–1945.* New York: Simon and Schuster, 2002.

Casey, Steven. *Cautious Crusade: Franklin D. Roosevelt, American Public Opinion, and the War against Nazi Germany.* Oxford: Oxford University Press, 2001.

Cave Brown, Anthony. *Bodyguard of Lies*, Vol. 1. New York: Harper and Row, 1975.

Edmonds, Robin. *The Big Three: Churchill, Roosevelt, and Stalin in Peace and War.* New York: Norton, 1991.

Fleming, Thomas. *The New Dealers' War: FDR and the War within World War II.* New York: Basic Books, 2001.

Hasegawa, Tsuyoshi. *Racing the Enemy: Stalin, Truman, and the Surrender of Japan.* Cambridge, MA: Harvard University Press, 2005.

Kersaudy, François. *Churchill and De Gaulle.* New York: Atheneum, 1982.

Klemperer, Klemens von. *German Resistance against Hitler: The Search for Allies Abroad, 1938–1945.* Oxford, UK: Clarendon, 1992.

Larabee, Eric. *Commander in Chief: Franklin Delano Roosevelt, His Lieutenants & Their War.* New York: Harper and Row, 1987.

Liddell Hart, Basil H. *History of the Second World War.* New York: Perigee Books, 1982.

Nash, George. *Freedom Betrayed: Herbert Hoover's Secret History of the Second World War and Its Aftermath.* Stanford, CA: Hoover Institution Press, 2011.

O'Connor, Raymond G. *Diplomacy for Victory: FDR and Unconditional Surrender.* New York: Norton, 1971.

Ritter, Gerhard. *The German Resistance: Carl Goerdeler's Struggle against Tyranny.* New York: Praeger, 1958.

Sherwood, Robert. *Roosevelt and Hopkins: An Intimate History.* New York: Universal Library, 1948.

Smith, Jean Edward. *FDR.* New York: Random House, 2007.

Snell, John L. *Wartime Origins of the East-West Dilemma over Germany.* New Orleans: Hauser, 1959.

Speer, Albert. *Inside the Third Reich.* New York: Avon Books, 1971.

Trevor-Roper, H. R. *The Last Days of Hitler.* New York: Macmillan, 1962.

Viorst, Milton. *Hostile Allies: FDR and de Gaulle.* New York: Macmillan, 1965.

von Hassell, Agostino, and Sigrid MacRae, with Simone Ameskamp. *Alliance of Enemies: The Untold Story of the Secret American and German Collaboration to End World War II.* New York: St. Martin's, 2006.

Weinberg, Gerhard L. *A World at Arms: A Global History of World War II.* New York: Cambridge University Press, 1994.

Zeiler, Thomas W. *Unconditional Defeat: Japan, America, and the End of World War II.* Wilmington, DE: Scholarly Resources, 2004.

Zentner, Christian, and Friedemann Bedürftig. *The Encyclopedia of the Third Reich.* New York: Macmillan, 1991.

41. Was Adolf Hitler the Primary Driving Force behind the Holocaust, or Would It Have Occurred without Him?

No name is more closely associated with the Holocaust than that of German chancellor Adolf Hitler. As the leader of the German state from 1933 until his death in 1945 near the end of World War II, the virulently anti-Semitic Hitler orchestrated the genocide of some 6 million Jews as well as approximately 5 million others—including Poles, Soviets, Romas, disabled people, and gay people—whom the Nazi Party labeled as Untermenschen *(subhumans). Safeguarding the purity of the "Aryan race" and removing the supposed racial, social, and economic threat posed by European Jewry were central to the ideology of both Hitler and his National Socialist Workers' (Nazi) Party.*

In the devastating wake of the Holocaust, world leaders, academics, and the general public questioned how such a monstrous tragedy had transpired and how best to prevent a similar event from happening in the future. Such discussions quickly bogged down, however, over the issue of who bore primary responsibility for the genocide. Some pointed to Hitler as the prime factor motivating the Holocaust, while others viewed the unique political, economic, and social circumstances in which Germany found itself in the decade preceding World War II (of which Hitler was a product) as the true cause of the Holocaust. Although Hitler's central role in the Holocaust is clear, the question of whether the genocide would have occurred without Hitler remains a topic for scholarly debate.

In the perspectives that follow, three scholars offer their own opinions on this enduring historical question. In his essay, Dr. Spencer C. Tucker argues that Hitler was absolutely instrumental to the Holocaust and that it very likely would not have occurred without his leadership. He points out that although there are no written orders from Hitler himself calling for the wholesale destruction of the Jewish people, it is clear from Hitler's own writings and the manner in which the German state functioned that the Holocaust could not have occurred without Hitler's knowledge and express direction. By contrast, Michael Nolte asserts that the Holocaust could not have happened without the support—at least passively so—of the German people. He suggests that although Hitler was indeed anti-Semitic, the Nazis' targeting of the Jews was done largely for political purposes precisely because Hitler knew that such a stance would serve as a powerful rallying point among a large segment of the German populace. In her essay, Dr. Alexis Herr traces the historical roots of anti-Judaism and anti-Semitism to demonstrate that the Holocaust was a product of long-standing prejudice and discrimination. She explores how views on Jews changed during the Middle Ages and the early modern period of European history.

Background Essay

The Holocaust was the organized operation by Nazi Germany to exterminate the Jews of Europe. Historians have developed different interpretations of the subject. While some see the Holocaust as the last most horrible manifestation of historical anti-Semitism, others view it as the outcome of factors inherent in Western civilization. Intentionalists see German chancellor Adolf Hitler, determined to destroy the Jews from the beginning, as the crucial factor in the Holocaust. Functionalists, on the other hand, see the persecution of the Jews as an incremental process, exhibiting no overall plan. Research during the past several decades seems to have largely settled in favor of the intentionalists. Attempts have been made to reconcile these positions, fusing anti-Semitism with bureaucratic techniques of mass extermination.

German chancellor Adolf Hitler, in a 1939 photograph. (Roger Viollet/Getty Images)

Hitler became the chancellor of Germany in 1933 and thereafter quickly consolidated power. The most notorious anti-Semite of the 20th century, he was born in Austria in 1889. A high school dropout, he spent his early adulthood living in a flophouse in Vienna, where he developed a virulent anti-Semitism. Moving to Bavaria, he served with zeal and distinction in World War I and was crushed by the Allied victory.

Soon active politically, Hitler blamed socialists and Jews for the defeat. By the early 1920s he was the leader of the ultranationalist

National Socialist German Workers' Party (popularly known as the Nazis). Briefly imprisoned for a bloody effort in 1923 to overthrow the Bavarian government, Hitler wrote *Mein Kampf* (My Struggle), a tirade full of race hatred and anti-Semitism. After he became chancellor, he and his supporters soon moved against the Jews.

Although scholars identify different events and dates for the start of the Holocaust—as early as 1938 with the Anschluss or (more commonly) Kristallnacht—it was not fully implemented until after the beginning of World War II in September 1939, when the Nazis found themselves in control of millions of Polish Jews.

The Nazi treatment of Poles and Jews, considered inferior races, was brutal. Head of the Schutzstaffel Heinrich Himmler on September 27 amalgamated all police and security services in the Reichssicherheitshauptamt (Reich Security Main Office) under Reinhard Heydrich. On September 21, Heydrich issued instructions to Einsatzgruppen (deployment groups) leaders in which he distinguished between the "final aim" (*Endziel*) of Jewish policy and the steps leading to it. Jews were to be moved from the countryside and concentrated in cities near rail lines.

The first major ghetto was established in Lodz in February 1940. The largest was in Warsaw. Ghettos were in older sections of cities, with inadequate living space, housing, and food. They were surrounded by walls and barbed wire, and attempts to leave were punished by death. Living conditions were deplorable.

Despite the mention of "final aim" and the brutality of these measures, most scholars do not believe that the Nazis had yet adopted the idea of mass extermination. Their main goals during 1940 were either fostering emigration by Jews or deporting them to a colony in Africa or the Near East.

In a speech to senior army officers on March 30, 1941, preceding the June 22 invasion of the Soviet Union, Hitler stated that the struggle against the Soviet Union would be a war of annihilation, a campaign to subjugate inferior Slavs and to exterminate Jewish Bolshevism. Subsequent orders calling for liquidation of the Bolshevik leadership without trial, reprisals against whole villages for partisan actions, and the freeing of military personnel from prosecution for crimes against civilians paved the way for military complicity in war crimes against Russian soldiers and civilians and especially against the Jews.

Following the German invasion of the Soviet Union, four Einsatzgruppen, each of 600–1,000 men, swept through the conquered territories after the invading armies, shooting Communist Party functionaries and male Jews. The German Army provided no obstacles to and in some cases actively cooperated with these activities. After their numbers were augmented in August, the Einsatzgruppen expanded their killing of Jews, including women and children. Between June and August they killed approximately 50,000 Jews and in the next four months some

500,000. Hitler had undoubtedly given the overall approval to widen the killing, and he regularly received reports of Einsatzgruppen activities.

Collaborators throughout Eastern Europe actively aided—and in some cases outdid—the Nazis in mass killings. In October following the blowing up of a Romanian military headquarters in Odessa that claimed 60 lives, Romanian Army units killed some 39,000 Jews in reprisal.

Although no written order has come to light and Hitler confined himself to murderous ranting about the Jews, there can be no doubt that the Holocaust proceeded with his express knowledge and desire. Scholars are divided, however, about when exactly the so-called Final Solution (*Endlösung*) was put into effect. Some authorities place the decision as early as the spring of 1941 during the planning for the invasion of the Soviet Union, but others argue that there was a gradual escalation of measures throughout the summer and fall of 1941.

On January 20, 1942, the Wannsee Conference, held for the purpose of coordinating activities by various agencies with regard to the Final Solution, took place in Berlin. Jews in German-controlled areas were to be "evacuated" to the east in a "final solution to the Jewish question." Deportation was to be replaced by systematic mass murder. Since execution by shooting was both inefficient and stressful for the executioners, the Nazis began gassing victims, based on the Nazi euthanasia program during 1939–1941.

In December 1941 Chelmno, near Lodz, was the first extermination center to begin operation. Three more death camps were then set up at Belzec, Sobibor, and Treblinka. Auschwitz, however, became the epicenter of the Holocaust. A conservative estimate puts the death toll there at 1.1 million Jews, 75,000 Poles, 21,000 Romas, and 15,000 Soviet prisoners of war.

Jews were rounded up throughout Europe, told they were being resettled to labor camps in the east, and packed into cattle cars. When those Jews still alive arrived at the camps, their few belongings were confiscated, and those selected for immediate execution, as opposed to those to be worked to death, were forced to undress and sent into gas chambers disguised as showers. The resulting corpses were buried in mass graves or incinerated in crematoria.

Between 1942 and early 1945, the Nazis extended the Holocaust to occupied Western, Central, and Southern Europe. Although exact numbers will never be known, it is estimated that 3.5 million to 4 million people died in the death camps. When victims of pogroms and the Einsatzgruppen and those who died of overwork, starvation, and disease in the camps and ghettos are added, the Holocaust claimed some 6 million lives, or two-thirds of the prewar Jewish population of Europe of 9 million. In Poland, some 45,000 Jews survived out of a prewar population of 3 million.

Donald E. Thomas Jr.

Perspective Essay 1. The Central Role of Hitler

Adolf Hitler was absolutely the driving force behind the Holocaust, and it is difficult to conceive of it occurring without him.

Of course, anti-Semitism had deep roots in Germany but had also been prevalent in much of Eastern Europe, notably in Poland and in Russia, as well as in Western Europe, as in France. Hatred of Jews was not a function of behavior or deeds. It was an irrational phenomenon, defying reasoned explanation. But with Jews being a small minority in Germany, it was possible to alienate them without major political cost, and Hitler made anti-Semitism a focal point of his National Socialist movement. This was for him both an ideological principle and a propaganda tactic. Jews were persecuted not for their religion but instead because Hitler presented them as having been part of an effort that had denied Germany its rightful victory in World War I (the "stab-in-the-back legend") and a counterrace of subhumans out to destroy Aryans by blood pollution. Either destroy the Jews or be destroyed by them, Hitler claimed.

After Hitler came to power in Germany in 1933, Jews were gradually excluded from German society, turned into untouchables in their own land. This was done at varying rates, not according to a precise, preconceived plan. Years later it became clear that the only way to save the Jews was through immigration to Palestine or overseas, but this was not evident in the early days of the Nazi regime when the authorities actually sought to encourage emigration. With other countries unwilling to admit the Jews, Hitler drew the appropriate conclusion: Jews were defenseless and had no way out of their predicament.

One of Hitler's cardinal goals was to reverse the outcome of World War I, even at the cost of a new and more terrible world war. Hitler blended hatred for the Jews and the Bolsheviks, choosing to regard them as one force. This conveniently justified German expansion in the east to secure lebensraum (living space). There was in fact an overriding concentration and consistency of Hitler's policy toward the destruction of the Jews.

There was no straight path to the Holocaust, however. As late as 1940 there was still talk of settling Jews in Madagascar, but it is difficult not to believe that executing the Jews was there from the beginning. The plan to exterminate the Jews began with Hitler, and despite the fact that there is no document bearing his signature ordering their extermination, there is a paper trail through his loyal Schutzstaffel (SS) leader Heinrich Himmler. Unlike Hitler, who gave his orders orally and in the most general terms, Himmler, the consummate bureaucrat, left a long paper trail.

In 1977 David Irving, a British military historian specializing in World War II, created a storm of protest when he stated unequivocally in his book *Hitler's War* that Hitler was unaware of the extermination of the Jews in Europe, at least until 1943. Irving contended that Himmler and the SS had instigated the Final Solution. A number of historians quickly took issue with Irving, but in the opinion of many the matter was settled once and for all by the late British historian Gerald Fleming at Surrey University in his 1984 book *Hitler and the Final Solution,* which was thereafter widely translated and published abroad.

Fleming marshaled an impressive amount of evidence from a wide variety of sources, including a horde of documents seized by the Soviets at the end of World War II and stored at Riga. Despite elaborate Nazi efforts to conceal or destroy evidence linking those at the top of the chain of command to the Final Solution, Fleming was able to assemble such a weight of circumstantial evidence as to prove conclusively that Hitler had full knowledge of the plan to exterminate the Jews, that it was in fact done at his express order, and that he went to considerable lengths to conceal his direct role.

As noted, there exists no written order with Hitler's signature on it ordering the killing of the Jews—a fact exploited by Irving and other Holocaust deniers. Most probably the order was given orally to either Hermann Goering or Himmler. This was Hitler's studied practice, with his secretary and head of the chancellery Martin Bormann forming these into written commands. When queried by his subordinates in regard to the so-called Final Solution to the Jewish question, Himmler repeatedly referred to a "very hard" Führer Order (which in the Third Reich had the force of law) as the justification for the extermination of the Jews. Himmler said that Hitler had ordered "without exception" the elimination of "whatever Jews we can reach" during the war.

From research in the archives at Riga, Fleming also established that the killing of 27,000 Jews there in November and December 1941 was not the decision of local authorities but was in fact carried out on orders from Berlin. Hitler must have been behind it, and he was certainly kept informed of all the work of the four SS Einsatzgruppen units (special units formed to carry out the execution of communist officials and Jews in Russia). There is conclusive proof that he was given totals of Jews executed in the winter of 1941 in Russia.

This is important because it precedes the so-called Wannsee Conference of January 20, 1942 in Berlin that is generally given as the impetus for the implementation of the Final Solution. By that date, 1 million Russian Jews had already been executed, Jews from Germany were being killed at Riga and Chelmno, construction of death camps had begun, and Zyklon-B gas was being tested at Auschwitz.

In any case, it is inconceivable that Reinhard Heydrich, the number two man in the SS and the spokesman at the Wannsee Conference, would have presented the Final Solution as policy to high-ranking SS and Reich officials without Hitler's express approval. There is simply no way Hitler could have been unaware of the Final Solution until 1943, as suggested by Irving. For Hitler, the Jewish question took priority over everything else, including conduct of the war. Nazi ideologue and self-proclaimed expert on the Soviet Union Alfred Rosenberg sought for tactical reasons to delay the massacre of Jews until the war with the Soviet Union had been won, but he was overruled. Indeed, freight trains that were badly needed to move supplies for the German Army were being diverted to carry Jews to the death camps. There is no way that such practices could have escaped the führer's notice, let alone occurred without his explicit order.

The only remaining issue to be resolved by historians concerning Hitler and the extermination of the Jews is whether he was intent on this from the very beginning or if it evolved as other options closed. The weight of evidence suggests the former, given Hitler's repeated references to the "elimination of the Jewish race in Europe." But since Hitler so deliberately concealed his true plans even from his closest subordinates, we may never know for certain.

Spencer C. Tucker

Perspective Essay 2. The Key Role of the German People

The question of whether the Germans would have murdered the Jews without Adolf Hitler's leadership cannot be answered. Since the Holocaust is an undisputed fact, any speculation that under different conditions the perpetrators would not have committed their crimes leads into the realm of fiction.

Although evoking unfounded assumptions, whether the Holocaust would have occurred without Hitler has a factual layer. It asks if a single person was capable of mobilizing millions of followers and using his power to orchestrate genocide. Hitler, the German chancellor who completely dominated the Nazi state, wielded enormous influence, yet his authority did not emerge from a vacuum. The majority of Germans supported him and his policies. Millions joined National Socialist demonstrations, accepted concentration and slave labor camps, and stood idly by as their *Volksgenossen* (racial comrades) escorted Jews to deportation trains. To put it another way, what was the relationship between the dictator and the population? Was Hitler the driving force behind the mass murder, or did the impetus come from below?

The support of ordinary Germans without a doubt was a key element in the implementation of the so-called Final Solution. Although anti-Semitic street violence and the vulgarity of anti-Jewish Nazi propaganda initially appalled many Germans, the social and economic segregation of Jews was carried out with widespread public approval. In his immensely important book *Backing Hitler: Consent and Coercion in Nazi Germany* (2002), historian Robert Gallately concludes that "by the beginning of the war at latest, most Germans agreed with Nazi anti-Semitism."

Yet only a small segment of society participated in mass murder. Scholars estimate that about 200,000 persons—no more than 0.25 percent of the Reich's inhabitants—were directly involved in the killings. Although the number of perpetrators was relatively small, the majority of German civilians provided crucial support for the Holocaust. Most Germans knew about the mass murder; still, they aligned themselves with the regime and at best passively supported National Socialism. They refused to associate with Jews, stole Jewish property, and denounced those who were then persecuted by the Nazis. Particularly during the last years of National Socialism, civilians played an active role. As the Germans evacuated the concentration camps at the end of the war, large parts of the population witnessed mass murder. Driven on long and exhausting marches, the prisoners passed cities, town, and villages. Ordinary Germans, who watched the guards shoot those who could not continue, frequently joined the killers. In April 1945 near the city of Celle, for instance, a group consisting of camp guards, Sturmabteilung personnel, soldiers, policemen, party members, and civilians hunted down fugitive prisoners. Among these German civilians, writes Israeli scholar Daniel Blatman, were boys aged 14–16 who did not hesitate to shoot their victims. German society was deeply involved in the crimes of the Nazi regime. The population, permeated by an anti-Semitic and racist consensus, generally endorsed National Socialist racial policies. Without such broad-based support from below, Hitler and his henchmen would have most likely been relegated to the role of insignificant hatemongers.

Even though the majority of Germans supported what became the Holocaust, whether actively or passively, they collectively denied culpability for Nazi crimes after the war. Already during the last months of the Third Reich, U.S. intelligence officer Saul Kussiel Padover observed the "tendency" of Germans "to put the whole burden of guilt and blame upon Hitler . . . psychologically." Writing about his experience in 1946, Padover noted that "The German people is now prepared to escape punishment and moral responsibility by offering the world a scapegoat who only a short while ago was a demi-god." Presenting themselves as reluctant bystanders, Germans sought to diminish their own role in the crimes of the regime. Even the legal system of the Federal Republic of Germany (West Germany) played into the myth of the almighty führer. For Holocaust perpetrators to be convicted, the prosecution had to demonstrate that they exhibited particular cruelty and malice. As long as the killers merely carried out orders, they were considered innocent. Not individual agency, German society maintained, but rather commands from above were responsible for the implementation of genocide.

Against this backdrop, it is not surprising that this view found its way into historical writing. German scholar Eberhardt Jackel, for instance, regarded Hitler as the driving force behind the Holocaust. This is not to say that Jackel discounted German civilian participation in National Socialism; on the contrary, he stressed the widespread support for the Nazi regime. Nonetheless, in claiming that a single person propelled the mass murder, this involuntarily falls in line with the German postwar campaign to reject individual accountability.

Hitler, without doubt, played a crucial role in both rallying Germans behind National Socialism and guiding the bureaucracy of genocide. The dictator was, to quote historian Christopher Browning, "not only 'champion and spokesman' [of the Final Solution] but also the necessary and pivotal decision maker." Reducing the Holocaust to an executive procedure orchestrated from above, on the other hand, ignores the social dimension of mass murder. Nazi decision making did not unfold in a vacuum. The German apparatus of power consisted of an unmanageable network of overlapping and conflicting agencies pertaining to ministerial bureaucracy, armed forces, industry, and party; although the führer stood on top, these structures were carried from below. "The Nazis," Gellately demonstrated, "did not act out of delusional or blind fanaticism in the beginning, but with their eyes wide open to the political and social realities around them. They developed their racist and repressive campaigns by looking at German society, history, and traditions." Hitler and his lieutenant knew that it would be impossible to carry out the Holocaust without societal backing. They were able to murder the Jews because the Germans accepted this decision. The führer and his followers, in other words, belong together. How the dictator would have acted without the support of the population is as much a matter of speculation as the question of what the Germans would have done without Hitler's leadership.

Michael Nolte

Perspective Essay 3. The Historical Roots of the Holocaust

The Nazi's annihilation of millions of European Jews in the Holocaust relied on centuries of prejudice and violent hatred to succeed. The Holocaust did not occur overnight. Instead, German chancellor Adolf Hitler capitalized on preexisting prejudice and managed to rally those around him in the wake of World War I. The murder of Europe's Jews speaks to society's deepest vulnerability: to embody evil and commit atrocity. The Holocaust shows us that the path to genocide is generally built over time. Hitler was part of the chain that linked the history of anti-Judaism to murderous anti-Semitism.

The history of the Jews in Europe is rooted in their separation from Christian society. By the Middle Ages the Catholic Church had managed to convert nearly all of Europe to Christianity, but the Jews were the exception. Theologians and philosophers in the Middle Ages purported that everyone had a place and position in society, and Jews were part of that social order. Jews, however, often dressed differently and spoke Yiddish. Those residing in cities were relegated to a specific neighborhood known as a ghetto, an enclosed space with a gate that locked Jews in and Christians out on high religious days such as Easter. Jewish separation from Christians afforded an unequal coexistence.

Christian othering of Jews was strengthened by elements of the Jewish faith. The Yiddish language, for example, was one way Jews failed to assimilate into Christian society, as many Jews could not speak the common tongue of their country of residence.

Political struggle often motivated pogroms (organized massacres of Jews) during the Middle Ages. These occurred not only in Poland and Russia but also in West European countries such as Spain. During this period kings and local noblemen were responsible for Jews, and Jews came to symbolize royal power and elitism, as they were the only members of the community permitted to lend money. Violent outbreaks in medieval Europe erupted from conflicts between religious and secular authorities. Because Jews fell under the nominal protection of the king or nobleman, Christians frustrated with the rigid class system often attacked Jews out of political discontent more than religious hatred.

In the 16th and 17th centuries centralized governments emerged, as did philosophers who called for political equality. The French Revolution was inspired by the drive for political equilibrium and aimed to abolish the old kind of society in which the elites had all the power.

Although a decree in the French Revolution in 1791 extended complete emancipation to Jews on the grounds that the Jews had to be given equality in order to complete the work of the revolution, there were nonetheless acts of violence against them. The French Revolution destroyed the Middle Age rhetoric that everyone had a place in society. The violent actions during the French Revolution introduced the notion that mass murder was an acceptable form of political expression. This time the nobles and royals were the victims, but who would come next?

During the 1700s and 1800s, nationalism emerged as a dominant force in Europe. As a result of French Revolution leaders' demand for political equality, societies came to view themselves as one nation of people—not classes or individuals—with a shared responsibility to ensure the success of their homeland.

With the obsession of nation came the idea of separate races and the thought that a nation was made up of a people with shared biological and genetic makeup. In this new racial conceptualization of nationalism and people, the Jews were left out. While in the Middle Ages their outsider status had much to do with political monarchies, in the 1700s and 1800s Jews were seen as something other on a biological level.

In the middle of the 19th century, anti-Judaism (political and economic hatred) changed into anti-Semitism. Anti-Semitism is prejudice toward Jews motivated by religious, racial, cultural, and ethnic biases. Jews were seen as an internal enemy and a scapegoat for a nation's misgivings. In Russia, for example, Christians blamed Jews for mass poverty and famine, which inspired widespread pogroms. Unlike pogroms of the Middle Ages, the pogroms of the 1800s had much to do with ethnic hatred.

World War I created another opportunity for disgruntled nations to blame Jews and further the obsession over the concept of race. The war was an explosion of death, carnage, and industrialized warfare. Violence and bloodshed saturated all of Europe, and mutilated corpses affronted Europeans at a new level. Men returned home with amputated limbs and other disfiguring injuries, which spurred scientists to study the body's place in racial thinking.

German military leaders sold the myth of the "stab in the back": that Germany had not been defeated militarily but had succumbed to a collapse of the home front caused by Jews, pacifists, and communists. With Jews being only a small minority of the population, it was easy to offend them politically.

Harsh economic restrictions and reparations imposed on Germany by the victorious Allies in the Treaty of Versailles of 1919 left many Germans in dire economic circumstances. This certainly helped bring Hitler to power in 1933.

Hitler's path to power had much to do with timing and the building anti-Jewish and anti-Semitic fever throughout Europe. The same can be said of the mass German support for the genocide. Hitler's ascent to power and the German consensus to Hitler's genocidal demands can only be understood by examining the historical patterns of violence, political strife, and racial thinking over the proceeding centuries.

It is impossible to say that Hitler was the driving force behind the Holocaust, because it is unknown whether he could have rallied support without centuries of anti-Jewish and anti-Semitic philosophies and politics. Hitler managed to turn anti-Semitic sentiment into an annihilationist policy supported by Germans. Without civilian participation, Hitler would not have been able to execute his murderous plans.

Alexis Herr

Further Reading

Arad, Yitzhak. *The Holocaust in the Soviet Union.* Nebraska: University of Nebraska Press, 2009.

Arendt, Hannah. *Eichmann in Jerusalem: A Report on the Banality of Evil.* New York: Penguin Classics, 2006.

Bartov, Omer, ed. *The Holocaust: Origins, Implementations, Aftermath.* London: Routledge, 2000.

Bauer, Yehuda. *A History of the Holocaust.* Revised ed. New York: Franklin Watts, 2001.

Breitman, Richard. *The Architect of Genocide: Himmler and the Final Solution.* New York: Knopf, 1991.

Browning, Christopher. *Ordinary Men: Reserve Police Battalion 101 and the Final Solution in Poland.* New York: Harper Perennial, 1993.

Burleigh, Michael. *The Third Reich: A New History.* New York: Hill and Wang, 2000.

Dawidowicz, Lucy S. *The War against the Jews, 1933–1945.* New York: Holt, Rinehart and Winston, 1975.

Fleming, Gerald. *Hitler and the Final Solution.* Berkeley: University of California Press, 1985.

Friedlaender, Saul. *Nazi Germany and the Jews,* Vol. 1, *The Years of Persecution, 1933–1939.* New York: HarperCollins, 1997.

Gellately, Robert. *Backing Hitler: Consent and Coercion in Nazi Germany.* Oxford: Oxford University Press, 2002.

Goldhagen, Daniel J. *Hitler's Willing Executioners: Ordinary Germans and the Holocaust.* New York: Vintage, 1997.

Gordon, Sarah. *Hitler, Germans, and the Jewish Question.* Princeton, NJ: Princeton University Press, 1988.

Heer, Hannes, and Klaus Naumann, eds. *War of Extermination: The German Military in World War II, 1941–1945.* New York: Berghahn Books, 2004.

Hilberg, Raul. *The Destruction of the European Jews.* 3rd ed. New Haven, CT: Yale University Press, 2002.

Hitler, Adolf. *Mein Kampf.* Translated by James Murphy. London: Imperial Collegiate Publishing, 2010.

Kershaw, Ian. *Hitler.* 2 vols. New York: Norton, 1998, 2000.

Laqueur, Walter, ed. *The Holocaust Encyclopedia.* New Haven, CT: Yale University Press, 2001.

Marrus, Michael R., ed. *The Nazi Holocaust: Historical Articles on the Destruction of European Jews.* 9 vols. Westport, CT: Meckler, 1989.

Megargee, Geoffrey P. *War of Annihilation: Combat and Genocide on the Eastern Front, 1941.* New York: Rowman and Littlefield, 2006.

Rossino, Alexander B. *Hitler Strikes Poland: Blitzkrieg, Ideology, and Atrocity.* Lawrence: University of Kansas Press, 2003.

United States Holocaust Memorial Museum. *Historical Atlas of the Holocaust.* New York: Macmillan, 1996.

Waller, James. *Becoming Evil: How Ordinary People Commit Genocide and Mass Killing.* Oxford: Oxford University Press, 2002.

Weinberg, Gerhard L. *Germany, Hitler, and World War II.* New York: Cambridge University Press, 1995.

Yahil, Leni. *The Holocaust: The Fate of European Jewry, 1932–1945.* New York: Oxford University Press, 1991.

42. Should the Allies Have Bombed Auschwitz?

Despite their intelligence networks possessing the knowledge of the extermination of European Jews at the hands of the Nazi regime, the Allies did not attempt to destroy the death mills at Auschwitz-Birkenau. Strategic considerations about the liberation of Europe did not include any plans to attack Nazi concentration camps. While the camps provided much of the slave labor that kept the German war machine going until the bitter end, Allied military strategists did not deem the bombing of these as crucial to the disruption of the enemy's overall war effort. The unconditional surrender of Germany was viewed as the only way to end the suffering of the various peoples under Nazi domination. However, there were Jewish groups in Great Britain and the United States that clamored for the destruction of the death camps, particularly Auschwitz, given its prominence in the stories that came out of Europe in relation to the Holocaust.

Could Allied bombings have put a stop to the murder of millions of Jews in the latter years of the war? There are critics of Allied policy who maintain that this is the case. They argue that the Allies had the military capability to strike and destroy the Nazi death camps and chose not to do so. Others maintain that the Allies could have done more damage to the lives of Jewish captives by attacking the camps and that at this point in the war, it was better to end Germany's ability to make war by winning the war. By doing so, more lives would be saved.

In her perspective essay, Alexis Herr states that the issue of whether the Allies, primarily Great Britain, the Soviet Union, and the United States, should have bombed Auschwitz is not an easy question to answer. Given their knowledge of the death camps, the Allies did not see them as a viable target for destruction in terms of the overall war strategy to defeat the Nazis. It was also gauged that attacking the camps would have caused more damage than lives saved. Moreover, the death camps were not the reason for going to war in the first place. Finally, Herr believes that attacking the rail lines into the camp would have been one way the Allies could have helped save the lives of Jewish victims.

In his perspective essay, Michael Berenbaum argues that the Allies did not prioritize the plight of the Jews in their grand strategy of winning the war. They lacked the political will to take on a humanitarian concern that would have doubtlessly saved lives. In this manner, the Allies proved that they sought the destruction of the Third Reich as the best way to improve the lot of the people of occupied Europe and thus devoted their resources to doing so. Despite having the knowledge of the death camps, the Allies rationalized that it would do more harm than good to the Jewish captives to attack Auschwitz.

This June 1958 image shows buildings behind a defunct high voltage electric fence at Auschwitz I camp in Poland. The four camps at Auschwitz constituted the largest German concentration and extermination centers during World War II. (AP Photo)

In his perspective essay, William D. Rubinstein sustains that no one proposed bombing Auschwitz until May 1944, and when it was finally proposed it was largely rejected as counterproductive to the war effort. Furthermore, contemporaries did not see the bombing of Auschwitz as something that should be done as part of the larger strategy of winning the war against the Axis. The priority was the defeat of Nazi Germany in order to end the occupation of Europe and thus liberate the oppressed masses. In his view, hindsight is not evidence given that people of the time viewed things differently in regard to military priorities.

Finally, in his perspective essay Roger W. Smith states that despite the humanitarian concerns, bombing Auschwitz would have diverted resources that could help end the war. The Allies calculated that the best way to end the suffering endured by the people living under the Nazi regime was the unconditional surrender of Germany. This rationale allowed the Allies the leeway to choose what were strategic targets in this pursuit. Auschwitz, despite its use of slave labor for the German war machine, was not one of these. As such, the Allies chose to overlook what was deemed but one humanitarian target for the larger goal of ending the war and liberating all of Europe from Nazi tyranny.

Background Essay

Auschwitz (Oswiecim in Polish) was the name given to a number of German concentration camps in eastern Poland that served as one of the epicenters of the Holocaust. More Jews were killed in Auschwitz during the war than in any other single location. Since the victims came from every part of Europe and because the camps were in operation longer than any other death camp, Auschwitz has come to symbolize the Nazi determination to destroy the Jews.

Understanding the history of Auschwitz is a challenge because of the complexity of its story. Initially Auschwitz was established as a concentration camp for Polish soldiers and political prisoners. After June 1941, Soviet prisoners of war were added to the prison population. During its first two years of operation, little distinguished Auschwitz from any other Nazi camp or indeed could predict the role it would play in the Holocaust. It must also be remembered that there was not a single Auschwitz but rather 3 main camps—Auschwitz I, Auschwitz II (Birkenau), and Auschwitz III (Monowitz)—along with some 50 satellite camps located over a wide geographical region. Thus, even at the height of the killings, Auschwitz concentration and work camps continued to exist next to the Auschwitz death camp of Birkenau.

In the winter of 1940–1941 the German chemical firm I. G. Farben, taking advantage of governmental tax breaks for industrialist building in the newly conquered territories, chose the Auschwitz area as the site for the construction of a new plant. The availability of a railroad junction and raw material, along with the chance to utilize cheap concentration camp labor, added to the allure of the area. A deal was struck between I. G. Farben and the Schutzstaffel (SS) whereby the latter would provide slave labor (drawn from Auschwitz inmates), and the company would pay the SS for the use of the workers. At the same time, SS chief Heinrich Himmler ordered the camp system expanded to accommodate over 100,000 inmates, probably in expectation of a massive number of Soviet prisoners.

In the fall of 1941 a local Nazi official, ordered to kill a number of Soviet prisoners of war, decided to experiment with the use of Zyklon-B (a cyanide gas used for delousing). A small farmhouse was sealed off, and thus the first tests with gassing prisoners was carried out on those considered subhuman (*Untermenschen*) by Nazi ideology.

The context for these tests reflects why the history of Auschwitz and thus Adolf Hitler's so-called Final Solution are sometimes so difficult to comprehend. Although Hitler ordered the extermination of the Jews, there was no straight chain of command from the chancellory to guards at Auschwitz to gas Jews. The story of Auschwitz thus reflects how policy was set by the Nazi hierarchy, with its implementation left to local officials. In September 1941 when Hitler ordered the slaughter of Europe's Jews, the gassing experiment at Auschwitz was being conducted independently of higher control.

Auschwitz seemed to be a logical site for the implementation of the Holocaust because it was remote from major population centers, and yet a rail line ensured that access was not subject to unreliable roads. When high-ranking Nazi officials learned of the effectiveness of Zyklon-B in killing Jews they adopted it as the execution method, thereby merging industrial production with mass slaughter.

While the first killings took place at Auschwitz I, Auschwitz II (Birkenau) became the focal point for the gassing of Jews brought from all over Europe. Initially, two converted farmhouses were employed in this task. By the middle of 1942, however, specially built gas chambers and crematoriums were in use, enabling the Germans to gas and then incinerate several thousand people per day. Indeed, at Birkenau alone, where the majority of the mass killings occurred, it is estimated that toward the end of the war some 12,000 people per day were being systematically slaughtered.

To clean the bodies out of the chamber and sort the clothes and valuables of those who were murdered, the Nazis created several groups of *Sonderkommando* (special squads) of prisoners. Periodically these *Sonderkommando* were culled, along with prisoners from the other camps, in a process known as selection. The SS (and I. G. Farben) hoped that by replacing weak and ailing prisoners with slightly healthier inmates, they would be able to maintain production levels. The killing of the *Sonderkommando* also helped remove witnesses to the actual mechanism of mass slaughter. On October 7, 1944, however, members of the *Sonderkommando* revolted not in any expectation of escape but instead to destroy as much of the gas chambers and crematoriums as possible. They were also hoping to buy time to bury manuscripts, evidence of the horrible work they were forced to carry out. More than 400 *Sonderkommando* were killed, along with some 15 SS guards. The hidden manuscripts were not discovered for more than a decade.

On January 6, 1945, four Jewish women who had smuggled gunpowder to the *Sonderkommando* for their revolt were executed in Auschwitz. They were among the last people killed in the camp, as the Nazis evacuated the area ahead of the advancing Red Army, destroying as much of the evidence of their genocide as they could. Many thousands of inmates whom the Nazis forced to march back to the Reich perished along the way. Only a few hundred were found alive in the camp when the Red Army arrived at the end of January.

Around 1.1 million people died at Auschwitz, some 90 percent of them Jews. This constituted 1 of every 6 Jews who perished in the Holocaust. Much of Auschwitz has been preserved, serving today as a grim reminder of the efficiency of the German machinery of death.

Frederic Krome

Perspective Essay 1. Allies Should Have Bombed Rail Lines

The question of whether the Allies (primarily Great Britain, the Soviet Union, and the United States) should have bombed Auschwitz is far from easy to answer. In order to best respond to this issue, it is prudent to ask four questions: What did the Allies know? Why did the Allies not bomb Auschwitz? What are the moral and ethical implications of inaction? Should the Allies have bombed Auschwitz? The answers to the first three questions inform the argument that the Allies should have, at the very least, bombed the railway lines leading to Auschwitz.

What did the Allies know? The Allies knew that the Auschwitz camp complex was murdering thousands of Jews daily and had some knowledge of the camp layout and railway access routes. News of the gas chambers and crematoria complexes of Auschwitz-Birkenau reached the Western Allies long before the end of the war. European Jews who had escaped Nazi-occupied Europe were some of the first to supply this information. Survivors shared their stories and rallied their communities to pressure their governments to halt the Auschwitz death factory. In the United States, the World Jewish Congress and the War Refugee Board sent proposals to the War Department in the summer and fall of 1944 urging that U.S. aircraft bomb Auschwitz immediately. The government denied their requests.

In addition to the stories shared by Jewish refugees fleeing Europe, the Allies had acquired aerial photographs of the Auschwitz complex and the railway lines funneling victims into the annihilation center. The last exhibit in the United States Holocaust Memorial Museum in Washington, D.C., shares these photos with visitors.

Why did the Allies not bomb Auschwitz? Scholars have offered a plethora of reasons as to why the Allies elected to not bomb Auschwitz-Birkenau. Some argue that the Allies did not possess the technical capacity to hit the camp with accuracy. Others suggest that bombing Auschwitz would have only emboldened Nazi Germany to take even more drastic measures against Jews and the Allies. Destroying the camp would have served propaganda value in the occupied territories and would have been manipulated to rally perpetrators. Historian Stuart G. Erdheim contends that the Allies failed to destroy the gas chambers in Poland because doing so would have accomplished little in the way of advancing their war efforts. The Allies might also have worried that bombing a facility housing Jews still alive might have been perceived as reckless behavior by Jews in the Allied countries. Also, the Allies may have feared that bombing the Auschwitz camp while it housed Jews only would have helped Adolf Hitler achieve his ultimate aim of killing all Jews.

What were the moral and ethical implications of inaction? While the true reason why the Allies did not destroy Auschwitz remains illusive, the implications of not having bombed the gas chambers are apparent. Despite having the ability and knowledge, the Allies did not pursue a line of action that would have stopped the death factory and in so doing possibly have prevented thousands of deaths.

The argument that bombing the camp would have only killed more Jews is a compelling one; however, this line of reasoning does not excuse the Allies' decision not to attempt to destroy the railway tracks delivering Jews to their deaths. As it stands now, it appears that the Allies did not attempt to destroy Auschwitz itself because it did not serve their own needs. With this said, it may be possible that the Allies chose to leave the railway lines intact because they would be needed to rebuild the country after the war. And yet one has to wonder about the logic of such a position, given the Allies' immense bombing campaign against cities throughout German-occupied Europe. In short, the Allies did not go to war with Germany to save Jews.

Should the Allies have bombed Auschwitz? This is a complex question to answer because we do not have all the facts, nor are we able to truly understand why government officials made the choices they did. Also, the word "should" seems to imply a moralizing question more than one in consideration of political motivations and war strategy. With that said, the Allies should have at least attacked the railway system, because this would have both stopped the flow of Jews into the death camp and interrupted German war supplies being shuttled by train to the front.

Alexis Herr

Perspective Essay 2. Bombing Auschwitz and Political Will

The question "why wasn't Auschwitz bombed?" is not only historical but has also become a moral issue emblematic of the overall Allied response to the plight of the Jews during World War II.

The question of bombing Auschwitz arose only in the summer of 1944, more than two years after the gassing of Jews had begun and by which time more than 90 percent of the Jews murdered in the Holocaust were already dead. It did not occur earlier for several reasons. Not enough was then known specifically about the camp, and the camps were beyond the range of Allied bombers until the spring of 1944. Only when the Allies captured Italian air bases could the issue be raised. U.S. authorities had also decided that they would not send pilots on a mission in which they would not have a good chance of returning to their bases. The question should be raised as to why the Soviets did not bomb Auschwitz or allow Allied bombers so engaged to land on Soviet territory.

Ever since Walter Laqueur published *The Terrible Secret: The Suppression of the Truth about Hitler's "Final Solution"* (1980), Holocaust scholars have distinguished between information and knowledge. By July 1944, reliable information regarding the function of Auschwitz was available—or could have been made available—to those undertaking such a mission. Furthermore, German air defenses were weakened, and the accuracy of Allied bombing was increasing. What was required was the political will to authorize the effort.

In March 1944, German forces had invaded Hungary. In April, Jews there were ghettoized. Between May 15 and July 7, more than 430,000 Jews were deported on 147 trains from Hungary. The vast majority went to Birkenau, the death camp of Auschwitz. Any interruption in the killing process might possibly have saved thousands of lives. Thus, even as late as the spring and summer of 1944, the Allies could have—and therefore should have—either bombed Auschwitz-Birkenau or the railway lines leading to the camp.

Bombing a death camp filled with an innocent, unjustly imprisoned civilian population posed a moral dilemma for the Allied side, which had to be prepared to sacrifice innocent civilians. It was essential to know that the sacrifices of those prisoners who would undoubtedly die in Allied bombings was worth interrupting the machinery of death in the camp. In short, one had to accept the fact that those in the camps would soon die. Such information was not available until the spring of 1944, when a full report on the camp complex was written by Alfred Wetzler and Walter Rosenberg (who took the name Rudolph Vrba), two Jews who had escaped from Auschwitz on April 7.

It is generally assumed that anti-Semitism or indifference to the plight of the Jews was the primary cause of the refusal to support bombing Auschwitz. The issue is in fact more complex. On June 11 the Jewish Agency Executive (JAE), meeting in Jerusalem, refused to call for the bombing of Auschwitz. David Ben-Gurion, chairman of the Executive Committee, said that "We do not know the true situation in Poland" and "we cannot take responsibility for a bombing that might cause the death of a single Jew." Rabbi Yehuda Leib Fishman concurred. The JAE soon reversed its June 11 decision, however. Yitzhak Grunebaum, who headed the JAE's Rescue Committee, cabled its representatives in London on June 27, 1944, to demand immediate Allied bombings. By June 30, officials of the JAE in London were forcefully calling for bombing.

Presumably this reversal was because the leaders of the Jewish community in Palestine had seen the report known as the Auschwitz Protocols, by Vrba and Wetzler. Anyone reading the Vrba-Wetzler report was patently aware of what was occurring in the Auschwitz complex and would therefore be much more willing to risk Jewish lives on the ground rather than permit the gassing to proceed unimpeded.

Moshe Shertok, head of the JAE's Political Department, and Chaim Weizman, president of the World Zionist Organization, appealed to British foreign secretary Anthony Eden, who took the issue to Prime Minister Winston Churchill. Churchill then told Eden on July 7 "Get anything out of the Royal Air Force you can and invoke my name if necessary." Yet the British never carried out the bombing. They turned the matter over to the Americans, who did nothing.

Requests were also made to American officials to bomb Auschwitz. In a letter of August 14, 1944, from Assistant Secretary of War John J. McCloy to Leon Kubowitzki of the World Jewish Congress, the Americans gave several reasons for their refusal: military resources could not be diverted from the war effort reaching its crescendo in the post D-day battles, bombing Auschwitz might prove ineffective, and bombing might provoke even more vindictive German action. Nowhere did American officials claim that Auschwitz was not within range of American bombers.

In fact, as early as May 1944, the U.S. Air Force had the capability to strike Auschwitz at will. The rail lines from Hungary were also well within bomber range, although in order that it be effective such bombing would have to be sustained. Also, it had to be undertaken by day in good weather and probably between July and October 1944. On July 7, 1944, American bombers flew over the railway lines to Auschwitz. On August 20, 127 B-17 Flying Fortresses dropped 1,336 500-pound bombs on the I. G. Farben synthetic oil factory less than five miles from Birkenau. The death camp remained untouched.

For three decades, the issue of bombing Auschwitz was a minor sidebar to the war and to the Holocaust. In 1978, American historian David Wyman wrote an article in *Commentary* magazine titled "Why Auschwitz Wasn't Bombed." The effect of that piece was reinforced by photographs published shortly thereafter by U.S. Central Intelligence Agency photo interpreters Dino Brugioni and Robert Poirier. These photographs, developed with technology available in 1978 but not in 1944, were given by President Jimmy Carter to Elie Wiesel when he visited the White House as chairman of the President's Commission on the Holocaust. In his memoir *And the Sea Is Never Full: Memoirs, 1969–* (1999), Wiesel recounts asking Carter whether these photographs reached President Franklin D. Roosevelt's desk, to which Carter replied in the affirmative. It seems unlikely that Carter would assent to something that he did not know and could not know, as his predecessor could not have seen these photographs except through a magnifying glass and then would not have understood what he was viewing. Seeing these same photographs when he visited Yad Vashem, President George W. Bush turned to Secretary of State Condoleezza Rice and said, "We should have bombed Auschwitz."

The photographs are a vivid demonstration of what American intelligence could have known about Birkenau if only it had been interested in data not directly related to military targeting. One photograph shows bombs dropping over the camp, owing to the apparent early release of bombs intended for the I. G. Farben plant. Another photograph shows Jews on their way to the gas chambers.

Historians are uncomfortable with the counterfactual speculation of "what if," but such is the debate over bombing Auschwitz. In the end, the pessimists won. They argued that nothing could be done—and nothing was done. The optimists did not even have their proposals considered. Auschwitz was not tasked for bombing. Given what occurred at Birkenau during the summer of 1944, the failure to bomb it has become a symbol of inaction due to priorities, which gave a relatively low priority to the fate of the Jews. Inaction aided the Germans in achieving their goals.

Michael Berenbaum

Perspective Essay 3. Gauging Success: What Would Bombing Auschwitz Have Accomplished?

It is understandable, and in the context of World War II perfectly justified, that the Allies did not bomb Auschwitz. The real questions that must be addressed in considering this topic are these: why was Auschwitz not bombed? Could a bombing raid on Auschwitz have been successful? And would this have made any difference to the unfolding of the Holocaust?

Probably the most important single point that might be made is that there was no discussion of an effort to bomb Auschwitz until May 1944, when this was proposed by Rabbi Michael Dov Weissmandel. He was a Slovakian rabbi who escaped from a train carrying Jews to Auschwitz and managed to make his way to Bratislava. There, Weissmandel sent a telegram to Swiss Orthodox Jewish leaders recommending the bombing of the railway line between Kosice and Preskov in Slovakia utilized by some trains to Auschwitz. There were, however, no such appeals to the Allies prior to May 1944 to bomb Auschwitz, the railway lines to Auschwitz, or any other Nazi extermination camp such as Treblinka or German concentration camps such as Dachau and Buchenwald (which were already in existence and notorious before the war began).

Two striking examples of the absence of any call to bomb Auschwitz can be given. In early 1944 the British National Committee for Rescue from Nazi Terror, headed by Victor Gollancz and Eleanor Rathbone, issued their "Ten Point Programme for Measures of Rescue from Nazi Terror." Tens of thousands of copies of this were produced, and it was widely discussed by British opinion makers. It included such virtually useless proposals as "Reconsideration of Regulations for

United Kingdom Visas" and "Increased Transport Facilities for Evacuation [of] Refugees." Of course, the Jews of Nazi-occupied Europe, if alive, were prisoners, not refugees free to flee their homelands. There was no mention in the program of bombing Auschwitz or any other extermination camp.

Even more telling, in early 1944 the newly formed U.S. War Refugee Board contacted every American Jewish and prorefugee body to request their proposals for rescuing Jews. It received about 120 separate and specific proposals, which it then summarized, about March 1944, in the "Digest of Suggestions Submitted to the War Refugee Board by Various Private Organizations in Response to a Circular Letter." None of the responses suggested bombing Auschwitz, the rail lines to Auschwitz, or any other extermination or concentration camp.

Why did it take so long to propose such action? Several reasons have been suggested. The extent of the vast machinery of death that constituted the Holocaust was largely unknown until after the war and the Nuremberg Trials of Nazi war criminals. The so-called Vrba-Wetzler Report that detailed the nature of Auschwitz as an extermination center, written in Slovak by two Jewish escapees in late April 1944, was not translated into English until November 1944. It was thus received too late to have impact on the thinking of Jewish and prorefugee groups prior to mid to late 1944. Also, it did not propose bombing Auschwitz.

Jewish and prorefugee groups in the West were extremely reluctant to recommend any specific form of military action to the U.S. and British governments. Military strategy was the responsibility of the most senior Allied leaders, political and military; civilian armchair strategists had no role in these matters. The first proposals to bombing Auschwitz also coincided with intense preparations for and carrying out the Normandy Invasion of June 1944, and no Jewish group would possibly have recommended diverting military resources away from it.

Jewish groups were also reluctant to recommend specific actions that would benefit only or mainly Jews, in preference to the tens of millions of other peoples who constituted the so-called captive nations under Nazi rule. In the early 1940s, these groups lacked the confidence, knowledge, or access to high governmental and military officials. Perceptions of widespread anti-Semitism in the English-speaking democracies also played a role, although it should be noted that Jewish groups, at least in the United States, did regularly hold rallies and demonstrations highlighting the suffering of Jews. Requesting significant changes in military strategy was another matter, however.

Also, Auschwitz was situated in southern Poland and was not reachable by Western Allied bombers until Foggia Air Base in Italy fell to the Allies in December 1943. Nor would any bombing raid have necessarily been successful. The gas chambers at Auschwitz were the size of two tennis courts. Allied bombing at the time was wildly inaccurate, and there would have been heavy casualties among the prisoner population. It is entirely possible that any bombing raid on Auschwitz would have been a fiasco in which Allied bombs missed their intended target of the gas chambers but killed thousands of Jews and others who might have survived the war.

Another point, not generally raised, is that Auschwitz and the other camps in Poland would presumably have required the approval of ever-suspicious Soviet leader Joseph Stalin. The attitude of Stalin and the Soviet government toward the genocide of the Jews remains largely unexplored, but it is difficult to believe that he would have agreed to divert military resources specifically to assist Jews and no one else.

When Rabbi Weissmandel's proposal to bomb the railway line from Kosice to Preskov reached Washington in June 1944, it became the basis of proposals to bomb Auschwitz itself. However, proposals to bomb Auschwitz met initial opposition from many key individuals and organizations. In particular, the Jewish Agency for Palestine (the governing body of the Jewish community there), headed by David Ben-Gurion, debated the suggestion on June 11, 1944, and then voted to oppose it on the grounds that any such bombing was likely to kill Jews. For the same reason, the U.S. War Refugee Board, including its head John Pehle, "flatly rejected as unfeasible" such a proposal. Pehle stated this on August 11, 1944, noting that many Jewish organizations had opposed bombing Auschwitz as likely to kill Jews. Pehle advocated bombing Auschwitz for the first time only on November 8, 1944, after reading eyewitness accounts of the camp. This was after the killings at Auschwitz had ceased. The destruction of the Hungarian Jews, who constituted the last major deportations to Auschwitz, had occurred during May 15–July 8, 1944.

The claim that the bombing of Auschwitz was an immeasurably tragic lost opportunity did not arise until many decades after the war, in particular until the publication of David S. Wyman's influential article "Why Auschwitz Was Not Bombed" in *Commentary* magazine in May 1978 and his considered study of this question titled *The Abandonment of the Jews* (1984). Contemporaries saw matters in a different light: no one proposed bombing Auschwitz until May 1944, and when it was finally proposed, it was largely rejected as impractical or counterproductive. Hindsight is not historical evidence.

William D. Rubinstein

Perspective Essay 4. Diverted Resources and Grand Strategy

Allied political and military leaders during World War II made the right decision not to bomb Auschwitz. Precision bombing was not possible at that time, and area bombing would have brought the deaths of many of those held prisoner at Auschwitz. Destroying the killing mechanisms—the gas chambers and crematoria ovens—would not have stopped the killing, as the Germans would have found other means to accomplish that end. There was also a strategic reason: the Allied goal was to defeat the Nazis and liberate Europe. This entailed using all of their resources, including aircraft and bombs, to end the war as soon as possible. Despite the humanitarian justification, bombing Auschwitz would have diverted resources that could help end the war soon, and accomplishing this could itself save many lives.

In March 1944, Germany occupied Hungary and demanded that the government deport Jews for "labor" to Germany. Auschwitz had been one of the major German killing centers for two years, but some 10,000 to 12,000 Hungarian Jews were deported daily during May 15–July 11, 1944. Out of the some 440,000 deported from Hungary, all but about 50,000 Jews were killed soon after arriving at Auschwitz. Then in late June 1944, major Jewish organizations proposed to the U.S. War Department that the rail lines leading from Hungary to Poland be bombed. Within days, the request had been rejected on the grounds that it was not feasible and would be ineffective and that all aircraft had to be directed against military and industrial targets helping to sustain the German war effort. In short, the goal was to end the war as quickly as possible. One must also keep in mind that only two weeks before the proposal to bomb Auschwitz the Western Allies had landed in Normandy, where they ran into stiff opposition from the German forces. It was clear to U.S. military commanders and political leaders alike that all efforts must be focused there.

Even before the demand to destroy the rail lines (which could have been repaired within days and thus would have required frequent raids), there was a proposal from a Jewish member of the U.S. War Refugee Board and others to bomb Auschwitz itself to stop the killing, the assumption being that with no killing center, there would be an end to the mass killing. There is some truth to that, but millions of Jews were killed in Ukraine and elsewhere by being shot to death and through forced starvation. In any case, most major Jewish organizations rejected the call for bombing on the grounds that it would end up killing the very people it was supposed to save from destruction. There were, for example, 50,000 prisoners in Auschwitz-Birkenau who were only a short distance from where the gas chambers and crematoria did their daily work. And when the Allies rejected the proposed bombing, again on the grounds of lack of feasibility and the need to win the war as quickly as possible, they also noted that there was no possibility in any case of precision bombing: any bombing would be by heavy bomber aircraft suitable only for area bombing. Thus, the death toll among the inmates would no doubt have been extremely high. Although the U.S. War Department did not mention this, Jewish organizations who opposed the attacks pointed out that it would offer Germany the opportunity to claim that those who died in Auschwitz were massacred by the Allies, not by Germany.

In the end, there was no bombing of Auschwitz or of the rail lines from Hungary. By mid-July deportations from Hungary had ended, and by January 1945 Auschwitz and other camps in the east were evacuated, with prisoners being marched toward camps in the Reich. According to historian Saul Friedlander, most of those evacuated "perished from exhaustion, freezing, shooting, or being burned alive." Some 250,000 of the prisoners from all the camps who died were Jews, many of them from the 56,000 who were evacuated from Auschwitz and its satellite camps.

The legacy of the proposals for bombing both the rails and the camp still goes on. There are many different perspectives: questions of evidence, military capacity, ethics, prudence, and what the priorities should have been and questions about sheer prejudice against Jews and other related issues, such as why only a small number of Jewish refugees who were fleeing persecution and death were admitted to the United States. David Wyman's *The Abandonment of the Jews* (1984) is perhaps the most important work on these matters. There are charges of anti-Semitism, particularly that U.S. president Franklin D. Roosevelt put politics above Jewish lives in not wanting to seem to be fighting a war for protection of Jews; of bureaucratic rigidity and lack of imagination; and of a military dedicated to taking lives but not saving them. These charges are false or at most only partly true. The context of the decisions is important. Normandy had just begun, and the war was far from over. Bombing Auschwitz and the rail lines to it as a humanitarian intervention to save lives had to be weighed against the Allied commitment to winning the war and stopping violence, which was also a commitment to humanitarian intervention. Such ethical discussions are never easy, and despite the many books on war, there is never justice in it.

Perhaps those who sought to have the Allies bomb the proposed targets thought in good faith that bombing in Hungary and Poland could proceed without negatively impacting the broader war effort. But most of the political and military leadership at the time thought that a choice, given their military situation and resources, had to be made, and this was to direct all resources to the military effort alone. The Holocaust was not at the center of what World War II was about; even the term "Holocaust" did not come into currency until the 1960s. The overriding goal was the necessity to defeat Nazi Germany and liberate Europe. Some of those who write today seem to forget that to privilege one set of lives above others ignores the ancient Jewish adage "Whose blood is redder?"

Roger W. Smith

Further Reading

Bartov, Omer, ed. *The Holocaust: Origins, Implementations, Aftermath.* London: Routledge, 2000.

Bauer, Yehuda. *A History of the Holocaust.* Revised ed. New York: Franklin Watts, 2001.

Breitman, Richard. *Official Secrets: What the Nazis Planned, What the British and Americans Knew.* New York: Hill and Wang, 1998.

Breitman, Richard, and Alan Kraut. *American Refugee Policy and European Jewry, 1933–1945.* Bloomington: Indiana University Press, 1987.

Dawidowicz, Lucy S. *The War against the Jews, 1933–1945.* New York: Holt, Rinehart and Winston, 1975.

Erdheim, Stuart G. "Could the Allies Have Bombed Auschwitz-Birkenau?" *Holocaust and Genocide Studies* 2(2) (1997): 129–170.

Feingold, Henry L. *Bearing Witness: How America and Its Jews Responded to the Holocaust.* Syracuse, NY: Syracuse University Press, 1995.

Gilbert, Martin. *Auschwitz and the Allies.* New York: Pimlico, 2001.

Gurock, Jeffrey S., ed. *America, American Jews, and the Holocaust.* New York: Routledge, 1998.

Hamerow, Theodor. *While We Watched: Europe, America, and the Holocaust.* New York: Norton, 2008.

Hilberg, Raul. *The Destruction of the European Jews.* New Haven, CT: Yale University Press, 2003.

Laqueur, Walter. *The Terrible Secret: The Suppression of the Truth about Hitler's "Final Solution."* Boston: Little, Brown, 1980.

Levi, Primo. *Survival in Auschwitz.* New York: Macmillan, 1993.

Levy, Richard. "The Bombing of Auschwitz Revisited: A Critical Analysis." *Holocaust and Genocide Studies* 18 (Winter 1996): 267–298.

Neufeld, Michael J., and Michael Berenbaum, eds. *The Bombing of Auschwitz: Should the Allies Have Attempted It?* New York: St. Martin's, 2000.

Rees, Laurence. *Auschwitz: The Nazis and the Final Solution.* New York: Random House, 2005.

Rubinstein, William D. *The Myth of Rescue: Why the Democracies Could Not Have Saved More Jews from the Nazis.* London: Routledge, 1997.

Wiesel, Elie. *And the Sea Is Never Full: Memoirs, 1969–.* New York: Knopf, 1999.

Wyman, David S. *The Abandonment of the Jews: America and the Holocaust, 1941–1945.* New York: New Press, 1998.

43. Were the Agreements Reached at the Yalta Conference an Unnecessary Giveaway to the Soviets?

During February 4–11, 1945, a little over a year after the Tehran Conference, the Big Three—U.S. president Franklin D. Roosevelt, British prime minister Winston Churchill, and Soviet leader Joseph Stalin—met again at the negotiating table, this time at the resort town of Yalta on the Crimean Peninsula's southern coast. On the agenda were a number of thorny issues, including the future of postwar Europe (specifically Germany and Poland), the outlines of the soon to be created United Nations (UN), the Soviet Union's representation in that body, postwar territorial changes, the forced repatriation of Soviet citizens residing in Europe, and the entrance of the Soviet Union into the Pacific war against Japan. The final wartime conference that occurred among the Big Three was in Potsdam, Germany, from July 17 to August 2, 1945. Some of the decisions reached at Yalta have subsequently proven to be quite controversial, and scholars continue to debate the necessity and wisdom of the concessions made to the Soviets during the conference.

The three perspective essays that follow demonstrate divergent opinions on the topic. In the first essay, Dr. George L. Simpson Jr. argues that the results of the Yalta Conference did indeed constitute an unnecessary giveaway to the Soviets. He suggests that the concessions made at Yalta and the inability of the Western Allies to present a unified front against Stalin helped bring about the Cold War. Dr. Lee W. Eysturlid, in the second essay, expresses a similar view. He posits that if Roosevelt and Churchill had made certain demands of Stalin, including adherence to the Declaration of Liberated Europe, no separate representation in the UN General Assembly for Belorussia and Ukraine, and truly free elections in Eastern Europe, these demands would likely have been ignored, but Roosevelt and Churchill would not have lost the valuable moral high ground. Dr. Spencer C. Tucker, however, takes the opposite view, suggesting that the decisions made at Yalta reflected the military situation on the ground in Europe and the resulting relatively weak bargaining position of the Western Allies. Indeed, by early 1945 Soviet troops had pushed the German Army all the way to the Polish-German border, in the process having essentially already occupied all of Eastern Europe and much of Central Europe. He also suggests that Yalta was not nearly as important as both its supporters and its critics allege; many of the decisions finalized at Yalta had already been formulated during previous diplomatic meetings.

Background Essay

In January 1944, the Allied Powers' European Advisory Commission on Germany began meeting in London. The commission decided that Germany's postwar government would be an Allied Control Council in Berlin, composed of commanders of the occupying forces of the various powers. But clarification was required from the Allied leadership on other matters. Between August and October 1944, delegates at the Dumbarton Oaks Conference in Washington, D.C., worked to draft proposals for a postwar United Nations international organization. They also needed decisions on several issues. To resolve these and other matters, a second meeting was scheduled of the Big Three of British prime minister Winston L. S. Churchill, U.S. president Franklin D. Roosevelt, and Soviet leader Joseph Stalin and their staffs (some 700 people in all). It occurred in the Soviet Union during February 4–11, 1945, at the former Livadia Palace near Yalta in the Crimea.

This meeting, also known as the Crimea Conference and code-named Argonaut, was less significant than either its supporters or detractors have alleged. Many of the decisions confirmed here had already been taken during the earlier Tehran Conference (November 28–December 1, 1943) and other lower-level meetings.

Regarding Germany, the Big Three agreed to government by the Allied Control Council. German occupation zones were also set, with France also allowed a zone. The three leaders also agreed on demilitarizing Germany and the punishment of war criminals. The Soviets insisted on exacting heavy reparations from Germany for the extensive damage suffered by the Soviet Union. The Western Allies refused to set a specific amount but tentatively agreed to discuss the sum of $20 billion, with the Soviet Union to receive half of any amount.

Regarding a postwar international organization to maintain the peace, the Big Three adopted recommendations from the Dumbarton Oaks Conference that the

British prime minister Winston L. S. Churchill (left), U.S. president Franklin D. Roosevelt (center), and Soviet premier Josef Stalin (right) at the Yalta Conference during February 4–11, 1945. (National Archives)

United Nations be organized along the lines of the old League of Nations, with a General Assembly, a Security Council, and a Secretariat. It also set the composition of the Security Council. Roosevelt agreed that the Soviet Union might have three votes in the General Assembly. The most difficult matter to resolve was that of the veto in the Security Council.

The disposition of Poland was especially difficult. Stalin demanded and succeeded in establishing the Curzon Line, with slight modifications, as Poland's eastern border. The Allies were more strenuous in objecting to the Oder-Neisse Line as Poland's western boundary, and there was no agreement on this matter at Yalta. Regarding the Polish government, Stalin agreed to broaden the Soviet-organized Lublin government on a "democratic basis" and promised to hold "free and unfettered elections as soon as possible on the basis of universal suffrage and secret ballot." Indeed, in the Declaration on Liberated Europe the three leaders pledged that the provisional governments of liberated European states would be "representative of all democratic elements" based on free elections.

Decisions reached regarding the Far East were kept secret from China. Stalin had already made it clear that the Soviet Union would enter the war against Japan sometime after the defeat of Germany. This was never in doubt. At Yalta, Stalin pledged to enter the war against Japan "two or three months" after the defeat of Germany. In return, the Soviet Union would receive South Sakhalin Island, concessions in the port of Dairen, Port Arthur as a naval base, control over railroads leading to these ports, and the Kurile Islands (which had never been Russian territory). Outer Mongolia would continue to be independent of China, but China would regain sovereignty over Manchuria.

Roosevelt, already in poor health, died in April 1945 and was widely blamed by detractors for concessions thought to be unnecessary made to Stalin at Yalta. The last wartime conferences occurred at Potsdam (July 17–August 2, 1945) and was attended by Stalin, Churchill (who was replaced halfway through by newly elected prime minister Clement Attlee), and Roosevelt's successor, President Harry S. Truman.

Spencer C. Tucker

Perspective Essay 1. The Yalta Agreement Was an Unnecessary Giveaway

When they met in the Crimea in February 1945, U.S. president Franklin D. Roosevelt and British prime minister Winston Churchill acquiesced to Soviet leader Joseph Stalin and allowed wartime exigencies to trump their support for democratic principles. The Big Three, as the triumvirate became known, imposed their decisions on lesser powers without the latter's concurrence and sometimes even without their knowledge. The result of all their convoluted machinations was not concord but enmity. Indeed, the unresolved disputes among the great powers, many of which had begun before Yalta, opened the door for the Cold War.

The Allied leaders each had different goals as they met on the eve of victory over Nazi Germany. From an American perspective, these included securing Soviet assistance in the war against Japan and the desire to get Stalin to join and work constructively with the new United Nations (UN) after the war. The British were eager to have the French included in the postwar European order and prevent the dismemberment of Germany so as to prevent the economic collapse of the continent. The Soviets had borne the brunt of the fighting on the Eastern Front for much of the conflict, and Stalin sought to enhance the strategic position of the Soviet Union much in the manner of the Russian Empire in the final years of the Romanov dynasty that ended in 1917. Thus, the communist dictator was keen to advance Soviet power into the heart of Europe, reconstitute his country's position in the Far East, and obtain reparations for damages inflicted on the Soviet Union.

There are many competing interpretations of what occurred at Yalta. Apologists for Roosevelt and Churchill emphasize how the requirements of waging a war in the European and Pacific theaters constrained the Western Allies at the Yalta Conference. Those who give a sympathetic account of what transpired at Yalta also underscore that the Red Army already occupied much of Eastern Europe and consequently had a great advantage in dictating terms of peace in that region. They further point out that Roosevelt was ill at the time of the conference. Other so-called realists go further and emphasize the "legitimate interests" pursued by the Soviet Union at Yalta. Revisionists place the blame on the breakdown of the wartime coalition not on the Soviet Union but instead on American and British capitalist interests and imperial ambitions.

Each of these interpretations is based on an element of truth and can offer evidence for its conclusions. Yet in the final analysis, what occurred at Yalta was appeasement. Stalin acted like a bully, and Roosevelt and Churchill gave in to him when they did not have to do so.

A central issue to be resolved at the Yalta Conference was the fate of Eastern and Central Europe. In particular, the Allies disagreed over the nature of Poland's future government and its borders. To Stalin, the Polish question was of vital importance to the security of the Soviet Union. He intended to impose the Soviet system on its territory and would brook no dissent from his command. As Great Britain and the United States could not find common ground on the issue, the two countries unwisely came to the crucial summit split on this important issue.

Thus divided, Roosevelt and Churchill gave in to Stalin's demands on Poland when they should not have done so and could have at least publicly expressed their disagreements with the Soviet leader. They allowed the Polish Committee of National Liberation, better known as the Lublin Committee, pride of place in the composition of the interim government of Soviet-occupied Poland. Unfortunately, the individuals who made up the Lublin Committee were handpicked Soviet collaborators who did not represent Poles. The Western Allies relied on the goodwill of Stalin, hoping somehow that he would put continued cooperation with his allies above unilaterally imposing his will on Poland.

Elsewhere in Eastern Europe, disagreements concerned what constituted the Soviet "sphere of influence." The Western Allies wanted "free and unfettered elections" based on universal suffrage with secret balloting that would allow for the self-determination of nations and unimpeded trade. Just as was the case in Poland, however, this desire came up against Soviet security demands of "friendly governments" in these countries.

The Allies were willing to accommodate Stalin by conceding that the foreign and defense policies of the countries of the region would comport with those of the Soviet Union so that they would serve as a buffer zone, but they expected that otherwise they would be autonomous with regard to purely domestic issues. Yet Stalin recognized that truly free elections were bound to create anti-Soviet governments. The Soviet leader would have none of it.

Another area of disagreement at Yalta about which the Western Allies made unwarranted concessions concerned reparations and forced labor. Again, Roosevelt parted with Churchill and acceded to Stalin's demand that the Soviet Union receive half of reparations for war damages from Germany. This occurred when Roosevelt accepted the Soviet leader's figure of $20 billion as the starting point for discussions to be held under the auspices of a Trilateral Reparations Commission, which would meet in Moscow. The accommodation opened the door and ultimately permitted the Soviet Union to exact punitive sanctions that amounted to the wholesale expropriation of the German industrial plant in the Soviet-occupied zone of that country. The reparations permitted the Soviets to coerce ordinary citizens into working for them and gave sanction to the continued exploitation of German prisoners of war as slave laborers.

Roosevelt and Churchill also acceded to Stalin's demands to accept the principle of border alterations and abetted the inhumane transfer and resettlement of millions of people who had no voice in the matter. Thus, the eastern border of Germany moved west to the Oder-Neisse Line, and Germany lost Silesia, Pomerania, part of Saxony, and West Prussia to Poland. East Prussia was annexed to the Soviet Union. The lands ceded to the Poles served as compensation due to a similar adjustment of their frontier with the Soviet Union. With these frontier adjustments came hardships and suffering due to the expulsion of more than 3 million Germans and the removal of nearly 1.5 million displaced persons in what had been eastern Poland. Hundreds of thousands of others chose to live in diaspora rather than come under the oppressive rule of the new Soviet order. According to historian Nikolai Tolstoy, some 2 million Soviet citizens who sought residence outside of the Soviet Union found themselves forcibly repatriated with British and American assistance under the Yalta agreements.

The concessions that Stalin obtained with respect to Northeast Asia were equally disturbing. Roosevelt, who was much more willing to work with Stalin than Churchill at the time, was particularly responsible for the covert deal he made with his Soviet counterpart. The Russo-American protocol essentially amounted to a return to the status quo in the region before the 1904–1905 Russo-Japanese War at a time when imperial Russia sought a position of preeminence in the Far East. In return for the Soviet Union's entry into the war against Japan within two or three months of the defeat of Germany, Roosevelt made a host of concessions. One was the Soviet annexation of South Sakhalin Island and the Kurile Islands. The Soviets also secured a lease on the naval base at Port Arthur as well as preeminence at the port of Darien and control of two Manchurian railways. Outer Mongolia would remain under Soviet authority, too. For his part, Stalin recognized Jiang Jieshi (Chiang Kai-shek), chairman of the Nationalist government of China; promised not to support the Chinese Communists; and recognized China's sovereignty in Manchuria.

Concerning the UN, the Allies resolved most of their differences early in the conference. The Soviets did not press their earlier expressed desire to exercise a veto on procedural issues presented before the UN Security Council. Likewise, they backed off of their contention that the 16 Soviet republics should also be individual members of the UN, although they persisted in arguing that the Soviet Union should have more than one UN representative. Roosevelt felt strongly that a new and improved UN would ensure the peaceful resolution of disputes and thus was willing to make compromises on other issues. The concessions he made, however, did anything but bring about a better world.

One of the arguments in favor of what Roosevelt and Churchill did contends that they had no choice in the matter. Concerning Eastern Europe, those who offer such an apology for the Western leaders stress the fact that the presence of the conquering Red Army made it impossible to reverse such a fait accompli. Unfortunately, such a contention misses the point. Whether they could have stopped Stalin from doing what he wanted is different than giving him sanction for his actions. Signing the agreement was an abnegation of moral responsibility and gave legitimacy to the assertion of brute power. The United States saw itself as the defender of democracy around the globe, and Great Britain had a similar notion of its place among "civilized" nations, yet both were aiding a tyrant.

Even the most rudimentary appreciation of what were then relatively recent events will underscore the folly of trusting in Stalin's benevolence. The Soviet leader killed more people than did Adolf Hitler. Furthermore, it had not yet been half a dozen years since the communist strongman had signed the Nazi-Soviet Nonaggression Pact with Germany. The agreement gave Hitler a free hand to attack Poland and start World War II. Less than three weeks later, the Red Army had captured the same territory Stalin was now getting the Western leaders to accept as his spoils. The Soviets had fed the Nazi war machine right until the moment Hitler turned on them. In the meantime, the Soviets ended the independence of the Baltic states and forced them to join the Soviet Union and fought a war of aggression against the Finns when they would not submit to Soviet dictates. There was no hint of self-determination in any of these conquered territories that the Soviets had ruled. How, then, could the Western Allies believe that there could be anything resembling "free and unfettered elections" or "democracies" anywhere Stalin ruled?

Yet another defense of the concessions of Yalta is that they were necessary to get Stalin to join the war against Japan. The Allies expected that Japan would fight to the bitter end and that there would be a terrible price to be paid in blood to bring about its defeat. Hence, it was necessary to make compromises at the Yalta Conference to get the Soviets to join in the battle. Yet as a good ally, shouldn't Stalin have come to the aid of his counterparts in the war with Japan? From what he demanded at Yalta, the Soviet leader clearly had ambitions in the Far East. Was it not in his interest to join in the defeat of the Japanese war machine? Besides, if Stalin did not do so, he would have had almost no say in the peace—and he knew it. Hence, it was unnecessary to give him so much.

In the final analysis, the concessions that the Western leaders made at the Yalta Conference were unnecessary and illegitimate. As a consequence, Yalta rightfully holds a unique and infamous place in the history of modern times.

George L. Simpson Jr.

Perspective Essay 2. Losing Moral High Ground at Yalta

For eight days in February 1945, the three principal Allied leaders, generally referred to as the Big Three, met in the Crimean resort town of Yalta. The United States was represented by President Franklin D. Roosevelt, the United Kingdom by Prime Minister Winston Churchill, and the Soviet Union by Premier Joseph Stalin. While the conference looked to create a plan to bring an end to the war with Germany and Japan, it also revealed what each power wanted from a postwar world. Although allies, all three sides were necessarily interested first in their own needs and positions, creating a competitive, if not combative, environment.

Roosevelt was far too indulgent of Stalin's demands during the conference and in the process undermined the creation of a peaceful postwar world. What Roosevelt and Churchill should have done in their dealings with Stalin is difficult to resolve. One must first examine the issues being discussed and then the circumstances in which they were resolved.

The Yalta Conference occurred just four months before the end of World War II in Europe. The first real conference of the Big Three had been held in Tehran, Iran, in late 1943. For that conference, the notion of a postwar world was secondary to the actual winning of the war. The defeat of Nazi Germany and imperial Japan was anything but obvious. This was not the case nearly two years later when the same three leaders met in Yalta. By February 1945 German and Japanese forces were in retreat on all fronts, although much difficult fighting remained. Also, the atomic bomb had not been tested and thus played no role in the negotiations.

Roosevelt envisioned a postwar world where all the major powers would cooperate on important issues, sidelining the need to resolve differences through war. His dedication to the United Nations (UN), the Declaration of Liberated Europe, and a democratic Eastern Europe is clear. Despite the special relationship between the United States and the United Kingdom, Roosevelt did not press at Yalta for an end to the colonial regimes of the British or French. Abandoning that topic surrendered some of the moral high ground that could be played against the Soviets, as it concerned their control of Eastern Europe.

From a military point of view, the Western Allies were anxious to retain the Soviet offensive against the Germans on the Eastern Front. By 1945 this effort was critical to completing the destruction of the German Army, often at great cost to the Soviets. Secondary was Roosevelt's emphasis on Stalin keeping his promise to go to war with Japan. Roosevelt regarded the Soviets as the key to avoiding a bloody, protracted invasion of the Japanese home islands. No one knew if the atomic bomb would work, and some projections for an invasion of the Japanese home islands suggested as many as 1 million American casualties.

Churchill, while also an ardent supporter of a free Eastern Europe and the creation of the UN, had a different focus. For him, UK interests included Britain's maintenance of empire, especially India and the Middle East, and the continuation of Britain as a major world power. To this end, he was clearly willing to enter into a more cynical view of the postwar world, readily making deals with Stalin aside from Roosevelt. Churchill also had a much more accurate assessment of Stalin than did Roosevelt.

Stalin was a tyrant, responsible—in part or whole—for the creation and continuation of the Soviet Union's system of political mass murder and repression. The Soviet Union maintained a large-scale political prison system, the gulag, into which millions had disappeared or would disappear or would spend long, gruesome sentences. Stalin was an ardent Marxist-Leninist who had made clear his belief that the war was merely a continuation of the climactic destruction of capitalism. His cynical alliance with Nazi Germany in 1939 demonstrated that he was always willing to make allies where convenient and would keep them only as long as they furthered his own interests. Stalin also believed that deception was simply a part of diplomacy; he never intended to honor anything he agreed to at Yalta unless it suited his purposes. Stalin intended to control as much of Europe as possible, allowing him to maintain his grip in the Soviet Union and create a substantial buffer zone of puppet states. To this end, he showed no concern for human rights, the rule of law, or international agreements.

The general structure of the UN, agreed to at Yalta, doomed that organization to gridlock and inaction. Roosevelt supported Soviet insistence that both Belorussia and Ukraine be given seats in the UN General Assembly. This is farcical, as both states were part of the Soviet Union. The concession gave the Soviet Union enhanced voting strength. The granting of the veto to each of the five permanent members of the UN Security Council meant that Stalin could block anything of substance. Finally, the call for all members to place into "trusteeship" any territories in dispute was an empty concept. Why would the Russians, who had invaded Finland and Poland without provocation in 1939, listen to such?

The Declaration of Liberated Europe was a failure. The declaration made clear the determination of the Big Three to ensure independent, freely elected governments in all the states now freed from German or Italian control and those states that had been ruled by a fascist government, such as Hungary and Romania. No mention was made of states freed from Japan, although Roosevelt looked for the same process for China.

The declaration was a failure, its intentions blocked from the outset by Stalin. The call for the "restoration of sovereign rights and self-government to those peoples who have been forcibly deprived them by the aggressor nations" fell flat. In fact, there was a striking difference between those states liberated by the Western Allies and those taken by the Soviets. Where U.S. and British forces had liberated Western states, democracy would return. Wherever Soviet forces were in control, communist regimes would come into being, economically tied to the Soviet Union.

The reparations agreement agreed to at Yalta for purposes of further discussion laid Germany open to being pillaged, if not economically destroyed, by the Soviet Union. Especially onerous on the part of the Americans and British was the agreement to allow for the use of "German labor." Since the Soviets were notorious for the use of their own citizenry in slave labor conditions, what could this mean except that millions of German civilians would be subject to Soviet slavery?

The Big Three's specific agreements on Poland and the rest of Eastern Europe in general were useless. While specific provisions were made as to what should be done concerning democratic voting and the return of Polish anticommunists,

Stalin provided only lip service. By the time of the Yalta Conference, the Soviets were already establishing a puppet regime in Poland, and those in opposition were being marginalized. Churchill bemoaned this abandonment of Poland; it was the German invasion of Poland that had triggered the British declaration of war against Germany. Now seemingly it was to be given up to a new conqueror.

In a similar vein were agreements on bringing the forces of the Soviet Union into the war with Japan. To secure Soviet participation, Roosevelt signed over Mongolia, South Sakhalin Island, and the Kuriles. These broad decisions concerning the post-war status of China were taken without consultation with Chinese Nationalist leader Jiang Jieshi (Chiang Kai-shek), although he was to be "consulted" later. Stalin's agreement to recognize the Nationalist government in China at Yalta was another promise that held no meaning for him. For all of this and for real access to China and Korea, the Soviets agreed to enter the Pacific war within three months after the defeat of Germany.

If Roosevelt's actions at Yalta were "sellouts" to the Soviets, what could he have done to change this? There is no easy answer. If the United States and the United Kingdom had been serious in their commitment to democracy and self-determination in Europe, could they have followed it up? To answer yes—that the Yalta Conference was the time and place to face down the next great menace to world peace and global cooperation—would have meant risking a new war, this time with the Soviet Union. It is not clear what Roosevelt could have gained from a hard-line approach to Poland and Eastern Europe and other contentious issues. In the end, the thought that Roosevelt and Churchill would have been willing to go to war with the Soviet Union over these issues is unrealistic. However, it is not unrealistic to believe that Roosevelt could have made a point of exposing the crimes and criminal intentions of the Soviet dictator for what they were—aggrandizement and repression. That failure made Yalta a byword for betrayal in Poland; *yowta*, the Polish word for "Yalta," means "betrayal" to this day.

Lee W. Eysturlid

Perspective Essay 3. Securing Soviet Cooperation against Japan

The agreements reached at the February 4–11, 1945, Yalta Conference were not an unnecessary giveaway to the Soviet Union; rather, many of the decisions confirmed there had already been made earlier and, in any case, were conditioned by the realities on the ground. At the time, the outcome of the conference generated considerable satisfaction. It was only later that it became contentious.

The bargaining position of the Western leaders had not appreciably improved since the conference of the Big Three leaders at Tehran (November 28–December 1, 1943). The situation on the ground found British prime minister Winston Churchill and U.S. president Franklin Roosevelt in a very weak bargaining position. They had just suffered the humiliation of the initial German successes in the Ardennes Offensive (Battle of the Bulge), which had caught American forces in Belgium completely by surprise. The Red Army, on the other hand, had recently destroyed German Army Group Center and was then only 50 miles from Berlin.

One factor at Yalta was certainly Roosevelt's determination to draw Joseph Stalin "out of his shell" and bring the Soviet Union into postwar cooperation with the Western powers. Roosevelt believed, falsely as it turned out, that Stalin was "getable." As a result, Roosevelt continued his mistaken conciliatory tactical approach of the Tehran Conference by making every effort to accommodate the Soviet leader. It certainly did not enhance the Western bargaining position when Roosevelt announced that U.S. troops were unlikely to remain long in Europe with the end of hostilities. Churchill had hoped, indeed expected, that he and Roosevelt would stand together on policy matters, but in another serious error Roosevelt continued his practice of distancing himself from Churchill most notably on colonial issues, even taking the form of making jokes at the British leader's expense. Another factor at work was that Roosevelt and U.S. planners had chosen to seek the speediest possible conclusion to the war with the least expenditure of American lives rather than wage the war for geopolitical objectives and advantage, as Churchill (and Stalin) desired.

These factors aside, the Western position was weak, and Stalin was well aware of it. The Soviet leader also knew exactly what he wanted, and he was determined to secure it. After World War I, the Western Allies had sought to construct a cordon sanitaire to contain Bolshevism, erecting a string of new states, largely carved out of former czarist Russia, that would wall in the new Soviet Union from the West. Stalin's goal was now essentially the reverse, a belt of East European satellites that would exclude Western influence. Russia had been invaded from the west three times in modern history—in 1812, during World War I, and now in World War II. Stalin was determined to provide territorial security against another invasion from the west, and he was equally set on protecting a severely wounded Soviet Union.

Although Staliun trumpeted Soviet suffering in the war, the actual toll for the Soviet Union was greater than even he was prepared to admit or that Western leaders believed at the time. Some 27 million Soviet citizens died in the war, and much of the western Soviet Union had been devastated by the shifting tides of battle. A great swath of the western Soviet Union had been devastated, with villages, towns, and cities destroyed.

There was another factor at work as well. Stalin wanted to keep out Western influence. In 1945, Soviet soldiers could see for themselves even in war-torn

Germany the far higher standard of living enjoyed by the peoples in the West, and they would now certainly expect improved conditions in their own country following the defeat of Germany. Stalin was determined to maintain firm control, however, and his vision of a postwar Soviet society was far different than that of the masses who assumed that peace would bring consumer goods and a higher standard of living.

Regarding Germany, the Big Three agreed to government by an Allied Control Council. German occupation zones were also set, and at the suggestion of the Western leaders, France was allowed a zone, although Stalin denigrated the French contribution to victory and insisted that its zone be carved from territory already assigned to Britain and the United States. The three leaders also agreed on steps to demilitarize Germany, dissolve the National Socialist Party, and punish war criminals (the "Three Ds" of demilitarization, democratization, and denazification). In what would later be regarded as a controversial decision, the leaders also agreed that all nationals accused of being "deserters or traitors" were to be returned to their countries of origin. This enabled the Soviets to secure numerous opponents of the regime who had sought asylum in the West even before the war.

The Soviets insisted on exacting heavy reparations from Germany for damages inflicted by that nation on the Soviet Union. The Western Allies, remembering the trouble caused by reparations after World War I and fearful that they would be subsidizing Soviet exactions (as indeed proved to be the case), refused to set a specific amount but tentatively agreed to discuss the sum of $20 billion. The Soviet Union was to receive half of any reparations. In the end, the Soviets literally took everything they could move, including entire factories, and shipped them back to the Soviet Union. According to Western calculations, the Soviets extracted from their zone of Germany alone reparations on the order of $14 billion, more than it had initially demanded from the whole of Germany. In addition, the Soviets confiscated properties held to be Nazi and extracted reparations from the other European states occupied by the Red Army.

As with President Woodrow Wilson after World War I, Roosevelt was keen to secure the establishment of a postwar organization of nations. Thanks to Soviet espionage, Stalin was well aware of Roosevelt's aspirations in this regard and, although not greatly interested in the organization himself, used this to secure concessions elsewhere. Roosevelt agreed that the Soviet Union might have three votes in the United Nations (UN) General Assembly, but the major issue to be resolved was the matter of a veto over decisions by the UN Security Council. This only became an issue in U.S. politics later, when the Soviet Union exercised that privilege so liberally. In fact, the U.S. Senate would likely not have approved American participation in the UN without the veto provision.

Poland was a a major issue to resolve. The invasion of Poland in September 1939 had begun the war, there was a large Polish American population in the United

States, and Poles had provided invaluable assistance to the Allied victory in code breaking and in the Battle of Britain and many other campaigns. But the Red Army already occupied Poland. Churchill made this a major issue, pointing out that Britain had gone to war in September 1939 because of the German invasion of that country. But, once again, the West had little or no leverage in the matter. Regarding boundaries, Stalin demanded and won the Curzon Line, with slight modifications, as Poland's eastern border. This was the line that had been set by the Western powers themselves after World War I, so they were hardly in position to oppose it in 1945. The Allies were more strenuous in objecting to the Oder-Neisse Line as Poland's western boundary and there was no agreement on this matter at Yalta. Regarding the Polish government, only a month before the Yalta meeting Moscow had recognized the Lublin Poles as the official government of Poland. Stalin agreed to broaden this puppet government on a "democratic basis," and he pledged to hold "free and unfettered elections as soon as possible on the basis of universal suffrage and secret ballot." In the Declaration of Liberated Europe, the Western Allies secured the same concessions for Yugoslavia, Romania, and Bulgaria. But events would prove that such lofty phrases would be subjected to completely different interpretations by the West and the Soviets. As it worked out, the Soviets excluded from the governments any parties they deemed "fascist" and interpreted "democratic" to mean only those political parties sympathetic to and supportive of communism.

The most controversial decisions taken at Yalta concerned the Far East. These were deliberately kept secret from China. Stalin had made it clear that the Soviet Union would enter the war against Japan sometime after the defeat of Germany. This matter was never in doubt. The problem lay in its timing. Here, Stalin was in the same position enjoyed by the Allies before the invasion of France across the English Channel. Tardy Soviet entry into the Pacific war might mean heavy U.S. casualties in an invasion of the Japanese home islands. No one knew whether the atomic bomb would work and, even if it did, whether it would be decisive in bringing about Japan's defeat.

In light of the heavy U.S. casualties sustained in the battles for Iwo Jima and Okinawa, it is easy to understand the reluctance of the U.S. Joint Chiefs of Staff to invade Japan. The Japanese military had available in its home islands 1 million troops, 3,000 Kamikaze aircraft, and 5,000 suicide boats. With a U.S. invasion scheduled for November 1, 1945, and well aware of the high cost of such an enterprise, the Joint Chiefs of Staff pressed Roosevelt at Yalta to get the Soviet Union into the war against Japan as soon as possible and at any cost.

At Yalta, Stalin pledged to enter the war against Japan "two or three months" after the defeat of Germany. The Soviet Union would receive in return South Sakhalin Island, concessions in the port of Dairen (now Dalian, China), a naval base at Port Arthur (today Lüshunkou, China), control over rail lines to these ports, and the Kurile Islands (which had never been Russian). Outer Mongolia was to remain independent of China, but China would regain sovereignty over Manchuria.

The concessions to the Soviets in the Far East created the greatest controversy. In effect, they replaced Japanese imperialism with that of the Soviet Union, but the Western leaders believed that they were necessary to secure the timing of the Soviet entry into the Pacific war. In future years, what Americans disliked most about Yalta was that these concessions turned out to be unnecessary. At the time, however, the outcome of the Yalta Conference generated considerable satisfaction. Only with the developing Cold War during the late 1940s and the realization that Soviet help had not been necessary in the Pacific war did Yalta become such a fractious issue in U.S. politics, with Republican Party leaders charging that there had been a Democratic Party "giveaway" to the communists.

Spencer C. Tucker

Further Reading

Buhite, Russell D. *Decisions at Yalta: An Appraisal of Summit Diplomacy.* New York: Rowman and Littlefield, 1992.

Feis, Herbert. *Churchill-Roosevelt-Stalin: The War They Waged and the Peace They Sought.* Princeton, NJ: Princeton University Press, 1957.

Fischer, Louis. *The Road to Yalta: Soviet Foreign Relations, 1941–1945.* New York: Harper and Row, 1972.

Gaddis, John Lewis. *The Cold War: A New History.* New York: Penguin, 2005.

Gaddis, John Lewis. *We Now Know: Rethinking Cold War History.* Oxford, UK: Clarendon, 1997.

Gardner, Lloyd C. *Spheres of Influence: The Great Powers Partition in Europe, from Munich to Yalta.* New York: Ivan R. Dee, 1994.

Graebner, Norman A., Richard Dean Burns, and Joseph M. Siracusa. *America and the Cold War: A Realist Interpretation.* Santa Barbara, CA: Praeger Security International, 2010.

Harbutt, Fraser J. *Yalta 1945: Europe and America at the Crossroads.* New York: Cambridge University Press, 2010.

Kennedy-Pipe, Caroline. *Stalin's Cold War: Soviet Strategies in Europe, 1943 to 1956.* New York: Manchester University Press, 1995.

Leffler, Melvyn P. "Adherence to Agreements: Yalta and the Experiences of the Early Cold War." *International Security* 11(1) (1986): 88–123.

Mastny, Vojtech. *Russia's Road to the Cold War: Diplomacy, Warfare, and the Politics of Communism, 1941–1945.* New York: Columbia University Press, 1979.

Plokhy, Serhii. *Yalta: The Price of Peace.* New York: Viking, 2010.

Rees, Laurence. *World War II behind Closed Doors: Stalin, the Nazis and the West.* New York: Pantheon, 2009.

Reynolds, David. *Summits: Six Meetings That Shaped the Twentieth Century.* New York: Basic Books, 2009.

Seton-Watson, Hugh. *Neither War nor Peace: The Struggle for Power in the Postwar World.* New York: Praeger, 1960.

Snell, John L. *The Meaning of Yalta: Big Three Diplomacy and the New Balance of Power.* Baton Rouge: Louisiana State University Press, 1956.

Stettinius, Edward R., Jr. *Roosevelt and the Russians: The Yalta Conference.* Edited by Walter Johnson. New York: Harold Ober Associates, 1949.

Szaz, Zoltan Michael. *Germany's Eastern Frontiers: The Problem of the Oder-Neisse Line.* Chicago: Henry Regnery, 1960.

Theoharis, Athan G. *The Yalta Myths: An Issue in U.S. Politics, 1945–1955.* Columbia: University of Missouri Press, 1970.

Thomas, Hugh. *Armed Truce: The Beginnings of the Cold War, 1945–1946.* New York: Atheneum, 1987.

Tolstoy, Nikolai. *Victims of Yalta: The Secret Betrayal of the Allies, 1944–1947.* New York: Pegasus, 2012.

Wandycz, Piotr Stefan. *The United States and Poland.* Cambridge, MA: Harvard University Press, 1980.

Zubok, Vladislav, and Constantine Pleshakov. *Inside the Kremlin's Cold War: From Stalin to Krushchev.* Cambridge, MA: Harvard University Press, 1996.

44. Was the United States Justified in Dropping Atomic Bombs on Hiroshima and Nagasaki?

By the summer of 1945, America's participation in World War II had been dragging on for nearly four years. The war in Europe had ended in May with the surrender of Nazi Germany, but the United States and Japan continued to slug it out in a brutal campaign in the Pacific. The American public was war weary and wanted the conflict to end. At the time, U.S. military planners were girding themselves for a potentially brutal campaign to assault and subdue the Japanese home islands, an endeavor that was expected to bring heavy U.S. casualties. Presented with an opportunity to end the war quickly, President Harry S. Truman authorized the use of atomic bombs against Japan. The Japanese death toll from the bombings was shockingly high. Some 70,000 people died almost instantly at Hiroshima on August 6, and more than 70,000 people died at Nagasaki on August 9; perhaps as many as 200,000 more were injured or later died from radiation poisoning or cancer. Japan surrendered unconditionally on August 15. But was the use of the atomic bomb justified? Were there other ways in which the Japanese might have been compelled to capitulate? And were there other motives at play in employing the atomic bombs?

In the first perspective essay, Dr. Conrad C. Crane argues that the use of atomic bombs was justified and was merely a natural extension of bombing tactics that had already been implemented, including the firebombing of German and Japanese cities that had killed tens of thousands of civilians. Thus, discussions concerning the use of the bombs revolved around how to employ them rather than if they should be employed in the first place. Dr. Spencer C. Tucker contends that the use of the atomic bombs was justified, as the United States did not have conclusive proof that Japan was ready to surrender unconditionally. Furthermore, a land invasion would have resulted in unacceptably high numbers of casualties. Dr. J. Samuel Walker takes issue with the arguments made by both traditionalists and revisionists, pointing out errors and oversimplifications made on both extremes of the debate. Instead, he opts for a middle ground that rejects the "atomic bomb or invasion" dichotomy. He argues that dropping the bombs was necessary to end the war quickly and save thousands (although not hundreds of thousands) of American lives, but it was not the only feasible alternative to an all-out invasion of the Japanese home islands. Finally, Dr. Gar Alperovitz is firm in his view that dropping the bombs was unnecessary and, further, that many if not most of the top U.S. military leaders are on record as having strongly agreed that it was unnecessary. He contends that Japan was on the brink of surrendering and that a coordinated Soviet attack, along with a readily acceptable modification of the surrender terms as advised by U.S. intelligence and other officials, would likely have brought an end to the war well before an invasion could begin. He also argues that U.S. policy makers elected to employ the bombs to intimidate the Soviet leadership.

Background Essay

The U.S. bombing of the Japanese city of Hiroshima on August 6, 1945, was the first use of an atomic bomb in warfare. On July 25, 1945, commander of U.S. Strategic Air Forces General Carl Spaatz received orders to employ the 509th Composite Group, Twentieth Air Force, in a "special bomb" attack on selected target cities in Japan, specifically Hiroshima, Kokura, Niigata, or Nagasaki. Following Japanese rejection of conditions promulgated by the Potsdam Proclamation on July 26, a declaration threatening Japan with total destruction if unconditional surrender was not accepted, U.S. president Harry S. Truman authorized use of the special bomb.

Assembled in secret and loaded on the Boeing B-29 Superfortress *Enola Gay*, the bomb consisted of a core of uranium isotope 235 shielded by several hundred pounds of lead encased in explosives designed to condense the uranium and initiate a fission reaction. Known as "Little Boy," the bomb possessed a force equivalent to 12,500 tons of TNT (12.5 kilotons).

The *Enola Gay*, commanded by Colonel Paul Tibbets, departed Tinian early on August 6, accompanied to Japan by two B-29s assigned as scientific and photographic observers. The flight to Japan was uneventful, and Tibbets was informed at 7:47 a.m. by weather planes that Hiroshima was clear for bombing. Japan's eighth-largest city (with about 245,000 residents in August 1945), Hiroshima was an important port of southern Honshu and headquarters of the Japanese Second Army.

The *Enola Gay* arrived over the city at an altitude of 31,600 feet and dropped the bomb at 8:15:17 a.m. local time. After a descent of some nearly 6 miles, the bomb detonated 43 seconds later some 1,890 feet over a clinic and about 800 feet from the aiming point, Aioi Bridge. The initial fireball expanded to 110 yards in diameter, generating heat in excess of 300,000 degrees Centigrade, with core temperatures over 50 million degrees Centigrade. At the clinic directly beneath the explosion, the temperature was several thousand degrees. The immediate concussion destroyed almost everything within 2 miles of ground zero. The resultant mushroom cloud rose to 50,000 feet and was observed by B-29s more than 360 miles away. After 15 minutes, the atmosphere dropped radioactive "black rain," adding to the death and destruction.

Four square miles of Hiroshima's heart disappeared in seconds, including 62,000 buildings. More than 71,000 Japanese died, another 20,000 were wounded, and 171,000 were left homeless. Some estimates place the number of killed at more than 200,000. About one-third of those killed instantly were soldiers. Most elements of the Japanese Second General Army were at physical training on the grounds of Hiroshima Castle when the bomb exploded. Barely 900 yards from the explosion's epicenter, the castle and its residents were vaporized. Also killed was an American prisoner of war in the exercise area. Radiation sickness began the next day and added to the death toll over several years.

Truman released a statement on August 7 describing the weapon and calling on Japan to surrender, but most Japanese leaders ignored his message as propaganda. Following the Japanese refusal to surrender, on August 8 the Twentieth Air Force headquarters directed that on the following day the second atomic bomb on Tinian Island be dropped on another Japanese city. Kokura was designated as the primary target, with Nagasaki, a city of some 230,000 persons, the alternate.

Early on August 9, the Boeing B-29 Superfortress bomber *Bockscar* (sometimes written as *Bock's Car*), commanded by Major Charles Sweeney, departed Tinian. Again, two other B-29s accompanied it as scientific and photographic observer

The ruins of the Japanese city of Hiroshima after the dropping of the atomic bomb on August 6, 1945. (Library of Congress)

aircraft. *Bockscar* carried a plutonium nuclear-fission bomb nicknamed "Fat Man." Its payload was greater than that of the Hiroshima bomb. The plutonium 238 isotope core consisted of two melon-shaped hemispheres surrounded by a ring of explosive charges designed to drive the sections together, achieving critical mass and a chain reaction releasing 22 kilotons of energy in a millionth of a second.

Sweeney flew *Bockscar* to Kokura but found it overcast and circled for 10 minutes, then decided to divert to Nagasaki, which was also partly obscured by clouds. A break in the clouds allowed a visual bomb run rather than employing radar. The aiming point was the Mitsubishi shipyards.

The bomb was dropped from 31,000 feet at 11:02 a.m. local time and detonated 53 seconds later, approximately 1,500 feet over the city, destroying everything within a 1,000-yard radius. An intense blue-white explosion pushed up a pillar of fire 10,000 feet, followed by a mushroom cloud to 60,000 feet.

Although the bomb exploded 8,500 feet from its intended aiming point, it leveled one-third of the city. Called the "Red Circle of Death," the fire and blast area within the Urakami Valley section destroyed more than 18,000 homes and killed 74,000 people. Another 75,000 were injured, with many of these dying from wounds or complications. Blast forces traveling in excess of 9,000 miles per hour damaged buildings 3 miles away, and the concussion was felt 40 miles from the epicenter. Ashes of death from the mushroom cloud spread radiation poisoning, killing those not taken outright within 1,000 yards of the epicenter. The bomb might have killed thousands more, but it detonated away from the city center in a heavy industrial area, vaporizing three of Nagasaki's largest war factories.

Critically low on fuel, the *Bockscar* landed on Okinawa, its gas tanks virtually empty, then flew back to Tinian. Included in the instrument bundle dropped from the observation plane was a letter addressed to Japanese physicist Professor F. Sagane (Sagane Ryokichi) urging immediate surrender and threatening continued atomic destruction of Japanese cities. Written by three American physicists, the letter was a bluff, as no other atomic bombs were then ready. Nonetheless, the second atomic attack, coupled with the August 8 declaration of war against Japan by the Soviet Union, provided Japanese emperor Hirohito with the excuse to end the war.

Mark E. Van Rhyn

Perspective Essay 1. The Decision to Employ the Bomb

Although there were extensive consultations about the employment of the atomic bomb, discussions always focused on how to use the new weapon rather than whether to use it. Its employment was a natural extension of bombing tactics already in use, including the firebombing of German and Japanese cities in which civilians perished in the tens of thousands.

Intelligence reports revealed that Germany was working to develop an atomic weapon, so during the first years of the top-secret Manhattan Project, military planners assumed that an American-made bomb would be used against the Germans. Germany surrendered before the U.S. bomb could be successfully tested, however. In the spring and summer of 1945, the primary aim of Allied decision makers was to achieve the surrender of Japan as quickly as possible at the lowest cost in lives, and all involved assumed that if the Manhattan Project could produce a workable weapon, it would be expended against an enemy target.

It could be argued that the decision to use the atomic bomb was made on December 6, 1941, when the first funds were approved for its development. At the time, American leaders assumed that the new invention would be a legitimate weapon in the war, and they never questioned that assumption afterward.

Although President Franklin D. Roosevelt's key advisers on the project concluded in May 1943 that the first operational bomb should be dropped on Japan, the choice of targets really did not receive systematic attention until two years later. A special Target Committee for the Manhattan Project began meeting in April

1945, and by the next month it had produced a short list of target cities, including Kyoto and Hiroshima. On May 31, the blue-ribbon Interim Committee appointed by Secretary of War Henry L. Stimson began meeting to discuss how best to use the new weapon. A suggestion made to try a warning and noncombat demonstration was quickly rejected. First, if this failed, it might serve to stiffen Japanese resolve rather than forcing surrender. Second, at the time, there were only two or three bombs under development; if one failed or did not impress the Japanese, this left only one or two bombs in the American arsenal. The committee thus recommended that the bomb be dropped without warning on a target that would have the largest possible psychological impact.

On July 16, 1945, the United States successfully detonated the world's first atomic bomb in the desert near Alamogordo, New Mexico. Eventually, military planners came up with a target list of Hiroshima, Kokura, Kyoto, and Nigata. Stimson persuaded the planners to substitute Nagasaki for the shrine city of Kyoto and then presented the list to President Harry S. Truman in late July. Truman approved the directive without consulting anyone and wrote in his diary that the bomb would be used between July 25 and August 10. The new weapon offered the possibility of ending the war sooner, and he saw no compelling reason not to employ it. Despite some historians' claims to the contrary, there was no reliable evidence of any imminent Japanese collapse or surrender. Although some leaders did perceive a display of the atomic bomb's power as a potential tool to intimidate the Soviet Union in the future, this was a secondary benefit of its employment and not a factor in operational decision making.

No single government document shows Truman's decision to use the bomb, but there were two relevant military directives from the Joint Chiefs of Staff to the U.S. Army Air Forces. The first, to Army Air Forces commander General Henry "Hap" Arnold on July 24, designated the four possible targets. The next day a similar order to General Carl Spaatz, commanding U.S. Strategic Air Forces in the Pacific, added a date: "after about August 3, 1945." That document also directed that other bombs were to be delivered against targets as soon as they were ready. On the basis of these orders, Spaatz selected Hiroshima and then Kokura to be the targets for the first and second atomic missions. Cloud cover on the day of the second raid caused the shift to the secondary target of Nagasaki.

Some critics have questioned why there was not more deliberation about whether to use the terrible new weapon. The main concern for decision makers was to win the war quickly while avoiding a costly invasion of the Japanese mainland or losing public support for unconditional surrender. Under the conditions in 1945, which had already produced fire raids that had killed far more Japanese civilians than did the attacks on Hiroshima and Nagasaki, no U.S. president or general could have failed to employ the atomic bomb.

Conrad C. Crane

Perspective Essay 2. Dropping the Bomb Saved Lives

Dropping the atomic bombs on Japan saved the lives of hundreds of thousands of U.S. soldiers and was the only way to end the war quickly. In the summer of 1945, American planners hoped that a naval blockade and a strategic bombing campaign of the Japanese home islands would bring the war to an end. The prospects for an actual invasion appeared dim, as Japanese leaders made major preparations to defend against such an attack. In light of the heavy casualties sustained by U.S. forces in the invasions of Iwo Jima and Okinawa earlier that year, the U.S. Joint Chiefs of Staff were reluctant to carry out Operation DOWNFALL, the planned land invasion of Japan. The Japanese military had 1 million soldiers, 3,000 kamikaze aircraft, and 5,000 suicide boats available to defend its home islands. Civilians were also being prepared to fight to the death. With the U.S. invasion scheduled for November 1, 1945, and well aware that the cost of such an enterprise was likely to be high, the Joint Chiefs of Staff pressed President Franklin D. Roosevelt at the February 1945 Yalta Conference to persuade the Soviet Union to enter the war against Japan at any cost.

Following the successful test detonation of an atomic bomb at Alamogordo, New Mexico, on July 16, 1945, sharp debate arose among advisers to U.S. president Harry S. Truman (who had succeeded Roosevelt as president on the latter's death in April) regarding whether to employ the new weapon against Japan. The terror threshold had already been passed in the firebombing of Japanese cities. Indeed, the most destructive single air raid in history was not the atomic bombing of Hiroshima or Nagasaki but rather the firebombing of Tokyo on the night of March 9–10, 1945. This was total war. It was always assumed that the bomb would be used if it became available. American planners believed that employing the bomb would in all likelihood bring the war to a speedy end, saving many American lives. It would also mean that the United States would not have to share occupation of Japan with the Soviet Union, and hopefully it would deter Soviet leader Joseph Stalin from future aggression. The atomic bomb was thus essentially a psychological weapon rather than a purely military tool, the use of which was designed to influence Japanese political leaders. Dropping it appeared to be the only way to realize the American goal of unconditional surrender.

Revisionist historians have held that the Japanese government was trying desperately to leave the war and that employing the bomb was unnecessary. Intercepts of diplomatic messages indicated, however, that Japan had not yet reached the decision to surrender when the first bomb was dropped. While Emperor Hirohito and his principal advisers had concluded that Japan could not win the war, they still held out hope for a negotiated settlement and believed that a last decisive battle would force the Allies to grant more favorable peace terms.

Post–atomic bomb estimates have claimed the possibility of up to 1 million casualties in a U.S. invasion of Japan. However, historian Ray Skates concludes in his authoritative study *The Invasion of Japan: Alternative to the Bomb* (1998) that Operation OLYMPIC, the first phase of the invasion of Japan (the conquest of the island of Kyushu planned for November 1945), would alone have taken two months and resulted in 75,000 to 100,000 U.S. casualties. Such losses, while they would not have affected the outcome of the war, might indeed have brought about the political goals sought by the Japanese leaders for more favorable surrender terms.

Prolonging the war would have meant a significantly higher cost in Japanese lives than those actually killed in the atomic bombings. During the war the Japanese lost 323,495 dead on the home front, the vast majority of them from air attack. With continued strategic bombing this total would have swelled, and many other Japanese would simply have died of starvation. By August 1945, Japan's largest cities had been largely burned out. Waterborne transportation had been interdicted by airborne mining and submarines, and the Japanese nation was close to starvation. The reduced food supply was highly dependent on railroad distribution, and the railroads would have been the next major strategic bombing target. In effect, dropping the bomb resulted in a net saving of both Japanese and American lives.

The first bomb fell on Hiroshima on August 6, 1945. On August 8, the Soviet Union declared war on Japan, with Stalin honoring to the day his pledge at Yalta to enter the war against Japan "two or three months after the defeat of Germany," which had occurred on May 8, 1945. On August 9, a second atomic bomb fell on Nagasaki.

After prolonged meetings with his advisers, Hirohito made the decision for peace. The U.S. dropping of the atomic bombs enabled him to take this difficult step in the face of a sharply divided cabinet. Even so, his decision was not without danger, for fanatics determined to fight on to the end plotted to assassinate the emperor to prevent announcement of the decision. To forestall this, Hirohito communicated the decision over radio. On the afternoon of August 15, 1945, in a voice never heard before by the Japanese people, Hirohito told his people that Japan would accept the Potsdam Declaration and surrender. In so doing, he specifically mentioned the atomic bomb: "Moreover, the enemy has begun to employ a new and most cruel bomb, the power of which to do damage is indeed incalculable, taking the toll of many innocent lives." World War II had come to an end, and the atomic bomb played a major role in it, saving both Japanese and American lives.

Spencer C. Tucker

Perspective Essay 3. A Necessary Action to End the War

The simple answer to the question "Was the United States justified in dropping the atomic bomb on Hiroshima and Nagasaki in World War II?" is *yes,* the United States was justified in using atomic bombs to end World War II in the Pacific at the earliest possible moment. The answer to a closely related question—"Was the use of the bomb necessary?"—is more ambiguous. In my view, the answer to this question is yes, it was necessary in some ways, and no, it was not necessary in other ways.

By the summer of 1945 after three and a half years of cruel and bloody war, American leaders knew that Japan was defeated. It was running desperately short of vital supplies and faced the prospect of mass starvation. But this did not mean that Japan was ready to surrender. Although its leaders recognized that they could not win the war, they fought on in hopes of securing surrender terms that they would find acceptable. President Harry S. Truman and his advisers considered various methods of forcing the Japanese to surrender including, in the worst case, an invasion of the Japanese home islands that would claim the lives of large numbers of U.S. soldiers, sailors, and marines. The invasion, if it became necessary, was scheduled to begin around November 1, 1945.

The success of the Manhattan Project in building atomic bombs that became available for the first time in the summer of 1945 greatly eased the dilemma that Truman faced. Here, he hoped, was a means to force the Japanese to quit the war without having to confront the ghastly prospect of an invasion or risk the major drawbacks of the other possible but highly uncertain alternatives. The alternatives included continuing the firebombing of Japanese cities that had already caused massive destruction and loss of life, modifying the U.S. demand for unconditional surrender by allowing the emperor to remain on his throne, and waiting for Soviet entry into the war against Japan. Those options might have brought about a Japanese surrender, but they ran the risks of prolonging the war in the first two cases and expanding Soviet influence in East Asia in the third.

Although some Japanese leaders sought to persuade Emperor Hirohito to surrender, he vacillated while the war continued. Therefore, the use of the atomic bomb was essential and justified to compel Japan to capitulate promptly. The shock of the bombing of Hiroshima, followed immediately by a Soviet attack on Japanese forces in Manchuria, finally convinced Hirohito that the war must end quickly. After agonizing deliberations in Tokyo, the Japanese government surrendered on the sole condition that the institution of the emperor be preserved.

For many years after the end of World War II, Americans embraced the view that the use of the bomb was necessary because the only alternative was an invasion of

Japan that would have cost hundreds of thousands of American lives. But this categorical position has been discredited by the opening of new American and Japanese sources. They show that neither the president nor top military advisers regarded an invasion as inevitable. Further, Truman was not told by his most trusted advisers that an invasion, if it became necessary, would cost hundreds of thousands of lives. The idea that Truman had to choose between the bomb and an invasion to defeat Japan is a myth that took hold in the United States after World War II.

Truman was committed to ending the war as soon as possible, saving as many American lives as he could. He did not need estimates of potential losses in the hundreds of thousands to authorize the use of the bomb, and in fact there is no contemporaneous evidence that he received projections of such staggering losses. For Truman, his advisers, and the vast majority of the American people, ending the war and sparing the lives of a smaller but far from inconsequential number of Americans was ample reason to drop atomic bombs. The Japanese government could have avoided the terrible effects of the atomic bombs by electing to surrender sooner than it did, but Japan was too divided and too indecisive to take the proper action.

There are many uncertainties and complexities surrounding the end of World War II. But the answer to the fundamental question of whether the use of the bomb on Hiroshima and Nagasaki was necessary appears to be: yes and no. Yes, it was necessary to end the war as quickly as possible. And yes, it was necessary to save the lives of American troops, perhaps numbering in the several thousands. But no, the bomb probably was not necessary to end the war within a fairly short time without an invasion, because Japan was in such dire straits. And no, it was not necessary to save the lives of hundreds of thousands of American troops.

J. Samuel Walker

Perspective Essay 4. Dropping the Bombs Was Not Justified

The United States was not justified in using atomic bombs against Japanese cities in 1945. U.S. and British intelligence had already advised that Japan was likely to surrender when the Soviet Union entered the war in early August and on terms that, in fact, would have been very close to those ultimately accepted by the United States. There are also reasons to believe that the decision had as much to do with geopolitics connected with the Soviet Union as it did with the war against Japan.

The conventional wisdom that the atomic bomb saved 1 million lives is so widespread that most Americans have not paused to ponder something rather striking to anyone seriously concerned with the issue: most American military leaders did not think that the bombings were either necessary or justified, and many were morally offended by what occurred at Hiroshima and Nagasaki.

Here is how General Dwight D. Eisenhower reacted when he was told by Secretary of War Henry L. Stimson that the atomic bomb would be used: "During his recitation of the relevant facts, I had been conscious of a feeling of depression and so I voiced to him my grave misgivings, first on the basis of my belief that Japan was already defeated and that dropping the bomb was completely unnecessary, and secondly because I thought that our country should avoid shocking world opinion by the use of a weapon whose employment was, I thought, no longer mandatory as a measure to save American lives." In another public statement the man who later became president was blunt: "It wasn't necessary to hit them with that awful thing."

General Curtis LeMay, the tough Army Air Forces general and hawk who directed the firebombing of Tokyo and other Japanese cities, was also dismayed. Shortly after the bombings, he stated that "The war would have been over in two weeks. . . . The atomic bomb had nothing to do with the end of the war at all." And Fleet Admiral Chester W. Nimitz, commander in chief of the Pacific Fleet, went public with this statement: "The Japanese had, in fact, already sued for peace. . . . The atomic bomb played no decisive part, from a purely military standpoint, in the defeat of Japan."

The reasons these and many, many military leaders felt this way are both clear and instructive: Japan was essentially defeated, its navy at the bottom of the ocean; its air force was limited by fuel, equipment, and other shortages; its army was facing defeat on all fronts; and its cities were subjected to bombing that was all but impossible to challenge. With Germany out of the war, the United States and Britain were about to bring their full power to bear on what was left of the Japanese military. Moreover, the Soviet Army was getting ready to attack on the Asian mainland.

American intelligence had broken Japanese codes and had advised as early as April 1945 that although a hard-line faction wished to continue the war, the expected Soviet Union attack, roughly in the first week of August, would likely force Japan to surrender as long as assurances were given concerning the fate of the emperor. Combined U.S. and British intelligence reaffirmed this advice a month before the bombings. One reason this option using the shock of the Soviet attack and giving assurances to the emperor appeared highly likely to work was that Japanese leaders feared the political consequences of Soviet power. Moreover, there was also little to lose: an invasion could not in any event begin until November, three months after the Soviet attack. If the war did no end as expected, the bomb could still be used.

Instead, the United States rushed to employ two bombs on August 6 and August 9 at almost exactly the time that the Soviet attack was scheduled. Numerous studies suggest that this was done in part because they "preferred," as Pulitzer Prize–winning historian Martin Sherwin has put it, to end the war in this way. Although the available evidence is not as yet absolutely conclusive, impressing the Soviets also appears to have been a factor.

Many military leaders were offended not only because the bombs were used in these circumstances but also because they were used against Japanese cities, essentially civilian targets. William D. Leahy, President Truman's friend, his chief of staff, and a five-star admiral who presided over meetings of both the U.S. Joint Chiefs of Staff and the Combined U.S.-British Chiefs of Staff, wrote after the war that "the use of this barbarous weapon at Hiroshima and Nagasaki was of no material assistance in our war against Japan. The Japanese were already defeated and ready to surrender. . . . [I]n being the first to use it, we . . . adopted an ethical standard common to the barbarians of the Dark Ages."

President Richard Nixon would recall that "[General Douglas] MacArthur once spoke to me very eloquently about it, pacing the floor of his apartment in the Waldorf. He thought it a tragedy that the Bomb was ever exploded. MacArthur believed that the same restrictions ought to apply to atomic weapons as to conventional weapons, that the military objective should always be limited damage to noncombatants. . . . MacArthur, you see, was a soldier. He believed in using force only against military targets, and that is why the nuclear thing turned him off."

Gar Alperovitz

Further Reading

Alperovitz, Gar. *Atomic Diplomacy: Hiroshima and Potsdam; The Use of the Atomic Bomb and the American Confrontation with Soviet Power.* New York: Simon and Schuster, 1994.

Asada, Sadao. "The Mushroom Cloud and National Psyches: Japanese and American Perceptions of the Atomic-Bomb Decision, 1945–1995." In *Living with the Bomb: American and Japanese Cultural Conflicts in the Nuclear Age,* edited by Laura Hein and Mark Selden, 173–201. Armonk, NY: East Gate Book, 1997.

Bernstein, Barton. "The Dropping of the A-Bomb." *Center Magazine* (March–April 1983): 7–15.

Bix, Herbert. "Japan's Delayed Surrender: A Reinterpretation." In *Hiroshima in History and Memory,* edited by Michael J. Hogan, 197–225. Cambridge: Cambridge University Press, 1996.

Bywater, Hector C. *The Great Pacific War: A Historic Prophecy Now Being Fulfilled.* Boston: Houghton Mifflin, 1991.

Craig, William. *The Fall of Japan.* New York: Dial, 1967.

Frank, Richard B. *Downfall: The End of the Japanese Empire.* New York: Random House, 1999.

Giangreco, D. M. *Hell to Pay: Operation Downfall and the Invasion of Japan, 1945–47.* Annapolis, MD: Naval Institute Press, 2009.

Hasegawa, Tsuyoshi. *Racing the Enemy: Stalin, Truman and the Surrender of Japan.* Cambridge, MA: Harvard University Press, 2005.

Hogan, Michael J. *Hiroshima in History and Memory.* Cambridge: Cambridge University Press, 1996.

Kagan, Donald. "Why America Dropped the Bomb." *Commentary* 100 (September 1995): 17–23.

Maddox, Robert James. *Weapons for Victory: The Hiroshima Decision Fifty Years Later.* Columbia: University of Missouri Press, 1995.

Malloy, Sean L. *Atomic Tragedy: Henry L. Stimson and the Decision to Use the Bomb against Japan.* Ithaca, NY: Cornell University Press, 2008.

Merrill, Dennis. *Documentary History of the Truman Presidency,* Vol. 1, *The Decision to Drop the Atomic Bomb on Japan.* Bethesda, MD: University Publications of America, 1995.

Miscamble, Wilson D. *The Most Controversial Decision: Truman, the Atomic Bombs, and the Defeat of Japan.* New York: Cambridge University Press, 2011.

Mosley, Leonard. *Hirohito, Emperor of Japan.* Englewood Cliffs, NJ: Prentice Hall, 1966.

Newman, Robert P. *Truman and the Hiroshima Cult.* East Lansing: Michigan State University Press, 1995.

Rotter, Andrew J. *Hiroshima: The World's Bomb.* Oxford: Oxford University Press, 2008.

Schaffer, Ronald. *Wings of Judgment: American Bombing in World War II.* New York: Oxford University Press, 1985.

Sherwin, Martin J. *A World Destroyed: Hiroshima and Its Legacies.* Stanford, CA: Stanford University Press, 2003.

Skates, John Ray. *The Invasion of Japan: Alternative to the Bomb.* Columbia: University of South Carolina Press, 1998.

Spector, Ronald H. *Eagle against the Sun: The American War with Japan.* New York: Free Press, 1987.

Toland, John. *The Rising Sun: The Decline and Fall of the Japanese Empire, 1936–1945.* New York: Penguin, 2001.

Wainstock, Dennis D. *The Decision to Drop the Atomic Bomb.* Westport, CT: Praeger, 1996.

Walker, J. Samuel. *Prompt and Utter Destruction: Truman and the Use of Atomic Bombs against Japan.* 2nd ed. Chapel Hill: University of North Carolina Press, 2004.

Walker, J. Samuel. "Recent Literature on Truman's Atomic Bomb Decision: A Search for Middle Ground." *Diplomatic History* 29 (April 2005): 311–334.

Watt, D. C. *How War Came: The Immediate Origins of the Second World War, 1938–1939.* London: Pimlico, 2001.

Wilmot, H. P. *The Great Crusade: A New Complete History of the Second World War.* New York: Free Press, 1991.

Zeiler, Thomas W. *Unconditional Defeat: Japan, America, and the End of World War II.* Wilmington, DE: Scholarly Resources, 2004.

PART VI

THE COLD WAR (1945–1991)

45. Which Power Bears Principal Responsibility for Starting the Cold War, the Soviet Union or the United States?

From July 17 to August 2, 1945, the heads of state of the major Allied powers met in the Cecilienhof Palace at Potsdam, near Berlin, Germany, for what became the final wartime conference of World War II. Issues discussed included the occupation of postwar Germany, the disposition of Eastern Europe, and the impending involvement of the Soviet Union in the war against Japan. Although agreements were reached on many of these topics, it was clear that with the end of World War II approaching, the wartime alliance between the Soviet Union and the Western Allies was breaking down. With the end of World War II, the shaky wartime alliance between the Western Allies and the Soviet Union quickly unraveled. By then, the United States and the Soviet Union had emerged as the world's two unparalleled military powers, a situation that seemed to invite conflict. U.S. president Harry S. Truman soon found himself and his country squaring off against Soviet premier Joseph Stalin and his seemingly expansionary brand of communism. Although the Cold War undoubtedly shaped global events for almost half a century, the question of which—if either—of the two superpowers bears responsibility for precipitating the conflict is not so easily answered.

Dr. Lee W. Eysturlid, in the first perspective essay, argues that responsibility for the Cold War lies squarely with the Soviets. He asserts that the ideological foundations of communism, coupled with Stalin's personal brutality and paranoia, precipitated the lengthy clash with the capitalist and democratic West. Dr. Paul G. Pierpaoli Jr., however, cites the United States as the chief instigator of the Cold War. He outlines numerous factors that support this claim, including U.S. policies toward the Soviet Union that date back to World War I, an American refusal or inability to recognize historic Soviet security needs and the devastation wrought by World War II, and the U.S.

A Nike anti-ballistic missile air defense battery near Providence, Rhode Island, 1963. During the Cold War, such air defense batteries had the task of defending U.S. territory against possible Soviet air and missile attacks. (Library of Congress)

decision to use its preponderant economic might to create a new postwar order that excluded the Soviets. Taking a different approach, Dr. Priscilla M. Roberts posits that it was the power vacuum created in Europe after World War II—rather than the actions of either the United States or the Soviet Union—that brought about the Cold War. She argues that neither superpower intended to start the conflict, but each sought to stabilize Europe to meet its own security goals. Dr. James I. Matray takes a similar stance, although he focuses more closely on the role played by Truman's and Stalin's personalities. Matray characterizes Truman as confrontational and blunt and Stalin as pragmatic and paranoid—character traits that, when coupled with domestic concerns, would lead both men to overreact to tense situations in the years following World War II.

Background Essay

The deadlock between East and West known as the Cold War was the single most momentous development in the post–World War II period and dominated the next half century. Put in simplest terms, it was the rivalry between the Soviet Union and the United States as each sought to fill the power vacuum left by the defeat of Germany and Japan. Leaders on each side believed that they were forced to expand their national hegemony by the "aggressive" actions of the other. Misunderstandings, bluff, pride, personal and geopolitical ambitions, and simple animosity grew until the struggle became the Cold War. Although there is no scholarly agreement on exact dates for the Cold War, the most likely starting date is the end of World War II in 1945, while the end date is usually given as the collapse of the Soviet Union in 1991.

At the end of World War II, Washington, D.C., and Moscow each had different views of the world. The United States sought a system based on democratic capitalism and the rule of law and placed high hopes on the new United Nations (UN).

Typically for the United States in wartime, its leaders had paid scant attention to trying to shape the postwar world. President Franklin Roosevelt had not greatly concerned himself with postwar political problems, working on the assumption that the UN could resolve these later. Washington's preoccupation throughout the conflict was winning the war as quickly as possible at the least cost in American lives. This frustrated British prime minister Winston Churchill, who, as with his Soviet counterpart Joseph Stalin, sought to establish spheres of influence. U.S. leaders claimed such as both outdated and immoral.

In 1945 a power vacuum existed throughout much of the world, for in defeating Germany and Japan the United States had destroyed traditional bulwarks against communist expansion, a fact largely unappreciated at the time. In Europe there was no single strong continental state able to bar Soviet expansion. In the Far East there was only China, which Roosevelt had expected to be one of the great powers and a guarantor of a peace settlement, but China had been badly weakened by its long war with Japan and was about to plunge into a full-scale civil war.

Americans assumed that wars ended when the shooting stopped, and thus domestic political considerations brought the rapid demobilization of the armed forces before the situation abroad had stabilized. Although the Soviet Union was actually much weaker in 1945 than was assumed at the time, Churchill expressed the view that only the U.S. nuclear monopoly prevented the Soviet Union from overrunning Western Europe.

In 1945, though, vast stretches of the western Soviet Union had been devastated. Twenty-five million people were homeless, and perhaps one-quarter of the national total property value had been lost. As many as 27 million people were dead. Certainly for the indefinite future whatever government held power in Moscow would be obsessed with security. This, rather than expansion, was the Kremlin's paramount concern in the immediate postwar years. Nonetheless, the Soviet Union emerged from the war in the most powerful international position in its history. The way seemed open to Soviet political domination over much of Eurasia and the realization of long-sought aims.

Stalin had seen the Western powers after World War I erect a cordon sanitaire in the form of a string of buffer states against communism. He now sought the same in reverse: a buffer to keep the West out. This was for security reasons, as Russia had been attacked from the west three times since 1812, but it was also to prevent the spread of Western ideas. Western leaders did not appreciate the extent to which concerns over security and xenophobia drove Soviet policy.

Finally, there was the ideological motivation behind Soviet policy. Although its leaders had soft-pedaled it during World War II, they had never abandoned the goal of advancing communism. It is thus inconceivable that Stalin would not have attempted to take full advantage of the opportunities that presented themselves at the end of the war.

A communist world seemingly encircled and threatened would also aid Stalin in enforcing authority and cooperation at home. With World War II at an end, Soviet citizens expected an improved standard of living. A new announced threat from abroad would cause them to close ranks behind their leaders. Playing the nationalist card would enable the Kremlin to mobilize public effort and suffocate dissent.

Washington's encouragement of the disintegration of the European colonial empires, while justified morally, nonetheless reduced the strength of U.S. allies such as Britain, France, and the Netherlands and helped ensure that the United States would carry most of the burden of defense of the noncommunist world.

Roosevelt's gamble that he could arrange a détente with the Soviet Union proved ill-founded. By mid-March 1945 it was obvious that the Soviets were taking over Poland and Romania and violating the Yalta agreements of February 1945 regarding multiparty systems and free elections.

Roosevelt died in April 1945. His successor, Harry S. Truman, insisted that U.S. forces adhere to previously set agreements and withdraw from areas they had occupied deep beyond the lines assigned to the Soviets for the occupation of Germany. The American public clearly did not want confrontation or a global economic and political-military struggle with the Soviet Union.

The Soviets, however, were already angry over Washington's abrupt termination of World War II Lend-Lease aid, regardless of the terms of the original law. Russian ill will was also generated by the close cooperation of the Anglo-Saxon powers and Moscow's belief that the two constantly combined against the Soviet Union. The U.S. monopoly on the atomic bomb also aroused fear in the Soviet Union, for a small but vocal group of Americans demanded a preventive war. Soviet concerns increased when the United States retained bomber bases within striking distance of Soviet industrial areas.

The Soviet Union, however, rejected a plan put forth by the United States to bring nuclear weapons under international control; instead, it proceeded with research and exploded its own atomic bomb in September 1949. The nuclear arms race was under way.

Certainly American and British attitudes toward Soviet activity in Eastern Europe and the Balkans exasperated Moscow. Having accepted Soviet hegemony there, why did the West continue to criticize? In countries such as Poland and Hungary, noncommunist parties were highly unlikely to ensure the security that the Soviet Union desired, and Moscow interpreted Western encouragement of these groups as a threat.

On the American side, the Soviet moves kindled exasperation and then alarm as the Soviet Union interfered in the democratic processes of one East European state after another. In addition, the UN seemed paralyzed as the Soviet Union made increasing use of its UN Security Council veto. Despite this, Western pressure in the UN did help secure a Soviet withdrawal from northern Iran in 1946.

This did not mean that the West was unified. In Britain, left-wing Labourites criticized American capitalism and wanted to work with the Russian communists. Interim French president Charles de Gaulle made vigorous efforts to build a third force in Europe as a counterbalance to the Anglo-Saxon powers and the Soviet Union. It is thus tempting to conclude that only Moscow could have driven the West to the unity achieved by 1949. As Belgian diplomat Paul-Henri Spaak put it, Stalin was the real founder of the North Atlantic Treaty Organization.

Spencer C. Tucker

Perspective Essay 1. The Belligerence of Soviet-Style Communism

The end of World War II in Europe is generally seen as the marker for the collapse of Allied cooperation and a lead-in to the inevitable conflict that became known as the Cold War. So, who provoked the nearly half century of covert conflict that would embrace far more of the globe then either of the world wars?

It was the Soviet Union under the leadership of Joseph Stalin that provoked a series of responses from the United States and other West European countries making peaceful coexistence impossible. First and foremost, the Cold War was to be a war not of territorial aggrandizement but instead of ideologies: totalitarian communism against democratic capitalism. It was in the nature of these two intellectual systems that the seeds of the conflict can be found. As Stalin would make clear in a speech given on February 9, 1946, he did not believe that the capitalist West and the communist East could, as his term "incompatible" made clear, get along for any period of time.

The reality was that the Soviet embrace of Marxism looked to spread world revolution. Stalin's "socialism in one country" of the 1930s would by 1946 fade into a considerable effort by the Soviet Union to spread an anticapitalist and anti-imperialist message worldwide. This fit with the ideals and long-term notions of major Marxist leaders Vladimir Lenin, Leon Trotsky, Nikolai Bukharin, and later Nikita Khrushchev and Mao Zedong. Therefore, the Soviet ideology itself mandated an effort to undermine Western imperialist and bourgeois (meaning capitalist) strength and control. It must also be remembered that Stalin had hoped, in private, that Adolf Hitler's imperialist National Socialist Germany would fight a wasting war with France and Great Britain, resulting in the West destroying itself and opening the path for Soviet liberation. Stalin's efforts to support this strategy can be seen in his August 1939 Pact of Steel with Nazi Germany.

Added to the Soviet ideology must also be the tyrannical leadership of Stalin, who retained absolute power in Russia until his death in 1953. Stalin's policies and lack of humanity caused great fear in the West. His willingness to carry out mass starvation campaigns (as in the Ukraine in the 1930s), his alliance with Germany in 1939, and the millions who died as a direct result of his purges paint a picture of a murderous and paranoid dictator.

Western ideology flowed from a general notion of capitalism and a strong adherence to democracy. For the United States and Great Britain, these two ideas had formed the core of the political life of their citizens. For this reason, one cannot really refer to President Harry S. Truman as the leader of the United States in the same way as when referring to Stalin as the leader of the Soviet Union. One was elected and subject to dismissal by ballot. The other kept every human in his country in mortal terror of his displeasure. Neither capitalism nor democracy called for a state to make any effort to spread these ideals, although capitalism certainly is in a constant search for new markets. This search for new markets in the middle of the 19th century had led to Britain and France acquiring substantial empires, but it would have been all but impossible to see these African or Asian holdings as direct threats to the Soviet Union. The African and Asian colonies would, however, be the battlegrounds of the Cold War and the place where both the democratic West and the Soviets would engage in a direct ideological battle.

The clear beginning of the Cold War and Soviet responsibility for the conflict can be seen in the events that came to pass between the Potsdam Conference in July–August 1945 and the end of the Berlin Blockade in May 1949. In the first year following the war, it quickly became apparent to some key leaders and analysts in the West that the Soviets had no intention of fulfilling promises made at Potsdam.

One of the most important and telling factors was Stalin's refusal to permit free elections in newly liberated Eastern Europe. This was especially true in Poland. There, opposition candidates were barred access, driven out, or murdered, and the press and other vital communication points were controlled by communist pro-Soviet parties. Stalin's promise of free elections, vague to begin with, was then seen by Truman as the sham that it was.

In 1946 the imminent intent of the Soviets was made clear by U.S. State Department analyst George Kennan, then in the Soviet Union. In a memorandum to the State Department that came to be known as the Long Telegram, Kennan emphasized that a peaceful and cooperative relationship with the Soviet Union was impossible and that Soviet efforts at ideological expansion would have to be "contained." Kennan's advice led to the policy of containment: that the United States must make use of financial and military resources to prevent the expansion of communism.

The first implementation came in the form of the Truman Doctrine of March 12, 1947. It can also be seen in the great humanitarian effort to rebuild the ruined economies of Europe that became known as the Marshall Plan. Stalin's paranoia and lack of concern for the lives of millions can be seen in his reaction to that plan. Convinced that U.S. economic assistance to Europe was essentially an effort to undermine Soviet influence especially in the Soviet sphere, he barred any acceptance of Marshall Plan money where he had control. Instead, East European states were "allowed" access to the Soviet Molotov Plan, a Potemkin village of empty promises that left half of the continent to linger in an industrial miasma for half a century.

It is clear that the Soviet Union intended to engage in a broad array of internationalism as well. To further these Soviet efforts, two organizations were established as a reaction to the Marshall Plan's perceived ideological imperative. The first was the Information Bureau of the Communist and Workers' Parties (known in the West as the Cominform), created at a meeting of representatives of all Soviet bloc members in Poland in September 1947. There, chairman of the Soviet Union Andrei Zhdanov announced that the notion of coexistence with the noncommunist world was at an end. Instead, he created the thesis of a "two-camp" world: the peace-loving, anti-imperialist communist camp and the warmongering and imperialist camp led by the United States. This rhetoric was meant to justify the spread of communist ideology and looked to the West like a revival of the prewar agency known as the Comintern. The second came in January 1949 with the creation of the Council for Mutual Economic Assistance (Comecon), the official part of the abovementioned Molotov Plan. It was a direct reaction to the success of the Marshall Plan and was meant to assist and control the economic reconstruction of Eastern Europe. In short order, the Comecon would also be extended to a communist China and North Korea. The agency, with the stated purpose of "socialist economic integration," looked to carry on the financial and economic fight with the West and bind the satellites closely to Moscow economically.

Having crushed any effort at democracy in Eastern Europe and assisting in the rise of communist dictatorships in China and North Korea, Stalin looked to test the resolve of the West in strategically critical Germany. Germany as well as Berlin had been divided into occupation zones, but the nation's long-term fate remained unresolved. As the West looked to revive the economy of its sectors—the future West Germany and West Berlin—the Soviets removed almost all of eastern Germany's industrial plants as war reparations. Assuming that the United States and its allies would not resort to force to prevent this, Stalin ordered a blockade of West Berlin, which was surrounded by Soviet-controlled East Germany. Having cut road access and train lines, the Soviets hoped by starving the western zones to force France, Britain, and the United States to quit their zones so that all Berlin would pass under communist rule.

An extensive Anglo-American airlift negated Russian efforts, and West Berlin remained out of Soviet hands. But the event had demonstrated outright Soviet belligerence and a willingness by Moscow to use military pressure on democratic elements in order to get its way.

In the several months that followed the end of the Berlin Blockade, the United States and its United Nations allies would be drawn into a war in Korea. Here, the two superpowers came very close to open conflict. From 1950 there was clearly an open, if not immediate or declared, war between the United States and its worldwide allies and the Soviet Union, the Eastern bloc states, and their growing number of allies worldwide. The animosities and heightened level of distrust that had been brought into existence in the previous five years were now beyond reconciliation.

Lee W. Eysturlid

Perspective Essay 2. A Pattern of U.S. Hostility

The United States bears the primary responsibility for precipitating the Cold War. There are eight primary factors that substantiate this claim. First among them were U.S. policies toward the Soviet Union prior to 1941, particularly during the period from 1918 to 1933. Second was American wartime diplomacy from 1941 to 1945, when the United States was part of an uneasy alliance with the Soviet Union. Third was the change in U.S. leadership upon President Franklin D. Roosevelt's death in April 1945 and the leadership style of new president Harry S. Truman. Fourth was the Americans' misapprehension of Russia's traditional security needs. Fifth was the U.S. unwillingness or inability to comprehend fully the vast level of destruction suffered by the Soviet Union during World War II. Sixth was the secrecy surrounding the Manhattan Project and America's atomic monopoly between 1945 and 1949. Seventh was the rabid anticommunism that suffused U.S. domestic politics and governmental policies after 1945. Last were the U.S. post-1945 foreign policies and the overwhelming economic power that the Americans wielded in the post–World War II period.

The history of U.S. policy toward the Soviets in the pre–World War II period greatly troubled many Russian leaders. In the early winter of 1918, Western leaders, including U.S. president Woodrow Wilson, decided to intervene militarily in Russia. Wishing to protect stocks of arms sent to Russia from falling into German hands and fearing that the success of a communist revolution might spread to other European countries, the West chose to intervene in what was essentially a domestic civil war. The first troop deployments from the West arrived in Russia in the spring of 1918, with U.S. forces arriving that summer.

Soviet leaders bitterly resented the intervention by the West and never entirely forgot it. As late as the early 1960s, Soviet leader Nikita Khrushchev made reference to the fact that American and Western troops had "violated" Russian sovereignty in the past. Also, between 1921 and 1933 the United States refused to recognize the Soviet regime, and the two nations had no formal diplomatic relations. Along with its West European partners, the Americans sought to isolate the Soviet Union diplomatically and economically and attempted to seal it off from the rest of Europe to prevent the spread of communism.

U.S. diplomacy during World War II clearly dismayed Soviet leaders. In early 1942, President Roosevelt assured Soviet leader Joseph Stalin that a second military front would be opened in Western Europe by year's end. Roosevelt not only failed to make good on his pledge but also acceded to British prime minister Winston Churchill's repeated attempts to postpone the second front, which was not opened until June 1944. This meant that the Soviets were forced to continue to bear the brunt of the German war machine. In addition, Roosevelt's so-called personal diplomacy, emphasizing charm versus hard-headed reality, ultimately led to unmet expectations and misunderstandings on the part of Soviet officials. Roosevelt's tendency to postpone tough decisions, especially for the postwar order, also troubled the Kremlin. Making matters even worse was the uncommonly close Anglo-American cooperation during the war that bred distrust of the West among the Kremlin leadership.

Roosevelt's death on April 12, 1945, significantly changed U.S.-Soviet relations and the dynamics of the wartime alliance. Unlike Roosevelt, Truman was completely inexperienced in foreign affairs and harbored a deep distrust of Stalin and of the Soviet Union. To make matters worse, Truman was largely ignorant of the content of Roosevelt's wartime discussions with Stalin, many of which had not been recorded or written down. Whereas Roosevelt's diplomacy had been personal and flexible, Truman's dealings with the Kremlin tended to be blunt, pragmatic, and increasingly inflexible. After the defeat of Germany in May 1945, Truman was far less willing to compromise with the Soviet Union.

Indicative of Truman's impatience and no-nonsense approach to U.S.-Soviet relations was a now-famous verbal exchange he had with Soviet foreign minister Vyacheslav M. Molotov. On April 23, 1945, Truman met with Molotov in the Oval Office and accused his government of duplicity, alleging that the Kremlin was not adhering to previous agreements it had made concerning Eastern Europe. Molotov stormed out of the meeting. Things did not get any better when Truman, Churchill, and Stalin met in Potsdam, Germany, during July–August 1945. Truman informed Stalin that the United States had developed a "new weapon of unusual destructive force" but gave no details. Stalin knew of the Manhattan Project and did not doubt that the first atomic bomb had been detonated just a few days before, but Truman's secretness led him to further distrust his allies' motives. At the end of August 1945 also, the United States suddenly cut off Lend-Lease aid to the Soviets, which caused even greater strain in U.S.-Soviet relations.

U.S. policy makers, including Truman, failed to understand the concern of the Soviets regarding national security, which had long historical antecedents. Indeed, the Americans viewed Soviet hegemony along its western border as strictly offensive in nature, when in fact it was more defensive. Russian history had been punctuated by invasions from outside forces. Russia's experience with foreign invasions dates at least to the 13th century. In more recent times, Russia had also been invaded by Napoleon in 1812, by the Germans in World War I, and then again by the Germans in 1941. Given this history, Stalin was most concerned about securing his nation against attack, so he sought a "security zone" along the Soviet Union's western flank. This meant controlling Eastern Europe. Stalin also sought to quarantine Soviet citizens from Western cultural and economic influences, which were considered hostile. Thus, the Soviets saw the construction of a "defensive" perimeter in the west as the best way to keep capitalist influences in check and to secure their nation from another attack.

U.S. leaders failed to comprehend fully the massive devastation and suffering visited upon the Soviet Union during World War II. They also failed to acknowledge how their wartime policies may have compounded that suffering. In fact, of all the World War II belligerents, the Soviet Union suffered the most destruction of any nation. Estimates now place Soviet war deaths at 26 million to 28 million, including 7 million to 8 million military dead and 19 million to 20 million civilians. An estimated 25 million Soviets were left homeless at war's end, and at least 25 percent of the total national wealth had been wiped out between 1941 and 1945. The Soviets believed that their nation would have suffered much less had their allies dedicated more money and resources to defeating Hitler.

By comparison, the United States suffered virtually no damage to its homeland, cities, industrial base, or civilian population. Its economy and national wealth grew tremendously between 1940 and 1945, and its industrial output dwarfed all other nations at war's end. Although the United States suffered 405,399 war-related casualties, this could not begin to compare with Soviet losses. Yet U.S. policy makers in the immediate post–World War II period did not seem to comprehend how the devastation of the Soviet Union might impact that nation's foreign policy. It is little wonder that the precipitous end of Lend-Lease and the increasingly belligerent stance of the Americans toward the Kremlin caused dismay and anger among the Soviet leadership.

The U.S. atomic monopoly most certainly helped provoke the Cold War. Surely Stalin figured that if the United States had employed the atomic bomb against Japan, it would have few qualms about using the bomb against the Soviet Union. And while it is true that the Soviet Army in the postwar period was much larger than that of the United States (and the West in total), the Americans had the atom bomb and a longer-range bombing capability as a trump card. Furthermore, the Soviets had no idea how large America's nuclear arsenal was. This kept the Soviets on the defensive and helped spark the nuclear arms race. In August 1949 the Soviets exploded their own atomic bomb.

The tenor of U.S. domestic politics and U.S. government policies in the immediate post–World War II period certainly contributed to the Cold War. Virulent anticommunism became a hallmark of U.S. politics after 1945, embraced by both Republicans and Democrats. The rhetoric and ensuing policies were alarming to Soviet leaders. Some U.S. politicians even spoke of launching a preemptive war against the Soviet Union, employing America's nuclear arsenal to destroy it. Although this was highly unlikely, such posturing certainly influenced Soviet foreign policy and military decisions.

Perhaps the most compelling cause of the Cold War was U.S. foreign policy after 1945, which was viewed by the Soviets as provocative, unreasonable, and even hostile. Compounding those policies was the economic preponderance of the United States, which the Americans used to intimidate the Kremlin and erect a world economic order that was antithetical to Soviet interests. The policy of containment was first enunciated by U.S. diplomat George Kennan in February 1946. As Kennan saw it, the Soviets were excessively paranoid, and their leaders could neither be trusted nor reasoned with. He urged a hard-line foreign policy of "containment" toward the Soviet Union, which soon became official policy and guided U.S. foreign relations for the next 45 years.

In the name of containment, the United States engaged in a multitude of unilateral and multilateral undertakings designed to limit Soviet influence and ensure Western economic preponderance. First came the 1947 Truman Doctrine, which pledged U.S. aid for any nation under threat from communism internally or externally. Next came the Marshall Plan (1947), which ultimately dispersed over $13.5 billion in aid to Western Europe. Also in 1947, the United States sponsored the General Agreements on Tariffs and Trade, the precursor to the World Trade Organization, that attempted to create a potent world economic order among non-communist industrialized nations. In 1949 the United States entered into the North Atlantic Treaty Organization, a military alliance among nations in North America and Western Europe designed to act as a bulwark against Soviet expansionism.

If these foreign policy initiatives were not enough to convince the Soviets that the United States was a dangerous adversary, American economic might surely was. Indeed, from an economic standpoint, in 1945 the United States was poised to rule the world through a liberal-capitalist world order. While virtually all World War II belligerents had witnessed catastrophic economic losses during that war, the United States had emerged from the conflict amid unprecedented industrial and economic might. With a 1945 gross national product of $211.9 billion, the U.S. economy constituted nearly 50 percent of the world's total productive output. Increasingly, especially after 1950, U.S. foreign aid was used to shore up the military establishments of noncommunist nations. Soviet leaders regarded U.S. economic hegemony as threatening as they viewed American military might.

The United States must shoulder the bulk of responsibility for the Cold War because of its anti-Soviet policies that date as far back as World War I. Despite the brief thaw in relations during World War II, the Americans viewed the Soviets with disdain and mistrust. They ignored historical imperatives and Soviet security concerns when it suited them, and they chose not to acknowledge the level of suffering and destruction that the Soviets had endured between 1941 and 1945. Finally, the United States used its economic power to create a postwar world that the Soviets perceived as bent on their destruction.

Paul G. Pierpaoli Jr.

Perspective Essay 3. Filling the European Power Vacuum

The principal responsibility for the Cold War might most accurately be placed not on the United States and the Soviet Union but instead on the international power vacuum prevailing when World War II ended and Soviet and American forces came face-to-face in Europe. Some trace the Cold War's origins back as early as 1918, shortly after Bolshevik revolutionaries established a communist government in Russia. The United States joined Great Britain, France, and Japan in sending troops to Siberia in an unsuccessful attempt to overthrow communist rule in Russia. Until 1933 the United States, unlike other Western powers, refused to recognize the Soviet government. Even after recognition, U.S.-Soviet relations remained cool throughout the 1930s. Most Americans feared and deplored Soviet communism.

It took a global war to bring the two powers into outright collision. The World War II alliance between the United States, Britain, and the Soviet Union was based decidedly on convenience, not mutual trust. In June 1941 German leader Adolf Hitler, having subdued most of Western Europe, chose to invade the Soviet Union. Britain and the United States, by this time virtual allies against Hitler even though the Americans had yet to declare war, immediately embraced Russia as a fellow combatant. After the Pearl Harbor attack of December 1941, when both Germany and Japan declared war on the United States, the Big Three powers were formally allied against Hitler.

Within each country many officials remained decidedly wary of their supposed friends. Until 1945 Joseph Stalin regularly suspected that Britain and France might make a separate peace, abandoning him to face Hitler's might unassisted. British prime minister Winston Churchill and U.S. president Franklin D. Roosevelt were similarly apprehensive that the Soviet Union might individually negotiate peace with Germany. Initially Stalin hoped that his Anglo-American allies would open a second front in France in 1942, thus relieving German pressure on the Soviet forces and populace. The eventual decision to defer this invasion until 1944 caused Stalin to believe that his allies had chosen to expend Russian lives to win the war.

The decision to postpone the West European invasion until June 1944 carried important consequences for postwar Europe. At the Tehran Conference in late 1943, the Allied leaders decided that Soviet troops would be left to defeat the German forces that controlled most East European countries, including Poland, Hungary, Czechoslovakia, Romania, Bulgaria, and Albania. By early 1945 these states were under effective Soviet control, as Soviet military conquest reached into eastern Germany. The Allies had little real leverage over Soviet behavior in Eastern Europe, an area whose control Stalin considered vital to Soviet security. At the Yalta Conference of February 1945, Stalin effectively won British and American acquiescence in his dominance of Eastern Europe, though he did promise to hold "free and unfettered elections" in Poland and elsewhere. Within two weeks the Soviets imposed a subservient government on Romania, evidence of how little weight their pledges carried.

When war ended in Europe, German and Italian power lay in ruins, and France lacked the economic and moral resources to replace them. Britain emerged from the war victorious but dependent on the United States economically. Although technologically backward, the Soviet Army was by far the largest military force in Europe. The violence and brutality with which Soviet officials imposed their rule on Eastern Europe, allowing troops to loot and rape at will, dispossessing many Poles and Germans, and summarily disposing of political opponents, made Russian domination appear even less attractive.

For West European nations, the United States was the only potential counterbalance available against a menacing Russian neighbor. The United States was the only power to end World War II with its international position both economically and strategically enhanced. The United States also had a monopoly on the atomic bomb.

Within and outside the U.S. government there existed a group of policy makers deeply committed to the belief that their country should be far more active in world affairs. Believing that international economic barriers and structural imbalances had largely triggered the Great Depression and the consequent emergence of authoritarian states, such officials strongly advocated the creation of a liberal world economic order based on free trade and convertible currencies. At the 1944 Bretton Woods Conference, the United States was instrumental in establishing the International Monetary Fund and the International Bank for Reconstruction and Development, institutions designed to finance postwar recovery. U.S. support was also crucial to the creation in 1945 of the United Nations.

From 1943 onward, Roosevelt envisaged a postwar world allocating to each of the great powers—the United States, Britain, China, and the Soviet Union—a sphere of influence: Latin America, the British Empire and Western Europe, Asia, and Eastern Europe, respectively. Each of the great powers would be primarily responsible for maintaining order within its sphere. After 1945 the United States rapidly reduced its military forces, particularly the European and Asian contingents. American officials hoped that their overseas commitments would be modest, while future international organizations would bear the primary responsibility of providing both military security and economic relief.

As World War II ended, Soviet-Western relations rapidly degenerated. The harshness with which Stalin imposed Russian rule contributed to broad Western distaste for the Soviets. When Roosevelt died suddenly in April 1945, tensions over Soviet behavior had already been mounting. His replacement by the less diplomatic Harry S. Truman further chilled relations. Perhaps most important, the American failure in the summer of 1945 to inform Stalin of just how destructive the atomic weapons it had successfully tested were intensified growing Soviet distrust of Western intentions. Stalin immediately instituted a crash program to develop a Russian bomb.

Soviet and American military power confronted each other directly in occupied Germany. At the Tehran Conference it was agreed that each nation would occupy part of Germany, which would ultimately be united under a government acceptable to all the occupying powers. To compensate for their own wartime deprivations, the Soviets were determined to extract heavy reparations from Germany, whereas the United States, anxious to facilitate German reintegration into Europe and mindful of the lengthy difficulties that Allied demands for German reparations precipitated after World War I, opposed their imposition. At the July 1945 Potsdam Conference the Allied leaders agreed to treat Germany as one economic entity, and initially the United States and Britain shipped reparations in kind from their zones to the Soviets. Suspecting that the Soviets were utilizing the reparations program to cripple the German economy permanently, in May 1946 the Anglo-Americans ceased such payments.

This decision coincided with growing tensions in Soviet-Western relations over Iran in the Middle East. During the war, Soviet and British troops occupied Iran to safeguard its rich oil holdings from German takeover. At Yalta, the Soviets unsuccessfully sought major Iranian oil concessions in exchange for withdrawing their troops, who remained in place until 1946. In January of that year renewed Soviet demands for such concessions, together with aggressive suggestions that Turkey allow Soviet warships unrestricted passage through the Dardanelles, the strategically vital outlet from the Black Sea to the Mediterranean, created new alarm. The United States responded forcefully by stating its strong backing of Iran, demanding the withdrawal of Soviet troops, and sending its most powerful warship to Turkish waters, whereupon the Soviets yielded on all points.

Despite the relative Russian caution demonstrated in these episodes, Western officials focused on what they viewed as the expansionist character of Soviet foreign policy. American and British policy makers bore very much in mind what they perceived as the "lessons" of the 1930s, especially the Munich Crisis of 1938, that yielding to dictators merely whetted their appetite for more, ultimately making war inevitable. Stalin stoked Western fears on February 9, 1946, when he publicly characterized the next Russian five-year economic plan as necessary preparation for inevitable conflict with the capitalist powers.

British and European leaders had good reasons to encourage American involvement. Aware that even united their countries could not match Soviet military strength and fearful that domestic economic weakness might make their nations easy prey to both internal communist subversion and external threat, Western politicians actively sought to persuade the United States to assume far greater European responsibilities than ever before. In the crucial early Cold War years, British officials took the lead in this process. Most dramatically, in March 1946 Churchill stated that an "iron curtain" had descended over Europe, with freedom on one side and totalitarian despotism on the other. British and Americans must unite to oppose its further extension.

In February 1947, British officials informed the American government that economic difficulties prevented them from continuing to aid Greece and Turkey, countries bordering the strategically important supply routes for Middle Eastern oil. During 1946–1947 Europe had its hardest winter in many years, closing factories and generating severe food and fuel shortages, rising inflation, and social unrest. Europe also faced an annual balance of payments deficit surpassing $5 billion. Severe strikes in France and the growing electoral strength of both French and Italian communist parties raised the specter that two major West European nations would move into the communist camp, shifting the European balance of forces immensely in Soviet favor. The British government took the lead in energetically seeking American assistance in all of these assorted problems. In March, President Truman not only publicly supported an extensive aid program for Greece and Turkey but also presented this in the context of an American commitment to assist any country where democracy was threatened.

The Truman Doctrine paved the way for Secretary of State George C. Marshall to announce a major economic aid program for all European nations. The Soviet Union and its satellites soon boycotted the Marshall Plan, while noncommunist nations participated in a coordinated four-year enterprise to enhance their economic performance and make the European economies once more self-sustaining. The Marshall Plan further divided Western Europe from Eastern Europe, intensifying the Cold War. Essential to successful West European recovery was German economic revival, at least in the Western-occupied sectors. It seems that one major Soviet preoccupation was to keep Germany weak, unable to start a third European war or invade Russia again. Soviet security concerns were incompatible with the West European quest for economic recovery, and Soviet-Western relations were so poor as to render any understanding or negotiated compromise unattainable. The Soviets responded by tightening control over Eastern Europe, and in 1948 communist coups overthrew predominantly democratic governments in Hungary and Czechoslovakia.

Hostilities came to a head over occupied Germany. In June 1948 after currency reforms were introduced in the now merged Western occupation sectors of Germany, the Soviet Union responded by cutting off land access to western Berlin, deep in the Soviet sector, where each of the three Western occupying powers—Britain, France, and the United States—had been assigned zones that were later merged. Soviet obduracy met American resolve; for 11 months, a massive airlift ferried all essential supplies into West Berlin. The Berlin Blockade contributed to the Western decision to abandon hope of German reunification and establish a separate state, the Federal Republic of Germany (West Germany), in the former Western-occupation sectors.

The Berlin Blockade also persuaded the United States to conclude a permanent military alliance with most West European states. In 1949 the United States, Canada, and 14 European countries formed the North Atlantic Treaty Organization (NATO). Under its terms, an attack on one signatory would automatically be considered an assault on all. The outbreak of the Korean War in June 1950, when the communist north sought to take over the noncommunist remainder of a comparably divided Asian nation, proved a spur to beginning West German rearmament and the incorporation of German troops into NATO units. In 1955 West Germany joined the alliance, prompting the Soviet Union in turn to establish the Warsaw Pact, a similar military grouping of its East European satellites.

Neither major player in the early Cold War apparently sought to initiate conflict. Facing a war-induced power vacuum in Europe, which brought their forces into direct contact and competition, each side, however, felt that it had nonnegotiable security interests at stake.

Priscilla M. Roberts

Perspective Essay 4. A Clash of Personalities

Competition and discord between the United States and the Soviet Union after World War II was a virtual certainty, because over five years of destructive warfare had devastated Europe, creating a political and military vacuum. Both nations had vital economic and security interests that justified postwar efforts to establish decisive influence over postwar European affairs. Conflicting ideologies exacerbated this rivalry, but what transformed this power struggle into the Cold War lasting almost 50 years was the clash of personalities between U.S. president Harry S. Truman and Soviet premier Joseph Stalin.

Truman had scant experience in foreign affairs when the sudden death of Franklin D. Roosevelt in April 1945 made him president of the United States. Truman had been elected to the U.S. Senate in 1934 and reelected in 1940 without Roosevelt's support. Truman had gained national prominence in World War II as chair of a Senate committee exposing corporate waste, incompetence, fraud, and labor abuse in the defense industry. However, he was a surprise choice to be the vice presidential candidate in Roosevelt's successful reelection in 1944. Now as president, Truman relied heavily on his advisers for information about most issues in world politics, but he jealously guarded his final authority and made decisions that were both decisive and impulsive. Truman was known for his hot temper and combativeness, and subtlety and diplomacy were not among his attributes.

Stalin was one of the most barbaric yet captivating figures in human history. He became a leading figure with the Bolshevik seizure of power in November 1917, holding the post of commissar for nationalities. In 1922 Stalin became secretary-general of the Communist Party. After the death of Vladimir Lenin in 1924, Stalin consolidated his authority and by 1929 was the unquestioned leader of the Soviet state. Thereafter he would supervise massive industrialization, forced collectivization of agriculture, and extensive purges of the party and the military. His harsh policies led directly to the deaths of tens of millions of Soviet citizens.

Stalin's primary goal in World War II was to ensure that military victory resulted in permanently weakening Germany, thereby eliminating it as a threat to Soviet national security. For further protection, he was determined to install governments in Eastern Europe closely allied to the Soviet Union, removing the potential for this area to be a future avenue for invasion, as it had been three times since 1812. Had he not been a communist, his wartime objectives would have been precisely the same. Pragmatic, cautious, and realistic, Stalin was a skillful practitioner of power politics who expected his wartime allies to accept a division of the postwar world into spheres of influence.

Roosevelt's vision of the postwar world order had little in common with that of Stalin, because Roosevelt's assumptions and expectations derived from a contrasting American historical experience. In August 1941 before Japan's attack on Pearl Harbor, Roosevelt announced his plan for peace, issuing the Atlantic Charter during a meeting with Churchill. Roosevelt's wartime objectives were identical to the goals that President Woodrow Wilson had specified in his Fourteen Points during World War I—committing the United States to the achievement of postwar national self-determination, economic cooperation, disarmament, and freedom of the seas. Roosevelt and Churchill also pledged not to seek territorial gains after the war.

Despite signing the Atlantic Charter, Churchill had not abandoned faith in power politics as the best method for creating the foundation for postwar peace as well as preserving the British Empire. During October 1943 he met in Moscow with Stalin, where the two like-minded leaders agreed to a division of Eastern Europe into spheres of influence. Roosevelt was aware of this deal but disregarded its legitimacy. In January 1945 at the Yalta Conference, he confirmed instead Allied endorsement for his vision when Stalin and Churchill joined him in pledging freedom of choice for all Europeans in choosing postwar governments. But as the Red Army advanced against Nazi forces, Roosevelt's anxiety grew because he was powerless to stop Stalin from imposing communist-dominated governments in Poland and Romania.

Roosevelt's death on April 12 delivered a fatal blow to hopes for postwar U.S.-Soviet cooperation because his productive partnership with Stalin ended. The Soviets recognized that collaboration with the United States was necessary to defeat the Axis, having received huge amounts of Lend-Lease aid. Stalin, however, was by nature distrustful of any nation or leader he did not control.

Stalin had good reason for defensiveness as World War II came to an end. Soviet and German military forces waged a brutal and desperate fight for more than three years, inflicting utter destruction on a huge area stretching from the Polish border to Moscow. The Soviet people suffered enormous hardship in a war that left roughly 27 million dead and almost as many homeless. For Stalin, Soviet economic weakness at the end of World War II made it imperative to create a string of buffer states on his western frontier to prevent penetration of Western values and political beliefs. Stalin's insecurity and xenophobia virtually eliminated the likelihood of continued Allied cooperation after the war.

Truman viewed the Soviet Union as an immediate threat to U.S. postwar interests, ignoring its weaknesses. Accordingly, he was far less inclined than Roosevelt to be conciliatory in his dealings with Stalin, not least because of Truman's personal predisposition toward being confrontational and belligerent. Certain of American altruism, Truman disliked and distrusted the Soviets. At their first meeting in April 1945, Soviet foreign minister Vyacheslav Molotov objected when Truman sternly reprimanded him for taking control of Poland.

Many of Roosevelt's advisers welcomed Truman's tough approach in dealing with Stalin, believing that Roosevelt had been too gentle in responding to Soviet expansionist behavior. The new president joined them in equating Stalin's actions with Hitler's aggression, concluding that appeasement was not an option. Soon only advocates of confrontation with the Soviet Union remained in Truman's administration, notably U.S. ambassador in Moscow W. Averell Harriman. After Germany surrendered on May 8, 1945, Truman acted on Harriman's advice and terminated Lend-Lease aid to the Soviet Union in the hope that Stalin would be more agreeable in return for economic assistance.

At the Potsdam Conference in July 1945 Truman and Stalin clashed on every major issue, especially German reparations and elections in Eastern Europe. While there Truman learned of the successful test explosion of an atomic bomb, but he only made a vague reference about this to Stalin, who was aware of the new weapon. Truman would order atomic attacks on two Japanese cities in August primarily to end the war and save lives, but Stalin likely saw intimidation as another motive. He also resented Truman's transparent attempt to preempt Soviet entry into the war in the Pacific to negate promised territorial rewards for participation. Just before Japan surrendered, the Soviets declared war and occupied strategic areas in East Asia. Adding to the distrust, Truman rejected Stalin's request for an occupation zone in Japan.

Failure to reach agreements at Potsdam resulted in Allied leaders deciding that their foreign ministers would meet to specify the terms of peace treaties for the Axis. The first meeting in London established a pattern of the Soviet Union opposing steps toward German reunification and recovery while refusing to allow free elections in Eastern Europe. Apparently, U.S. secretary of state James F. Byrnes decided that since Moscow would not budge, it would be best to retreat. At Moscow in December 1945, he agreed to U.S. recognition of the communist regimes installed along the Soviet western border in return for concessions elsewhere. When Byrnes reported this, Truman was furious.

Stalin ascribed sinister intent to Truman's criticism of Soviet domination of Eastern Europe. On February 9 he reaffirmed in an election speech the validity of Marxist-Leninism, declaring that the continued existence of capitalism made a future war inevitable. After initially permitting parties other than the communists to run for political office in Eastern Europe, Moscow now began eliminating dissenters as Hungary and Bulgaria joined Poland and Romania as Soviet satellite states. In March 1946, Churchill delivered his famous "Iron Curtain" speech, which escalated bilateral tensions. Rejecting appeasement, he called for Anglo-American action to counteract the Soviet threat. Almost immediately, Truman's refusal to consider further compromise with Stalin was apparent.

In February 1946 George F. Kennan, U.S. foreign service officer in Moscow, recommended a policy of containment of Soviet expansionism. Early in 1947, the first implementation of containment came in response to Soviet demands on Turkey for territorial concessions and the communist insurgency in Greece. In his Truman Doctrine speech on March 12, the president declared that worldwide democracy was in grave peril, and Congress quickly approved $400 million in economic and military aid to the two countries. As a result the Greek insurgency was ended, and Turkey resisted Soviet demands.

Less exaggerated was Truman's response to Stalin's presumed intent to dominate Western Europe, where infrastructures had not recovered from wartime devastation and persistent economic distress encouraged rising public support for communist parties, especially in France and Italy. In response, on June 5, 1947, Secretary of State George C. Marshall pledged U.S. financial aid to promote a sustained reconstruction of all of Europe. Complying with Marshall's conditions, European leaders jointly devised a plan for economic recovery, but Moscow and its East European clients rejected the terms and refused to participate in the Marshall Plan. Congressional appropriations of $13.15 billion stimulated after 1948 a robust economic recovery that ended the threat of communist electoral victories.

Truman's initiation of containment against the Soviet Union constituted essentially a formal declaration of cold war, to which Stalin reciprocated with three provocative actions. First, he ordered communists in Western Europe to stage strikes protesting acceptance of U.S. help, alienating the local populace. This only motivated Truman to join Britain in the fall of 1947, after uniting their occupation zones, in promoting economic recovery of a separate West German state, seen as vital to Western Europe's prosperity.

Creation of a united anti-Soviet bloc in Western Europe including a revived Germany elicited Stalin's second sharp response. In late 1947 he had created the Communist Information Bureau (Cominform) to replace the old Communist International (Comintern) as the new agency to propagate communism globally. Then in February 1948 communists seized power in Czechoslovakia in a coup d'état that shocked U.S. and European leaders, igniting fears of imminent war and silencing lingering congressional opposition to the Marshall Plan. Further proof that Stalin intended to replicate his aggressive expansion in Western Europe came in June when the Soviets terminated road access through the zone to West Berlin.

Stalin initiated the Berlin Blockade because he thought it would force the Western powers to quit their zones of Berlin. Instead it solidified Truman's resolve and inflexibility, as he ordered a massive airlift of food, clothing, and coal to the 2 million residents of West Berlin. In May 1949, Stalin admitted defeat and lifted the blockade. By then, however, the United States had joined Canada and 10 West European nations in signing the North Atlantic Treaty, agreeing that an attack on one was an attack against all. Formation of the North Atlantic Treaty Organization followed, with the United States committing itself to the military defense of Western Europe.

Europe was now divided into two hostile camps and faced the likelihood of renewed conflict. A postwar U.S.-Soviet confrontation was inevitable, because each nation saw its own future security and prosperity as dependent upon extending its social, economic, and political systems into liberated areas. But it was not at all preordained that this quarrel should escalate into the Cold War. Domestic concerns on both sides encouraged this outcome. While Soviet leaders thought they were confronting a new threat from encircling enemies, they also exploited the Cold War to reinforce authority and cooperation at home. Similarly, U.S. leaders manipulated the Soviet threat to unite Congress and the American public behind an admired foreign policy.

That Washington and Moscow studiously avoided a resort to force during their first direct brawl over Berlin raises, however, the question of whether the differences between the two nations were grave enough to justify the emergence of the Cold War. In fact, a clash between two antagonistic personalities was what transformed this struggle into an intractable dispute reaching extreme levels of tension and danger.

James I. Matray

Further Reading

Acheson, Dean. *Present at the Creation: My Years at the State Department.* New York: Norton, 1969.

Ball, Simon J. *The Cold War: An International History, 1947–1991.* New York: St. Martin's, 1998.

Byrnes, James F. *Speaking Frankly.* New York: Harper and Brothers, 1947.

Crockatt, Richard. *The Fifty Years' War: The United States and the Soviet Union in World Politics, 1941–1991.* New York: Routledge, 1995.

Donovan, Robert J. *Conflict and Crisis: The Presidency of Harry S. Truman, 1945–1948.* New York: Norton, 1977.

Feis, Herbert. *Between War and Peace: The Potsdam Conference.* Princeton, NJ: Princeton University Press, 1957.

Fontaine, Andre. *History of the Cold War, 1917–1966.* 2 vols. New York: Pantheon, 1968.

Gaddis, John Lewis. *The Long Peace: Inquiries into the History of the Cold War.* New York: Oxford University Press, 1989.

Gaddis, John L. *The United States and the Origins of the Cold War.* New York: Columbia University Press, 1972.

Gaddis, John Lewis. *We Now Know: Rethinking Cold War History.* New York: Oxford University Press, 1997.

Kennan, George F. *Memoirs, 1925–1950.* Boston: Little, Brown, 1967.

Kuniholm, Bruce R. *The Origins of the Cold War: Great Power Conflict and Diplomacy in Iran, Turkey and Greece.* Princeton, NJ: Princeton University Press, 1994.

LaFeber, Walter. *America, Russia, and the Cold War, 1946–1996.* 8th ed. Columbus, OH: McGraw-Hill College, 1996.

Leffler, Melvyn P. *A Preponderance of Power: National Security, the Truman Administration, and the Cold War.* Stanford, CA: Stanford University Press, 1992.

McCormick, Thomas J. *America's Half-Century: United States Foreign Policy in the Cold War and After.* Baltimore: Johns Hopkins University Press, 1995.

Nogee, Joseph L., and Robert H. Donaldson. *Soviet Foreign Policy since World War II.* New York: Macmillan, 1992.

Painter, David S. *The Cold War: An International History.* New York: Routledge, 1999.

Reynolds, David. *From World War to Cold War: Churchill, Roosevelt, and the International History of the 1940s.* New York: Oxford University Press, 2006.

Seton-Watson, Hugh. *Neither War nor Peace: The Struggle for Power in the Postwar World.* New York: Praeger, 1960.

Thomas, Hugh. *Armed Truce: The Beginnings of the Cold War, 1945–1946.* New York: Atheneum, 1987.

Volkogonov, Dmitri. *Stalin: Triumph and Tragedy.* New York: Grove Weidenfeld, 1988.

Walker, J. Samuel. "The Origins of the Cold War in United States History Textbooks." *Journal of American History* 81(4) (March 1995): 1652–1661.

Walker, Martin. *The Cold War: A History.* New York: Henry Holt, 1994.

Yergin, Daniel H. *Shattered Peace: The Origins of the Cold War.* New York: Penguin, 1990.

Zubok, Vladislav M., and Constantine Pleshakov. *Inside the Kremlin's Cold War: From Stalin to Khrushchev.* Cambridge, MA: Harvard University Press, 1996.

46. Have Nuclear Weapons Prevented Another Catastrophic War since 1945?

The nuclear era began in July 1945, when the United States tested the world's first atomic bomb. The following month America dropped two atomic bombs on Hiroshima and Nagasaki, Japan, which ended World War II. The United States enjoyed an atomic monopoly until September 1949, when the Soviets detonated their own atomic bomb. Thereafter, a nuclear arms race ensued between both Cold War superpowers. First came hydrogen (thermonuclear) bombs, which were many times more destructive than atomic bombs. Short- and intermediate-range missiles were soon outfitted with nuclear weapons, and by 1960 both the Soviets and the Americans possessed nuclear-tipped intercontinental ballistic missiles (ICBMs), which could unleash destruction across the globe within minutes. By the late 1960s the concept of mutual assured destruction had emerged, which held that neither side would launch nuclear bombs against the other for fear of a catastrophic retaliatory strike, thus depriving both sides of victory. Mutual assured destruction, some historians have argued, prevented a major war between the Americans and Russians.

Dr. Brian Madison Jones, in the first perspective essay, argues that nuclear weapons have indeed contributed significantly to the absence of a catastrophic war since 1945. He notes that despite the myriad smaller wars waged since then, the overall number of lives lost in the second half of the 20th century was drastically lower than the number of lives lost in the first half of the century, a development brought about by the presence of nuclear weapons. In the case of the 1956 Suez Crisis, he asserts that both the Americans and Soviets prevented a wider war from developing precisely because both possessed nuclear arms. Nevertheless, he concedes that nuclear weapons have made smaller wars more likely. In the second essay, Dr. Michael Kraig posits that nuclear weapons alone have not prevented another world war. Instead, he argues, politics have also played a critical role in preventing a major war. In the end, he says that the nuclear threat both increased the likelihood of a major war and prevented a global holocaust at the same time. In the third essay, Dr. Paul J. Springer asserts that a number of intersecting factors prevented a major war and that crediting nuclear weapons alone is reductionist thinking. Indeed, he sees diplomacy, economic imperatives, and changes in the dominant form of warfare as having thwarted catastrophic conflict. Economic partnerships and globalism have reduced the likelihood of a major conflict because war ultimately damages or destroys economic prosperity. In the last half century modern warfare has tended toward civil wars and insurgencies, which are considerably less likely to escalate into a full-blown war. Even proxy wars such as the Korean War and the Vietnam War did not become global conflagrations, even though all of the players did not possess nuclear weapons.

Background Essay

Nuclear weapons have played a major role in international diplomacy and national defense policies since World War II. During the Cold War (1945–1991) both the

United States and the Soviet Union sought to ensure that the other power did not gain a measurable advantage in nuclear-strike capability. Also at play was the evolving concept of nuclear deterrence, which held that a nation must retain adequate nuclear capabilities to deter the enemy from launching a preemptive nuclear attack. This concept became known as mutual assured destruction, which held that any preemptive attack would result in an overwhelming and catastrophic retaliatory strike. The threat of this has imposed great caution on those making decisions of war and peace.

During World War II, the Allied side became aware that Germany had the capacity to build an atomic bomb and was working toward that end. Spurred by this threat, the United States in cooperation with Britain and Canada undertook a major effort in the Manhattan Project to develop a nuclear weapon. The first test explosion occurred in July 1945, and the first atomic bombs were employed against the Japanese cities of Hiroshima and Nagasaki in August 1945. For a time the United States possessed a monopoly, and leaders of the Soviet Union, with which the Americans found themselves increasingly at odds, understandably feared the American nuclear threat, especially given the demonstrated capability of the United States to conduct strategic bombing. The Soviets were determined to develop their own nuclear weapons and, aided by espionage, detonated their own such weapon in September 1949.

The United States sought to retain its nuclear lead and, in an action-reaction cycle that typified the nuclear arms race, pursued the next step of developing a far more powerful thermonuclear (or hydrogen) bomb. Success in this occurred in 1952, and the Soviets followed suit in 1955. Both sides continued to pursue weapons that were smaller in size and more powerful as well as increasingly accurate and more difficult to detect in terms of delivery systems.

During the late 1940s and early 1950s, the primary delivery vehicle for nuclear weapons was the strategic bomber. Both sides developed intercontinental bombers capable of delivering large nuclear payloads to multiple targets. Advances in rocketry also led to the development of ballistic missiles. The first U.S. intercontinental ballistic missile (ICBM), the Atlas D, was deployed in October 1959. The Soviets followed suit with their own ICBM, the SS-6 Sapwood (NATO designation), in January 1960. ICBMs were a step up from their cousins, medium-range ballistic missiles and intermediate-range ballistic missiles, and became the most popular delivery system because of their range and relative invulnerability to enemy air defenses. ICBMs had a maximum range of 10,000 miles and could be launched on the other side of the world from their targets.

In the 1950s, both superpowers came to rely on nuclear weapons as the primary weapon for any major Cold War engagement. The nuclear arms race created larger and larger arsenals and increasingly effective delivery systems. As a result, both sides became vulnerable to enemy attack. It was this vulnerability that perpetuated

The first explosion of a hydrogen bomb by the United States at Enewetak Atoll in the Marshall Islands on November 1, 1952. (National Archives)

the arms race throughout the decade and beyond. Neither side has been willing to give up its weapons, and the newer weapons meant that the nation that launched a first strike might be able to avoid a retaliatory strike if its nuclear advantage was sufficient to allow it to destroy most of the enemy's nuclear forces in the first blow. Any large gap in nuclear arms made one nation vulnerable, with nuclear stability only ensured by nuclear parity. As a result, scientific advances by one nation had to be matched by the other.

This situation was aggravated in the 1960s with the evolution of the counterforce doctrine. Advocates of counterforce, or "no cities" doctrine, suggested a general agreement between the superpowers to use nuclear weapons only against military installations, sparing population centers. Adopting this policy meant accepting the reality that in order to sustain the ability to launch an effective counterstrike, a nation must deploy enough weapons to ensure that the enemy cannot destroy them all in a preemptory strike. Thus, better and more weapons were needed.

The existence first of a so-called bomber gap, then a missile gap, later an antiballistic missile gap, and later still a missile throw-weight gap kept nuclear weapons manufacturers in perpetual development. In November 1960, the United States deployed the world's first nuclear-powered ballistic-missile submarine. The Soviets followed suit in 1968. Ballistic-missile submarines heightened the danger of the arms race and were potentially even more deadly than ICBMs, as they were capable of avoiding retaliatory strikes because of their ability to hide deep beneath the ocean. Computer technology also advanced the nuclear arms race.

The United States maintained strategic superiority. In the late 1960s and into the 1970s, however, the Soviet Union took the lead in ICBM production and in the development of antiballistic-missile (ABM) technology. Soviet ABMs were designed primarily to protect major cities, such as Moscow, and were less effective against a full attack against Soviet military installations. Multiple independently targeted reentry vehicles (MIRVs) complicated matters. MIRVs meant that each ICBM could deploy a dozen or more warheads, each programmed for a separate target. MIRVs promised to overcome any ABM system.

Arms control talks and treaties in the 1970s and arms reduction agreements during the 1980s have slowed but not stopped the threat of nuclear weapons. Indeed, despite efforts to prevent their spread, more and more nations have nuclear weapons. Today the list includes not only the United States and the Soviet Union but also Great Britain, France, China, India, Pakistan, Israel, and North Korea. The latter has been a particular concern, since it has repeatedly defied international treaties and routinely threatened to employ its nuclear arsenal.

Brian Madison Jones and Spencer C. Tucker

Perspective Essay 1. The Threat of Nuclear Destruction

In the turbulent years since the end of World War II, nuclear weapons and the threat of global nuclear war have alone prevented the outbreak of another catastrophic global war similar to those that consumed the first half of the 20th century. Indeed, the 20th century, by many statistical renderings, was the bloodiest in human history, and the killing began less than two decades into the millennium. But the preponderance of the lives lost occurred between 1914 and 1945, and the flow slowed considerably after the bombings of Hiroshima and Nagasaki. Still, the postwar period saw terrible acts of violence and warfare. Nation-states and occasionally stateless actors across the world killed millions in the name of ethnicity, religion, borders, resources, reciprocity, and beyond. But on any chart that depicts global deaths from warfare in the modern era, the line drops precipitously after 1945, and nuclear weapons are the reason.

A decade before the outbreak of the Great War in 1914, Englishman Norman Angell posited that future major wars were impossible. Economies, industries, markets, and indeed families were too intertwined to allow for modern war between nations. Nations, he reasoned, would lose too much in any serious conflict. Angell was proven wrong, of course, and the history of the first half of the 20th century shows that national leaders will often not be restrained in contests regarding territory, markets, or national rivalries. They will allow political situations to escalate into avoidable military confrontations, and they will also allow those confrontations to escalate into global war. Leaders will describe external threats as both persistent and fatal, their enemy as unyielding in desire and increasing in strength. They will send the young and the poor to fight and die for the cause of righteousness, and the military-industrial complex will earn vast sums manufacturing and selling the instruments of death. All of these factors increase the likelihood of conventional war.

Where Angell miscalculated was that he overestimated the resulting damage possible from a conventional war in the early 20th century. He did not recognize that a world war in 1914 would leave so much of life and livelihood intact as to prompt the reasonable view that the national risk was not what happens if the country goes to war but what happens if the country does not. In the nuclear age the circumstances are different, as the risk of global nuclear war precludes a semblance of victory for either side.

There is no question that during the Cold War of 1945–1991, nuclear deterrence worked. As both the United States and the Soviet Union developed increased capacity to deliver ever more powerful nuclear weapons on target, nuclear deterrence evolved, and the major competitors became aware of the risk involved with any major military confrontation. In the Cuban Missile Crisis of 1962, for example, the great powers avoided war precisely because the nuclear weapon promised them nothing but their own destruction at best and the destruction of civilization at worst. A different deterrent scenario unfolded in Egypt in 1956. In that case, smaller regional powers were constrained by their larger, wealthier, and better-armed allies to avoid escalation; when small powers could not be swayed, the great powers dissociated themselves from the conflict to avoid being drawn into an uncontrollable military situation from which the catastrophic war might follow. In both cases, the risk of nuclear war deterred a larger conflict. The metaphor of two scorpions in a bottle, neither able to kill the other without putting themselves in mortal danger, remained true throughout the Cold War.

Of course, since 1945 nuclear weapons have not prevented all warfare, and one might argue that they make possible and more likely smaller-scale conflicts among nation-states and other combatant groups. Civil wars in China and the Sudan, anti-imperial wars in Indochina and Algeria, ethnic cleansing in Rwanda and the Balkans, and the numerous flashpoints in the Middle East, including the Six-Day War, the Soviet-Afghan War, the Iran-Iraq War, the Persian Gulf War, and the growing virulence of international terrorist groups, all resulted in considerable loss of life and destruction on a wide scale. Nevertheless, catastrophic general war was avoided, and so was the global World War II–type conflict characterized by a protracted struggle between industrialized nations on multiple continents including land, air, and sea battles.

To those individuals and families who fall victim to such violence, the consequences are always catastrophic. But the argument is not that nuclear attack is not terrible, for it is. The argument is not that nuclear weapons are dangerous; they must be. The argument is not that nuclear weapons pose tremendous risk in their testing and their use; of course they do. The question is whether they work as intended. Those who suffered the atomic bombings of imperial Japan and others who avoided an amphibious military landing on the island of Kyushu in November 1945 might say yes, while revisionist historians in the United States would say no. All of those who avoided the fate of Lawrence, Kansas, in the fictional television drama *The Day After* (1983) could argue that these weapons served a great deterrent purpose as well. Sadly, nuclear deterrence has proven so effective in deterring a catastrophic conflict that the preponderance of examples of the world on the brink of nuclear war are circumstances in which failures of technology or interpretation nearly brought accidental war. That is both upsetting and terrible but is also irrelevant to this question.

Even Ward Wilson in his persuasive study *Five Myths about Nuclear Weapons* cannot claim that nuclear deterrence has not worked to avoid catastrophic war. Wilson attempts to argue that the absence of evidence is not proof with regard to nuclear weapons. Although this may be true for other things, it is not true for the deterrent value of nuclear weapons. The absence of global catastrophic war is not a myth perpetuated by the nuclear elites but instead is the reality of geopolitics since 1945 rooted in the terrible destructive power of the nuclear weapon and the powerful instinct to self-preserve among the humans who control those weapons.

Brian Madison Jones

Perspective Essay 2. Mutual Assured Destruction Is No Guarantee of Peace

In the context of the Cold War, the promise of mutual destruction by nuclear weapons did not ease existential fears. Instead, nuclear arsenals became an integral part of these fears, acting as both their source and a tool with which to wage the Cold War. Cold War nuclear competition consistently intensified worst-case beliefs that each side held about the other's strategic intentions, which often made war more rather than less likely. This lasted until the late 1980s. It is my contention that nuclear weapons alone have not guaranteed the peace since 1945.

There are two implicit, and overly simplistic, assumptions about human conflict that drive the argument that nuclear weapons have been responsible for the long peace in major power relations. First, large-scale warfare between major powers is virtually inevitable otherwise. Second, nuclear weapons do not by themselves appreciably inflame superpower tensions and instead consistently induce mutual caution and moderation.

This view of international security is incomplete. Left out of the equation is politics itself and how arms races often play into and dramatically worsen relations between two adversaries. First, cooperation among competitors is nearly always possible with the right leadership, although it is admittedly difficult in cases of radically divergent social and political values. Second, it is indeed politics that drives decisions on war and peace, defined in turn by beliefs and values emanating from deeply ingrained cultural worldviews. Third, as cognitive and emotional psychological theories suggest, it is usually fears of imminent loss, in turn based on worst-case assumptions of enemy intent, that drive aggressive behavior rather than purposeful designs to dominate. Fourth, research has shown that nations do not respond to perceived unequal relationships by backing down. Rather, they often respond to hostilities through actions meant to restore a sense of equality, whether physically (e.g., increasing arms capabilities) or psychologically (e.g., asserting symbolic principles).

This means that in international politics, the perceived fairness of the status quo matters as much as the physical reality of potential mutual destruction. Although they might induce caution, nuclear weapons can also be seen as providing evidence for worst-case threat assessments, thereby fueling extreme perceptions about enemy intent. This ultimately undermines stability between competing nations.

In this regard, historians now recognize that the reasons for the Soviets' clandestine missile deployments that precipitated the 1962 Cuban Missile Crisis were tethered to goals of strategic defense. These involved both military and symbolic aspects. Soviet motivations included a number of often interconnected goals. First, they sought to protect their Cuban ally from a (perceived) imminent U.S. invasion threat, based on intelligence about sustained contingency planning and proxy operations by the U.S. Central Intelligence Agency. Second, they hoped to overcome their 17 to 1 inferiority in deliverable nuclear warheads at a time when many Soviet warheads were still limited to European targets because of performance issues and underproduction of long-range missile systems. Third, they were reacting to a massive strategic missile buildup undertaken by the John F. Kennedy administration that promised far faster annihilation of Soviet targets than America's extensive bomber force. Finally, the Soviets were trying to protect Premier Nikita Khrushchev's plans to grow the moribund Soviet agricultural and consumer goods economic sectors so as to deliver tangible socioeconomic rewards to the Soviet population.

Crucially, Khrushchev's grand domestic development effort was in danger of being overridden by a Soviet establishment that felt compelled to answer U.S. nuclear superiority with a new Soviet military buildup to maintain destructive parity. Given the political as well as military concerns driving Soviet behavior, it should come as no surprise that the final "solution" to the above-mentioned dilemmas was a geopolitical deal based on hard bargaining. Indeed, the crisis was ended when both sides made concessions. The United States agreed not to invade Cuba and to deactivate its Jupiter missile systems in Italy and Turkey, while the Soviet Union agreed to withdraw its missiles from Cuba peacefully.

However, the threat of mutual annihilation would continue to escalate in the years that followed. There was a brief easing of superpower tensions in the 1970s, which was based on the complex diplomatic achievement of the 1972 Strategic Arms Limitation Treaty. However, a subsequent surge in technological capabilities on both sides and extreme threat assessments came to define a "second Cold War," beginning in the early 1980s.

This latter period witnessed a major buildup of new Soviet missiles with multiple-warhead capabilities in their land- and submarine-based delivery forces. This gave them the ability to launch surprise strikes against a majority of U.S. command-and-control centers and land-based weapons systems. This was paralleled by a steady modernization of U.S. first-strike nuclear capabilities, including cruise missiles and stealth bombers that could avoid radar detection as well as precision-strike warheads for land- and sea-based ballistic missile forces. Together, these developments promised increasingly prompt and accurate destruction of Soviet military targets with little warning, potentially undermining Soviet retaliatory capabilities.

Soviet missile warhead capacity deeply concerned nuclear arms expert Paul Nitze, who fretted about a strategic "window of vulnerability" beginning in the late 1970s. This drove fears that a preemptive Soviet missile blitz might neutralize U.S. retaliatory capability, a prospect that might lead to Soviet political hegemony during peacetime. At the same time, Soviet leaders now doubted America's commitment to détente. This perception was driven by U.S. deployments of Pershing II missiles and ground-launched cruise missiles in Europe, which were more accurate and deadly than the arms they replaced. These new systems offered the ability to incapacitate Soviet leadership with so little warning that the United States might conceivably succeed in its own preemptive attack.

For the Soviets, these developments signaled American rejection of nuclear deterrence as the primary basis for international peace and stability. Worse yet, underlying all of this was a sharp escalation in American political-ideological rhetoric that vilified the Soviet bloc at nearly every turn and seemed to call into question America's earlier commitments to peaceful coexistence.

As it turns out, repeated attempts by the United States to sound and act tough in the periods of perceived "windows of vulnerability" (1957–1962 and 1981–1985), including surges in nuclear weapons quantity and quality, were in no small part an effort to shore up the credibility of nuclear threats. But in so doing, these actions raised fears of a nuclear exchange so that nuclear threats both increased the likelihood of and prevented a global holocaust at the same time.

The latter paradox was especially apparent during the North Atlantic Treaty Organization's Operation ABLE ARCHER, a war games exercise staged in November 1983. At the time, Soviet leaders came to believe that the Ronald Reagan administration intended to initiate—and win—a nuclear war. During this period, Soviet KGB agents were spread across the globe to watch for any signs that a massive nuclear attack was imminent. Soviet leaders feared that the period 1981–1983 was a historical juncture not unlike Adolf Hitler's invasion of the Soviet Union in 1941. ABLE ARCHER thus nearly drove the Soviets toward preemptive military action to forestall a perceived and imminent U.S. nuclear blitz. Thus, nuclear capabilities and threats had the effect of worsening negative beliefs of enemy strategic intent, creating the very grounds for all-out war, which nuclear weapons were then depended on in the last minute to prevent.

Given these obviously contradictory effects, one cannot look to technology alone to explain peace in the nuclear age. Conflict is ultimately avoided by human decision makers reaching beyond their self-defined worldviews in order to empathize with the other side's security perceptions and need for self-defense. These points were made by President Kennedy during his historic address at American University after the Cuban Missile Crisis, sentiments eventually incorporated by the 1975 Helsinki Accords, which promised better relationships between East and West in return for the West's promise to accept Soviet geopolitical hegemony in Eastern Europe.

Nuclear weapons did not save humanity from itself. Rather, humanity was ultimately saved by the recognition that neither side wanted to destroy the other by a preemptive nuclear strike. This was made clear as the Cold War began to thaw in the mid-1980s, when President Reagan and Mikhail Gorbachev, the new and dynamic Soviet leader, began to communicate and negotiate face-to-face. As soon as this thoroughly political understanding was embraced by senior strategic decision makers on each side, the perceived need for an offensive version of nuclear deterrence abated with astonishing speed. Nuclear weapons avoided a major conflict on multiple occasions but only alongside mutual compromises that attempted to mitigate and even transcend the underlying sources of East-West conflict.

Michael Ryan Kraig

Perspective Essay 3. A Number of Factors Are at Play

It is ludicrous to solely credit nuclear weapons for the prevention of catastrophic wars since 1945 precisely due to the complicated underpinnings of human conflict. War is and always has been one of the most complex of human undertakings. The development and proliferation of nuclear weapons has done nothing to alter this simple fact. Just as no war can be traced to a single cause, the prevention of wars also comes down to a number of factors. While nuclear weapons may deserve some credit for preventing the escalation of warfare to the levels seen during World War II, diplomacy, economics, and changes in the dominant form of warfare also deserve credit for limiting the size and scope of more recent wars.

The term "catastrophic" carries a significant amount of baggage into the discussion. After all, wars are always catastrophic to the unfortunate populations caught up in them. There is no standard for which wars should be deemed catastrophic beyond the vague suggestion that if they do not rival World War II, they are somehow unworthy of the term. Yet in the immediate aftermath of the deadliest war in human history the Chinese Civil War resumed, resulting in the deaths of millions of Chinese citizens. The Korean War claimed at least 1 million lives, while the Vietnam War cost at least twice as many. Should these wars not be classified as catastrophic?

The prospect of a full-scale nuclear exchange has certainly altered our perception of how terrible a modern war might rage. Were two nuclear nations to launch an all-out attack on one another, the death toll would easily rise into the tens of millions. In that regard, all wars since 1945 have failed to include the detonation of nuclear devices and are therefore considered less destructive when compared to the awful potential possessed by nuclear states. Yet, this sets an incredibly low bar for success if it is to be declared when the worst possible consequences do not come to pass. Nuclear-armed nations have fought a number of direct conflicts as well as dozens of proxy wars without the use of nuclear weapons, and perhaps the nuclear deterrent possessed by these belligerents served to some degree as a mitigating factor, preventing escalation for fear of a devastating retaliation. However, fear alone cannot suffice to prevent conflict escalation—rather, the fear of enemy nuclear weapons might precipitate a first-strike strategy in the hope of disabling an enemy's nuclear capabilities before they can be employed.

In 1945 the world's leading states formed the United Nations (UN), an organization primarily dedicated to the prevention of future warfare. Embedded in the organizational charter is a strict prohibition on warfare between member states and an expectation that members will rally to the defense of any nation unlawfully attacked. The principle was put to the test in 1950, when North Korea invaded South Korea. Sixteen UN members sent troops to aid in South Korea's defense. Despite a stalemated situation on the Korean Peninsula, the UN Command there did not employ nuclear weapons, even though North Korea and its ally, the People's Republic of China, did not have the ability to retaliate in kind. In the seven decades since World War II the UN Charter's defense requirements have been tested dozens of times, and the international responses have not been flawless. But nuclear weapons have not been used in anger at any point in the UN's existence, and wars have at least been relatively contained.

Another major factor preventing the outbreak of catastrophic war is the growth of global economic partnerships. The world's largest military powers have developed interconnected systems of trade, which ensure that any open conflict would almost immediately devastate both national economies. These complex relationships continue to expand and diversify, making any direct conflict between global powers into an economic suicide pact. In short, it would be impossible for a nation to attack a fellow major power without destroying its own power base. Without the participation of at least two of the world's largest military powers, all of whom engaged in World War II, no future war is likely to be dubbed catastrophic.

A final major factor limiting the devastation of modern wars is a fundamental though possibly temporary shift in the conduct of warfare. Prior to World War II, wars were mostly conventional and were conducted with an aim of territorial conquest. The victor could expect to claim some or all of the territory of the vanquished. However, one significant part of the UN system is a guarantee of the territorial integrity of member states. Again, the record has not been perfect, but it has far surpassed any expectations derived from an understanding of pre–World War II conflicts. Modern war is far more often characterized by insurgency or civil war—both of which have a natural tendency to remain contained within a single nation. While these types of wars can produce enormous bloodshed, their failure to include cross-border conflict makes them far less likely to escalate into massive coalitions of combatants struggling for regional or global hegemony.

As the World War II generation gradually passes, they take with them the last living memory of the deadliest conflict in history. It is possible that as memories fade the horror of full-scale warfare will also recede, and conflict may again erupt. If so, the existence of nuclear weapons is less likely to minimize the chances of catastrophic warfare and more likely to massively escalate its costs. Despite postwar efforts to protect civilians in wartime, largely by demanding that belligerents act with discrimination and proportionality, some nations continue to develop nuclear arms. These weapons are the least discriminatory and proportionate devices in modern arsenals, and the mere contemplation of their use indicates a willingness to abandon the laws of armed conflict and throw away all of the progress made in averting catastrophic wars. To credit their existence as the sole preventative measure regarding catastrophic war is to embrace the most likely method of those wars actually occurring in the future.

Paul J. Springer

Further Reading

Anderson, Robert, and Annelise Anderson. *Reagan's Secret War: The Untold Story of His Fight to Save the World from Nuclear Disaster.* New York: Crown, 2009.

Borawski, John. *Avoiding War in the Nuclear Age: Confidence-Building Measures for Crisis Stability.* Boulder, CO: Westview, 1986.

Bundy, McGeorge. *Danger and Survival: Choices about the Bomb in the First Fifty Years.* New York: Vintage Books, 1990.

Cimbala, Stephen J. *The New Nuclear Disorder: Challenges to Deterrence and Strategy.* Burlington, VT: Ashgate, 2015.

Dobbs, Michael. *One Minute to Midnight: Kennedy, Khrushchev, and Castro on the Brink of Nuclear War.* New York: Knopf, 2008.

Fleron, Frederic J., Erik P. Hoffman, and Robbin F. Laird, eds. *Soviet Foreign Policy: From Brezhnev to Gorbachev.* Hawthorne, NY: Aldine de Gruyter, 1991.

Freedman, Lawrence. *Deterrence.* Malden, MA: Polity, 2004.

Freedman, Lawrence. *The Evolution of Nuclear Strategy.* 3rd ed. New York: Palgrave Macmillan, 2003.

Gaddis, John Lewis. *We Now Know: Rethinking Cold War History.* New York: Oxford University Press, 1997.

Goldstein, Joshua S., and John R. Freeman. *Three-Way Street: Strategic Reciprocity in World Politics.* Chicago: University of Chicago Press, 1990.

Graebner, Norman A., Richard Dean Burns, and Joseph M. Siracusa. *Reagan, Bush, Gorbachev: Revisiting the End of the Cold War.* Westport, CT: Praeger Security International, 2008.

Hansen, Chuck. *The Swords of Armageddon: U.S. Nuclear Weapons Development since 1945.* Sunnyvale, CA: Chukelea Publications, 1995.

Hoffman, David E. *The Dead Hand: The Untold Story of the Cold War Arms Race and Its Dangerous Legacy.* New York: Anchor Books, 2009.

Jervis, Robert. *The Meaning of the Nuclear Revolution: Statecraft and the Prospect of Armageddon.* Ithaca, NY: Cornell Studies in Security Affairs, 1989.

Jervis, Robert, ed. *Psychology and Deterrence.* Baltimore: Johns Hopkins University Press, 1989.

Keeney, L. Douglas. *15 Minutes: General Curtis LeMay and the Countdown to Nuclear Annihilation.* New York: St. Martin's, 2011.

Lebow, Richard Ned, and Janice Gross Stein. *We All Lost the Cold War.* Princeton, NJ: Princeton University Press, 1994.

Lieber, Keir A. *War and the Engineers: The Primacy of Politics over Technology.* Ithaca, NY: Cornell University Press, 2005.

McMahon, Robert J. *The Cold War: A Very Short Introduction.* Oxford: Oxford University Press, 2003.

Mueller, John. "The Essential Irrelevance of Nuclear Weapons: Stability in the Postwar World." *International Security* 13 (Fall 1988): 58–79.

Mueller, John. *Retreat from Doomsday: The Obsolescence of Major War.* New York: Basic Books, 1989.

Rudig, Wolfgang. *Anti-Nuclear Movements: A World Survey of Opposition to Nuclear Energy.* New York: Longman, 1990.

Schwartz, Stephen, ed. *Atomic Audit: The Costs and Consequences of U.S. Nuclear Weapons since 1940.* Washington, DC: Brookings Institution Press, 1998.

Sherwin, Martin J. *A World Destroyed: Hiroshima and Its Legacies.* Stanford, CA: Stanford University Press, 2003.

Smoke, Richard. *National Security and the Nuclear Dilemma: An Introduction to the American Experience in the Cold War.* 3rd ed. New York: McGraw-Hill, 1993.

Walker, Martin. *The Cold War: A History.* New York: Henry Holt, 1994.

Weart, Spencer. *The Rise of Nuclear Fear.* Cambridge, MA: Harvard University Press, 2012.

Weart, Spencer. *Nuclear Fear: A History of Images.* Cambridge, MA: Harvard University Press, 1988.

Zagare, Frank C. "Reconciling Rationality with Deterrence: A Re-Examination of the Logical Foundations of Deterrence Theory." *Journal of Theoretical Politics* 16(2) (2004): 107–141.

47. Why Did the Communist Side Defeat the Nationalists in the Chinese Civil War?

In the aftermath of World War II and upon the withdrawal of occupying Japanese forces from China, the Chinese Communist Party (CCP), under the leadership of Mao Zedong, and the Chinese Nationalist Party (Guomindang, GMD), under the leadership of Jiang Jieshi, vied for control of the country. The CCP-GMD rivalry had long predated World War II, however, and so the renewed postwar hostility between the two factions in fact represented a continuation of a civil conflict that had been under way since 1927. Despite the initial advantages enjoyed by the GMD, including aid and support from the United States, Mao Zedong's forces were eventually able to overcome the odds in the civil war, emerging victorious in October 1949 with the establishment of the People's Republic of China. Jiang Jieshi and the GMD leadership meanwhile fled mainland China and established a separate regime on the offshore island of Formosa (modern-day Taiwan). Scholars continue to examine the factors that enabled the Communists to persevere over the Nationalists in the Chinese Civil War and ultimately achieve victory, an outcome that significantly altered the course of modern Chinese and Asian history, not to mention the evolving Cold War.

Hong Zhang explains the Communist victory in the Chinese Civil War by comparing the political and military shrewdness of the Communist leadership with the political and military ineptitude of the Nationalist leadership. Despite the fact that the Nationalists enjoyed superiority in both numbers and equipment for much of the conflict, Zhang explains that the Communist forces fared better on the battlefield for a variety of reasons, including superior military leadership and better morale. Also crucial to the Communist victory were Mao Zedong's effective political mobilization and social reform campaigns, which resulted in ever-growing support among the Chinese peasant population. At the same time, Jiang Jieshi squandered the advantages enjoyed by the Nationalists through poor military leadership, political corruption, and mismanagement of urban and economic affairs. The resulting domestic crises only fueled frustration and disillusionment among the Chinese population, who saw the GMD at the root of their suffering. Dr. Meredith Oyen credits the Communist victory to the CCP's revolutionary and nationalistic appeal as well as the uncanny flexibility of its leadership in three key areas: social and economic policies, diplomacy, and battlefield tactics. On the other hand, she argues that Jiang Jieshi's inflexibility and rigid adherence to certain ideas, many of them outmoded and ineffective, led to political and military blunders that undermined domestic and international support for the Nationalists, thereby helping to make a Communist victory possible.

Background Essay

The Chinese Civil War began in 1927 and ended in 1949 and was fought between China's Guomindang (GMD, Nationalist) government and supporters of the Chinese Communist Party (CCP). The war ended with the establishment of the People's Republic of China. The roots of the Chinese Civil War went back as far as the late 1920s. After the foundation of the CCP in 1921, Soviet Comintern representatives advised its members to collaborate with other political groups supporting the Chinese revolution, especially the GMD founded by Sun Yixian, the revered revolutionary leader who was elected provisional president of the new Republic of China in 1911. After Sun's death in 1925, military leader Jiang Jieshi won power within the GMD and began to eliminate all potential rivals. In 1926 Jiang, alarmed by abortive but bloody Communist uprisings in several industrial cities, began to purge Communist Party members from GMD institutions and to suppress them elsewhere. In mid-1927 he made the Communist base in the Jiangxi Province of south-central China the new target of the Northern Expedition that he had launched the previous year against northern warlords and suppressed several further Communist insurrections.

Led by Mao Zedong and fortified by several former GMD military units whose commanders defected to the Communists, this rural base developed into the Jiangxi Soviet Republic, whose military forces numbered 200,000 by 1933. Chinese Communists also mounted several further urban and rural insurrections, and Jiang regarded them as the greatest threat to his government, more serious than even the

In this May 2, 1949, photo, a column of Chinese Communist light tanks enter Beijing during the Chinese Civil War. In Beijing on October 1, 1949, Communist leader Mao Zedong proclaimed the establishment of the People's Republic of China. (AP Photo)

Japanese troops who in 1932 established the client state of Manzhouguo in Manchuria and constantly sought to enhance Japan's influence in northern China. Between 1930 and 1934 Jiang waged annual campaigns against the Ruijin base in Jiangxi, in the last of which he succeeded in forcing the Communists to undertake the famous Long March of some 6,000 miles to the remote northwestern province of Shaanxi.

During 1935–1936 Jiang ordered troops commanded by his loyal ally, Manchurian warlord Zhang Xueliang, to attack and, he hoped, eliminate the remaining Communists. The soldiers rejected his orders, arguing that all Chinese should unite to fight the Japanese, not each other. In the December 1936 Xi'an Incident, Zhang kidnapped Jiang and forced him to form a united anti-Japanese front with the Communists. The GMD-CCP relationship remained strained, as the Communists developed their own military forces, the Eighth Route Army, commanded by Zhu De, and the New Fourth Army, under Lin Biao, and retained control of northern Shaanxi.

In 1937 a minor clash between Chinese and Japanese troops at the Lugouqiao Marco Polo Bridge, near Beijing, quickly escalated into full-scale warfare between the two countries. During the next 18 months Jiang gradually retreated to Chongqing in the far southwestern province of Sichuan, abandoning northern and eastern China to protracted Japanese occupation. The Communists controlled northwestern China. For 3 months in late 1940, the Communists launched the Hundred Regiments Campaign against Japan, but their defeat by the better-equipped Japanese convinced them to switch to guerrilla warfare behind Japanese lines in northern and central China. This policy provoked ferocious Japanese reprisals against both the Communists and the civilian population, but it proved effective in disrupting Japanese control and in enhancing the Communists' reputation as dedicated opponents of Japanese rule. It was insufficient to defeat Japanese rule, however.

In late 1941 GMD forces attacked and defeated the Communist New Fourth Army in the lower Changjiang (Yangtze) Valley. This marked the fundamental breakdown of CCP-GMD collaboration, although an uneasy alliance continued until 1944. GMD forces possessed superior equipment and funding, but Jiang's abandonment of much of China to Japanese rule and his reliance on a protracted strategy of attrition, together with the corruption that characterized many top officials of his regime, eroded his hold on popular loyalties. Communist morale was high. Their idealistic rhetoric, the Spartan living conditions at their Yan'an base in Shaanxi, their attractive and charismatic leaders, and their dangerous though small-scale partisan operations all caught Chinese popular imagination and impressed many visiting Western journalists and officials.

World War II ended in August 1945 with Japanese forces still in place in China. CCP membership had reached 1.2 million people, plus military forces of 900,000, and the Communists controlled an area whose population numbered 90 million. Despite Jiang's objections, Soviet forces entering Manchuria transferred captured Japanese equipment to Communist units. U.S. leaders, especially Ambassador Patrick J. Hurley in late 1945, sought to strengthen Jiang's regime, promote reform from within, and encourage Nationalist-Communist reconciliation and the formation of a coalition government in which Communists would have some influence, albeit as junior partners.

The most sustained such effort was the 13-month (December 1945–January 1947) mission to China of former U.S. Army chief of staff General George C. Marshall, who in January 1946 arranged a temporary cease-fire in the developing civil war, broken later that spring when, as Soviet units withdrew, GMD forces attacked Communist troops in Manchuria, winning control of that region in late May. That same month the Communists rechristened their military forces the People's Liberation Army (PLA).

It proved impossible to devise any further agreements acceptable to both sides, and full-scale civil war resumed on June 26, 1946, when Nationalist units launched an offensive against Communist-held areas in Hubei and Henan Provinces. The United States continued to provide massive loans and quantities of military hardware to the GMD but prudently refused to commit American troops. As the Cold War rapidly developed, Soviet and American officials clearly backed different parties in the evolving Chinese Civil War, but neither was prepared to run great risks to assist its side.

By 1947 as inflation and corruption both ran rampant, Chinese businessmen and the middle class began to desert the GMD, and many fled overseas. As they had against the Japanese, the Communists frequently employed guerrilla tactics against Nationalist forces. The Communist introduction of land reform persuaded many peasants to support them. These tactics supplemented full-scale military campaigns that they soon launched.

In mid-May 1947 Lin and the New Fourth Army opened a major offensive in northeastern China, and six weeks later another large army commanded by Liu Bocheng moved southwest across the Huanghe River (Yellow River), into Shandong Province. In September 1948 Lin began a massive campaign in Manchuria, capturing Shenyang in Liaoniang Province in November; soon afterward 300,000 GMD troops surrendered to him. In north-central China, the Communist Huai River campaign ended victoriously on January 10, 1949, after PLA troops surrounded 66 regiments—one-third of the existing GMD military forces. That same month Lin's troops captured Beijing, China's symbolic capital, followed by the southern city of Guangzhou (Canton) in Guangdong in October. The GMD government fled to Taiwan as Communist forces gradually consolidated their hold over the entire country. On October 1, 1949, Mao proclaimed the new People's Republic of China.

Priscilla M. Roberts

Perspective Essay 1. Military and Political Shrewdness

The Chinese Civil War between the Chinese Guomindang (GMD, Nationalists) led by Jiang Jieshi and the Chinese Communist Party (CCP) under the leadership of Mao Zedong was one of the largest wars fought in modern times. When fighting between the two sides resumed in earnest following the end of World War II, the Communists decisively defeated the GMD forces, which were both numerically superior and better equipped at the inception of the civil war. The Communist victory forced GMD leader Jiang Jieshi, his remaining army, and his bureaucracy to seek refuge on Taiwan. On October 1, 1949, in Beijing, Communist leader Mao Zedong proclaimed the establishment of the People's Republic of China. The crushing defeat of the GMD resulted from both the military and political shrewdness exercised by the CCP and the military and political blunders committed by Jiang and his government.

Fighting between the CCP and the GMD can be traced to 1927, although the beginning of the Second Sino-Japanese War (1937–1945) brought about the formation of the united front between the two political parties against Japanese aggression and officially ended their open hostility. Distrust continued, however. Then when Japan surrendered in August 1945, this prompted a frantic race between the CCP and the GMD to seize Japanese-occupied territory, weapons, and supplies. With the prospect of civil war looming and amid heightened concerns regarding Soviet intervention, the U.S. government sought to secure a negotiated political solution.

The Harry S. Truman administration dispatched former U.S. Army chief of staff General George C. Marshall to China. The Marshall Mission (December 1945–January 1947) secured a temporary cease-fire, but the effort to avert full-scale warfare failed owing to continuing U.S. assistance to the GMD, its wartime ally, and the insincerity of both sides in attempting to achieve a lasting political settlement.

After Marshall criticized both parties for the breakdown of the peace negotiations and left China in early 1947, full-scale warfare commenced. GMD forces enjoyed a superiority in weapons and material, supplied largely by the United States, and numbered about 3 million men. They thus enjoyed a clear advantage over the poorly armed Communist military forces of about 1 million when the civil war erupted.

Early in the fighting the Nationalist side won a number of seemingly easy battles. In March 1947 they even captured Yanan, which had been the CCP capital since 1935. However, the seizure of Yanan was merely a symbolic victory, as Mao and other Communist leaders and troops had already evacuated the area and withdrawn to new rural bases farther north to continue their war efforts. Mao also dismissed the GMD battlefield victories by claiming that the key to winning a war was through solving the agrarian problem and not by losing or taking a city. By the end of 1946, GMD forces had gained control of the major cities and rail lines in Manchuria. However, the CCP preserved its troops by simply withdrawing and avoiding battles and casualties when in a disadvantageous military position, a strategy firmly espoused by Mao.

The Communist victory was amazingly swift. Enjoying initial military advantages in both manpower and weaponry, the GMD squandered its superiority. The CCP demonstrated political astuteness and employed a flexible and practical military strategy. Its troops had capable military leaders, strong discipline, and high fighting morale. Furthermore, the CCP's political work dovetailed closely with its military effort. While its forces engaged the Nationalists on the battlefield, Communist political organizers sought to transform the countryside by launching land redistribution programs and working on mass mobilization. Its attention to the needs of the peasantry allowed the CCP to gain mass support and ensured its army of a steady inflow of recruits. In contrast, Jiang demonstrated strategic ineptitude, while his generals often failed to coordinate their military efforts. In the end, the Nationalist troops suffered from poor command, poor discipline, demoralization, insufficient training, and massive desertions and defections.

The ultimate CCP triumph was achieved on the battlefield. The military showdown occurred in Manchuria. This vast region located in northeastern China beyond the Great Wall turned out to be pivotal to the outcome of the civil war. Confined largely to southwestern China when Japan surrendered, the United States facilitated, at Jiang's insistence, the transport there of GMD forces. As soon as the Marshall Mission ended, fighting became intense. Having committed half a million of his best-trained and -equipped troops in Manchuria to retain control over a region with industrial and strategic importance, Jiang blundered by overextending his forces before he could consolidate control of the area south of the Great Wall.

Meanwhile, the CCP had already penetrated the Manchurian countryside, winning peasant support and establishing rural bases. The CCP was also able to take advantage of the Soviet defeat of Japanese forces in Manchuria in terms of Japanese weapons and equipment captured by the Soviets. Lin Biao, an outstanding general, commanded the Communist forces, renamed the People's Liberation Army (PLA) in late 1946. After a number of initial military setbacks, Lin's army seized control of rail lines and besieged the Nationalist-held cities. In a desperate move to relieve his troops entrapped in the cities, Jiang ordered airdrops, to little avail. The ensuing Liao-Shen Campaign (September–November 1948) launched by the PLA eliminated some 470,000 Nationalist soldiers, sealed the fate of Manchuria, and marked the beginning of the end for the GMD.

Seizing the momentum of the Manchurian victory, Lin's forces proceeded to the north China plain and launched the major offensive known as the Ping-Jin Campaign (Beijing-Tianjin region), which lasted from November 1948 to January 1949. After the PLA captured Tianjin, one of the largest cities in northern China, and encircled Beijing, the Nationalist commander in control of the city surrendered the ancient Chinese capital without putting up a fight. The massive battles fought in northeastern and northern China cost Jiang 1 million men through death, desertion, and defection.

At the same time, Communist military attention had already focused on central China, where the third major campaign of the civil war, the Huaihai Campaign, occurred. Both sides committed large numbers of troops to it. The climactic battle, at Xuzhou in northern Jiangxu for control of the vital rail junction there, lasted some two months, during which GMD military commanders often had to deal with confusing and contradictory orders from Jiang, who directed the campaign from a distance. The Communist generals utterly outmaneuvered their Nationalist counterparts and routed the GMD forces, many of which simply defected. The Nationalist armored corps, Jiang's trump card in the Huaihai battles, was immobilized by tank traps dug by peasants mobilized by the Communists. The PLA also benefited from large quantities of arms and equipment taken from its enemy. The GMD defeat in this campaign shifted the balance of power to the Communist side and allowed it to threaten the Yangzi River Valley.

Facing this bleak situation, the GMD requested cease-fire talks. Mao then produced an eight-point proposal that essentially demanded complete surrender. Impatient with further negotiations, on April 21, 1949, Mao ordered 1 million Communist troops to cross the Yangzi. This move culminated in the collapse of GMD resistance. During the next few months the PLA captured one Nationalist-held city after another, and by the end of 1949 the Chinese Civil War was over.

Although the battlefield delivered the ultimate victory for the CCP, a number of other factors facilitated this outcome. The Japanese invasion of China in 1937 affected the political fortunes of the two sides in different ways. It shook the foundation of the Nationalist government. Having lost several major battles to the Japanese at the beginning of the war, the Nationalists were forced to retreat to the remote mountainous city of Chongqing in western China, and consequently they lost control over coastal cities that had served as their main financial and political sources of support. The absence of GMD authority in the northern and central countryside enabled the Communists to expand their political and military influence there. During World War II, the CCP greatly benefited from Mao's policies of guerrilla warfare and peasant mobilization through land reform and organized resistance against Japanese aggression. The Communists won peasant support by either reducing peasants' rent or returning land to poor peasants. Soldiers also assisted in harvesting crops. These wise policies allowed CCP membership to jump from about 40,000 in 1937 to 1.2 million in 1945. This enormous popular support for the CCP from the countryside proved critical for the ultimate Communist victory in 1949.

Mao also proved to be far superior to Jiang as a military strategist. Mao instructed his troops to "fight no battle unprepared, and fight no battle not sure of winning, and make every effort to ensure victory in the given set of conditions as between the enemy and ourselves." By the second half of 1947, CCP forces had grown to some 2 million through Nationalist defections and recruitment from the rural bases. As the war tide began to favor the CCP, Mao went over to large-unit conventional offensives. He directed the PLA to "concentrate an absolutely superior force (two, three, four and sometimes even five or six times the enemy's strength), encircle the enemy forces completely, strive to wipe them out thoroughly," and not to "let any escape from the net." Following Mao's strategy, the PLA launched and won a series of offensives that routed their opponents and secured not only defections but also considerable quantities of military supplies.

Paralleling the GMD's poor handling of the battles was its mismanagement of urban affairs. When Japan surrendered, Jiang was heralded as a war hero, and his government received a warm welcome when it resumed control over the previously Japanese-occupied areas of urban China. However, the policies pursued by the GMD and its officials soon disillusioned the urban populations, and popular support dissipated. Widespread official corruption undermined civilian morale. Commandeering Japanese-held property, mishandling factories and businesses, and allowing those who had collaborated with the Japanese to retain their jobs were some of the charges leveled at GMD officials. Preoccupied with fighting the civil war, the Nationalist government failed to tackle the urgent task of reconstructing a badly ravaged economy.

The official solution to the severe shortage of revenue was to print paper money, which resulted in spiraling inflation. Growing unrest marked the years 1947 and 1948 in urban China, where the political and economic situations provided fertile soil for political activities. Besides economic distress, the Nationalist government's corruption and maladministration, repression of dissent, purge of Communist sympathizers and student leaders, and suppression of student political activities all worked to intensify swelling discontent with the GMD. Indeed, the widespread student protests against the Nationalist government during the years of the civil war induced Mao Zedong to conclude that the student movement in the Nationalist-controlled cities constituted a "second front." Thus, the GMD lost both the war on the battlefield and that on the home front.

Hong Zhang

Perspective Essay 2. Flexibility Was the Key

On October 1, 1949, Chairman Mao Zedong of the Chinese Communist Party (CCP) announced the establishment of the People's Republic of China. The day marked an end to the civil war against the Nationalist Party (Guomindang, GMD). Although there were many factors leading to the CCP victory in 1949, the most critical factor was the flexibility of the CCP and its leader, Mao. When contrasted with the rigidity of GMD policies, that flexibility allowed the CCP to overcome difficult odds and win a victory. This critical difference between CCP and GMD actions is visible in three discrete areas: social and economic policies before, during, and after World War II; the management of international powers in China in the immediate postwar period; and tactical military decisions during the civil war.

Although it began as a revolutionary party that overthrew the Qing dynasty in 1911 and brought the establishment of the Republic of China (ROC), the GMD transformed into a rigid structure more in line with former dynasties than modern democracies. During the two decades that followed the revolution, the Nationalists struggled to unify the country, especially in peripheral areas with a long history of warlord control. Many new political voices came onto the scene, including the CCP, which held its first formal meeting in Shanghai in 1921.

Although opposed on many political principles, the two parties managed to reach a united front agreement in 1922, which led to the GMD accepting CCP members into the party and culminated with the Northern Expedition to unite China against warlord rule. In short order, however, the attempt at cooperation broke down as mutual suspicion and conflicting goals divided the two parties. In 1927, Nationalist leader Jiang Jieshi purged the GMD ranks of Communists in what became known as the White Terror.

The increasingly inflexible nature of GMD party politics was also visible in the contrast between GMD and CCP social policies. The center of GMD power rested in major port cities along the long Chinese coastline. As leader of the party, Jiang abandoned some of his early experiments with democracy in favor of a government that was strikingly similar to that of the former Qing Empire. He held dictatorial power, did not permit real participation from other parties in decisions of government, and made it the main goal of the GMD to remain in power and unify the country, not to reform existing systems.

While the GMD worked to shore up its power and economic base, the CCP was developing its own base of support in the villages. Adjusting traditional Marxist-Leninist theories to the Chinese countryside required placing the focus on the peasants instead of on the urban industrial workers. Early experiments with Soviet-style collectives in Jiangxi Province were cut off by GMD raids, leading to the Long March of 1934–1935 when the CCP relocated some 6,000 miles from Jiangxi to Shaanxi and in the process created an enduring mythology about the party and its leaders. Throughout this period, the CCP placed the strength of the party over communist ideology, only pursuing radical reforms when it could help build the party's base. The Japanese invasion of Manchuria in 1931 limited CCP efforts at agricultural reform, as the party opted to place a greater focus on the survival of the Chinese state. During the course of the 1940s, the CCP developed a reputation for following through on promises of reform and being willing to correct mistakes, attitudes that would help it to win popular support, even from those wary of communist ideology.

The formal start of the Second Sino-Japanese War in 1937 further undermined GMD power, and the CCP made good use of the changing circumstances. During the long eight-year conflict that followed Japanese attacks weakened GMD power, but the Nationalist side also made significant mistakes that inhibited its ability to survive after the war. First, the GMD reacted to the Japanese conquest of the ROC capital, Nanjing, by withdrawing and moving the seat of the ROC government to the peripheral city of Chongqing. Far removed from both its tax base and its greatest support, the ROC government also had to contend with the traditional influence of warlords in the region. A second mistake developed in fiscal policy: the ROC had taken China off the silver standard in 1935, in part to fight off the impact of the global international depression. During the Second Sino-Japanese War the ROC simply issued more money when funds dried up in direct contrast to the CCP, which looked to local resources and farming to survive the lean years.

During the conflict itself, the GMD enacted measures that had the effect of losing the support of the general public and failed to correct its course when CCP policies proved more successful. The GMD depended on military conscription, heavy taxes, and strong-arm tactics to force the public to support the ROC Army. Both during the war and afterward, the government was plagued by corruption. The decision to work with former Japanese collaborators for the sake of stability further alienated the general public. Meanwhile, the CCP courted support from the people around its wartime base area at Yan'an through a series of experiments with agrarian reforms.

Although efforts at land reform made little lasting impact during the war, revised tax policies and agrarian reforms did allow the CCP to gain crucial ideological support from the peasants. Moreover, land reform efforts during the war were more strategic than ideological: Mao was mindful of not wanting to alienate small landlords who had long given support to the CCP base areas. This assistance was confined to areas on the periphery in the north and northwest of the country, but even though CCP wartime revolutionary policies did not secure widespread cooperation from peasants, GMD policies by contrast sparked numerous peasant rebellions.

The GMD also demonstrated weakness in the public perceptions of its resistance to Japan. During the war, the two parties once again attempted to coexist under a second United Front agreement. For the purpose of fighting the Japanese, CCP forces became divisions under the command of the general commander of the ROC Army: the New Fourth Army and the Eighth Route Army were Communist. The CCP won a propaganda coup by presenting itself to the public as the more active patriotic troops endeavoring to fight the foreign invaders, although in reality both Nationalist and Communist troops fought the Japanese. However, after the war it was hard for Jiang to fight against the general impression that he had spent the war more interested in fighting Communists than the Japanese. While the CCP adjusted its information campaigns to improve its image, Jiang remained steadfastly focused on his anti-Japanese goals and especially his anticommunist goals.

Despite these missteps, by the end of World War II in August 1945 the GMD continued to hold a substantial advantage over the CCP as the party in power. In addition to superior numbers and war matériel, the GMD had a tax base, troop conscription, authority over much of the territory of China, and, importantly, international standing as the recognized government of China. Some of that advantage was misleading, however, as the GMD forces were larger and better equipped, but by the end of the war they were also frustrated and war weary. Those drafted were anxious to return home, and those who had fought the war in their home province were reluctant to leave it. Nationalist forces were also unquestionably stretched too thin across the vast country. At the same time CCP troops contained conscripts, but some fought voluntarily for the social changes they had seen in CCP-controlled areas, and as time wore on the latter's numbers increased.

Although the conflict that emerged after 1945 was civil in nature, international forces had a substantial impact on the direction it took, and in this area Jiang's inflexibility relative to Mao also proved to be an important factor. The controversial agreement between the United States, Great Britain, and the Soviet Union at Yalta in February 1945 contained an important advantage for Jiang's efforts to stay in power: it ensured Soviet recognition of the ROC and in theory prevented Soviet support for the CCP. At the end of the war, the Soviet Union occupied Manchuria and agreed to hold the territory until the ROC troops were in position to accept the Japanese surrender. Jiang assumed that the United States would remain committed to his government and, as a result, allowed his strong anticommunism to get in the way of a productive relationship with the Soviet Union. At his request, the United States helped move Nationalist troops around the country and even landed U.S. marines in northern China to help the GMD establish control over the region around Beijing.

Despite this direct aid to the Nationalists, the United States remained interested in a negotiated joint government, and given the unequal balance of power between the parties, an opportunity existed for a compromise that would have kept the GMD in power but given the CCP a role in government. U.S. ambassador Patrick Hurley tried to facilitate such an agreement, but his pro-GMD bias gave Mao and his second-in-command Zhou Enlai the impression that the United States was less than neutral. Hurley resigned in late 1945, and the temporary emissary, former U.S. Army chief of staff General George C. Marshall, proved far more sympathetic to the CCP. During the Marshall Mission, the GMD, the CCP, and representatives of other parties met for a political consultative conference and worked out an agreement for shared representation in government and in the National Assembly and limited powers for the president. Jiang recommended alterations to the agreement to ensure that the GMD would retain control. The CCP had been willing to use the agreement as an opportunity to increase its influence in the government slowly but would not agree to the revisions.

Throughout this process, Jiang had maintained his rigid anticommunist and anti-Soviet attitudes but also added to them an unshakable faith in U.S. interest in preventing a Communist victory in China. By 1947, however, the view from Washington was to avoid getting overtly involved in a conflict that it increasingly believed the Nationalist side could not win, and there was little chance of the United States committing militarily to preventing the fall of the GMD. Jiang's attitudes and beliefs prevented the GMD from adopting a more flexible policy. As a result diplomacy failed, and the two sides moved closer to war.

Still, the GMD would not have lost the Chinese Civil War without a series of tactical missteps that allowed Mao and the CCP to emerge victorious. The most crucial of these was Jiang's focus on reestablishing ROC authority in Manchuria long before ensuring a firmly established base in the rest of the country. In response to a second assault on Manchuria in July 1946, the CCP adjusted its tactics and withdrew from the cities into the surrounding countryside, from which it tried to gain peasant support. Jiang had invested his army and his own prestige in his ability to retake Manchuria, but holding only urban islands surrounded by Communist-dominated rural territory while the economic strength of the nation in central and southern China quickly became a losing proposition. Jiang ignored advice to regroup south of the Great Wall, and this stubbornness would prove nearly fatal to the GMD.

Meanwhile, the CCP learned to adapt to the changing circumstances. Starting in 1947, General Lin Biao converted the CCP divisions of the Nationalist Revolutionary Army into the People's Liberation Army (PLA) and prepared the forces to fight conventional battles in addition to guerrilla actions. Lin and the PLA largely reserved fighting for when victory was ensured and in so doing managed to gain the upper hand and secure masses of deserting Nationalist troops and their weapons. By maintaining good discipline within troop ranks, the PLA also won another propaganda victory relative to the unruly GMD troops, a factor that contributed to the CCP's increasing popular support near the end of the conflict. By 1949 the situation in China had drastically shifted from that in 1945, with the CCP growing steadily in numbers of troops and weaponry and controlling increasing amounts of territory. Jiang resigned as president of the ROC in January 1949 as the military losses mounted, and by the end of the year he and the rest of the ROC government fled the mainland to regroup on the island of Taiwan.

In the end, the CCP victory in the Chinese Civil War can be credited in part to its revolutionary and nationalistic appeal, its strategic choices on how and when to fight, and its strong leadership but also in large part to its innovation. Though they made their share of mistakes in developing strategy and fighting the war, Mao's ability and that of his commanders to adjust to changing circumstances and seize opportunities to improve the narrative was what finally brought a Communist victory. CCP flexibility was matched by GMD rigidity, as Jiang became too attached to specific ideas that proved to be his downfall.

Meredith Oyen

Further Reading

Bianco, Lucien. *Origins of the Chinese Revolution, 1915–1949.* Stanford, CA: Stanford University Press, 1971.

Chen, Jian. *Mao's China and the Cold War.* Chapel Hill: University of North Carolina Press, 2001.

Crozier, Brian. *The Man Who Lost China: The First Full Biography of Chiang Kai-shek.* New York: Scribner, 1976.

Dreyer, Edward L. *China at War, 1901–1949.* New York: Longman, 1995.

Eastman, Lloyd E., ed. *The Nationalist Era in China, 1927–1949.* Cambridge, MA: Harvard University Press, 1991.

Elleman, Bruce A., and S. C. M. Paine. *Modern China: Continuity and Change, 1644 to the Present.* New York: Prentice Hall, 2010.

Fairbank, John King. *China: A New History.* Cambridge, MA: Harvard University Press, 1994.

Fairbank, John King. *The Great Chinese Revolution, 1800–1985.* New York: Harper Perennial, 1987.

Fairbank, John K., and Albert Feuerwerker, eds. *The Cambridge History of China,* Vol. 13, *Republican China 1912–1949,* Part 2. Cambridge: Cambridge University Press, 1986.

Feigon, Lee. *Mao: A Reinterpretation.* Chicago: Ivan R. Dee, 2002.

Fenby, Jonathan. *Chiang Kai-shek: China's Generalissimo and the Nation He Lost.* New York: Carroll and Graf, 2004.

Furuya, Keiji. *Chiang Kai-shek: His Life and Times.* New York: St. John's University Press, 1981.

Hsiung, James C. *China's Bitter Victory: The War with Japan, 1937–1945.* New York: M. E. Sharpe, 1992.

Hutchings, Graham. *Modern China: A Guide to a Century of Change.* Cambridge, MA: Harvard University Press, 2001.

Lary, Diana. *China's Republic.* New York: Cambridge University Press, 2007.

Liu, F. F. *The Military History of Modern China, 1924–1949.* Princeton, NJ: Princeton University Press, 1956.

Lynch, Michael. *The Chinese Civil War, 1945–49.* Oxford, UK: Osprey, 2010.

Lynch, Michael J. *China: From Empire to People's Republic, 1900–49.* London: Hodder and Stoughton, 2006.

Lynch, Michael J. *Mao.* New York: Routledge, 2004.

Pepper, Suzanne. *Civil War in China: The Political Struggle, 1945–49.* 2nd ed. Lanham, MD: Rowman and Littlefield, 1999.

Pogue, Forrest C. *George C. Marshall,* Vol. 4, *Statesman, 1945–1959.* New York: Viking Penguin, 1987.

Short, Philip. *Mao: A Life.* New York: Henry Holt, 2000.

Spence, Jonathan. *The Search for Modern China.* New York: Norton, 1990.

Spence, Jonathan D. *Mao Zedong.* New York: Viking, 1999.

Tanner, Harold. *The Battle for Manchuria and the Fate of China.* Bloomington: Indiana University Press, 2012.

Tanner, Harold. *Where Chiang Kai-shek Lost China: The Liao-Shen Campaign, 1948.* Bloomington: Indian University Press, 2015.

Taylor, Jay. *The Generalissimo: Chiang Kai-shek and the Struggle for Modern China.* Cambridge, MA: Harvard University Press, 2009.

Terrill, Ross. *Mao: A Biography.* Revised and expanded ed. Stanford, CA: Stanford University Press, 1999.

Truman, Harry S. *Memoirs,* Vol. 2, *Years of Trial and Hope, 1946–1953.* New York: Doubleday, 1956.

Westad, Odd Arne. *Cold War and Revolution: Soviet-American Rivalry and the Origins of the Chinese Civil War, 1944–1946.* New York: Columbia University Press, 1993.

Westad, Odd Arne. *Decisive Encounters: The Chinese Civil War, 1946–1950.* Stanford, CA: Stanford University Press, 2003.

Westad, Odd Arne. *Restless Empire: China and the World since 1750.* New York: Basic Books, 2012.

Zarrow, Peter Gue. *China in War and Revolution, 1895–1949.* London: Routledge, 2005.

48. How Has the Debate over the "Right" to Palestine Shaped the Arab-Israeli Conflict?

Since the beginning of the 20th century, tensions have mounted between the Arab and Jewish populations living in the area once known as Palestine. Traditionally, Palestine has consisted of an area on the eastern coast of the Mediterranean Sea bordered by the Jordan River Valley to the east, the Negev Desert to the south, and Lebanon to the north. Arab-Jewish turmoil morphed into full-scale warfare upon Israel's declaration of independence on May 14, 1948. But rather than conclusively ending the conflict, the Israeli War of Independence only deepened both sides' determination to lay claim to Palestine and added a new dimension to hostilities, as hundreds of thousands of Palestinian Arabs now became refugees. Since that time, mutual distrust, incendiary rhetoric, armed clashes, terrorism, and actions taken by both sides have created an Arab-Israeli conflict that is both immensely complex and deeply emotional for all involved. What is more, the Arab-Israeli conflict has been adversely affected by larger geopolitical and regional developments, most notably the Cold War, Arab nationalism, and the war on terror. With the establishment of a cooperative and inclusive peace between Arabs and Israelis proving elusive, the debate over Palestine has frequently turned to the question of which side—Arab or Jewish—has the greater claim to the area.

The essays that follow explore this issue from two very different perspectives. In the first essay, Dr. Sherifa Zuhur posits that Palestinians—a group that includes Muslims, Christians, and some Jews—have a legitimate claim to land in Palestine based on historical precedent and continuous ownership. She argues that the Israelis, by contrast, gained territory through conquest and the illegal seizure of land and property previously owned by Palestinians. The territorial ambitions of Israel during several wars and the nation's continued unwillingness to recognize the legitimacy of Palestinian claims and even a Palestinian identity have only fueled the ongoing Arab-Israeli conflict. In the second perspective essay, Dr. David Tal asserts that as the birthplace and epicenter of the Jewish identity and the site of its first religious and political institutions, Eretz Israel (Land of Israel) continued to serve as a spiritual anchor for the world's Jewish population even after the great diaspora in the early years of the first millennium. Tal points out that with the development of the modern nation-state and increased anti-Semitism, it was only logical that Zionists would turn to Palestine to fulfill their desire for self-determination and safety within the modern world.

Background Essay

Few peoples have been as violently displaced as the Jews. Palestine was their ancient home, but a series of expulsions occurred. These took place at the hands of the Assyrians during 733–722 BCE and during the Babylonian exile in 597 BCE for 70 years. In 63 BCE following the siege of Jerusalem, the kingdom became a Roman protectorate, and in 6 CE it was made the Roman province of Judea. A Jewish revolt in 66 brought the First Jewish-Roman War (66–73), during which the Romans took Jerusalem and destroyed much of the city and its Second Temple. This ended with the Roman or Edom exile, when Jewish leaders and elites were killed, sold into slavery, or exiled. In 132 Bar Kokhba led another revolt against Rome. It was crushed in 135, and all semblance of Jewish independence was lost. The name of Jerusalem was changed, and Jews were no longer permitted to live there. Judea and Samaria became Syria Palaestina.

By 635 the Arabs had conquered most of Palestine. Arab rule was followed by that of the Ottoman Turks beginning in 1516. Modern times thus found only a remnant of Jews remaining in their original homeland. This began to change with modern nationalism, the concept that each people of distinct origin should have their own nation-state.

Jews had been subjected to widespread discrimination, segregation, and even savage persecution. Their manner of dress, language, and religious customs set them apart, and non-Jews found it easy to discriminate against them. As a result many Jews embraced Zionism, the movement calling for the creation of a Jewish state or homeland in Palestine. Only when this was achieved, they believed, would Jews be safe from persecution.

The word "Zionism" comes from "Zion," the name of a hill in Jerusalem. Justification for it sprang from the account in the Old Testament of the Bible wherein God is described as having given the Land of Israel to the Israelites in perpetuity. Diaspora Jews held that one day they would return to their Holy Land. Zionists held that Jews had a national identity and as such should live together in a Jewish state. Great pogroms in Russia and anti-Semitism elsewhere in Europe provided impetus to the movement in the last two decades of the 19th century and led to efforts to settle Jewish farmers and artisans in Palestine.

Zionism became a political force under Theodor Herzl, an Austrian Jew who in 1896 published *The Jewish State,* in which he argued for a Jewish state in Palestine. In August 1897 Herzl convened the First Zionist Congress. It voted in favor of a "publicly recognized, legally secured homeland" for the Jews in Palestine. Efforts to negotiate the establishment of a Jewish state within the Ottoman Empire failed but did not prevent a steadily increasing Jewish immigration to Palestine, supported by wealthy European Jews. In 1914 Palestine had a population of some 657,000 Muslim Arabs, 81,000 Christian Arabs, and 59,000 Jews.

World War I brought great change to the Middle East. Ottoman leaders decided to join the war on the side of the Central Powers, and this had a profound effect. In May 1916 British Middle Eastern expert Sir Mark Sykes and French diplomat François Georges Picot concluded a secret agreement to partition much of the Middle East between their two states. Palestine was to fall within the British sphere. This flew in the face of a British demarche to the Arabs, which brought the Arab Revolt against Ottoman rule. Nonetheless, in November 1917, to attract Jewish support for the Entente war effort, the British government issued the Balfour Declaration. Named for Foreign Secretary Arthur James Balfour, it proclaimed British government support for a "national home" (although not a state) for the Jews in Palestine.

By 1931, however, the number of Palestinian Jews had sharply increased to 174,606, while the Arab population was 858,788. Tensions grew not only from this population influx but also because of Jewish land purchases. Often the land was purchased from wealthy absentee Arab landowners and brought the eviction of Arab tenants.

The real rise in Jewish immigration to Palestine came, however, with the virulent and rampant anti-Semitism of the 1930s, the Holocaust of World War II, and the influx of surviving Jewish refugees immediately thereafter. The official census of 1945 shows the dramatic increase in the Jewish population, with 553,660 Jews and 1,211,100 Arabs (1,061,270 Muslims and 149,830 Christians), or some 31 percent of the population, up from 11 percent in 1922.

The British government soon had cause to regret its League of Nations mandate of Palestine. British rule during 1920–1948 failed to keep the peace between Arabs and Jews. The escalating violence was the inevitable result of the impossible British policy of permitting Jewish immigration while at the same time attempting to safeguard Arab rights. Continued immigration brought more Jewish land purchases, and these led in turn to Arab violence and riots. The British would suspend Jewish settlement and land purchases but, under pressure from world Jewry, reverse this.

In 1920 Arabs began sporadically attacking Jewish settlements, and in response Jews formed Haganah, a clandestine defense organization. The British attempted to create a legislative council of Arabs and Jews, but the Arabs believed that this would signal their acceptance of the mandate and refused to participate. In 1936, a full-fledged Arab revolt began. Lasting until 1939, it forced the British to dispatch 20,000 additional troops and resulted in the deaths of some 5,000 Arabs and many more injured. It also brought a temporary alliance between the British and the Jews.

In 1937, the British government considered partitioning Palestine into separate Arab and Jewish states but then rejected this as not feasible. In 1939 the British announced that Palestine would become an independent state within 10 years. They also sharply curtailed Jewish immigration and restricted the sale of Arab land to Jews. This policy continued during World War II, when the British even diverted naval assets to intercept and turn back ships carrying Jews attempting to escape the

British troops searching residents of Jaffa in Palestine for weapons, 1936. A three-way struggle developed in Palestine between the British, Arabs, and the Jews. (Library of Congress)

Holocaust. Jewish extremists then took up arms against the British, and a three-way war ensued.

News of the Holocaust resulting in the deaths of more than 6 million Jews dramatically changed attitudes throughout most of the world in favor of Jewish settlement in Palestine and even the creation of a Jewish state there. Probably most Jews now believed that the only way to prevent a new Holocaust was a nation-state capable of safeguarding their interests. Jewish terrorist organizations were also increasingly at war with the British administration, which was refusing to allow the resettlement in Israel from Europe of more than 250,000 Jewish survivors of the Holocaust. For their part, the Arabs could not understand why they should be made victims for something not of their doing.

On February 14, 1947, exasperated by its inability to solve the Palestinian problem, the British government turned it over to the newly created United Nations (UN). That August the United Nations Special Commission of Palestine (UNSCOP) recommended the termination of the British mandate and granted Palestine its independence on the basis of separate Arab and Jewish states. Although the Arab population was 1.2 million and the Jewish population just 600,000, the Jews would have had some 56 percent of the land. Jews supported the plan; understandably, the Arabs did not. Desperate to quit Palestine, the British government announced acceptance of the UNSCOP recommendation and declared in September 1947 that the mandate of Palestine would terminate on May 14, 1948.

On November 29, 1947, the UN General Assembly officially approved the partition of Palestine according to the UNSCOP report. This ensured the establishment of a Jewish state in Palestine, and in January 1948 the Arab Liberation Army invaded. Although the Arab forces enjoyed initial success, Jewish forces took the offensive in the spring of 1948 and by design and/or circumstance caused many Arabs to flee their homes and land. Then on May 14, 1948, the Jews of Palestine declared the establishment of the State of Israel. The next day Arab armies invaded, beginning the Israeli War of Independence (May 15, 1948–March 10, 1949).

Spencer C. Tucker

Perspective Essay 1. Palestinians' Right to Their Land, Property, and National Sovereignty

The Palestinians can trace their ancestry back to the ancient Canaanites referred to in the Old Testament, who predated the Hebrew tribes in the land of Canaan.

Palestinians are also descended from other groups that invaded or settled Palestine and intermarried with the inhabitants. The Palestinian common identity was based on continuous tenure and residence in the territory of Palestine. Palestinians, who were not allowed to identify themselves by this name and were simply dubbed "Arabs" by the Israeli government, may be Muslims, Christian, or Druzes (who consider themselves Muslim). Under the Palestinian definition of national identity, the members of the small Jewish community that was able to return to Jerusalem in ancient times and resided there prior to World War I are also considered Palestinian, like their Muslim and Christian counterparts. However, the many Jews who traveled to and settled in Palestine as part of the work of Zionist organizations were not natives of this land.

Palestinians' claim to their land and property is religious as well as historic. Palestine contains many places holy to Muslims and Druzes, including the tombs of various holy and historic Muslim figures. Palestinians, who cannot move freely around historic Palestine, are denied access to many sites, including the tomb of Abu Huraira, while others are closed. Some, such as the tomb of the prophet Abraham (from whom Muslims, like Jews, claim descent), are shared and uneasily used by the two religious groups. No place is more sacred in Palestine to Muslims than Jerusalem. From there, Prophet Muhammad ascended to visit Heaven, and subsequent Muslim Umayyad rulers who conquered the city in the seventh century established the Dome of the Rock and al-Aqsa Mosques on that site. Palestinians were denied control of this area, known as Haram al-Sharif, until the signing of the 1993 Oslo Accords, and their legal control over the walkway leading to the Wailing Wall, which was a religious endowment, was wrested from them. To Palestinian Christians, the Via Dolorosa down which Jesus walked to his crucifixion at Golgotha, his birthplace in Bethlehem, the site of Mary's annunciation in Nazareth, and various locations near the Sea of Galilee are all sacred. In addition to homes, farms, and land, many other public areas of Palestine were legally owned by Palestinians (and in some cases other Arab Muslims) as *waqf*, or endowed property created for religious purposes. These endowments were never supposed to be claimed or appropriated by governments, yet they were seized and administered by Israeli officials and councils.

Israel, which accords full citizenship rights only to Jews, claimed rights to Palestine through conquest: first in 1948 and then through occupation of the West Bank and Gaza after 1967. A constant multidimensional policy of illegal land appropriations has negatively impacted Palestinians. The Palestinians who fled their properties in terror after the massacre at Deir Yassin in April 1948 or who were physically forced out of their neighborhoods and villages retained keys and deeds to their properties and lands, yet they were never allowed to return, despite legal judgments in their favor. Additional lands were systematically taken from the Palestinians by military force, military law, and other forms of appropriation. These actions followed decades of Zionist efforts during the British mandate period to acquire lands possessed by absentee landlords. Other methods included Israeli seizure of peasants' land held in a legal form of collective tenure and of lands irregularly registered or not occupied, continuously tilled, or belonging to the many large Bedouin tribes. While Palestinians were forced into a diaspora by the State of Israel and never permitted to return, under the 1951 Law of Return any Jew in the world, even some of dubious religious background, could claim Israeli citizenship and rights superior to those of Palestinians.

Meanwhile, Palestinian refugees remained in a nebulous legal status, unable to return to their lands and prevented from becoming citizens of Arab states (a policy intended to bolster their legal rights to their own land). This situation persisted even after Israel signed the Oslo Accords. Thus far, Israelis have not acknowledged the right of any Palestinian, even UN-registered refugees, to return to their lands, even in symbolic or token numbers. Nor have they considered providing reparations. In sum, the Palestinians' claim to their own land and to national sovereignty is based on history, religious claims, international law, and, notably, continuous tenure.

The disposition of the so-called Jewish question—the plight of Jews in Europe who were discriminated against and subjected to pogroms and genocide under Adolf Hitler—was "solved" by creating an enormous humanitarian problem. A Jewish diaspora should not have been replaced with a Palestinian one. The British recognized this dilemma, as did the United Nations (UN). The British supported the Zionists' quest for a homeland but stipulated that this should not be at the expense of the native inhabitants of Palestine. They noted the unequal resources of the Zionists compared to the increasingly poorly developed Palestinian areas and tried to limit Jewish immigration. The UN proposed a partition that neither side would agree to. Then during the 1948 war (known as "the Catastrophe" among Palestinians), Jewish military forces depopulated many areas of historic Palestine and subsequently focused on obtaining territories and property in other key areas. A series of UN resolutions declared the illegality of Israeli actions particularly during the 1967 Six-Day War, when Israel seized control of the West Bank from Jordan, Gaza from Egypt, and the Golan Heights from Syria. Palestinians' despair over the situation, coupled with the treatment they received from Israel, was the cause of terrorist activities in the late 1960s and 1970s, political organizing toward diplomatic efforts after 1974, popular uprisings in the First and Second (al-Aqsa) Intifadas, and suicide attacks and factional violence between Palestinian factions. Palestinians have been imprisoned in huge numbers for political activities, which has only embittered them or hardened their resolve to seek justice.

The crystallizing of modern-day Palestinian identity, recognizable in dialect, music, and historic and contemporary cultural output, owes much to the national crisis. Certain Israelis have refused to recognize any separate Palestinian identity because this would support the latter's national claim. Yet Palestinian identity has become ever more distinct as refugees struggle to survive and as Palestinians in Israel and the occupied territories are increasingly cut off from contact with the Arab world.

Sherifa Zuhur

Perspective Essay 2. The Jewish People's Historical Right to Palestine

The Jewish people became a nation some 3,000 years ago in the area on the eastern shores of the Mediterranean they called Eretz Israel (Land of Israel), also known as Palestine. It was in the Land of Israel that the Jews created and developed their unique identity. That identity was based on their adherence to monotheism and Judaism, which led spiritually to the composition of the Bible and politically to the creation of their own national institutions. These materialized around the two temples built in Jerusalem, the first by King Solomon and the second by those who returned from Babylon.

Jerusalem and the temples were the spiritual center of the ancient kingdoms of Judah and modern-day Israel. The first temple was destroyed by Nebuchadnezzar in 586 BCE, and many Jews were exiled to Babylon. Seventy years later, the Persian king Cyrus the Great permitted exiled Jews to restore the temple, and later a Jewish independent entity was re-created. Between the 66 BCE and 130 CE, generals of the Roman Empire were engaged in fighting against the Jews. In the year 70 BCE, the Romans destroyed the Jewish temple and forced tens of thousands of Jews to leave the country. The Bar Kokhba Revolt (132–135 CE) led to the final Roman offensive against the Jews. With the defeat of the rebels, the Romans reduced Jerusalem to shambles. Wishing to completely obliterate the Jewish entity, an atypical act on their part, the Romans renamed Jerusalem Aelia Capitolina and called the rest of the country Syria-Palestine after the Philistines, a tribe that lived to the south along the coast.

The attempts to erase the Jewish identity, however, failed. Judaism had a strong territorial dimension, but with the loss of their homeland the Jews transformed, now basing their identity on spirituality. They made religion alone the center of their lives, while Eretz Israel became a source of spiritual longing. For centuries, Jewish communities maintained their identity through adherence to their ancient texts and traditions, praying the same prayers in the same language and thereby preserving the memory of their homeland.

Resorting to spiritualism allowed the Jews to preserve their identity even without having their own homeland. For centuries, a certain political reality made such an existence in foreign territories possible. Even when they were subjected to persecution as the result of varying degrees of anti-Jewish sentiment (particularly prevalent in the Christian world), the nature of medieval and early modern political institutions enabled Jews to live among non-Jews. Two major developments, however, forced the Jews to reevaluate their position. The first was the emergence of the modern nation-state, and the second was the emergence of modern anti-Semitism.

In a process that had begun in the 16th century in Western Europe and had reached its peak in the 19th century, a new sociopolitical structure and ideology had emerged: the modern nation and nationalism. The emerging centralized and bureaucratic nation-state became a source of identity for the people living within its boundaries, giving rise to the concept of nationalism. Concurrently, a new form of hatred toward Jews emerged, one that was based on pseudoscience. Modern anti-Semitism presupposed that people could be divided along racial lines and that Jews were a distinct race rather than the bearers of a common religion.

These two developments had a major effect on Jewish history in several ways. It was no longer possible to keep the rigid and exclusive social structure that had characterized Jewish communities since the departure into exile. The modern bureaucratic nation-state undermined the authority of Jewish leaders (rabbis), as did the growing urbanization of the modern industrialized nation. It became harder and harder to maintain the tight structure of the Jewish community, but the alternative proved to be just as difficult. While some Jews resisted the trends of change and tried to adhere to their traditional ways of life, others tried to assimilate through the abandonment of the unique characteristics of Jewish communal life. This latter course of action gave rise to the expression "be a Jew in your home and a man in the street." Both choices proved problematic. Attempts to maintain the Jewish social structure in Central and Eastern Europe were stymied by the growing power of bureaucratic states. Anti-Semitism proved to be a major obstacle preventing assimilation, as evidenced by events such as the pogroms in czarist Russia during the second half of the 19th century and the Dreyfus Affair in France during the 1890s.

One reaction to this state of affairs was the emergence of Zionism. Because nationalism and the nation-state had become the proper—and only—way for people with a common history and heritage to live their lives in the 19th- and early 20th-century world, it was only natural for the Zionists to endorse this same path as a means to solve "the Jewish problem." Through the League of Nations, the international community endorsed the Zionist solution and acknowledged the Jewish right to self-determination.

The natural place for the Zionists to actualize their dream of self-determination was the Land of Israel, the place where Jews had first lived as an independent people. Following the dismemberment of the multinational Ottoman Empire after World War I and the British occupation of the region in 1917, the Zionist movement sought to materialize Jewish spiritualism. Palestine was defined as being *res nullius* (without a ruler), and the League of Nations provided the British Empire with a mandate over the area, commissioning it with the task of helping the Jews build their national home in Palestine.

The Jewish right to Palestine is thus based on Jewish history. The Jews became a nation in the Land of Israel, long before the modern term was known. Although forced into exile, the Jews had never spiritually abandoned their homeland. The history of the Jews and of the Land of Israel converged again with the rise of nationalism and the concept of self-determination. With the approval and support of the international community, Jews could once again live as an independent and free people in the place where they first formed their unique identity and established their political and religious institutions.

David Tal

Further Reading

Ahlstrom, Gosta W. *The History of Ancient Palestine.* Minneapolis: Augsburg, 1993.

Aruri, Naseer Hasan, ed. *Palestinian Refugees: The Right of Return.* London: Pluto, 2001.

Ateek, Naim, Hilary Rantisi, and Kent Wilkens. *Our Story: The Palestinians.* Jerusalem: Sabeel Ecumenical Liberation Theology Center, 2000.

Avi-Yonah, Michael. *The Jews of Palestine: A Political History of Palestine from the Bar Kokhba War to the Arab Conquest.* New York: Schocken Books, 1984.

Ayaad, Abdelaziz A. *Arab Nationalism and the Palestinians, 1850–1939.* Jerusalem: Passia, 1999.

Bickerton, Ian J. *A Concise History of the Arab-Israeli Conflict.* Upper Saddle River, NJ: Prentice Hall, 2005.

Bright, John. *A History of Israel.* 4th ed. Louisville, KY: Westminster John Knox, 2000.

Cohen, Aharon. *Israel and the Arab World.* New York: Funk and Wagnalls, 1970.

Dimont, Max. *Jews, God and History.* New York: Simon and Schuster, 1962.

Dowty, Alan. *Israel/Palestine.* Malden, MA: Polity, 2005.

Farsoum, Samih K., and Naseer H. Aruri. *Palestine and the Palestinians: A Social and Political History.* 2nd ed. Jackson, TN: Westview, 2006.

Ginat, Joseph, Edward J. Perkins, and Hassan bin Talal, eds. *Palestinian Refugees: Traditional Positions and New Solutions.* Norman: University of Oklahoma Press, 2002.

Harris, Ron. *The History of Law in a Multi-Cultural Society: Israel, 1917–1967.* Aldershot, UK: Ashgate, 2002.

Hertzberg, Arthur, ed. *The Zionist Idea: A Historical Analysis and Reader.* Philadelphia: Jewish Publication Society, 1997.

Kamrava, Mehran. *The Modern Middle East.* Berkeley: University of California Press, 2005.

Lenczowski, George. *The Middle East in World Affairs.* Ithaca, NY: Cornell University Press, 1952.

McCarthy, Justin A. *The Population of Palestine: Population History and Statistics of the Late Ottoman Period and the Mandate.* Institute for Palestine Studies Series. New York: Columbia University Press, 1990.

Pappe, Ilan. *A History of Modern Palestine: One Land, Two Peoples.* Cambridge: Cambridge University Press, 2003.

Pappe, Ilan. *The Israel/Palestine Question: Rewriting Histories.* Minneapolis: Augsburg, 1999.

Parkes, James. *A History of Palestine from 135 AD to Modern Times.* Elibron Classics Replica Edition. Brighton, MA: Adamant Media, 2005.

Russell, Michael. *Palestine or the Holy Land from the Earliest Period to the Present Time.* Kila, MT: Kessinger Publishing, 2004.

Sachar, Howard M. *A History of Israel: From the Rise of Zionism to Our Time.* New York: Knopf, 1976.

Sanders, Ronald. *The High Walls of Jerusalem: A History of the Balfour Declaration and the Birth of the British Mandate for Palestine.* New York: Holt, Rinehart and Winston, 1983.

Schneer, Jonathan. *The Balfour Declaration: The Origins of the Arab-Israeli Conflict.* New York: Random House, 2010.

Shepherd, Naomi. *Ploughing Sand: British Rule in Palestine, 1917–1948.* New Brunswick, NJ: Rutgers University Press, 1999.

Smith, Charles D. *Palestine and the Arab-Israeli Conflict: A History with Documents.* New York: Bedford/St. Martin's, 2000.

United Nations. *The Right of Return of the Palestinian People.* New York: United Nations, 1979.

49. How Should Responsibility Be Apportioned for the Start of the Korean War?

Only five short years after the close of World War II, the Korean War erupted when North Korean forces attacked South Korea on June 25, 1950. Not surprisingly, the conflict soon became almost inextricably entangled within the larger Cold War. Although the resulting Korean War did not, as feared, become a global conflict, it eventually expanded to include Chinese and American-led United Nations (UN) forces. It was a conflict of many firsts. The Korean War was the first major conflict of the nuclear age, the first hot war within the Cold War, and the first war fought under the auspices of the UN. It was also the Cold War's first proxy war, with North Korea being aided by China, which in turn was being aided by the Soviet Union. South Korea was directly aided by the United States and many of its allies within the United Nations

Command (UNC). Although the war remained a limited one, it nevertheless wrought much destruction. The UNC suffered 40,534 deaths; South Korea suffered more than 250,000 military deaths and perhaps an additional 900,000 civilian deaths. North Korean and Chinese death tolls are not at all precise, but perhaps as many as 2 million to 2.5 million North Koreans and Chinese died of all causes during the conflict (both military and civilian). While the North Korean invasion clearly marked the beginning of open hostilities on the Korean Peninsula, scholars continue to debate which nations bear responsibility for the conditions that precipitated the Korean War.

In the first perspective essay, Dr. George Kallander contends that no single country bears the full burden of having started the Korean War; it was a complex conflict brought about by a number of causes and players. He does, however, pay particular attention to the role of imperial Japan and the emerging Cold War tensions between the United States and the Soviet Union. By contrast, Dr. James I. Matray argues that the Korean War was caused by the United States and reflected the consequences of the historic pattern in U.S. policy of subordinating Korea's interests in pursuit of American objectives elsewhere in the world. He traces the long and often contentious relationship between the United States and Korea from the 1800s through the start of the Cold War. In her essay, Dr. Priscilla Roberts asserts that North Korea bears primary responsibility for beginning the Korean War but points out that the Soviet Union, China, and the United States each had a role to play in facilitating and broadening the conflict. She highlights the fact that North Korean leader Kim Il Sung saw a window of opportunity to reunite the peninsula in June 1950, a window that he believed would soon be closed.

Background Essay

Situated as it is between the major powers of China, Russia, and Japan, Korea seemed fated to have a stormy history. Indeed, it was long the nexus of big-power confrontation and war, first between China and Japan and then between Japan and Russia. After having defeated both China in 1894–1895 and Russia in 1904–1905, Japan annexed Korea in 1910. Korea has been a single entity during its modern history, however. The 38th parallel between the present Democratic People's Republic of Korea (DPRK, North Korea) and the Republic of Korea (ROK, South Korea) is simply an arbitrary political line dividing a country that forms a single geographic, ethnic, and economic unit.

At the Yalta Conference (February 4–11, 1945), U.S. president Franklin Roosevelt secured a pledge from Soviet premier Joseph Stalin that the Soviet Union would enter the war within three months after the defeat of Germany. U.S. military leaders were anxious to get such a timetable in order to reduce anticipated heavy American casualties in an anticipated invasion of the Japanese home islands. Negotiations led to concessions, however. Regarding Korea, Roosevelt secured an agreement from Stalin for a postwar international trusteeship for Korea under the United States, Great Britain, China, and the Soviet Union. Although there was consensus that Korea become "independent in due course," there was no agreement on specifics.

On August 10, 1945, with the Soviet Union having declared war on Japan and the Red Army having invaded Manchuria (only 60 miles from Korea, with the nearest U.S. troops then 600 miles distant in Okinawa), U.S. Army colonels Dean Rusk and Charles Bonesteel were told to define an American occupation zone in Korea. They chose the 38th parallel because it divided Korea approximately in half but left the capital of Seoul in the American zone. No Korean experts were consulted. Harry S. Truman, who had succeeded Roosevelt as president on the latter's death in April, approved this proposal on August 15, and it was cabled to the Soviets, who accepted it without discussion the next day. Tokyo had already agreed to the Allied surrender terms, and on September 8 U.S. occupation forces began arriving in Korea.

The occupiers, both north and south, found a land seething with pent-up political frustration and rampant nationalism, all fueled by returning exiles. Koreans of whatever political stripe had suffered nearly a half century of Japanese occupation and wanted immediate independence, not a trusteeship or occupation. Certainly they did not want a divided nation. But few outside of Korea thought of the occupation zones as anything other than temporary.

The Soviets and the Americans each installed Korean administrators in their two zones. These individuals were strongly conservative and hardly democratic in the American zone and staunchly procommunist in the Soviet zone. In December 1946 a legislative assembly opened in the American zone.

In September 1947, frustrated with the failure to settle the future of Korea by direct negotiation with Moscow, Washington referred the matter to the United Nations (UN). The UN General Assembly recognized Korea's right to independence, foreseeing a unified government and withdrawal of the occupation forces, and also established the United Nations Temporary Commission on Korea (UNTCOK). In January 1948 UNTCOK representatives arrived in Seoul to supervise elections for a national constituent assembly.

Refused admission to the Soviet zone, UNTCOK recommended elections in South Korea for a new national assembly. These were held, and the assembly convened in May 1948; its invitation that North Korea send representatives was ignored. In August 1948 the ROK was officially proclaimed in South Korea with a strong presidential regime headed by the staunchly conservative former exile Syngman Rhee. Many of the ROK's key figures, including military leaders, had served the Japanese. Washington sought stability, but its slavish support of Rhee brought the enmity of many Korean radicals. The U.S. military government was then terminated, and the new Korean government entered into an agreement with the United States for the training of its military. In September 1948 the DPRK was inaugurated in North Korea under the presidency of veteran communist Kim Il Sung. The DPRK also claimed authority over all of Korea.

In December 1948 the UN General Assembly recognized the ROK as being Korea's only lawfully elected government. That same month the Soviet Union announced that it had withdrawn all its forces from North Korea. The United States completed withdrawal of its occupation forces in June 1949.

In September 1949, UNTCOK reported its failure to mediate between the two Korean states and warned of impending civil war. Beginning in April 1948, there had been sporadic fighting. Indeed, the Korean War may actually have begun on April 3, 1948, in the Jeju Island (Cheju-do) Rebellion in which communist guerrillas mounted attacks against the South Korean government. Estimates of the dead in the rebellion during 1948–1950 range from 30,000 to as many as 100,000. There were also clashes along the 38th parallel involving battalion-size units on both sides that claimed hundreds of lives. Two of the largest were launched by the DPRK south of the 38th parallel in the Ongjin Peninsula in May and August 1949.

Both Rhee and Kim Il Sung were fervent nationalists determined to unify their country during their lifetimes. Indeed, Rhee's support for a possible military solution to the reunification question led President Truman in April 1948 to approve a policy statement that the United States should not become so irrevocably involved that an action taken by any faction in Korea or by any other power there could be considered a cause for war for the United States.

This U.S. government's attempt to adopt a hands-off policy no doubt encouraged Kim in his belief that the United States would not fight for Korea. On January 12, 1950, U.S. secretary of state Dean Acheson further distanced the United States when, in the course of a speech to the National Press Club, he specifically excluded both Korea and Taiwan from the Asian "defensive perimeter" of vital strategic interests that the United States would fight to defend. The U.S. Joint Chiefs of Staff reached the same conclusion. In two separate interviews in 1949, U.S. commander in the Far East General Douglas MacArthur outlined a defense perimeter for the United States that excluded Taiwan as well as Korea. Republicans in Congress then demanded U.S. defense for Formosa, but no such move was made regarding Korea.

The timing of June 1950 for the North Korean invasion was caused by the need to plant rice in March and then harvest it in September. At the time many observers believed that this was a diversionary effort by the communist bloc to divert U.S. attention away from Europe, where the Soviet Union had just suffered a rebuff in the Berlin Blockade (1948–1949). Others considered it to be "soft-spot" probing to test U.S. resolve or a demonstration to show the world that America was a paper tiger. Some even saw it to be part of an elaborate plot by Stalin to unseat Mao Zedong in China. Most Americans believed that Moscow had initiated events in Korea as part of some global chess move.

But the reasons behind the invasion were local, not global. Rhee's government had suffered a major reversal in what was a relatively free election. Kim Il Sung judged that Rhee might be about to fall from power, and given the announced American position and his own attitude, the moment seemed ripe. As early as September 1949 Kim had sought Soviet support for a military operation to seize the Onjin Peninsula and perhaps territory south of the 38th parallel all the way to Kaesong. The Soviets demurred, believing that this would result in a protracted civil war that would be disadvantageous to the DPRK and the Soviet Union.

Kim met secretly with Stalin in Moscow in April 1950 concerning an invasion and presented what turned out to be wildly exaggerated prospects of a quick North Korean military success. He promised Stalin a concurrent communist revolution in South Korea and insisted that Washington would not intervene. Stalin himself concluded that even if the United States did move to defend South Korea, it would come too late. Soviet military aid was substantial, and Soviet military personnel took on a key role in planning the invasion.

Stalin's approval had been contingent on the support of Chinese leader Mao Zedong, and indeed Stalin insisted that Kim meet with Mao and secure his support. As a result Kim's Korean People's Army (KPA) included at least 16,000 members of the People's Liberation Army, Korean volunteers who had fought against the Japanese in World War II and in the Chinese Civil War thereafter. They joined the KPA with their weapons and equipment and played a key role in the subsequent invasion. Certainly both Moscow and Beijing were actively involved in preparations for the invasion as early as the spring of 1949.

On June 25, 1950, the DPRK's armed forces mounted a massive conventional invasion of South Korea across the 38th parallel. The communist bloc claimed that the war had begun in a South Korean attack of North Korea and that North Korean, Soviet, and Chinese policy was merely reactive. This is false, as border clashes diminished in the period from October 1949 to the spring of 1950 on Soviet insistence of preventing hostilities developing before the DPRK was completely ready. In any case, the war was on.

Spencer C. Tucker

Perspective Essay 1. Imperialism, Nationalism, and the Cold War

During the Cold War, the communist and anticommunist nations held opposing views about the start of the Korean War. North Koreans have blamed the war on the United States. Known by North Koreans as the "Fatherland Liberation War," the conflict is viewed as a counteroffensive against an "unprovoked" invasion by South

United Nations Command forces, driven south by the massive Chinese intervention in the war, recross the 38th Parallel in December 1950. (Interim Archives/Getty Images)

Korea, the "puppets" of Washington. China supported this interpretation, as that nation rallied to fight the "War to Resist America and Support Korea." Soviet propaganda characterized the war as a U.S. plot by "the beasts of Wall Street." On the opposing side, South Koreans blamed North Korea, calling the war "June 25," the day North Korea launched an "unprovoked" invasion. The United States and the West referred to the war as the Korean War, a struggle against communism in which the United Nations intervened to oppose a Soviet-backed invasion of a "peaceful and democratic" South Korea. Today, research unambiguously points to a North Korean invasion as the trigger for the war. However, many countries, including Japan, the United States, and the Soviet Union, were responsible for creating conditions on the peninsula that led to the conflict.

Five years after its victory in the Russo-Japanese War (1904–1905), Japan annexed Korea in 1910, ending centuries of independent Korean rule. In 1919 Koreans launched a nationwide protest against Japan's harsh colonial occupation. While this failed to free the country, it spurred Korean nationalism and calls for independence.

In the 1920s, two groups of nationalists emerged that would impact the post-1945 period. The first, the cultural nationalists, believed that Korea should be free from Japan but that the nation was unprepared for independence. These nationalists, most of whom were older and well respected in business and the arts, believed that Koreans should prepare themselves by becoming more modern through education. The second group, the radical nationalists, opposed this approach. Younger and more left-leaning in their political views and including socialists and communists, they agreed that Korea should be free but also believed that independence should be immediate and, if necessary, secured through violence.

With the U.S. defeat of Japan in 1945, it appeared that Korea would soon be independent. Nationalist leaders began building a government in the capital city of Seoul. This government, "the Preparation of Korean Independence," was soon renamed the "Korea People's Republic." This was a national-level government involving groups from across the political spectrum. Local government also emerged as leaders in villages and towns began forming People's Committees. These provided security but also distributed land to farmers and conducted trials of Koreans who had collaborated with the Japanese.

The rivalry between the United States and the Soviet Union that became the Cold War soon touched Korea. Two U.S. Army officers in Washington, D.C., charged with the task arbitrarily divided Korea at the 38th parallel, with Soviet forces to take the Japanese surrender north of the line and with U.S. forces handling the surrender south of the line. The Soviets promptly agreed with the dividing line. No Koreans took part in the decision. The line gave more territory to the Soviet Union occupiers but left the capital in the U.S. zone.

In short order, both the United States and the Soviet Union had established control of their zones, appointed Korean advisers, and began to develop political systems that reflected their ideological point of view. No matter their political leaning, Koreans did not welcome the division of their country or being told how they should be governed.

The Soviets established a government in Pyongyang that reflected their social and political policies, installing in power there veteran communist guerrilla leader Kim Il Sung, who had fought with the Soviets against the Japanese in Manchuria. With Soviet assistance, Kim carried out a revolution in which pro-Japanese collaborators, landlords, and anyone else who opposed the communist regime were purged.

As part of the U.S. policy to protect Japan, a country that was deemed vital to U.S. national defense interests in 1945, Washington sought to turn South Korea into a staunchly anticommunist state. U.S. troops arrived in Korea in September 1945 and established a military government. One of the first orders was the disbanding of the Korea People's Republic, which was too leftist in appearance for the occupiers. Indeed, any opposition to U.S. efforts was seen as pro-Soviet and suppressed accordingly. The occupation government reconstituted the former colonial-era police force, including rehabilitated former pro-Japanese Korean collaborators. U.S. authorities selected the staunch anticommunist Syngman Rhee to lead the government. Rhee and his associates violently suppressed any resistance.

U.S.-Soviet intervention amplified Korean nationalism. The leadership of both regimes consisted of nationalists who strove to legitimize their governments by denouncing the "puppets" of the other side and espousing unification through military action. Rhee advocated striking north, but Washington opposed this. Kim had the same intentions regarding South Korea and approached both the Soviets and the Chinese for permission to launch an invasion.

With the formal establishment of both Korean states in 1948, the United States and the Soviet Union withdrew their forces, leaving behind two hypernationalist regimes, each denying the legitimacy of the opposing regime and determined to unify the peninsula under its system. The North Korean consolidation of power took place in a climate where the population welcomed the moves to uproot colonial legacies, punish landowners, and implement various socialist policies to correct the injustices of the colonial era. South Korea experienced resistance to the government policy of employing pro-Japanese sympathizers and the return of colonial-era landlords and the colonial police. Both Koreas faced off across the 38th parallel. Sometimes North Korea prodded South Korea, while at other times South Korea launched raids against North Korea. The leaders on both sides sought a war to unify the country under their brand of nationalism, but only North Korea was preparing for and capable of launching a full-scale invasion to overcome the Japanese colonial legacy and bring about a resolution to the U.S. and Soviet division of the country and its people.

George Kallander

Perspective Essay 2. A Conflict of U.S. Creation

Relations between Korea and the United States commenced in conflict. In August 1866, the U.S.-owned armed merchant steamer *General Sherman* proceeded up the Taedong River toward Pyongyang in an attempt to open trade. When it ran aground, Koreans quickly attacked and destroyed the immobile target, killing survivors who had reached shore. In May 1871, U.S. envoy Frederick F. Low with a flotilla of U.S. ships arrived off Korea's coast to negotiate a treaty for protection of shipwrecked seamen. After Koreans fired on a survey team, the U.S. ships initiated a massive naval bombardment of Korean shore fortifications and then, in an amphibious assault, captured several Korean forts, but the Koreans still refused to sign a treaty. Five years later, Japan imposed a treaty on Korea. To preserve dominance over its tributary state, China mediated a U.S. treaty with Korea in May 1882. "If other Powers deal unjustly or oppressively with either Government," Article 1 declared, "the other will exert their good offices . . . to bring about an amicable arrangement, thus showing their friendly feelings."

Soon it became clear that the U.S. government had made its pledge of support only to gain favor with Koreans to facilitate economic penetration of their nation. Americans in Seoul continued, however, to give the impression that the United States would act to protect Korea's independence. A self-serving and disingenuous inconsistency thus came to characterize U.S. policy toward Korea from an early date. After the Sino-Japanese War of 1894–1895 left Korea vulnerable, U.S. ambassador Horace N. Allen allowed King Kojong to believe that Washington would intervene to prevent either Japan or Russia from ending Korea's independence. But when Japan easily triumphed in the Russo-Japanese War of 1904–1905, U.S. president Theodore Roosevelt brokered the treaty that gave Tokyo control over the Korean Peninsula. Rather than coming to Korea's aid, in July 1905 he endorsed the Taft-Katsura Memorandum, in which the United States sanctioned Japanese control of Korea in return for a pledge from Tokyo not to contest U.S. control in the Philippines. In 1908, Roosevelt affirmed this betrayal when he approved the same terms in the more formal Root-Takahira Agreement.

After forcing King Kojong to abdicate, Japan formally annexed Korea in August 1910. Admittedly the United States could not have saved Korea, but because it had encouraged and then endorsed Japan's aggression, the United States was complicit in the tragedy. Thereafter, U.S. officials continued to give Koreans reasons to think that Washington intended to fulfill prior pledges of patronage and protection. In January 1918 during World War I, President Woodrow Wilson advocated postwar national self-determination for all people in his Fourteen Points, but he did nothing do compel Japan to end its rule over Korea at the Paris Peace Conference.

Nonetheless, Wilson's words inspired and motivated many Koreans to demand freedom. In 1919 thousands joined in the March First Movement, a nationwide demonstration protesting Japanese rule. Japanese troops violently suppressed the uprising, killing nearly 2,000 Koreans and jailing countless others. That spring Korean patriots met in Shanghai and formed the Korean Provisional Government, but the United States ignored its lobbying efforts thereafter for support and recognition.

For the next quarter century, the U.S. government was silent as Koreans endured ruthless political repression, economic exploitation, and cultural suppression. Korean nationalists fought Japanese colonialism as exiles in the United States, China, and Soviet Siberia but disagreed on strategy and purpose. Korea regained importance for the U.S. government on December 7, 1941, when the Japanese attack on Pearl Harbor gave the nation value in advancing American strategic interests in Asia. President Franklin D. Roosevelt soon adopted trusteeship as the best way to achieve eventual independence for Korea. At the Cairo Conference in 1943 he gained British and Chinese support for a declaration, stating that the Allies, "mindful of the enslavement of the people of Korea, are determined that in due course

Korea shall become free and independent." In February 1945 at the Yalta Conference, Soviet premier Joseph Stalin endorsed a four-power trusteeship plan that would provide protection for Korea while it developed the political experience necessary to maintain its own independence.

Roosevelt's death in April 1945 set in motion a series of events that would climax in the outbreak of the Korean War. Harry S. Truman was now president, and Soviet expansion into Eastern Europe alarmed U.S. leaders. Almost immediately, Truman began to search for an alternative to trusteeship in Korea. He adopted a strategy to use the atomic bomb to achieve Japan's swift surrender before the Soviets entered the Pacific war, thereby permitting the United States to occupy Korea alone. The failure of Truman's gamble would lead to a civil conflict rather than liberation. When Stalin declared war on Japan after the first atomic attack on August 6 and sent the Red Army into Korea, Washington secured Moscow's approval for a presumed temporary division of the peninsula into Soviet and American zones of military occupation at the 38th parallel. After Soviet and U.S. forces occupied Korea, the partition became permanent because the emerging Soviet-American Cold War in Europe meant that neither side would permit Korea's reunification under a government closely aligned with its adversary.

Washington referred the Korean dispute to the United Nations in September 1947, which led to elections in South Korea alone and creation of the Republic of Korea in August 1948. Moscow responded in kind, sponsoring establishment in September of the Democratic People's Republic of Korea. Soviet troops withdrew in December, and U.S. forces followed suit in June 1949. That summer, major border clashes occurred at the 38th parallel. Fearing that South Korea might initiate an offensive to achieve reunification, the United States rejected its requests for tanks, heavy artillery, and warplanes. Top American leaders issued statements suggesting that the United States would not protect South Korea. These events emboldened North Korean leader Kim Il Sung, who persuaded a reluctant Stalin and Chinese leader Mao Zedong to approve the invasion of South Korea on June 25, 1950. Ultimately, Korea's war was a conflict of U.S. creation reflecting the consequences of the historic pattern in U.S. policy of subordinating Korea's interests in pursuit of American objectives elsewhere in the world.

James I. Matray

Perspective Essay 3. Kim Il Sung and the Road to the Korean War

North Korea bears primary responsibility for the outbreak of the Korean War in June 1950. Kim Il Sung, premier (later president) of the Democratic People's

Republic of Korea (DPRK, North Korea), was determined to reunite his country, an ambition that impelled him to invade the southern Republic of Korea (ROK, South Korea). The Soviet Union, China, and the United States each, however, played a significant part in facilitating or broadening the war.

Korea had been annexed by Japan in 1910. As World War II ended in 1945, Soviet troops entering from Manchuria liberated northern Korea, while American forces arriving by sea took over the country's southern half. The boundary between occupation zones was set at the 38th parallel of longitude. Initially, Allied wartime agreements called for a united Korean state. Growing hostility in Europe between the Soviet Union and the Western Allies meant that prospects for Korean unification quickly vanished, however. The competing military occupation governments each backed ideologically sympathetic Korean political forces.

In 1948 the United Nations (UN) approved the establishment of the ROK in the South; held elections in which Syngman Rhee, an authoritarian but strongly anticommunist Korean aristocrat, won an overwhelming majority as president; and promptly recognized his government. Meanwhile, with strong Soviet encouragement, in September 1948 Kim Il Sung, leader of the communist Workers' Party in North Korea, declared the DPRK a Soviet ally. The UN declined to recognize the DPRK and declared the ROK the sole legitimately elected Korean government. In late 1948, the last Soviet forces left North Korea. Early in 1949 the United States withdrew its remaining troops from South Korea.

Both Korean governments shared at least one objective: the elimination of the rival regime and their country's eventual reunification under their own control. Documents from former Soviet, East European, and Chinese archives reveal that the initial impetus for war against South Korea came from Kim, who sought to overthrow the still relatively weak southern government before it could consolidate its position. From March 1949 onward, he requested permission from Soviet president Joseph Stalin to invade South Korea, for which Soviet economic and military aid was essential. Stalin, fearful that the United States might assist South Korea and thereby possibly embroil the Soviet Union in a major war, initially refused. Eventually a January 12, 1950, speech by U.S. secretary of state Dean Acheson, affirming that South Korea fell outside the "defensive perimeter" of vital strategic interests in Asia that the United States would defend militarily, led Kim and Stalin to believe that should North Korea invade South Korea, the United States would not intervene. The two communist leaders ignored Acheson's qualification that South Korea should instead seek protection from the UN.

The establishment in China in October 1949 of a communist government after a lengthy civil war between the Chinese Communist Party, led by Mao Zedong, and the American-backed Nationalist government may also have emboldened Stalin. Mao, now head of the new People's Republic of China, visited Moscow in January 1950 for talks with Stalin. When the two discussed the Korean situation, Mao told

Stalin that while U.S. behavior was not entirely predictable, he largely shared Kim's view that if North Korea moved fast and overran South Korea quickly, the United States was unlikely to intervene. In April 1950, Kim visited the Soviet Union. Stalin endorsed his plans, provided that Mao also approved. Stalin made it clear that although Kim would receive Soviet military aid, no Russian ground forces would be committed to Korea. Should the United States intervene and the war turn against North Korea, the Soviet Union would not openly enter the conflict, and Kim would have to rely on whatever assistance China might provide.

The Korean War began on June 25, 1950, when North Korean forces crossed the 38th parallel. Defying the communist leaders' predictions, as DPRK military forces advanced rapidly into South Korean territory, within a week the U.S. government decided to commit major ground forces to Korea. The Americans acted under the auspices of the UN, which quickly passed a resolution condemning the North Korean invasion and demanding that all DPRK forces withdraw back above the 38th parallel. Why, given American officials' earlier dismissal of South Korea's strategic significance, did Washington take such quick and decisive action? Broader Cold War preoccupations intersected with a changing and dynamic Asian situation to persuade U.S. president Harry S. Truman that the United States could not simply acquiesce in a North Korean takeover of South Korea. Ignoring evidence that the Korean conflict was primarily a civil war, American officials firmly believed that North Korean troops were acting primarily as surrogates for the Soviet Union, which was masterminding a long-term global crusade to extend international communism worldwide. Having recently successfully faced down the Soviet Union during the lengthy Berlin Blockade of 1948–1949, U.S. policy makers were determined to prevent any American client state from succumbing to communist takeover. They feared that unless they acted in Korea, other U.S. allies, particularly those West European nations that in 1949 had joined the North Atlantic Treaty Organization, would question the American government's resolve to fulfill its military commitments to themselves. American leaders therefore perceived the Korean conflict as a test of broader U.S. international credibility.

Within months, success in reversing the North Korean assault caused American leaders to expand their objectives from mere restoration of the status quo to launching a drive across the 38th parallel intended to conquer North Korea and unite all of Korea under a southern-dominated, presumably Western-oriented regime. The momentum of victory was difficult to resist, generating a sense of hubris that soon brought its own nemesis. When a shocked Kim begged Stalin in September 1950 for Soviet intervention, Stalin rejected his plea, recommending that Kim seek Chinese aid instead. On October 1, Stalin suggested to Mao that China's leaders should dispatch "volunteers" to Korea. Otherwise, Stalin intended to abandon North Korea, evacuating Kim and his supporters to Soviet territory.

In September and October 1950 American officials ignored successive Chinese warnings, conveyed through Indian diplomats, that should UN forces cross the

38th parallel, Chinese forces would enter the war. After some internal debate, the Chinese, facing the unpalatable prospect of a U.S.-backed Korean state adjoining China's own border in Manchuria, eventually decided to fight.

On October 19, 1950, massed units of the Northeast Border Defense Army began to cross China's Yalu River border into North Korea, where they quickly turned the tide of battle and drove UN forces back beyond the 38th parallel. After initial sweeping Chinese gains, UN forces recovered lost ground. From the late spring of 1951 the war settled into a stalemate, with each side holding approximately the territory under its control in early June 1950. Negotiations for an armistice opened in July 1951 and dragged on inconclusively for two years before a settlement was reached in July 1953.

Priscilla M. Roberts

Further Reading

Acheson, Dean. *Present at the Creation: My Years at the State Department.* New York: Norton, 1969.

Allen, Richard C. *Korea's Syngman Rhee. An Unauthorized Portrait.* Rutland, VT: Charles E. Tuttle, 1960.

Armstrong, Charles. *The North Korean Revolution 1945–1950.* Ithaca, NY: Cornell University Press, 2003.

Bai, Bong. *Kim Il Sung: A Political Biography.* 3 vols. New York: Guardian Books, 1970.

Barnes, Robert. *The US, the UN and the Korean War: Communism in the Far East and the American Struggle for Hegemony in America's Cold War.* New York: I. B. Tauris, 2014.

Beckmann, George, and Okubo Genji. "Revolutionary Socialism in Japan, 1898–1921." In *The Japanese Communist Party, 1922–1945,* 1–29. Stanford, CA: Stanford University Press, 1969.

Cho Soon-sung. *Korea in World Politics, 1940–1950: An Evaluation of American Responsibility.* Berkeley: University of California Press, 1967.

Cumings, Bruce. *The Korean War: A History.* New York: Modern Library, 2010.

Cumings, Bruce. *Korea's Place in the Sun: A Modern History.* New York: Norton, 1997.

Cumings, Bruce. *The Origins of the Korean War.* 2 vols. Princeton, NJ: Princeton University Press, 1981, 1990.

Gaddis, John Lewis. *We Now Know: Rethinking Cold War History.* New York: Oxford University Press, 1997.

Goncharov, Sergei N., John W. Lewis, and Xue Litai. *Uncertain Partners: Stalin, Mao, and the Korean War.* Stanford, CA: Stanford University Press, 1993.

Goodrich, Leland M. *Korea: A Study of U.S. Policy in the United Nations.* New York: Council on Foreign Relations, 1956.

Halliday, Jon, and Bruce Cumings. *Korea: The Unknown War.* New York: Pantheon, 1988.

Kim, Jinwung. *A History of Korea: From "Land of the Morning Calm" to States in Conflict.* Bloomington: Indiana University Press, 2012.

Lowe, Peter. *The Origins of the Korean War.* 2nd ed. New York: Longman, 1997.

Matray, James I. *The Reluctant Crusade: American Foreign Policy in Korea, 1941–1950.* Honolulu: University of Hawaii Press, 1985.

McCune, George M., and Arthur L. Grey Jr. *Korea Today.* Cambridge, MA: Harvard University Press, 1950.

Meade, E. Grant. *American Military Government in Korea.* New York: King's Crown, 1951.

Merrill, John. *Korea: The Peninsular Origins of the War.* Wilmington: University of Delaware Press, 1989.

Millett, Allan R. *The War for Korea, 1945–1950: A House Burning.* Lawrence: University of Kansas Press, 2005.

Robinson, Michael. *Cultural Nationalism in Colonial Korea, 1920–1925.* Seattle: University of Washington Press, 1988.

Shen Zhihua. *Mao, Stalin and the Korean War: Trilateral Communist Relations in the 1950s.* New York: Routledge, 2012.

Shin, Gi-Wook. *Ethnic Nationalism in Korea: Genealogy, Politics, and Legacy.* Stanford, CA: Stanford University Press, 2006.

Stueck, William W., Jr. *Rethinking the Korean War: A New Diplomatic and Strategic History.* Princeton, NJ: Princeton University Press, 2002.

Stueck, William W., Jr. *The Road to Confrontation: American Foreign Policy toward China and Korea, 1947–1950.* Chapel Hill: University of North Carolina Press, 1981.

Suh, Dae-Sook. *Documents of Korean Communism, 1918–1945.* Princeton, NJ: Princeton University Press, 1970.

Truman, Harry S. *Memoirs.* 2 vols. Garden City, NY: Doubleday, 1955.

Weathersby, Kathryn. "Korea, 1949–50: To Attack or Not to Attack; Stalin, Kim Il Sung, and the Prelude to War." *Cold War International History Project Bulletin* 5 (Spring 1995): 1–9.

50. Was President Truman Justified in Removing General Douglas MacArthur as Commander of United Nations Forces during the Korean War?

When North Korea attacked South Korea on June 25, 1950, President Harry S. Truman named General Douglas MacArthur commander of United Nations (UN) forces, which were tasked with reversing the North Korean invasion and occupation of South Korea. After the successful September 15 Inchon landing, the Truman administration changed its war aim, now hoping to defeat North Korea completely. However, as UN troops drove deep into North Korea, China entered the war in late November 1950. Supported by the Soviet Union, the Chinese wanted to preserve a communist North Korea and refused to accept UN troops along its southern flank. After the Chinese intervention Truman reversed his policy again, fearing that a wider conflict might escalate into a full-blown war with the Soviet Union. UN troops would now be limited to protecting the status quo in South Korea. General MacArthur, however, wanted no part of a limited war. This set him on a collision course with Truman, who harbored a visceral dislike of the self-important general. Truman relieved MacArthur of his commands in April 1951, triggering a political uproar among MacArthur's many fans and supporters.

Dr. Paul J. Springer, in the first perspective essay, asserts that while Truman's action was legally sanctioned by the U.S. Constitution, MacArthur's firing was inadvisable and was based more on domestic politics than it was on military imperatives. Springer argues that Truman's firing of the general was mishandled and proved needlessly humiliating to MacArthur. Furthermore, Springer points out, Truman's war policies were too vague, and firing MacArthur deprived the military of a great commander. In the second essay, Walter F. Bell argues that the firing was entirely justifiable because MacArthur had attempted to act unilaterally and outside the official chain of command. Furthermore, past precedents, such as President Abraham Lincoln's firing of General George B. McClellan in 1862, lent legitimacy to Truman's decision. Bell also points out that Truman's decision received the full backing of the Joint Chiefs of Staff. Dr. Paul G. Pierpaoli Jr. contends that Truman had little choice but to fire MacArthur if the president wished to uphold the constitutional mandate that makes the president commander in chief of the armed forces. MacArthur's decision to set his own strategic policies and to ignore warnings that he not expand the war made it appear as if U.S. leadership was divided against itself. Furthermore, MacArthur's actions ignored Truman's Europe-first strategy and threatened to place too much power in the hands of the military establishment. The Truman administration's only mistake in this case was its inability to clearly articulate war goals or its rationale for removing MacArthur from his command.

Background Essay

On April 11, 1951, during the Korean War (1950–1953), President Harry S. Truman relieved General of the Army Douglas MacArthur of commands of U.S. forces in the Far East and as commander of the United Nations Command (UNC) forces in Korea. Truman's action came at a pivotal moment in the Korean conflict. The People's Republic of China had openly entered the Korean War in late 1950 after UNC forces advanced beyond the 38th parallel, deep into North Korea. The Soviet Union was already providing substantial military aid to both North Korea and the Chinese, and there were fears in Washington that Moscow might directly enter the war.

General MacArthur saw the Korean War in the wider prism of the Cold War and was reluctant to exclude the possibility of the conflict expanding beyond the Korean Peninsula. Apprehensive about a deadlock along the 38th parallel, in February 1951 he urged the U.S. Joint Chiefs of Staff (JCS) to authorize air strikes on Najin (Rashin), a harbor close to Soviet territory, and electric installations on the Yalu River. The general opposed a strategy of limited, static warfare, lamenting to newspapermen on March 7, 1951, about the "savage slaughter" of Americans that was sure to result from attrition combat. Openly censuring those who supported a pause at the 38th parallel, MacArthur asked the JCS to authorize the use of atomic weapons with which to defend Japan and bomb the Chinese–North Korean border. Despite knowledge of Truman's readiness to negotiate at this juncture, he advised against military restraints, and on March 24 he made known his own scheme to

General Douglas MacArthur addresses a crowd of some 50,000 people at Soldier Field in Chicago in April 1951, after his relief from command by President Harry Truman. (National Archives)

end hostilities. This included an ultimatum to China that it immediately cease all military activity or risk a UNC attack against its forces and homeland.

MacArthur's challenge not only undercut Truman's planned peace bid but also defied the constitutional supremacy of civilian policy making and greatly alarmed U.S. allies. Following a conference with Secretary of State Dean G. Acheson, Deputy Secretary of Defense Robert A. Lovett, and Assistant Secretary of State Dean Rusk, Truman sent MacArthur a subtle rebuke, reminding him of a directive dated December 6, 1950, that obligated commanders to refrain from public statements respecting delicate military and diplomatic subjects.

In the meantime, an ongoing Chinese and Soviet military buildup in Asia concerned U.S. military leaders. Having already forwardly deployed U.S. atomic weapons toward Asia, Truman and his advisers fretted that MacArthur's rash conduct might spark a wider war and that U.S. allies would never authorize retaliation with nuclear weapons as long as MacArthur was UNC commander.

Matters came to a head on April 5 when U.S. representative Joseph W. Martin, Republican Party minority leader, made public a letter from MacArthur in which the general applauded Martin's criticism of strategic limitations. MacArthur also praised Martin's belief that the Far East was the major theater of the Cold War and that Chinese Nationalist forces on Taiwan should be unleashed against the Chinese mainland. MacArthur concluded that there should be "no substitute for victory." Truman, on the other hand, always believed that Europe was the most important Cold War theater. London's *Daily Telegraph* also reported an interview with MacArthur in which the general complained about restrictions on his military options, while *The Freeman*, a conservative American journal, printed a remark credited to MacArthur saying that "political judgments" prevented enlargement of the Republic of Korea Army (South Korean Army).

Given all this, on April 6 Truman met with his top military and civilian advisers to determine what action to take, but there was no decision at that time. Later, Secretary of Defense George C. Marshall, on Truman's insistence, examined recent communications between the JCS and MacArthur. When the same group met with the president the next day, it found him incensed regarding *The Freeman* article. The group then recommended the general's dismissal, a determination that Truman waited to disclose until April 9, once he learned that the entire JCS concurred from "a military point of view only."

Truman signed the recall orders on April 10. He hoped to have Secretary of the Army Frank Pace convey the dismissal to MacArthur in person, with the White House announcement coming thereafter. But the message failed to reach Pace, and when Truman learned that the *Chicago Tribune* planned to break the news, his press secretary reported the decision on April 11. MacArthur learned of his relief while at his residence, where he was entertaining guests at lunch.

Reaction by the U.S. public to the news was extraordinarily emotional. Public opinion strongly supported the general. Congress invited him to speak to a joint session on April 19. While the Hearst, McCormick, and Scripps-Howard newspapers portrayed the general as a victim and Truman as a scoundrel, such prominent papers as the *New York Times* and the *Washington Post* defended the president's decision. A Gallup poll found most respondents opposed to MacArthur's relief, yet the bulk of American reporters assigned to Washington, D.C., as well as East Asia and the United Nations sided with Truman. Republican conservatives condemned the president, and Republican senator William E. Jenner of Indiana called for his impeachment. In the end, however, after a series of raucous hearings, Congress determined that Truman was within his constitutional authority to fire MacArthur. Furthermore, MacArthur's strategic vision had been exposed by military professionals as foolhardy and dangerous.

Rodney J. Ross

Perspective Essay 1. The Removal Was Unjustified

On April 11, 1951, U.S. president Harry S. Truman exercised his authority as the commander in chief and removed General Douglas MacArthur from his commands, including that of the United Nations (UN) forces in Korea. Ostensibly, the removal was because MacArthur had publicly disagreed with the president's foreign policy regarding the ongoing Korean War, specifically on the question of whether the combat zone should be extended to include parts of China. The removal, while legal, was an inadvisable decision that significantly complicated an already tenuous military situation and emboldened enemy combat forces and diplomatic negotiators. It also disregarded MacArthur's unique skill set regarding conflict in the region. The removal was motivated more by domestic U.S. politics than any effort to improve the war situation. In addition to Truman's decision being unjustified by the military realities on the Korean Peninsula, the act itself was terribly mismanaged and unnecessarily humiliating to an American hero. It also introduced a chilling new level of political influence into U.S. civil-military relations. In hindsight, it signaled that the United States had abandoned pursuit of any war aims beyond a return to the status quo ante bellum. It also firmly cemented the U.S. obsession over Europe as the most important potential Cold War battleground, virtually guaranteeing further communist aggression in other parts of the world.

Truman was the first U.S. president in nearly a century to remove a theater commander in wartime. President Abraham Lincoln did so on several occasions during the American Civil War, but in each case he was able to point to major failures in the field as the primary reason for changing the Union Army general in chief. Had

Truman removed MacArthur five months earlier, when a surprise Chinese attack sent UN forces reeling south in disarray, he could have followed Lincoln's precedent. Instead, Truman realized that MacArthur, the architect of the Inchon landings, offered the best hope for stabilizing and even reversing the situation and left him in command.

When MacArthur was removed from command, he had amassed nearly two decades of direct experience conducting military operations in Asia. This personal knowledge could not be replicated by any successor, a fact that deeply undercut the prospects of victory in Korea. In general, most wartime presidents have chosen to defer to their field commanders on military matters while offering explicit guidance on the broad objectives of a war. Truman failed to establish a clear policy or guidance regarding the military situation. When MacArthur broached the topic of nuclear weapons, Truman asserted control over their utilization but then suggested that they might be released for MacArthur's use. While publicly Truman remained ambiguous on this matter, he also secretly authorized the transfer of nine atomic warheads from their storage depots in the continental United States to an advanced air base in Okinawa. MacArthur, knowing that the transfer had been made, reached the natural conclusion that he would soon have operational control over a limited number of atomic weapons. Contrary to popular opinion, the general had no desire or intent to use them against enemy population centers, although he was willing to threaten such use. Instead, he saw them as a last line of defense should the communist side seek to move large columns quickly down the peninsula. When Truman fired MacArthur, he not only threw away decades of experience but also squandered any possibility of coercing the enemy through fear of a nuclear attack, essentially conceding that the war would remain entirely conventional.

When Truman removed the most experienced U.S. military commander in the Pacific, he clearly demonstrated to the communist side that the United States, and by extension the UN, would not pursue an effort to win the war via the unification of Korea under a democratic government.

The removal of MacArthur was undertaken without consulting the other members of the United Nations Command. Replacing the commander who publicly suggested aerial attacks against Chinese cities did nothing to reduce the Chinese zeal for aggression in the Korean Peninsula. Instead, it emboldened the Chinese leadership with the knowledge that the United States feared an expansion of the war, despite its massive military advantages.

There is substantial evidence to demonstrate that domestic political factors played a significant role in Truman's decision. The Democratic Party had held the White House for nearly two decades, but early polling for the 1952 presidential election showed an increasing level of support for a Republican candidate. MacArthur was a darling of the conservative wing of the Republican Party and had flirted with declaring his candidacy in 1948. By 1951, Truman was considering his own legacy and the direction of U.S. politics after his administration and certainly considered MacArthur a likely potential successor. Truman's abrupt removal of MacArthur undercut any political ambitions the general might have entertained. Although Truman was eventually succeeded by a Republican candidate, it was the far more moderate General Dwight Eisenhower rather than MacArthur.

Truman allowed his own personal dislike of MacArthur to influence his judgment not only in the decision to remove the general but also in the manner of the removal. Unfortunately, this compounded the error at hand. To Truman, it became extremely important that MacArthur be publicly terminated from his position rather than being allowed to save face and resign from his command. Despite MacArthur's decades of dedicated service to the nation and his status as both a five-star general and a Medal of Honor winner, he was unceremoniously cast aside by a vengeful president. The administration did not even give MacArthur the courtesy of directly informing him of his removal. MacArthur learned of his removal from the media. This mechanism for informing the general poisoned civil-military relations and greatly increased the distrust and enmity between military officers and political leaders.

In hindsight, President Truman traded a stalemate in warfare for a fleeting domestic political gain. He allowed the Soviet Union to regain the initiative in the Cold War despite the massive U.S. advantage in nuclear stockpiles and delivery systems, in large part by demonstrating that the United States did not have the will to use all of the tools at its disposal. He ignored the importance of non-European conflict zones in the long-term Cold War struggle, in large part because MacArthur had argued the point. This virtually guaranteed that future overt communist aggression would follow in Asia, Africa, and elsewhere. By almost any objective measure, Truman was unjustified in removing General Douglas MacArthur even though he had the legal right to do so.

Paul J. Springer

Perspective Essay 2. An Entirely Correct Decision

On April 11, 1951, U.S. president Harry S. Truman relieved General of the Army Douglas MacArthur of his military commands. This essay argues that Truman was entirely justified in this action.

The Truman-MacArthur controversy occurred in an environment growing out of the Korean War and the complex history of civil-military relations in the United States. Although the U.S. Constitution does not clearly define the relationship between the civilian authorities and the uniformed military, it does establish the president as commander in chief of the armed forces and the maker of foreign policy. In addition, the uniformed military's separation from the political sphere is firmly established by precedent and practice in U.S. history.

This relationship has been tested by radical changes in the structure of the American military establishment and the country's international role. The founding fathers deeply distrusted standing armies as a possible threat to civilian government. Until the 20th century (except for the American Civil War) the U.S. leadership was content to rely on volunteer formations raised by the states and a small regular army, which served as a cadre for larger forces when needed and as a frontier police force.

Truman's confrontation with MacArthur was not the first quarrel between civilians and the uniformed military regarding the coordination of military operations with political goals. President Abraham Lincoln's action in relieving Major General George B. McClellan as commander of the Union Army during the Civil War and asserting his own control of the war set a precedent that firmly established civilian supremacy in conducting war and defining war aims—concepts that remained in place with the growth of the U.S. military establishment through both world wars and into the early Cold War years of the late 1940s.

Communist North Korea's invasion of South Korea and the U.S. intervention with the support of the United Nations (UN) in June 1950 came close upon a series of unsettling events of the late 1940s. These included the Soviet Union's testing of an atomic bomb and the victory of the Communists in China. American diplomatic and military strategy was still in some flux, with the onset of the Korean War only adding to this. The decision to appoint General MacArthur, who was already supreme commander of Allied powers in Japan and commander of U.S. armed forces in the Far East, as commander in chief of the United Nations Command (UNC) on July 10, 1950, seemed a logical step. MacArthur's role in the Pacific theater during World War II (and his flair for publicity) had made him a national icon. Truman appointed MacArthur to the new post with the unanimous recommendation of the Joint Chiefs of Staff (JCS).

The potential for conflict between MacArthur and his superiors predated June 1950. The general held decidedly rightist political views and had ties to the Republican Party. He had publicly criticized the Truman administration for allowing the "loss" of China to the Communists and giving priority to Europe in foreign policy, aligning himself with Truman's Republican "Asia first" opponents. In July 1950 MacArthur, without notifying Washington, flew to Taiwan in a show of support for the Chinese Nationalists. Furious, Truman sent representatives to Tokyo to ensure that it would not happen again.

The war's shift in favor of the UNC with the successful landing of American forces at Inchon in September (widely regarded as MacArthur's master stroke) and the accompanying Busan (Pusan) Perimeter breakout should have lessened tensions between Tokyo and Washington, but this was not the case. Truman reluctantly took the step to order the pursuit of the surviving North Korean forces across the 38th parallel. Worried over a military confrontation with the Chinese, he urged MacArthur to allow only South Korean troops to advance to the Yalu River. Truman also sought to ensure MacArthur's understanding of his policies by meeting the general at Wake Island in October 1950. Still, MacArthur acted unilaterally, sending U.S. forces deep into North Korea and dismissing any prohibitions on their advancing to the Yalu as "appeasement." MacArthur's actions at this point reflected strategic incompetence, an arrogant attitude toward his superiors, and a dangerous underestimation of Chinese forces facing his troops on the ground.

The Chinese military intervention in November 1950 and their initial spectacular success in driving UNC forces into headlong retreat brought tensions between Truman and MacArthur into the open. MacArthur's alarmist claims that U.S./UN forces might have to evacuate the peninsula unless Washington accepted his recommendations suggest that he was trying to pressure Washington into widening the war. Specifically, MacArthur urged a blockade of the Chinese mainland, removal of restrictions on aerial reconnaissance over Manchuria, and support for Nationalist military operations against mainland China. Even after the Chinese advance was halted and UNC forces resumed offensive operations, MacArthur sent an open letter to Republican Party and House of Representatives minority leader Joseph Martin criticizing what he saw as administration timidity.

The final break came in March 1951. At this point, Washington had decided to seek a cease-fire and negotiate a settlement of the war based on the status quo ante. The JCS notified MacArthur of the policy change. Nevertheless, on March 24 MacArthur, without consulting Washington, issued a public statement amounting to an ultimatum, warning the Chinese that the United States would escalate the war militarily unless China sued for peace. MacArthur thus openly defied his superiors and sabotaged Truman administration diplomacy.

MacArthur's actions touched off a round of intense discussions involving Truman, U.S. allies, and the U.S. State Department and the JCS. All concluded that MacArthur had to go. It was not an easy decision given MacArthur's status, but in the end Truman had no other choice.

MacArthur's relief touched off a political firestorm. Ultimately the Truman administration rode it out, with the JCS testifying that widening the conflict would be "the wrong war in the wrong place at the wrong time." Even so, Truman never recovered his popularity.

The political cost notwithstanding, Truman's relief of MacArthur was unquestionably the correct decision. MacArthur's behavior was arrogant and unprofessional and reflected contempt for his superiors. By attempting to impose his own policies in Korea, he challenged the constitutional authority of the president as commander in chief. The Truman-MacArthur controversy was the product of two differing concepts of war. MacArthur saw only complete victory. His vision of war was the product of another time. MacArthur did not understand that wars are fought for political aims and that only the president has the authority to set those aims. Some analysts argue that MacArthur should never have been appointed UNC commander and instead should have retired when he reached his 70th birthday in March 1950. The only problem with Truman's relief of MacArthur was that the decision was not taken sooner.

Walter F. Bell

Perspective Essay 3. The Sanctity of Civilian Control of the Military

On April 11, 1951, President Harry S. Truman relieved General Douglas MacArthur as head of the United Nations Command (UNC) then fighting in Korea. This action effectively ended the general's long military career. Truman was amply justified in his decision; in fact, based on MacArthur's repeated insubordination, Truman was constitutionally obliged to fire him. In sacking MacArthur, Truman also upheld a long-standing American tradition of an apolitical military establishment charged with executing strategic decisions rather than devising them. In this case, the general not only challenged the president's constitutional authority but also attempted to establish his own strategic imperatives—which were at odds with official government policy—and became unabashedly involved in the political arena. In the end, Truman had little choice.

Truman's action was not without precedent. Indeed, President Abraham Lincoln famously fired General George B. McClellan as general in chief in 1862 during the American Civil War. Other military commanders have been relieved since. President Barack Obama relieved General Stanley A. McChrystal of his command in 2010 after he criticized the president and his policies.

General MacArthur's insubordination began in earnest on August 20, 1950, when in the course of a speech to the Veterans of Foreign Wars he stridently urged that the United States establish a military alliance with the Chinese Nationalists on Taiwan (then known as Formosa). He also intimated that the Nationalists should be permitted to undertake military action against the People's Republic of China (PRC) to prevent the Chinese from aiding North Korea. The Truman administration had already made it quite clear that the United States would not seek a formal alliance with the Nationalists. Furthermore, U.S. officials hoped to prevent a wider war in Asia so they could focus their attention on bolstering anti-Soviet defenses in

Europe, which they believed was America's top military priority. In short, MacArthur saw Asia as the chief theater of Cold War action, while the Truman administration saw Europe as the chief theater. Truman promptly refuted MacArthur's comments, but the damage had already been done, and the contretemps seemed to indicate that U.S. leadership was divided against itself. Truman later wrote that this was when he first considered firing MacArthur.

MacArthur's missteps only grew in number after the successful UNC Inchon counteroffensive of September 1951. Clearly buoyed by his success, on October 1 MacArthur issued a surrender ultimatum to North Korea without clearing it with Washington. This too irked Truman, but the scent of potential victory led him to downplay MacArthur's unauthorized action. On October 15, Truman and MacArthur met on Wake Island. There MacArthur greatly discounted the likelihood of direct Chinese military intervention in Korea and assured the president that if such a scenario were to occur, it would be promptly defeated. The general seemingly ignored the massed Chinese troops along the Manchurian-Korean border, not to mention their ability to intervene en masse. Within days, Chinese Communist troops undertook probing actions against UNC forces in North Korea.

At the same time, MacArthur flagrantly ignored a United Nations (UN) mandate—backed by Truman—that had instructed the general to prohibit non-Korean troops from moving deep into North Korea. By late November the Chinese mounted a massive military intervention in Korea, threatening all UNC forces. In a December 1950 UNC military report, MacArthur blamed flawed "political intelligence" for the Chinese intervention and complained bitterly that UNC restrictions on air operations in southern Manchuria had prevented him from properly gauging Chinese troop movements, despite the fact that PRC officials had repeatedly warned of a military intervention. In a March 1951 UNC report, MacArthur publicly groused about bombing restrictions for southern Manchuria even though by then the Truman administration had decided to limit the war and seek a negotiated settlement with China.

On March 7, 1951, MacArthur issued his "Die for Tie" statement. MacArthur's comments were completely at odds with official U.S. and UN policies that sought to avoid a larger Asian conflagration. Coming on the heels of Operation KILLER (February 1–March 5, 1951), which had stabilized the battle lines and pushed most communist forces out of South Korea, MacArthur suggested that the only way forward was to pursue the communists north, toward the Yalu River, and to lift bombing restrictions against Chinese supply lines in southern Manchuria. MacArthur complained about "abnormal military inhibitions" and opined that the people of South Korea were being needlessly sacrificed to fight the enemy to a draw rather than achieving a clear-cut victory. By now, Truman was deeply angered and embarrassed by MacArthur's lone-wolf actions and incendiary rhetoric.

Frustrated by what he believed to be Washington's unwillingness to seek an unambiguous victory in Korea, on March 24 MacArthur issued his infamous pronunciamento, which was an unauthorized ultimatum to China. The general stipulated that the Chinese must cease military operations and engage in peace talks immediately or risk a massive UNC attack against their troops in Korea or even an attack against mainland China. This diktat was the proverbial straw that broke the camel's back. It served to torpedo Truman's plans to open truce talks with China and threatened to open a much wider conflict in Asia. Truman now began to seek advice on MacArthur's removal, which was backed by virtually all of his advisers, both military and civilian.

Just days later on April 5, 1951, Congressman Joseph Martin (R-MA) revealed to the national press a letter written to him by MacArthur two weeks earlier. In that missive, the general made clear his disdain for Truman's policies and further stated that he had no use for limited war in Korea. The letter not only saw the general becoming directly involved in the political arena but was also a direct violation of a December 1950 gag order issued by the U.S. Joint Chiefs of Staff (JCS) prohibiting such activity. Furthermore, MacArthur never asked that the letter's contents remain private. This final act of insubordination convinced Truman that he had to act quickly. On April 11, 1951, with the concurrence of his chief advisers, he relieved MacArthur of his command.

President Truman's decision to fire MacArthur was based on the general's repeated insubordination and his penchant for issuing sweeping statements that had not been authorized and in fact did not represent U.S. policies, his vocal opposition toward America's Europe-first strategy, his refusal to abide by certain JCS and UN directives, and his meddling in the political arena while still in uniform. Moreover, Truman administration officials were fearful that the rash MacArthur might become involved in a decision to use nuclear weapons in Korea and China. Indeed, a number of these weapons had already been forwardly deployed to Asia, mainly as a deterrent to a larger Asian war.

Although Truman was lambasted politically for his firing of MacArthur, mostly by conservatives and Republicans who viewed the general as a hero, the president was fully empowered to take such action. Article II of the U.S. Constitution clearly states that the president "shall be commander in chief of the Army and Navy . . . and of the Militia of the several states, when called into service . . . of the United States." As commander in chief, the president is empowered to exercise full and complete control of the military establishment, which includes the promotion and removal of officers in the armed forces.

Truman was thus upholding the supremacy of civilian control of the military, not to mention the constitutionally enumerated powers of the executive branch of government. Indeed, Truman knew that civilian control of the military was an unalterable tenet of American democracy and that the military establishment must implement—and not formulate—strategic military policies. This was particularly important at the start of the Cold War, when U.S. forces were deployed in numerous areas around the world and when a large permanent standing army was becoming the rule rather than the exception. Allowing MacArthur to set his own agenda without civilian input would have meant placing the United States on the slippery slope to military dictatorship.

In the end Truman's action was vindicated by Congress, which acknowledged that the president was within his constitutional authority to sack MacArthur. General Omar Bradley, chairman of the JCS, also believed Truman's decision to be the correct one. Bradley famously stated that MacArthur's determination to wage a wider war in Asia would have been the "wrong war, in the wrong place, at the wrong time, and with the wrong enemy." Bradley went on to stress that MacArthur's policies would have "wrecked our global strategy" in pursuit of success in a localized conflict. Clearly, by the spring of 1951 the Truman administration was focused on European reconstruction and defense, not the defeat of communism in East Asia. A number of historians have argued that Truman's only mistake in the relief of MacArthur was his failure to explain it adequately to the American people.

Paul G. Pierpaoli Jr.

Further Reading

Acheson, Dean. *The Korean War.* New York: Norton, 1971.

Acheson, Dean. *Present at the Creation.* New York: Norton, 1969.

Alexander, Bevin. *MacArthur's War: The Flawed Genius Who Challenged the American Political System.* New York: Berkley Caliber, 2013

Blair, Clay. *The Forgotten War: America in Korea, 1950–1953.* New York, Times Books, 1987.

Blair, Clay. *MacArthur.* New York: Times Books, 1977.

Bradley, Omar M., and Clay Blair. *A General's Life: An Autobiography.* New York: Norton, 1969.

Caridi, Ronald J. *The Korean War and American Politics: The Republican Party as a Case Study.* Philadelphia: University of Pennsylvania Press, 1968.

Cumings, Bruce. *The Korean War: A History.* New York: Modern Library, 2011.

Halberstam, David. *The Coldest Winter: America and the Korean War.* New York: Hyperion, 2007

James, D. Clayton. *The Years of MacArthur,* Vol. 3, *Triumph and Disaster, 1945–1964.* Boston: Houghton Mifflin, 1985.

Kaufman, Burton I. *The Korean War: Challenges in Crisis, Credibility, and Command.* 2nd ed. New York: McGraw-Hill, 1997.

Lewis, Adrian R. *The American Culture of War: The History of U.S. Military Force from World War II to Operation Iraqi Freedom.* New York: Routledge, 2007.

MacArthur, Douglas. *Reminiscences.* New York: McGraw-Hill, 1964.

Manchester, William. *American Caesar: Douglas MacArthur, 1880–1964.* New York: Little, Brown, 1978.

Martin, Joseph. *My First Fifty Years in Politics.* New York: McGraw-Hill, 1960.

Millett, Allan R. *The War for Korea, 1950–1951: They Came from the North.* Lawrence: University Press of Kansas, 2010.

Neustadt, Richard E. *Presidential Power and the Modern Presidents: The Politics of Leadership from Roosevelt to Reagan.* New York: Free Press, 1991.

Pearlman, Michael D. *Truman & MacArthur: Policy, Politics, and the Hunger for Honor and Renown.* Bloomington: Indiana University Press, 2008.

Pierpaoli, Paul G., Jr. *Truman and Korea: The Political Culture of the Early Cold War.* Columbia: University of Missouri Press, 1999.

Reeder, Red. *Omar Nelson Bradley: The Soldier's General.* Champaign, IL: Garrard, 1969.

Rovere, Richard H., and Arthur Schlesinger Jr. *The General and the President, and the Future of American Foreign Policy.* New York: Farrar, Straus and Young, 1951.

Schaller, Michael. *Douglas MacArthur: The Far Eastern General.* New York: Oxford, 1989.

Steuck, William W., Jr. *Rethinking the Korean War: A New Diplomatic and Strategic History.* Princeton, NJ: Princeton University Press, 2004.

Truman, Harry S. *Memoirs.* 2 vols. Garden City, NY: Doubleday, 1956.

Wainstock, Dennis D. *Truman, MacArthur, and the Korean War.* New York: Enigma Books, 2011.

Weintraub, Stanley. *MacArthur's War: Korea and the Undoing of an American Hero.* New York: Free Press, 2000.

Wilz, John E. "The MacArthur Hearings of 1951: The Secret Testimony." *Military Affairs* 39(4) (December 1975): 167–173.

51. Was the Eisenhower Administration Justified in Relying on Massive Retaliation as a Defensive Posture in the 1950s?

When President Dwight D. Eisenhower took office in 1953, he inherited a war in Korea, a defense budget approaching $60 billion per year, budget deficits, and price and wage controls. As a Republican, Eisenhower was a fiscal conservative who abhorred budget deficits and intrusive government regulation over the economy. Thus, he was committed *to ending the war in Korea, reducing defense spending, eliminating budget deficits, and liquidating economic controls. Price and wage controls were suspended in the spring of 1953, and the Korean War ended that July. Reining in defense spending proved to be more complex, however. Reflecting the president's fears of a military-industrial complex run amok, the Eisenhower administration devised the concept of massive retaliation, which diminished the need for huge and expensive standing armies. Instead, the United States would use its nuclear might as a deterrent to foreign aggressors, employing nuclear weapons in the event of any Soviet advance, be it nuclear or conventional. Nuclear weapons, so the theory went, were cheaper than maintaining large standing armies.*

In the first perspective essay, Raymond D. Limbach asserts that massive retaliation was completely justified, given the era in which it was invoked. Indeed, massive retaliation reflected the enormity of the Soviet threat and was in fact dictated by the Cold War. Furthermore, Eisenhower's nuclear diplomacy was successful in ending the Korean War, and massive retaliation was a cost-effective defense strategy. By 1954, Limbach points out, massive retaliation was de-emphasized as tactical nuclear weapons proliferated. The second essay, by Dr. Paul G. Pierpaoli Jr., argues that massive retaliation was justified for several reasons. First, it was virtually demanded by the fiscally conservative Republican majority in Congress, which sought to reduce defense spending and balance the federal budget. Second, massive retaliation was in keeping with Eisenhower's reinterpretation of the containment policy, which refocused America's defense efforts on areas only of vital interest. Third, it was demonstrably cheaper than maintaining large standing armies. And fourth, it reflected Eisenhower's fears of an American garrison state in which the military-industrial complex would wield too much power. In the third essay, Dr. Paul J. Springer asserts that reliance on massive retaliation was a mistake. It left the Eisenhower administration with too few options in the face of crisis. Because Eisenhower sought to eschew limited wars such as the one in Korea, massive retaliation meant that any conflict—large or small—might well escalate into a nuclear conflagration between the Soviet Union and the United States. Thus, America's military options were very circumscribed—either nuclear war or capitulation. Furthermore, Springer argues that massive retaliation flew in the face of modern concepts guiding ethical warfare and military engagement. Indeed, it violated the concept of proportionality as well as the concept of discrimination. Certainly, nuclear bombs are among the most indiscriminate weapons ever created.

Background Essay

Massive retaliation was a U.S. defense posture adopted by the Dwight D. Eisenhower administration in the early 1950s. It was actually part of the larger multidimensional

New Look defense policy. When Eisenhower took office in January 1953, the annual defense budget—driven by the Korean War and the Harry S. Truman administration's decision to engage in a massive rearmament program enumerated in the National Security Council (NSC) policy document NSC-68—was close to $60 billion. The new president did not believe that such expenditures were desirable or sustainable over the long haul and thus sought to reduce defense spending. Realizing that maintaining large standing armies with which to counter the communist threat was extremely expensive, U.S. policy makers eventually concluded that the size of the U.S. Army could be reduced by relying on nuclear weapons as the principal deterrent to a Soviet offensive, particularly in Western Europe.

Embraced by President Dwight D. Eisenhower's administration on October 30, 1953, through the policy document NSC-162/2, the New Look defense policy was designed to implement U.S. military policy in a more cost-effective way without losing any ground in the Cold War. During the 1952 presidential election, Eisenhower had criticized Truman's administration for both being soft on communism and risking the economic health of the nation due to high defense expenditures, costly economic controls, and budget deficits. Once in office, the Eisenhower administration sought a new policy that would fulfill its election pledges and address world events that unfolded during 1953.

Dwight D. Eisenhower, 1952. General Eisenhower was supreme commander of the Allied Expeditionary Forces in the European Theater of Operations during World War II. He was subsequently the first commander of North Atlantic Treaty Alliance (NATO) forces, then president of the United States during 1953–1961. (Library of Congress)

Working with his treasury secretary, George Humphrey, and his director of the Bureau of the Budget, Joseph Dodge, President Eisenhower promptly proposed a policy of fiscal conservatism that would help balance the budget and allow the nation to wage the Cold War without risking its economic well-being. This would at once allay Eisenhower's deep concern that the U.S. government was ceding too much power and influence to the military establishment and address the Republican Party's traditional insistence that the size of the federal government be reduced and that the annual budget be balanced. Eisenhower and his advisers also knew that eliminating economic controls that had been put in place under Truman could be successfully and quickly accomplished only by shrinking defense spending.

The need for a new defense posture was highlighted further when the policy-making apparatus of the Eisenhower administration ground to a halt as its leading protagonists were racked by indecision in the wake of Soviet leader Joseph Stalin's death in March 1953 and the East German uprising in June of the same year. Leading members of the NSC argued over how best to exploit these situations and whether the United States should seize the initiative and attempt to roll back communism.

In May 1953 Eisenhower launched Operation SOLARIUM, which established three task forces to study and debate the future of American military and defense policies. Task Force A was headed by George Kennan, the principal architect of the containment policy, and advocated a scenario loosely based on the containment policy already in place; Task Force B, led by Major General James McCormack, proposed a more muscular type of containment that would emphasize nuclear deterrence (massive retaliation); and Task Force C, headed by Admiral Richard L. Conolly, examined the potential of a policy that would liberate Eastern Europe by rolling back communism. By July 1953 all three task forces had reported their findings to the NSC, although they were unable to reach consensus on the preferred course of action. Ultimately, the approach chosen would borrow from all three recommendations.

Discounting the 1950 NSC-68 policy document's presumption that 1954 would be the "year of maximum danger," NSC-162/2 instead outlined a plan that would see the United States prepare for a long-haul struggle, perhaps lasting for many decades. The document, which laid out the primary features of the New Look, called for greater use of propaganda, covert operations, and psychological warfare; an increase in military and nonmilitary aid to European and Asian allies; the establishment of regional defense pacts; more reliance on indigenous military forces to secure the periphery; and a readiness to employ nuclear weapons as a first response to any Soviet aggressive action, be it conventional or nuclear. At the same time, the New Look would decrease reliance on conventional U.S. forces, which, it was hoped, would bring down defense expenditures. The document was initialed by Eisenhower on October 30, 1953.

The New Look was soon put into place, and defense spending fell by some 20 percent between 1953 and 1956 before rising slightly during the late 1950s. Meanwhile, the number of combat-ready personnel was reduced by about 30 percent between 1953 and 1958. And within months of taking office, the Eisenhower administration had virtually liquidated all price, wage, credit, and material controls that had been in place since early 1951. Nevertheless, Eisenhower continued to remain wary of the defense establishment, and in his 1961 farewell address, he pointedly warned of the dangers of the "military-industrial complex."

Bevan Sewell and Paul G. Pierpaoli Jr.

Perspective Essay 1. A Correct Defense Policy Decision

The Dwight Eisenhower administration was certainly justified in relying on its policy of massive retaliation. World War II brought in the Atomic Age when the United States dropped two nuclear bombs on Japan in August 1945. This ushered in an era of previously unimagined capabilities of mass destruction. At the same time, the end of the war saw the emergence of two superpowers, the United States and the Soviet Union, each with its own political ideologies. One embraced capitalist democracy, and the other embraced socialist authoritarianism. These and geopolitical differences led to the worldwide confrontation that became known as the Cold War.

As supreme commander of the Allied Expeditionary Force for the invasion of Northwestern Europe, General Dwight D. Eisenhower oversaw the successful effort by the Western Allies against Germany in World War II. In 1951 he was recalled to active service as the first commander of the North Atlantic Treaty Organization (NATO) forces. In this latter post, he witnessed the Soviet Union establish an "iron curtain" around its European sphere of influence. Indeed, by 1948 the Soviets seemed poised to unleash aggression in Western Europe, which led to greatly increased tensions between the two superpowers. Based on his previous military experience, Eisenhower was certainly able to accurately assess the nature of the threat posed by a nuclear-armed Soviet Union.

During the early post–World War II era, aircraft were the primary delivery system for nuclear weapons. With the heightened tensions that accompanied the Berlin Blockade (1948–1949), the United States methodically incorporated increasing numbers of more powerful atomic bombs into its defense plans. The Soviet Union could field a considerably superior number of ground force divisions against NATO forces in Western Europe, and so atomic weapons were considered necessary to serve as a counterbalance. The Soviet Union's detonation of its own atomic bomb in 1949, followed by the Korean War (1950–1953), led to the Harry S. Truman administration's National Security Council Report 68 (NSC-68) and the development of the hydrogen (thermonuclear) bomb in an effort to preserve the U.S. strategic advantage. The Korean War also saw political restraints set by the United Nations

(UN) that would override U.S. strategic military plans by restricting the use of nuclear strikes against Soviet or Chinese sanctuaries.

Eisenhower became president of the United States in January 1953. One of his first actions was to break the deadlocked armistice talks in Korea in part by the suggestion that his administration might resort to the use of nuclear weapons to end the war. This marked the successful use of nuclear diplomacy. Eisenhower also realized that America's nuclear superiority at this time was a credible deterrent to Soviet manpower, which the West could not match or afford. On January 12, 1954, Secretary of State John Foster Dulles spoke openly about deterring Soviet aggression by dependence on retaliation with nuclear weapons. This concept became known as "massive retaliation."

Eisenhower knew that the maintenance of a large standing army was cost prohibitive and that it could in any case not be maintained in perpetuity. Therefore, NSC-162/2, which was approved on October 30, 1953, called for the forward deployment of tactical nuclear weapons that, coupled with strategic nuclear forces, would permit a reduction in the size of the army. It would also change the rules of engagement for general war. These policies ushered in the New Look defense plan. But NSC-162/2 was more than just a military strategy; it also embraced political, psychological, economic, and diplomatic responses to the Soviet threat, particularly in the so-called Developing World countries. Forging these ties would not be easy. Political initiatives coupled with patient diplomacy and aid would be necessary to form a "sense of mutuality" critical to countering "communist appeals."

A balanced national budget could be had at the expense of defense programs. Eisenhower believed that military programs should be analyzed and restructured to fit the country's requirements. He advocated a reexamination of the whole philosophy of defense. If these issues were not addressed and changed, the costs would be unsupportable, leading to inflation and massive debt.

Although emphasizing massive retaliation, Eisenhower planned to keep the door open to negotiations as both sides reached parity in nuclear capabilities. He also planned to secure approval from U.S. allies for the deployment on their soil and the use if need be of nuclear weapons. This deployment of tactical nuclear arsenals to the NATO nations, including their locations, would not be made public without approval by the NSC.

Eisenhower wrote that within the first two years of his presidency, his nuclear policies had brought about the end to the conflict in Korea. Defenses within the United States and the NATO alliance had also been strengthened against possible communist aggression. Requests for new appropriations had been reduced by $13 billion, and tax reductions were made financially feasible by substantial reductions in expenditure enacted by Congress.

On December 8, 1953, Eisenhower delivered a speech to the UN in an effort to get the Soviet Union to work with the United States in joint efforts in the atomic field rather than simply nuclear weapons for purposes of mass destruction. Eisenhower believed that nuclear energy for peaceful purposes might help end the suspicion and fear of war. With the death of Soviet leader Joseph Stalin in March 1953, U.S., British, and French diplomats met with their Soviet counterparts in Geneva and spoke urgently of the need for creating a "just and durable peace."

Another major change in nuclear strategic policy occurred on February 14, 1955, when the Killian panel (Technological Capabilities Panel) reported on the vulnerability of the United States and the Strategic Air Command to a first strike by the Soviet Union. The report also revealed major weaknesses in U.S. continental defenses and ability to mount a retaliatory strike. In response, the U.S. Department of Defense accelerated the ballistic missile program.

Events in the Far East influenced U.S. and Soviet nuclear strategies. In the spring of 1954, the French were facing defeat in Indochina by the communist Viet Minh at Dien Bien Phu. There was strong sentiment among Eisenhower's advisers for the possible employment of nuclear weapons to assist the French, but Eisenhower was opposed to any U.S. intervention unless the British concurred, and they did not. French forces at Dien Bien Phu went down to defeat, and the danger of nuclear attack now seemingly assumed a diminished credibility. Mutual deterrence and the use of nuclear weapons only for the purpose of responding to a direct attack shaped strategy. A new New Look, NSC-5440, in December 1954 de-emphasized massive retaliation and instead recommended tactical nuclear response as deemed appropriate.

Also in September 1954, the People's Republic of China precipitated the Quemoy and Matsu Crisis. Eisenhower again employed nuclear brinkmanship, threatening to employ nuclear weapons to keep the Chinese at bay, which helped end the crisis in May 1955.

Brinkmanship took on a new dimension when the Soviets launched the world's first successful Earth-orbiting satellite, Sputnik I, on October 1, 1957. Many Americans now believed that the Soviets led in the development of ballistic missiles and that the United States was falling behind in the arms race. Eisenhower, however, knew that this was not the case, thanks to secret U.S. reconnaissance overflights of the Soviet Union, and was unconcerned. But fears of perceived Soviet technological superiority persisted.

In January 1959, Albert Wohlstetter of the Rand Corporation published an article that represented the views by many civilian academics in various scientific fields that caught public attention. Wohlstetter was concerned about Soviet first- and second-strike capability, or a "nuclear Pearl Harbor," and advanced the debate of preemption and vulnerability. His article had a profound effect on strategic analysis.

Employing long-range ballistic missiles as the primary vehicles with which to deliver nuclear warheads became the chief military goal during Eisenhower's second term. The emphasis on nuclear delivery was not the only agenda for the president, however. He realized that Developing World countries were also vulnerable to communist encroachments, so he advocated policies that would employ covert action, psychological warfare, and economic assistance to countries opposing communist infiltration, as specified previously in the New Look.

With Stalin's death in 1953, however, tensions between East and West began to slowly subside. Stalin's immediate successor, Georgi Malenkov, stated that disputes could be settled peacefully. His successor, Nikolai Bulganin, let it be known that he was ready for agreements with the United States and the West. This spirit of détente led to a summit conference between Eisenhower and Bulganin at Geneva in July 1955. There they agreed to never engage in an aggressive action against the other, and the Soviets subsequently reduced their armed forces by 640,000 men. But a year later, internal Soviet affairs saw the renewal of Soviet polarization and mounting tensions between East and West.

Nikita Khrushchev followed Bulganin as Soviet premier. Khrushchev talked incessantly about coexistence and settling outstanding issues. He traveled extensively around the world, even including the United States in 1959. In the spirit of détente, a major conference involving the United States, the Soviet Union, Britain, and France was to be held in the summer of 1960 in Paris, followed by a visit to the Soviet Union by Eisenhower. Much preparation and fanfare went into the summit and visit by the Soviets.

On May 1, 1960, however, a U.S. U-2 reconnaissance aircraft was shot down over the Soviet Union. Believing that the plane had been destroyed and the pilot killed, the Eisenhower administration asserted that it had been a weather aircraft that had gone astray. Khrushchev then revealed that the pilot, Francis Gary Powers, was very much alive and produced evidence of the nature of the flight. Khrushchev demanded an apology from Eisenhower, who refused. Khrushchev went to Paris, but the summit quickly broke up, which would probably have been the case even without the U-2 incident. In any case, talks regarding arms control were put aside, and tensions between the two superpowers sharply escalated. Eisenhower left office shortly afterward. Having eased the Cold War toward détente, the Paris Summit was a deep disappointment in his presidency.

Eisenhower clearly understood Soviet military strategy and effectively employed nuclear brinkmanship to help end the Korean War and then keep China at bay. Furthermore, he understood that the U.S. economy could not maintain large conventional military forces around the world and that nuclear deterrence was required. Eisenhower also believed that all avenues of negotiation had to be pursued. Some would say that after the death of Stalin there had been some missed opportunities for success in this area, but with the uncertainty of Soviet leadership, the threats of massive retaliation and tactical nuclear strikes helped to check Soviet aggression. It was not until Khrushchev's rise to power that détente again seemed possible. Eisenhower's actions and policies kept the United States out of war at a time when many Americans prospered as never before. In Eisenhower's own words,

"Though force can protect in emergency, only justice, fairness, consideration and cooperation can finally lead men to the dawn of eternal peace."

Raymond D. Limbach

Perspective Essay 2. The Reinterpretation of Containment

When Dwight D. Eisenhower became president in January 1953, he inherited the long-stalemated Korean War and defense budgets approaching $60 billion per year. Determined to downsize the U.S. Army, shrink defense spending, eliminate budget deficits, liquidate economic controls, end the Korean War, and reevaluate the prosecution of containment policy, the Eisenhower administration developed the so-called New Look defensive posture out of which the concept of massive retaliation emerged. Massive retaliation placed the primary burden of U.S. defenses on nuclear weapons, which were cheaper to deploy and maintain than large standing armies. President Eisenhower was certainly justified in ushering in the era of massive retaliation. Indeed, he and his secretary of state, John Foster Dulles, adapted U.S. military and foreign policies to address the particular political and economic exigencies of the 1950s. They also based U.S. defenses on a fundamental reinterpretation of containment doctrine. Furthermore, Eisenhower, a professional soldier, harbored a distinct aversion to war that made him highly reluctant to engage U.S. ground troops in another major conflict; he also feared ceding too much power and too many resources to the military establishment.

From a political standpoint, Eisenhower was duty-bound to address the Republican Party's insistence that economic controls be promptly ended (price, wage, credit, and strategic materials controls had been instituted during the Harry S. Truman administration as a result of the Korean War). With the Republicans controlling Congress from 1953 until 1955, the Eisenhower administration could not ignore its supporters on Capitol Hill. Furthermore, economic controls during a period of relative peace were antithetical to Republican ideology that extolled the virtues of limited government and free markets. Eisenhower lifted most economic controls by the spring of 1953. In order to do so successfully, however, the White House had to pare back the defense budget and slow the military procurement process.

This development certainly jibed with Eisenhower's fiscal conservatism and his determination to downsize the number of military personnel. Furthermore, many Republicans simply did not subscribe to the military Keynesianism embraced by many of Truman's advisers, who helped formulate National Security Council Report 68 (NSC-68) in 1950. That seminal document had underwritten the massive increase in military spending between 1950 and 1953, with the defense budget quadrupling during that short period. Military Keynesianism implied that an ever-expanding economy, fueled in part by defense spending, would be able to sustain high military expenditures practically in perpetuity. It also suggested that short-term budget deficits were permissible so long as long-term economic growth proceeded apace.

The Republicans, including Eisenhower, simply did not buy into this freewheeling economic philosophy. Instead, they believed—with substantial justification—that the economic pie was finite and that more guns meant less butter, and vice versa. Republican ideology embraced the concept that governing meant making choices—that spending more on defense would result in less spending in other vital areas. Absent that, budget deficits and the national debt would continue to rise, which the Republicans also viewed as anathema. The repudiation, at least in part, of military Keynesianism was viewed by most Republicans as a moral as well as economic imperative.

The New Look, which was substantially articulated by Dulles in early 1954, would not only address these pressing fiscal concerns but would also fundamentally reassess how the United States applied containment policy. First and foremost, the New Look would de-emphasize meeting the Soviet threat everywhere and anywhere. Instead, America's resources would be used chiefly to protect its absolutely vital interests, which included Western Europe, Japan, and the Middle East. Peripheral areas would be defended largely by indigenous military forces. Second, the New Look would come to rely more directly on regional alliances, such as the Southeast Asia Treaty Organization, to defend the periphery. Third, the new defense doctrine would emphasize the increased use of covert and counterinsurgency operations instead of the direct employment of U.S. ground troops. Finally, more propaganda programs, psychological operations, and even direct talks with the Soviets would round out the nonmilitary tools of containment.

The New Look allowed the Eisenhower administration to shrink the military (and defense expenditures) and to refocus containment only on areas of vital interest. It did so principally through the increased reliance on nuclear weapons as the principal antidote to Soviet power. Thus, a large (and expensive) U.S. ground force in Western Europe was supplanted in part by the threat to employ U.S. nuclear might in the event of any Soviet advance in the region—conventional or nuclear. This, of course, meant that much of the defense budget would be allocated to air assets, strategic nuclear weapons, and theater (tactical) nuclear weapons. Strategists at the time trumpeted this approach as "more bang for the buck."

In fact, the Truman administration had already made a decision to emphasize airpower and nuclear forces; thus, part of the New Look was in fact not so new. What Eisenhower and Dulles did was to rationalize and codify defense decisions that had already begun under their predecessors. Indeed, it was Truman who authorized the development of hydrogen (thermonuclear) weapons, nuclear artillery shells, and nuclear-tipped long-range ballistic missiles. He also gave the green light to the Boeing B-52 long-range bomber, which became fully operational after Eisenhower took office. Thus, viewed from afar, a number of Eisenhower's defense decisions reflected a natural progression of military strategies that had begun before he took office.

As a career military officer who had seen combat in two world wars, Eisenhower was particularly cognizant of the horrors and risks attendant with ground combat and total war. He ardently sought to avoid situations that might have resulted in a major ground war or might have placed U.S. soldiers in harm's way. To his way of thinking, the New Look and massive retaliation made both of these scenarios less likely.

At the same time, Eisenhower was acutely aware that perennially high military budgets could skew the U.S. economy, leading to a garrison state in which the federal government and defense contractors would wield too much power and influence. Massive retaliation was cheaper than maintaining large standing armies and thus might preclude such a development. Indeed, Eisenhower's famous January 1961 farewell address warned of the dangers of a "military-industrial complex" even though the complex was already in existence and robust when he gave the speech.

For those who argue that Eisenhower relied too heavily on nuclear weapons and the threat of massive retaliation, one must consider that his administration's policies were more cautious and nuanced than its rhetoric might have otherwise suggested. Indeed, on only three occasions did the Eisenhower administration warn that it might resort to nuclear warfare. Ironically, all related to crises in Asia. In the spring of 1953, the U.S. government intimated that it might employ nuclear weapons to force an end to the Korean War. That conflict ended in July 1953. A year later, the White House obliquely warned China that it might launch a nuclear attack on that country if the Chinese intervened directly during the Battle of Dien Bien Phu in Vietnam. In March 1955, the U.S. government again hinted that it might resort to nuclear warfare against communist China during the Quemoy and Matsu Crisis. After the latter episode Eisenhower never again rattled the nuclear sword, perhaps realizing that such threats might ultimately dilute their inherent deterrent value.

And for those who assert that Eisenhower permitted the Soviets to achieve strategic military advantage over the United States in the 1950s, in reality American defenses were more than adequate to quash a Soviet offensive. By 1955, the United States enjoyed a wide lead in the number of deployable hydrogen bombs and was spending as much as $10 billion per year on the development and deployment of all sorts of tactical nuclear weapons. Indeed, America enjoyed a strategic defense advantage for the entire decade, including in the development of long-range ballistic missiles. The so-called missile gap that John Kennedy alluded to in the 1960 presidential campaign was in fact a complete fallacy. Eisenhower's New Look never degraded or threatened America's strategic advantage.

The Eisenhower administration relied on massive retaliation for a variety of important reasons. Some were practical and political and were tied to Republican ideology concerning the role and scope of the federal government. Other reasons were viewed as moral imperatives—the Truman's administration's free-wheeling military spending was deemed unsustainable and a long-term threat to U.S. solvency and security. Still others were more personal, such as Eisenhower's aversion to war and his deep desire to prevent the outbreak of another major conflict and keeping the United States out of regional wars such as the one in Korea.

Paul G. Pierpaoli Jr.

Perspective Essay 3. Reliance on Massive Retaliation Was a Mistake

Every presidential administration in the United States defines its own defense policy, and as long it does not violate the Constitution, that policy can take almost unlimited forms. Although the United States is justifiably proud of being an open society, it is not required or even advisable for an administration to be completely transparent regarding its military preparedness and intentions. When President Harry S. Truman's administration enumerated nations within the U.S. sphere of influence and, by extension, under U.S. protection, South Korea was left off the list. North Korea and its Soviet patron interpreted this as an invitation to act with impunity on the Korean Peninsula, a factor in triggering the Korean War.

Truman's successor, Dwight D. Eisenhower, campaigned on a promise to end the Korean War and implied that his administration would not allow itself to become embroiled in limited conflicts. Upon election, Eisenhower announced a defense policy dubbed the "New Look" that relied heavily on airpower and nuclear weapons to contain communist expansion. In January 1954, Secretary of State John Foster Dulles proposed "massive retaliation" against any Soviet aggression, suggesting the possibility of immediate nuclear escalation in a crisis. Three years before Eisenhower entered office the Soviet Union detonated its first atomic weapon, ending the U.S. nuclear monopoly. Both the United States and the Soviet Union soon developed hydrogen bombs. These weapons had 1,000 times the force of their atomic predecessors, greatly increasing the destructive potential of each nation's arsenal. Both nations also tested their first intercontinental ballistic missiles in the decade, guaranteeing that either one could wreak devastation on the enemy's homeland in a matter of minutes.

One of the fundamental questions of massive retaliation is whether the United States would actually carry out a nuclear first strike. Perhaps Eisenhower's stance was a bluff, and if so it offered a means to deter enemy aggression without devoting a ruinous portion of the federal budget to the military. By only pursuing one form of military strategy, Eisenhower could focus on the development of nuclear weapons and their delivery mechanisms without enormous investments in land and sea forces. During his tenure Eisenhower managed to shrink the military budget and devoted the savings to other national priorities, including massive infrastructure improvements. There is the possibility, though, that the massive retaliation stance was precisely what it purported to be, a threat to immediately escalate any military conflict to nuclear war at its very outset.

The international laws of armed conflict are designed to set fundamental limits on the permissible acts of belligerents in warfare. Likewise, the established ethics of warfare provide boundaries for acceptable behavior in conflicts. Both have gradually developed over decades, and often their development has accelerated in the aftermath of major wars.

Essentially, the laws and ethics of war rely on a few key principles, namely proportionality, discrimination, and military necessity. The principle of proportionality seeks to prevent rapid escalations in the use of force. Discrimination requires a belligerent to differentiate between military and civilian targets as much as possible. Military necessity means that a belligerent should inflict the absolute minimum amount of destruction and suffering required to achieve a military objective.

Massive retaliation, by definition, deliberately abandoned any pretense of proportionality. By not defining what level of aggression might provoke a nuclear attack and suggesting that any level of violence could trigger a nuclear strike, the United States threatened to escalate to the maximum extent in a war. Such an attack would almost guarantee a Soviet retaliation in kind against American and European targets, meaning that any conflict would immediately become the deadliest war in history. Such an unconscionable disregard for the catastrophic consequences of any miscalculation should have immediately invalidated the doctrine of massive retaliation as anything but an idle threat.

Nuclear weapons are one of the most indiscriminate weapons ever constructed, rivaled only by biological weapons in their inability to distinguish between military and civilian targets. Any nuclear detonation has the potential to destroy a city, wiping out all of the inhabitants in an instant. Once again, using such a military strategy abandons any attempt to adhere to the legal and ethical constraints of warfare, particularly for the first nation to do so.

Only in the realm of military necessity might the massive retaliation doctrine offer some rational defense as a justifiable position. However, massive retaliation only became a military necessity if all other forms of resistance had no chance of achieving victory. By reducing the size, equipment, and training of conventional forces, the Eisenhower administration essentially deliberately left itself no other options in the event of a conflict—only nuclear weapons might stave off a Soviet attack into Western Europe. By forcing these conditions on the United States and its North Atlantic Treaty Organization allies, Eisenhower took an enormous gamble not just with the U.S. military position but also with the population as a whole. In effect, the massive retaliation policy shifted the risk of warfare from the U.S. uniformed military to the entire American population.

While the United States avoided any direct confrontations with the Soviet Union during the Eisenhower administration, the same can be said of all subsequent presidential administrations, none of which saw fit to rely on a one-size-fits-all policy of national defense. Threats of massive retaliation may very well have given pause to Soviet premier Joseph Stalin and his successors when presented by a retired general. On the other hand, it might also have encouraged the Soviets to devote more effort to subversion campaigns and support for insurgencies. If so, the policy ironically served as an incentive for a transformation of modern warfare away from open, conventional wars, at which the United States had proven extremely proficient, and into irregular warfare. This unconventional style of conflict, which has dominated American wars for the past six decades, has proven far more challenging to American political and military leaders while at the same time eliminating any real opportunity for the effective use of nuclear weapons. Due to changes in the norms of international behavior, American presidents cannot even credibly threaten the use of nuclear weapons in the 21st century, making a renewed policy of massive retaliation, thankfully, almost an impossibility.

Paul J. Springer

Further Reading

Ambrose, Stephen E. *Eisenhower,* Vol. 1, *Soldier, General of the Army, President Elect, 1890–1952.* New York: Simon and Schuster, 1983.

Ambrose, Stephen E. *Eisenhower,* Vol. 2, *The President.* New York: Simon and Schuster, 1984.

Bowing, Robert, and Richard Immerman. *Waging Peace: How Eisenhower Shapes an Enduring Cold War Strategy.* New York: Oxford University Press, 1998.

Brodie, Bernard. *Strategy in the Missile Age.* Princeton, NJ: Princeton University Press, 1959.

Dockrill, Saki. *Eisenhower's New Look National Security Policy, 1953–1961.* New York: St. Martin's, 1996.

Eisenhower, Dwight D. *The Eisenhower Diaries.* Edited by Robert H. Ferrell. New York: Norton, 1981.

Freedman, Lawrence. *The Evolution of Nuclear Strategy.* New York: St. Martin's, 1981.

Gaddis, John Lewis. *Strategies of Containment: A Critical Appraisal of American National Security Policy during the Cold War.* Revised ed. Oxford: Oxford University Press, 2005.

Gaddis, John Lewis, ed. *Cold War Statesmen Confront the Bomb: Nuclear Diplomacy since 1945.* New York: Oxford University Press, 1999.

Immerman, Richard H. *John Foster Dulles: Piety, Pragmatism, and Power in U.S. Foreign Policy.* New York: Rowman and Littlefield, 1998.

Kahn, Herman. *Thinking about the Unthinkable.* New York: Horizon, 1962.

Kaplan, Fred. *The Wizards of Armageddon.* Redwood City, CA: Stanford University Press, 1991.

Kinnard, Douglas. *President Eisenhower and Strategy Management: A Study in Defense Politics.* Lexington: University Press of Kentucky, 1978.

Larres, Klaus, and Kenneth Osgood, eds. *The Cold War after Stalin's Death: A Missed Opportunity for Peace?* Lanham, MD: Rowman and Littlefield, 2006.

Leighton, Richard M. *History of the Office of the Secretary of Defense,* Vol. 3, *Strategy, Money, and the New Look, 1953–1956.* Washington DC: Historical Office of the Secretary of Defense, 2001.

Levine, Alan J. *The Missile and the Space Race.* Westport, CT: Praeger, 1994.

Paret, Peter, ed. *Makers of Modern Strategy: From Machiavelli to the Nuclear Age.* Princeton, NJ: Princeton University Press, 1986.

Pierpaoli, Paul G., Jr. *Truman and Korea: The Political Culture of the Early Cold War.* Columbia: University of Missouri Press, 1999.

Powaski, Ronald E. *March to Armageddon: The United States and the Nuclear Arms Race, 1939 to the Present.* New York: Oxford University Press, 1987.

Riasanovsky, Nicholas V., and Mark D. Steinberg. *A History of Russia.* 8th ed. Oxford: Oxford University Press, 2011.

Richardson, Elmo. *The Presidency of Dwight D. Eisenhower.* Lawrence: Regents Press of Kansas, 1979.

Schilling, Warren R. "The H-Bomb Decision: How to Decide without Actually Choosing." *Political Science Quarterly* 76 (March 1961): 24–46.

Sherry, Michael S. *In the Shadow of War: The United States since the 1930s.* New Haven, CT: Yale University Press, 1995.

Sherry, Michael S. *The Rise of American Air Power: The Creation of Armageddon.* New Haven, CT: Yale University Press, 1987.

Smith, Jean Edward. *Eisenhower in War and Peace.* New York: Random House, 2012.

Statler, Kathryn C., and Andrew L. Johns, eds. *The Eisenhower Administration, the Third World, and the Globalization of the Cold War.* Lanham, MD: Rowman and Littlefield, 2006.

Watson, Robert J. *History of the Office of the Secretary of Defense,* Vol. 4, *Into the Missile Age, 1956–1960.* Washington, DC: Historical Office of the Secretary of Defense, 1997.

Weigley, Russell F. *The American Way of War: A History of United States Military Strategy and Policy.* Bloomington: Indiana University Press, 1978.

52. Has President Eisenhower's Warning about the Military-Industrial Complex Come True?

When presidents leave office, they tend to give vent to concerns that they found harder to express while still in office. George Washington provided a thoughtful and often prophetic farewell address written by Alexander Hamilton, thereby making it more partisan than he may have intended. Andrew Jackson announced on departing the presidency that he regretted only that he had not shot Henry Clay or hanged John Calhoun. By contrast, President Dwight D. Eisenhower's farewell address warning about the growth and potential pitfalls of the military-industrial complex seems timid in comparison, but his words have gained resonance with the passage of time and the wisdom of hindsight. When he spoke on January 17, 1961, the Cold War was three decades from its conclusion, and the United States was already involved in a series of intense competitions with the Soviet Union—for superiority in weapons and alliances, on the ground geopolitically and in outer space, and even in the Olympics. Since then, the Cold War ended and the United States went on to become the world's lone military superpower, but the military-industrial complex seems every bit as embedded in our economy and psyche as Eisenhower feared more than a half century ago. Indeed, while U.S. defense spending has generally trended downward—at least as a percentage of gross domestic product (GDP)—since the end of the Cold War, it still remains much higher than it did in the late 1940s, when defense spending had reached its nadir after World War II. From 1950 to 1953, chiefly as a result of the Korean War and the geopolitical tensions it engendered, U.S. defense spending nearly quadrupled, and it never again returned to pre–Korean War levels.

Dr. Chris Magoc, in the first perspective essay, asserts that the military-industrial complex is not only alive and well in the 21st century but that it has taken on "monstrous dimensions" that have gone largely unrecognized by the American citizenry. These dimensions include war profiteering, wasteful spending on unneeded or unwanted weapons systems, an increasingly militarized foreign policy, and the privatization of national security procedures. In the second essay, Dr. Jolyon Girard essentially agrees about the existence and scope of the military-industrial complex at the time Eisenhower spoke. He goes on to point out, however, that the exigencies of the Cold War made the military-industrial complex virtually unavoidable and that defense spending as a percentage of GDP actually fell for decades after peaking in the early 1950s. Girard concludes that the alternatives to the military-complex would have been far worse and that its existence actually had a long history, dating at least to the 1890s.

Background Essay

The military-industrial complex is an interlocking alliance among the U.S. military establishment, defense industries, and research-oriented universities that during the Cold War created a virtual and separate stand-alone economy dedicated to national security and defense imperatives. President Dwight D. Eisenhower, in his January 1961 farewell address, was perhaps the first public official to warn explicitly of the dangers of the burgeoning complex, thereby raising awareness of a process that had begun in earnest some two decades before. Eisenhower, like others who worried about this phenomenon, feared that the military-industrial complex had the potential to wield great power by absorbing vast amounts of the nation's resources, granting undue influence to nonelected government officials and corporate executives, and perhaps subverting the democratic process as a result. Eisenhower's warning was in fact somewhat ironic, however, considering that his administration had been instrumental in the growth of the complex.

The military-industrial complex arose in response to the needs of World War II but accelerated rapidly beginning in the early 1950s. This occurred in large part because of the 1950–1953 Korean War and the Harry S. Truman administration's decision to engage in a massive long-term rearmament program designed to bolster America's global containment policy. In America's fight against communism, resources had to be harnessed to develop new military and defense technologies. Much of the research for these endeavors was conducted at large research-intensive universities. Defense-oriented industries often provided much of the capital and additional resources to fund research and development. In turn, they were usually rewarded with sizable government contracts to produce military hardware and weapons systems, many of which had originated in university laboratories. In many cases, the U.S. Department of Defense initiated both university and industrial research and development. Thus, a tightly connected military-industrial-academic reciprocal relationship resulted.

Between 1950 and 1953 the U.S. defense budget increased almost fourfold, from $13.5 billion in 1950 to more than $52 billion in 1953. The vast majority of those funds did not go to the war in Korea but instead were earmarked for long-term rearmament programs designed to keep the United States one step ahead of its Soviet Cold War rival.

Even after Eisenhower tried to rein in defense spending in the mid-1950s, the defense budget fell by only 20 percent and remained nearly three times as high as the pre–Korean War level. The Korean rearmament program essentially gave teeth to the National Security Council's seminal NSC-68 report of early 1950 that envisioned a huge military buildup. Pivotal in fueling the military-industrial complex was the 1950 decision to create a permanent industrial base that would provide the

United States with excess industrial capacity that could swing into high gear at the first sign of war. Such a decision resulted in the government-sponsored construction of a military-oriented industrial sector that was of little use for civilian applications.

It is important to note that Eisenhower did not object to the military, big industry, or academia. In fact, he was a proponent of all. As a former five-star army general, he appointed mostly businessmen and industrialists to his cabinet. He was also supportive of the scientific community, establishing the new post of special assistant to the president for science and technology in 1957. It was also his administration that embarked on the rapid deployment of intercontinental ballistic missiles, the U-2 reconnaissance plane, and orbiting satellites, all of which utilized the military-industrial complex.

But if Eisenhower encouraged the development of these relationships, why did he alert the nation to the dangers inherent in a scientific-technological-industrial elite? The answer to that may be that Eisenhower's address was directed at what science adviser Herbert York called the "hard-sell technologists and their sycophants" who invented the illusory missile gap and tried to exploit the 1957 Sputnik I launch and the 1957 Gaither Report to instill fear that America was losing ground to the Soviets. Clearly, what Eisenhower was warning against was not so much his own science advisers or programs but rather the special interest groups that had sprung from the emphasis on military research and development in industry and universities.

The test flight of an LGM-118A Peacekeeper intercontinental ballistic missile from Vandenberg Air Force Base in California, November 13, 1985. (Department of Defense)

After Eisenhower left office, the military-industrial complex remained a potent force in America's political economy. It received a boost during the Vietnam War and then waned a bit during the mid to late 1970s but grew appreciably again during the defense buildup of the 1980s. After the Cold War ended in 1991 the complex retreated once more, only to advance again after the September 11, 2001, terror attacks and the resulting wars in Afghanistan and Iraq.

The military-industrial complex has provided many benefits to society. Superior weapons technology, satellites, nuclear reactors, silicon chips, chemotherapies, molecular genetics, and particle physics have all benefited from the military-industrial-academic alliance.

On the down side, however, the military-industrial complex has resulted in the creation of a separate economy whose products, such as nuclear weaponry, are not likely to be used commercially and add little or nothing to long-term economic productivity. It also had made some industries too reliant on defense contracts, the results of which were glaringly apparent in the early 1990s when the end of the Cold War brought about sharp cuts in defense spending, fueling unemployment and an industrial downturn. Finally, many of the jobs in the defense-oriented sector are ones requiring advanced education and training, meaning that America's working class has largely been left out of the military-industrial complex's largesse. All in all, the phenomenon first brought to light in the early 1960s has been a mixed blessing.

Valerie L. Adams

Perspective Essay 1. The Disastrous Rise of Misplaced Power

In more than two centuries of American presidential speech making, few words have rung truer than the farewell address of President Dwight David Eisenhower in January 1961:

> In the councils of government, we must guard against the acquisition of unwarranted influence, whether sought or unsought, by the military industrial complex. The potential for the disastrous rise of misplaced power exists and will persist. We must never let the weight of this combination endanger our liberties or democratic processes. We should take nothing for granted.

Eisenhower concluded that the national security developments of the early Cold War era—pressure for ever larger military budgets, increasing capture of the nation's scientific and intellectual resources by a hypersecretive national security state, and a citizenry perpetually girded for war—were inherently at odds with the intent of the country's founders and with republican liberty and were ultimately dangerous for the nation's well-being. If Eisenhower could return more than 50 years later, the 34th president would discover that the military-industrial complex he spoke of has assumed monstrous dimensions and become such a force that most citizens fail to recognize the transformational role it has had over the past two generations.

The former five-star general had himself presided over the enormous growth of the military-industrial complex during his eight years as president. Eisenhower nevertheless feared the growing influence of powerful interests in and out of government that were increasingly shaping America's national security policy and leading the United States toward a permanent war footing. The president saw his authority overwhelmed by forces controlling the military budgeting and weapons procurement process: defense contractors led by the aerospace industry; high-ranking generals, retired military men now employed in the defense industry; and congressmen representing districts that were home to major weapons makers.

The tension between the president and the military establishment peaked in the fall of 1957. First came the Soviet Union's dramatic launch of Sputnik, which put the Eisenhower administration on the defensive regarding its commitment to space and rocket technology. Shortly thereafter current and former defense officials issued the Gaither Report, declaring that the United States had fallen behind the Soviet Union in intercontinental missile and nuclear fallout shelter development. Eisenhower considered the report to be alarmist, selfishly motivated, and based on faulty or contrived evidence (on this point he was aided by secret U-2 plane surveillance data regarding the Soviet Union's true capabilities).

Eisenhower's insistence on restrained military spending was at odds with the military-industrial complex, which by the end of his presidency he had concluded had already become problematic. His address therefore is best understood as a warning to his countrymen of the dangers that lay ahead.

That warning has gone unheeded. War profiteering, a concern of Eisenhower's as early as the 1930s when he served in an administrative capacity in the War Department, has continued. During the Ronald Reagan era (1981–1989), the military budget nearly doubled. With exceedingly lax oversight, the soaring profits of top defense contractors were fueled by the kind of malfeasance that would have aggrieved Eisenhower. Every one of the nation's top 10 military contractors was either convicted of or pleaded guilty to multiple offenses, and the vast rearmament program of the 1980s coincided with forces that both enlarged profit margins and invited deeper levels of greed and corruption.

At the center of the military-industrial complex, the U.S. Congress had played the central role in authorizing spending for national defense—including, on occasion, weapons systems not even desired by the Pentagon. When the Cold War ended in 1991, fiscal conservatives called for cuts in the military budget, including the B-2 Stealth Bomber. Rendered unnecessary by the Soviet Union's demise and the development of other more effective aircraft, the B-2 appeared doomed. But with components of the B-2 built in 46 states across 88 percent of the nation's congressional districts, contributions from Northrup, the plane's producer, poured into the coffers of congressmen and senators. The B-2 survived.

Following the dissolution of the Soviet Union, U.S. military spending fell nearly in half by the mid-1990s. However, the military-industrial complex simply retooled and constructed a new brand of American militarism, which the news media and the corporate culture reinforced. Further bolstering the newly militarized cultural atmosphere of the mid-1990s, an increasingly conservative media echoed calls from politicians and think tanks for the United States to fear "rogue states" such as North Korea, Iraq, Iran, and Libya—the combined military spending of which totaled less than $9 billion annually at a time when the U.S. military budget topped $250 billion.

Increasing privatization of U.S. national security since the 1990s has brought new concerns, with official privatization of military and security services beginning in the Balkan wars of the 1990s. This was fueled by a broader push to downsize government and by the broadly shared belief (often proven fallacious) that government services are always performed more efficiently by the private sector. In 2007 the United States had 160,000 uniformed military personnel in Iraq, outnumbered by an estimated 200,000 private contractors doing work formerly carried out by U.S. soldiers—and getting paid more (some a lot more) than rank-and-file soldiers.

A shocking lack of accountability inherent in privatized military security services has continually undermined the U.S. effort to establish an image of a nation that believes in the rule of law. In Iraq, Afghanistan, and elsewhere, U.S. companies such as L-3 Services, CACI, and Blackwater Security have been directly implicated in human rights abuses, including torture and, in the case of Blackwater, the unprovoked killing of 17 unarmed Iraqi civilians in 2007.

In fixing his eye on the unprecedented nature and scope of America's permanent military establishment, Eisenhower opened the door to a range of more challenging and disturbing concerns. This more expansive critique of the military-industrial complex centers on the deployment of the entire national security state to protect U.S. multinational corporate interests abroad. This more profoundly disturbing interpretation of the complex was reinvigorated with the U.S.-led invasion of Iraq in 2003—an event that had been advocated since shortly after the end of the Persian Gulf War by neoconservatives personally linked to the complex's economic interests.

American militarism has penetrated the national psyche and fortified the power of the military-industrial complex. When President George W. Bush called on Americans to support the preemptive Iraq invasion in 2003, the complex's relationship to the news media and the corporate culture at large was well positioned to respond. Even without the horrific terror attacks of September 11, 2001, direct military interventions over the previous half century had Americans ready to follow the commander in chief into battle. This tacit consent was reinforced by privatized military forces, which enabled the country to avoid broader sacrifices on the part of most of its young men and women. Moreover, after 2001 when taxes were being cut and not raised (even as the national debt soared), few Americans were asking how these major military engagements were being funded.

The only questions being asked were rhetorical ("How could anyone hesitate to remove Saddam Hussein?") or technological ("Where would the U.S. strategy of 'shock and awe' first be implemented?"). The questions were left to military experts such as retired four-star general Barry McCaffrey, whose interests in defense companies, military security firms, and security-related global private equity firms run deep. McCaffrey epitomizes the larger problem of systemic media complicity in the insidious reach of the military-industrial complex into virtually every corner of American society.

Although President Eisenhower's views of the military-industrial complex were informed mostly by events of his lifetime and his presidency in particular, at some point he must have encountered these words of President James Madison written in 1795, decades before he became embroiled in the War of 1812:

> Of all the enemies of public liberty, war is perhaps the most to be dreaded, because it comprises and develops the germ of every other. War is the parent of armies. From these proceed debt and taxes. And armies, debts and taxes are the known instruments for bringing the many under the domination of the few. . . . The same malignant aspect in republicanism may be traced to the inequality of fortunes and the opportunities of fraud growing out of a state of war, and in the degeneracy of manners and of morals engendered by both. No nation could preserve its freedom in the midst of continual warfare.

Sadly, Madison's words have been as ignored as those of Eisenhower.

Chris J. Magoc

Perspective Essay 2. Serious Threat or Security Necessity?

President Dwight D. Eisenhower delivered his farewell address to a national television audience on January 17, 1961. In that talk, he devoted time and attention to his concerns regarding the development of an emerging "military-industrial complex" in the United States. Since the conclusion of World War II in 1945, in which he had served as commanding general in Europe, Eisenhower sensed that a growing relationship had developed between American industry and the U.S. military as a result of the evolving Cold War confrontation with the Soviet Union. That alliance concerned the president, and he advised the public and its political representatives to remain aware and thoughtful regarding its potential impact on American political, economic, and even "spiritual" life:

> The conjunction of an immense military establishment and a large arms industry is new in the American experience. The total influence—economic, political, even spiritual—is felt in every city, every State house, every office of the Federal government. We recognize the imperative need for this development. Yet we must not fail to comprehend its grave implications. Our toil, resources and livelihood are involved; so is the very structure of our society. . . . In the councils of government, we must guard against the acquisition of unwarranted influence, whether sought or unsought, by the military-industrial complex. The potential for the disastrous rise of misplaced power exists and will persist.

Since that speech, scholars, pundits, and politicians have debated the intent and significance of Eisenhower's warning. Critics of America's military-industrial complex argued that the president recognized the dangers of the alliance between business and the defense establishment. Excessive military budgets and constantly expanding weapons systems, they believed, sparked a global arms race that threatened world peace. Critics of U.S. arms growth and the collaboration between business and defense in that process portrayed Eisenhower as being apprehensive and opposed to the evolution of the military-industrial complex, and they cite his address as evidence of that conviction.

Yet, the president never elaborated on his remarks in the 1961 address, nor did his words in the address support the thesis of those who question U.S. defense policies or the growth of the military-industrial complex. In fact, Eisenhower suggested that the emerging relationship appeared necessary in the dangerous international environment of the Cold War. The president may not have liked the growing military-industrial relationship, but he noted clearly that it was essential and would remain so in the future.

Since Eisenhower's speech, an objective analysis of U.S. defense spending and its relationship to an overreaching military-industrial complex indicates that the nation did not fall victim to a perverse or dangerous alliance. At the same time, the realistic national security threat that the Soviet Union posed during the Cold War made extensive military preparedness necessary in order to protect the strategic interests of the United States.

When President Eisenhower gave his speech, the United States faced a Cold War with the Soviet Union that was nearly 15 years in the making. America had also concluded a bloody conflict on the Korean Peninsula against North Korean and Chinese communist forces, both of whom had Soviet support. Many American policy makers believed that the United States faced a global contest between international communism and the free world, and they saw the United States as the only nation capable of confronting the Soviet menace.

Since 1945, the Soviets had maintained an extensive military force that eventually included nuclear weapons in their growing arsenal. With the Soviets maintaining a massive edge in conventional forces, most stationed in Eastern Europe, and given their large manpower reserves, American leaders concluded that the only way to meet the Soviet threat was by building a superior nuclear weapons arsenal and developing advanced military technology.

Eisenhower's secretary of state, John Foster Dulles, and others concluded that the threat of massive nuclear retaliation against a conventional Soviet military attack would also force the Soviets to eschew a first-strike nuclear attack. Beginning in the late 1940s the United States had entered into a number of regional security agreements, including in Southeast Asia. The costs of those pacts created an unusual commitment of U.S. military forces during an era of relative peace, something the United States had not done prior to World War II. As a result, the growth in peacetime defense spending created a significant but not ominous expansion in defense budgets.

The 1960 federal budget allotted to defense amounted to $53.3 billion. The Pentagon budget made up 35 percent of the total budget and about 10 percent of gross national product (GNP). Since procurement and research and development amounted to approximately one-third of the defense budget, the military-industrial complex accounted for about $17.5 billion.

Between 1960 and 1975 as the United States continued to pursue a similar defense posture and engaged in a lengthy and costly war in Vietnam, the defense budget, as related to GNP, remained relatively static. In 1975, two years after the United States exited Vietnam, the defense budget amounted to $110.2 billion, encompassing 6.73 percent of GNP and 20 percent of the entire federal budget. While the total amount of defense spending has increased since 1975, both its portion of the overall national budget and its percentage of GNP have declined.

It would seem difficult to argue, given the numbers, that a vast military-industrial complex has exercised an undue fiscal impact on U.S. government spending. In fact, since President Eisenhower's address, while the dollar amounts for defense allocations have increased, the percentages of GNP and the federal budget representing defense spending have fallen significantly once inflation is factored into the equation. The so-called defense establishment certainly plays a role in the American economy but not to an extent that may have concerned President Eisenhower.

Did the United States become paranoid regarding the Soviet threat? Did that paranoia propel defense spending to an unwarranted degree? If one concludes that Soviet capabilities were unrealistic or exaggerated, then an argument could be made that any major expenditures to support a military-industrial complex were unnecessary. This was not, however, the case. From the establishment of Soviet control of Eastern Europe after World War II through the Berlin Blockade of 1948–1949 to the Cuban Missile Crisis of 1962, aggressive Soviet foreign policies and military actions indicated a clear challenge to U.S. interests. The most significant aspect of Soviet military policy concentrated on maintaining and enhancing a huge standing military force and nuclear weaponry.

In the preamble to the U.S. Constitution, its framers included "to provide for the common defense" as a basic responsibility of government. In the early years of the republic, repeated European conflicts and the politics of internal expansion had led American leaders to stay largely aloof from matters outside the continental United States. So long as the great powers in Europe contested with each other and so long as an ocean prevented their quick access to the United States, the nation could develop with limited commitments to military defense.

In 1890 Captain Alfred Thayer Mahan, the prominent naval historian and strategist, wrote *The Influence of Sea Power upon History, 1660–1783*. In that seminal work, he argued that the development of a large modern navy was essential to protecting a nation's commercial interests and projecting national power abroad. In subsequent work, Mahan warned that modern European naval vessels and weapons posed a serious threat to the United States. They could, with impunity, arrive off America's coasts or control commercial sea-lanes in any future conflict. Unless the United States committed itself to an extensive naval buildup with modern warships, he argued, it ran the risk of jeopardizing its industrial success and stature within the international community. Mahan's influence led to the development of a modern U.S. battle fleet, tested successfully in the 1898 Spanish-American War.

Following World War I, American public opinion, along with many political leaders in America, rejected the nation's responsibility to provide adequate defenses. In 1922 the United States signed the Washington Naval Treaty, greatly limiting is capital ships. Then in 1928, U.S. secretary of state Frank Kellogg and French minister Aristide Briand initiated the General Treaty for the Renunciation of War (Kellogg-Briand Pact) in an effort to promote peaceful diplomacy and prevent future wars. Noble in their intent, those measures failed to prevent the rise of authoritarian governments in Germany, Italy, and Japan, and all three states commenced a major arms buildup that ultimately brought about World War II.

As late as 1934, Senator Gerald P. Nye of North Dakota chaired a Senate committee that concluded that the "munitions industry" in the United States had led the nation into World War I in order to increase its profits. That indictment played a key role in the passage of the subsequent Neutrality Acts and encouraged a dangerous lack of defense preparedness prior to World War II. While the robust industrial capacity of the United States enabled the nation to begin a major arms buildup during that war, the late start cost time, money, and lives.

Modern military technology and weaponry developed during and after World War II legitimized Mahan's warnings, just as did the emerging threat of the Soviet

Union. For the United States to have pursued a Cold War defense policy that had not made use of the evolution of a military-industrial complex would have been dangerous and would have threatened the nation's global security interests. President Eisenhower's concerns may be worth examining, but his stress that some sort of military-industrial partnership was necessary seems to remain more pertinent and realistic.

Jolyon P. Girard

Further Reading

Alexander, David. *Military-Industrial Complex: The Pentagon Goes to War.* Los Angeles: Triumvirate Non-Fiction, 2010.

Ambrose, Stephen E. *Eisenhower: Soldier and President.* New York: Simon and Schuster, 1990.

Bacevich, Andrew J. "The Tyranny of Defense, Inc." *Atlantic Monthly* 307(1) (January–February 2011): 74–79.

Boggs, Carl, and Tom Pollard. *The Hollywood War Machine: U.S. Militarism and Popular Culture.* Boulder, CO: Paradigm Publishers, 2007.

Divine, Robert. *Eisenhower and the Cold War.* New York: Oxford University Press, 1981.

Ettinger, Aaron. "Neoliberalism and the Rise of the Private Military Industry." *International Journal* 66(3) (2011): 731–752.

Hartung, William. *Prophets of War: Lockheed-Martin and the Making of the Military Industrial Complex.* New York: Nation Books, 2012.

Hogan, Michael J. *A Cross of Iron: Harry S. Truman and the Origins of the National Security State, 1945–1954.* New York: Cambridge University Press, 1998.

Hossein-Zadeh, Ismael. *The Political Economy of U.S. Militarism.* New York: Palgrave Macmillan, 2006.

Janiewski, Dolores E. "Eisenhower's Paradoxical Relationship with the Military-Industrial Complex." *Presidential Studies Quarterly* 41(4) (2011): 667–692.

Ledbetter, James. *Unwarranted Influence: Dwight D. Eisenhower and the Military Industrial Complex.* New Haven, CT: Yale University Press, 2011.

Leslie, Stuart. *The Cold War and American Science: The Military-Industrial-Academic Complex at MIT and Stanford.* New York: Columbia University Press, 1993.

Lynn, William J. "The End of the Military-Industrial Complex: How the Pentagon Is Adapting to Globalization." *Foreign Affairs* 93(6) (November–December 2014): 104–110.

Maddow, Rachel. *Drift: The Unmooring of American Military Power.* New York: Crown Books, 2012.

Markusen, Ann, Peter Hall, Scott Campbell, and Sabina Dietrick. *The Rise of the Gunbelt: The Military Remapping of Industrial America.* New York: Oxford University Press 1991.

Markusen, Ann, and Joel Yudken. *Dismantling the Cold War Economy.* New York: Basic Books, 1992.

Martino-Taylor, Lisa. "The Military-Industrial-Academic Complex and a New Social Autism." *Journal of Political and Military Sociology* 36(1) (Summer 2008): 37–52.

Pavelec, Sterling Michael, ed. *The Military Industrial Complex and American Society*. Santa Barbara, CA: ABC-CLIO, 2010.

Pierpaoli, Paul G., Jr. "Corporatist and Voluntarist Approaches to Cold War Rearmament: The Private Side of Industrial and Economic Mobilization, 1950–53." *Essays in Economic and Business History* 15 (April 1997): 263–275.

Pierpaoli, Paul G., Jr. "Gerrymandering America's Industrial Base: Defense Contractors, the Pentagon, and Civic Boosters in the Korean War." In *The Korean War at Fifty: International Perspectives,* edited by Mark Wilkinson, 178–189. Lexington: Virginia Military Institute, 2004.

Pierpaoli, Paul G., Jr. *Truman and Korea: The Political Culture of the Early Cold War.* Columbia: University of Missouri Press, 1999.

Swanson, David, ed. *The Military Industrial Complex at 50.* Charlottesville: University of Virginia Press, 2011.

Thorpe, Rebecca U. *The American Warfare State: The Domestic Politics of Military Spending.* Chicago: University of Chicago Press, 2014.

53. Was Media Coverage of the Tet Offensive the Primary Reason It Was Viewed as a Major U.S. Defeat for the United States?

Media coverage of the Vietnam War remains a source of continuing controversy in the United States. Nowhere is that controversy more evident than in discussions of the media's coverage of the Tet Offensive, which began on January 31, 1968. Until that point, the U.S. media had mostly provided the American people with fleeting glimpses of the North Vietnamese forces in action, because the People's Army of Vietnam (North Vietnamese Army) and the Viet Cong had remained mostly in the dense jungles or rice paddies of South Vietnam. During the Tet Offensive, however, much of the fighting took place in urban areas, providing ample opportunity for the media to capture graphic footage of the fighting. In particular, the attack on the U.S. embassy in Saigon received an inordinate amount of attention from the media because the Western press was stationed nearby. Back in the United States, millions of Americans watched scenes and viewed photographs of the embassy attack and the bloody Battle of Hue, witnessing the tenacity of the enemy perhaps for the first time. The Tet Offensive—or at least how it was portrayed in the media—seemed to have flown in the face of U.S. policy makers' repeated assurances that the war in Vietnam was going well and that a reduction in U.S. participation might be in the offing. Doubts about U.S. progress toward winding down the war were heightened after the Tet Offensive and ultimately compelled President Lyndon B. Johnson not to seek reelection in 1968.

Dr. Jerry Morelock, the author of the first essay, asserts that the media missed the big picture of the Tet Offensive, instead focusing on individual combat actions. He points out that the attack on the U.S. embassy in Saigon was a minor failed action that received a disproportionate amount of attention from journalists stationed nearby. In addition, he states that the nearly monthlong Battle of Hue provided the media with numerous opportunities to take gruesome photographs of dead soldiers and civilians, obscuring the fact that U.S. forces achieved a major military victory at Hue. Dr. Clarence R. Wyatt, the author of the second essay, argues that the Tet Offensive was not the major turning point in the public's opinion toward the war. He asserts that support for the war had been steadily eroding since 1965 and that by October 1967, three months before Tet, polls indicated that the majority of Americans believed that U.S. involvement in Vietnam was a mistake.

Background Essay

By 1967, the war in Vietnam had become a bloody stalemate. In June of that year a U.S. public opinion poll revealed that for the first time, more Americans opposed the war than supported it. At the same time, President Lyndon Johnson's popularity had dropped to below 40 percent. Faced with this situation, the beleaguered president initiated a "success campaign" to convince the American people that U.S. forces were making headway in the war. As part of that effort, Johnson brought General William Westmoreland, commander of all U.S. forces in Vietnam, home in late 1967 to make the administration's case before Congress and the American people. Stepping off the plane in Washington, D.C., an optimistic Westmoreland told reporters "I have never been more encouraged in the four years that I have been in Vietnam. We are making real progress." Later in a speech before the National Press Club, Westmoreland announced that "we have reached a point where the end begins to come into view." For the time being, Westmoreland's pronouncement helped calm a restive American public.

However, as Westmoreland made his assurances in the United States, the communist side was finalizing preparations for a massive offensive that would prove to be the turning point in the long war. By mid 1967, the leadership in Hanoi had decided that something had to be done to regain the initiative in South Vietnam. After a contentious debate among the military and political leadership about how to proceed, the decision was made to launch a general offensive to break the stalemate. The new campaign was designed to shatter the South Vietnamese armed forces, provoke a general uprising among the people in South Vietnam, and convince the United States that the war was unwinnable.

The offensive would be launched in early 1968 during Tet, Vietnam's most important holiday, which marks the start of the lunar new year and when most of the South Vietnamese soldiers would be visiting family members away from their units. General Vo Nguyen Giap, commander of the People's Army of North Vietnam (PAVN, North Vietnamese Army), although not originally a supporter of the decision to launch the offensive, was given responsibility for planning the campaign. The plan he devised called for simultaneous attacks on American bases and South Vietnamese cities and towns. Priority targets would be previously untouched urban centers, such as Saigon, Da Nang, and Hue.

During the fall of 1967 as part of Giap's deception plan, his forces attacked allied positions in the remote regions along South Vietnam's borders with Cambodia and Laos to draw U.S. forces away from the urban areas that would be struck during the offensive. Concurrent with this phase, a massive propaganda campaign was launched in South Vietnam to set the conditions for a popular uprising by the South Vietnamese population once the offensive was launched. The next phase of Giap's deception began on January 21, 1968, when 20,000 North Vietnamese troops surrounded and attacked the U.S. Marine Corps base at Khe Sanh. With this move, Giap hoped to further divert American attention away from the urban areas as his forces moved to their attack positions. General Westmoreland, convinced that Khe Sanh would be the target of the enemy offensive, quickly reinforced the marines there and mounted a major aerial campaign against the attackers.

With Westmoreland and the White House focused on Khe Sanh, communist forces made last-minute preparations for the main offensive, which was set to commence early on January 31. However, despite Hanoi's careful preparations, there was confusion over the timing of the attack, and the offensive was launched prematurely on January 30 in Viet Cong (VC) Region 5, with attacks against Da Nang, Pleiku, Nha Trang, and nine other cities in central South Vietnam. These attacks provided advance warning for American and South Vietnamese defenders, who went on alert and moved to blocking positions in key areas.

In the early morning hours of January 31, the remaining VC and North Vietnamese forces launched a massive countrywide attack on the cities and towns of South Vietnam. During the initial 48 hours of the offensive, more than 80,000 communists troops mounted near-simultaneous assaults on 36 of 44 provincial capitals, 5 of 6 major cities, 64 district capitals, and more than 50 hamlets. Even with the warning provided by the premature attacks, the allies were not prepared for the scope and ferocity of the offensive.

Saigon, which had not seen much combat before 1968, was attacked from several different directions, with 11 battalions comprising more than 4,000 troops focusing on key targets in the city's urban center while additional forces targeted the surrounding allied units and installations. The heaviest fighting in Saigon was in the Cholon district, but the most spectacular attack in the city was launched against the U.S. embassy, located only a few blocks from the Presidential Palace. A VC squad of 19 sappers blew a hole in the embassy wall and poured into the embassy grounds. During the six-hour battle that ensued, the VC were all killed or captured, and embassy security was reestablished. Although the attack on the embassy had failed, this small VC squad had demonstrated in dramatic fashion that no place in Vietnam was secure from attack.

Some of the fiercest fighting of the offensive took place in the battle to recapture the old imperial city of Hue. On January 31 a force of 7,500 VC and North Vietnamese soldiers seized the city, which contained the Citadel, an ancient fortress. U.S. marines and South Vietnamese forces counterattacked to retake the city. The bloody house-to-house fighting lasted for 25 days, resulting in heavy casualties for both sides and leaving most of Hue in ruins.

Even though the Tet Offensive took the Americans and South Vietnamese by surprise, U.S. and Army of the Republic of Vietnam troops recovered quickly. With the exception of Hue, Cho Lon, and a few other places, the communist forces were driven back in just a few days of intense fighting, and even where the fighting lasted longer, the allies prevailed in the end. At Khe Sanh, the marines held against the North Vietnamese and VC onslaught, inflicting heavy casualties on the attackers.

By the end of March, the initial phase of the offensive was over. There had been no spontaneous revolt by the South Vietnamese. The communists had failed to capture or hold on to any of the major objectives they had attacked. During the heavy fighting, the North Vietnamese Army and VC had suffered more than 40,000 killed and 5,800 captured. By any measurement, the VC and North Vietnamese Army had sustained a major defeat, one from which the VC would never fully recover.

Despite the clear outcome of the offensive on the battlefield, the media coverage of the intense fighting and destruction had a tremendous impact in the United States on the president, Congress, and the American people, ultimately prompting a reevaluation of the nation's commitment in Vietnam. The American people were stunned that the communists could launch such a widespread offensive, when only a few months before the White House and Westmoreland had assured them that U.S. forces were "turning the corner." Pictures of the close-quarter fighting that appeared on television screens and in newspapers clashed with the administration's

Journalists photograph a body in the Saigon area during the Communist 1968 Tet Offensive. While considered a military defeat for the Communist side, it sharply altered American attitudes regarding the Vietnam War. (AP Photo/Nick Ut)

optimistic reports, widening the credibility gap and shaking the confidence of the American people in their government and its efforts in Southeast Asia.

President Johnson, beset by the antiwar movement and challenged politically within his own party, was informed by his newly appointed secretary of defense, Clark Clifford, that there was "no end in sight." On March 31, still reeling from the impact of the offensive, a demoralized Johnson went on national television, announced a unilateral halt to the bombing of North Vietnam, and called for negotiations to end the war. Then he stunned the nation by saying that he would not run for reelection.

In military terms, the Tet Offensive had been a disaster for the communists, but it illustrated only too clearly that the enemy appeared to have an inexhaustible supply of men and women willing to fight for the overthrow of the South Vietnamese government. In the end, the Tet Offensive achieved a psychological victory at the strategic level, hounded a president from office, and proved to be the turning point of the war, after which the problem was not how to win the war but rather how to disengage.

James H. Willbanks

Perspective Essay 1. Media Coverage Turned Tet into a Defeat

How would you characterize a battlefield fiasco in which the attacking forces were totally defeated, every objective they captured was retaken, and the attackers lost 40,000 of their best troops killed, with tens of thousands more wounded? In 1968, the media represented North Vietnam's disastrous Tet Offensive to the American public as a "victory" for the People's Army of North Vietnam (PAVN, North Vietnamese Army).

Hanoi planned the 1968 Tet Offensive to precipitate a general uprising among South Vietnam's presumably disaffected population that would force Saigon to accept a coalition government. Yet, the savagery wreaked by PAVN general Vo Nguyen Giap's countrywide attack dismally failed to evoke the expected popular uprising. However, battlefield success is no guarantor of final triumph in war, as the aftermath of the Tet Offensive so starkly demonstrated. Although U.S. and South Vietnamese forces weathered and then overcame Giap's assault, the shock that reverberated through the American public precipitated a downward spiral in popular domestic support for the war that turned the communists' battlefield defeat into a public relations victory that arguably won the war for Hanoi.

No one can or should question the veracity of media reporting of the Tet Offensive or for that matter the truthfulness of its coverage of the Vietnam War in general. With rare exceptions, the reporting was factual and accurate. Contrary to what some may claim, the media did not intentionally lie about what they saw, heard, and reported from Vietnam. Yet, getting the facts right did not ensure that reporters got the story right. Media coverage of the Tet Offensive is likely the most egregious example of reporting the facts of individual combat actions while missing the more important story of the big picture that those combat actions represented. Out of the hundreds of combat actions that occurred during Tet, two in particular garnered excessive media coverage that, in turn, produced an unexpected domestic political impact far beyond the modest scope and size of the forces involved and the relatively small body count in each case: the Viet Cong (VC) sapper attack on the U.S. embassy in Saigon and the Battle of Hue.

The Tet attack on the U.S. embassy in Saigon was a minor unsuccessful assault by a small group of VC sappers that became a sensationalized media icon, hyped as symbolizing the failed U.S. strategy in Vietnam. The embassy was added to the VC target list almost as an afterthought, and only 19 enemy soldiers took part. In fact, all VC attackers were eliminated, and none actually made it inside the embassy building. Yet, what one U.S. participant characterized as "a piddling platoon action" took place only a short distance from the main quarters for the Western press corps, a proximity that virtually guaranteed extensive media coverage by reporters who were either too shocked or too timid to venture very far afield. When Americans picked up their morning papers a few hours after the last VC sapper was killed, the first inklings they had of the Tet Offensive were inaccurate headlines stating that the U.S. embassy had been "captured." The panicked, often confused news reports coming on the heels of claims by President Lyndon Johnson and U.S. Vietnam commander William Westmoreland that America was winning the war delivered a shock from which the public never recovered.

The battle for Vietnam's ancient imperial capital of Hue, in contrast to the failed six-hour "piddling" action at the embassy in Saigon, lasted 26 days, the longest sustained infantry combat of the war to that point. A major PAVN Tet objective, Hue was quickly captured by PAVN regulars supported by VC main force units, thereby precipitating brutal house-to-house fighting by U.S. forces to retake a city that was essentially a fort. The nearly monthlong battle for Hue provided ample opportunity for reporters to illustrate their coverage with gruesome photographs of dead marines, soldiers, and civilians, many showing bodies grotesquely stacked in trucks and hauled away under heavy fire. Although American forces recaptured the city, killing 5,000 North Vietnamese while losing 216 U.S. dead, the lopsided body count tally could never overcome the 26 days of pessimistic reporting and the barrage of bloody, negative images. By February 26, 1968, the American public was shell-shocked by the intense media coverage.

These two combat actions and how reporters chose to present them, more than any other events reported by the media from Vietnam, exerted a negative and lasting influence on the American public's opinion about and attitude toward the war. Reporters may have gotten their facts right, but they clearly missed Tet's big-picture story, with ultimately tragic results for the people of South Vietnam. Beyond its influence on public perceptions about the Vietnam War, media reporting also had an unintended and long-lasting secondary impact that is still felt today. Soldiers' experience with how they perceived what the media reported about Vietnam left many veterans of the conflict wary and distrustful of reporters. Many, particularly army officers who later reached high rank, became embittered and resolved to keep reporters at arm's length, providing only information that they were required to hand over and even then often reluctantly and grudgingly. Although the recent program of embedding reporters within military units in combat is a belated attempt to reestablish an atmosphere of trust and openness, it may be too little, too late for military personnel who trace their roots back to the Vietnam War generation. They had assumed that their war in Vietnam would be reported by Ernie Pyle; instead, they got Dan Rather.

Jerry D. Morelock

Perspective Essay 2. Blaming the Media Is an Oversimplification

On the morning of February 1, 1968, a Viet Cong (VC) agent, a small man in a plaid shirt, was seized by South Vietnamese marines in central Saigon. Soon, General Nguyen Ngoc Loan, chief of the National Police, approached the man, drew his pistol, and without a word fired a single round into the man's head. The man in the plaid shirt collapsed, his life pouring out onto the dirty Saigon street.

This death was not memorable because of the prominence of either the killer or the killed. It didn't change the tide of battle. Rather, it is memorable because Associated Press photographer Eddie Adams and NBC cameraman Vo Suu captured the event. Within hours, the photo and the film had been seen by millions of people around the globe; millions of people had witnessed the last moment of life for the man in the plaid shirt.

The photo and the film have also become part of the mythology that has grown up around the 1968 Tet Offensive and its coverage, a mythology that encapsulates the controversy over the press's role in the Vietnam War. This myth says that Tet was a watershed in public support of the war. It portrays public opinion before the event as supportive of or at least apathetic toward the war and claims that afterward public opinion swung against the war. Those who view Tet this way point to press coverage as one of prime catalysts if not *the* prime catalyst of this shift. They blame the press for distorting the character of the offensive, exaggerating both VC and North Vietnamese success and American and South Vietnamese desperation. In his memoirs, General William Westmoreland attacked the press for misrepresenting the actual course of events. Robert Elegant, a former correspondent for *Newsweek,* in 1981 cited Tet as a particularly grievous example of how the press sapped the public's will to pursue the war. Most of these critics ascribe the press's actions to gross incompetence, liberal bias, or outright disloyalty.

But this view fails to understand what shaped the actions and coverage of the war by mainstream American news organizations, most especially coverage of the Tet Offensive. Journalists in Vietnam especially from the major news organizations were some of the best the profession had to offer. Just as was the case for young military officers, a tour in Vietnam was considered an essential boost for up-and-coming reporters, many of whom went on to become some of the biggest names in American journalism for the next generation.

This perception of the press also does not recognize the challenges of covering American involvement in Vietnam. Most of the military action in Vietnam involved relatively small units, lasted for anywhere from a few minutes to a few hours, and took place all across a difficult landscape. Also, military action represented just one aspect of a conflict that involved important political, social, and economic issues crucial to success or failure. At the height of the press presence in Vietnam some 600 individuals held press credentials, a small number to cover such a widespread and complicated story. The nature of the challenge becomes even starker when one realizes that of those 600 or so people, only about 125–150 were actual news-gathering journalists; the remainder were drivers, couriers, and office personnel.

These logistical challenges led to the development by 1965 of a largely cooperative relationship between news organizations and the U.S. government and military on the ground in Vietnam. The press needed steady access to information in order to cover the war; the government and the military realized that if they provided the press that information, this could have a significant influence on coverage. Thus, news organizations came to depend on official sources to cover a complex and far-flung conflict, and the government and the military were able to use the news media to feed that information to the American public.

Finally, those who contend that incompetent or biased coverage shattered the American people's confidence in the war effort fail to see that support had been declining steadily since the commitment of American ground troops in large numbers in the spring and summer of 1965. The changes of opinion associated with Tet in 1968 had long been in the works. Editorial opinion, even of news organizations that had long supported Vietnam policy, was growing openly skeptical by the fall of 1967. Concern in Congress also grew steadily, and senior administration officials became increasingly doubtful. Defense Secretary Robert McNamara had grown so concerned that earlier that year he had authorized the secret study that came to be known as the Pentagon Papers. Even President Lyndon B. Johnson, who announced his withdrawal from the presidential race on March 31, had been contemplating retirement for some time.

However, the strongest repudiation of the view that the Tet Offensive turned the public against the war comes from the American public itself. From July 1965 to late 1972, the up-or-down measure of public support for the war effort was the question "Do you believe United States involvement in the Vietnam War to have been a mistake?" Well before Tet, in October 1967 for the first time more Americans answered "yes" than "no" to that question in the wake of a significant increase in American casualties and the imposition of a 10 percent income tax surcharge to pay for the war.

The scale and audacity of the Tet Offensive startled the American public, just as it did American leaders in Saigon and Washington. Tet also pushed the press's fragile logistical base to the limit, resulting in some confused coverage in the attack's earlier hours, as Peter Braestrup ably described in *Big Story.* But the public had come to question the government's effort in Vietnam months before. The American people did not need the press or the government to tell them that the cost of the war, in blood and in money, had reached a price that they were increasingly unwilling to pay and that their sons, husbands, and brothers continued to die in a confusing, inconclusive war. In March 1968, the weekly paper in the small town of Brewton, Alabama, turned from its previous support of the war after two young soldiers from the town died during the fighting. "Like hundreds of other communities across the country," the paper's editor said, "the war came too close when it got to Brewton."

Clarence R. Wyatt

Further Reading

Arnold, James R. *The Tet Offensive 1968: Turning Point in Vietnam.* London: Osprey, 1990.

Blood, Jake. *The Tet Effect: Intelligence and the Public Perception of War.* London: Routledge, 2005.

Braestrup, Peter. *Big Story: How the American Press and Television Reported and Interpreted the Crisis of Tet in Vietnam and Washington.* New Haven, CT: Yale University Press, 1983.

Bui Tin. *From Enemy to Friend: A North Vietnamese Perspective on the War.* Annapolis MD: Naval Institute Press, 2002.

Clifford, Clark, and Richard Holbrooke. *Counsel to the President: A Memoir.* New York: Random House, 1991.

Gilbert, Marc Jason, and William Head, eds. *The Tet Offensive.* Westport, CT: Praeger, 1996.

Hammel, Eric. *Fire in the Streets: The Battle for Hue; Tet 1968.* Chicago: Contemporary Books, 1991.

Johnson, Lyndon B. *The Vantage Point: Perspectives on the Presidency, 1963–1969.* New York: Holt, Rinehart and Winston, 1971.

Karnow, Stanley. *Vietnam: A History.* New York: Viking, 1983.

Lind, Michael. *Vietnam: The Necessary War.* New York: Free Press, 2002.

Macdonald, Peter. *Giap: The Victor in Vietnam.* London: Fourth Estate, 1994.

Military History Institute of Vietnam. *Victory in Vietnam: The Official History of the People's Army of Vietnam, 1954–1975.* Translated by Merle L. Pribbenow. Lawrence: University Press of Kansas, 2002.

Nolan, Keith W. *The Battle for Hue: Tet 1968.* Novato, CA: Presidio, 1983.

Nolan, Keith W. *The Battle for Saigon: Tet 1968.* New York: Pocket Books, 1996.

Oberdorfer, Don. *Tet!* Baltimore: Johns Hopkins University Press, 2001.

Palmer, Dave R. *Summons of the Trumpet.* Novato, CA: Presidio, 1978.

Pisor, Robert. *The End of the Line: The Siege of Khe Sanh.* New York: Norton, 1982.

Schmitz, David F. *The Tet Offensive: Politics, War, and Public Opinion.* Westport CT: Praeger, 2004.

Smith, George W. *The Siege at Hue.* Boulder, CO: Lynne Rienner, 1999.

Summers, Harry G. *On Strategy: The Vietnam War in Context.* Carlisle Barracks, PA: U.S. Army War College, Strategic Studies Institute, 1981.

Warr, Nicholas. *Phase Line Green: The Battle for Hue, 1968.* Annapolis, MD: Naval Institute Press, 1997.

Westmoreland, William C. *A Soldier Reports.* New York: Doubleday, 1976.

Willbanks, James H. *Abandoning Vietnam: How America Left and South Vietnam Lost Its War.* Lawrence: University Press of Kansas, 2004.

Willbanks, James H. *The Tet Offensive: A Concise History.* New York: Columbia University Press, 2007.

Wirtz, James J. *The Tet Offensive: Intelligence Failure in War.* Ithaca, NY: Cornell University Press, 1994.

Woodruff, Mark W. *Unheralded Victory: The Defeat of the Viet Cong and the North Vietnamese Army, 1961–1973.* New York: Ballantine, 1999.

Wyatt, Clarence R. *Paper Soldiers: The American Press and the Vietnam War.* New York: Norton, 1993.

Zaffiri, Samuel. *Westmoreland.* New York: William Morrow, 1994.

54. Could the United States Have Won the Vietnam War?

The Vietnam War began in 1957 and was in many ways a direct result of the Indochina War (1948–1954), which witnessed the defeat of French forces and the loss of France's Indochinese colony. When Ngo Dinh Diem established the Republic of Vietnam (RVN, South Vietnam) in October 1955, Vietnam was officially bifurcated, with the communist-controlled Democratic Republic of Vietnam (DRV, North Vietnam) controlling the region north of the 17th parallel. When Diem refused to hold elections in 1956, which were supposed to determine the future of all of Vietnam, the U.S. government backed his decision. Wedded as they were to the containment policy and the domino theory, American policy makers refused to permit the DRV from ruling all of Vietnam. Instead, they sought to prop up and aid the increasingly despotic and inept Diem regime. By the early 1960s as Diem's hold on power became more tenuous, U.S. aid to the RVN increased, including the positioning of nearly 17,000 military "advisers" in South Vietnam by 1963. After Diem's deposition and death in November 1963, the political situation in the RVN continued to deteriorate. The Lyndon B. Johnson administration then decided to gradually escalate U.S. participation in the war, and by late 1968 there were some 550,000 U.S. ground troops in Vietnam. Nevertheless, the United States proved unable to resoundingly defeat DRV forces or their allies in South Vietnam, the Viet Cong. In the meantime, antiwar protests in the United States were growing in both frequency and violence, and public opinion had turned against continued U.S. involvement in Vietnam.

In the first perspective essay, Dr. Jeremy Bonner makes the crucial point that the United States never understood Vietnam or the people for whom it was fighting and failed to learn from the mistakes made in the Indochina War. He also points out that America's reliance on conventional military operations was ineffective against the DRV's emphasis on political infiltration and guerrilla warfare. Dr. James H. Willbanks asserts that U.S. policy makers tied their own hands during much of the Vietnam War because they opted to keep it a limited conflict. North Vietnam, on the other hand, fought a total war that was bent on Vietnamese unification. Willbanks also argues that the United States never made the South Vietnamese Army truly self-sufficient. In the third essay, Dr. Sean McLaughlin approaches the question by using the arguments of those who contend that the United States could indeed have won the war and lays out how and why each of these arguments has fatal flaws—much like the U.S. policy toward Vietnam as a whole. Finally, Dr. Spencer C. Tucker demonstrates that while the United States theoretically could have won the war, American policy makers ignored two vital realities that doomed their efforts: Vietnam's geography and history. Furthermore, he argues that America's lingering fear of provoking a Chinese intervention in the war, which had occurred during the Korean War in the early 1950s, prevented U.S. policy makers from invading North Vietnam. Thus, the U.S. war effort in Vietnam remained a limited and defensive operation that doomed the entire affair to failure.

An American soldier readies his M60 machine gun in preparation for an assault during the Vietnam War. (U.S. Army Center of Military History)

Background Essay

The Vietnam War (1957–1975) grew out of the Indochina War (1948–1954). The 1954 Geneva Conference ending that war between France and the nationalist/communist Viet Minh provided for the independence of Cambodia, Laos, and Vietnam. Vietnam was temporally divided at the 17th parallel, pending national elections in 1956. In the meantime, Viet Minh military forces were to withdraw north of that line and French forces south of it. The war left two competing entities, the northern Democratic Republic of Vietnam (DRV) and the southern French-dominated State of Vietnam (SV), each claiming to be the legitimate government of a united Vietnam.

In June 1954, SV titular head Emperor Bao Dai appointed as premier Roman Catholic Ngo Dinh Diem. His support was narrow but strengthened by the addition of some 800,000 northern Catholics who relocated to the south. Then in October 1955 Diem swept Bao Dai aside and established the Republic of Vietnam (RVN), with himself as president. The United States provided substantial support to Diem, with most aid going to the RVN military budget. As Diem consolidated his power, U.S. military advisers reorganized the RVN armed forces. Known as the Army of the Republic of Vietnam (ARVN), it was designed to fight a conventional invasion from the north rather than deal with an insurgency.

Fearing a loss, Diem refused to hold the scheduled 1956 elections. This jolted veteran communist and DRV leader Ho Chi Minh, who believed that he would win the elections. Fortified by the containment policy, the domino theory, and the belief that the communists, if they came to power in Vietnam, would never allow democracy, the Dwight D. Eisenhower administration backed Diem's defiance of the Geneva Agreements.

Diem's decision led to a renewal of fighting, which became the Vietnam War. Fighting resumed in 1957 when Diem moved against the Viet Minh political cadres left in the south to prepare for the 1956 elections. They began the insurgency on their own initiative but were subsequently supported by the DRV government. The insurgents came to be known as the Viet Cong (VC, for "Vietnamese Communists"). In December 1960 they established the National Front for the Liberation of South Vietnam. Supposedly independent, it was completely controlled by Hanoi.

In September 1959 DRV defense minister Vo Nguyen Giap began sending supplies and men south along what came to be known as the Ho Chi Minh Trail, much of which ran through supposedly neutral Laos. At first the infiltrators were native southerners who had relocated in the north in 1954. Meanwhile, VC sway gradually expanded, fed by the weaknesses of the RVN central government, by the use of terror and assassination, and by Saigon's appalling ignorance regarding the VC. By mid-1961 the Saigon government had lost control over much of rural South Vietnam. Isolated from his people and relying only on trusted family members and a few other advisers, Diem resisted U.S. demands that senior officials and officers be appointed on the basis of ability and that he pursue the war aggressively.

Increased U.S. involvement was inevitable, given Washington's commitment to resist communist expansion and the belief that all of Southeast Asia would become communist if South Vietnam fell. Domestic political considerations also influenced the decision. In May 1961 President John F. Kennedy sent several fact-finding missions to Vietnam. These brought the Strategic Hamlet program, part of a general strategy emphasizing local militia defense, and the commitment of additional U.S. manpower. By the end of 1961 U.S. strength in Vietnam had grown to around 3,200 men, largely in helicopter units and advisers. In February 1962 also, the Military Assistance and Advisory Group was replaced by the Military Assistance Command, Vietnam (MACV) to direct the enlarged American commitment. This aid probably prevented a VC military victory in 1962, but the VC soon learned to cope with the helicopters, and again the tide of battle turned.

Meanwhile, a crackdown on Buddhists brought increased opposition to Diem, and South Vietnamese generals planned a coup. After Diem rejected reforms, Washington gave its approval. On November 1, 1963, the generals overthrew Diem, murdering him and his brother. Within three weeks Kennedy was also dead, succeeded by Lyndon B. Johnson. A military junta took power in South Vietnam, but coups and countercoups followed. Not until General Nguyen Van Thieu became president in 1967 was there a degree of political stability.

Both sides steadily increased the stakes, apparently without foreseeing that the other might do the same. In 1964 Hanoi decided to send south units of its regular army, the People's Army of Vietnam (North Vietnamese Army, PAVN). Hanoi also decided to rearm its forces in the south with modern communist bloc weapons, giving them a firepower advantage over the ARVN, and to order direct attacks on American installations, provoking a U.S. response.

On August 2, 1964, in the so-called Gulf of Tonkin Incident, DRV torpedo boats attacked a U.S. destroyer in international waters in the Gulf of Tonkin. A second attack on the same and another U.S. destroyer reported two days later probably never occurred, but Johnson believed that it had and ordered retaliatory air strikes against DRV naval bases and fuel depots. Also, a near-unanimous congressional vote for the Gulf of Tonkin Resolution gave Johnson authority to use whatever force he deemed necessary to protect U.S. interests in Southeast Asia.

Johnson rejected withdrawal, apparently fearing possible impeachment if he did so. At the same time, he refused to take the tough decision of fully mobilizing the country and committing the resources necessary to win, concerned that this would destroy his cherished domestic social programs. At the same time, however, he feared a widened war involving the People's Republic of China.

By 1965, Ho and his generals expected to win the war. Taking their cue from Johnson's own pronouncements, they mistakenly believed that Washington would not commit ground troops. Yet, Johnson did just that. Faced with Hanoi's own escalation, U.S. marines arrived at Da Nang in March 1965. Meanwhile, the United States also undertook bombing raids against North Vietnam.

Johnson hoped to win the war on the cheap, relying heavily on airpower. Known as ROLLING THUNDER and paralleled by BARREL ROLL, the secret bombing of Laos (which became the most heavily bombed country in the history of warfare), the air campaign was pursued during the next three and a half years. Its goals were to force Hanoi to negotiate peace and to halt infiltration into South Vietnam. The United States dropped more bombs than in all of World War II, but the campaign failed in both objectives.

In the air war Johnson decided on graduated response rather than the massive strikes advocated by the military. Gradualism became the grand strategy employed by the United States in Vietnam. Haunted by the Korean War, at no time would Johnson consider an invasion of North Vietnam, fearful of a Chinese intervention.

By May and June 1965, with PAVN forces regularly destroying ARVN units, MACV commander General William Westmoreland appealed for U.S. ground units, which Johnson committed. During October–November 1965, the 1st Cavalry Division (Airmobile) formed around some 450 helicopters won one of the war's rare decisive encounters in the Battle of the Ia Drang Valley and may have derailed Hanoi's hopes of winning the war before full American might could be deployed.

Heavy personnel losses on the battlefield were entirely acceptable to the DRV leadership. Washington never did understand this. From 1966 on Vietnam was an escalating military stalemate, as Westmoreland requested and received increasing numbers of men. In 1968, U.S. strength was more than 500,000 men. Johnson also secured some 60,000 troops from other nations (most of them from the Republic of Korea). Terrain was not judged important. The goals were to protect the population and kill the enemy with success measured in terms of body counts, which in turn led to abuses.

Hanoi meanwhile had reached a point of decision, with casualties exceeding available replacements. Instead of scaling back, North Vietnam prepared a major offensive that would employ all available troops to secure a quick victory. The result was a massive offensive during Tet, the lunar New Year holidays, called the General Offensive–General Uprising, for the communists believed that it would lead people in South Vietnam to rise up and overthrow the RVN government. In a major intelligence failure, U.S. and RVN officials misread both the timing and the strength of the attack.

The Tet Offensive (January 31–February 24, 1968) failed. ARVN forces generally fought well, and most South Vietnamese did not support the attackers. Half of the 85,000 VC and PAVN troops who took part in the offensive were killed or captured. It was the worst military setback for North Vietnam in the war. Paradoxically, it was also North Vietnam's most resounding victory, in part because the Johnson administration and Westmoreland had trumpeted prior allied successes, and the intensity of the fighting came as a profound shock to the American people who now turned against the war. At the end of March, Johnson announced a partial cessation of the bombing and withdrew from the November 1968 presidential election.

Hanoi persisted, however. In the first six months of 1968, communist forces sustained more than 100,000 casualties, and the VC was virtually wiped out; 20,000 allied troops died in the same period. All sides now opted for talks in Paris in an effort to negotiate an end to the war.

American disillusionment with the war was a key factor in Republican Richard Nixon's razor-thin victory over Democrat Hubert Humphrey in the November 1968 presidential election. Nixon embraced Vietnamization, actually begun under Johnson, or turning more of the war over to the ARVN. U.S. troop withdrawals were begun. Peak U.S. strength of 550,000 men occurred in early 1969; by the end of 1971, there were 157,000. Massive amounts of equipment were also turned over to the ARVN, including 1 million M-16 assault rifles and sufficient aircraft to make the RVN Air Force the world's fourth largest. Extensive retraining of ARVN was begun, and training schools were established. The controversial counterinsurgency Phoenix Program operated against the VC infrastructure, but PAVN forces remained secure in sanctuaries in Laos and Cambodia.

Nixon sought to limit outside assistance to Hanoi and pressure Hanoi to end the war. For years, American and RVN military leaders had wanted to attack the sanctuaries. In March 1970 a coup in Cambodia replaced Prince Noradom Sihanouk with General Lon Nol, and operations against the PAVN Cambodian sanctuaries soon began. Despite widespread opposition in the United States to these, the so-called Cambodian Incursions raised allied morale, allowed U.S. withdrawals to continue on schedule, and purchased additional time for Vietnamization.

By 1972 PAVN forces had been substantially strengthened with new weapons, including heavy artillery and tanks from the Soviet Union. Hanoi planned a major conventional invasion of South Vietnam, believing that the United States would not interfere. Giap had 15 divisions. He left 1 division in the DRV and 2 divisions in Laos and committed the remainder to the invasion.

The PAVN Spring (Easter) Offensive began on March 29, 1972, with a direct armor strike across the demilitarized zone at the 17th parallel. Again allied intelligence misread its scale and precise timing. Giap risked catastrophic losses but hoped for a quick victory before ARVN forces could recover. At first it appeared that the PAVN would be successful, but in May President Nixon authorized B-52 bomber strikes on Hanoi's principal port of Haiphong and the mining of its harbor. This new air campaign was dubbed LINEBACKER and involved new precision-guided munitions, or smart bombs. The bombing cut off much of the supplies for the invading PAVN forces. Allied aircraft also destroyed hundreds of PAVN tanks, and in June and July the ARVN counterattacked. The invasion cost Hanoi half its force—some 100,000 men died—while ARVN losses were only 25,000.

With both Soviet and Chinese leaders anxious for better relations with the United States to obtain Western technology, Hanoi gave way and switched to negotiations. An agreement was finally hammered out in Paris that December, but President Thieu balked and refused to sign, whereupon Hanoi made the agreements public. A furious Nixon blamed Hanoi and, in December, ordered a resumption of the bombing, dubbed LINEBACKER II. Although 15 B-52s were lost, Hanoi had expended virtually its entire stock of surface-to-air missiles and now agreed to resume talks.

After a few cosmetic changes, an agreement was finally signed on January 23, 1973, with Nixon forcing Thieu to agree or risk the end of all U.S. aid. The United States recovered its prisoners of war and departed Vietnam. The Soviet Union and China continued to supply arms to Hanoi, however, while Congress refused to honor pledges made by Nixon and constricted U.S. supplies to Saigon. Tanks and planes were not replaced on the promised one-for-one basis as they were lost, and spare parts and fuel were both in short supply. All of this had a devastating effect on ARVN morale.

Both sides violated the cease-fire, and fighting steadily increased. In January 1975 communist forces attacked and quickly seized a province on the Cambodian border north of Saigon. Washington took no action. The communists then moved against the Central Highlands, and in mid-March President Thieu decided to abandon the northern part of his country. Confusion became disorder and then disaster, and six weeks later PAVN forces controlled all of South Vietnam. Saigon fell on April 30, 1975. Vietnam was finally reunited but under a communist government.

Spencer C. Tucker

Perspective Essay 1. A Domino Too Far

American intervention in South Vietnam from the mid-1950s to the mid-1970s remains one of the most controversial decisions of modern U.S. foreign policy. During the early years of the Cold War, most American policy makers believed that the encouragement of communist movements in the Third World by the Soviet Union and communist China had to be countered both militarily and through the economic and political support of anticommunist regimes in vulnerable countries. A key battleground was French Indochina, where the struggle for Vietnamese independence between 1945 and 1954—itself a continuation of prewar nationalist unrest—saw the Communist Party of Indochina increasingly assume the mantle of nationalist leadership. The conferees at the 1954 Geneva Conference that ended the Indochina War agreed that Vietnam, Laos, and Cambodia were to be independent but temporarily divided Vietnam at the 17th parallel, with elections to take place to reunify the country in 1956. Washington, fearing a communist electoral victory, sought to build up a government in South Vietnam committed to an anticommunist agenda.

The appointment of Ngo Dinh Diem as premier of the State of Vietnam in 1954 (in 1955 he proclaimed the Republic of Vietnam, with himself as president) soon demonstrated the limitations of the southern nationalist experiment. A Catholic in a largely Buddhist country, Diem had not been an active participant in the anticolonialist movements of the 1940s. Despite efforts to institute a comprehensive program of economic reform, moreover, American aid frequently distorted existing economic relationships, and American construction of new roads and port facilities did little to encourage industrialization or improve the lot of those in the countryside. By 1960 Vietnam, which had previously been a net food exporter, was incapable of feeding itself. Land reform—which would have addressed the needs of the peasant majority—was not something that the Diem regime, with its base in the cities, chose to embrace.

Diem favored a form of government that served those elements most personally supportive of his agenda, and he had little interest in promoting democratic accountability. He proved to be incapable of exercising leadership that resonated with the mass of the South Vietnamese population. In the countryside, where most Vietnamese lived, Diem's officials were an alien presence, detached from the traditional and familial networks of authority. Even the Strategic Hamlet Program, which sought to protect the rural population by concentrating them in fortified villages, not only disrupted agricultural production but actually made ordinary villagers more vulnerable to communist attack. After Diem's fall in 1963, the succession of military rulers who oversaw South Vietnam could claim even less of a connection between the people and the government in Saigon.

If the Diem regime was fundamentally divided against itself, the success of his opponents in the National Front for the Liberation of South Vietnam (NLF) stemmed from their ability to work with the grain of Vietnamese society. Where Diem's American advisers promoted economic development from above, the NLF focused on the village substructure with which the majority of South Vietnamese were most familiar. Founded in 1960 as an alternative government for South Vietnam, the NLF refrained from creating a massive underground bureaucracy and focused instead on educating and empowering village communities. Over time, however, it sought to promote within village communities a desire to move beyond family-based relationships to a more structured form of rural life in which agricultural cooperation, military support, and political education were seamlessly integrated.

During the John F. Kennedy administration, despite the commitment of roughly 16,000 U.S. military personnel, the counterinsurgency strategy conducted mostly by the South Vietnamese forces had little success. Following the Gulf of Tonkin Incident in August 1964, however, U.S. president Lyndon Johnson secured from Congress an unprecedented degree of executive discretion in conducting the war. This resulted in a shift that involved the commencement of a campaign of bombing North Vietnam and the introduction of significant numbers of American ground troops under the overall command of General William Westmoreland. Westmoreland's military strategy emphasized large search-and-destroy operations and increased reliance on artillery and air support.

For geopolitical reasons, however, the ground war could not be extended into North Vietnam, which proved to be incredibly resilient to an American bombing campaign that was restricted in its targeting. While U.S. forces in South Vietnam dominated in pitched battles, they proved far less effective in the jungles into which the communist fighters retreated. The Americans might boast that they had won every major military encounter, but this did not translate into control over the territory gained by the Army of the Republic of Vietnam (ARVN).

In January 1968 the communist forces launched the Tet Offensive, seeking to inflict a decisive military defeat on American and South Vietnamese forces that would bring about a popular uprising and win the war. Militarily a failure and with no popular uprising, the Tet Offensive nevertheless constituted a political defeat for the United States, as it turned the American public against the war.

As long as public trust in the Johnson administration endured, the protests of antiwar activists had little impact, but by late 1967 media coverage and the costs of conducting the war had taken their toll. Challenged by dissidents from within his own party, President Johnson suspended the bombing of North Vietnam in March 1968. His successor, President Richard Nixon, initially resumed the bombing campaign and even carried out attacks against North Vietnamese bases in neutral Cambodia but also embraced Johnson's new strategy of Vietnamization that sought to turn more of the burden of fighting over to the ARVN. Nixon finally secured a peace settlement in January 1973 that ended American involvement. When North Vietnam launched its final assault on an already demoralized South Vietnam in 1975, President Gerald Ford's administration in Washington could do nothing to assist South Vietnam.

The failure of the United States to succeed in Vietnam can be attributed to an emphasis on conventional military operations against an enemy who favored political infiltration and guerrilla warfare and also to an inability to appreciate that the anticommunist regime that it supported was incapable of winning the hearts and minds of many South Vietnamese.

Jeremy Bonner

Perspective Essay 2. Too Many Missteps along the Way

The words "winning in Vietnam" beg definition. From the U.S. perspective, the desired end was clearly stated in National Security Action Memorandum 288 of March 17, 1964 as "an independent, non-Communist South Vietnam." The end goal may have been clear, but how to obtain it was another matter.

Each side saw the war differently. For North Vietnamese leaders in Hanoi, the war was a total war to achieve national unification. Therefore, they placed no restrictions or limitations on the ways and means to achieve their desired end state, a reunited Vietnam under communist control. Successive American presidents saw the war in Vietnam as a limited conflict in the broader context of the Cold War between East and West. The United States could not afford to prosecute a total war against North Vietnam because such an escalation could lead to a massive Chinese military intervention and perhaps even a nuclear confrontation.

Thus, the hope in Washington under successive presidents was to stem the spread of communism in Southeast Asia by fighting a limited war in Vietnam, imposing limitations and restrictions on what the military could and could not do there. This meant that there were limitations on attacking North Vietnam directly. While a number of successive bombing campaigns were launched against North Vietnam, there was never any attempt to strike directly at it with ground forces. This meant that North Vietnamese leaders could continue the struggle as long as North Vietnam could survive the bombing while being sustained logistically by China and the Soviet Union.

Given that reality, the United States made a number of other errors that contributed to the final outcome. Washington sought a viable noncommunist government in South Vietnam and should have early on taken measures to insist that government build support in the countryside in order to promote stability and meet the needs of the people. Instead, the John F. Kennedy administration gave a green light to a bloody coup that removed Republic of Vietnam (RVN) president Ngo Dinh Diem from power and ushered in a period of political chaos that further destabilized South Vietnam.

When the South Vietnamese government proved incapable of providing security against an ever-growing externally supported insurgency, Kennedy's successor, President Lyndon Johnson, committed U.S. ground troops. Johnson saw the war in Vietnam as a limited conflict within the larger Cold War. He insisted on numerous restrictions and limitations on military action in Vietnam.

Geography played a key role in the war. Vietnam was a long S-shaped country with a 1,200-mile border shared with Laos and Cambodia. The Ho Chi Minh Trail, which ran out of North Vietnam and then southward through Laos and Cambodia, provided the means for Hanoi to insert men and matériel into South Vietnam almost at will. Worried about the potential entry of China into the war, Johnson forbade the use of U.S. ground troops in Cambodia and Laos. This meant that the only answer to restricting Hanoi's use of the Ho Chi Minh Trail was airpower. Despite the dropping of thousands of tons of ordnance on the trail network, it was never effectively shut down. At the same time, Johnson imposed restrictions against striking the port of Haiphong, through which most of the war matériel flowed into North Vietnam from China and the Soviet Union. As a result, Hanoi could sustain the fighting in South Vietnam almost indefinitely.

Other U.S. policy decisions virtually precluded a satisfactory outcome in the war for the United States. First, when Johnson committed U.S. ground troops to Vietnam in force, the original effort to train and improve the South Vietnamese armed forces became a lesser priority. Left to their own devices, the South Vietnamese armed forces never addressed and overcame the intrinsic weaknesses that had existed since they were formed in the early days of the republic and would continue to exist all the way to the day Saigon fell in 1975. When President Richard Nixon succeeded Johnson in 1969 and instituted large-scale troop withdrawals, he also intensified the Vietnamization program begun by Johnson that shifted more of the burden to South Vietnamese armed forces, but this proved to be too late. In effect, American withdrawal from the war and the survival of the South Vietnamese government were always contradictory objectives.

Still, the other side made its own mistakes. The decision to launch the Tet Offensive of January 1968 proved ill-advised, at least at the tactical level. The communists sustained more than 50,000 killed in the bitter fighting that extended into the fall. In most areas, the failure of the Tet Offensive at the tactical level left the Viet Cong severely weakened, and only in a few selected areas did they ever recover. The absence of the Viet Cong in the countryside enabled a renewed RVN pacification effort to register gains.

However, this proved largely irrelevant as the war continued. The only difference was that fighting fell increasingly on the regular North Vietnamese forces. Despite renewed attempts to disrupt the communist supply system in Cambodia in 1970 and in Laos in 1971, the North Vietnamese were still able to sustain their military effort in South Vietnam.

In 1972, Hanoi launched a massive conventional invasion of South Vietnam in what it hoped would be a war-winning effort. Army of the Republic of Vietnam forces, initially caught by surprise, rallied and fought well, however. Greatly aided by American airpower, they blunted and then rolled back the gains made by the People's Army of Vietnam (North Vietnamese Army) gains. President Nixon proclaimed Vietnamization a success and intensified peace talks begun in Paris under Johnson. By October, a tentative agreement had been reached. RVN president

Nguyen Van Thieu balked at the agreement. Nixon blamed Hanoi for the impasse, and to force its negotiators back to the bargaining table he instituted punishing bombing of North Vietnam in Operation LINEBACKER II. Hanoi then agreed to resume the talks, resulting in the Paris Peace Accords of January 27, 1973, essentially the same agreement reached earlier but this time with Washington forcing Thieu to sign.

Perhaps there was a window of opportunity during LINEBACKER II for the United States to have secured meaningful concessions from Hanoi, but it was not seized. By this point, Nixon was more interested in disengaging from the war and securing American prisoners of war held by North Vietnam than securing a lasting and viable peace for South Vietnam. The agreement merely established a cease-fire in place for the opposing forces in South Vietnam.

To secure Thieu's agreement, Nixon made extensive pledges of assistance for the RVN, which were then never honored. Indeed, the Paris Accords proved to be the RVN's death warrant. Little more than two years after the cease-fire went into effect, North Vietnamese forces initiated a lightning offensive and had won the war.

Might the United States and the RVN have won? Driven by the demands of fighting a limited war, the restrictions and limitations that Washington placed on U.S. involvement sharply limited the possibility of this. Decisions taken by Washington certainly worked against this. Hanoi was prepared to expend all the resources at its disposal, while the United States fought a limited war for limited objectives. In the end, the war was not winnable at a price the United States was prepared to pay. The result was a massive failure for the United States and the end of the Republic of Vietnam as a sovereign nation.

James H. Willbanks

Perspective Essay 3. An Unwinnable War? The U.S. Military Experience in Vietnam

America's failed military campaign to prop up the anticommunist government of the Republic of Vietnam (South Vietnam) came at such cost that most historians argue that it was a massive strategic blunder. However, some revisionists counter that U.S. intervention was indeed justified and that the communist forces could have been defeated. They argue that politicians in Washington made victory impossible by preventing the military from using more aggressive measures against North Vietnam, which was fueling the insurgency in the South, or expanding the war to communist sanctuaries in neighboring countries. This essay will argue that although alternative military strategies existed, they were not feasible because they would have resulted in an even bloodier expanded war involving China and had a devastating effect on U.S. relations elsewhere.

In 1954, war-ravaged Vietnam was granted independence but was temporarily divided along the 17th parallel, with elections to reunify the country to be held in 1956. Ho Chi Minh, a veteran communist who had led the fight against the French, consolidated his control in northern Vietnam, while anticommunist Ngo Dinh Diem took power in southern Vietnam. Both claimed to represent all of Vietnam, but Diem refused to allow the elections that would have reunified the country. In the years that followed partition an insurgency began in South Vietnam, which North Vietnam supported. The Kennedy administration responded by ramping up aid to South Vietnam and committed 16,000 American military advisers in an effort to defeat the insurgency without American forces directly participating in combat. The communist insurgents, known as the Viet Cong (Vietnamese Communists) continued to gain ground, which led to U.S. president Lyndon Johnson's decision to commit U.S. ground forces in 1965. Within three years more than half a million American military personnel were serving in South Vietnam, prompting North Vietnam, assisted by the Soviet Union and communist China, to also increase its already substantial material and manpower support in South Vietnam. The Johnson administration launched a massive air campaign against North Vietnam in Operation ROLLING THUNDER in a bid to stanch the flow of manpower and supplies into South Vietnam. While this inflicted considerable damage on North Vietnam, it failed to convince the government in Hanoi to withdraw its support for the southern insurgency.

Escalating the war in the form of a ground assault on North Vietnam must have been tempting to U.S. military leaders in the Pentagon, but it would likely have brought about disastrous consequences. In June 1950, the American-led United Nations Command (UNC) came to the defense of noncommunist South Korea following an invasion by communist North Korea. After driving North Korean forces from South Korea, UNC troops invaded North Korea in an effort to reunify the country. This triggered a massive military intervention by the People's Republic of China and a decision in June 1953 to halt the fighting with essentially a restoration of the status quo ante bellum. Beijing had demonstrated a willingness to accept staggering casualties to prevent a pro-American regime on its border.

Chinese leaders threatened the same in the case of the Vietnam War. Beijing backed this threat up by deploying more than 320,000 troops to North Vietnam to man antiaircraft batteries, rebuild infrastructure destroyed by American bombs, and, most important, free up North Vietnamese forces for combat in South Vietnam. The Johnson administration understood that taking the ground war to North Vietnam would in all likelihood mean war with a now nuclear-armed China. This would have required a major increase of American manpower at a time of widespread resistance to the draft and likely would have produced an intolerable number of casualties as the general public was growing increasingly disillusioned with the course of the war in South Vietnam.

Other revisionists have suggested that American forces should have launched ground attacks on communist sanctuaries on the Ho Chi Minh Trail across the border in neutral Laos and Cambodia. North Vietnam took advantage of the weakness of the postindependence regimes in both countries, which shared sparsely populated frontiers with South Vietnam, by carving out the 600-mile-long supply route of the so-called Ho Chi Minh Trail in Laos. U.S. air strikes targeted the trail beginning in December 1964, but the communists continually rebuilt and even expanded it. By 1967 it had expanded to the point where it could accommodate trucks.

When President Richard Nixon did launch an attack on Cambodia against the communist sanctuaries there in April 1970, the communist military units withdrew mostly intact into the interior. U.S. and South Vietnamese forces did capture sufficient food, supplies, and weapons to disrupt communist offensive action for the better part of a year, but this merely postponed the eventual communist victory. At home, American college campuses responded to Nixon's expansion of the war with a fresh wave of antiwar protests that saw bloodshed at Kent State University in Ohio and Jackson State University in Mississippi. As much as some hawks would have liked to take the war to the Ho Chi Minh Trail, doing so probably would have led to an intolerable reaction on the U.S. home front.

In the end, America should not have gone to war in Vietnam. Most Americans considered the cost of victory too high, as the Vietnamese nationalists absolutely dedicated to expelling American troops they perceived as foreign invaders and rival superpowers took measures that effectively blocked more robust American military action.

Sean J. McLaughlin

Perspective Essay 4. U.S./Republic of Vietnam Victory Virtually Impossible

While it was theoretically possible for U.S., South Vietnamese, and other allied forces to have won the Vietnam War, a number of factors made that quite unlikely. Washington policy makers ignored two realities. The first was geography. While nearly the size of Germany, Vietnam has been called two rice baskets at the ends of a pole, for it is long and narrow for much of its expanse, with a north-south coastline of some 2,100 miles. It is bordered by China to the north and Laos and

Cambodia to the west. Isolating Vietnam means controlling the entire coastline as well as the interior borders. The problem posed by geography played a key role in the war and should have been clear from the outset. The second factor was history. The Vietnamese had fought tenaciously for their independence against China during many centuries. Vietnamese fear of Chinese domination, had it been understood, might have been turned to good account. Even under communist rule, it was quite realistic to assume that Vietnam might have been akin to Yugoslavia.

U.S. involvement in Vietnamese affairs really commenced in 1940 when, during the Second Sino-Japanese War (1937–1945), Japanese forces took advantage of the defeat of France by Germany to send troops into northern French Indochina in order to cut off foreign military aid to the Chinese. Worried about the threat this might pose to the Philippines, the Theodore Roosevelt administration insisted that Japan withdraw from both China and Indochina. When the Japanese refused, the United States froze Japanese assets and embargoed strategic materials, including oil. The latter was a major blow, as Japan had no oil of its own. This action led the Japanese military, then running Japanese affairs, to undertake war with the United States, beginning with a preemptive strike at the U.S. Pacific Fleet at Pearl Harbor.

After the war, Vietnamese communist leader and ardent nationalist Ho Chi Minh sought the support of the United States for independence from France. France, however, was determined to hold on to its colonies, because only thus would it still be regarded as a great power. In Europe, the end of World War II found the Soviet Union in a seemingly commanding position. With the start of the Cold War and with Germany prostrate, the United States needed a rearmed France to stand against the Soviets. The price of this was that Washington support the French in Asia.

When the French reneged on their agreements with Ho and actively sought to crush the nationalists, fighting broke out in 1946. At first Washington provided little aid, but with the start of the Korean War (1950–1953), Washington bought into the argument that Korea and Indochina were interconnected fronts in the struggle to contain communism, entirely ignoring the nationalist sentiment driving the insurgent Viet Minh. Washington swallowed the French government lie that it had given Vietnam independence when it proclaimed the State of Vietnam in 1949, although the French continued to control its affairs. With the communist victory in China in 1949. the Indochina War was lost, for the Chinese could, and did, provide considerable military assistance to the Viet Minh across their common border.

Fighting continued, with the United States ultimately paying most of the bill, but French defeat in the Battle of Dienbienphu brought a decision by Paris to cut its losses. The 1954 Geneva Conference ending the war established the independence of Vietnam, Cambodia, and Laos but also temporarily divided Vietnam at the 17th parallel, pending national elections to be held in two years that would reunify the country. In effect, there were now two states claiming to represent all of Vietnam:

the Democratic Republic of Vietnam (DRV) in the north and the State of Vietnam in the south.

With a larger population in the north and having largely crushed opposition to communist rule there, and with Viet Minh political cadres active in the south, Ho was confident of an election victory. South Vietnamese leader Ngo Dinh Diem, meanwhile, consolidated his own hold on the south and in 1955 transformed the State of Vietnam into the Republic of Vietnam (RVN), with himself as president. Diem, measuring his own chances of success, refused to hold the referendum, and Washington supported him in his stance, buttressed by the fact that once they had taken power the communists had never permitted democratic rule.

Actual fighting commenced in South Vietnam by 1957, when Diem moved against the Viet Minh political cadres allowed there under the Geneva Accords. They fought back and formed the National Front for the Liberation of South Vietnam. Hanoi then decided to support the southern insurgency, although its assistance was only a small fraction of that given the RVN by the United States. Washington meanwhile had made its first major mistake in military policy by insisting that the Army of the Republic of Vietnam (ARVN) be a conventional force designed to stop an invasion across the demilitarized zone at the 17th parallel rather than one capable of rapid movement and able to deal with guerrillas, which is where the threat lay.

The United States firmly supported the Diem government. This was owing to U.S. domestic politics, the Cold War, the doctrine of containment, and the domino theory (the belief that if one state of Southeast Asia became communist, the others would soon surely follow). Massive amounts of U.S. aid now flowed to the RVN government, freeing it from having to answer to its own people. This aid rarely reached the countryside, where the bulk of the population lived. Diem, a Catholic in a largely Buddhist country, increasingly relied on a small coterie of advisers, including family members, who told him what he wanted to hear. His appointments, including those of senior military officers, were on the basis of loyalty rather than ability. Diem also insisted that commanders keep their own casualties low, preventing aggressive action. He also rejected American calls for meaningful reform pending establishment of full security. Touted pacification efforts such as the Strategic Hamlet Program failed to work, owing largely to vast corruption. Perhaps the greatest mistake made by Washington was not imposing strict control over how its aid was expended.

In these circumstances, the Vietnamese Communists (known as the Viet Cong, or VC) registered solid gains. They benefited from more dedicated and effective leadership and did not hesitate to employ terror tactics, including widespread assassinations. They also received an increasing flow of supplies from North Vietnam. These came by sea but primarily by means of a long land transportation network begun in 1959 and known as the Ho Chi Minh Trail, most of which was in supposedly neutral Laos.

Diem meanwhile was increasingly isolated, and his policies directly antagonized the Buddhists. With the VC apparently winning the war, President John F. Kennedy increased aid primarily in the form of advisers and helicopters and their crewmen. This probably prevented a communist victory in 1962.

ARVN generals, frustrated over Diem's conduct of the war, approached the United States about a coup, and somewhat grudgingly Washington gave the green light. Diem was toppled and he and his brother were killed, which was followed by a rapid succession of inept leaders. South Vietnam was not to enjoy a stable government until President Nguyen Van Thieu took office in 1965, but Thieu never had Diem's standing and had his own failings.

Lyndon Johnson succeeded Kennedy on the latter's assassination shortly after that of Diem. Johnson was determined not to be the first U.S. president to "lose a war." He also apparently feared possible impeachment if he attempted to withdraw from the war. Johnson greatly expanded U.S. involvement, his war powers buttressed by the August 1964 Tonkin Gulf Resolution that gave him virtual carte blanche authority. But Johnson never did take the steps necessary to produce victory. Thus, he refused to fully mobilize the country by calling up the military reserves, concerned that this would destroy his cherished domestic Great Society social programs.

Both sides escalated in 1965. Indeed, the entire war was one of gradual escalation. Sensing victory, Hanoi, which had long before assumed direction of the war, dispatched southward native northerners of its regular army, the People's Army of Vietnam (North Vietnamese Army, PAVN), along with up-to-date weaponry. Hanoi also ordered direct attacks on American forces in South Vietnam. Johnson replied with extensive bombing of North Vietnam and dispatched first marines and then increasing numbers of regular army ground troops, all under General William Westmoreland. Although Johnson had authorized the bombing of the Ho Chi Minh Trail in Laos in 1964, bombing of the DRV was always restricted in target selection, with Washington having the final word. Thus, key targets that might have been attacked in World War II, such as the cities of Hanoi and Haiphong and the dike system in North Vietnam, were off limits.

Haunted by the Korean War and the prospect of Chinese intervention, Johnson also rejected a U.S. invasion of North Vietnam. Perhaps the best option was an invasion of Laos at the demilitarized zone then holding that territory in order to cut the Ho Chi Minh Trail. To accomplish this, however, would have required a massive investment of manpower in relatively stationary positions. A sizable yet far more modest ARVN incursion into Laos in 1971 proved to be a fiasco. And as the U.S. Central Intelligence Agency concluded, few supplies were required to sustain an insurgency.

U.S. forces now assumed more of the ground combat in South Vietnam. Westmoreland was obsessed with "body count" as a measure of success. Killing sufficient numbers of the enemy to cause North Vietnam to end its support for the insurgency in South Vietnam was the key. This led to major abuses in inflated counts and the frequent inclusion of civilians as military dead. Large search-and-destroy operations ensued, but as soon as U.S. and ARVN forces cleared an area and departed, the VC and the PAVN returned. The communists could also make use of sanctuaries in Laos and Cambodia. Washington never did understand the terrible costs that Hanoi was prepared to bear in order to achieve the goals of national reunification under communist control. What would have been totally unacceptable to the American public in terms of casualties was quite tolerable for the DRV leadership. Ho remarked at one point that the DRV could absorb an unfavorable loss ratio of 10 to 1 and still win the war.

It was only after the 1968 Tet Offensive (a communist military failure but a political victory, as it turned American public opinion against the war), when Westmoreland was replaced by General Creighton Abrams, that more effective tactics were instituted. Although Abrams could not change the impact of geography or procedural constraints, he immediately did away with body count as a measure of success and instituted population control. "Clear and hold" replaced "search and destroy." Small unit tactics replaced large multidivisional operations. Abrams also stressed "One War," with pacification and improvements in South Vietnamese forces on a par with combat operations. Had this been followed from the beginning, the war might possibly have had a different outcome. Johnson also fully embraced Vietnamization, or turning more of the war over to the Vietnamese themselves, but this came too late.

In spite of growing antiwar sentiment in the United States, Johnson's successor, Richard Nixon, continued the war, determined to secure "peace with honor." With the goal of buying time for Vietnamization he also expanded the war into Cambodia. At the same time Nixon began U.S. troop withdrawals, throwing away his bargaining power with Hanoi.

The Paris Peace Accords of January 1973 brought the withdrawal of the remaining U.S. fighting forces, but the war continued. Nixon had promised Saigon that if Hanoi violated the cease-fire provisions the United States would reenter the war, that the United States would replace on a one-to-one basis any combat systems lost in fighting, and that substantial economic assistance would continue. These promises were never kept, and the collapse of RVN morale was a major factor behind the rapid communist victory campaign in the spring of 1975. Given the panoply of U.S. mistakes, it is unlikely that the war would have had any other outcome.

Spencer C. Tucker

Further Reading

Berman, Larry. *Lyndon Johnson's War: The Road to Stalemate in Vietnam.* New York: Norton, 1999.

Berman, Larry. *No Peace, No Honor: Nixon, Kissinger, and Betrayal in Vietnam.* New York: Free Press, 2001.

Brocheux, Pierre. *Ho Chi Minh: A Biography.* Cambridge: Cambridge University Press, 2007.

Carter, James M. *Inventing Vietnam: The United States and State Building, 1954–1968.* New York: Cambridge University Press, 2008.

Currey, Cecil B. *Victory at Any Cost: The Genius of Viet Nam's General Vo Nguyen Giap.* Washington, DC: Brassey's, 1997.

Dommen, Arthur J. *Conflict in Laos: The Politics of Neutralization.* Revised ed. New York: Praeger, 1971.

Dong Van Khuyen. *The Republic of Vietnam Armed Forces.* Washington, DC: U.S. Army Center of Military History, 1980.

Duiker, William J. *The Communist Road to Power in Vietnam.* 2nd ed. Boulder, CO: Westview, 1996.

Edmonds, Anthony O. *The War in Vietnam.* Westport, CT: Greenwood, 1998.

Fitzgerald, Frances. *Fire in the Lake: The Vietnamese and the Americans in Vietnam.* Boston: Little, Brown, 1972.

Halberstam, David. *The Best and the Brightest.* New York: Random House, 1972.

Herring George C. *America's Longest War: The United States and Vietnam, 1950–1975,* 3rd ed. New York: Wiley, 1979.

Hess, Gary H. *Vietnam: Explaining America's Lost War.* Malden, MA: Blackwell, 2009.

Karnow, Stanley. *Vietnam: A History.* New York: Viking, 1983.

Lind, Michael. *Vietnam, the Necessary War: A Reinterpretation of America's Most Disastrous Military Conflict.* New York: Free Press, 1999.

Logevall, Frederick. *Choosing War: The Lost Chance for Peace and Escalation of the War in Vietnam.* Berkeley: University of California Press, 1999.

Maclear, Michael. *The Ten Thousand Day War, Vietnam: 1945–1975.* New York: St. Martin's, 1981.

McMaster, H. R. *Dereliction of Duty: Johnson, McNamara, the Joint Chiefs of Staff and the Lies That Led to Vietnam.* New York: Harper Perennial, 1998.

McNamara, Robert S., and Brian VanDemark. *In Retrospect: The Tragedy and Lessons of Vietnam.* New York: Vintage Books, 1996.

O'Ballance, Edgar. *The Wars in Vietnam, 1954–1960.* New York: Hippocrene Books, 1981.

Oberdorfer, Don. *Tet! The Turning Point in the Vietnam War.* Baltimore: Johns Hopkins University Press, 2001.

Palmer, Bruce, Jr. *The 25-Year War.* Lexington: University Press of Kentucky, 1984.

Prados, John. *Vietnam: The History of an Unwinnable War, 1945–1975.* Lawrence: University Press of Kansas, 2009.

Preston, Andrew. *The War Council: McGeorge Bundy, the NSC and Vietnam.* Cambridge, MA: Harvard University Press, 2006.

Pribbenow, Merle L., and William J. Duiker. *Victory in Vietnam: The Official History of the People's Army of Vietnam.* Lawrence: University Press of Kansas, 2002.

Schandler, Herbert Y. *America in Vietnam: The War That Couldn't Be Won.* New York: Rowman and Littlefield, 2009.

Sorley, Lewis. *A Better War: The Unexamined Victories and Final Tragedy of America's Last Years in Vietnam.* Boston: Houghton Mifflin Harcourt, 1999.

Tucker, Spencer C. *Vietnam.* Lexington: University Press of Kentucky, 1999.

Tucker, Spencer C., ed. *The Encyclopedia of the Vietnam War: A Political, Social, and Military History.* 4 vols. Santa Barbara, CA: ABC-CLIO, 2011.

Willbanks, James H. *Abandoning Vietnam: How America Left and South Vietnam Lost Its War.* Lawrence: University Press of Kansas, 2004.

Zhai, Qiang. *China and the Vietnam Wars, 1950–1975.* Chapel Hill: University of North Carolina Press, 2000.

55. What Was the Significance of the Soviet-Afghan War in the Context of the Cold War?

The Soviet-Afghan War began in December 1979, when Soviet troops invaded Afghanistan to prop up the pro-Moscow communist government there and to keep the nation at least nominally within the Soviet sphere of influence. The conflict soon devolved into a decade-long insurgency. With victory elusive, the Soviets withdrew the last of their troops in early 1989, having suffered some 15,000 military deaths and another 50,000 wounded. The Soviet-Afghan War cost the Soviet treasury some $70 billion and left Afghanistan in political and economic shambles. What's more, the conflict derailed détente and contributed to a marked increase in Cold War tensions between the East and the West. Meanwhile, the Central Intelligence Agency's (CIA) backing of the anti-Russian mujahideen during the war became the largest and most successful covert operation in history. U.S. involvement also transformed Afghanistan into another Cold War battlefield similar to the Korean War in the early 1950s and the Vietnam War in the 1960s and 1970s. Afghanistan proved to be the last Cold War chess piece, however, because the Soviet Union fell within three years of withdrawing from the country. The extent to which the Soviet-Afghan War precipitated the dissolution of the Soviet Union remains an interesting topic for discussion.

In the first perspective essay, Dr. Paul Doerr evaluates U.S. involvement in the Soviet-Afghan War and questions the extent to which the financial and military aid provided by the CIA contributed to the eventual Afghan victory. He begins by addressing the initial U.S. reaction to developments in Afghanistan toward the end of the 1970s, subsequently charting the evolution of the support provided to the mujahideen by the CIA. Doerr also discusses contributions made to the Afghan resistance by other countries throughout the course of the war as well as the limitations of U.S. assistance. In the second essay, Dr. Stefan M. Brooks begins by addressing the preexisting problems affecting the Soviet Union on the eve of the Afghanistan invasion and the ways in which they were aggravated by the conflict. Brooks then examines the reasons why the Soviet occupation ultimately failed, focusing in particular on geography, tactics, and foreign assistance. He also provides a discussion of the political, economic, and social impact of the war on the Soviet Union before offering a final assessment of the extent to which the conflict contributed to the collapse of the Soviet Union in 1991.

Background Essay

Having signed a mutual friendship treaty in 1919, Afghanistan and the Soviet Union enjoyed good relations over the next several decades. Then as the rivalry with the United States intensified during the Cold War, the Soviets invested in the Afghan relationship by providing that country with extensive financial aid. Political developments in the 1970s, however, ultimately led to the outbreak of the Soviet-Afghan War in 1979.

In April 1978, Afghan president Mohammad Daud Khan was overthrown and killed during a Soviet-supported coup, known as the Saur Revolution. While Daud Khan had preferred to remain nonaligned during the Cold War, the coup brought to power a new pro-Soviet government headed by Nur Mohammad Taraki of the communist People's Democratic Party of Afghanistan (PDPA), which Taraki had helped found in the 1960s. Once in power, he closely aligned Afghanistan with the Soviet Union, signing in December 1979 the Afghanistan-Soviet Union Friendship Treaty with Soviet premier Leonid Brezhnev.

The new regime received little support from the largely anticommunist and conservative Afghan population, however. This prompted Taraki and the PDPA to initiate a ruthless campaign of purging the domestic opposition. Radical economic and social reforms were also enacted that compounded resentment among Islamic conservatives and the rural population. Armed rebel resistance soon emerged and increasingly threatened the new government. After governmental infighting led to another coup in which Taraki was overthrown and killed in September 1979, the Soviet Union decided to intervene militarily in order to maintain its influential grip on Afghanistan.

In December, the Soviets sent airborne forces to seize the Afghan capital of Kabul as thousands of Soviet ground troops crossed the Afghan border from the north by land. Having secured Kabul, the Soviets installed procommunist Babrak Karmal as the new leader of Afghanistan.

The vast assortment of insurgent groups that had resisted Taraki's regime responded to the Soviet invasion by forming the Islamic Alliance of Afghan Mujahideen, a loosely organized militia dedicated to driving out the foreign occupier. The mujahideen (freedom fighters) effectively employed guerrilla warfare to combat Soviet troops throughout the 1980s, operating from bases located in Afghanistan's remote mountainous regions and across the border in neighboring Pakistan. Many Muslim supporters of the Afghan cause characterized the conflict as a jihad (holy war), and the mujahideen thus benefited greatly from an influx of volunteers from other Muslim nations.

The Soviet Army enjoyed the advantage of better equipment, training, and organization during the conflict, and Soviet airpower posed one of the greatest challenges to the mujahideen. In particular, the Soviets deployed helicopter gunships capable of delivering immense close-support firepower, and the Afghan fighters initially lacked weapons that could be used effectively against them. Over time, military weapons, supplies, and financial aid provided by the United States, Britain, and neighboring Islamic nations were smuggled into Afghanistan from neighboring Pakistan. That support helped level the playing field and thus played an important role in the eventual Afghan victory.

Covert U.S. involvement in the war was initially quite limited, and Washington's reluctance to become extensively involved was enhanced by the congressional backlash surrounding the Iran-Contra Scandal in the mid-1980s. Thanks in part to the behind-the-scenes efforts of Texas congressman Charles Wilson, however, the Central Intelligence Agency gradually increased its level of support and eventually supplied the mujahideen with U.S. Stinger missiles. Those surface-to-air missiles proved to be an equalizing factor in the conflict by enabling the mujahideen to effectively counter Soviet airpower. Having been fought to a standstill and with the war's high financial cost and casualties, new Soviet leader Secretary-General Mikhail Gorbachev agreed to a United Nations (UN) proposal providing for a phased Soviet withdrawal. It was completed in February 1989.

The war claimed more than 40,000 Soviet and close to 2 million Afghan casualties. In addition, millions of Afghans fled the country, most of them into Pakistan. Afghanistan's infrastructure was left in ruins, and the government in place at the end of the war, headed by Soviet-installed president Mohammad Najibullah, was largely ineffective. Najibullah was overthrown in April 1992, and Afghanistan subsequently slid into civil war as rival factions vied for control of the government during the next several years. A fundamentalist militia known as the Taliban, led by former mujahideen commander Mohammed Omar, ultimately rose to power after capturing Kabul in September 1996. The Taliban established a new regime strictly based on sharia (Islamic law).

An Afghan mujahid demonstrates the firing of a surface-to-air missile in 1988. The United States supported the Afghan resistance against the Soviets, who had occupied Afghanistan. U.S. Stinger surface-to-air missiles proved an important weapon against the Soviet helicopter gunships. (U.S. Department of Defense)

The rise of the Taliban did not bring stability to the scarred nation, however. While many war-weary civilians supported the Taliban, violent resistance to the new regime remained, especially in the north. There, the Northern Alliance opposition militias (consisting of many former mujahideen fighters) had long resisted the domination of the Pashtuns, who formed the core of the Taliban, and continued armed resistance against them. Within the international community, only Pakistan, Saudi Arabia, and the United Arab Emirates established diplomatic links with the Taliban government.

Many scholars have cited the unpopular Soviet-Afghan War as an underlying issue that contributed to the collapse of the Soviet Union in December 1991. Economic problems in the Soviet Union were compounded by the fact that the government spent approximately $80 billion on the failed occupation, and the unpopular war also traumatized the Russian national psyche, a development that helped facilitate the acceptance of internal reform measures instigated by Gorbachev toward the end of the decade.

Ironically, some of the Islamic rebels who fought the Soviets with U.S. aid later became sworn enemies of the United States, as evidenced by Osama bin Laden's orchestration of the crippling terrorist attacks of September 11, 2001. Since the Taliban harbored bin Laden and allowed terrorist training camps to operate in Afghanistan and refused to take action against Al-Qaeda, the United States began bombing Taliban and Al-Qaeda targets in the country on October 7, 2001, followed by the insertion of U.S. ground forces. U.S. and Northern Alliance forces quickly took control of much of the country, and in December UN-sponsored talks led to the formation of a new interim government led by Hamid Karzai. A major milestone was reached on October 9, 2004, when Afghanistan's first-ever direct presidential election was held. Despite that progress, the Taliban continued to fight coalition forces in Afghanistan.

Gregory Wolf

Perspective Essay 1. The United States Helped Defeat the Soviets

On December 24, 1979, the Soviet Red Army invaded Afghanistan to prop up a crumbling communist regime. The U.S. Central Intelligence Agency (CIA) had already been providing assistance to the mujahideen, the anticommunist rebels in Afghanistan. During the next 10 years until the Soviet withdrawal from Afghanistan in 1989, the CIA extended at least $2 billion in aid to the mujahideen, with some estimates placing the total as high as $3 billion. How significant was the CIA's role in the eventual Afghan victory?

The armed coup d'état that brought the Afghan communist party, known as the People's Democratic Party of Afghanistan (PDPA), to power in April 1978 was an unwelcome surprise to the West. But the PDPA's heavy-handed policies soon triggered a nationwide revolt. We now know that the CIA began extending assistance to the mujahideen six months prior to the Soviet invasion. With the Soviet Red Army soon bogged down in a guerrilla war against the mujahideen, some in Washington, especially President Jimmy Carter's national security adviser Zbigniew Brzezinski, saw an ideal opportunity to trap the Soviet Union in a quagmire similar to that of the United States in the Vietnam War.

After Ronald Reagan won the presidential election of 1980, assistance to the mujahideen continued. Much of the aid took the form of military equipment, including rifles, antitank grenade launchers, heavy machine guns, mortars, antiaircraft guns, and multiple rocket launchers, but humanitarian assistance was also provided. Initially the CIA limited its support out of fear that the Soviets might retaliate against Pakistan, which distributed material and provided sanctuary to the mujahideen. By 1985 such fears appeared groundless, and the amount of assistance was substantially increased. The biggest step was taken in 1986, when the CIA began shipping Stinger surface-to-air missiles to the mujahideen and provided training on how to operate them. In addition to the United States and Pakistan, Israel, Egypt, China, the United Kingdom, and especially Saudi Arabia all provided the group with financial backing. Thousands from across the Islamic world volunteered to fight alongside the mujahideen.

The rallying of international support was important for mujahideen morale and convinced the Afghan people that they were not alone in resisting Soviet domination. The weapons provided by the CIA gave the mujahideen the combat capability to carry on the fight. Humanitarian assistance provided shelter for Afghan refugees and medical aid for the wounded, while financial assistance proved important as well.

Many observers have pointed to the Stinger missiles as a crucial contribution to the mujahideen war effort. By 1986, the mujahideen fighters were under great pressure from the Soviet Red Army and Afghan government forces. Soviet aerial supremacy threatened to overwhelm them. Soviet jet fighters and helicopter gunships pounded the mujahideen with impunity. In addition, helicopter transports provided mobility and logistical support to Soviet and progovernment ground forces. The introduction of Stinger missiles jeopardized Soviet aerial supremacy. To avoid being shot down, Soviet aircraft had to fly above the range of the Stinger missiles, which reduced their bombing accuracy considerably. The Stinger missiles gave the mujahideen a fighting chance against Soviet helicopters.

Were there limitations to CIA assistance? Despite CIA urgings, the mujahideen remained a deeply divided movement split into seven major groups and many smaller ones. A national leader for the mujahideen never really emerged, and the resistance groups bickered constantly among themselves. The CIA chose Pakistan's Inter-Services Intelligence (ISI) agency to distribute the aid, but the ISI distributed the aid to groups that it felt would advance Pakistan's influence in Afghanistan after the war ended. Some of the most effective Afghan resistance groups, such as Shah Ahmed Massoud's fighters in the Panjshir Valley, complained bitterly that they saw scarcely any CIA aid simply because they were not interested in doing the bidding of the ISI. Many of the Stinger missiles distributed to the mujahideen were never recovered after the war, despite the offer of substantial CIA cash rewards for their return.

In terms of military effectiveness, it is perhaps worth remembering that despite all the aid, the mujahideen never launched a nationwide offensive, never captured a major urban center, and never defeated a major Soviet offensive. When the Soviets withdrew in 1989, they did so for political reasons to smooth diplomatic relations with the West and China, not because the military situation in Afghanistan had taken a turn for the worse.

On the other hand, one could say about the mujahideen in Afghanistan the same thing that has been said about the communists in Vietnam: they lost every battle but still ended up winning the war. CIA assistance bolstered the mujahideen resistance, kept it going, contributed to the public's perception in the Soviet Union that the war could not be won, and therefore led to the Soviet decision to withdraw. Finally, we should remember that all the aid in the world would not have mattered had the Afghan people not made the decision to resist and keep fighting through impossibly difficult times. Although exact numbers are unknown, the Soviet invasion of Afghanistan may have cost over 1 million Afghan lives, this in addition to somewhere between 5 million and 7 million refugees out of a prewar population of only 15 million, a sobering reminder of the cost of war.

After the Soviets departed Afghanistan in 1989, the U.S. government and the CIA lost all interest in Afghanistan. Mujahideen infighting and factionalism after the final defeat of the PDPA in 1992 led to a brutal civil war that saw the Taliban take power in 1996. The Taliban in turn invited Osama bin Laden and his fundamentalist anti-Western Al-Qaeda terrorist organization to set up bases in Afghanistan, with dire consequences for the United States.

Paul Doerr

Perspective Essay 2. Precipitating the Collapse of the Soviet Union

The Soviet invasion of Afghanistan in 1979 not only failed in its objective to stabilize a friendly communist regime in that country and secure the Soviet Union's south-southwestern borders against Islamic fundamentalism but also contributed to, if not accelerated, the existing decline in Soviet economic and military power and prestige, ultimately culminating in the collapse of the Soviet Union itself in 1991, thus bringing an end to the Cold War.

Throughout the 1970s and early 1980s, the Soviet Union seemed to be at the height of its power and prestige as it eagerly exploited and sought to fill the power vacuum in the world following the U.S. defeat and withdrawal from South Vietnam. Owing to the secretive and repressive nature of its political infrastructure and, admittedly, its powerful and intimidating military, the Soviet government was nonetheless able to conceal the depth of its problems, which included a rapidly declining economy and standard of living, a scarcity of consumer goods, an increasingly corrupt and ineffective Communist Party, and a disenchanted population. Yet at the same time, the Soviet government maintained a massive military that may have consumed as much as one quarter of its shrinking gross domestic product.

It was in this environment of economic, political, and social malaise that the Soviet Union fatefully invaded Afghanistan and became entangled in a 10-year quagmire that claimed the lives of some 15,000 Soviet soldiers, injured and permanently maimed tens of thousands of others, and drained its economy, all while struggling to compete with the United States in a renewed arms race following President Ronald Reagan's massive military buildup to challenge the Soviet Union. By draining or bleeding the Soviet Union of scarce resources in a conflict it failed to win, Afghanistan has been called "the Soviet Union's Vietnam" or, in the words of a title of a book on this conflict, "The Bear Trap"—the bear being the symbol of Russia.

The 10-year war in Afghanistan (1979–1989) aggravated the deep economic, political, and social problems plaguing the Soviet Union. The Soviet Union proved unable to achieve its stated goals for invading Afghanistan for a variety of reasons, including the unfamiliarity of the Soviet military with fighting in rugged and treacherous mountainous terrain, its utter inexperience in counterinsurgency warfare, and the lack of even a counterinsurgency plan. Perhaps reflective of the deep economic problems plaguing the Soviet Union, no more than 100,000 troops were ever deployed to Afghanistan—an insufficient force to even try to control most of the country, which, not surprisingly, the Soviets were never able to do.

The insurrection or insurgency the Soviets faced consisted of Afghan and foreign Muslim, mostly Arab, guerrillas adept at ambush, sabotage, and hit-and-run tactics, thereby denying the Soviet Army the ability to bring to bear its superior firepower and wipe out the guerrillas in open and head-on battles. The mobility of the guerrillas and their ability to blend in and hide from Soviet forces by not only seeking shelter and refuge in the many deep caves of the mountains of Afghanistan but also among the villages and towns of the local population—many if not most of whom supported the guerrillas—prevented the Soviets from ever eliminating or marginalizing the guerrilla forces. Owing to the geography and inaccessibility by land, Soviet tanks proved to be of limited use in neutralizing the guerrillas such that the Soviets relied heavily on artillery and airpower, particularly helicopters. Nonetheless, the geography undermined even the effectiveness of artillery and helicopters.

Moreover, the United States armed the Afghan guerrillas with surface-to-air missiles (SAMs) that proved highly effective in shooting down hundreds of Soviet aircraft and helicopters. In addition, the bulk of the Soviet troops deployed to Afghanistan were draftees and therefore of limited if not poor quality and suffering from low morale, and their frequent rotation out of Afghanistan—some 600,000 troops served in Afghanistan, but never more than around 100,000 were ever deployed in the country at any one time during the 10-year war—resulted in a military force that was never really able to act on their battlefield combat experience. Finally, the combination of the lack of Soviet experience in waging a counterinsurgency war and the absence of a counterinsurgency strategy only further embittered the local population and further legitimized the insurrection against the Soviet Union; indeed, because conventional or traditional military tactics are of limited utility in combating a guerrilla force, Soviet military operations often inflicted significant casualties among the local population, including damaging and destroying local villages and towns.

A 1985 report by the Central Intelligence Agency (CIA) titled "The Soviet Invasion of Afghanistan," declassified in 1999, concludes that "the Soviets have been bogged down in a guerrilla war of increasing intensity . . . [and] have had little success in reducing the insurgency or winning acceptance by the Afghan people, and the Afghan resistance continues to grow stronger and to command widespread popular support." Also discussed is the heavy toll of the war on the Soviet military in terms of deaths and injuries and also heavy equipment losses, including the destruction of over 600 Soviet helicopters and aircraft by SAMs, along with thousands of armored vehicles and trucks. The CIA report shockingly revealed that poor medical care in the field made the Soviet killed-to-wounded ratio of one death for every two wounded comparable to the U.S. experience in World War II. Owing to an inadequate water supply, poor medical care, and unsanitary living conditions, it is revealed that Soviet troops suffered from a high incidence of disease, estimated to be three times the number of combat casualties sustained. The CIA report also offers some evidence of public Soviet opposition to the war. First, the lack of media coverage in the government-controlled press regarding casualties indicates that the regime was sensitive to the effect that such reporting would have on the population. Second, the government received thousands of letters from citizens complaining about the casualties and demanding an explanation of Soviet policy in Afghanistan. Finally, the same report also revealed that a military post or commissariat in Kazan, 450 kilometers east of Moscow, was burned by relatives of dead Soviet soldiers, and in 1983 a Moscow radio announcer, Vladimir Danchev, altered official news broadcasts to denounce the war in Afghanistan.

Despite Soviet military opposition to invading Afghanistan, which included an accurate prediction that deploying approximately 100,000 troops would be insufficient to secure the factional and unpopular Marxist People's Democratic Party of Afghanistan, the Soviet-Afghan War delegitimized not only the Communist Party of the Soviet Union (CPSU) but also the Soviet military, which came to be viewed as an invader and an aggressor, thereby demoralizing it and undermining its role as a source of national pride and unity. Indeed, both the CPSU and the Soviet military were marginalized by Soviet society, as were the veterans of the war. The famed political dissident Andrei Sakharov, who seized on the unpopularity of the war and the atrocities committed by the Soviet military to denounce the war, was exiled to Gorky.

While the Soviet Union in the 1970s and early 1980s had seemed to the United States and the world quite strong and resilient and while the 1979 invasion of Afghanistan was viewed at the time as a sign of Soviet power and confidence, the quagmire that the Soviet Union quickly found itself in not only undermined these impressions, thereby increasing the resolve and morale of the United States, but also made worse the already deep economic, political, and social problems plaguing the Soviet Union. In so doing, the Soviet-Afghan War precipitated the decline and ultimately the collapse of the Soviet Union in 1991.

Stefan M. Brooks

Further Reading

Alexiev, Alex. *The United States and the War in Afghanistan.* Santa Monica, CA: Rand, 1988.

Allen, Robert, C. "The Rise and Decline of the Soviet Economy." *Canadian Journal of Economics* 34(1) (November 2001): 859–881.

Arnold, Antony. *The Fateful Pebble: Afghanistan's Role in the Fall of the Soviet Empire.* Novato, CA: Presidio, 1993.

Barfield, Thomas. *Afghanistan.* Princeton, NJ: Princeton University Press, 2010.

Bhargava, G. *South Asian Security after Afghanistan.* Lexington, MA: Lexington Books, 1983.

Borovik, Artyom. *The Hidden War: A Russian Journalist's Account of the Soviet War in Afghanistan.* New York: Grove, 2001.

Bradsher, Henry S. *Afghan Communism and Soviet Intervention.* Oxford: Oxford University Press, 2000.

Braithwaite, Rodric. *Afgansty: The Russians in Afghanistan, 1979–89.* New York: Oxford University Press, 2011.

Brown, Archie. *The Gorbachev Factor.* Oxford: Oxford University Press, 1997.

Brzezinski, Zbigniew. *The Grand Failure. The Birth and Death of Communism in the 20th Century.* New York: Scribner, 1989.

Coll, Steve. *Ghost Wars: The Secret History of the CIA, Afghanistan, and Bin Laden, from the Soviet Invasion to September 10, 2001.* New York: Penguin, 2004.

Cook, Linda J. "Brezhnev's 'Social Contract' and Gorbachev's Reforms." *Soviet Studies* 44(1) (1992): 37–56.

Faringdon, Hugh. *Strategic Geography.* London: Routledge, 1989.

Galeotti, Mark. *Afghanistan: The Soviet Union's Last War.* London: Frank Cass, 1995.

Galeotti, Mark. *Gorbachev and His Revolution.* New York: St. Martin's, 1997.

Goldberg, David, and Paul Marantz. *The Decline of the Soviet Union and the Transformation of the Middle East.* Boulder, CO: Westview, 1994.

Gorbachev, Mikhail. *Perestroika: New Thinking for Our Country and the World.* New York: Harper and Row, 1987.

Gorodetsky, Gabriel, ed. *Soviet Foreign Policy, 1917–1991.* London: Frank Cass, 1994.

Grau, Lester W. *The Soviet-Afghan War: How a Superpower Fought and Lost.* Lawrence: University Press of Kansas Press, 2002.

Grau, Lester W., ed. *Bear Went over the Mountains: Soviet Combat Tactics in Afghanistan.* Darby, PA: Diane Publishing, 1996.

Harasymiw, Bohdan. "The CPSU in Transition from Brezhnev to Gorbachev." *Canadian Journal of Political Science* 21(2) (June 1988): 249–266.

Hauner, Milan, and Robert L. Canfield, eds. *Afghanistan and the Soviet Union; Collision and Transformation.* Boulder, CO: Westview, 1989.

Hyman, Anthony. *Afghanistan under Soviet Domination, 1964–91.* 3rd ed. Houndmills, UK: Macmillan Academic and Professional, 1992.

Jalali, Ali Ahmad. *Afghan Guerilla Tactics: In the Words of Mujahideen Fighters.* Osceola, WI: Zenith, 2001.

Laqueur, Walter. *The Dream That Failed: Reflections of the Soviet Union.* New York: Oxford University Press, 1996.

Laqueur, Walter. *The Long Road to Freedom: Russia and Glasnost.* New York: Collier Books, 1989.

MacKenzie, David. *From Messianism to Collapse: Soviet Foreign Policy, 1917–1991.* Fort Worth, TX: Harcourt Brace, 1994.

Maley, William. *The Afghanistan Wars.* Basingstoke, UK: Palgrave Macmillan, 2002.

Odom, William E. *The Collapse of the Soviet Military.* New Haven, CT: Yale University Press, 1998.

Reuveny, Rafael, and Aseem Prakash. "The Afghan War and the Breakdown of the Soviet Union." *Review of International Studies* 25 (1999): 693–708.

Riasanovsky, Nicholas V. *A History of Russia.* 6th ed. New York: Oxford University Press, 2000.

The Russian General Staff. *The Soviet-Afghan War: How A Superpower Fought and Lost.* Edited and translated by Lester W. Grau and Michael A. Gress. Lawrence: University Press of Kansas, 2002.

Suny, Ronald Grigor. *The Soviet Experiment: Russia, the USSR, and the Successor States.* Oxford: Oxford University Press, 1998.

United States Central Intelligence Agency, Directorate of Intelligence. *At Cold War's End: U.S. Intelligence on the Soviet Union and Eastern Europe, 1989–1991.* Edited by Benjamin B. Fischer. Reston, VA: Central Intelligence Agency, 1999.

Valenta, Jiri, and Frank Cibulka. *Gorbachev's New Thinking and Third World Conflicts.* New Brunswick, NJ: Transaction Publishers, 1990.

Yousaf, Mohammed, and Mark Adkin. *The Bear Trap.* South Yorkshire, UK: Pen and Sword Books, 2002.

56. Were Ronald Reagan's Policies Responsible for the Collapse of the Soviet Union and the End of the Cold War?

After the end of World War II, the United States and the Soviet Union became powerful adversaries. For more than 40 years, the two nations engaged in the Cold War that encompassed virtually every region of the world. The two superpowers jockeyed for dominance on the world stage with diplomacy, bluster, and strategic maneuvering. To ensure their continued power, both nations built up huge nuclear arsenals and engaged in a series of proxy wars. By 1985 when the reform-minded Mikhail Gorbachev assumed leadership of the Soviet Union, thousands of nuclear warheads were spread around the globe, capable of wiping out human life on Earth in a matter of minutes. But by 1990—just a year after President Ronald Reagan left office—the Soviet Union was nearing collapse. In December 1991, the Soviet Union dissolved peacefully. The world was stunned: the Cold War was over. How did the world situation shift so dramatically in little more than half a decade? And what role did the Reagan administration play in the changes? Many historians are in disagreement as to what set of events were critical in ending the Cold War and who, if anyone specifically, was responsible for the demise of the Soviet Union. Since 1991, a clear political divide has emerged in this argument. Generally, more liberal historians have seen the collapse as inevitable, while conservatives see Reagan's administration as the vital factor in the demise of the Soviet Union.

In the first perspective essay, Dr. Lee W. Eysturlid argues that Reagan's hard-line stance toward the Soviets in the early 1980s caused them to hasten their own demise. Eysturlid believes that Reagan's repudiation of "peaceful coexistence" and his decision to increase military spending forced the Soviets into an arms race they could neither afford nor win. Eysturlid also suggests that it was Reagan's policies that prompted the appointment of Gorbachev—a relative unknown—as head of the Communist Party of the Soviet Union in 1985. By contrast, Dr. Spencer C. Tucker asserts that the collapse of the Soviet Union was inevitable and would have occurred independently of the Reagan administration. Tucker cites a myriad of causes, including the Soviets' command economy, corruption, inability to forge a unified Soviet state, discouragement of initiative and innovation (particularly in the fields of science and technology), and the ongoing war in Afghanistan. Tucker also dismisses the claim that Gorbachev's policies brought about the Soviet Union's demise as shortsighted, arguing that the collapse would have happened regardless—although perhaps years later and amid much greater violence.

Background Essay

With the end of World War II, the shaky alliance between the West and the Soviet Union quickly dissolved. As what former British prime minister Winston Churchill described as an "Iron Curtain" fell across Eastern Europe, the United States and the Soviet Union found themselves opponents in a conflict that would last for almost half a century. Much of the tension between the two superpowers was ideological. U.S. containment policy, developed by George F. Kennan of the State Department in the late 1940s, demanded that the country take actions to halt the spread of communism and check its international influence. At the same time, Soviet leader Joseph Stalin took a hostile stance toward capitalism and the West. Even after Nikita Khrushchev, Stalin's successor, adopted the principle of peaceful coexistence between the communist and capitalist systems, tensions remained.

Jockeying for political and strategic advantage only widened the rift between the two nations. Shortly after the end of World War II, two mutual defense organizations—the North Atlantic Treaty Organization and the Warsaw Pact—were created in order to safeguard the superpowers' spheres of influence. Throughout the 1950s and 1960s, both countries engaged in a massive competitive buildup of nuclear weapons and delivery systems and engaged in a number of military actions around the world in order to advance their political and economic agendas. The nuclear arms race was slowed but not stopped during the 1970s with the evolution of détente and the signing of the Strategic Arms Limitation Treaty (SALT) I Interim Agreement and the Anti-Ballistic Missile Treaty in 1972 and SALT II in 1979.

When Republican president Ronald Reagan took office in January 1981, he ended the decade-long period of détente by accelerating a U.S. military buildup. During his first five years as president, the defense budget rose by 119 percent. On March 23, 1983, Reagan unveiled his Strategic Defense Initiative (SDI), popularly known as "Star Wars," an extremely expensive defense system that would use such high-tech components as lasers stationed on satellites with the goal of making the United States invulnerable to missiles launched by the Soviet Union. Although never fully completed or launched, the SDI, which was projected to cost from hundreds of billions of dollars to as much as $1 trillion, remained an important aspect of Reagan's defense strategy. Reagan administration officials hoped that this buildup in military force would oblige the Soviet Union to do the same, thereby weakening the already strained Soviet economy.

Reagan's strategy also involved using direct economic pressure on the Soviet Union. In 1982 and 1983, he worked to prevent the Soviets from receiving Western trade, loans, and technological aid. He also used dramatic rhetoric to create support for his policies within the United States, labeling the Soviet Union an "evil empire" in the course of a speech before the British Parliament on June 8, 1982. Reagan projected an eternally optimistic view regarding the eventual downfall of the Soviet Union and the triumph of the American way of life. Less than a year after identifying the Soviet Union as an "evil empire," on March 8, 1983, Reagan confidently stated, "Let us pray for the salvation of all of those who live in that totalitarian darkness—pray they will discover the joy of knowing God. . . . I believe that communism is another sad, bizarre chapter in human history whose last pages even now are being written."

Yet despite his public image as a strident anticommunist who would not hesitate to use force when dealing with the Soviet Union, Reagan also exhibited a cautious, practical side. Perhaps intending to use the negative effect that the military buildup was having on the Soviet economy as leverage, Reagan approached the Soviets regarding arms limitation talks in September 1984. Reagan suggested that all major ongoing negotiations, which had stalled for years, be combined into one package, a proposal the Soviet leadership accepted. A major breakthrough came on December 8, 1987, when Reagan and Secretary-General Gorbachev signed the Intermediate-Range Nuclear Forces (INF) Treaty. The INF Treaty was the first of its kind, banning completely all conventional and nuclear ground-launched cruise and ballistic missiles with a range of 300 to 3,400 miles.

On the other side of the globe, the situation in the Soviet Union was steadily deteriorating. During the course of the Cold War, a number of domestic economic and social problems led to tumultuous conditions within the nation. Although the state-run command economy could produce impressive weaponry, aircraft, and satellites, it did not provide the average citizen with a variety of high-quality consumer products. Shortages and rationing of even the most basic goods, such as meat and fresh produce, were not uncommon. In addition to these economic hardships, the Soviet Union experienced significant class stratification, racism, and a floundering sense of national identity. Discontent grew among the Soviet citizenry, who were generally powerless to affect the policies of their government. These internal problems were compounded by extensive censorship and a corrupt and inefficient bureaucracy.

U.S. president Ronald Reagan, right, shakes hands with Soviet leader Mikhail Gorbachev after the two leaders signed the Intermediate-Range Nuclear Forces Treaty to eliminate intermediate-range missiles during a ceremony at the White House in Washington, D.C., on December 8, 1987. (AP Photo/Bob Daugherty)

By the 1980s, the Soviet Union was also suffering as a result of its international policies. Supporting communist actions around the world and a war in Afghanistan that would last the entire decade funneled money away from domestic programs. Voices of dissent within the Soviet Union and in Eastern Europe grew louder. Gorbachev, who came to power in 1985, sought to reform and thereby strengthen certain aspects of the Soviet system. His policies of glasnost (openness) and perestroika (restructuring) included steps toward decentralization, increases in freedom of speech and dissent, and the allowance of private ownership and foreign investment in the Soviet Union. These measures, however, were too little, too late. In 1989 the government of East Germany fell, and along with it the Berlin Wall tumbled. The two Germanies were formally reunited in October 1990.

Earlier that year several Soviet states, including Lithuania and Estonia, declared independence from the Soviet Union. An August 1991 coup against Gorbachev was foiled (largely with the support of Boris Yeltsin), but Gorbachev's power was now gone. In December 1991, the Commonwealth of Independent States replaced the Union of Soviet Socialist Republics. Gorbachev resigned as president on December 25, and by December 31 the Soviet Union was officially dissolved, bringing the Cold War to an end.

Maxine Taylor

Perspective Essay 1. Reagan's Policies Hastened the Soviet Collapse

U.S. president Ronald Reagan's policies and tough diplomatic stance were key factors in causing the Soviet Union—through its spending and adoption of glasnost—to hasten its own collapse. In 1981 Reagan, addressing an audience at Notre Dame University, stated that "The West won't contain communism. It will transcend communism. It will dismiss it as some bizarre chapter in human history whose last pages are even now being written." This prophetic assertion was dismissed at the time as wishful thinking at best, and many felt that Reagan was undermining the current status quo of a stagnant, détente-oriented world. But within 10 years the Soviet Union, which in 1981 appeared to be winning the Cold War, broke apart.

When Reagan became president, he inherited a significantly compromised situation. The old notion of parity between the Soviet Union and the United States had been slowly collapsing under pressure from without and from within. The Brezhnev Doctrine, the idea that once a state entered into the Soviet sphere it would remain there, even if by force, had seen Ethiopia, Kampuchea, Angola, Mozambique, Yemen, Grenada, Nicaragua, and Afghanistan fall to communist insurgencies between 1974 and 1980. Soviet military spending had exceeded 20 percent of gross domestic product, and the Russians and the Warsaw Pact countries had moved ahead of the West in numbers of both conventional and nuclear weapons. Internally, America was suffering from what historian Paul Johnson has labeled a serious effort at "national suicide." The U.S. economy, suffering from stagflation, or the double burden of high unemployment and soaring inflation, had stalled. President Jimmy Carter's administration talked of shaken American self-confidence and the need for citizens to expect less in the future.

Much to the shock of liberals, conservatives, and the Soviet leadership, Reagan immediately charted a different course than that of his predecessor. He made it clear that he felt that the policy of détente was finished and that the United States would reassert itself with a substantial arms buildup, both in conventional and nuclear weapons. At the same time, he also managed to gain substantial tax cuts and deregulation that, following a brief recession, saw the revival of the U.S. economy.

Reagan initiated a $1.5 trillion military spending program, the largest ever in American peacetime history. His intention was clearly to draw the Soviets into an arms race that he was certain they could not match, let alone win. This paved the way for the advent of a high-tech weapons arsenal still in use today, including the M-1 tank, stealth fighters, and laser-guided bombs.

Concerning nuclear arms, Reagan found allies in the European leadership of the United Kingdom (Margaret Thatcher) and West Germany (Helmut Kohl) that resulted in a new generation of nuclear weapons for forward deployment. Reagan secured approval for the placement of 108 Pershing II and 404 Tomahawk cruise missiles in Europe to counter Soviet medium-range SS-20s. At the same time, Reagan dropped the moribund Strategic Arms Limitation Talks idea for a new "zero option" Strategic Arms Reduction Treaty. Combined with his March 1983 announcement of a new antimissile program called the Strategic Defense Initiative (SDI), the idea of reducing nuclear weapons became an option for the first time.

Soviet leaders found themselves facing an economic crisis that originated from a failed economic system and overextended military spending. At the same time they faced the Reagan Doctrine, as it came to be called, which asserted that the United States would support anticommunist movements worldwide with money and weapons. Reagan also worked with the Vatican and the international branch of the AFL-CIO to support the Polish trade union Solidarity. Finally, Reagan ordered the surprise invasion of Grenada in October 1983, where the democratically elected government had been overthrown by communist insurgents aided by Cuba. This military operation, a successful assertion of U.S. willingness to use force, started the decline of communist guerrilla movements that was to continue throughout the 1980s.

That the Soviets saw what they were up against is clear. Experienced diplomat Andrei Gromyko stated that "behind all of this [military buildup] lies the clear calculation that the USSR will exhaust its material resources and therefore will be forced to surrender." Yuri Andropov, secretary-general when the SDI was announced, stated that the program was intended as "a bid to disarm the Soviet Union." By 1985 the normally ultraconservative Soviet leadership, unable to sustain its economy and an arms buildup, chose a relative unknown, Mikhail Gorbachev, to head the government.

It soon became clear to Reagan that this shift in leadership gave him someone he could deal with, and the two leaders entered into a series of meetings that culminated in agreements for serious reductions in nuclear weapons. This was only possible because the Soviets understood that they could no longer count on weak Western leadership. Gorbachev, fighting a losing Vietnam-style war in Afghanistan and faced with a failed economy and demand for reform, had little choice but to cooperate. These reforms, given the general title "glasnost," would lead in 1989 and 1991 to the collapse of the Soviet Union, Gorbachev's removal from power, the end of the Soviet domination of Eastern Europe, and the end of the Cold War.

Certainly, Reagan's policies were not the only reason for the demise of the Soviet Union and the end of the Cold War. Further, the successes came at the cost of soaring federal deficits and intense bitterness between liberals and conservatives. Yet it is also clear that Reagan's leadership played an absolutely key role in resurrecting U.S. confidence and power while fatally undermining the Soviet Union.

Lee W. Eysturlid

Perspective Essay 2. Soviet Collapse Was Inevitable

While the massive defense buildup of Ronald Reagan's administration undoubtedly had an influence, it was not the principal reason for the 1991 collapse of the Soviet Union and its empire and thus the end of the Cold War. Indeed, the Soviet Union had been tottering toward collapse for some time, although U.S. officials and the military had failed to recognize the signs.

One factor was certainly the vast corruption and inefficiency of the Soviet economy. The Soviet Union had a command economy, in which the government bureaucracy determined exactly what and how much of it would be produced. The West, on the other hand, had a demand economy, driven by consumers. The latter produced far better goods. If its leadership threw considerable resources at a problem, the Soviet Union could produce spectacular successes, as with some of its military hardware or in 1957 with Sputnik, the first satellite placed in Earth's orbit. But even in the space race, the Soviets were soon far outdistanced by the United States.

Most of what the Soviets produced in their state-run factories, particularly in the area of consumer goods, was shoddy. Health care was declining, and the average life span was actually decreasing, not increasing as in the West (the Soviet Union was the only developing nation where this was occurring). Despite government efforts to keep the truth from the Soviet people, the average citizen knew that life was far better in the West.

Far from a classless society, the Soviet Union was as riven by economic division as under the czars. The elite lived very well, while the average citizen found it difficult to get by. Corruption was rampant, and bribes were a way of life. The judiciary was not independent but instead was an arm of the government charged with carrying out its policies. The lack of free flow of ideas and information was part of the problem. The Soviet leadership was afraid of the truth and sought to control this area, and yet it impacted every aspect of national life, including the economy. Cybernetics had become vital, yet in 1985 the Soviet Union had an estimated 50,000 personal computers, while in the United States there were 40 million.

Another factor was the failure of the Soviet Union to create a unified nation. Despite the claim of a classless society free of discrimination, ethnic Russians predominated and controlled key government and military posts. There was rampant discrimination against minorities, who had been drifting back into their national republics. These minorities, especially in Central Asia, had higher birth rates than the Russians, who were about to become a minority within the union. Prescient sociologists were pointing out these democratic trends decades before the end of the Cold War.

Another factor was certainly the restlessness of the Soviet empire. On several important occasions—East Germany in 1953, Hungary in 1956, Czechoslovakia in 1968, and Poland in 1981—the Central and East European states had demonstrated their desire for full independence. Perhaps only Bulgaria really desired close ties with the Soviet Union at the end of World War II. The rest of the empire would bolt, given the opportunity.

Finally, there was above all Mikhail Gorbachev, the leader of the Soviet Union from 1985 to 1991. Today, many Russians blame him for the dramatic loss of national power. This is unfair, for it was inevitable. Thanks to Gorbachev, the dissolution of Soviet power was a peaceful process. True, he would have to worry about keeping the Soviet Union strong militarily (and, not incidentally, keep an eye on the powerful military establishment should it seek to take power), but much more important was the need to modernize the economy and make communism actually work. Gorbachev was one of the few who truly believed in the communist ideal. He was also fully aware of the need to reform his nation economically. This was not only because he genuinely wanted to improve the lot of the Soviet people but also because he knew that the Soviet Union could not continue to fall further and further behind the West and hope to compete. He was undoubtedly the best-informed leader in the history of the Soviet Union.

Gorbachev at first tried to impose discipline on his people in an effort to make the system really work for their benefit as it was supposed to. When that failed, he introduced perestroika in order to make the Soviet bureaucracy accountable and modernize the economy. When the Soviet bureaucrats, virtually all of whom had a vested interest in maintaining the status quo, balked at Gorbachev's reforms, he responded with glasnost. This meant open criticism and democratization but also led to full revelations that the Soviet Union was really the emperor with no clothes. And once the Soviet people were allowed full freedom of expression, many turned their backs on failed communism. Gorbachev, in essence, had failed. The hole he opened became a massive breach, and he could not control the ensuing rushing torrent.

Gorbachev's foreign policy was also revolutionary, for he sought a new international era based on cooperation, rather than competition, with the West. If the cost of keeping up with the Americans militarily was a burden, so too was the bleeding wound of the senseless war in Afghanistan. What had begun in 1979 as an effort to maintain a communist regime became a quagmire that threatened to endure indefinitely with no resolution. The economic and human costs of this effort were heavy. Gorbachev withdrew Soviet forces in 1989, and he also determined that the Soviet Union could not afford to prop up communist regimes elsewhere in the world, from Vietnam to Cuba to Eastern Europe. The natural consequence of the withdrawal of Soviet aid, coupled with Gorbachev's reluctance to use force to maintain communism, led to the inevitable collapse of communism in Eastern and Central Europe. By November 1989, the Berlin Wall had been toppled.

Without Gorbachev, the Soviet Union would not have collapsed in 1990. If the members of the Politburo had chosen a communist hard-liner or if the August 1991 coup against Gorbachev had succeeded, there is little doubt that increased defense spending or no, communism would have continued for at least another decade or so, until the same factors of economic inefficiency and demographics simply overwhelmed it. Probably the end would have come violently in a breakup of the member republics. Thanks to Mikhail Gorbachev, what was inevitable occurred earlier and was peaceful.

Spencer C. Tucker

Further Reading

Ball, S. J. *The Cold War: An International History, 1947–1991*. London: Hodder, 1997.

Beschloss, Michael R., and Strobe Talbott. *At the Highest Levels: The Inside Story of the End of the Cold War*. Boston: Little, Brown, 1993.

Blum, William. *Rogue State: A Guide to the World's Only Superpower*. Monroe, ME: Common Courage, 2005.

Brzezinski, Zbigniew K. *The Grand Failure: The Birth and Death of Communism in the Twentieth Century*. New York: Macmillan, 1989.

Brzezinski, Zbigniew K. *Ideology and Power in Soviet Politics.* Westport, CT: Greenwood, 1976.

Crockett, Richard. *The Fifty Years' War: The United States and the Soviet Union in World Politics, 1941–1991.* New York: Routledge, 1996.

D'Encausse, Hélène Carrère. *Decline of an Empire: The Soviet Socialist Republics in Revolt.* Translated by Martin Sokolinski and Henry A. La Farge. New York: Newsweek Books, 1979.

Diggins, John Patrick. *Ronald Reagan: Fate, Freedom and the Making of History.* New York: Norton, 2007.

English, R. D. *Russia and the Idea of the West: Gorbachev, Intellectuals and the End of the Cold War.* New York: Columbia University Press, 2000.

Fischer, Beth A. *The Reagan Reversal: Foreign Policy and the End of the Cold War.* Columbia: University of Missouri Press, 1997.

Fitzgerald, Francis. *Way Out There in the Blue: Reagan, Star Wars, and the End of the Cold War.* New York: Simon and Schuster, 2000.

Fontaine, Andre. *A History of the Cold War, 1917–1966.* 2 vols. New York: Pantheon, 1968.

Gaddis, John L. *The Cold War: A New History.* New York: Penguin, 2005.

Gaddis, John L. *The Long Peace: Inquiries into the History of the Cold War.* New York: Oxford University Press, 1989.

Gaddis, John Lewis. *The United States and the End of the Cold War.* Oxford: Oxford University Press, 1992.

Gaddis, John Lewis. *What We Now Know: Rethinking the Cold War.* Oxford: Oxford University Press, 1997.

Gorodetsky, Gabriel, ed. *Soviet Foreign Policy, 1917–1991: A Retrospective.* London: Frank Cass, 1994.

Hosking, Geoffrey Alan. *The Awakening of the Soviet Union.* Cambridge, MA: Harvard University Press, 1991.

Kowalski, Ronald. *European Communism, 1848–1991.* New York: Macmillan, 2006.

Kyvig, David E. ed. *Reagan and the World.* Westport, CT: Greenwood, 1990.

Lafeber, Walter. *America, Russia, and the Cold War, 1945–2006.* New York: McGraw Hill, 2006.

MacKenzie, David. *From Messianism to Collapse: Soviet Foreign Policy, 1917–1991.* Fort Worth, TX: Harcourt Brace, 1994.

Malia, Martin. *The Soviet Tragedy: A History of Socialism in Russia, 1917–1991.* New York: Free Press, 1994.

Mann, James. *The Rebellion of Ronald Reagan: A History of the End of the Cold War.* New York: Penguin, 2009.

Matlock, Jack F. *Autopsy of an Empire: The American Ambassador's Account of the Collapse of the Soviet Union.* New York: Random House, 1995.

McCormick, Thomas J. *America's Half-Century: United States Foreign Policy in the Cold War and After.* Baltimore: Johns Hopkins University Press, 1995.

Painter, David S. *The Cold War: An International History.* New York: Routledge, 1999.

Prados, John. *How the Cold War Ended: Debating and Doing History.* Washington, DC: Potomac Books, 2011.

Reagan, Ronald. *An American Life: The Autobiography.* New York: Simon and Schuster, 1990.

Reagan, Ronald. *The Reagan Diaries.* New York: HarperCollins, 2007.

Seton-Watson, Hugh. *Neither War nor Peace: The Struggle for Power in the Postwar World.* New York: Praeger, 1960.

Smith, Joseph. *The Cold War, 1945–1991.* 2nd ed. Oxford, UK: Blackwell, 1998.

Ulam, Bruno Adam. *Understanding the Cold War: A Historian's Personal Reflections.* Piscataway, NJ: Transaction Publishers, 2002.

Walker, Martin. *The Cold War: A History.* New York: Henry Holt, 1994.

Zubok, Vladislav, and Constantine Pieshakov. *Inside the Kremlin's Cold War: From Stalin to Khrushchev.* Cambridge, MA: Harvard University Press, 1996.

PART VII

THE NEW MILLENNIUM (1991–PRESENT)

57. Should the U.S.-Led Coalition Have Removed Saddam Hussein from Power before Ending the Persian Gulf War?

Iraqi forces invaded neighboring Kuwait on August 2, 1990, and imposed a brutal occupation on the small oil-rich nation. Almost immediately, the George H. W. Bush administration decided to compel Iraqi dictator Saddam Hussein to withdraw his troops from Kuwait. Several months of negotiations with and ultimatums to Iraq followed as U.S. and coalition forces massed in Saudi Arabia. Hussein remained defiant, however, and refused to withdraw from Kuwait. On January 17, 1991, Operation DESERT STORM *commenced as a withering allied air campaign against Iraqi targets. The ground campaign began on February 24 and lasted just 100 hours. On February 27, combat ended, Kuwait had been liberated, and Hussein's forces had suffered a significant defeat. The main U.S. military objective in the Persian Gulf War was to eject Iraqi forces from Kuwait, not to remove Hussein from power. After the outbreak of the Iraq War (2003–2011), some critics alleged that had Hussein been removed from power in 1991, subsequent events in Iraq would have not occurred, and the second war would have been unnecessary.*

In the first perspective essay, Dr. John Gentry argues that at the time of the Persian Gulf War, the restoration of Kuwait's sovereignty was the principal goal of U.S. war policy, not the overthrow of Hussein. Indeed, the United Nations Security Council Resolution of November 29, 1990, had authorized the use of "all necessary means" to force Iraqi troops from Kuwait—it said nothing about effecting regime change in Iraq. Gentry further argues that the United States could have sought a diplomatic means by which to oust Hussein after the war, but such an effort could have led to factional insurgencies similar to those experienced in the more recent Iraq War. In the second essay, Dr. Alexander Mikaberidze claims that Hussein's regime had perpetrated enough human rights violations by 1991 to merit his removal from power and that the Persian Gulf War was a lost opportunity to end his dictatorship. However, the limited war objectives of the United States and its allies did not consider regime change in Iraq and only sought to restore Kuwait's independence. In the third essay, Dr. John Kuehn asserts that Hussein's removal from power was not a consideration at the time of the Persian Gulf War because the conflict was intended from the start to be a limited engagement. Kuehn states that U.S. allies in the Middle East, most notably Saudi Arabia and Egypt, would not have found a lengthy U.S.-led occupation of Iraq palatable and would not have agreed to participate in the Persian Gulf War if regime change had been a war goal.

Background Essay

On August 2, 1990, Iraqi president Saddam Hussein sent Iraqi forces into the small neighboring oil-rich country of Kuwait. Within a few days, the Iraqis had completely occupied the country. Hussein had long been angry with Kuwaiti leaders regarding what he perceived as the refusal of Kuwait to adequately assist Iraq financially for the considerable expenses incurred in the Iran-Iraq War (1980–1988). Hussein also was upset that Kuwait had been exceeding oil production quotas set by the Organization of Petroleum Exporting Countries, thus driving down the price that Iraq received for its own oil. There was also the matter of alleged Kuwaiti slant-drilling into rich southern Iraqi oil fields. Hussein, however, had long insisted that Kuwait was actually a lost Iraqi province and was intent on annexing it. After his elite Iraqi Republican Guard divisions had overrun their neighbor, Hussein proclaimed Kuwait to be part of Iraq. He then waited for the world to accept the reality of the situation.

U.S. president George H. W. Bush took the lead in opposing the Iraqi takeover and demanding that Hussein withdraw his forces from Kuwait. Bush's chief concern was that if Iraq's occupation was allowed to stand, Iraq would exert undue influence over and might even invade Saudi Arabia, possessor of the world's largest oil reserves, and that influence alone could severely impact the U.S. and world economies. Bush assembled an impressive international coalition that even included the prominent Arab states of Egypt and Syria. U.S. forces were dispatched to Saudi Arabia in Operation DESERT STORM to protect that nation from Iraqi attack, and then, with the full support of United Nations Security Council resolutions, Bush demanded that Iraq withdraw its forces. When Iraq refused, coalition forces commenced Operation DESERT STORM. It began with an air campaign against Iraq on January 17, and then a month later there was a ground campaign that liberated Kuwait in only a few days.

With the Iraqi Army beaten and withdrawing from Kuwait, U.S. forces penetrated only a little way into Iraq, permitting the withdrawal of most of the Iraqi Republican Guard before Bush declared a unilateral cease-fire on February 28. His goal had been achieved. The Iraqis had been expelled from Kuwait. A full-scale

Iraqi president Saddam Hussein, center, accompanied by aides, tours Iraqi-occupied Kuwait in January 1991. (AP Photo/INA)

invasion of Iraq would undoubtedly have alienated a number of Arab states and split the coalition. It would also have entailed a lengthy occupation of Kuwait, with unknown consequences. Thus, despite an uprising of the majority Shiite Muslims in southern Iraq that had been encouraged by the United States as well as that of Kurds in the north of the country, Hussein was able to retain power. There were many at the time and since who believed that an opportunity had been lost and that if this brutal dictator, who had ridden roughshod over his own people for so long, had been removed from power, a more stable and democratic Iraq would have emerged.

The Persian Gulf War restored Kuwaiti sovereignty and prevented Iraq from perhaps controlling the world price of oil. Certainly it was profoundly satisfying to most Americans, who in the words of President Bush believed that they had "kicked the Vietnam syndrome once and for all" and restored the prestige of the American military. Be that as it may, the war unfortunately did not resolve many issues. Many claimed that it was stopped too early. Hussein remained in power, with his Republican Guard divisions largely intact and able to hold his people in check. Hussein was determined to continue as a major player in the region and pursue his own ambitions at the expense of most of the Iraqi population.

Frustrated by Hussein's refusal to abide by international weapons inspections set by the United Nations and apparently convinced that Iraq possessed weapons of mass destruction and was actively seeking to secure more, President George W. Bush, son of president George H. W. Bush, took the United States into a new war with Iraq in 2003, this time without the widespread support of the Persian Gulf War. Although Hussein was quickly overthrown, the war destabilized Iraq and led to a prolonged insurgency. That war's negative effects continue to play out today.

Historians still disagree over what might have happened had Hussein been removed from power a decade earlier in the Persian Gulf War.

Spencer C. Tucker

Perspective Essay 1. Not an Objective in the Persian Gulf War

The narrower goal of restoring Kuwait's sovereignty after Iraq's conquest was far more legally legitimate and militarily achievable than deposing Iraqi president Saddam Hussein. The former was also essential to assembling and maintaining the broad coalition that achieved a rapid and decisive military victory. A change in U.S. goals in midwar would have fractured the coalition with major negative consequences for U.S. diplomacy and the war effort, and an effort to remove Hussein probably would have produced an insurgency similar to the one that plagued the United States in 2003–2011. The U.S. government could have made more effective diplomatic and military moves to weaken Hussein during and immediately after the military campaign of 1991, however. Regrets should focus there, not on a foregone chance to march on Baghdad.

In the aftermath of his decisive defeat in the Persian Gulf War, Hussein continued to hold a tight rein on power, refused to obey United Nations (UN) Security Council resolutions, sought to assassinate former president George H. W. Bush when the latter was in Kuwait in April 1993, and treated much of the Iraqi population brutally. Many Americans therefore argued that if only the United States had overthrown Hussein in 1991, these and other problems would not have happened, and the painful and costly invasion of Iraq in 2003 could have been averted. But such wishful thinking ignores many key aspects of the global and U.S. domestic situation in 1990 and 1991 as well as the challenges of deposing Hussein—which might have been even greater than those of 2003.

Iraq's invasion of Kuwait on August 2, 1990, surprised most of the world and led to criticism of the U.S. intelligence community about another intelligence failure and of U.S. ambassador to Iraq April Glaspie for her alleged failure to persuasively warn Hussein that Washington firmly opposed Iraq's use of force to resolve its simmering dispute with Kuwait. Iraq's attack was so swift, unjustified, and brutal that it galvanized world opinion and ultimately led the UN Security Council to pass 12 resolutions calling on Iraq to withdraw from Kuwait. An ultimatum in Resolution

678 on November 29, 1990, authorized UN member states to "use all necessary means" to uphold previous resolutions—that is, to expel Iraq from Kuwait by force. This authorization, which gave command of UN forces to the United States and amounted to a veritable blank check regarding military strategy and tactics, was consistent with core principles of the UN Charter that no country may aggressively threaten or attack any other state.

Despite the unusually clear nature of Iraq's crime against Kuwait, the American people and the U.S. Congress were divided regarding the advisability of going to war to defend the principle of state sovereignty and to rescue the Kuwaiti people. While the debate raged, the United States dispatched some 500,000 troops to the Middle East in late 1990 as part of what the Department of Defense called Operation DESERT SHIELD. But under terms of the War Powers Act of 1973, Bush needed congressional authorization to employ U.S. military forces in combat, and he used his position as president to cajole Congress into giving him that power. Finally on January 14, 1991, Congress barely passed a joint resolution authorizing the use of U.S. armed forces pursuant to UN Security Council Resolution 678. The Senate passed the resolution largely along party lines by a vote of 52 to 47, with 45 Democrats voting no. The House of Representatives passed it by a vote of 250 to 183, with 179 Democrats voting no.

Encouraged by the United States, 33 other countries accepted the UN's call to contribute troops to free Kuwait, including seven Arab states: Saudi Arabia, Egypt, Syria, Oman, Qatar, the United Arab Emirates, and Morocco. The United Kingdom ultimately sent a large force, and France committed an army division. About 950,000 allied troops eventually deployed to the region.

When coalition commander U.S. Army general H. Norman Schwarzkopf concluded that preparations were adequate, he launched what the Americans called Operation DESERT STORM, which began with an extensive air campaign that started on January 17, 1991. On February 24, conventional coalition ground troops crossed into Iraq in a 100-hour-long ground campaign that shattered the Iraqi Army in Kuwait and southern Iraq and liberated Kuwait. Bush ended the war when he received what turned out to be inaccurate advice from Schwarzkopf that all military objectives had been achieved. Bush also wanted to bring a halt to the bloodshed even of Iraqi troops.

Coalition casualties were much lighter than expected—482 total deaths, of which Iraqi actions directly caused only 190. Accidents and friendly fire were responsible for the rest. The United States suffered 279 fatalities, 114 of which were due to hostile action. By comparison, battle-related deaths of U.S. Defense Department personnel in Iraq in 2003–2011 during Operation IRAQI FREEDOM were 3,489, and total fatalities of Defense Department personnel even tangentially connected to the war were 4,422.

The narrow goal of reestablishing the independence of Kuwait also led to minimal financial costs for the United States. Saudi Arabia, worried that Iraq might advance farther south into its territory, provided basing and paid the U.S. government some $36 billion. Japan and Germany gave $10 billion and $6.6 billion, respectively, to the United States. Thus, allies paid for most of the roughly $60 billion financial cost of the U.S. part of the war. In contrast, the financial cost of Operation IRAQI FREEDOM is variously estimated between several hundred billion and several trillion dollars.

Let us imagine what a scenario involving a regime change mission might have looked like in 1991 and compare likely consequences of these hypothetical events to what actually happened in 2002 and 2003, when President George W. Bush used military force to remove a leader he viewed, in the post-9/11 world, as a threat to Americans as well as the Iraqi people. Congressional Democrats, many of whom were embarrassed by their votes in 1991 and aware of the low costs of Operation DESERT STORM, also were angry at 9/11 terrorist attacks; they temporarily bought Bush's arguments that Hussein might have ties with Al-Qaeda and wanted to acquire nuclear weapons and, as a result, approved Operation IRAQI FREEDOM. But they quickly returned to their traditional antiwar positions as the war bogged down and used antiwar arguments effectively against Republicans in the 2006 and 2008 election cycles.

Given the extended domestic political struggle in 1990–1991 to gain legislative approval of the clearly legitimate nature of President George H. W. Bush's proposed military action, it is hard to imagine that Congress would have approved a more ambitious and far less normatively and legally justifiable plan to conquer Iraq—the only sure way of deposing Hussein. Any change in war aims in midstream surely would have provoked legitimate allegations that President George W. Bush flaunted the will of Congress and violated the War Powers Act—perhaps provoking a constitutional crisis.

International reaction to a more aggressive plan also would surely have been negative. The Soviet Union or China might have vetoed one or more of the UN Security Council resolutions, including the critical Resolution 678. In late 2002, the United States could not convince Russia, China, or even NATO ally France to agree to a resolution authorizing "all necessary means" to force Iraq to comply with other Security Council resolutions, which exposed Washington to charges that it illegally attacked Iraq, thereby sharply reducing the size of the so-called coalition of the willing from that of 1990–1991. Had Washington publicly announced plans to take out Hussein by conquering Iraq in 1991, most Arab states probably would have defected, putting enormous pressure on Saudi Arabia to limit cooperation with the U.S.-led coalition. Many Arab states had been under Western control of various sorts during the previous century, and public opinion in these countries was very sensitive to perceived external aggression. Iraqi propaganda messages designed to exploit this sensitivity failed to gain much traction because the UN operation in 1990–1991 was so clearly a response to Iraq's aggression against its Arab neighbor.

Nevertheless, several Arab countries allowed their troops to fight Iraqi soldiers in Kuwait, although not in Iraq. In 2003, no Arab military forces accompanied American troops into Iraq. Only Kuwait provided direct basing support, and Saudi Arabia, Japan, and Germany contributed no funds to the United States.

While the U.S. military force assembled for DESERT STORM was numerically larger than the U.S. force that invaded Iraq in 2003, the Iraqi military that survived the 1980–1988 Iran-Iraq War was more powerful in 1991 than in 2003. The Iraqi military in 1991 also had chemical weapons; it used them against Iran repeatedly in the 1980s and against Iraqi Kurdish civilians at Halabja in 1988. Moreover, the Iraqis would have had a set of military options similar to those they used in 2003 and later—including abandoning conventional fighting and turning to irregular warfare in such forms as guerrilla attacks and the use of roadside bombs, which bedeviled the U.S. military for eight years during Operation IRAQI FREEDOM. The U.S. military did not in 1991 or 2003 anticipate or prepare to fight an insurgency in Iraq.

It is thus quite probable that the U.S. military would have been as inept in counterinsurgency operations in 1991 as it was in 2003 and later had there then been a serious plan to conquer Iraq. But there was not. Some military planners contemplated in general terms an attack on Hussein that would have involved a small conventional force that stopped short of Baghdad and a smaller force of special operations troops and Iraqi insurgents that would have entered the city to hunt Hussein. But U.S. military commanders strongly opposed the idea and quickly killed it, precluding the development of a detailed war plan. The limited territorial reach of the proposed search area suggests that U.S. forces would have had at least as much trouble finding Hussein as they had in 2003, when coalition troops occupied the entire country. After an extensive search, U.S. troops finally captured Hussein on December 13, 2003, in his tribal homeland well north of Baghdad eight months after the end of large-scale conventional fighting.

Military and civilian leaders in 1991 might have done more to actualize a key political hope of the war—that defeat would lead Iraqi elites to oust their disgraced leader or enable disgruntled groups, especially Shia Arabs in the south and Kurds in the north, to overthrow him. First, American leaders recognized that the Republican Guard was a bulwark of the regime. Yet the American-led coalition allowed some Republican Guard units in the south to escape by making the command-and-control mistake that led President Bush to prematurely terminate hostilities. Coalition air forces also did not bomb Republican Guard units throughout the country during the air campaign, which would have been reasonable given that the relatively mobile units might have moved south to threaten coalition forces. Second, the United States encouraged Hussein's opponents to overthrow him but gave little tangible support to the rebellions by Shias and Kurds that began almost immediately after the coalition stopped fighting. Iraqi security forces smashed the uprisings by April at a very large cost in insurgent and civilian lives.

More generally, neither the Bush administration nor the U.S. military had any real plan for postwar Iraq. The U.S. government, and Bush personally, simply expected a weakened Hussein to topple and a better Iraq to emerge, presumably accounting largely for the vague instructions Washington gave Schwarzkopf for ending the war. The general wanted to get his troops home quickly, not run an occupation. Therefore, while regrets over the costs and partial success of the war of 2003–2011 are understandable, there was no good alternative to the limited goals of Operation DESERT STORM in 1991. Indeed, an exercise in imagining what-ifs suggests that Operation IRAQI FREEDOM was the major mistake the United States wisely avoided 12 years earlier.

John A. Gentry

Perspective Essay 2. Human Rights Violations Warranted Hussein's Removal

Iraqi president Saddam Hussein was a flagrant violator of international humanitarian law, and his massive human rights violations alone warranted his removal.

On August 2, 1990, the international community was faced with the massive Iraqi invasion of the neighboring state of Kuwait. In response to the Iraqi aggression, the United Nations (UN) acted with a rare unanimity, with the UN Security Council passing Resolution 660 condemning the invasion and demanding an immediate withdrawal of Iraqi troops from Kuwait. Subsequent resolutions imposed economic sanctions and created an international coalition to expel Iraqi forces from Kuwait should diplomacy fail. Led by the United States, a coalition of more than 30 nations—the largest since World War II—launched Operation DESERT STORM on January 17, 1991. The coalition liberated Kuwait and even invaded some of southern Iraq before the declaration of a cease-fire. In April 1991, the UN Security Council laid out formal cease-fire terms that remained in place for more than a decade.

After the United States declared a cease-fire on February 28, the UN adopted Resolution 687 that dealt with a wide range of issues, but regime change was not one of them. Despite violating international law and then suffering a major military defeat, Hussein's government survived the war, and no direct international action was taken to remove him from power. The UN resolutions were intended only to dislodge Iraqis from Kuwait and were silent on toppling Hussein. In his later writings, President George H. W. Bush argued that overthrowing Hussein not only would have been in contravention of the UN resolution but would have also fractured the fragile alliance, which included several Muslim states providing combat troops and aircraft. It would also have led to many unnecessary human and political costs. Furthermore, the United States did not want to create a political vacuum with all its possible attendant problems that might result from the fall of Hussein. Coalition leaders were also acutely aware of the threat posed by a belligerent Iran and were reluctant to create circumstances that would facilitate the spread of Iranian influence attendant in a weakened or splintered Iraq.

Yet Hussein should have been removed on the grounds of mass abuses of human rights, ethnic cleansing, and genocide. The international community had the moral obligation to undertake intervention to end grave violations of fundamental human rights and suffering among the inhabitants of Iraq. Prior to 1991 there had been several examples of interventions undertaken on humanitarian grounds: for example, the Belgian and UN involvements in the Congo in 1960–1964, Indian forces in East Pakistan in 1971, the Vietnamese invasion of Cambodia in 1978, and the Tanzanian invasion to overthrow Idi Amin's brutal regime in Uganda in 1979.

The core underlying idea of protecting innocent civilians from abuse and mistreatment is well established in international humanitarian law. Indeed, the justification for the existence of the modern state is for the protection and enforcement of the natural rights of its citizens. The failure of a state to protect its citizens and their rights makes intervention permissible. The strongest justification for this is that intervention is morally permissible, even obligatory, based on the need to protect basic human rights. Thus, the UN Charter, while upholding states' absolute sovereignty and territorial integrity, also strives to uphold its other primary goal: the protection of human rights and freedoms. Discussion of intervention can be framed as a simple choice between upholding the law (and thereby sanctioning mass abuse or killings) or defending basic moral values. Facing ethnic cleansing in Kosovo, the NATO leaders, including the U.S. State Department, argued that the situation represented a dire moral emergency that justified intervention without UN Security Council authorization.

Furthermore, there is another line of justification for humanitarian intervention, originally developed to explain NATO's involvement in Kosovo but applicable to Iraq as well. It is that humanitarian intervention needs to be undertaken not only to deal with a dire moral emergency but also with the aim of developing a new morally progressive rule of international law. This argument calls for violating existing international law in order to initiate a moral improvement in the international legal system. Thus, NATO intervention in Kosovo was needed to prompt changes in the international legal system so it could better serve one of its core missions: the protection of human rights.

Under Hussein, Iraq was among the worst national offenders of human rights. Hussein came into power in a coup in 1968 by a group of army officers affiliated with the Baathist Party. Just 31 years old at the time, Hussein became vice president of the Iraqi Revolutionary Command Council and assumed control of foreign affairs. Gradually increasing his influence, he built and maintained his base of political power through intimidation, effectively consolidating this by 1979. Hussein's government fostered a cult of personality that was buttressed by secret police, intelligence services, and military security that maintained a thoroughly oppressive rule with little respect for human rights.

The tyrannical nature of the Iraqi government was not unique in the region, but it was singular in its violent assault on tens of thousands of individuals. The Assyro-Chaldeans became the victims of ethnic cleansing that sought to destroy their very identity and history. Hussein's government, composed of Sunni Muslims, undertook the displacement of the so-called Shiite Marsh Arabs from their lands in the southern provinces of Iraq and gravely mistreated them. The Kurds in the north, even though Sunnis, were also brutally oppressed with mass arrests and wanton killings. In 1982 following an assassination attempt on Hussein in the Shia town of Dujail, the Iraqi government responded by levying a collective punishment on the entire community, arresting over 600 residents, subjecting many of them to torture and abuse, and executing more than 140 people.

In 1980 Hussein instigated what became an eight-year-long and costly war with Iran, which was fought over territorial, ethnic, and religious issues but also because Hussein was determined to play the dominant role in the Arab world. During the war he established a chemical weapons program and employed chemical weapons against Iran as well as his own Iraqi Kurdish minority in the north.

The worst of these atrocities took place in 1987–1988 when Hussein and his regime launched a military campaign against the Kurds. Embroiled in a war with Iran, the Iraqi government considered the Kurds to be a major domestic threat and potential "fifth column" for Iran because of the Kurdish demands of autonomy in northern Iraq. In the early spring of 1987 the Iraqi government launched a series of attacks on Kurdish villages, destroying settlements and resettling thousands in detention centers in other regions of Iraq. The Kurds resisted this forcible relocation, and clashes erupted between them and government forces. In response, Hussein's government sanctioned the mass killing of anyone refusing to leave their villages. Code-named AL-ANFAL, this campaign consisted of eight major stages that lasted between February 23 and September 6, 1988, and featured ground offensives, aerial attacks, firing squads, and widespread use of chemical warfare. An estimated 100,000 to 150,000 Kurds suffered from the regime's brutality, many of them gassed to death. Some 4,000 Kurdish villages and towns, more than 1,700 schools, and hundreds of mosques were destroyed. The SF/4008 directive, issued by the Iraqi government in June 1987, specified that "all persons captured in [Kurdish] villages shall be detained and interrogated by the security services and those between the ages of 15 and 70 shall be executed after any useful information has been obtained from them."

The AL-ANFAL campaign was not the only example of mass abuse of human rights perpetrated by the Iraqi government. In 1989, the international human rights watch group Amnesty International reported gruesome stories about hundreds of Iraqi children whose eyes had been gouged out in order to force confessions from their adult relatives.

The defeat in the Persian Gulf War contained the Iraqi dictator's external ambitions but barely affected his repression within Iraq. After Iraq's military defeat in the war, Hussein took immediate revenge on those who had threatened or might potentially threaten his authority. His primary target was the uncoordinated uprisings by Shiite Arabs in the south and the Kurds in the north, fueled by the perception that Hussein's regime was vulnerable as well as by misplaced encouragement from the Western states, especially the United States. Although the rebellions began successfully and secured several key Iraqi cities, internal divisions and the lack of anticipated Western support resulted in their utter defeat. Hussein's regime brutally suppressed the rebellions, killing tens of thousands of people; nearly 2 million more became refugees.

The Iraqi government's actions represented gross violations of international humanitarian law and constituted a variety of crimes against the people of Iraq, including torture, assassination, extrajudicial executions, forcible relocation of residents, genocide, use of chemical weapons, and crimes against humanity. The vast scope of these wrongdoings could have been interpreted as a threat to international peace and constituted legal grounds for intervention. The UN in fact had done this shortly after the Persian Gulf War, and its interventions in Somalia (1992), Rwanda (1994), and Haiti (1994) were sanctioned under Chapter VII of the UN Charter to use military force to end massive human rights abuses.

In 1991, the situation at the end of the Persian Gulf War offered conditions that could have allowed democracy to take root in Iraq. A U.S.-led advance to Baghdad in the spring of 1991 would have been unstoppable, and overthrowing the oppressive regime would have paved the way for democratic reform. There were several precedents of UN acquiescence to foreign interventions in sovereign states' affairs, and considering Iraq government's crimes, the United States and its allies could have secured UN consent for intervention. The international coalition could have then established a meaningful dialogue with the Iraqi opposition and found a way to ensure a peaceful transition of power. This could have involved a new Security Council resolution sanctioning deployment of an international contingent; in fact, in 1991 the UN effectively did this when it acquiesced in silence to the British, French, and U.S. forces being sent to the Kurdish regions of northern Iraq. This was preceded by a Security Council condemnation of Iraqi repression of Kurds that produced a steady stream of refugees into neighboring Turkey and Iran. Invoking Chapter VII, the Security Council did declare Iraqi repression a threat to international peace and security. The coalition could provide substantial military and financial support for the Iraqi opposition movements as long as they sought outside help and wished to use it benevolently.

Iraq might have been transformed into a confederation where three Shia, Sunni, and Kurdish sides enjoyed broad leeway in domestic affairs but collaborated on foreign policy and defense issues. Western-style democracy would not have been the immediate next step, but had the coalition toppled Hussein in 1991 and began working on democracy and reform, Iraq's civil society would have had ample time to mature.

Yet the international coalition, led by the United States, had little desire to bring about change in Iraq. Regional powers such as Saudi Arabia, Syria, and Egypt also had little interest in seeing a prosperous and democratic Iraq, as they were all apprehensive of Iran and concerned about their own power. Aspirations of millions of the Iraqis were thus trampled by geopolitical considerations.

Alexander Mikaberidze

Perspective Essay 3. Removing Hussein Would Have Unhinged the Coalition

On March 3, 1991, representatives of Saddam Hussein met at Safwan, Iraq, with coalition generals led by General H. Norman Schwarzkopf, commanding general of the U.S. Central Command and commander of coalition forces in the Persian Gulf War, and signed a permanent cease-fire ending the war. This agreement was signed three days after an interim cease-fire had been declared by the United States. The cease-fire signaled the end of the conflict between Iraq and a coalition of nations led by the United States that had expelled Iraqi forces from Kuwait.

Following the termination of the conflict, many pundits, with 20-20 hindsight, criticized the George H. W. Bush administration and its generals for not having pressed on to Baghdad and overthrown Hussein's Baathist regime. After the terrorist attacks of 9/11, this viewpoint intensified and led to the misconception that the first Bush administration should have continued military operations until the Hussein regime had been removed, even if it meant going all the way to Baghdad to do so. As such, it became one of the factors that led to the decision taken by the George W. Bush administration to invade Iraq in 2003 to "finish the job." However, this sort of second-guessing ignores the facts on the ground in 1991. There were valid concerns that the U.S.-led coalition, which included such Arab nations as Syria and Egypt, would not hold together, never mind the substantial effort it would take to overthrow Hussein and to deal with rebuilding Iraq once he was overthrown.

The argument for continuing the war also fails to consider the limited set of war aims that had been adopted by the George H.W. Bush administration and approved by the United Nations (UN). A better basis for such criticisms includes the mistakes made in terminating the conflict to achieve the stated objectives. These errors allowed Hussein to retain significant military power and remain a threat to stability in the Persian Gulf region.

To understand the termination of the first war between Iraq and the United States and why it proved unsatisfactory, one must first examine the principal war aims identified by the Bush administration. Iraq's invasion and conquest of Kuwait in August 1990 provided the first and most easily identifiable war aim—the removal of all Iraqi military forces from that occupied nation. This objective was supported by UN Security Council Resolution 660 and was initially addressed by a variety of diplomatic moves by the United States and international economic sanctions against Iraq. When Hussein defiantly refused to remove his forces from Kuwait, the UN Security Council passed Resolution 668, which authorized the use of force by the U.S.-led coalition if Iraq had not removed its troops by January 15, 1991. However, the United States also had at least one other objective in the war, aimed at limiting Hussein's ability to further destabilize the region. U.S. war planners wanted to eliminate the primary sources of Hussein's military power—his army (including the Republican Guard) and his ability to produce and employ weapons of mass destruction (WMD). In particular, they wanted to eliminate Iraq's ability to conduct offensive operations. When Hussein put the bulk of his military in Kuwait and along the adjacent Saudi-Iraqi border, this gave the Bush administration the opportunity to destroy much of Hussein's military establishment, especially the mechanized and armor divisions of the elite Republican Guard. The air campaign, which was a key element of this effort, could also simultaneously be used to weaken Iraq's ability to develop WMD.

However, the Bush administration had hopes that an overpowering air and ground attack that weakened Iraq and, by extension, Hussein's military base of power would also have other fortuitous results. It was hoped that the liberation of Kuwait and the destruction of the Iraqi Army would combine with economic sanctions, the unrest of both Kurds in northern Iraq and Shiites in southern Iraq, and the results of a concurrent air campaign that targeted leadership, WMD, and command-and-control facilities to loosen Hussein's grip on power. There was also the advantage of potentially doing so without any ground forces going into Iraq for any significant distance or extended duration. However, none of these things could happen if the Iraqi Army escaped from Kuwait with sufficient combat power to put down potential rebellions in the northern and southern parts of the country. As it turned out, this is precisely what the still viable Iraqi military did after significant portions of the Republican Guard were allowed to escape from a trap—closing on the Republican Guard units in Kuwait and southern Iraq.

The great error of the Bush administration's military strategy was not its failure to push on to Baghdad but rather the failure of the air-ground war to destroy the bulk of the Iraqi Army, deployed to defend Kuwait. Although Kuwait was easily liberated, Hussein's best divisions escaped with over half of their equipment intact owing to the early cease-fire declared on February 28, 1991. The agreement to cease military operations was the result of a communications breakdown in the U.S. chain of command, sensational and misleading press coverage of the so-called Highway of Death leading from Kuwait City north to Iraq, and the failure of Schwarzkopf, President Bush, and chairman of the Joint Chiefs of Staff General Colin Powell to understand that the second major objective of the war had not been accomplished. Most accounts hold that even 24 additional hours of combat would have severely crippled the Iraqi Army. Furthermore, Schwarzkopf made the critical error during the cease-fire negotiations of allowing Iraqi attack helicopters to fly under its terms so that they could "transport personnel." Instead, they would be used to attack rebelling Shia Marsh Arabs, who, responding to the Bush administration's appeals, had rebelled against the Iraqi government.

Shortly after the cease-fire had been signed at Safwan, several senior policy makers inside the Bush administration pushed for the creation of a demilitarized zone in southern Iraq to both help the Shia rebels and retrieve some of the advantages conferred by the seemingly successful war. At the same time, certain military officers secretly laid out the plans for what would be required to continue operations by U.S. forces all the way to Baghdad. However, Schwarzkopf expressed the view that U.S. forces should be removed from the theater as quickly as possible and should avoid tarnishing the victory with either an extended occupation of southern Iraq (which probably would not have been supported by the Arab coalition members) or a much more involved and risky march on Baghdad to overthrow Hussein. Without support from the generals, these initiatives went nowhere.

In leaving the details to Schwarzkopf and Hussein's representatives, Bush also allowed the critical error of letting the Iraqi dictator disassociate himself with the terms of the cease-fire and portray himself as a defiant survivor of the best the United States could throw at him. He also later portrayed his defeat in Kuwait as a fighting withdrawal and victory. As the cease-fire took effect, Hussein reorganized his disorganized but still largely intact Republican Guard divisions and unleashed them (and his attack helicopters) against the Marsh Arabs in the south who had revolted at the urging of President Bush. After brutally crushing that rebellion, Hussein turned north to deal with the Kurds. It was this action that led to the establishment of a no-fly zone in the northern third of Iraq some months later. Too late, almost 18 months after the war did Bush implement a no-fly zone (Operation SOUTHERN WATCH) in southern Iraq to protect the already defeated rebel Shiites. If Bush and his generals had simply finished executing their existing operations plan, they would have destroyed the Iraqi main forces in and around Basra and greatly aided the Shia revolt. If this had succeeded, Iraq might have broken into three de facto states—a Shia south, a Sunni Arab center, and a Kurdish north.

The real problem with the critics of the Bush administration's decision to settle for an incomplete victory in Iraq in 1991 is their failure to imagine what the likely outcome that pressing on to Baghdad to oust Hussein would have been. It is very likely that the coalition would have fractured had coalition forces pushed deliberately up the Tigris and Euphrates Rivers in March 1991. In the confusion of the last phase of the war, Egypt, Syria, Saudi Arabia, and the other associated Arab members of the coalition would have almost certainly countenanced a vigorous effort to pursue and destroy Hussein's fleeing army inside southern Iraq, especially the Republican Guard.

On the other hand, it is almost certain that these same nations would have halted their forces and perhaps even demanded that the United States cease operations or lose logistical bases in the Persian Gulf region had the offensive pressed on to Baghdad. In this scenario the United States would have been embarrassed on the international stage and also would have been unable to continue the offensive. Its forces were, after all, operating out of numerous foreign facilities as guests, especially in Saudi Arabia but also in Bahrain and Qatar. This situation involved even more risk because the United States had the very unfriendly regime of Iran located along its lengthy lines of communications through the Persian Gulf region should these states (except Kuwait) pull the plug on supporting further U.S. offensive operations.

The second great weakness in the argument of those who claim that the United States should have pressed on to remove Hussein has been informed by the problematic U.S. invasion and subsequent counterinsurgency in Iraq during 2003–2011. Assuming that the United States had been able to overthrow Hussein, it would have found itself in the same situation as 2003, in the midst of a counterinsurgency with various recalcitrant Arab communities. Even if an insurgency against U.S.-led forces had not occurred, there is every reason to believe that the United States and whoever supported its operations inside Iraq would find themselves in the same difficult civil war and sectarian violence that plagued Iraq after 2003 and still plagues it today. Additionally, U.S. forces, especially the U.S. Army, were no better prepared to conduct counterinsurgency operations in 1991 than they were in 2003. In fact, according to some observers, they were less prepared and certainly much less capable in 1991. The army fought the kind of conventional mechanized war it wanted to fight and for which it had developed doctrine after the Vietnam War, hardly putting any effort into training for the counterinsurgency and stability operations that it found itself struggling to learn and implement during 2003–2007. It seems unlikely that the military establishment of 1991 would have done any better, and there are valid reasons to believe that it would have done worse.

Finally, there is the issue of congressional support and U.S. public opinion. Both had been lukewarm to the use of armed force, and once hostilities began neither had seen large casualties incurred yet by U.S. forces. Ironically, there was more of an antiwar effort in 1990–1991 than in 2003, and the American public was ready for a peace dividend after the recent successful termination of the Cold War with the Soviet Union. In 1991 most Americans still had very strong negative memories of the Vietnam War experience. In all likelihood public and congressional support for an ongoing war would have soured quickly if the conflict had lasted any length of time or bore any resemblance to the quagmire of a counterinsurgency similar to what occurred Vietnam.

In summary, it is hard to imagine anything good coming from a U.S. push to Baghdad in 1991. Yes, the Bush administration made real errors in terminating the conflict in a way that had some promise of neutralizing Hussein's troublesome influence in the region or leading to a rebellion inside the country to displace him. But it avoided the much greater error that George H. W. Bush's son made in 2003 by going back to "finish the job."

John T. Kuehn

Further Reading

Atkinson, Rick. *Crusade: The Untold Story of the Persian Gulf War.* Boston: Houghton Mifflin, 1993.

Black, George, ed. *Genocide in Iraq: the Anfal Campaign against the Kurds.* New York: Human Rights Watch, 1993.

Bolger, Daniel P. "The Ghosts of Omdurman." *Parameters* 26 (Autumn 1991): 28–39.

Bush, George H. W., and Brent Scowcroft. *A World Transformed.* New York: Vintage, 1999.

Cohen, Eliot, and Thomas A. Keaney, eds. *The Gulf War Air Power Survey.* Washington, DC: U.S. Government Printing Office, 1993.

Crist, David. *The Twilight War: The Secret History of America's Thirty-Year Conflict with Iran.* New York: Penguin, 2012.

Daaldor, Ivo H., and Michael E. O'Hanlon: *Winning Ugly: NATO's War to Save Kosovo.* Washington, DC: Brookings, 2000.

Gordon, Michael R., and Bernard E. Trainor. *Cobra II: The Inside Story of the Invasion and Occupation of Iraq.* New York: Pantheon Books, 2006.

Gordon, Michael R., and Bernard E. Trainor. *The General's War: The Inside Story of the Conflict in the Gulf.* New York: Little, Brown, 1995.

Hufbauer, Gary Clyde, Jeffrey J. Schott, and Kimberly Ann Elliott. *Economic Sanctions Reconsidered: History and Current Policy.* 2 vols. 2nd revised ed. Washington, DC: Institute for International Economics, 1990.

Kelly, Michael J. *Ghosts of Halabja: Saddam Hussein and the Kurdish Genocide.* Westport, CT: Praeger, 2008.

Makiya, Kanan. *Republic of Fear: The Politics of Modern Iraq.* Berkeley: University of California Press, 1998.

Marr, Phebe. *The Modern History of Iraq.* Boulder, CO: Westview, 2011.

Randall, Jonathan. *After Such Knowledge, What Forgiveness? My Encounters with Kurdistan.* New York: Farrar, Straus and Giroux, 1997.

Ricks, Thomas E. *Fiasco: The American Military Adventure in Iraq.* New York: Penguin, 2006.

Sassoon, Joseph. *Saddam Hussein's Ba'th Party: Inside an Authoritarian Regime.* Cambridge: Cambridge University Press, 2011.

Scales, Robert H., Jr. *Certain Victory: The U.S. Army in the Gulf War.* Washington, DC: Brassey's 1994.

Schwarzkopf, H. Norman. *It Doesn't Take a Hero.* New York: Bantam, 1992.

Woods, Kevin M., David D. Palkki and Mark E. Stout, eds. *The Saddam Tapes: The Inner Workings of a Tyrant's Regime, 1978–2001.* Cambridge: Cambridge University Press, 2011.

Woodward, Bob. *The Commanders.* New York: Pocket Books, 1991.

58. Was the International Community Justified in Initially Avoiding Military Action to Prevent Ethnic Cleansing in Bosnia?

Despite the knowledge of genocidal incidents occurring in Bosnia and Herzegovina in the early 1990s, the international community did not immediately move to quell Serbian and Bosnian Serbian atrocities. Instead, the United States, the European Union (EU), the North Atlantic Treaty Organization (NATO), and the United Nations (UN) responded cautiously to the events in Bosnia, forcing Bosniaks to endure displacement, massacres, and various war crimes amid the cover of the Bosnian War (1992–1995). However, as Bosnian Serb violence against Muslims increased, the international community finally decided to take action. This included the deployment of UN peacekeeping troops, NATO bombings of Bosnian Serb key positions, and the invocation of stiff international economic and political sanctions. However, these actions were arguably too little too late, as most of the ethnic cleansing campaign instigated by Serb and Serb-affiliated forces in Bosnia had occurred prior to international intervention. The international community's initially tepid response to events in Bosnia was indicative of the major world powers' limited interests in the region. Given the foreign policy interests of these nations (e.g., the United States, Britain, France, Russia, etc.), there was little incentive to act decisively early on. Direct intervention finally came when Serbian ethnic cleansing policies had become far too extreme to overlook or justify.

Dr. Mary Hampton, in the first perspective essay, argues that the international response to the breakup of Yugoslavia was "slow and unsure." Hampton explains that as the post–Cold War world began to take shape, the major powers were reluctant to engage militarily in the Balkans. Assumptions about the role of other powers or the UN as well as a lack of national interests in the region led to hesitation on the part of the United States and the EU. Involvement came later as events rapidly escalated to the point of genocide. In contrast, in his perspective essay Dr. Brian G. Smith argues that the international community's involvement in Bosnia was limited from start to finish. Complex questions concerning the specifics of military intervention tied the hands of the major powers and the UN. While a more timely response could have halted the worst of the violence, caution and hesitancy prevented the United States, the EU, and NATO from acting in a timely fashion. By the time military intervention took place, ethnic cleansing policies had already taken a significant toll on the Bosniak population. Finally, Dr. Henry Carey demonstrates that although the United States had the ability to become more involved in the Bosnian situation early on, domestic politics had a significant impact on the Bill Clinton administration's reluctance to take a more proactive stand in the growing crisis. While the administration had indeed considered more concerted U.S. action in the region in the early days of the war, political considerations and limitations at home ultimately took precedence and led to a delayed response.

Background Essay

The campaigns of ethnic cleansing committed throughout the 1990s in the former Yugoslavia, particularly in Bosnia-Herzegovina at the hands of Bosnian Serbs and Serbian nationals, appalled a world community certain that the excesses committed during the Holocaust would never again plague Europe. The surge of nationalist sentiment unleashed by the end of the Cold War created the conditions that allowed this process, which ultimately led to the deaths of an estimated 200,000 Bosnian Muslims, Serbians, and Croatians. The ambivalent behavior of international organizations, including the United Nations (UN) and the North Atlantic Treaty Organization (NATO), in responding to policies of ethnic cleansing emboldened the Serbians to engage in genocidal actions. The attempt at ethnic cleansing in the province of Kosovo several years later, in a Serbian attempt to cleanse the area of

A Srebrenica survivor who lost 13 family members in a massacre by Serb forces in Bosnia in July 1995 is shown protesting in front of UN offices in Sarajevo in 1998. More than 8,000 Bosniak (Bosnian Muslim) men and boys died in the massacre. (AP Photo/Hidajet Delic)

Kosovar Albanians, also triggered international outrage but resulted in a prompt assertive military response by NATO.

The conciliatory policies of former Yugoslav leader Josip Broz Tito had maintained a fragile unity within the post-1945 multinational communist Republic of Yugoslavia. Upon his death the devolutionist nationalist tendencies became unleashed, and his tactics of playing the major ethnic groups against each other no longer worked. In 1989 Serbian president Slobodan Milosevic proceeded to eliminate the autonomous position of the Yugoslavian provinces of Kosovo and Vojvodina. His continued attempts to assert Serbian domination over Yugoslavia triggered the secession of Slovenia, Croatia, Macedonia, and Bosnia-Herzegovina in 1992. This angered Milosevic, triggering his deployment of the Yugoslavian military, composed primarily of Serbians, to reclaim the newly independent nations and unleashing a civil war. The attempts to create ethnically heterogeneous nation-states on the part of each former Yugoslavian republic, with the exception of Slovenia, resulted in various campaigns of ethnic cleansing in the midst of the Yugoslav Wars.

The ethnic cleansing pursued by various actors within Bosnia-Herzegovina was a result of its multicultural character. The tenuous constitutional structure of newly independent Bosnia-Herzegovina rested on the supposed cooperation of its various component nationalities. Unlike the other former Yugoslavian republics, it had no majority ethnic group but instead was composed of substantial pluralities of different nationalities. In 1991 a census estimated that Muslims accounted for 43.7 percent of the population, Serbians accounted for 31.4 percent, and Croatians accounted for 17.3 percent, with others accounting for 7.6 percent.

Determined to maintain its political and cultural hegemony, the Serbia population of Bosnia proceeded to create the Republika Srpska under the leadership of Radovan Karadzic. Bosnian Serb paramilitary formations, with covert assistance from Serbia, then proceeded to ethnically cleanse Bosnia-Herzegovina of non-Serbs, primarily Muslims. The age-old antagonisms based on religious hatred emerged in the midst of the Bosnian Civil War. The resulting exterminations of Muslims with the associated tactics of widespread massacres, shootings, and mass rapes led to a massive death toll. Concentration camps and mass killings characterized the Bosnian Serbs' effort to exterminate the culture and populations of Bosnian Muslims. Armed groups of Bosnian Muslims retaliated by conducting their own campaigns of genocide against Bosnian Serbs. In the midst of the carnage, Serbia maintained official neutrality while supplying the Bosnian Serbs with arms and supplies.

Bosnian Croatians and Muslims also enacted policies of attrition against the Serbs and each other in an attempt to eliminate each other from territories where a respective ethnic group constituted a demographic majority. Croatian forces concentrated their persecutions of Muslims in central Bosnia and most of Herzegovina. In the Bosnian town of Ahmici, Croatian militants perpetrated a massacre of Muslims by locking them in cellars and setting them afire. The smaller Muslim guerrilla force managed to commit small-scale massacres against both Croatians and Serbians. A mass grave containing hundreds of Serbian civilians murdered by Muslim authorities near Sarajevo and abuses committed against Serbian prisoners at a Bosnian camp in Celibici are examples of Bosnian Muslims' actions against their opponents. While Serbian genocide created a larger death toll, Croatian and Muslim actions also characterized the chaotic acts of ethnic cleansing on all sides.

The tactics involved in ethnic cleansing in the former Yugoslavia involved very crude methods of extermination and torture. Accounts of such actions involve shooting en masse, stabbing or knifing victims to death, torturing to death by various means, and starvation in concentration camps. The dehumanization of rival groups resulted in acts of mass rape, torture, and death. The participation of both paramilitary groups and civilians characterized many of these genocidal acts.

Knowledge of these events troubled NATO and the UN in particular, which eventually sent in peacekeepers. Some accounts allege that inaction on the part of the peacekeepers encouraged genocide in some instances. Allegations of corruption and misconduct among UN peacekeepers and their role as mere bystanders have also proven controversial.

Following the 1995 Dayton Agreement, which brought an end to the bloodletting, Milosevic proceeded to focus on affairs within Serbia. The province of Kosovo, which had a considerable Muslim Albanian population, became the next target of Serbian exclusionary legislation targeting non-Serbs. However, NATO and the UN were paying close attention to these actions on the part of Serbia. While Milosevic maintained that this was an internal affair and that he was merely responding to the actions of Muslim terrorist groups, NATO commenced aerial bombardment of key Serbian positions and the city of Belgrade in 1998 in retaliation for Serbian aggression in Kosovo.

In early 1999 U.S. president Bill Clinton promulgated the so-called Clinton Doctrine, which advocates a policy of military engagement in nations where internal ethnic strife has the potential of escalating into genocide. Diplomacy and the eventual granting of autonomy to Kosovo eventually diffused the crisis. Milosevic, however, was indicted as a war criminal in 2000.

Abraham O. Mendoza

Perspective Essay 1. Slow and Unsure Military Action

The international response to the violent breakup of Yugoslavia in the early 1990s was slow and unsure. The Yugoslav Wars that began in 1991 represented one of the first international crises of the emerging post–Cold War world and the first in Europe. It is therefore no surprise that the international community took no immediate military action. American academic Samantha Power (later U.S. ambassador to the United Nations [UN]) and many others have argued that the international community, but especially the United States and Europe, "stood by" while approximately 200,000 Bosnians were killed and another 2 million were displaced.

A number of factors contributed to the delayed decision by the international community to employ military force to halt ethnic cleansing in Bosnia, where the process of Serb-targeted violence against and displacement of Croats, but especially against Bosnian Muslims, began in late 1991. The reasons for the delayed response were hard to justify morally, but the delay was politically and strategically justifiable considering the still murky realities of the post–Cold War world.

In the early portions of the post–Cold War era, the parameters of great power interests and the boundaries of their spheres of influence were not yet known and were still in flux in 1991, when Slovenia and then Croatia declared independence. There was no consensus in Europe concerning the political and security roles of the newly emerging European Union (EU), whose restated mission included political and security policy coordination. The lack of international consensus regarding the post–Cold War security role of the UN and the concomitant absence of a clearly defined post–Cold War mission for the North Atlantic Treaty Organization (NATO) were key elements in the less than slow international response to the unfolding nightmare of ethnic cleansing and brutality in Bosnia. In short, Yugoslavia's eruption into civil and then transnational war was a severe aftershock of the Cold War's collapse. The international community had no blueprints, guidelines, or courses of action to respond with military force to the wars and accompanying brutal practices of ethnic cleansing.

The first factor that contributed to the outbreak of war in Yugoslavia and the delayed international response to abuses in Bosnia was the collapse of the bipolar Cold War international order. The Soviet Union and the United States had managed a world divided into two blocs for nearly half a century. By the 1950s, the United States and the West basically ceded Eastern and Central Europe to Soviet dominance. Although Yugoslavia remained somewhat of an outlier because of the uncanny capability of its leader, Josip Broz Tito, to keep Yugoslav interests largely independent of Soviet dominance, it was still considered within the Soviet sphere of influence. Further, Russia and then the Soviet Union long considered itself the guardian of Slav identity and interests, a phenomenon that underscored Soviet interest and influence, especially in Serbia. Partly for these reasons, the George H. W. Bush administration was not interested in intervening in what it determined to be a domestic political squabble as Yugoslavia began imploding in 1991. Secretary of State James Baker famously opined that the United States had "no dog in this fight," a colloquialism broadcasting that American interests were not in play.

The Bush administration also kept its distance from the emerging crisis in Yugoslavia because the end of the Cold War witnessed the formal emergence of the EU in 1992, which was accompanied by a wide-eyed optimistic belief by many that Europe could now handle events in its own backyard. For Pan-Europe advocates, the demise of the Cold War opened new opportunities for managing European affairs independently of U.S. influence. The breakup of Yugoslavia seemed to offer Europeans the chance to take responsibility for events on their continent. Jacques Poos, then foreign minister of Luxembourg and an activist for European unity, stated that "This is the hour of Europe." Further, he stated, "It is not the hour of the Americans." The fact was, however, that there actually was no European consensus on how to respond to the situation in the dissolving Yugoslavia. There was no EU military force, and no concerted policy had yet emerged. A leadership vacuum therefore prevailed in the West.

The other two institutions that could have responded with military force to halt ethnic cleansing were the UN and NATO. The UN did in fact act, but it acted by sending peacekeepers, the United Nations Protection Force, into a situation that required a different response. While UN peacekeepers, backed by the European states, attempted to protect declared safe areas and to safeguard humanitarian aid being sent to Bosnians from abroad, they often found themselves helplessly standing by while violence continued. At one point in 1994, the Serbs held many peacekeepers themselves hostage.

In the face of ineffective UN protection and nonexistent U.S. and EU military intervention, the institution that might have made a real difference in halting Serb aggression was NATO. But NATO members were virtually the very same European states that could not bring themselves to intervene militarily. During 1994 and early in 1995, NATO air strikes were used in a limited capacity to deter Serb behavior, but they did not stop Serb aggression. Not until August 1995 in the aftermath of the Serb massacre of between 6,000 and 8,000 Bosnian Muslims at Srebenica, and while Croat and Bosnian ground forces were actually beginning to have some success in repelling Serb forces, did the Bill Clinton administration decide that the time had come to put NATO's reputation on the line. The administration successfully advocated for a NATO military air campaign of bombing Serb targets. The campaign, code-named Operation DELIBERATE FORCE, was instrumental in halting the war, paving the way for the Dayton Accord of December 1995.

In conclusion, democracies generally do not take lightly the use of military force. The pooled resources and collective decision making necessary for international organizations to employ military force is even more complex. While the norm of humanitarian intervention in the name of human rights has been steadily gaining credibility and acceptance since the Holocaust of the 1930s and 1940s, there was certainly no Western consensus in 1992 concerning when to use military force and how to stop ethnic cleansing. The fact that it took the West until 1995 to mount an effective military response to the genocide being carried out by the Serbs was morally shameful but understandable and even justifiable given the complexities created by the conflict in the wider context of the undefined post–Cold War international order.

Mary Hampton

Perspective Essay 2. Limited Intervention Justifiable and Understandable

The international community's response to the Yugoslav Wars in general and the Bosnian War in particular was one of limited intervention. Not until the fall of 1995 did the intervention escalate to include significant air assets and bombing. Large numbers of ground forces were put in place only after conclusion of the 1995 Dayton Accords. Would an earlier overwhelming military intervention have been more legal, moral, and wise than limited intervention? On each point, the international community was justified in not undertaking early and overwhelming military action against the ethnic cleansing in Bosnia.

There is an ongoing debate among international law scholars concerning the legality of humanitarian military intervention in the face of genocidal acts and human rights violations. The issue is at best murky. There are many contradictory elements in the United Nations (UN) Charter concerning when force may be used, the inviolability of national sovereignty, and the requirement to promote and protect human rights. Much of the debate boils down to the requirements to respect national sovereignty, enshrined in much of the UN Charter, versus the human rights elements of the charter and the requirements to prevent and punish genocide through proper UN channels under the 1948 Genocide Convention. Since the genocides of the 1990s, the UN and human rights organizations have attempted to put in place "responsibility to protect" as a suggested addition to international conventions, which would largely eliminate legal questions and allow humanitarian intervention when a sovereign state fails to protect its own citizens from atrocities and genocide. Without the adoption of such a clause, even limited military intervention can be seen as pushing the bounds of what is legally justified.

On a related matter, was NATO's delay in intervening with airpower in the Bosnian Civil War justified from a moral standpoint? Most theories of morality as they relate to military action are based on some version of the doctrine of just war, which suggests when countries are morally justified in going to war. Most modern just war doctrine focuses on self-defense as the only morally justifiable cause of war. Humanitarian military intervention rests on the assumption that the morality of self-defense can be extended to the citizens of other countries when their own governments cannot provide protection or are themselves supporting or committing genocide. That assumption sets aside the critical ethical question of interventions undermining the international order designed to prevent war. This is further complicated by the lack of universal agreement as to the principles under which states have the moral duty to intervene. Finally, some scholars have moral reservations about the high financial cost of military intervention when those expenditures could be employed to combat chronic health and hunger problems.

The moral imperative to protect civilians during dangerous situations is clear. The goal of any intervention would be to reduce civilian deaths and avoid or mitigate atrocities. Many organizations and states are attempting to create a moral norm mandating the duty to intervene in a way that does not undermine global peace and security. This thinking assumes that no response at all would be morally unjustifiable, given current capacities to intervene and the timely dissemination of information that can alert the international community to mass atrocities. However, the use of overwhelming military power in response to a multisided civil war that included ethnic cleansing of both city neighborhoods and entire regions could not necessarily guarantee fewer casualties or atrocities. Simply put, an unrestrained military intervention in the Balkans by hundreds of thousands of troops and an indefinite occupation would not necessarily have produced a more moral outcome judged solely by deaths and civilian suffering.

Even assuming that nonintervention is morally unjustifiable, limited intervention cannot be considered morally unjustified. Limited ground forces from the UN mission in Croatia moved into Bosnia before the fighting there even started. Furthermore, an arms embargo was put into place to avoid escalation, and diplomatic efforts produced numerous cease-fires. As early as May 1992 the UN, in an effort to reach a negotiated end to the war, imposed broad economic, travel, and financial sanctions on the Federal Republic of Yugoslavia, which was supporting the actions of the Serbs in Bosnia. In 1993 the UN established five major safe havens in Bosnia, supported with limited airpower to protect the relatively few and very vulnerable UN peacekeeping troops on the ground. Military force was employed to create safe corridors for civilians fleeing active areas of the war. Aid convoys and airlifts were ongoing throughout the civil war, while aid workers labored on the ground, all in an effort to protect civilian lives. In May 1993, a special international criminal tribunal was created as a way to minimize atrocities by holding individuals responsible for war crimes and crimes against humanity committed during the conflict. Some of these efforts had unintended consequences, such as possibly aiding the process of ethnic cleansing. Others can be considered clear failures in execution or concept. None of them, however, can be considered a morally unjustified failure to act.

Finally, was the decision by the international community not to intervene militarily early a wise one? Military intervention early in 1992 would have meant the commitment of substantial ground forces amid intense hostility from Russia and China and would have involved enforcing a peace in the face of hostile elements within the population. Furthermore, the intervention would have come at a time when the international community was intensely concerned over continued instability in Russia. Finally, there were serious concerns about expanding the role of NATO in the early post–Cold War period.

When NATO finally applied overwhelming airpower in 1995, the situation was quite different. The international community had brokered an alliance between the Bosnian government and the Croatians. The Croatian military had obtained equipment and had received training in NATO tactical doctrine through the hiring of retired U.S. officers working for an American private consulting firm. Economic sanctions on Serbia had destabilized President Slobodan Milosevic's regime, pressuring him to cut off aid to the Bosnian Serbs and forcing him to reach a negotiated settlement. The Bosnian Serb forces fractured after the Croatian Army quickly overran Serbian-held Krajina in Croatia in early August 1995, forcing some 200,000 Serbs from Croatia in the process. The effectiveness of the late intervention therefore did not rest simply on newfound political will.

The international community was justified in not initially taking overwhelming military action as a means to put an end to the ethnic cleansing in Bosnia. This does not mean that delay is always justified. There is a tendency to move toward extreme positions concerning the efficacy of humanitarian military intervention. At one extreme, there can be too much emphasis on prompt military interventions that can supposedly provide a quick and moral solution to human rights abuses. At the other extreme, there can be a tendency to spurn intervention in the belief that intervening once will set a precedent for constant interventions. Humanitarian military intervention can only be evaluated as legal, moral, or wise on a case-by-case basis that takes into consideration the individual, idiosyncratic realities of an emerging conflict.

Brian G. Smith

Perspective Essay 3. Domestic Politics Delayed Military Action

While understandable, the international community's failure to prevent the Bosnian Genocide was not morally or legally justified, given the United Nations (UN) Genocide Convention's requirement that genocide be halted. The fighting brought the deaths of some 200,000 civilians and displaced another 2 million people. The international inaction was, however, entirely predictable. Decisions by the International Criminal Tribunal for the Former Yugoslavia, such as the *Krstic* and *Popovic et al.* cases, established that criminal acts of genocide occurred. The judgment of the International Court of Justice (*Bosnia v. Serbia,* 2007) also established that genocide occurred in Bosnia, with the Serbian government guilty of failing to prevent the genocide (though not guilty of direct collaboration).

The delay in the North Atlantic Treaty Organization (NATO) intervention is understandable, given that states tend to intervene militarily only in cases involving their national interests. No state, including the United States, had ever before intervened to stop a genocide. The UN, NATO, and the United States all faced a much more difficult challenge in Bosnia than they did in the 1994 humanitarian intervention in Haiti and during the Rwandan Genocide, when there was no international intervention. If the international community was reluctant in Rwanda, then it would only be more reluctant to face a better-armed and more ferocious opponent in the Serbs in Bosnia, even if the latter held more strategic value for the West.

Still, it was obvious to many that halting genocide, and the war that facilitated it, was in the self-interest of NATO and the United States. However, fear of casualties and the so-called CNN effect during the October 1993 Battle of Mogadishu in Somalia, which resulted in numerous U.S. casualties and the end of the U.S. humanitarian mission there, made future American interventions very complicated. The perceived political risks to the United States from humanitarian intervention were once more realized in the U.S.-Canadian peacekeeping mission in Haiti in 1994, which did not go well. The political embarrassment resulting from these earlier interventions clearly weighed heavily on U.S. policy makers.

The belated major NATO intervention in Bosnia in June–August 1995 and Croatia's retaking of the Western Krajina region of Bosnia induced the Dayton Peace Accord by year's end, which ended the war and the genocide. The intervention was motivated as much by security concerns as humanitarian ones. Neither the UN Security Council, the United States, nor NATO were willing and able to take significant military action until 1995 and only minimal military action until 1994, two years after the genocide began.

Part of this delay was attributable to what turned out to be unsuccessful peace negotiations that could have also halted the genocide, but these and primarily the Vance-Owen initiative were also not undertaken in earnest until 1993. Economic and military sanctions were also imposed to induce negotiations, but these were applied to the entire former Yugoslavia and thus gave a military advantage to Serbia. That was not conducive to an environment that might have induced negotiations. It was NATO military force that finally ended the genocide: UN-sanctioned airpower combined with covert U.S. operations to sponsor the successful Croatian invasion of the Western Krajina region of Bosnia.

Another factor in the delayed reaction was the early development of what has come to be viewed in recent years as the responsibility to protect doctrine, which would legally permit UN Security Council authorizations for force inside countries, such as Bosnia, that did not present any clear "threat to international peace" and before all peaceful alternatives had been exhausted first.

U.S. domestic politics also played a key role. Public opinion bears directly on decisions to intervene, because presidents weigh the effects on their own political fortunes in upcoming elections. Presidential approval ratings are the best predictors of election prospects, even more so than the perceived state of the economy, and hence strongly influence presidential decision making. In 1994, President Bill Clinton's general approval ratings declined to the lowest level of any U.S. president to that time. The situations in Haiti and Bosnia, with the constant images of starving refugees, mass killings, and U.S. inaction, contributed heavily to low public perceptions of his performance as president. This motivated Clinton to change policy. Less than two months before the 1994 congressional midterm elections, Clinton made the decision to invade Haiti. Bosnia's Dayton talks took place during the Democratic primary season, less than a year before the 1996 presidential election. Clinton's approval rating specifically in foreign affairs also reached a nadir in 1994, standing at 40 percent positive and 55 percent negative in a September poll. Clinton's stand on the use of force in Bosnia largely mirrored the ups and downs of U.S. public opinion polls. In May 1992, 55 percent of those polled opposed U.S. air strikes against the Serbs, and 61 percent of women—the base of swing votes that had brought Clinton victory in 1992—opposed them. Even Clinton's own putative base of Democratic voters opposed U.S. armed intervention by 55 percent to 36 percent. By July 1992, just 35 percent of respondents favored the United States taking the lead with air strikes against the Serbs.

Thus, the U.S.-led response, legally sanctioned by the UN Security Council in 1995 and implemented by NATO in Bosnia, reflected political calculations by President Clinton that were politically motivated and not based on either international legal mandates or moral responsibilities. The European Union (EU) was so divided that the newly instituted effort to create a military branch of the EU was doomed to failure. The United States, regarded as the only superpower after the end of the Cold War, was the only nation capable of leading a major military intervention in what was a very difficult environment.

Henry (Chip) Carey

Further Reading

Anzulovic, Branimir. *Heavenly Serbia: From Myth to Genocide.* New York: New York University Press, 1999.

Bull, Hedley, ed. *Intervention in World Politics.* Oxford, UK: Clarendon, 1984.

Burg, Steven L., and Paul S. Shoup. *The War in Bosnia-Herzegovina: Ethnic Conflict and International Intervention.* London: M. E. Sharpe, 2000.

Cohen, L. J. *Broken Bonds: The Disintegration of Yugoslavia.* 2nd ed. Boulder, CO: Westview, 1995.

Denitch, Bogdan. *Ethnic Nationalism: The Tragic Death of Yugoslavia.* Minneapolis: University of Minnesota Press, 1994.

Feher, Michel. *Powerless by Design: The Age of the International Community.* Durham, NC: Duke University Press, 2000.

Gibbs, David N. *First Do No Harm: Humanitarian Intervention and the Destruction of Yugoslavia.* Nashville: Vanderbilt University Press, 2009.

Honing, Jan Willem, and Norbert Both. *Srebrenica: Record of a War Crime.* New York: Penguin, 1997.

Judah, Tim. *The Serbs, History, Myth and the Destruction of Yugoslavia.* New Haven, CT: Yale University Press, 1997.

Leydesdorff, Selma. *Surviving the Bosnian Genocide: The Women of Srebrenica Speak.* Translated by Kay Richardson. Bloomington: Indiana University Press, 2011.

Mertus, Julie. *Kosovo: How Myths and Truths Started a War.* Berkeley: University of California Press, 1999.

Nikolic, Milos. *The Tragedy of Yugoslavia.* Baden-Baden, Germany: European Trade Institute Press, 2002.

Petersen, Roger D. *Western Intervention in the Balkans: The Strategic Use of Emotion in Conflict.* New York: Cambridge University Press, 2011.

Ramet, Sabrina. *Balkan Babel: The Disintegration of Yugoslavia from the Death of Tito to the Fall of Milosevic.* 4th ed. Boulder, CO: Westview, 2002.

Rieff, David. *Slaughterhouse: Bosnia and the Failure of the West.* London: Vintage, 1995.

Rohde, David. *Endgame: The Betrayal and Fall of Srebrenica, Europe's Worst Massacre since World War II.* Boulder, CO: Westview, 1997.

Sacirby, Nedzib. "The Genesis of Genocide: Reflection on the Yugoslav Conflict." *Brown Journal of World Affairs* 3(1) (Winter–Spring 1996): 341–352.

Schabas, William A. *Genocide in International Law: The Crime of Crimes.* Cambridge: Cambridge University Press, 2000.

Scheffer, David. *All the Missing Souls: A Personal History of the War Crimes Tribunals.* Princeton, NJ: Princeton University Press, 2011.

Sell, Louis. *Slobodan Milosevic and the Destruction of Yugoslavia.* Durham, NC: Duke University Press, 2002.

Silber, Laura, and Allan Little. *The Death of Yugoslavia.* London: Penguin and BBC Books, 1995.

Symynkywicz, Jeffrey B. *Civil War in Yugoslavia.* New York: Dillion, 1997.

Toal, Gerard, and Carl T. Dahlman. *Bosnia Remade: Ethnic Cleansing and Its Reversal.* New York: Oxford University Press, 2011.

Weiss, Thomas, and Don Hubert. *The Responsibility to Protect: Research, Bibliography, Background.* Ottawa: International Development Research Centre, 2001.

Woodward, Susan L. *Balkan Tragedy: Chaos and Dissolution after the Cold War.* Washington, DC: Brookings Institution, 1995.

59. Was the 2003 U.S.-Led Coalition Invasion of Iraq Justified?

On March 20, 2003, a "coalition of the willing," led by the United States and Great Britain, invaded Iraq and promptly overthrew the Saddam Hussein regime. The succeeding occupation and rebuilding of Iraq went awry, however, after the nation was convulsed by a potent politically and sectarian-based insurgency. U.S. and coalition forces thus remained in Iraq for years, and the last American troops did not depart the country until late 2011. Prior to the Iraq War, the George W. Bush administration instituted a new muscular national security policy to deal with terrorism in the aftermath of the September 11, 2001, terrorist attacks against the United States in which 2,974 people died. The linchpin of this policy was the so-called Bush Doctrine, which justified the use of preemptive U.S. military force against any nation that threatened American interests or that possessed weapons of mass destruction (WMD), which could threaten the United States. The justification for invading Iraq was based on the assumption that Hussein possessed WMD and that his regime had ties to Al-Qaeda, the terrorist group that perpetrated the September 11 attacks. This assumption had allegedly been confirmed by various intelligence agencies in the run-up to the war. Using these intelligence reports as justification for war, the United States and its allies invaded Iraq, despite pushback from some of its closest and oldest allies as well as significant international disapproval. Further complicating matters, the Iraq War occurred while the United States and its allies were still involved in the Afghanistan War, which had begun in October 2001.

In the first perspective essay, Dr. Jonathan M. House asserts that the United States was not justified in attacking Iraq, given that it had not finished its military mission in Afghanistan. Moreover, in 2003 he argued that Iraq did not present a clear and present danger to U.S. national security, despite manufactured evidence to the contrary. In the second essay, Dr. John T. Kuehn demonstrates that the United States lacked solid evidence that Hussein had ties to Al-Qaeda or that he had the capability of transferring WMD to Al-Qaeda or other terrorist organizations. In addition, Kuehn points out that the invasion of Iraq was not consistent with international law and therefore was not justified. In the third essay, Dr. Phillip Pattee suggests that the United States was indeed justified in invading Iraq in 2003 based on a series of resolutions passed by the United Nations Security Council and the U.S. Congress. With the virtual blessing of these institutions, the United States was legitimately acting within the bounds of international law, given existing evidence that rationalized the invasion of Iraq.

Background Essay

The September 11, 2001, attacks against the United States changed U.S. military policy, as seen in the 2002 National Military Strategy draft whereby the United States shifted from a "shape, respond, and prepare" posture to one in which it vowed to "assure, dissuade, deter forward, and decisively defeat" enemies or potential enemies. This was significant in that it restored clear-cut victory as primacy in military doctrine as opposed to the ongoing post–Cold War philosophy that had sought merely to manage existing situations. The draft also showcased U.S. willingness to launch military operations in a preemptory—rather than a reactive—fashion, something that came to be called the Bush Doctrine. Although initially after the terrorist attacks many in the intelligence community suspected an Iraqi link, no such proof emerged, and Iraq was put on the back burner as the administration pursued Operation ENDURING FREEDOM in Afghanistan in October 2001.

General Tommy Franks, head of U.S. Central Command who directed ENDURING FREEDOM, was told to bring all his war plans up to date, including those dealing with North Korea and Iraq. By December 2001, he had already briefed President George W. Bush and Secretary of Defense Donald Rumsfeld on several plans covering war with Iraq.

By then, Bush was convinced that Iraq had the potential to provide weapons of mass destruction (WMD) to Al-Qaeda and other terrorist organizations. Intelligence coming out of Iraq was thin, much of it supplied by émigrés who had a vested interest in the toppling of President Saddam Hussein's totalitarian regime. Most of the evidence was either in the "probable" category or in the "common sense" category: Hussein had possessed these weapons in the past and had used them in the Iraq-Iran War. He had become infamous in many circles for having employed poison gas against his Kurdish population, and there was little hard evidence that he had completely dismantled these programs. Although the Central Intelligence

U.S. Marines on patrol near Iraqi dictator Saddam Hussein's presidential palace in Baghdad, April 18, 2003. (Department of Defense)

Agency qualified its language in reports to Bush, most officials—especially Vice President Richard Cheney, Rumsfeld, National Security Advisor Condoleezza Rice, and General Franks—all believed that the intelligence community tended to underestimate threats and misjudge how quickly enemy attacks could be launched. With that in mind, Bush began a yearlong campaign to either determine that Hussein did not have WMD or, if he did, to remove him from power. In his January 2002 State of the Union address, the president invoked the term "axis of evil" to describe the three nations he believed to be in possession of "the world's most dangerous weapons": specifically Iraq, Iran, and North Korea.

General Franks had already begun to develop war plans. In part because of opposition to a war with Iraq from key U.S. allies, Franks realized that a massive buildup on the scale of the Persian Gulf War simply would not be possible. Despite the opinions of a number of knowledgeable military leaders that these numbers would be inadequate, Franks planned on a much smaller force of approximately 150,000 to 200,000 troops. The military buildup occurred over a period of several months in Kuwait. Franks determined that an opening air campaign of several weeks—as had been the case in the 1991 Persian Gulf War—might not be the best approach, and he formed separate plans for simultaneous ground and air operations.

Having secured authorization from the U.S. Congress for war should he believe it necessary and having had Secretary of State Colin Powell make the case before the United Nations that Iraq possessed WMD, Bush moved toward war. After Hussein rejected Bush's demand that he and his sons give up power, Bush approved a "decapitation strike" on Hussein and senior Iraqi leadership on the night of March 19, 2003. While this strike failed in its primary objective of removing Hussein, it did effectively sever him from his command structure. The U.S. invasion of Iraq, dubbed Operation IRAQI FREEDOM by the Bush administration, was on.

By that time the United States had 241,500 troops in the region, joined by 41,000 British, 2,000 Australian, and 200 Polish forces along with smaller or ancillary commitments from Spain, Italy, Ukraine, Denmark, and other countries for peacekeepers after the official end of hostilities. The actual invasion force numbered some 183,000 troops. Coalition forces began moving into Iraq on March 21.

Larry E. Schweikart

Perspective Essay 1. Manufactured Intelligence Brought War

There are two standard explanations for the 2003 U.S. invasion of Iraq. On the one hand, many critics accuse the George W. Bush administration of lying to justify an attack that was motivated by a desire to secure oil. Others blame the intelligence agencies for incompetence, misleading the administration as well as the public. While the intelligence community was by no means perfect, these two versions overlook a third explanation: that a group of officials were so convinced that Iraq constituted a threat that they rejected intelligence reports that contradicted their preconceived notions, instead manufacturing their own "intelligence" to support those notions.

After the 1991 Persian Gulf War, the United Nations (UN) Security Council demanded the destruction of all Iraqi weapons of mass destruction (WMD) and all missiles with a range of more than 150 kilometers. Under the supervision of the UN Special Commission on Iraq, President Saddam Hussein's Iraqi regime destroyed more than 38,000 filled and unfilled bombs as well as 690 tons of lethal chemical agents. Meanwhile, the International Atomic Energy Commission carried out inspections designed to prevent any Iraqi efforts to create nuclear weapons. The Iraqi government repeatedly "certified" that it had destroyed all forbidden materials, only to have inspectors find additional weapons. The Iraqis increasingly impeded these inspections, which ground to a halt in 1998. Meanwhile, the Iraqi regime manipulated the UN Oil-for-Food Programme, designed to aid the Iraqi people, in order to obtain some $1.8 billion that it used to purchase unauthorized materials abroad.

This record gave rise to a belief among analysts, reporters, and politicians that Hussein would never surrender a WMD capability and that he appeared to be waiting for UN sanctions to expire so he could resume weapons production. The United States and its coalition partners therefore used the no-fly zones of Operations NORTHERN WATCH and SOUTHERN WATCH to strike various Iraqi targets possibly associated with these programs.

Hussein was a secular dictator not associated with religious extremism. In fact, some terrorists considered him to be their enemy. In the wake of the September 11, 2001, terrorist attacks against the United States, however, many Americans in and out of office drew the emotional conclusion that America's adversaries must be cooperating with each other. In his 2002 State of the Union address, President Bush described the three dissimilar states of secularized Sunni Iraq, radical Shia Iran, and communist North Korea as an "axis of evil" and warned that these states might provide WMD to terrorists. Defense Secretary Donald Rumsfeld accused Hussein of supporting terrorism because, as a public relations ploy, Iraq paid compensation to the families of Palestinian suicide bombers.

The U.S. intelligence community's efforts to track down nonstate terrorists depended heavily on human sources, Middle Easterners who claimed unique access to the terrorists. The reports of such sources were by definition difficult to confirm or deny. Therefore, various individuals—Ahmed Chalab being a prime example—whether seeking personal gain or wanting the United States to invade told the Bush administration what it obviously wished to hear. U.S. intelligence agencies received various allegations concerning contacts between the Baghdad government, Al-Qaeda, and other enemies of America or reports of new WMD in Iraq. Most experienced Middle East analysts were extremely skeptical of these allegations, but unfortunately not everyone read these reports with the same critical eyes. In fact, when the intelligence agencies did not provide the expected confirmation of their beliefs, some political appointees apparently decided that those agencies were politicizing the process and so decided to bypass them and create their own "intelligence."

Even before 9/11, U.S. undersecretary of state for arms control John Bolton insisted that he and his staff must have access to the raw intelligence reports normally filtered by analysts with experience in the subject matter. Deputy Defense Secretary Paul D. Wolfowitz created the Office of Special Plans, which combined such reports with the input of Iraqi exiles such as Chalabi; many of these exile assertions were later discredited. Yet, without conclusive evidence to the contrary, there was no way for intelligence analysts to reject the claims, especially when policy makers led by Vice President Dick Cheney were so insistent upon believing those allegations.

U.S. undersecretary of defense for policy Douglas Feith organized the Policy Counter Terrorism Evaluation Group within Wolfowitz's organization. This group claimed, contrary to the opinion of several intelligence agencies, that there was a cooperative relationship between Iraq and Al-Qaeda. Feith not only circularized these allegations to the White House as if they were finished intelligence products but also criticized the intelligence community for its analysis to the contrary. The result was an obvious conflict of interest, with policy makers generating "intelligence" to justify their own recommended courses of action. The Defense Department inspector general later described Feith's actions as "improper."

By July 2002 the Bush administration, influenced by "intelligence" reports that confirmed its own expectations, had decided that it must overthrow Hussein in order to eliminate a range of perceived threats. The United States persuaded the UN Security Council to declare Iraq in breach of its obligations, putting the onus on Baghdad to prove that it had complied with previous restrictions on WMD. As UN inspectors again entered the country, U.S. intelligence agencies received dozens of reports of Iraqi efforts at concealment. Just what was being concealed was unclear, but seen in context, many analysts assumed that this included additional unreported WMD components.

One final factor should be noted. To coerce Iraq into accepting renewed inspections, the United States began to build up its forces in the region. As a practical matter, the United States could not maintain such forces indefinitely, yet any withdrawal would appear to be backing down to Hussein. Therefore, the U.S. government was inclined to use those forces, preferably before the extreme heat of the Middle Eastern summer.

Thus, by early 2003 the Bush administration had backed itself into a corner regarding Iraq. Having repeatedly announced that the Baghdad regime was concealing WMD and aiding terrorist organizations, the administration felt compelled, by its own logic and its sincere but flawed perception of the situation, to eliminate that regime.

Jonathan M. House

Perspective Essay 2. Evidence Was Lacking

Five disappointing years after the U.S. invasion of Iraq in 2003, a study by the National Defense University concluded that "Measured in blood and treasure, the war in Iraq had achieved the status of major war and a major debacle." The decision to invade Iraq in 2003 was not justified based on what was known at the time about Saddam Hussein's chemical and nuclear weapons of mass destruction (WMD) programs as well as his alleged links with terrorists who posed a threat to the United States. Nor was the invasion consistent with international law.

The backdrop for the decision to invade Iraq was the devastating September 11, 2001, attacks on the World Trade Center and the Pentagon mounted by the Al-Qaeda terrorist organization. It was this context that caused the George W. Bush administration to marginalize the constraints in place and conflate two conflicts, one against terrorists and their sponsors in Afghanistan and an ongoing conflict with but not in Iraq.

A cold war with Iraq had begun 10 years earlier with the end of the Persian Gulf War in 1991. The American people hardly realized that the conflict with Iraq existed. Occasionally the United States employed air strikes to punish Hussein for his actions, but other than that most Americans were unaware of the deterioration of the U.S. measures supporting United Nations (UN) resolutions against Iraq. By 2000 this cold war had turned into a shooting war, although the relatively limited casualties were on the Iraqi side.

The U.S.-UN regime of sanctions led both France and Russia to apply pressure to reduce these measures. U.S. policy makers were on the defensive, and UN officials benefited from secretly colluding with Iraq in circumventing the Oil-for-Food Programme. Hussein used this extra money not for medicine and food as specified but instead to make purchases to refurbish his military in violation of the sanctions. Some U.S. intelligence assessments failed to understand that Hussein's ability to produce WMD had been damaged by the combination of air strikes and UN sanctions.

The 9/11 attacks, however, cast an entirely new light on the Iraqi situation. First, the supposed threat of Iraqi WMD gained new significance, given the innovative actions of terrorists such as Al-Qaeda. What if they managed to get WMD munitions from Hussein and then employed them against U.S. targets, as had been done on 9/11?

Another factor contributing to the context for the decision was the ongoing campaign in Afghanistan. The terrorists who had attacked the United States had been trained in that country and supported by the Taliban regime in power in Kabul. Despite a successful campaign that toppled the Taliban, Osama bin Laden escaped efforts to capture him, and U.S. forces and intelligence had still not located him.

The contrary position, against an invasion of Iraq, was perhaps best summed up by President Bush's father, former president George H. W. Bush, and Brent Scowcroft in their 1998 book *A World Transformed:*

> Going in and occupying Iraq [in 1991], thus unilaterally exceeding the United Nations' mandate, would have destroyed the precedent of international response to aggression that we hoped to establish. Had we gone the invasion [of Iraq] route, the United States could conceivably still [in 1998] be an occupying power in a bitterly hostile land.

Thus, from the standpoint of international law, UN support was required to invade Iraq.

The chief impetus for an invasion of Iraq in 2003 came from a cabal led by Vice President Dick Cheney and other so-called Neocons (neoconservatives) inside the government. They tended to reject the caution espoused by Secretary of State Colin Powell and formed their own intelligence cell to assess intelligence regarding WMD and terrorists. It is still unclear as to just what their objectives were beyond neutralizing or confirming the absence of Hussein's WMD, since most of them had been critical of perceived nation-building efforts by President William Clinton's administration.

Hussein's claim to have WMD when he did not was in all likelihood (and later confirmed by him during his interrogations following his capture by U.S. forces) to have been a bluff to convince Iranian leaders that Iraq was far more a threat than was actually the case. However, the second part of any threat involves demonstrating its use—and in Hussein's case he had not used chemical weapons outside his own nation following the end of the 1980–1988 Iran-Iraq War. The air of mystery surrounding whether he had any operational WMD and was following a more robust program to develop them served his purposes as long as he believed that U.S. forces would never invade Iraq for this reason. After the UN failure to authorize the use of force, he must have believed that U.S. forces would not carry out such a threat.

In 2002 as the Bush administration prepared the case to justify an invasion of Iraq, the ongoing air war in the no-fly zones changed focus. One of the key items in the timing of the invasion of Iraq hinged on the destruction of the Iraqi air defense network. Operation SOUTHERN WATCH was secretly renamed Operation SOUTHERN FOCUS, and the United States began to attack Iraqi air defense targets. Thus, these air operations prior to the invasion of Iraq further degraded the primary reason for the war in the first place—the threat of Iraqi WMD. A bellicose U.S. stance, along with the international perception of the United States as the victim of terrorism, had reversed much opposition in the international community to a U.S.-led aggressive containment policy. Hussein had seen U.S. military action and aid to anti-Taliban forces in Afghanistan crush the Taliban there in a matter of weeks.

In 2003 Hussein thus was contained, his WMD facilities targeted and his ability to deliver WMD both critically damaged. Additionally, his air defense system was in ruins. He could continue to be managed with airpower and UN sanctions. Instead, the United States invaded Iraq.

In conclusion, the invasion was clearly unwarranted because by early 2003 the objectives to be accomplished by an invasion had mostly been achieved by an air campaign and the nearly unassailable American diplomatic position after 9/11 and collapse of the Taliban regime in Afghanistan.

John T. Kuehn

Perspective Essay 3. There Was Legal Justification

The United States was justified in invading Iraq in 2003. A series of United Nations (UN) resolutions dating back to 1990 and laws passed in the United States provided the legal basis for the invasion.

In August 1990, Iraqi forces invaded and occupied Kuwait. Resolutions passed by the UN Security Council demanded immediate withdrawal and imposed sanctions on Iraq. UN Security Council Resolution (UNSCR) 678 demanded that Iraq comply by January 15, 1991, noting that legal justification for international action had been met, and authorized member states "to use all necessary means to uphold and implement Resolution 660 and all subsequent relevant resolutions and to restore international peace and security in the area." Justification for the U.S.-led coalition's action in the 1991 Persian Gulf War was predicated on that resolution and congressional authorization granted by Public Law 102-1 of January 14, 1991.

The UNSCR 678's key phrase, "all subsequent relevant resolutions," indicated that member states were authorized to act on future resolutions provided that each is linked to the original. New resolutions with language "recalling" or "reaffirming" previous resolutions by number and approval date establish that they are "relevant subsequent resolutions."

At war's end, the UNSCR 687 of April 3, 1991—specifically recalled and linked to UNSCR 678—established that Iraq must unconditionally accept dismantling and destruction of its chemical, biological, and nuclear weapons (weapons of mass destruction, or WMD) programs and any missile program exceeding 150 kilometers in range. The UN would lift sanctions when Iraq met those conditions and weapons inspectors, known as the UN Special Commission (UNSCOM), had verified compliance.

During the next several years Iraq stonewalled UNSCOM inspectors, periodically ejecting them but then allowing their return when the United States and the United Kingdom threatened military force. Finally in December 1998 when threats had no effect, U.S. and British aircraft conducted four days of strikes throughout Iraq. Known as Operation DESERT FOX, these were intended to disrupt Saddam Hussein's WMD program. The governments justified their actions with UNSCRs 678 and 687. Without inspectors, however, assessing the damage to Iraq's WMD capability was impossible.

In January 2001 when George W. Bush became U.S. president, the status of Iraq's WMD programs remained unknown, so Bush still considered Iraqi leader Hussein a threat. Hussein continued to forestall weapons inspections, so by April 2002 British prime minister Tony Blair and President Bush concluded that Hussein must be overthrown. White House legal experts advised Bush that he had the same legal justification for an invasion as had been employed in Operation DESERT FOX based on UN resolutions and his authority as commander in chief. Bush acknowledged this but knew that Russia, France, and Germany had opposed DESERT FOX. UN support and congressional authorization would strengthen his position.

Bush met congressional leaders to explain his rationale, and Congress approved. Public Law 107-243 authorized the president to employ force in order to enforce the UN resolutions. Within the UN, France insisted on new inspections, then upon receipt of the weapons inspector's report the UN Security Council would consider the situation to determine if Iraq had made false declarations and failed to cooperate or whether the UN had achieved its purposes and Iraq was in full and verified compliance. In the latter case, UN-imposed sanctions could be lifted. After some haggling, the Security Council passed UNSCR 1441 unanimously.

UNSCR 1441 clarified that Iraq had a final opportunity for compliance with UNSCR 687 with the goal of achieving full and verified completion. As in previous resolutions, UNSCR 1441 recalled UNSCRs 678 and 687—reiterating the authorization of member states to use all necessary means to uphold and implement the original UNSCR 660 and all subsequent relevant resolutions—and thus was linked to them with their embedded authority. In fact, UNSCR 1441 stated plainly that Iraq had been and remained in material breach of UNSCR 687, having failed to meet its obligation to disarm. Paragraph 9 provided that Iraq must demonstrate immediate, unconditional, and active cooperation with the UN Monitoring, Verification and Inspection Commission (UNMOVIC).

On November 26, 2002, Hussein agreed to allow new weapons inspections. The next day, UNMOVIC commenced its activities. On January 27, 2003, lead inspector Hans Blix reported to the Security Council covering the first 60 days of inspections. He concluded that Iraq had not come to a genuine acceptance of the WMD disarmament demanded of it. Iraq had made false declarations and was less than fully cooperative. Blix could not guarantee that Iraq no longer possessed WMD, but he also could not definitely state that Iraq had them. Bush's cabinet concluded that UNMOVIC's report provided all the justification required to show that Iraq had squandered its final chance.

Because the governments of France, Russia, and China remained unmoved by Blix's report, U.S. secretary of state Colin Powell appeared at the UN and detailed the Bush administration's case against Iraq. Response to Powell's speech was mixed. But Hussein was clearly feeling the pressure. His agents made contact with the Egyptian government to explore the possibility of Hussein and his family going into exile. French president Jacques Chirac, aware of the idea, spoke with Bush about it because he thought it could avoid war. However, after Chirac met with German chancellor Gerhard Schröder and Russian premier Vladimir Putin, the three insisted on extended inspections in Iraq and declared war unjustified. With clear opposition to the use of force from Security Council permanent members France and Russia, Hussein's plans for possible exile evaporated.

Although the Bush administration worked diligently to gain French support, Chirac remained unwilling to either reaffirm use of force or certify that Iraq had met the UN demands. Meanwhile, Great Britain showed its support for Bush's position by passing its own resolution authorizing force against Iraq.

Ultimately a U.S.-led coalition invaded Iraq on March 20, 2003. Bush and coalition members were confident that the invasion was justified. Iraq had failed to cooperate with UNMOVIC inspectors, thus violating UN Resolutions 1441, 687, and 678. The invasion was legal because it was authorized based on Public Law 107-243 in the United States and by UN Resolution 1441.

Phillip G. Pattee

Further Reading

Anderson, Terry H. *Bush's Wars.* Oxford: Oxford University Press, 2011.

Art, Robert J., and Patrick M. Cronin. *The United States and Coercive Diplomacy.* Washington, DC: United States Institute of Peace, 2003.

Blix, Hans. *Disarming Iraq.* London: Bloomsbury, 2004.

Bush, George H. W., and Brent Scocroft. *A World Transformed.* New York: Knopf, 1998.

Carlisle, Rodney P., and John S. Bowman, eds. *Iraq War.* Updated ed. New York: Facts on File, 2007.

Collins, Joseph J. "Choosing War: The Decision to Invade Iraq and Its Aftermath." Occasional Paper, Institute for National Strategic Studies. Washington, DC: National Defense University, 2008.

Crist, David. *The Twilight War: The Secret History of America's Thirty-Year Conflict with Iran.* New York: Penguin, 2012.

Duelfer, Charles. *Hide and Seek: The Search for Truth in Iraq.* New York: PublicAffairs/Perseus Group, 2009.

Feith, Douglas J. *War and Decision: Inside the Pentagon at the Dawn of the War on Terrorism.* New York: HarperCollins, 2008.

Gordon, Michael, and General Bernard Trainor. *Cobra II: The Inside Story of the Invasion and Occupation of Iraq.* New York: Pantheon Books, 2006.

Hamza, Khidhir, with Jeff Stein. *Saddam's Bombmaker: The Terrifying Inside Story of the Iraqi Nuclear and Biological Weapons Agenda.* New York: Scribner, 2000.

Hannay, David. "Three Iraq Intelligence Failures Reconsidered." *Survival* 51(6) (December 2009–January 2010): 13–20.

Hersh, Seymour M. "Selective Intelligence Annals of National Security." *New Yorker* 79(11) (May 12, 2003): 44–51.

Lambeth, Benjamin S. *The Unseen War: Allied Air Power and the Takedown of Saddam Hussein.* Annapolis, MD: Naval Institute Press, 2013.

Mullaney, Craig. *The Unforgiving Minute.* New York: Penguin, 2010.

Pollack, Kenneth. *The Threatening Storm: What Every American Needs to Know before an Invasion in Iraq.* New York: Random House, 2002.

Woods, Kevin M., with M. R. Pease, Mark E. Stout, Williamson Murray, and James Lacy. *Iraqi Perspectives Project: A View of Operation Iraqi Freedom from Saddam's Senior Leadership.* Norfolk, VA: Joint Center for Operational Analysis and Lessons Learned, 2006.

Woodward, Bob. *Plan of Attack.* New York: Simon and Schuster, 2004.

60. Was the U.S. Goal of Constructing a Stable, Democratic Regime in Post-2003 Iraq Realistic?

After the September 11, 2001, Al-Qaeda terror attacks against the United States, the George W. Bush administration formulated the Bush Doctrine, which held that the United States reserved the right to use preemptory force against any nation or group that threatened American interests or possessed weapons of mass destruction (WMD). The doctrine also embraced the idea of exporting democratization to other parts of the world. In the run-up to the Iraq War, the Bush administration insisted that Iraqi dictator Saddam Hussein had links to Al-Qaeda and possessed WMD. Thus, preemptive war against Iraq was justified. With Hussein gone, U.S. policy makers hoped to transform postwar Iraq into a beacon of democracy that would serve as a model for other nations in the Middle East. The first months of the Iraq War went well—Hussein's government was quickly toppled, and coalition troops secured Iraq's major cities in short order. However, a series of missteps and miscalculations on the part of U.S. occupation officials along with rising sectarian strife soon resulted in a potent insurgency that threatened millions of Iraqi civilians as well as coalition troops. By 2005, the country was involved in a full-blown civil war. Coalition troops were trapped in Iraq until late 2011, and Iraq was nearly as unstable as it had been eight years earlier. The country is now involved in another insurgency with Islamic extremists, and violence remains endemic.

In the first perspective essay, Dr. Lance Janda believes that America's goal of constructing a stable, democratic Iraq after 2003 was not realistic. He points out that Iraq lacked many of the prerequisites of democracy, including governmental bodies designed to protect civil liberties, a commitment to the rule of law, a tradition of respecting minority rights, experience with freedom of the press and religion, a history of political compromise, and national unity. Furthermore, the United States had too few troops to stabilize Iraq, and its policy makers had little understanding of Iraqi history and culture. In the second essay, Dr. Michael Kraig asserts that America's mission in Iraq was well intentioned but doomed to failure. He points out that forced democratization and mass marketization in countries such as Iraq are bound to fail because these nations lack any experience with democratic pluralism and free market capitalism. They also lack a commitment to the rule of law. Kraig goes on to argue that America's de-Baathification program hamstrung efforts to bring democracy to Iraq and that American values could not be summarily imposed on Iraq. In the end, he concludes that democratization is a product—and not a producer—of social stability in places such as Iraq.

Background Essay

For the United States at least, the Iraq War ended in December 2011 when the last U.S. forces left the country, but the effects of the war continue to impact Iraq and the entire region. There can be little doubt that the conflict has had a profound impact on regional security. The war changed the nature and stability of the Iraqi state and that of some of its neighbors, most notably neighboring Syria. Since the withdrawal of U.S. troops, Iraq is still plagued by sectarian strife and general violence.

Far from the easy victory the George W. Bush administration promised, the war was prolonged and costly, and it created a power vacuum filled first by lawlessness and then by an intractable insurgency. The resulting destruction of property and infrastructure, coupled with unemployment that at its peak topped 60 percent, greatly diminished the Iraqi standard of living. Resentment of Americans only fueled the insurgency. The conflict further damaged Iraqi infrastructure and delayed economic and social recovery. Indeed, the country is still struggling to rebuild and regain its prewar standard of living.

Operation IRAQI FREEDOM did deliver on its promise to remove Hussein from power and replace his brutal regime with a democratic one. Iraqi democracy is, however, still on very shaky ground, for Iraq is a nation profoundly divided by religion and ethnicity. Iraq's population totals some 35 million. Arabs constitute some 75–80 percent, Kurds make up 15–20 percent, and Turkomen and Assyrians constitute some 5 percent. Religion has played a central role in postinvasion Iraq. Some 97 percent of the population is Muslim, while Christians are perhaps 3 percent. (The ancient Christian community of Iraq has been subject to considerable persecution since the stated end of the war in 2011.)

The great divide, however, is between Shia and Sunni Muslims. Shias constitute perhaps 60–65 percent of the total Iraqi population, while Sunnis make up 32–37 percent. For some time before the U.S.-led invasion, the Sunnis had dominated the life of the country, controlling all aspects of its government and its military establishment. There had also been severe persecution of both the Kurds and the Shias under President Saddam Hussein, himself a Sunni. In the process many Shias and Kurds had died. Among the Kurds in northern Iraq there was great distrust of both the Sunnis and the Shias. The Kurds therefore have sought their own state or at least autonomy. The Shias, however, particular thirsted for revenge; the change to majority rule wrought by the United States following the 2003 invasion gave them the opportunity, and they seized it. With the Sunni population dominating in northern and western Iraq, the Kurds dominating in the far north, and the Shias dominating in the south, the country seemed ripe for a split into three states along ethnic lines, a danger that had been pointed out to and ignored by the Bush administration when it undertook the invasion.

The United States and its partners were determined to preserve the territorial integrity of a state the borders of which had been artificially created after World War I. But despite efforts to preserve minority representation through proportional representation and regional autonomy, instituting majority rule in effect led to a purge of Sunnis from positions of influence throughout the country and to a fierce insurgency that has yet to be quelled today. The coalition led by Shiite politician Nuri al-Maliki, who was Iraqi premier during 2006–2014, proved a particular disaster. Al-Maliki simply ignored all appeals from the United States to form a more inclusive government and even engaged in repression of the Sunnis, which both fed the Sunni insurgency and abetted the influence of Al-Qaeda and the rise of the

Iraq's prime minister–designate Nuri al-Maliki during a news conference in Baghdad on May 9, 2006. Al-Maliki was officially sworn in as the country's new prime minister on May 20, 2006. (AP Photo/Ali Haider)

Islamic State of Iraq and Syria (ISIS). Al-Maliki's successor, Haider al-Abadi, has at least expressed his desire for a more inclusive democracy and has appointed both Kurds and Sunnis to positions of influence, but much more needs to be done in a country where religious animosities remain strong.

Even if Iraq can avoid a civil war and dismemberment, these problems threaten to keep the Iraqi state weak for years to come. The insertion of ISIS into this complicated equation has only made Iraq's long-term viability even more remote. Iraq's future thus remains very much in question.

Spencer C. Tucker and Thomas R. Mockaitis

Perspective Essay 1. No Chance of Securing Democracy in Iraq

In 100 years, scholars will wonder with abject dismay how intelligent people in the United States convinced themselves that constructing a stable democracy in Iraq through force of arms was possible. Few other military or foreign policy efforts in American history combined good intentions, arrogance, ignorance, wishful thinking, staggering incompetence, abject corruption, and poor planning on such a massive scale. None was ever more preventable or absolutely destined for failure.

Consider that in 2003 Iraq had virtually none of the prerequisites considered essential for democracy. There existed no large group of elites committed to democratic rule, no state institutions devoted to protecting civil liberties, no cultural or social commitment to a rule of law to which all citizens answered, limited national unity, no tradition of respecting majority rule or minority rights or pluralism, no freedom of speech or of the press, limited freedom of religion, no widespread commitment to individual liberties or women's rights, and no experience with negotiation or compromise in the political culture.

Instead, after thousands of years and dozens of civilizations and after decades of colonial rule and British interference, Iraq endured monarchy, revolution, and ultimately despotism under Sadaam Hussein. Iraq existed as a deeply fractured state, riddled with tribal and sectarian divisions and dominated by a Sunni Muslim minority that held sway over a bitter Shiite majority and a Kurdish population eager for independence. Already weakened by the Iran-Iraq War in the 1980s, by an American invasion in 1991, and by years of international sanctions, the country was held together only by the brutal subjugation and tyrannical rule of a police state. In short, it was absolutely poised to break apart in sectarian fighting if the government ever collapsed and not to come together in a moment of Jeffersonian democracy if only Hussein were removed from power.

Collectively, those challenges made the creation of a viable democracy in Iraq virtually hopeless, particularly given the proximity of Iran, which had no interest in seeing a pro-U.S. democracy emerge on its western border, and the decisive nature of the Sunni/Shiite hatred in Iraq. Shiites were a majority of the population, yet they were repressed for decades by a Sunni minority led by Hussein that held all major leadership positions. In any true Iraqi democracy the Shiites would rule as a majority party, and they were likely to be eager for payback. Sunnis were just as likely to refuse to accept political and cultural marginalization, and that fact alone likely doomed efforts at democratic reform before they could even began.

The United States compounded these problems by invading with too few troops to maintain order and, after brilliant tactical and operational success, found itself in a strategic wilderness. Few provisions had been made for long-term stability operations or nation building, and following a brief period of euphoria after the capture of Hussein the country gradually broke apart due to an emerging insurgency and a breakdown of law and order. That breakdown was accelerated by the Coalition Provisional Authority (CPA), the first post-Hussein government created by the United States. Under the leadership of Paul Bremer, the CPA excluded all members of the Baath Party (which Hussein had led) from positions of leadership and disbanded the Iraqi Army. These actions practically guaranteed an insurgency led by alienated Sunnis who had dominated the Baath Party and the Iraqi Army and had the military training to become opposition leaders almost immediately. Looting, murders, and ambushes became commonplace, foreign fighters flooded the country, and the deteriorating security situation made democratic reforms difficult because Iraqis were often afraid to vote or speak out against abuse for fear of reprisals.

Legions of American civilians sent to Iraq to assist in the difficult transition to democracy often worsened the situation because they were chosen for their ideology and commitment to the Republican Party rather than for their expertise. Most had little or no knowledge of Iraqi history and culture and did not possess Arabic-language skills, and they were arrogantly and tragically idealistic and naive. Their well-intentioned efforts at building free institutions and infrastructure almost all met with failure, alienated Iraqis, and cost billions of U.S. dollars.

By 2006, Iraq had deteriorated to the point that an Iraq Study Group recommended a large-scale American withdrawal. President George W. Bush countered with a troop surge instead and by changing tactics and paying off disparate insurgent groups was able to significantly lower the intensity of the fighting. However, the Iraqi government under Prime Minister Nouri Kamil Mohammed Hasan al-Maliki persecuted Sunnis and provoked more fighting, particularly after the United States withdrew troops in 2011. It was also his government, responding to popular pressure (a reminder that a truly democratic Iraq might not be pro-U.S.), that refused to sign a status of forces agreement with the United States and therefore prevented the long-term presence of U.S. forces that could have supported the Iraqi Army. Dozens of disparate terrorist and insurgency groups flocked to or emerged from the almost constant chaos in Iraq until 2014, when the Islamic State of Iraq and the Levant became so powerful and captured so much equipment from an incompetent and ineffective Iraqi Army (trained at great expense by the United States) that American troops were forced to return to prop up the government.

In 2016 the Iraqi government remained largely inept and seemingly incapable of creating unity among Kurds or Shiite and Sunni Muslims and was also unable to police its border with Iran, with which many see Iraq as being aligned. Indeed, Iran seems to have strengthened its power in the region, which Washington had sought to prevent.

Whether all of this could have been averted is a highly charged political topic. Most scholars agree that the 2003 invasion was a catastrophic mistake that destabilized the region and that any hopes of building a stable democracy in Iraq were misplaced. Some, however, argue that there was hope for a time, that many opportunities were lost, and that the surge demonstrated that U.S. forces needed to stay longer. The mistake, in their view, was withdrawing in 2011 rather than invading Iraq in 2003 in the first place.

Despite those arguments, it remains difficult to conceive of a scenario in which a stable democracy could have emerged in Iraq, given the overwhelming sectarian, historical, cultural, and regional obstacles in place within the time frame allotted by the United States. With no meaningful indigenous prodemocracy movement to build on, the idea of democracy remained stronger in the minds of Americans than it ever was in the minds of most Iraqis. And with trillions of American dollars now lost, between 150,000 and 500,000 Iraqi dead, and the region in chaos, it is an idea that seems destined to remain elusive.

Lance Janda

Perspective Essay 2. Noble Intent That Was Doomed to Failure

America's stated political (and economic) project in Iraq was unobtainable because it did not understand or admit the strong *social* engineering aspect of any attempt to create a modern, viable nation-state. The key word here is "nation," which is the *cultural* component of any functioning country.

In this regard, any assessment of this latest modernizing effort is incomplete if it views 2003 onward as a purely unique case of Iraq, the Middle East, and the George W. Bush administration's handling of the aftermath of military invasion. Far beyond Iraq alone, since 1991 democratic and free market policies have had their day not just in the Middle East but also across the most conflict- and poverty-ridden states of Central America, Africa, and Asia. Such structures have been purposefully and repeatedly instituted in societies recovering from violent internal conflicts via the United Nations (UN) in various development organizations, the European-dominated Organization for Economic Cooperation and Development, the U.S.-dominated International Monetary Fund (IMF) and World Bank, the new World Trade Organization, and countless bilateral development programs, all directed by wealthy states toward poor ones. And the paradigm of quick democratization and mass-marketization has often been found wanting.

Exhaustive research efforts across regions and continents have now shown that the collective, societal rule of law—based on a widely held civic identity—has proven far more difficult to establish than relatively straightforward election, legal, and financial procedures. And as seen perhaps most dramatically in Iraq, without both the rule of law and a firm national-level identity that is meaningful (with one complementing the other), democratization and marketization can be a recipe for rampant violence, criminality, and substate conflict.

To understand Iraq's outcomes—and similar outcomes across continents since the early 1990s—one must understand the larger civilizational history from which U.S. occupation policy was formed. From the start, the U.S. effort was predicated on widely held American assumptions about human nature that ultimately are fundamentally acultural in content and origin. U.S. assumptions have basically been derived from the European Enlightenment tradition, traceable to philosophers such as Jean-Jacques Rousseau, John Locke, Thomas Hobbes, Charles-Louis Montesquieu, Immanuel Kant, and later John Stuart Mill. A thread shared by all of these founding fathers of modern civic thought is that there is something called a "universal human being" or "human nature" with ultimately broadly similar wants, needs, desires, and drivers, all in turn exerted outward from the individual via the use of *reason* and *free will* in an ideally free society. And what is meant by "a free society" is both an economic and a political environment in which there is a minimum of "artificial" or "corrupted" skewing of natural, individual capabilities and desires. The "natural condition of man" that they all agreed on was one of individual freedom that allowed individuals to exert to the utmost their own gifts, with societal and governmental structures alike existing only to improve the chances of those gifts being realized in harmony with others.

Notably, these grand European thinkers did *not* look kindly on inherited cultural worldviews. Instead, they looked around them and saw individual reason, will, and abilities chronically short-changed or blocked—and even actively punished—by societies based instead on unequal, arbitrary, inherited structures, whether those corrupting structures were racial or ethnic, religious, tribal, aristocratic, and so on. In short, Western philosophers saw the pristine reasoning individual as being unjustly challenged by the historical and ultimately accidental development of corrupt, oppressive, and overly hierarchical government and economic elites. The goal then was to have a revolution that decisively overturned the one in favor of the other.

This philosophic foundation has driven U.S. policies since 1945. It was originally seen quite explicitly in the efforts of a whole generation of new sociological scholars in the 1950s and 1960s, who together were heavily funded by the then-new Social Science Research Council, with strong ties to Cold War security goals. Their mutually supportive research and theoretical efforts eventually involved actual measurement of universal social categories across the globe, with finely defined metrics that filtered away cultural dissimilarities to expose the (presumed) core universal constants in the *modernization of the human race.*

Perhaps inevitably, these scholars, particularly Harvard professor and sociologist Talcott Parsons, came to the conclusion that the way to avoid overly radical, oppressive, failed nationalisms such as German and Japanese fascism (and of course Soviet communism) was to have guided middle-class revolutions. The latter, in turn, were to be predicated on the values of the American New Deal: democratic vote, high employment, free market fiscal and monetary policies, public education, and so forth in which competition for relative individual gain would be moderated in the context of an attachment to the modernizing state as its own entity, apart from preexisting "nonrational" cultural categories. These scholarly and advocacy efforts, via strong networking connections to policy makers in Washington, D.C., became ultimately channeled, defined, and packaged as "modernization theory." The final product of this fundamentally Enlightenment theory of the betterment of humankind was offered by MIT scholar Walt Whitman Rostow in *The Economic Stages of Growth: A Non-Communist Manifesto* (1960). In due time Rostow was himself adopted into the highest levels of President Lyndon Johnson's cabinet, after having previously remarked that Vietnam should be viewed as the core test case for halting the perceived communist advance in a fragile, still largely primitive Third World.

According to this theory, as a society became modernized, preexisting and "parochial" taboos, worldviews, and practices—including potentially deadly divisions of "us" versus "them" based on religion, tribe, or ethnicity—would inexorably give way to the free-reasoning individual favored already in the West. This would lead in turn via orderly market and political competition to an equally self-determining nation. Thus, a genuinely new *civic identity* would make up the nation within the state, with the key idea being the overall state as the provider of social belonging and cooperation. The goal, in short, was to produce amid the helter-skelter of thousands of competing lingual, ethnic, tribal, and religious identities in the Third World a far more homogenous, individualist, and abstract "civic self" that would be paired with an equally abstract civic community, ultimately defined by the bounded territorial nation-state. The goal was to fight the Cold War not with just bombs and guns or straight economic payoffs to unsavory regimes but instead by using American values, material largesse, and sense of purpose to engineer the "right kind of revolution" throughout the postcolonial world.

This focus did not disappear with the end of the Cold War; indeed, it has become mainstreamed. IMF and World Bank reforms in fiscal, monetary, and financial institutions have become the new normal in weak and fragile states seeking to recover from armed conflict, along with purposefully parallel efforts at political democratization.

Iraq in turn has been an especially tragic case of the limited success of this intellectual and policy consensus. Actual data from early UN and Western efforts in the 1990s to build market democracies from Central America to Africa to the Middle East have often shown that in the absence of a functioning, noncorrupt system of domestic law and security alongside the empowerment of local cultures and economic actors, the immediate institution of free-for-all competition in both politics and economics creates not peace but instead a heightened and even severely intensified version of us-versus-them, winner-take-all competition. An unfiltered, abstract imposition of Western modernization tends to create a doubling down along preexisting cultural fault lines, producing the opposite of the rule of law: the "capturing of the state" by one or two favored identity groups at the expense of all others. The result is often rampant criminality and corruption of state institutions, as fast-tracked market and democratic institutions become skewed toward preexisting cultural boundaries that already provide their own version of communal identity, prosperity, and security.

Apparently, an abstract, all-inclusive, *purely civic* definition of "I" and "us" is hardly natural to the human condition and cannot be instantly engineered. Before heated electoral and free market competition, there must be a more pragmatic rule of law—in short, a republic rather than a democracy. This means a strong but noncorrupt judiciary, police, and penal systems and subsidized help to major traditional sectors of the economy, building up from preexisting cultural groupings toward a functioning state. A national identity then slowly materializes over time in this safe, predictable environment, leading eventually to a true national identity that can support complex, multiparty democracy.

In the case of Iraq, this would have meant accepting some version of the preexisting Baathist army, police, and civilian institutional and educational infrastructure as a given from the start (albeit without Hussein's cliques leading it). The goal, then, would have been the slow incorporation of all social actors into the Baathist political structure over time, with steady work toward making Baathist institutions more transparent, more open, and as corruption-free as possible. Eventually, a fully formed free market democracy might have been possible. President George W. Bush's policies might have succeeded had the Iraq War's creators accepted contemporary empirical studies that have together shown democratization to be the *product*, not the *producer*, of national social stability in a modernizing state.

Michael Ryan Kraig

Further Reading

Al-Ali, Zaid. *The Struggle for Iraq's Future: How Corruption, Incompetence and Sectarianism Have Undermined Democracy.* New Haven, CT: Yale University Press, 2014.

Allawi, Ali A. *The Occupation of Iraq: Winning the War, Losing the Peace.* New Haven, CT: Yale University Press, 2007.

Anderson, Terry H. *Bush's Wars.* New York: Oxford University Press, 2011.

Baker, James A., III, and Lee Hamilton. *The Iraq Study Group Report.* New York: Vintage, 2006.

Barnett, Michael. "Building a Republican Peace: Stabilizing States after War," *International Security* 30(4) (Spring 2006): 87–112.

Bolger, Daniel. *Why We Lost: A General's Inside Account of the Iraq and Afghanistan Wars.* New York: Houghton Mifflin, 2014.

Brazinsky, Gregg. *Nation Building in South Korea: Koreans, Americans, and the Making of a Democracy.* Chapel Hill: University of North Carolina Press, 2007.

Bull, Carolyn. *No Entry without Strategy: Building the Rule of Law under UN Transitional Administration.* New York: United Nations University Press, 2008.

Call, Charles T., ed. *Constructing Justice and Security after War.* Washington, DC: United States Institute of Peace Press, 2007.

Caraley, Demetrios James. *American Hegemony: Preventive War, Iraq, and Imposing Democracy.* New York: Academy of Political Science, 2004.

Chandrasekaran, Rajiv. *Imperial Life in the Emerald City: Inside Iraq's Green Zone.* New York, Vintage Books, 2007.

Cheeseman, Nic. *Democracy in Africa: Successes, Failures, and the Struggle for Political Reform.* Cambridge: Cambridge University Press, 2015.

Diamond, Larry. *Squandered Victory: The American Occupation and the Bungled Effort to Bring Democracy to Iraq.* New York: Holt Paperbacks, 2006.

Dodge, Toby. *Inventing Iraq: The Failure of Nation and a History Denied.* New York: Columbia University Press, 2005.

Feldman, Noah. *What We Owe Iraq: War and the Ethics of Nation Building.* Princeton, NJ: Princeton University Press, 2006.

Fukuyama, Francis. *Nation-Building: Beyond Afghanistan and Iraq.* Baltimore: Johns Hopkins University Press, 2005.

Fukuyama, Francis. *State-Building: Governance and World Order in the 21st Century.* Ithaca, NY: Cornell University Press, 2004.

Gilman, Nils. *Mandarins of the Future: Modernization Theory in Cold War America.* Baltimore: Johns Hopkins University Press, 2007.

Gordon, Michael R., and Bernard E. Trainor. *Cobra II: The Inside Story of the Invasion and Occupation of Iraq.* New York: Pantheon Books, 2006.

Gordon, Michael R., and Bernard E. Trainor. *The Endgame: The Inside Story of the Struggle for Iraq, from George W. Bush to Barack Obama.* New York: Vintage, 2013.

Isakhan, Benjamin. *Democracy in Iraq: History, Politics, Discourse.* Farnham, Surrey, UK: Ashgate, 2013.

Kirmanj, Sherko. *Identity and Nation in Iraq.* Boulder, CO: Lynne Rienner, 2013.

Latham, Michael E. *Modernization as Ideology: American Social Science and "Nation Building" in the Kennedy Era.* Chapel Hill: University of North Carolina Press, 2000.

Latham, Michael E. *The Right Kind of Revolution: Modernization, Development, and U.S. Foreign Policy from the Cold War to the Present.* Ithaca, NY: Cornell University Press, 2010.

Packer, George. *The Assassins' Gate: America in Iraq.* New York: Farrar, Straus and Giroux, 2005.

Paris, Roland. *At War's End: Building Peace after Civil Conflict.* Cambridge: Cambridge University Press, 2004.

Phillips, David L. *Losing Iraq: Inside the Postwar Reconstruction Fiasco.* New York: Basic Books, 2009.

Pollack, Kenneth. *The Threatening Storm: What Every American Needs to Know before an Invasion in Iraq.* New York: Random House, 2002.

Rayburn, Joel. *Iraq after America: Strongmen, Sectarians, Resistance.* Stanford, CA: Hoover Institution, 2014.

Record, Jeffrey. *Wanting War: Why the Bush Administration Invaded Iraq.* Dulles, VA: Potomac Books, 2009.

Ricks, Thomas E. *Fiasco: The American Military Adventure in Iraq.* New York: Penguin, 2006.

Rostow, Walt Whitman. *The Economic Stages of Growth: A Non-Communist Manifesto* 1960. Cambridge: Cambridge University Press, 1960.

Rotberg, Robert I., ed. *When States Fail: Causes and Consequences.* Princeton, NJ: Princeton University Press, 2004.

Sky, Emma. *The Unraveling: High Hopes and Missed Opportunities in Iraq.* New York: Public Affairs, 2015.

Tripp, Charles. *A History of Iraq.* Cambridge: Cambridge University Press, 2007.

Wood, Trish. *What Was Asked of Us: An Oral History of the Iraq War by the Soldiers Who Fought It.* New York: Little, Brown, 2006.

Woodward, Bob. *Plan of Attack.* New York: Simon and Schuster, 2004.

Zinmeister, Karl. *Dawn over Baghdad: How the U.S. Military Is Using Bullets and Ballots to Remake Iraq.* New York: Encounter Books, 2004.

61. Is It Accurate to Draw Parallels between the Crusades of the Middle Ages in the Holy Land and the Afghanistan and Iraq Wars of the Early 21st Century?

The Crusades encompassed a sequence of religious wars officially sanctioned by the Roman Catholic Church beginning in 1096 CE. They were waged in an attempt to wrest control of the Holy Land from Muslim control. The Holy Land was defined as an area generally between the Jordan River and the Mediterranean Sea. At its heart was Palestine, an area generally considered sacred by Jews, Christians, and Muslims. By 1291 the Crusades were over, and Muslims retained control of the area. Recent U.S.-led wars in Afghanistan and Iraq, both predominantly Muslim nations, have often been labeled as latter-day crusades waged under the general rubric of the war on terror. For a variety of reasons, however, this comparison remains problematic given the religious, cultural, and racial connotations involved. Nevertheless, its use in the West and by Muslims in the Middle East alike demonstrates that a sizable number of people believe that these conflicts are indeed shaped by religious undertones and are therefore a continuance or resumption of the medieval Crusades. It is not surprising, then, that the 1991 Persian Gulf War, the 2001–2014 Afghanistan War, and the 2003–2011 Iraq War, not to mention the decades-long Israeli-Palestinian conflict, have all been shaped and conditioned to some extent by the religious rhetoric associated with the Crusades.

Dr. Karl Yambert, in the first perspective essay, asserts that the recent wars are indeed direct continuations of a millennium of religious conflict that began with the medieval Crusades. Like the Crusades, the modern conflicts under discussion pitted East against West, involved military expeditions against peoples of another faith, and represented an attempt to create new states amid the largely Muslim Middle East. In contrast, the essay by Dr. Skip Knox emphasizes that it is problematic to draw parallels between the Crusades and the U.S.-led wars in Afghanistan and Iraq of the early 21st century given that these conflicts differed greatly at every level. Even in instances where they appear to be similar, drawing such comparisons is misleading. The war on terror, he points out, is not a religious crusade; rather, it is a conflict fought among nation-states and against stateless groups largely in the name of national security and democracy. In the last perspective essay, Dr. James B. McNabb argues that while significant differences do exist between the Crusades and more recent wars in Afghanistan and Iraq, there are certain patterns and dynamics present in both that show why the term "crusade" can arguably still be applied. Chiefly, this includes efforts to "frame the strategic narrative" of war to each belligerent's own interests. Today we tend to refer to this as propaganda, and although the term did not exist in medieval times, the notion nevertheless was operational during the Crusades.

Background Essay

The ideology of the crusade becomes apparent in all kinds of historical sources about crusading, most clearly in texts concerned with the definition, regulation, and promotion of crusades. Crusade ideology was based on both legal theory and theology. In legal and institutional terms, the idea of crusade rested on the twin pillars of the theory of holy war and the model of pilgrimage, which represented the collective and individual aspects characterizing the activity of crusading. These motivations shaped the medieval worldview of crusaders and make this a unique historical movement specific to the two centuries that spanned the Crusades.

The traditions of holy war and pilgrimage reach far back in the history of Christianity, its intellectual foundations and pastoral practice. Both played important roles during the 11th century, the period leading up to the First Crusade (1096–1099). In theological terms, crusading was couched in both Old and New

Testament thought. Whereas crusades were presented as parallels to the wars fought by the people of Israel in the Old Testament with the help and on the instigation of God, the spirituality of the individual crusader was based on New Testament theology and seen in Christocentric terms as forming a personal relationship with Christ.

The ideology of the crusade thus rested on four principal elements: holy war theory, the model of pilgrimage, Old Testament history, and New Testament theology. Early on in the history of the crusade movement, these four elements were fused into one more or less coherent cluster of ideas, giving the crusade a firm intellectual foundation, which among other factors accounted for the dynamism and longevity of the institution of the crusade and the activity of crusading.

The perception of the crusade as a holy war was set against the background of historical parallels with the wars of the Israelites in the Old Testament. This combined the idea of a war led by the church for the good of Christianity with the concept of a war initiated by divine authority and fought by God's chosen people. The idea of pilgrimage as a devotional activity imbued in New Testament theology contributed toward the definition of a specific crusader spirituality. In ideal terms, the crusader was seen as a special pilgrim who carried arms or actively supported a military venture and whose spiritual journey in the act of crusading was aimed at salvation by forming a closer relationship with God or Christ.

From the beginning of the movement, crusading was closely associated with the recovery of Jerusalem and the Christian holy places in Palestine. The symbolic significance of Jerusalem in Christian history, in particular as the setting for Christ's act of redemption, was pivotal in bringing about the First Crusade and successfully establishing the institution of crusading. This explains why throughout the Middle Ages crusades to the Holy Land always met with the greatest enthusiasm and support and gave the most forceful expression to the idea of the crusader as a soldier fighting on Christ's behalf.

Crusade ideology was surprisingly uniform throughout the centuries spanned by the crusade movement. Its formation, vitality, and survival were ultimately dependent on two principal factors: the idea of Christendom as a geopolitical reference and the penitential practice of the medieval church. The rise and fall of the idea of Christendom represented by one church led by the pope, which was actively promoted by the Gregorian Reformers of the 11th century and died down in the aftermath of the Reformation, mirrored the beginning and end of the idea and the practice of crusading.

By the same token, the universal acceptance of penitential practice and the belief in the effectiveness of the indulgence enshrined in Roman Catholic doctrine, which were preconditions for creating and sustaining the ideology of the crusade, gained momentum with the crusade movement and were dealt a serious blow during the Reformation. Even though the ideology of the crusade was kept alive after the

16th century, most notably in the aspirations of the military orders, its impact dwindled as the arrival of other forms of religious wars led to the formation of new ideologies. Despite the use of religious rhetoric in later wars, particularly in the context of the current U.S.-led war on terror, the motivations in these latter conflicts by Western forces do not necessarily mirror the intentions of European crusaders of centuries' past.

Christoph T. Maier

Perspective Essay 1. A Direct Continuation of Centuries of Struggle

Is it accurate to draw parallels between the Crusades and the Afghanistan and Iraq conflicts of the early 21st century? Yes, particularly to many Muslims, the 21st-century conflicts in Afghanistan and Iraq are not just parallels but direct continuations of a millennium of West-East conflict that began with the Crusades.

In the seventh century, desert nomads swept out of Arabia in an irresistible wave of conquest. They established the new religion of Islam across the Middle East and North Africa and even into Europe's Iberian Peninsula (modern-day Spain and Portugal). The Arabs assumed control of Palestine, or what Christians call the Holy Land. In 1095, Pope Urban II of the Roman Catholic Church called upon European Christians to take up arms in a crusade to restore Christian control of the Holy Land.

The First Crusade (1096–1099) successfully recaptured the holy city of Jerusalem and led to the establishment of crusader states in Palestine. All of the crusader states were back in Muslim hands within 200 years, but the states were tangible evidence of the Christian West's intent to subordinate Muslim peoples and lands to their control.

Three main attributes, then, define the Crusades. First, the Crusades pitted the West against the East: European kingdoms formed coalitions to assault Muslim states in the Middle East. Second, the Crusades were religiously sanctioned expeditions against people of a different faith. Third, a primary goal of the Crusades was to establish new states to consolidate Christian control over Muslim lands and peoples.

The theme of Western aggression against the East, and vice versa, is a long one. Urban II's call to arms in 1095 is relevant to wars of the 21st century, because by some arguments the Crusades have never truly ended. Military campaigns to recapture the Holy Land continued to the 13th century. The Muslim empire of the Ottomans expanded into Europe, prompting an exhausting series of West-East wars, some explicitly sanctioned by popes and called Crusades, until as late as the 20th century. Napoleon's invasions of Egypt and Syria (1798–1801), the British occupation of Egypt (1882–1952), the partitioning of the Ottoman Empire among the victorious European powers after World War I (1914–1918), and the coup backed by the U.S. Central Intelligence Agency in 1953 against the government headed by Iranian prime minister Mohammad Mosaddegh likewise all continue the theme of war, occupation, and foreign control of local government that the West has exerted against the East over the centuries. The Persian Gulf War (1991) led by U.S. president George H. W. Bush and the Afghanistan War and the Iraq Wars of President George W. Bush may be seen by many Muslims as continuations of 1,000 years of ongoing West-East struggle in which Muslim states have been targeted by coalitions of Western powers.

A member of the U.S. Army's 3rd Armored Cavalry Regiment on patrol next to a Christian church in Tal Kaeef, Iraq, November 11, 2008. Iraqi Christians became a target for Islamic extremists who labeled them "crusaders." (AP Photo/Petros Giannakouris)

The invasion of Iraq in 2003 defies easy geopolitical explanation. Neither the United Nations (UN) nor the North Atlantic Treaty Organization (NATO) found compelling reasons to attack Iraq. Instead, the American insistence on invading Iraq bore the mark of a personal animus of President George W. Bush toward Iraqi president Saddam Hussein, grounded in Bush's Christian worldview. The specifically Christian motivation underlying the wars in Afghanistan and Iraq is a second parallel with the earlier Crusades. In the immediate aftermath of the 9/11 attacks on America, Bush declared a new war on terror that he specifically characterized as a "crusade." Bush's use of the term provoked strong reactions from many Muslims who believed that crusades, old or new, were not wars to gain territory but instead were wars on the religion of Islam.

As a born-again Christian, Bush viewed the world in terms of a monumental struggle of good versus evil. In his 2002 State of the Union address, Bush declared the Democratic People's Republic of Korea (North Korea), Iraq, and Iran members of an "axis of evil." He confided to friends and foreign diplomats, such as Palestinian president Mahmoud Abbas, that his decisions to go to war in Afghanistan and Iraq stemmed from directives to him from his Christian God. Bush initiated a forceful response against the perpetrators of the 9/11 attacks—Osama bin Laden, Al-Qaeda, and the Taliban in Afghanistan—but he also chose to invade "evil" Iraq, led by Hussein. In this new crusade, not a medieval pope but rather the modern leader of the free world entered into a Middle East war on religious impulses.

A third parallel to the early Crusades is the real or imagined intent of the Christian West to establish new states amid the Islamic East, comparable to the early crusader states. The dismemberment of the Ottoman Empire after World War I supports Middle Eastern suspicions of Western intentions to colonize the East. Rather than granting independence to former Ottoman domains, the League of Nations (a forerunner of the UN) assigned certain of the territories to France and Great Britain as mandates, essentially colonies controlled by the European powers.

The founding of the State of Israel is undoubtedly the most problematic issue concerning a new Western enclave in the Muslim world. The UN proposed partitioning Palestine into separate Arab and Jewish states following World War II. The UN-developed plan assigned some 56 percent of the land to the Jews, who had only one-third of the population. While the Jews accepted the plan, the Arabs understandably rejected it. When Israel declared its nationhood in 1948 just before the British mandate was to expire, the Arab states went to war in what would be only the first of a number of Arab-Israeli military confrontations.

Compared to its neighbors, Israel is a Western-oriented nation. In the thinking of many Muslims, Israel serves as a bridgehead through which the West seeks to control and exploit the Muslim world. The West and Israel are therefore inextricably linked as "crusader-Zionists" in the minds of those such as Osama bin Laden, the founder of Al-Qaeda, the terrorist organization responsible for the attacks of 9/11.

In a 1998 statement urging jihad (holy war) against "Jews and Crusaders," bin Laden objected strenuously to "crusader armies" that remained in the Arabian Peninsula following the Persian Gulf War. Furthermore, though the puritanically devout bin Laden held no love for the secularist regime of Hussein, he opposed the invasion of Iraq because he believed the coalition to be a "crusader-Zionist alliance" that had effectively declared war against Allah, Muhammad, and all Muslims.

Times have changed. Wars are now fought with manned aircraft, unmanned drones, and cyberattacks. News and propaganda are spread instantly around the world via social media. Popes predictably plead for peace rather than proclaim wars against unbelievers. But from the perspective of Islamist activists, the Crusades have never ended.

Karl Yambert

Perspective Essay 2. The War on Terror Is Not a Crusade

The parallels between the Crusades and the Afghanistan and Iraq Wars are easy to draw, but they are also misleading. The combatants appear to be the same, and the battles take place in more or less the same geographic area. The conflict can be cast as a struggle between Christianity and Islam. Certainly people in the modern wars on both sides have made explicit reference to the Crusades. For example, U.S. president George W. Bush on September 16, 2001, referred to "this war on terrorism" as a "crusade." On the other hand, Iraqi dictator Saddam Hussein had posters made showing himself together with Saladin, and many Islamist militants call all Western powers "crusaders."

These comparisons are superficial and mainly political, not historical. The differences are much more significant. For example, the Crusades cover a span of centuries, while the modern conflicts are only a decade or so long. The one is an epoch, a movement, while the other is simply a single war.

The combatants are different. The modern war is between professional armies, with the addition of guerrilla fighters on the Muslim side. The Crusades were fought with knights and nobles, along with conscripted armies of foot soldiers. In other words, both sides had similar fighting forces.

They differed ethnically as well. The Crusades were dominated by the French, along with Italians and Germans on the one side, while the Muslim forces were mostly Egyptians and Turks. The modern war involves Americans with a few other European nations on the one side fighting against Iraqis and Afghans, with some Arab peoples joining as volunteers. In other words, not the same peoples at all.

Finally, the Crusades were called into existence by popes and were led by kings and nobles. The Muslim armies were led by sultans with the support of caliphs. Despite Hussein's attempt to cast himself as a modern Saladin, Islam is no longer led by sultans.

Motives are always tricky to identify, even with modern wars, but we can assert that religion was a major motivating factor in the Crusades on both sides. This cannot be said for the modern wars, where nationalism and ideology play a far more important role. Only among the radical Islamist insurgents do we find a clear religious factor in the desire to die a martyr's death. This can motivate individuals, but it does not put armies in the field. The medieval conflict was profoundly religious with practical overtones, while the modern conflict is essentially political with religious overtones.

The differences are most noticeable when it comes to objectives. The objective of the Crusades was clear and limited: the liberation of Jerusalem. Even when the immediate objective was different (Egypt, for example), the ultimate goal was always to free Jerusalem of Muslim rule. For the Muslims, even though individual leaders might squabble and refuse to cooperate with each other, the ultimate goal was consistent: to drive the invaders into the sea.

The objectives of the Western powers in Iraq and Afghanistan are to restructure existing states along the lines of Western ideals and to root out a perceived direct threat to those Western powers. Jerusalem is not being contested directly, and there is no goal of destroying Muslim power in Afghanistan or in Iraq.

On the Muslim side, there has been no unified purpose. The radical Islamists want all Western influence out of the Middle East; this is the closest to the medieval goal of driving the Christians into the sea. There are other players, though, including the Afghan government, supporters of the former Hussein regime, the new Iraq, the Taliban, and so on. Each of these has its own local goals.

The key here is that the modern objectives are stated in terms of nation-states: democracy, national identity, elections, and peace treaties. The medieval objectives centered on religious shrines (e.g., the Holy Sepulcher and the Dome of the Rock) as well as on castles and cities as strategic centers. Finally, the intent of the crusaders was always not merely to liberate Jerusalem and, in support of this, other cities and sites in the Holy Land but also to occupy those places and to live there. Jerusalem was to become a Christian city. So too were Antioch, Tyre, Acre, and the other crusader strongholds. Occupation has never been the goal of the Western armies in Iraq or in Afghanistan; on the contrary, the goal has always been to pull their forces back out again.

In the Middle Ages, the two contending sides were rather evenly matched. In terms of absolute numbers the Muslims were potentially far more powerful, but they rarely were sufficiently united to field large armies. In fact, most of the time the two sides were roughly comparable in numbers. The tactics and arms used by both sides, while different, came out to be likewise a fairly even match. The result was a back-and-forth conflict that stretched out across 200 years.

In the modern conflicts the Western powers hold an overwhelming military advantage, both in numbers and in firepower, while the Muslims have relied mainly on guerrilla warfare. Their one attempt at fighting a pitched battle was undertaken by Hussein, with disastrous results. In other words, the wars themselves, the actual fighting, are radically different from their medieval counterparts.

If the points of comparison are so few and if the differences are so numerous and evident, why even raise the question? Parallels are frequently drawn but mostly by people other than historians. By invoking the medieval Crusades, individuals and groups on both sides are evoking a stereotype, an image of something that never actually happened but whose image was deeply embedded in the consciousness of societies during the 19th century and reinforced by events in the 20th century. The Crusades became a symbol of something, a kind of shorthand in political rhetoric, and have remained a potent symbol ever since. The political sentiments are powerful, but they reflect modern times and modern concerns.

Ellis L. (Skip) Knox

Perspective Essay 3. Recurring Patterns in Space and Time

While significant differences exist between the medieval Crusades and the modern conflicts in Afghanistan and Iraq, there are fundamental and recurring dynamics present in both the Crusades and the U.S.-led campaigns in Afghanistan and Iraq. History is replete with examples of leaders, rulers, and governments attempting to sway the masses to their cause by virtue of a carefully managed information campaign. Accordingly, the process of "framing the strategic narrative" has been employed for centuries, including the years following the establishment of Islam and extending through the era of the Crusades. Strategic information management (sometimes referred to as public diplomacy) was also conducted by the participants in both the Iraqi and Afghan conflicts of the early 21st century.

The most significant differences between the Crusades and the modern era conflicts in Iraq and Afghanistan were the presence of medieval weapons during the Crusades versus the advanced technologies in the conflicts of the early 21st century. During the Crusades military leaders referred to battlefields, while in the contemporary era commanders often refer to battle space in order to reflect the impact of sea, air, land, space, and cyber domains on modern war. Additionally, the concept of holy or religious war, which featured prominently in the minds of many participants fighting on both sides during the Crusades, was featured neither by the regime of Saddam Hussein in Iraq nor the U.S. government during Operation IRAQI FREEDOM. In U.S. operations against Al-Qaeda and its Taliban supporters in Afghanistan following the attacks on September 11, 2001, only the two Muslim groups considered themselves as conducting a holy war, or jihad. The United States was not at war with Islam in either Iraq or Afghanistan, as there were and are millions of practicing Muslim citizens living peacefully in the United States. Americans went to war against those who attacked their country (Al-Qaeda) or provided support for the planning of the attacks (the Taliban government in Afghanistan) on the U.S. homeland on 9/11.

In terms of the similarities or parallels, throughout much of history individuals and groups have attempted to influence the behavior of societies by orchestrating well-managed information campaigns in which those behind the campaign attempt to frame the strategic narrative in a manner most conducive toward their own aims and interests and with scant regard for the interests of the common people. Unfortunately, much of the world's population during the Crusades and in many underdeveloped regions of today was and continues to be illiterate and uneducated. During the time of the Crusades in both the West and within the Middle East, elite centers of power (or small groups of powerful individuals) within a country found it much easier to create a story or frame the strategic narrative in order to incite the masses to fight other countries or groups for what often were elite-specific economic aims and objectives.

Often religion was used by an elite group to further its interests in having the common people fight another society over land or resources. The German (Prussian) philosopher Immanuel Kant (1724–1804) argued that as people learn to read and become more educated, they create governments of and for the people or, more commonly, modern democracies. Eventually as reading and education become more prevalent across the globe, people will be less susceptible to the spurious attempts at manipulation by a self-interested elite, which traditionally has driven many of the strategic information management campaigns that often led to great violence and suffering. Certainly, not all wars were fought for the narrow, specific interests of an elite few, and many conflicts arose as people defended themselves against violent attack from external groups and in defending their rights, internally or within a nation, against overly oppressive regimes. However, many wars in history have been fought for narrow, elite interests, and those who did the fighting, the common man, bore the burnt of the violence and ended up sharing only marginally in any rewards. As men in the modern area have become increasingly literate and educated, they have sought not only greater control over how they are governed but also greater clarity, transparency, and input on questions regarding war and peace.

In the West, while democracy has taken hold and people have the opportunity to weigh in through their elected representatives on matters regarding war, there remains considerable maneuvering behind the scenes by economic actors attempting to benefit from military operations. As U.S. president Dwight D. Eisenhower cautioned the nation in a speech during the 1950s, Americans should be on alert against undue influence from what he called the military-industrial complex, which, given so much power, had the potential for controlling events regarding war and peace rather than these being determined by the nation's citizenry. That questions regarding war and peace should be vested with the people through their elected representatives is a primary principle of U.S. constitutional government. Thus, strategic information campaigns, even in a nation where the public is widely literate, can at times be conducted to further narrow economic interests. In the United States, the military consistently ranks as the most trusted national institution. Nevertheless, heeding Eisenhower's advice, it is incumbent upon citizens to be aware of events and their implications and demand that matters of war and peace be weighed carefully, rationally, and transparently.

In the Afghanistan War (Operation ENDURING FREEDOM), the Taliban had taken control of a country where barely 20 percent of the population were able to read and write. The Taliban was able to carry out a strategic information campaign to buttress its authority. In sum, the United States and coalition forces were essentially unable to reach the bulk of the population through written communication. The lack of education among the Afghan people made it much more difficult for the United States and its coalition partners to secure the support of an already suspicious and largely illiterate Afghan population.

In certain respects, the Western message was muted if not outright blocked by Taliban advantages in strategic communication. The Taliban, enforcing its version of fundamentalist Islam, created a harsh and unforgiving environment that effectively coerced and compelled the citizenry to bend to their leaders' wills. The wishes of the leadership were packaged and presented as being "God's will." Thus, the strategic information campaign centered on two assertions: (1) "If you go against the Taliban, you go against God" and (2) "Even if you do not accept our religious message, the Americans will leave eventually, and you will have to deal with us again." This type of strategic management campaign, which has been conducted for centuries, animated much of the era of the Crusades and has been utilized by the Taliban in Afghanistan in outlasting a militarily superior United States in the modern era. However, as Napoleon aptly observed, "There are but two powers in the world, the sword and the mind. In the long run the sword is always beaten by the mind." In the long run, freedom and a people's desire for it create an irresistible force inevitably overcoming totalitarian and repressive governments doing their utmost to contain it. It is a parallel that connects much of human political, military, and economic history with the contemporary world. It is also a parallel that is likely to continue and in doing so drive events well into the future.

James Brian McNabb

Further Reading

Abulafia, Anna Sapir. "The Interrelationship between the Hebrew Chronicles on the First Crusade." *Journal of Semitic Studies* 27 (1982): 221–239.

Anderson, Terry H. *Bush's Wars.* New York: Oxford University Press, 2011.

Armstrong, Karen. *Holy War: The Crusades and Their Impact on the World Today.* New York: Anchor Books, 1988.

Asbridge, Thomas. *The Crusades: The Authoritative History of the War for the Holy Land.* New York: HarperCollins, 2010.

Claster, Jill. *Sacred Violence.* Toronto: University of Toronto Press, 2009.

France, John. *Victory in the East: A Military History of the First Crusade.* Cambridge: Cambridge University Press, 1974.

Gabrieli, Francesco. *Arab Historians of the Crusades.* Translated by E. J. Costello. Berkeley: University of California Press, 1969.

Haddad, Yvonne Yazbeck. "Islamist Perceptions of U.S. Policy in the Middle East." In *The Middle East and the United States: History, Politics, and Ideologies,* edited by David W. Lesch and Mark L. Haas, 467–490. 5th ed. Boulder, CO: Westview, 2012.

Hall, M. Clement. *The History of Afghanistan, 1600–2012.* Mansfield, MA: Charles River, 2012.

The Iraq Study Group Report. Washington, DC: United States Institute for Peace, 2006.

Maalouf, Amin. *The Crusades through Arab Eyes.* Translated by Jon Rothschild. New York: Schocken Books, 1983.

MacAskill, Ewen. "George Bush: 'God Told Me to End the Tyranny in Iraq.'" *The Guardian,* October 6, 2005.

Mackey, Sandra. *Reckoning: Iraq and the Legacy of Saddam Hussein.* New York: Norton, 2003.

Maier, Christoph T. *Crusade Propaganda and Ideology: Model Sermons for the Preaching of the Cross.* Cambridge: Cambridge University Press, 2000.

Mansfield, Stephen. *The Faith of George W. Bush.* New York: Jeremy P. Tarcher/Penguin, 2003.

Mayer, Hans Eberhard. *The Crusades.* Oxford: Oxford University Press, 1988.

Mayer, Hans E. *The Crusades.* London: Oxford University Press, 1972.

Murray, Williamson, and Robert H. Scales Jr. *Iraq War: A Military History.* Cambridge, MA: Belknap Press of Harvard University Press, 2003.

Philips, Jonathan. "Why a Crusade Will Lead to a Jihad." *The Independent,* September 18, 2001.

Ricks, Thomas E. *Fiasco: The American Military Adventure in Iraq.* New York: Penguin, 2006.

Riley-Smith, Jonathan. *The Crusades.* New Haven, CT: Yale University Press, 2005.

Riley-Smith, Jonathan. *The Crusades, Christianity, and Islam.* New York: Columbia University Press, 2008.

Riley-Smith, Jonathan. *The First Crusade and the Idea of Crusading.* London: Athlone, 1986.

Rock, Stephen R. *Faith and Foreign Policy: The Views and Influence of U.S. Christians and Christian Organizations.* New York: Continuum International Publishing Group, 2011.

Runciman, Sir Steven. *A History of the Crusades.* 3 vols. Cambridge: Cambridge University Press, 1951–1954.

Stark, Rodney. *God's Battalions: The Case for the Crusades.* New York: HarperCollins, 2009.

Tucker, Spencer C., ed. *The Encyclopedia of Middle East Wars: The United States in the Persian Gulf, Afghanistan, and Iraq Conflicts.* 5 vols. Santa Barbara, CA: ABC-CLIO, 2010.

Tyerman, Christopher. *God's War: A New History of the Crusades.* Cambridge, MA: Belknap Press of Harvard University Press, 2006.

West, Francis J. *The Wrong War: Grit, Strategy and the Way Out of Afghanistan.* New York: Random House, 2011.

62. Did Post–Cold War Policies Pursued by the United States and Other Nato Powers Contribute to Russia's Increasingly Aggressive International Policies in the 2000s?

After waging the all-encompassing Cold War for nearly 45 years, the United States and Russia embarked on a remarkably new path in bilateral relations during the late 1980s and early 1990s. As the Cold War thawed in the late 1980s, the Americans and Soviets negotiated treaties that significantly reduced nuclear arsenals and the number of ground troops and conventional arms situated in Europe. When parts of the Soviet Union began to break down into constituent and autonomous republics and Soviet satellite states in Eastern Europe declared independence from Soviet control, the world hailed these developments as the definitive end of the Cold War. In December 1991, the Soviet Union was officially dissolved and replaced by the Russian Confederation. At the time, many believed that the Cold War's demise would usher in a new era of global cooperation and superpower relations. By the late 1990s, however, America and Russia were again at loggerheads, as disagreements over the Bosnian War and the Kosovo War and Russia's economic collapse drove the two former Cold War rivals apart. U.S.-Russian relations continued to deteriorate during the George W. Bush administration as the North Atlantic Treaty Organization (NATO) expanded to Russia's borders and Bush's unilateralist foreign policy antagonized the Kremlin. These developments coincided with a more belligerent Russian foreign policy, which included the Russian invasion of part of the Republic of Georgia in 2008, Russia's annexation of the Crimean Peninsula in 2014, and Russia's intervention in the Syrian Civil War in 2015.

Robert Broadwater argues in the first perspective that the West's post–Cold War policies did contribute to Russian aggressiveness but only because they were spun by conservative leaders such as Vladimir Putin and used as potent propaganda tools. Broadwater goes on to assert that Russia's current policies are not much different from Soviet policies and that the Cold War never actually ended. Ascendant Russian nationalism and a tanking economy led conservative Russian officials to portray Western policies in the worst possible light. In the second essay, Dr. Michael Kraig credits Western policies for Russia's belligerence, particularly in regard to the eastern expansion of NATO. This threatened Russia's historic national identity, which is intertwined with traditional Russian imperialism. Russia's top-down authoritarian leaders viewed the West's policies as threatening and managed to convince many Russians that the West was a serious threat to Russian interests. Dr. Paul G. Pierpaoli Jr. asserts that Western policies played a major role in Russian aggressiveness in the 2000s. He cites lackluster economic aid and advice, an overemphasis on human rights as a prerequisite to economic assistance, the western expansion of NATO and the European Union, and U.S. unilateralism as the most troublesome policies, at least from the Russian perspective. Those policies stoked Russia's historic security fears, threatened Russia's traditional sphere of influence in Eastern Europe, and impeded Russia's economic progress and transition to free market capitalism. In the end, the West failed to take into account Russia's historic security concerns.

Background Essay

For some 40 years, the United States and its West European allies were engaged in a global Cold War with the Soviet Union. By 1985, however, the Cold War began to thaw, and by late 1989 the conflict was essentially over. The last Soviet leader, the dynamic reformer Mikhail Gorbachev, had sought to rehabilitate his country and relax control over its East European satellites. That process, however, precipitated unforeseen consequences. After the Berlin Wall fell in November 1989, numerous Soviet-allied satellites overthrew their communist governments and declared independence from Moscow. During 1990 and 1991, Soviet republics such as Estonia, Latvia, and Lithuania likewise declared their independence, and in December 1991 the Soviet Union was officially dissolved.

The surviving Russian Federation, the successor state to the Soviet Union, was a mere shadow of its former self. Its economy was in shambles—it had lost a quarter of its land area and half of its population. The new Russia lacked the institutions to transition toward a market-based economy, and the Russian people experienced severe economic deprivations.

The United States and the other Western democracies responded fitfully to the resulting Russian economic crisis, which endured for the better part of a decade. While some efforts were made to aid Russia, by and large these measures were inadequate to the task at hand, and some actually made the economic morass worse. The result by the late 1990s was an oligarchic Russian economic system that was rife with corruption and bore little resemblance to a free market economy. By then, Russian politics seemed to be democratic in name only. At the same time, the West seemed unsure of how it should deal with a post-Soviet Russia, which remained a large and potentially powerful nation.

The first real fissures in the West's post-1991 relations with Russia appeared as early as 1994, when the North Atlantic Treaty Organization (NATO), an alliance initially intended to defend the West from Soviet aggression, intervened militarily in the Bosnian War, over strenuous Russian objections. Moscow was angered that NATO acted virtually unilaterally against its traditional Serbian allies. Another NATO intervention in the 1998–1999 Kosovo War, which again saw NATO wage war against Serbians, outraged Moscow and forced the Russians to insist that they play a direct role in postwar peace operations.

Meanwhile, the West criticized the Kremlin for having waged the First Chechen War (1994–1996) in an effort to prevent the Chechen region from seceding. In 1999, a second conflict with Chechnya began and did not end until 2009. Russia was repeatedly rebuked by the West for its prosecution of that war and the attendant human rights violations that accompanied it.

When Vladimir Putin assumed power as Russia's leader on the last day of December 1999, he inherited a war with Chechnya and an economy ravaged by years of mismanagement and neglect. That same year, NATO had expanded to the

Russian president Vladimir Putin shown addressing veterans of World War II on May 7, 2000, during a commemoration of the end of the war in Europe. (AP Photo/Mikhail Metzel)

east by granting membership to Poland, Hungary, and the Czech Republic. Russian leaders claimed that the move broke an earlier pledge that the alliance would not expand east of Germany. The West claimed that no such assurance had ever been made. NATO continued to expand eastward so that by 2009 it included nine more nations, some of them former Soviet republics. Several of these same countries also joined the European Union beginning in 2004. Putin was now convinced that NATO was encircling Russia and posed a significant threat to his nation.

The advent of the George W. Bush administration and the start of the war on terror in 2001 triggered an even steeper plunge in Western relations with Moscow. Washington's increased unilateralism and its embrace of preemptive war deeply concerned Kremlin policy makers. Putin spoke out sharply against Bush's 2002 decision to withdraw from the Anti-Ballistic Missile (ABM) Treaty and roundly denounced the U.S.-British–led invasion and occupation of Iraq in 2003. To counter U.S. hegemony in the Middle East, Russia increased aid to both Iran and Syria, which further destabilized the region. In 2007, the U.S. government announced plans to erect an ABM system in Poland and the Czech Republic; the Kremlin viewed this as a brazen attempt to negate its nuclear deterrence in Europe.

In 2008 Putin, emboldened by high oil prices that had revived Russia's economy and taking advantage of the West's preoccupation with Iraq, invaded Georgia to support pro-Russian separatists in South Ossetia and Abkhazia. The Bush administration responded with rhetoric but no substantive action. Putin now asserted that NATO's repeated eastward expansion had forced Russia to secure its western and southern flanks with more vigor. As Western-Russian relations continued to deteriorate, both sides traded barbs and criticized the other for human rights abuses. In August 2013, President Barack Obama abruptly cancelled a summit with Putin because of the Edward Snowden affair, and U.S.-Russian relations became even more troubled.

In early 2014, the Russians invaded the Crimean Peninsula under the guise of protecting ethnic Russians there; after annexing it outright, they have since backed pro-Russian separatists fighting in eastern Ukraine. That conflict has been simmering ever since. Meanwhile, the West has imposed punishing sanctions on Russia, which so far have not reversed Russia's latest moves. By mid-2015, the West's relations with Russia had reached lows not seen since the Cold War of the early 1980s. Russia's September 2015 intervention in the ongoing Syrian Civil War added even more potential danger to the Russian-NATO relationship, as the Western democracies sought to oust Syrian president Bashar al-Assad from power, while the Kremlin sought to prop him up. Turkey's rash November 2015 decision to shoot down a Russian fighter jet after it momentarily strayed into Turkish airspace showcased this very peril. And NATO's December 2015 decision to admit Montenegro into NATO certainly did not play well in Moscow.

Paul G. Pierpaoli Jr.

Perspective Essay 1. The Cold War Continues

Actions and policies of the United States and its NATO partners contributed to the escalating aggressiveness of Russia in the post–Cold War era only to the extent that they provided propaganda platforms for Russian leadership to pursue an already established military and political agenda. In fact, it can be argued that the Cold War era never really ended but instead merely observed a short-lived truce during the rule of Mikhail Gorbachev.

It has been said that a country's allies may change but that its own national interests remain constant. Such has been the case with Russia, stretching back from its takeover by the communists and the formation of the Soviet Union through to the modern-day Russian Federation. Russian actions and policies have always been in the best interest of Russia and have largely been based on a mentality of fear and distrust of the outside world. This is to be expected, given the history of Russia in the 20th and 21st centuries. During World War I Russian lost as many as 3.3 million of its citizens dead from all causes before the country bowed out of the war in 1917. Russia immediately entered into a civil war between the communist and noncommunist factions of the country in which nearly 1 million more soldiers died. In addition, estimates of civilian deaths, largely conducted as summary executions of "enemies of the people" by one side or the other, range as high as another 1 million. American intervention on the side of the losing noncommunist faction did little to inspire confidence of the communist regime in the outside world. The droughts and famine of 1920–1921 led to widespread disease in Russia, accounting for 3 million more deaths from typhus alone. During World War II, a failed diplomatic and military partnership with Adolf Hitler's Nazi Germany led to Russia becoming one of the Allies, and though the country emerged on the winning side in the war, more than 22 million of its citizens had died or been killed. The staggering loss of Russian lives in the 20th century was combined with the ideology of Vladimir Lenin and Joseph Stalin that the Soviet Union was a socialist island surrounded by a hostile capitalist encirclement, leading to a suspicious and isolated mentality for Soviet leadership and citizens. Politics and diplomacy were viewed as a means to keep Soviet enemies divided in a world that was seen as bipolar between the capitalist nations and those gravitating toward socialism.

In 1988, the glasnost policies of Mikhail Gorbachev led to the dissolution of the Soviet Union and promised the end of the Cold War division of Europe. While several former Eastern bloc countries in Europe prospered and thrived amid the new democratic freedoms, Russia's post–Cold War economy tanked in the wake of reduced military spending. Hundreds of millions of Russian workers lost their jobs, and the Russian economy experienced a recession worse than the Great Depression. The grave economic situation combined with a diminishing influence of the former Soviet Union in regional and world affairs led to the government being controlled by politicians more conservative and traditionalist in their values than Gorbachev had been and signaled a shift of the government's policies back toward state control. The administration of current president Vladimir Putin has even gone so far as to declare Gorbachev's government as having been illegitimate and its actions therefore unlawful and not binding to the Russian people. As such, the Russians have openly questioned the legality of the independence of Latvia, Lithuania, and Estonia and have based the Russian takeover of the Crimea on the claim that the previous government had no legal right to cede that land to Ukraine in the first place. Russia's increasing incursions of military aircraft into Baltic airspace and submarines in the Baltic Sea point to the fact that the Russian government is posturing to test the resolve of NATO to defend the Baltic states while at the same time demonstrating a show of force to Baltic leaders.

Russia has withdrawn within itself, becoming more closely associated with the old communist Soviet Union than with the democratic Russian Federation of Gorbachev's vision. Under Putin's leadership, joblessness, which was once as high as nearly 50 percent, has been significantly reduced, and Russian industry has begun to thrive. As a result, Putin and his government won the widespread acclaim and support of the Russian people. His People's Front party urges Russians to care about the "fate" and "victory" of Russia and advocates that those who want "access to participation in power" join up. Just as with the old Soviet Union, Russia is depicted as being surrounded by hostile forces, intent on its destruction, and fear and distrust of the outside world have once more become the basis of political dialogue, as diplomacy is used to keep those countries viewed as enemies separated and divided.

Clearly, the Cold War never ended. It merely took a vacation of a few years during the period of glasnost and perestroika before resuming along the borders of a slightly altered world map. Russia is pursuing its own national interests and agenda in a fashion similar to that of the old Soviet Union, and this includes a severe distrust of the capitalistic and democratic nations of the West and the NATO alliance. Any actions taken by the United States or its NATO partners are viewed with suspicion by the government in Moscow and as such are subject to becoming the political fodder that can be used as propaganda to justify Russia's increasingly aggressive actions. Have the actions of the United States and the NATO nations contributed to the aggressive tendencies of Russia in the post–Cold War era? Absolutely, but that contribution has largely been to the extent that Russian leaders have twisted and convoluted those actions to make them fit with their own nationalistic agenda.

Robert P. Broadwater

Perspective Essay 2. The United States Broke Its Promise Not to Expand NATO

In the period 1989–1990 as the Berlin Wall fell and the communist regimes in Eastern Europe were about to collapse, U.S. secretary of state James Baker, followed by West German chancellor Helmut Kohl, promised in separate high-level bilateral talks with Soviet president Mikhail Gorbachev that the North Atlantic Treaty Organization (NATO) would not "expand one inch" or "take advantage" if Moscow allowed Germany to peacefully reunite. While U.S. president George H. W. Bush quickly changed this to allow NATO expansion to at least include East Germany (with strict provisions against immediate military deployments there), this verbal promise, though never constituting a true legal commitment, was important, especially given the still strong Russian memories of some 27 million deaths in World War II. However, in just two short decades, 12 new states had joined NATO in a sweeping arc from far Northern Europe (the Baltics) to its southeast (Romania, Bulgaria), with both Georgia and Ukraine encouraged by the George W. administration before it left office in 2008 to apply for eventual membership.

It is thus not surprising that longtime senior Russian diplomat Sergei Lavrov argued in 2008 that NATO had violated one diplomatic promise after another: to wit, not to enlarge the alliance, not to deploy substantial forces on the territories of new NATO members once enlargement in fact took place, and then not to move NATO infrastructure to the Russian border.

What matters more than such promises, however, is why and how the receiver of that promise views it as centrally important in interpreting the tenor of interstate relations. On this, what is of central importance is Russia's long historical evolution as not just a state within set boundaries or just an inward-looking Russian cultural nation. During the course of centuries, the Russian ruling elite have fostered a Russian national identity with several transnational elements that bode poorly for passive acceptance of the rapid expansion of NATO alliance commitments and political boundaries. This long history should have been plain to Western decision makers, particularly in regard to decisions that went well beyond the first three new NATO states of Poland, the Czech Republic, and Hungary, to include lands that had for longer centuries been viewed somehow, in some way, as intimately connected to Russian power, purpose, identity, and security.

The path started with an aristocratic, dynastic land empire based on a top-down hereditary czar tied firmly to a "divine" mission of spreading Orthodox Christianity. It then eventually evolved, with incredible revolutionary violence, into an even larger utopian-ideological land empire based on a "secular religion" (Marxist-Leninist communism). When this transnational imperial edifice failed just like that of the earlier dynastic orthodox czarist effort, the present Russia emerged, purporting to be a modern nation-state along the same lines as those adopted by Western powers a century earlier.

The problem is that the path from an imperial to a nation-state identity is hardly so simple in economic, cultural, or political terms. In practice, the state and its primary ruling class can and does define what the nation is and what it means, both territorially and culturally. In Russia, this has traditionally taken on the extreme of a national identity that puts the population in total unquestioned service to state institutions and the ruling class, rather than vice versa. The czars in particular (and later the communist Politburo) stood over and above a decidedly imperial all-Russian land empire based on the steady spread of a divine, transcendent ideology—first Orthodox Christianity and then communism. In both cases, this was practically ensured via the spread of Russian language and culture.

The dynastic leadership also stood above and apart from the normal Russians themselves. It claimed a mystical edict for mass rule that, while informed by Russian popular culture, was neither beholden to a popular mandate nor defined in its values solely by the core Russian heartland alone. Indeed, after the czars, the Soviet imperial class brutally suppressed the two main bastions of core Russian identity, the village peasantry and the Orthodox Church, in favor of a civilizing mission that went well beyond the borders of Russia proper.

Thus, Russian national identity from the days of Peter the Great in the early 1700s to the end of the Soviet Union in 1991 was often inseparable from its identity as an imperial power. Moreover, Russian identity, insofar as it can be separated and identified in narrow ethnic terms apart from its land-based imperial role over neighbors, has been steadily defined since the 1800s as "Slavic" or "Pan-Slavic"—that is, as involving all of those peoples resting upon a Russian language and broader civilizational history that has been called "ancient Rus."

Notably, the Romanov dynasty first started as a Kiev-based land empire in today's Ukraine before eventually moving to Moscow. And Soviet dictator Joseph Stalin eventually fused this 19th-century ethnic-nationalist notion with communist ideals, pulling history in the desired direction in the three Baltic nations and in the Caucasus via brute blunt-force deportations. This involved massive post–World War II movements of millions of peoples of "non-Russian" ethnic histories (and suspect nationalist leanings and loyalties) to far eastern or far southern more Asian holdings of the Soviet empire. These western areas were then to be repopulated with perceived durable and trustworthy Slavs from the Russian heartland, which in Stalin's time also meant ideological purity, as decided by the notorious and all-powerful interior political police, the People's Commissariat for Internal Affairs. The result of this massive, perhaps globally unprecedented mass movement of peoples at gunpoint succeeded in creating sizable Russian-language and Russian-ethnic enclaves that cross any easy conception of true national boundaries today.

One might reply that democracy in Russia itself, or the slightly larger Russian Federation (including perhaps similar moves in Belorussia), will solve these old-style historical mind-sets. However, historical patterns do not lend easy confidence in a final peaceful outcome, largely because popular ownership of what it means to be Russian does not mean an end to expansive mind-sets.

Czarist attempts at modernization, together with Soviet purges and such asging up of millions of former rural people into urban, educated existence, has meant the progressive creation of a professional, bureaucratic, and ultimately truly Russian middle class focused on a sense of ethnic Slav identity. In the 1960s, this trend was augmented by popular histories with mass readership, academic writings, and even popular fictional literature by Soviet-era intellectuals, which reinterpreted history to divine a truly Russian national ethos apart from czarist aristocratic values.

This "found" identity was both narrower than and separate from the purely top-down elite identities once fostered by either the czars or the communists—but nonetheless still decidedly different from the West and still based on a strong sense of ethnic pride, heritage, and greatness in European affairs that stood apart from Western forms of power and prestige. Thus, whether dynastic, Slavic, communist, or federated, whatever the formal status of outlying areas, Russian elites and peoples alike have only felt truly secure and in cultural terms truly Russian if the political and cultural status of neighboring lands have preserved and supported the uniqueness of the Greater Russian heartland.

Such historical patterns have positioned Russian political culture to interpret and react negatively to any attempts by another nation-state to advance territorially, even economically, into lands viewed as part of the "true" Russian identity. Russia cannot possibly hope to join the rule-based Western conception of international order when what Russia actually is remains so naturally unstable and dynamic at this point in its long historical evolution.

It is unrealistic to assume that borders of what were once czarist and Soviet imperial holdings would be indeed the inviolable state borders for all time, absent further conflict and friction. Broad principled language in senatorial debates, followed by massive inclusion of new states in a web of alliance commitments, can hardly be said to decide all of these complex historical realities. History is still unfolding in this area of the world. Reality portends only two possible outcomes: increased military conflicts or some level of negotiated appeasement by the original core NATO nations that first started the eastward march of militaries and democratic values.

Michael Ryan Kraig

Perspective Essay 3. Missteps and Lost Opportunities

Since the late 1990s, the West's relations with Russia have charted a precipitous decline, and Western policies over the past 25 years appear to be one of the principal reasons why Russia's foreign and military policies have become increasingly aggressive in recent years. The West's failure to adequately aid the Russians in their transition to democratic capitalism, America's overemphasis on human rights as a prerequisite to economic aid, Western unilateralism (particularly since 2001), and the eastward expansion of both the North Atlantic Treaty Organization (NATO) and the European Union (EU) have all prompted Russian president Vladimir Putin to become markedly more bellicose in his external policies. Indeed, from Russia's perspective, many Western policies appear to be a direct threat to its strategic interests and traditional sphere of influence, which for decades had included large portions of Eastern Europe and the Baltic states.

When the Soviet Union imploded in 1991, the new Russian Federation, which partly replaced it, faced staggering economic challenges. As former Soviet satellites declared independence, Russia lost some 24 percent of its territory, 50 percent of its population, 55 percent of its economic activity, and nearly 70 percent of its military personnel. Compounding these losses was the complete absence of political and economic institutions capable of aiding Russia's transition to a market-based economy.

The West responded haphazardly to Russia's plight and seemed not to fully grasp the enormity of the Kremlin's economic challenges. The U.S. government, along with the International Monetary Fund, recommended economic "shock treatment" for Russia. This included the forced and hasty reformation of existing economic and political systems into ones that would accommodate the transition to a market economy. However, the changes were implemented too quickly and without mechanisms in place to blunt their harsh effects on Russian citizens. The West also focused too much attention on Russian debt reduction, which caused even more economic chaos.

In 1992 the G-7 nations pledged a $1 billion aid package for Russia, but it was tied to future economic reform that never occurred. Other Western aid was often tied to Russia's human rights record, which similarly stalled forward economic momentum. Furthermore, the amount of economic aid offered to Russia was simply too small to help that nation out of its economic straitjacket or to aid it in a transition to a liberal market-based economic system.

The unfortunate result of these developments was a Russian economy in free fall during the 1990s. Russia's gross domestic product and industrial production plunged by 50 percent during 1990–1995. At the same time, the poverty rate more than tripled. Flawed attempts at privatization in Russia created oligarchs who formed monopolies and transferred billions of dollars of assets to other nations, which further sank Russia's economy. Worse still, massive budget deficits, some of which may be blamed on wrongheaded policies prescribed by the West, precipitated a grave Russian financial crisis in 1998. By 2000 when Putin came to power, the Russians were weary of more "help" from the West and were bitterly disillusioned with the promises of liberal capitalism.

America's preponderance of geopolitical power and the West's turn toward unilateralism have also badly strained relations with Moscow. Indeed, U.S. and NATO intervention in the 1992–1995 Bosnian War (Moscow backed the Bosnian Serbs, its traditional allies, while the West supported the Bosniaks and Croats) angered Moscow, as did NATO's unilateral military intervention in the 1998–1999 Kosovo War. The latter intervention was not sanctioned by the United Nations and again involved NATO fighting Russia's Serbian allies.

The George W. Bush administration augured an even more profound shift toward unilateralism particularly with the 2003–2011 Iraq War, which Putin sharply denounced and presciently warned would destabilize the entire Middle East. An unintended consequence of the Iraq War was a major spike in long-term oil prices, which greatly benefited Russia, a major oil-producing nation. High oil prices buoyed the Russian economy, enabling Putin to rebuild his military and emboldening him to invade Georgia to help pro-Russian separatists in South Ossetia and Abkhazia in 2008. In early 2014, Russia invaded the Crimean Peninsula and soon annexed it; Russia is also currently aiding pro-Russian rebels fighting for autonomy in eastern Ukraine and has become involved in the internecine Syrian Civil War.

Meanwhile, in 2002 the Bush administration unilaterally withdrew from the 1972 Anti-Ballistic Missile Treaty (ABM Treaty). This elicited howls of protest from the Kremlin, which believed that any future U.S./NATO ABM system that was to be based in Eastern Europe would imperil Russian security and potentially weaken or destroy its nuclear deterrence. The White House claimed that the system would protect against missiles from "rogue nations or groups"; from the Kremlin's perspective, however, the system would imperil Russian security. Neither NATO nor the U.S. government ever seriously sought Russian input on the proposed ABM system, nor did they invite Russia to participate in its implementation.

Perhaps nothing has wounded the West's relations with Russia more than the eastward expansion of NATO and the EU. Between 1999 and 2009, NATO welcomed into its ranks 12 new member states. All are in Central and Eastern Europe, and several—including Estonia and Latvia—were former Soviet republics that now directly border Russia. In similar fashion, since 2004 the EU has also expanded eastward to include such nations as Slovakia, Poland, Romania, and Latvia. In December 2015 NATO issued a formal membership invitation to Montenegro, which is expected to join the alliance in 2017.

Moscow now faces rivals—if not adversaries—lined up along its western flank and interconnected by potent military and economic alliances. These developments have only stoked the Kremlin's penchant for paranoia, which is far from baseless when one considers that Russia was invaded from the west by foreign forces in 1812, 1914, and 1941.

Making matters worse, for nearly a quarter of a century the Russians have insisted that as the Cold War wound down the West made assurances that NATO would not be expanded any farther to the east. Many U.S. and NATO officials, however, claim that no such assurance was ever made. Russian leaders, on the other hand, assert that American and NATO leaders did indeed imply that NATO would not expand, and they further state that the issue was first discussed during 1990 talks involving the reunification of Germany. The Soviet Union's last leader, Mikhail Gorbachev, who was a participant in those discussions, has repeatedly claimed that he acquiesced to German reunification in large part because he had been assured that NATO would remain within its 1990 borders.

Western officials have asserted that they promised only that NATO troops would not be stationed in the former East Germany. Nevertheless, Jack Matlock, the last U.S. ambassador to the Soviet Union, has claimed that the Soviets were indeed given the impression that NATO membership would not be extended to nations situated to the east of Germany. While no definitive document has yet been revealed concerning NATO expansion, there is general agreement among a number of international diplomats that the Russians were permitted to believe that there was an implicit pledge not to expand NATO in order to secure their acceptance of German reunification.

EU and NATO expansion has clearly unnerved the Kremlin and has led Russian leaders to conclude that the West cannot be trusted. Indeed, President Putin has invoked NATO expansion as a primary justification for his moves against Georgia and Ukraine. If the West wished to expand these institutions, it would have been better served to include Russia. At the very least, Russia could have been involved in them as an associate member, with the promise of full membership once it had met all of the qualifications of membership. This might well have allayed Russia's security fears and helped it progress more rapidly toward a functional capitalist democracy. As political scientist Joseph S. Nye Jr. has argued, membership in international military and economic alliances makes a country much less likely to engage in aggressive or militaristic foreign policies against other members. In short, the failure to integrate Russia into multilateral institutions has only served to isolate it and rekindle its historic security fears.

Western policies have failed to take into account Russia's security needs and have in fact forced the Kremlin onto the defensive. Instead of looking toward the West, Russian officials are increasingly looking toward the East—China in particular—while aggressively defending their western flank. The West's ineffectual attempts to aid Russia economically in the years following the demise of the Soviet Union have resulted in a Russian economy that is far too dependent on oil and gas exports and is vexed by widespread monopolies, rampant corruption, endemic cronyism, and abundant graft. To add insult to injury, Western unilateralism, particularly on the part of the United States, has been justifiably perceived by the Kremlin as a palpable menace. And the Bush Doctrine of preemptive war only deepened Russia's growing insecurity. Finally, the West's triumphalist post–Cold War rhetoric and U.S. cultural and economic hegemony have led many Russian leaders to conclude that their nation has no place within the Western orbit.

Paul G. Pierpaoli Jr.

Further Reading

Ambrosio, Thomas. *Challenging America's Global Preeminence: Russia's Quest for Multipolarity.* Aldershot, UK: Ashgate, 2005.

Applebaum, Anne. *Iron Curtain: The Crushing of Eastern Europe, 1944–1956.* New York: Anchor Books, 2012.

Asmus, Ronald. *A Little War That Shook the World: Georgia, Russia, and the Future of the West.* New York: New York University Press, 2010.

Bowker, Mike, and Cameron Ross. *Russia after the Cold War.* New York: Routledge, 2000.

Brooks, Stephen G. *World Out of Balance: International Relations and the Challenge of American Primacy.* Princeton, NJ: Princeton University Press, 2008.

Brudny, Yitzhak. *Reinventing Russia: Russian Nationalism and the Soviet State, 1953–1991.* Cambridge, MA: Harvard University Press, 1998.

Brzezinski, Zbigniew. *Second Chance: Three Presidents and the Crisis of American Superpower.* New York: Basic Books, 2007.

Gow, James. *Defending the West.* Cambridge, UK: Polity, 2005.

Hooks, Steven W. *U.S. Foreign Policy: The Paradox of World Power.* 3rd ed. Washington, DC: CQ Press, 2010.

Kanet, Roger E. *Russian Foreign Policy in the 21st Century.* London: Palgrave Macmillan, 2010.

Kaplan, Lawrence S. *NATO Divided, NATO United: The Evolution of an Alliance.* Westport, CT: Praeger, 2004.

Kennedy, Paul. *The Rise and Fall of the Great Powers: Economic Change and Military Conflict from 1500 to 2000.* New York: Vintage Books, 1987.

Korinman, Michel, and John Laughland. *Russia: A New Cold War?* Portland, OR: Valentine Mitchell Books, 2008.

Krastev, Ivan, Mark Leonard, and Andrew Wilsons, eds. *What Does Russia Think?* London: European Council on Foreign Relations, 2010.

Laqueur, Walter. *Putinism: Russian and Its Future with the West.* New York: Thomas Dunne Books, 2015.

Longworth, Peter. *Russia: The Once and Future Empire from Pre-History to Putin.* New York: St. Martin's, 2006.

Mandelbaum, Michael. *The Case for Goliath: How America Acts as the World's Government in the Twenty-First Century.* New York: PublicAffairs, 2005.

Mankoff, Jeffrey. *The Russian Economic Crisis.* New York: Council on Foreign Relations, 2010.

Matlock, Jack. *Superpower Illusions.* New Haven, CT: Yale University Press, 2010.

Molchanov, Mikhail A. *Eurasian Regionalisms and Russian Foreign Policy.* Aldershot, UK: Ashgate, 2015.

Nalbandov, Robert. *Not by Bread Alone: Russian Foreign Policy under Putin.* Dulles, VA: Potomac Books, 2016.

Norloff, Carla. *America's Global Advantage: U.S. Hegemony and International Cooperation.* Cambridge: Cambridge University Press, 2010.

Nye, Joseph S., Jr. *The Future of Power.* New York: PublicAffairs, 2011.

Pomerantsev, Peter. *Nothing Is True and Everything Is Possible: The Surreal Heart of the New Russia.* New York: PublicAffairs, 2014.

Prezel, Ilya. *National Identity and Foreign Policy: Nationalism and Leadership in Poland, Russia, and Ukraine.* Cambridge: Cambridge University Press, 1998.

Sakwa, Richard. *Frontline Ukraine: Crisis in the Borderlands.* London: I. B. Tauris, 2015.

Satter, David. *It Was a Long Time Ago, and It Never Really Happened Anyway: Russia and the Communist Past.* New Haven, CT: Yale University Press, 2013.

Sergi, Bruno S. *Western Views of Putin and His Presidency.* London: Bloomsbury Academic, 2011.

Smith, Martin A. *Power in the Changing Global Order: The US, Russia and China.* Cambridge, UK: Polity, 2012.

Stent, Angela E. *The Limits of Partnership: U.S. Russian Relations in the Twenty-First Century.* Princeton, NJ: Princeton University Press, 2014.

Tsygankov, Andrei P. *Russia's Foreign Policy: Change and Continuity in National Identity.* 3rd ed. Lanham, MD: Rowman and Littlefield, 2013.

Wilson, Andrew. *Ukraine Crisis: What It Means for the West.* New Haven, CT: Yale University Press, 2014.

63. Should Women Be Allowed to Serve in Combat Positions in the U.S. Military?

Women have served in military capacities, including combat, since ancient times, although this was the exception rather than the rule. Some fought alongside their spouses, while others fought disguised as men. Women did not begin serving legally in the U.S.

military until World War II. Even then, however, they served in noncombat support positions or in medical units. Nevertheless, by the end of World War II several hundred thousand women had served in the uniformed armed forces. In the postwar years, attitudes toward women in America underwent profound changes as women sought equal treatment and equal pay and began to make inroads into traditionally male-dominated fields. These changes also affected the U.S. military. In 1976 for the first time in history, women were permitted to attend the U.S. service academies, and in 1979 military enlistment requirements for men and women became identical. But women in combat roles still lay in the future. Beginning in the 1990s, the debate over the inclusion of women in combat came to be dominated by the assertion that women do not meet the physical requirements necessary for combat and by the conflicting viewpoint that the military had to adapt to contemporary societal changes and evolving gender norms. Finally, in 2013 the ban prohibiting women from serving in most combat roles was lifted, and in 2016 the Pentagon opened all combat positions to women.

In the first perspective essay, Dr. Jerry Morelock argues that women should not participate in combat, given that some studies indicate that they do not meet the physical requirements necessary for battle. Morelock further states that despite changes made by the U.S. military to adapt to changing gender norms in society, the issue of physical abilities of soldiers remains an important factor that should be carefully considered to ensure the best performance by the U.S. military. In contrast, Rosemarie Skaine asserts in her essay that women should indeed be allowed to participate in frontline combat positions, because historically they have served in various U.S. conflicts dating back to the American Revolutionary War. Furthermore, she points out, permitting women to take combat positions enhances overall military preparedness, aids in ending gender discrimination, and helps curb problems of sexual abuse within the ranks.

Background Essay

Women have played a key role in wars throughout history but most usually on the home front. While men were off doing the actual fighting, women were busy maintaining the family unit, tending to farms and fields, and, more recently, working in factories and other jobs in order to release men for combat service.

Women serving in combat and indeed as battlefield leaders is not new in history, however. In the 1st century BCE Queen Boudioca led the Celts in England against the Roman invaders; in the 3rd century Queen Zenobia, ruler of the Palmyrene Empire, led armies against the Roman Empire, and Trieu Thi Trinm of Vietnam led forces in the field against the Chinese; Tomoe Gozen distinguished herself in combat in 12th-century Japan; and in the 15th century Joan of Arc took to the field against the English.

Through the 18th century many women openly accompanied their husbands in the field and occasionally fought alongside them in combat. There are also examples of women who disguised themselves as men and enlisted to serve in the military, as in the American Revolutionary War and the American Civil War, but for most of human history women have not been accorded a regular combat role.

Women became more important in warfare in the modern era, with total national mobilizations. Thus, during World War II in the Soviet Union, 1 million women worked in industrial jobs by December 1941, and before the war ended they constituted 55 percent of the overall civilian workforce. By 1945, women made up 92 percent of the Soviet agricultural workforce. In Great Britain, 80,000 women joined the Women's Land Army and worked in agriculture to release men for war services between 1939 and 1945. In the United States, "Rosie the Riveter" became an icon of the American women's contribution to the war effort.

Whereas during World War I when women served as auxiliaries, largely in medical services, in World War II women also actually joined the military, although in most countries in noncombat roles. In Great Britain, more than 470,000 women served in the armed forces or in uniformed auxiliary units, while in the United States women joined the Women Accepted for Voluntary Emergency Service (WAVES), the Women Airforce Service Pilots (WASPs), the Women's Army Corps (WAC), the women's Coast Guard arm known as the SPARS (from the Coast Guard motto "Semper Paratus," or "Always Ready"), and the Women Marines. At its height, the WAVES numbered 8,000 officers and 76,000 enlisted women, most of whom were stationed in the continental United States. A 1944 study concluded that WAVES then in service released from noncombat duties sufficient male personnel to man 10 battleships, 10 aircraft carriers, 28 cruisers, and 50 destroyers.

WASP pilots ferried military aircraft from factories to bases and filled aviation support roles stateside. Despite an outstanding record, the WASP was disbanded late in 1944 because of protests from Congress and male pilots who feared competition with women during and after the war. Some 150,000 women served in the WAC during 1942–1978 performing support work. Many served overseas. Women's units were rounded out by the SPARS, which enlisted almost 11,000 women to help free men for sea duty with the Coast Guard, and the Women Marines. By 1945, 800 officers and 14,000 enlisted Women Marines were in uniform, and their service freed enough men from support duty to form the 5th Marine Division. All told, more than 350,000 U.S. women served in uniform during the war.

Although most countries eschewed combat roles for women, the Soviet Union was a notable exception. More than 800,000 women served in the Red Army, including approximately 400,000 in the Air Defense Forces and another 400,000 in ground units. Women maintained antiaircraft batteries, formed tank and artillery crews, and worked as mechanics and cooks as well as in medical and headquarters units. The most famous women were those who fought as snipers or as fighter and light bomber pilots.

Neither Germany nor Japan utilized auxiliaries or women in the military to the same extent as the Allies. Historians have pointed to this as a major factor in the defeat of the Axis in the war.

Early in the 21st century, however, for the most part women have largely been excluded from combat roles. Israel has a high percentage of women in the military as a consequence of a relatively small overall population vis-à-vis its larger neighbors. Yet despite a regulation in 2000 that opens all roles in the Israel Defense Forces (IDF) to women, in 2014 fewer than 4 percent of women in the IDF were serving in combat positions, such as infantry, tank crews, artillery, and pilots. The rest were in combat support roles.

In the United States, in 1979 qualifications for military enlistment were made the same for men and women, but women were nonetheless prohibited from direct combat roles and assignments. Indeed, in 1994 the Defense Department officially prohibited women from serving in combat. This ban was lifted in January 2013. Although a few women have completed the U.S. Marine Corps Infantry Training Battalion Course, women are still not permitted in infantry units barring studies that demonstrate that they are physically capable of such service. A few women

Coalition forces deployed some 40,000 women during the Persian Gulf War, although they were largely restricted to non-combat roles. (Corel)

have also completed the U.S. Army's grueling ranger training, but they have yet to be assigned to ranger units. The first enlisted female Navy SEALs would be assigned to units in 2017. In December 2015, U.S. defense secretary Ash Carter stated that in 2016 all combat positions would be open to women. Chairman of the Joint Chiefs of Staff general Joseph Dunford of the U.S. Marine Corps demurred, seeking to keep some combat positions, including that of infantry, closed to women. Another issue that has been raised is whether women should now be subject to Selective Service registration.

Spencer C. Tucker and Lance Janda

Perspective Essay 1. Physical Requirements and Combat Duty

Women should not be assigned to direct combat infantry and special operations forces, as these specific combat positions demand the absolute highest possible prolonged levels of strength, stamina, and endurance that women, in general, are physically incapable of attaining and sustaining. This has nothing to do with any lack of courage, motivation, or effort on the part of military women; it is due to the substantial and measurable physical differences between men and women. It is unreasonable to expect that any more than a handful of military women can achieve the demanding physical standards required of direct combat infantry—and even fewer, if any, the much more rigorous special operations forces standards—unless current physical standards are significantly lowered, which would seriously compromise combat effectiveness.

Typically, the proponents of women in combat primarily present this issue as a question of ensuring equality of career opportunities for military women. Those opposing women in combat often choose to rest their argument on the dubious claim that women somehow inherently lack the aggressiveness and so-called warrior spirit vital for succeeding in combat. Both of these positions miss the mark, since neither of them directly addresses the only valid criteria that should be permitted to be the deciding factor in this question—making absolutely certain that the direct frontline combat units of the U.S. armed forces contain only the best-qualified personnel in order to attain and maintain the maximum achievable level of combat effectiveness that will ensure accomplishment of their mission to fight and win the nation's wars. These direct frontline combat duties involve exposure to battlefield conditions that are so difficult, prolonged, and physically demanding that assignments must be based solely on the uncompromising application of the existing stringent physical standards. If these high standards are adhered to few women will qualify, and it seems extremely improbable that those women who might be able to meet the minimum physical standards will be the best-qualified personnel to perform these duties.

Given the reality that 21st-century military operations put all personnel at some degree of risk, the "women in combat" debate must be more narrowly focused to address the main point of contention separating those on each side of the issue: should women be assigned to direct frontline ground combat positions in the infantry (the U.S. Army and the U.S. Marine Corps) and special operations forces (Army Special Forces and Rangers, Marine Recon and Special Operations regiments, Navy SEALs, etc.)? In a June 1994 memorandum to the secretary of defense, Army Secretary Togo D. West Jr. provided a definition of this type of combat that still remains a valid description:

> Direct ground combat is engaging an enemy on the ground with individual or crew-served weapons, while being exposed to hostile fire and to a high probability of direct physical contact with the hostile force's personnel. Direct ground combat takes place well forward on the battlefield while locating and closing with the enemy to defeat them by fire, maneuver, or shock effect.

Even when not actually engaging an enemy force, the physical stresses placed on infantrymen and special operations forces personnel in sustained field operations are exceptionally severe. To focus on only one example, while conducting extended ground patrols or executing special operations missions, each individual typically carries a load (body armor, helmet, weapon, ammunition, food, water, squad supplies, radios, etc.) weighing 70–80 pounds and sometimes as heavy as 90–125 pounds. Infantry squad machine-gunners have the added burden of lugging the M240 "Light" Machine Gun that weighs 22 pounds, not counting the weapon's basic load of 70 pounds of ammunition divided among squad members. When infantry mortar section personnel must move dismounted, they break down the 91-pound M252 81mm mortar into the weapon's three major components (weighing 27, 29, and 35 pounds) and distribute the load to three section members—the remaining mortarmen have to carry the weapon's ammunition, the total weight of which greatly exceeds that of the mortar itself.

Moreover, the physical stresses of carrying such loads over rugged terrain (and, in Afghanistan, often at high altitude) already have created serious long-term musculoskeletal medical problems. A Johns Hopkins University researcher found that nearly one-third of all medical evacuations from Iraq and Afghanistan from 2004 to 2007 resulted from musculoskeletal, connective tissue, or spinal injuries—twice the number of evacuations for combat injuries. From 2003 to 2009, the number of U.S. Army soldiers medically retired with at least one musculoskeletal condition increased tenfold. Since the typical combat load of about 70 pounds represents

35 percent of average male body weight but 50 percent of average female body weight, the risk to women service members' health is substantially increased. Even in the services' basic training during which the loads that personnel carry are far less than what ground combat infantrymen routinely carry, women sustain injuries at a higher rate than men.

On average, military women are half a foot shorter and 20–30 pounds lighter than their male counterparts, possess only half of the upper body strength of men, and have 37 percent less muscle mass as well as 25–30 percent less aerobic capacity than male service members. Indeed, these significant physical differences are clearly acknowledged by the U.S. armed forces, as confirmed in the uniformed military services' annual physical fitness tests (PFT), which accommodate women through physical standards that are significantly lower than those required of male service members. The services call this "gender norming," but it is in fact preferential treatment of military women, since few would qualify to serve if required to achieve male physical fitness standards. For example, in order to pass the U.S. Army PFT, men must do at least 40 push-ups and run two miles in 16.5 minutes, while women need only do 17 push-ups and run two miles in 19.5 minutes.

Proponents of allowing women in combat units frequently support their position by citing two historical examples: Soviet units in World War II (1941–1945) and Israeli forces during the 1948 Israeli War of Independence. In both instances the countries were in grave danger of being overrun by invading enemy forces, and some women served alongside men in direct combat. Although most of the Soviet women who served in World War II—proportionately about the same percentage as American women served in the U.S. armed forces in the war—were in noncombat assignments (such as medical personnel, radio operators, and administrative duties), some Soviet women did fight in combat as snipers, tank drivers, machine-gunners, and pilots (about 0.7 percent of Soviet pilots were women). Yet, as historian Martin van Creveld has pointed out, the actions of both the Soviet Union and Israel after their respective wartime emergencies passed are revealing—both countries banned women from direct combat duties. Although in 2000 the Israel Defense Forces (IDF) established what it calls a "mixed-gender" combat infantry battalion—the Caracal Battalion—by 2009 the battalion was 70 percent female, and it is employed as a border patrol unit on the Israeli-Egyptian border in the Sinai, not as a ground combat infantry unit.

Another fact often pointed out by proponents of women in combat is that about a dozen countries worldwide allow women to be assigned to combat units. These countries include the military forces of New Zealand, Canada, Denmark, Finland, Italy, Germany, Norway, Serbia, Sweden, Switzerland, Taiwan, and, as noted, the IDF Caracal Battalion. However, simply assigning women to combat units is somewhat of a moot point for nearly all of these countries. With the possible exception of Israel, the likelihood that any of these listed countries will actually be in a war requiring direct infantry ground combat is essentially zero. The last time Sweden fought a major war, for example, was 200 years ago. In addition to those countries, Great Britain—whose oft-demonstrated willingness to engage in armed conflicts makes it likely that its military forces will continue to face ground combat—has been under political pressure for years to open combat assignments to women as a gender equality measure. The British Ministry of Defense has studied the issue for over a decade, and in the ministry's study "Women in the Armed Forces" (presented to Parliament on May 22, 2002) it was found that after a two-year assessment of women's ability to complete routine ground combat tasks (such as lifting and carrying gear over distances), only 0.1 percent of female applicants and 1 percent of trained female soldiers "would reach the required standards to meet the demands of these [combat] roles." As of this writing, the British government has not chosen to open combat assignments to women.

Military women have continued and will continue to accomplish every task assigned to them that they are physically capable of performing. But until human evolution catches up to the utopian ideals of those who prefer to see no difference in men and women beyond their gender, the incredibly demanding physical requirements of direct combat infantry and special operations should bar women from assignment to these specific military positions. It is in fact the duty of the U.S. armed forces to ensure that the military maintains the highest level of combat effectiveness by assigning only the best-qualified personnel to these units.

Jerry D. Morelock

Perspective Essay 2. Female Participation in Combat

The U.S. Department of Defense's decision to allow women to serve in all U.S. military combat positions beginning in January 2016 was the correct one. Women should be involved in all phases of the military, including combat.

Women have served in the military for centuries. They served even when they were officially restricted from doing so. Women dressed as men and served in the American Revolutionary War and the American Civil War. During the Civil War, the government recruited women to serve as nurses but without military status. In 1901, the Army Reorganization Act established the Army Nurse Corps and made nurses an official part of the military. In World War I and World War II, the roles of women in the military were expanded. In World War II, women support staff and nurses were stationed near the front lines.

In 2013, women made up 14.5 percent of total service members and 9–11 percent of the military personnel who had served in Afghanistan and Iraq. In these two wars women had served more than 285,000 tours of duty, and since many women served more than one tour, this number exceeds the total number of women who served. As of January 2013, 43 had died in Operation ENDURING FREEDOM in Afghanistan, including 22 from hostile fire. In Operation IRAQI FREEDOM that ended on August 31, 2010, 107 women were killed; 62 were from hostile fire. Purple Hearts were awarded to more than 865 servicewomen for wounds acquired through enemy action. Two women received the Silver Star for heroism: one in Iraq and one in Afghanistan.

In spite of their distinguished service in combat, U.S. military regulations continued to exclude women from 7.3 percent of U.S. Army positions, mostly in infantry, armor, and special forces. In addition, the policy limited women's career opportunities, including promotion, and contributed to gendered stereotypes about war.

Ending combat exclusion policies will enhance the readiness of the military when women are integrated into combat units. Combat exclusion policies are sometimes thought of as being designed to protect women by not putting them in harm's way, but the real reasons were the issues of readiness, unit cohesion, and ability. The argument was that women in combat zones would weaken the military's readiness, unit cohesion, and ability to fight. Thus, the risk rules were put in place. The military learned that excluding women by law from serving in combat did not enhance readiness. In fact, as more women served in the military and were increasingly involved in combat, they caused the exclusion provisions to be modified because the military found that the involvement of women actually improved readiness.

Including women in the military was formalized through the 1948 Women's Armed Services Integration Act. This legislation created a permanent corps of women in all military departments but limited the number of women to 2 percent of total service members and excluded women from combat. The 1988 Risk Rule excluded women from being assigned to noncombat units that were positioned close to combat units. The services were required to compare the risk of exposure to direct combat, hostile fire, or capture present in noncombat units associated with combat units, and if the risks were equal to or greater than those occurring in combat units in the same theater of operations, those units and positions would be closed to women. The 1988 Risk Rule did not work, because in the 1991 Persian Gulf War women demonstrated that they were essential to military readiness and were required in combat. In the war, 41,000 women were exposed to combat. It was a watershed event that supported the justification for women in combat. After the war, Congress repealed the U.S. Air Force and U.S. Navy exclusion laws but did not remove the exclusion policies of the U.S. Army and the U.S. Marine Corps.

In 1994, the Department of Defense rescinded the 1988 Risk Rule and opened almost all positions, units, and assignments for which women were qualified; however, units below brigade level were not opened because their primary mission was direct ground combat. The new policy defined ground combat as:

> Engaging the enemy on the ground with individual or crew-served weapons, while being exposed to hostile fire and to a high probability of direct physical contact with the hostile force's personnel. Direct ground combat takes place well forward on the battlefield while locating and closing with the enemy to defeat them by fire, maneuver, or shock effect.

In addition, the services could close positions to women if they are required to be physically close and remain with direct ground combat units.

The policies to exclude women from combat proved to be unenforceable in practice, because more women were required in positions in the combat zones. In Islamic countries men are forbidden to search women, and because of that in Iraq in 2003 the U.S. Army organized Lioness teams of servicewomen to accompany the all-male ground combat teams to operate at entry control points. In April 2004, a Lioness team accompanied a U.S. Marine Corps unit on a mission to arrest insurgent leaders in Ramadi. A firefight occurred, and the women returned fire. In 2004, Female Engagement Teams in Afghanistan also engaged in combat missions.

Even when the battlefields were symmetrical—that is, when the battle lines are clearly drawn—women found themselves in combat. As modern warfare has become increasingly asymmetrical, with no clearly drawn battle lines, women have been increasingly involved in combat situations alongside men.

On May 14, 2012, the collocation clause of the policy was eliminated and resulted in opening over 13,000 positions and six additional specialties to U.S. Army women. An exception to the provision of the 1994 memorandum that delineated occupations and units closed to women became effective. The exception allowed women to be assigned to some battalion-level ground combat unit staffs and opened 1,186 positions to women from the U.S. Army, the U.S. Navy, and the U.S. Marine Corps. By prohibiting women from ground combat roles, the military realized that it was limiting firepower. Commanding officers were aware of this fact, so they did not apply the exclusion policy and assigned women to serve in combat in times of crisis and, when these subsided, returned women to their noncombat positions. The policy could not keep up with the change on the battlefield and the need to deploy women to combat zones, so it had to change.

Excluding women from combat units prevented them from advancement to high-level positions. Excluding women from combat roles excluded them from serving in the units from which officers at high ranks are routinely promoted. Highly capable women were not even considered for promotion. Opening combat units to women will provide military women the opportunity to compete with men for command positions. The face of the U.S. Army and the U.S. Marines Corps should change, as has happened in the U.S. Air Force, the U.S. Navy, and the U.S. Coast Guard, where women have a fairer opportunity for promotion to higher ranks.

Two lawsuits filed in 2012 played a role in expediting combat inclusion. The first of these, *Baldwin et al. v. Panetta et al.,* was filed in May. It alleged that the exclusion of women from combat units violated Fifth Amendment rights of equal protection and the Administrative Procedure Act. Then in November, the American Civil Liberties Union (ACLU) filed a lawsuit against the Department of Defense on behalf of servicewomen. The suit claimed that the exclusion from combat was discriminatory and unconstitutional. The ACLU says that one of the plaintiffs, Major Mary Jennings Hegar, an Air National Guard helicopter pilot, was shot down in Afghanistan and returned fire and was wounded. She could not seek combat leadership positions because the Defense Department did not officially acknowledge her experience as combat.

Another point to make is that sexual abuse and discrimination of military women will be reduced when high-ranking officers include women and the officers are fully integrated. Military women are facing what has been called an epidemic of sexual abuse and discrimination. This includes sexual assaults, including rape, that deny a woman her right to control her body and exposes her to the risks of infection and the danger and discomfort of abortion or pregnancy. According to the Department of Defense 2012 annual report on sexual assault in the military, 26,000 service members claimed that they were sexually assaulted in 2012. It is significant that only 11 percent of these assaults were reported. The Pentagon counted only 3,374 formal allegations. Of these, 88 percent were against women; 2,558 were unrestricted, and 816 were restricted. Unrestricted reporting results in a referral to a military criminal investigation organization, while restricted reporting allows the victim to receive confidential care.

The sexual assault, abuse, and discrimination are abetted by the military's male-dominated, female-subordinate culture. This culture does not discourage sexual assaults at the enlisted level and above. It does not discourage discriminatory treatment of females. The military justice policies give commanders, who are almost all male, the power to make the final decision in military court cases and even to override the verdict of a military court that might have decided in favor of a woman.

Military culture has produced a history of discriminatory treatment of women in cases of sexual harassment, assault, rape, and murder. The culture has a history of discriminating against women even in sexual issues that involve consensual sexual relationships, such as pregnancy and same-sex relations. The situation is so bad that in one case a military woman was declared to have committed suicide when she was shot in the back of the head, so no further investigation was launched.

The military culture has its roots in the combat exclusion rules. As long as women have been denied access to the avenues for promotion to the top ranks, the male culture has flourished. As women are admitted to the top ranks and become a major force in deciding the nature of the culture, women will have a greater chance to receive fair and nondiscriminatory treatment. The Department of Defense is acknowledging the impact of placing women in positions dedicated to the elimination of sexual assault. The recently appointed officers in charge of Sexual Assault Prevention and Response offices are women.

Women in combat increase military readiness, enhance unit cohesion, and add to the quality of performance of the military.

Rosemarie Skaine

Further Reading

Biank, Tanya. *Undaunted: The Real Story of America's Servicewomen in Today's Military.* New York: NAL Hardcover, 2013.

Brown, Kingsley. *Co-Ed Combat: The New Evidence That Women Shouldn't Fight the Nation's Wars.* New York: Sentinel HC, 2007.

Campbell, D'Ann. *Women at War with America: Private Lives in a Patriotic Era.* Cambridge, MA: Harvard University Press, 1984.

Fenner, Lorry, and Marie deYoung, *Women in Combat: Civic Duty or Military Liability?* Washington, DC: Georgetown University Press, 2001.

Higonnet, Margaret Randolph, ed. *Behind the Lines: Gender and the Two World Wars.* New Haven, CT: Yale University Press, 1987

Holmstedt, Kristen. *Band of Sisters: American Women at War in Iraq.* Mechanicsburg, PA: Stackpole Books, 2008.

Hurrell, Margaret C., and Laura Miller. *New Opportunities: Effects upon Readiness, Cohesion, and Morale.* Santa Monica: Rand, 1997.

Maginnis, Robert L. *Deadly Consequences: How Cowards Are Pushing Women into Combat.* Washington, DC: Regnery Publishing, 2013.

Morelock, Jerry D. "Gender Wars—Army Utilization of Women in World War II." Chapter 3 in "A Single Soldier: World War II Mobilization, Manpower, and Replacement Policies and Their Influence on the Conduct of U.S. Army Operations in Northwest Europe, 1944–45." Unpublished PhD dissertation, University of Kansas, 2000.

Pennington, Reina. "Offensive Women: Women in Combat in the Red Army in the Second World War." *Journal of Military History* 74(3) (July 2010): 775–820.

Pennington, Reina. *Wings, Women, and War: Soviet Airwomen in World War II Combat.* Lawrence: University Press of Kansas, 2001.

Sanborn, James K., and Andrew deGrandpre. "4 Female Marines Will Graduate Enlisted Infantry Training This Week." *Marine Corps Times,* November 18, 2013.

Saywell, Shelley. *Women in War.* Markhan, Canada: Viking, 1985.

Scarborough, Rowan. "Army May Train Women for Rigor of Front Lines." *Washington Times,* July 30, 2012.

Skaine, Rosemarie. *Women at War: Gender Issues of Americans in Combat.* Jefferson, NC: McFarland, 1999.

Skaine, Rosemarie. *Women in Combat: A Reference Handbook.* Santa Barbara, CA: ABC-CLIO/Greenwood, 2011.

Springer, Barbara A., and Amy E. Ross. *Musculoskeletal Injuries in Military Women.* Borden Institute Monograph Series. Edited by Paul J. Dougherty. Washington, DC: U.S. Government Printing Office, 2011.

Treadwell, Mattie E. *United States Army in World War II: Special Studies; The Women's Army Corps*. Washington, DC: U.S. Government Printing Office, 1954.

U.S. Department of Defense, Office of the Under Secretary of Defense (P&R). *Report to Congress on the Reviews of Laws, Policies and Regulations Restricting the Service of Female Members in the U.S. Armed Forces*, February 2012.

U.S. Department of Health and Human Services, Centers for Disease Control and Prevention. "Anthropometric Reference Data for Children and Adults: United States, 2007–2010." *Vital and Health Statistics*, Series 11, Number 252, October 2012.

Van Creveld, Martin. *Men, Women & War: Do Women Belong in the Front Line?* London: Cassell, 2002.

Women's Research & Education Institute. *Women in the Military: Where They Stand*. 8th ed. Washington, DC: Women's Research & Education Institute, 2012.

64. Should the U.S. Government Reinstate the Draft?

Background Essay

During the American Revolutionary War, the Continental Army fluctuated between 6,000 and 20,000 troops and was small for the colonial population of 2.5 million people. One-year enlistments were the norm. General George Washington finally prevailed on Congress to allow three-year enlistments, but most Americans believed that everyone should take their turn. As time went on and conditions of service deteriorated, it became increasingly difficult to recruit soldiers, however.

Militia constituted perhaps half of the Patriot forces. Militia forces are distinct from those of the regular army and consist of private individuals formed largely for local defense. In American myth, the militia triumphed over the British. In truth, it was the Continental Army and the French forces who won the war. The poorly trained militiamen were unable to stand against hardened regulars and often broke and ran during battle.

When the war ended in 1783, there was much debate over the type of military establishment for the nation. Washington and the Federalists favored a permanent standing army, while Thomas Jefferson and the Democratic-Republicans saw such a force as a threat to liberty and wanted only a citizen militia. In June 1784, Congress directed that all remaining troops be discharged except for 80 privates and an appropriate number of officers. The navy was totally disbanded.

In 1792 Congress passed the Militia Act, which required that "every free white able bodied male citizen" between the ages of 18 and 45 enroll in their state's militia. Militiamen were to be ready to supplement the small regular army in the event of national emergency. Individuals were also expected to provide their own weapons, hence the "right to bear arms" in the Second Amendment to the U.S. Constitution. Militia service was limited to three months, which ensured their uselessness in all but the briefest of conflicts, and militiamen could not be compelled to fight outside U.S. territory.

The U.S. Army slowly increased in size, and in 1794 Congress created a navy. Still, on the eve of the War of 1812 the army numbered only 7,000 men. The nation again counted heavily on militia, and the same problems of the American Revolutionary War reappeared. The most glaring example of militia failure came during the British advance on Washington, D.C., in August 1814. The government called up 95,000 militia, but only 7,000 appeared. Although they still greatly outnumbered the British, they broke and ran in the Battle of Bladensburg on August 24, allowing the British to capture Washington.

So-called volunteers emerged during the War of 1812 and were in effect a mix of regulars and militia. Congress authorized the formation of these units, drawn from the militia, to augment the regular army. Volunteers had the advantage of being able to serve for longer periods than militiamen and also were not bound by state boundaries and could also serve abroad.

After the War of 1812, the United States reverted to its dual-track military system of a small professional establishment and a citizen militia. The outbreak of the Mexican-American War in 1846 found the U.S. Army with only about 8,000 men, a fourth the size of that of Mexico. As militia could not legally serve in Mexico, to supplement the regulars the national government again chose to rely on volunteers. A total of 104,000 Americans served in the war: 60,000 volunteers, 32,000 regulars, and 12,000 militiamen.

During the American Civil War, both sides relied heavily on volunteers. At the onset, the U.S. regular army numbered only about 16,300 men, and it remained small throughout the war. The bulk of the troops were in volunteer units. In March 1861, Confederate president Jefferson Davis called for 100,000 volunteers to serve for 12 months. In April, U.S. president Abraham Lincoln called for 75,000 volunteers, to serve for just 3 months. The war went on far longer than anticipated, and the cost in lives was heavy. As a result, the South, with far less manpower, adopted conscription in 1862; the North enacted it a year later.

The military shrank dramatically after the Civil War. From 1 million men under arms in 1865, the U.S. Army went to only 25,000 by the end of 1866, where it remained for 30 years. During the Spanish-American War in 1898, the army retained the dual-track system of regulars and volunteers. Fully 150,000 volunteers served during the war. In 1903, the Dick Act repealed the old Militia Act of 1792 and in effect created two militias, with the new wholly volunteer National Guard to be the first-line military reserve. Under the 1903 act, all other adult males between the ages of 18 and 45 constituted the second militia.

Troubles with Mexico and World War I in Europe were the impetus behind the National Defense Act of 1916. It authorized army expansion to 175,000 officers and men over a five-year period, with the National Guard to increase from 100,000 men to 400,000. The act also stated that the National Guard could be federalized for the duration of a war rather than the previous maximum of three months. In addition, the act created the Reserve Officers' Training Corps (ROTC) as well as army officer and enlisted reserves.

In April 1917, the United States entered World War I. At the time, the U.S. Army numbered 127,000 men; an additional 66,000 National Guardsmen were in federal service along the border with Mexico. In May 1917 Congress passed the Selective Service Act, requiring all males between the ages of 21 and 30 to register (in 1918 it was extended to ages 18 to 45). Ultimately 24 million men were registered, and the army grew to 3.7 million men. Of this total almost 2.2 million were conscripts, but most of those who saw combat were volunteers.

Following World War I the United States withdrew into isolation, and the army shrank back to near its prewar size. When World War II began in Europe in September 1939, the U.S. Army ranked 19th in size in the world, with only 190,000 men. In September 1940 Congress approved the Selective Training and Service Act, the nation's first peacetime draft. During the war the army grew to 8.2 million men and women, of whom 1.8 million were in the 16 Army Air Forces. The marines expanded to more than 485,000 men and women. Total navy personnel strength grew to 3.4 million men and women.

Following the war, the U.S. military went from 12 million men and women in 1945 to only 1.6 million in 1950. That situation changed with the Korean War (1950–1953). Again the United States rearmed, and the American force that fought in Korea was essentially formed of draftees.

In 1965, the United States sent ground troops to the Republic of Vietnam. The army that fought in Vietnam was essentially a draftee force led by professional army officers and those fulfilling ROTC obligations. More affluent Americans obtained deferments from serving while they attended college. Enlisted men served a one-year combat tour, but men departed when it ended, and the resulting lack of unit cohesion was a serious liability in fighting the war. Because the war was so unpopular, President Lyndon B. Johnson refused to mobilize the reserves.

In the early 1970s, President Richard Nixon embraced the concept of an all-volunteer military as a means to remove middle-class opposition to his Vietnam policies. The draft was abolished in 1972. A year later, the U.S. armed forces were all volunteer. This new all-volunteer military preformed well in the Persian Gulf War in 1991 and the current Iraq War.

The active-duty U.S. military has gone from a force of 2.4 million men and women in 1969 to only 1.4 million in 2015. There are some 1.1 million in the active

Selective Service Director U.S. Army lieutenant colonel Lewis B. Hershey draws the last capsule from the goldfish bowl during the first U.S. peacetime Selective Service lottery, October 15, 1940. (Library of Congress)

reserves. The army has been the hardest hit, as civilian leaders in the Department of Defense believed that they could shrink the size of the army though reliance on new high-tech weaponry and mobility at the expense of boots on the ground. However, the demands of the Afghanistan War and the Iraq War forced the army to rely heavily on the National Guard. The strains of the Iraq War in particular on both the army and the National Guard prompted a number of members of Congress to call for a reexamining of the entire U.S. military force structure. Another question to be resolved is whether women, now eligible to serve in U.S. combat units, should be required to register for the draft.

Spencer C. Tucker

Perspective Essay 1. In Defense of an All-Volunteer Force

The debate over whether to return to a draft or to maintain the current American military all-volunteer force continues as a key political point of discussion in spite of conscription ending over three decades ago. Such politicians as U.S. congressman

Charles Rangel (D-NY) have called for a return to conscription, and the topic gains more attention given the current active deployment tempo of U.S. military forces. Indeed, supporters make strong arguments for the reinstatement of the draft as the shared sacrifice of service among American citizens, the much-needed reinvigoration of civic virtue, and, in Rangel's argument, a more discriminating use of military force by the government, given its more socially inclusive composition. However, arguments regarding a return to the draft need to address two key issues: military necessity and civic obligation.

From a practical standpoint, the Department of Defense is not in need of a World War/Cold War–size military that requires the enlistment of every military-age American for a minimum service requirement. Even with the unpopularity of the Iraq War, all services met enlistment quotas for volunteers, including record numbers of reenlistments from veterans. Statistics indicate that reinstatement of a draft would lower, not raise, the standards of education, skills, and ability of the average service member. Most analysts agree that commanders would rather keep the intelligent, educated, and capable volunteer soldier of today in this technologically sophisticated military rather than sacrifice quality for numbers. The current operational environment makes a call for a *levée en masse* (mass conscription) both impractical and undesirable.

The battlefield success of the all-volunteer force in the conflicts in the Middle East erased post–Vietnam War reservations regarding projected lack of military effectiveness of individual soldiers (because of anticipated lower quality) and the entire institution. The performance of the American military in Operation DESERT STORM and the wars in Afghanistan and Iraq demonstrated a highly motivated, well-trained, professional all-volunteer force to have equal, if not better, success in combat. Indeed, it remains a subject of admiration by America's global allies and rivals.

Proponents of conscription argue that a draft results in greater equality in the burden of military service by compelling all adult citizens to serve. The history of the draft in America, however, does not support that claim, at least in its perception by the greater populace. Since the American Revolution, the wealthy and well connected of American society were able to avoid compulsory military service through a variety of means: hiring substitutes, paying commutation fees, deferments (educational, medical, etc.), and conscientious objection. Regardless of attempts to make service obligations socially equitable, the system traditionally left the privileged class a means of evasion, often ironically leading to social unrest rather than civic cohesiveness. Traditionally, during the world wars in particular, the American government used the draft more as a device to invigorate volunteerism in recruiting, pushing those conscriptable men to willingly enlist to avoid the stigma of being coerced draftees. Moreover, recent statistics debunked fears that an all-volunteer military places a greater burden on the poor and less educated. Studies demonstrate today's all-volunteer force as demographically illustrative of greater American society than the previous conscript military, with more equitable representation from minorities and a high participation of women (nearly nonexistent in the old draftee military).

The conflicts in Iraq and Afghanistan, and more broadly the war on terror, has seen the U.S. government trying to keep the people distanced from war rather than asking them to make major personal sacrifices, as in wars past. This is especially true in the case of mobilizing the entire society. Instead, the government asked citizens to proceed with their lives as normal, maintaining a strong economy and society to send a message to the enemy that its tactics cannot shake the American fabric and resolve. Resurrecting conscription would contradict that strategy and sends a mixed message.

The war on terror also shows that military service may not be the ultimate demonstration of citizenship in homeland defense. After 9/11, American society identifies first responders (police, fire fighters, etc.), federal agency employees, and security personnel as being as important as military service members in maintaining the nation's safety.

The sociopolitical/civil-military landscape has changed over the last 50 years, and with it, conceptions of republicanism and civic sacrifice have shifted. Perception, not necessarily reality, of conscription remains key. The post–Vietnam War generations continue to view the draft as punishment or the device of a coercive, apathetic government, not the ultimate application of civic duty. Most Americans today view the primary function of national government as protecting rights and freedoms of individuals, particularly since the United States serves increasingly as the model for a liberal, capitalistic society.

Volunteerism remains the hallmark of both military and civic virtue. The all-volunteer force has distinguished itself on the battlefield and still maintains the highest sense of trust among the American people. Having an all-volunteer force demonstrates a more equitable distribution of service and continues to embody the values and traditions of this great nation.

Bradford A. Wineman

Perspective Essay 2. Many Good Reasons to Reinstate the Draft

When the United States ended the draft in 1973 and created the All Volunteer Force (AVF), supporters heralded the arrival of a more just era in which high-quality recruits would be attracted to the military by better pay and benefits. They argued that armed services consisting only of those who wished to serve would be better motivated, more cohesive, and more equitable and that the fighting prowess of our soldiers, sailors, airmen, and marines would therefore be enhanced. We would, they said, move past the turbulent Vietnam War era and reduce the conflict and tension between civilians and the armed forces and find that returning to volunteers would prove more just, more sustainable, and more equitable in the long run. In a democratic society centered on individual rights, they said, it was the logical thing to do.

And they were wrong. More than 40 years later, the empirical evidence is overwhelming that the AVF has failed on multiple fronts and that reinstatement of the draft—particularly if it includes an option for nonmilitary national service—is absolutely necessary. Indeed, the current all-volunteer force is fiscally unsustainable, ethically and morally indefensible, and strategically bankrupt.

On the financial front, the available data is damning. To support approximately 1.4 million members of the armed service in 2015, the Department of Defense allocated $598.5 billion. Yet in 1985 it supported more than 2.1 million personnel for only $405 billion, meaning that the higher costs associated with recruiting, reenlisting, paying, training, and equipping the AVF require the United States to spend 48 percent more money to field a force that is one-third smaller. Note that this utterly unsustainable rate of increase does not include supplemental allocations to fund ongoing wars overseas. If it did, the total outlays for military activity would be even higher.

Rising gross domestic product and weapons costs mitigate and/or explain much of the rise in costs, but there is no denying the explosion in personnel expenditures in an era when recruiting is expensive and the armed forces must compete with the private sector for skilled people. The U.S. Army has raised pay and allowances 90 percent since 2000; it offers room, board, health care, a salary, and $78,000 in college fees and professional training plus bonuses (which totaled $860 million in 2008) in 46 job specialties to each and every recruit, yet it still struggles to meet annual recruiting goals. That struggle is bound to continue, as the nation finds itself in a period of low-intensity yet seemingly endless wars when press coverage of the military is often negative and the labor market is strong enough to attract young people to the private sector. Worse, so many young people are obese, academically limited, or have criminal records that only 30 percent of the nation's 21 million 17–21-year-olds would be eligible to enlist even if they were willing, which means that the competition for a dwindling pool of qualified young people will only drive costs higher.

There is simply no way the United States can support the recent rate of increase in the long run or afford to raise a genuinely large force in the event of another major conflict without a galvanic shock to the economy in terms of radically adjusted spending or higher taxes. The affordable alternative is a draft that would require national service at reasonable salaries for a limited period of time.

Moreover, a draft would help address the astonishing gap between civilians and the armed forces. Fewer than 1 percent of Americans serve in uniform, which is perhaps ironic in a society that pays such exorbitant and ostentatious obeisance to all things military, from national holidays to generous government benefit packages to discounts at local and national businesses. Yet Americans seem to prefer paying for military service than doing it themselves, and over the last 40 years the military has steadily faded from the lives of most people. In 1990, 40 percent of young Americans had at least one parent who had served, and in 2014 the rate was 16 percent.

Few young people today have any connection to the armed forces, and among elites, few serve the armed forces in any capacity at all. The result is a morally reprehensible situation in which an indifferent, self-indulgent, largely obese and generally poorly educated majority are defended and served by the tiny minority who are willing to serve if the price is right, and that miniscule fraction of the population comes disproportionately from working-class and minority families.

Almost half of all recruits are African American or Latino, and less than 10 percent of recruits have college degrees, meaning that the well-to-do have progressively left military sacrifice to the poor. The result is that the idea of collective sacrifice on behalf of something greater than oneself is steadily being lost to a mantra of me-first, passive citizenship that evokes the latter decades of the Roman Empire, when native Romans simply refused to serve in the legions and brought in outsiders to fight on their behalf (much as the United States increasingly recruits foreign nationals). A draft would help to close the dangerous gap between civilians and the armed forces; unite Americans across boundaries of race, class, and ethnicity; and reinvigorate a sense of national purpose and citizenship in the same way it did for previous generations.

Finally, by reconnecting the American people to the armed forces, a draft might bring public attention back to foreign and military policy, where greater scrutiny is long overdue. Since 2001 the United States has waged expensive and largely fruitless wars with minimal public debate or congressional oversight, tolerated successive presidents who waged war without congressional approval, and used military force at a rapidly expanding rate. Between 1933 and 1973, for example, the United States used military force abroad 27 times. In the 40 years between the end of the draft and 2014, it did so 175 times. Surely part of the explanation for that disturbing and empirically counterproductive trend is the fact that few American in or out of Congress have a vested interest in what happens to the military. In 1981, 64 percent of Congress was composed of veterans. In 2015, the rate was 18 percent. And while no one would argue that veterans have a monopoly on strategic insight, it is certainly true that vigorous public scrutiny and debate, the kind that would ensue if every American had served or was expected to serve in some capacity, is the best check on reckless military ventures.

Military leaders today have too much power and too little oversight because so few people understand what they do, and voters and Congress are hesitant to criticize the armed forces as a result. This is a dangerously out-of-balance situation that lends itself to further alienation of the armed forces and more strategic blunders in the future. The solution is to restore full membership in the political community to all Americans by connecting them to the nation and giving them a stake in what happens to the armed forces through a draft.

Ironically, the draft ended in part in 1973 because it became so virulently controversial during the Vietnam War, a war that popular pressure helped end. At the time, critics argued that the draft was too controversial to keep as an institution, which is a shame, because by connecting the people to the armed forces and thereby prompting the people to care about the Vietnam War in the first place, the draft did one of the things it was supposed to do. Perhaps without the draft we might still be in Vietnam, fighting with a tiny volunteer army largely forgotten by the people, just as we are in Iraq and Afghanistan.

Lance Janda

Further Reading

Anderson, Martin. *The Military Draft: Selected Readings on Conscription.* Stanford, CA: Hoover Institution Press, 1982.

Baskir, Lawrence M., and William A. Strauss. *Chance and Circumstance: The Draft, the War, and the Vietnam Generation.* New York: Random House/Vintage, 1978.

Brown, John Sloan. *Kevlar Legions: The Transformation of the U.S. Army, 1989–2005.* Washington, DC: U.S. Army Center of Military History, 2012.

Carr, Caleb. "Storm Warning." *Lapham's Quarterly* 1 (Winter 2008): 211–219.

Flynn, George Q. *Conscription and Democracy: The Draft in France, Great Britain, and the United States.* Westport, CT: Greenwood, 2001.

Flynn, George Q. *The Draft, 1940–1973.* Lawrence: University Press of Kansas, 1993.

Geva, Dorit. *Conscription, Family, and the Modern State: A Comparative Study of France and the United States.* Cambridge: Cambridge University Press, 2013.

Halstead, Fred. *GIs Speak Out against the War: The Case of the Ft. Jackson 8.* New York: Pathfinder, 1970.

Hawkins, Williams. "Draft Duplicity." *Washington Times,* October 21, 2004.

Hilderman, Walter C., III. *They Went into the Fight Cheering! Confederate Conscription in North Carolina.* Boone, NC: Parkway, 2005.

Keith, Jeanette. "The Politics of Southern Draft Resistance, 1917–1918: Class, Race, and Conscription in the Rural South." *Journal of American History* 87(4) (2001): 1335–1361.

Kerber, Linda. *No Constitutional Right to be Ladies: Women and the Obligations of Citizenship.* New York: Hill and Wang, 1999.

Leach, Jack F. *Conscription in the United States: Historical Background.* Rutland, VT: Tuttle, 1952.

Mjøset, Lars, and Stephen Van Holde, eds. *The Comparative Study of Conscription in the Armed Forces.* Amsterdam: JAI Press/Elsevier Science, 2002.

Moore, Albert Burton. *Conscription and Conflict in the Confederacy.* Columbia: University of South Carolina Press, 1996.

Mullen, R. W. *Blacks in America's Wars.* New York: Monad, 1975.

Reeves, Thomas, and Karl Hess. *The End of the Draft: A Proposal for Abolishing Conscription and for a Volunteer Army.* New York: Random House, 1970.

Simon, Rita J., and Mohamed Alaa Abdel-Moneim. *A Handbook of Military Conscription and Composition the World Over.* New York: Lexington Books, 2011.

Sutherland, John. "Draft Dilemma." *The Guardian,* May 31, 2004.

Warner, John T., and Beth J. Asch. "The Record and Prospects of the All-Volunteer Military in the United States." *Journal of Economic Perspectives* 15(2) (2001): 169–192.

Wheeler, Kenneth H. "Local Autonomy and Civil War Draft Resistance: Holmes County, Ohio." *Civil War History* 45(2) (1999): 147–159.

About the Editor and Contributors

Editor

Spencer C. Tucker, PhD, has been senior fellow in military history at ABC-CLIO since 2003. He is the author or editor of 61 books and encyclopedias, many of which have won prestigious awards. Tucker's last academic position before his retirement from teaching was the John Biggs Chair in Military History at the Virginia Military Institute, Lexington, Virginia. He has been a Fulbright scholar, a visiting research associate at the Smithsonian Institution, and, as a U.S. Army captain, an intelligence analyst in the Pentagon. Tucker's recently published works include *Wars That Changed History: 50 of the World's Greatest Conflicts, U.S. Conflict in the 21st Century: Afghanistan War, Iraq War, and the War on Terror,* and *Modern Conflict in the Greater Middle East: A Country-by-Country Guide,* all published by ABC CLIO.

Contributors

Thomas Adam is a professor of history at the University of Texas at Arlington, where he teaches undergraduate courses in German history and graduate courses in modern transatlantic history. He received his PhD from the University of Leipzig in 1998. Adam's publications include *Buying Respectability: Philanthropy and Urban Society in Transnational Perspective, 1840s to 1930s* (2009), *Stipendienstiftungen und der Zugang zu höherer Bildung in Deutschland von 1800 bis 1960* (2008), *Traveling between Worlds: German-American Encounters* (coedited with Ruth Gross, 2006), the three-volume encyclopedia *Germany and the Americas: Culture, Politics, and Society* (2005), and *Philanthropy, Patronage, and Civil Society: Experiences from Germany, Great Britain, and North America* (2004).

Valerie L. Adams is an assistant professor at Embry-Riddle Aeronautical University. She earned her PhD in history from the University of New Hampshire. Adams is the author of *Eisenhower's Fine Group of Fellows: Crafting National Security Policy to Uphold the "Great Equation"* (Lexington Books, 2005) and has contributed essays to several other works, including *The Uniting States: The Story of Statehood* (Greenwood, 2004) and *The Red Scare after 1945* (Manley, 2004).

Gar Alperovitz, the Lionel R. Bauman Professor of Political Economy at the University of Maryland, is also the founder of the university's Democracy Collaborative, a research center working on economic policy and democratic institutional reconstruction. He is former fellow of Kings College, Cambridge University, and of the Institute of Politics at Harvard and a previous guest scholar at the Brookings Institution, and his work encompasses both diplomatic history and political-economic theory and its applications. A major ABC television documentary on the 50th anniversary of the decision to use the atomic bomb drew heavily on Alperovitz's work, and two BBC television documentaries on the subject have been based almost exclusively on his publications. His latest book on the atomic bomb was a distinguished finalist for the Lionel Gelber Prize. Alperovitz has also served as a legislative director in both the U.S. House of Representatives and the U.S. Senate and as a special assistant for international organization affairs in the State Department.

James R. Arnold is a military historian, cofounder of the website on Napoleon Bonaparte, and the author of more than 20 books. Some of his works include *Grant Wins the War: Decision at Vicksburg* (Wiley, 1997), *Jungle of Snakes: A Century of Counterinsurgency Warfare from the Philippines to Iraq* (Bloomsbury, 2009), and *The Moro War: How America Battled a Muslim Insurgency in the Philippine Jungle, 1902–1913* (Bloomsbury, 2011). Arnold's book *Napoleon Conquers Austria: The 1809 Campaign for Vienna* (Praeger, 1995) won the International Napoleonic Society's Literary Award in 1995.

Ralph Ashby received his PhD from the University of Illinois at Chicago in 2003. He has taught at Barat College of DePaul University, the University of Illinois at Chicago, and Truman College in Chicago. He is a U.S. Army veteran of the Persian Gulf War. Dr. Ashby currently teaches at Eastern Illinois University. His publications include *Napoleon against Great Odds: The Emperor and the Defenders of France, 1814* (Praeger, 2010).

Rolando Avila is a lecturer in American heritage in the History and Philosophy Department at the University of Texas–Pan American (UTPA). He received an MA in history (1999) and an EdD in educational leadership (2013) from UTPA. He has published more than 100 articles in various historical and educational works.

Walter F. Bell has retired as a historian. During his career he authored several publications, including *The Philippines in World War II, 1941–1945: A Chronology and Select Annotated Bibliography of Books and Articles in English* (Greenwood, 1999).

Michael Berenbaum is a professor of Jewish studies at the American Jewish University in Los Angeles and the director of the Sigi Zieirng Institute: Exploring the Ethical and Religious Implications of the Holocaust. Among the 20 books he has authored and edited is *The Bombing of Auschwitz: Should the Allies Have Attempted it?* (University Press of Kansas, 2003), coauthored with Michael Neufeld, a dialogue between military historians and Holocaust historians. Berenbaum was also the executive editor of the second edition of the *Encyclopaedia Judaica*. He was project director overseeing the creation of the United States Holocaust Memorial Museum and the first director of its research institute and later served as president and CEO of the Survivors of the Shoah Visual History Foundation, which took the testimony of 52,000 Holocaust survivors in 32 languages and 57 countries. Berenbaum's work in film has won Emmy Awards and Academy Awards.

Jeremy Bonner graduated from the Catholic University of America in Washington, D.C. He was the J. Franklin Jameson Fellow at the Library of Congress from 2001 to 2002 and has taught at Robert Morris University and Duquesne University. Dr. Bonner is the author of two books and various scholarly articles exploring the relationship between religious belief, the state, and society.

Wayne H. Bowen is a professor in and chair of the Department of History at Southeast Missouri State University, where he is also the director of university studies. He is the author of six books and many articles on modern Spain, the Middle East, and military history. Bowen received his BA in history from the University of Southern California and his MA and PhD in history from Northwestern University. His research focuses on Spanish history, with ongoing projects on Hispanic-U.S. diplomacy, relations between the Spanish and Ottoman Empires, and the Reformation in the Spanish Empire.

Lee L. Brice is a professor of ancient history in the History Department at Western Illinois University. He has won awards for his teaching and for mentoring students' undergraduate research. Brice's primary research specializations are in discipline in ancient armies and Greek numismatics. Brice recently held a prestigious Tytus Fellowship at the University of Cincinnati and has won a Franklin Grant from the American Philosophical Society. Among his publications are *Greek Warfare from the Battle of Marathon to the Conquests of Alexander the Great* (ABC-CLIO, 2012) and "Armada from Athens: Case Study of the Sicilian Expedition 415–413 BCE" in *The Oxford Handbook of Warfare in the Classical World c. 700 B.C.–A.D. 602,* edited by Lawrence Tritle and Brian Campbell (Oxford University Press, 2012).

Robert P. Broadwater is an independent scholar and historian. He has authored or contributed to more than 30 books on the American Revolution and the American Civil War, including ABC-CLIO's *William T. Sherman: A Biography* and *Ulysses S.*

Grant: A Biography as well as *Civil War Special Forces: The Elite and Distinct Fighting Units of the Union and Confederate Armies* (Praeger, 2014).

Stefan M. Brooks is an assistant professor at the Institute for Regional Analysis and Public Policy at Morehead State University. He received his PhD in political science from the University of Houston and his MA in international relations from St. Mary's University. Brooks is the author of *The Webster-Hayne Debate: An Inquiry into the Nature of Union* (2008) and is a regular contributor to ABC-CLIO print and electronic publications, including *World at War: Understanding Conflict and Society* and *The Encyclopedia of the Arab-Israeli Conflict: A Political, Social, and Military History.*

Eric Dorn Brose is a professor at Drexel University in Philadelphia. He is the author of several books, including *A History of the Great War: World War One and the International Crisis of the Early Twentieth Century* (Oxford University Press, 2009) and *A History of Europe in the Twentieth Century* (Oxford University Press, 2004). He received his PhD and MA from Ohio State University and his BA from Miami University of Ohio.

Henry (Chip) Carey is an associate professor of political science at Georgia State University. He has published several books, including *Privatizing the Democratic Peace: Policy Dilemmas of NGO Peacebuilding* (Palgrave Macmillan, 2012) and *Reaping What You Sow: A Comparative Examination of Torture Reform in the United States, France, Argentina, and Israel* (Praeger, 2012). In addition, Dr. Carey is coeditor of *Trials and Tribulations: International Criminal Tribunals and the Challenges of International Justice* (Lexington Books/Rowman and Littlefield, 2013).

Jessica M. Chapman is an assistant professor of history at Williams College. She specializes in the United States and the world, with particular emphases on U.S. foreign relations, Southeast Asia, modern European diplomacy, and decolonization. She is currently revising her dissertation, "Debating the Will of Heaven: South Vietnamese Politics and Nationalism in International Perspective, 1953–1956," into a book manuscript. Chapman received her PhD in history from the University of California at Santa Barbara in 2006.

Paul A. Cimbala is a professor of history at Fordham University and received his BA from St. Joseph College in Philadelphia and his MA and PhD from Emory University. He has held an editorial appointment with the Black Abolitionist Papers Project at Florida State University and has taught at the University of South Carolina at Aiken. He teaches undergraduate and graduate courses on the American Civil War and Reconstruction, war and American society, the American South, and African American history to 1877. Dr. Cimbala has published articles and essays on slavery, Civil War soldiers, and the Freedmen's Bureau. He is the author of *Under the Guardianship of the Nation: The Freedmen's Bureau and the Reconstruction of Georgia, 1865–1870* (1997, 2003), which received the Malcolm and Muriel Barrow Bell Award of the Georgia Historical Society.

Jessica H. Clark is an assistant professor of classics at Florida State University. Her primary area of study is the history and historiography of the Roman Republic. She is the author of *Triumph in Defeat: Military Loss and the Roman Republic* (Oxford University Press, 2014). Dr. Clark received her PhD from Princeton University in 2008.

Conrad C. Crane has authored and edited numerous books and articles on topics including the Korean War, the American Civil War, World War I, and World War II. He was a professor of history at the U.S. Military Academy, a researcher at the Strategic Studies Institute, and the director of the U.S. Military History Institute.

Malcolm Crook is a professor of French history at Keele University in Staffordshire, England, where he has taught for the past 30 years. He specializes in the 18th- and 19th-century history of France, with particular emphasis on the French Revolutionary and Napoleonic periods. His books include a study of elections during the French Revolution and Napoleon's rise to power. Crook has recently stepped down as editor of the journal *French History* but continues to write articles for a variety of reviews and magazines in addition to lecturing widely.

Lawrence Davidson is a professor emeritus of history at West Chester University in West Chester, Pennsylvania. He specializes in Middle East history with a particular emphasis on the evolution of U.S. foreign policy toward that region. Davidson has traveled extensively in the Middle East and neighboring areas. Countries visited include Egypt, Morocco, Israel, Palestine, Syria, Jordan, Lebanon, Sudan, and Iran. In most of these countries he has met and interviewed governmental leaders, academics, students, and leaders of civil society. Dr. Davidson's publications include *America's Palestine: Popular and Official Perceptions from Balfour to Israeli Statehood* (University Press of Florida, 2001) and *Cultural Genocide* (Rutgers University Press, 2012).

Paul K. Davis is a military historian. He obtained his PhD from King's College in London. Davis has lectured at St. Mary's University, the Alamo Colleges, and the University of Texas. He has served as a consultant in military history for the BBC and National Public Radio. Davis has published a number of books, including *Masters of the Battlefield: Great Commanders from the Classical Age to the Napoleonic Era* (Oxford University Press, 2013), *100 Decisive Battles: From Ancient Times to the Present* (Oxford University Press, 2001), and *Besieged: An Encyclopedia of Great Sieges from Ancient Times to the Present* (ABC-CLIO, 2001).

James Daybell was educated at Hertford College, Oxford, and the University of Reading in the United Kingdom. He has taught history at the University of Reading and at Oxford University in the United Kingdom and Central Michigan University in the United States and is currently a professor of early modern British history at the University of Plymouth. Daybell has been awarded fellowships at the Folger Shakespeare Library and Huntington Library, California, and is a fellow of the Royal Historical Society. He is the editor of two collections of essays published by Palgrave Macmillan: *Cultures of Correspondence in Early Modern Britain, 1580–1640* (2012) and *Gendered Correspondence in Early Modern Britain* (2015). Daybell is also the series editor (along with Adam Smyth, Birkbeck College, University of London) for the new Ashgate book series Material Readings in Early Modern Culture.

Richard L. DiNardo is a professor for National Security Affairs at the U.S. Marine Corps Command and Staff College at Quantico, Virginia. He has been a member of the Command and Staff College faculty since 1998. Dr. DiNardo also spent two years as a visiting professor at the Air War College at Maxwell Air Force Base, Alabama. He has written on a wide variety of subjects in military history. Dr. DiNardo's publications include *Breakthrough: The Gorlice-Tarnow Campaign, 1915* (Praeger, 2010) and *Invasion: The Conquest of Serbia, 1915* (Praeger, 2015).

Paul Doerr teaches European, diplomatic, and military history at Acadia University in Nova Scotia, Canada. He has a PhD in history from the University of Waterloo. Dr. Doerr is the author of *British Foreign Policy 1919–1939: Hope for the Best, Prepare for the Worst* (1998) and is currently writing a study of war from 1945.

Timothy C. Dowling has been teaching history at the Virginia Military Institute (VMI) since August 2001. Before moving to VMI, he taught at the Vienna International School in Austria and served as an adjunct assistant professor at Old Dominion University in Norfolk, Virginia. Dr. Dowling earned his doctoral degree from Tulane University in New Orleans, Louisiana, in 1999. From 1989 to 1993 he worked at the American embassy in Moscow, Russia, and traveled extensively through the former Soviet Union. Dr. Dowling received his master's degree in history from the University of Virginia (1987) and a bachelor's degree in journalism and public relations from Texas Christian University (1985). His publications include *The Brusilov Offensive* (Indiana University Press, 2008). He is also the editor of ABC-CLIO's *Russia at War: From the Mongol Conquest to Afghanistan, Chechnya, and Beyond* (2014).

James B. Tschen-Emmons received his PhD in history from the University of California, Santa Barbara. He also holds an MA in library science and a BA in classical archaeology. His major research field is early medieval Ireland, most especially the relationship between native and imported narratives about holy people. Outside of the hagiography of early Christian Ireland, Emmons is interested in medieval European conceptions of borderlands, identity, and the ways in which people navigated between cultures. He currently teaches for Northern Virginia Community College's Extended Learning Institute.

Lee W. Eysturlid is a history instructor at the Illinois Mathematics and Science Academy in Aurora, Illinois. He also serves as an adjunct professor for Northwestern University's School of Continuing Studies program. Dr. Eysturlid earned his PhD in history from Purdue University, where he specialized in intellectual military history and the Habsburg and Ottoman empires. He is a member of the Citadel Historical Association and is an ABC-CLIO history fellow. Dr. Eysturlid's published works include *The Formative Influences, Theories, and Campaigns of the Archduke Carl of Austria* (Praeger, 2000). He also served as the editor of *Philosophers of War: The Evolution of History's Greatest Military Thinkers* (Praeger, 2013).

Garrett G. Fagan is a professor of ancient history at Penn State University, where he has taught since 1996. His primary research interests are Roman history and archaeology. Fagan has published several books, including *Bathing in Public in the Roman World* (University of Michigan Press, 1999) and *The Lure of the Arena: Social Psychology and the Crowd at the Roman Games* (Cambridge University Press, 2011), and has written several academic articles and book chapters. Dr. Fagan received his BA and MA from Trinity College, Dublin, and his PhD from McMaster University, Canada.

Bruce Farcau holds a BA in history from the University of California, Los Angeles (UCLA); an MA in international relations from Boston University; and a PhD in comparative government (Latin American studies) from Georgetown University. He retired after a career of nearly 25 years in the U.S. Foreign Service, spent mostly in Latin America and Western Europe. Farcau currently teaches international relations at the University of Central Florida. He has a dozen books to his credit, both fiction and nonfiction, including *The Coup: Tactics in the Seizure of Power* (Praeger, 1994), *The Chaco War* (Praeger, 1996), *The Transition to Democracy in Latin America: The Role of the Military* (Praeger, 1996), *A Little Empire of Their Own* (Vandamere, 2000), and *The Ten Cents War: Chile, Peru, and Bolivia in the War of the Pacific, 1879–1884* (Praeger, 2000).

Carole Fink, distinguished humanities professor in the Department of History of Ohio State University, is a specialist in European international history and historiography. Her books include *Defending the Rights of Others: The Great Powers, the Jews, and International Minority Protection, 1878–1938* (2004), which was awarded the George Louis Beer Prize of the American Historical Association for the best book in European international history; *Marc Bloch: A Life in History* (1989), the first biography of France's soldier-patriot-historian, which has been translated into six languages; *The Genoa Conference: European Diplomacy, 1921–22* (1984, 1993), which was also awarded the George Louis Beer Prize; an introduction to and translation of *Bloch's Memoirs of War, 1914–15* (1980, 1988); seven edited volumes; and more than 50 articles.

John France is a professor emeritus at Swansea University, Wales, and held the Charles Boal Ewing Chair in Military History at the U.S. Military Academy West Point for 2011–2012. He has published extensively on the Crusades, notably with *The Crusades and the Expansion of Catholic Christendom, 1000–1714* (Routledge, 2005) and *Victory in the East: a Military History of the First Crusade* (Cambridge University Press, 1994). *Western Warfare in the Age of the Crusades, 1000–1300* (Routledge, 1999) is an analysis of medieval warfare, while *Perilous Glory: The Rise of Western Military Power* (Yale University Press, 2011) discusses conflict from ancient times to the present day. His *Battle of Hattin* is forthcoming from Oxford University Press.

Richard A. Gabriel, PhD, is a professor emeritus of military history. He has served on the faculty of the Department of History and War Studies at the Royal Military College of Canada and the Department of Defense Studies at the Canadian Forces College in Toronto and as a professor of history and politics at the U.S. Army War College. In addition to regular appearances on the History Channel, Gabriel is the author of numerous articles and books, including *Hannibal: The Military Biography of Rome's Greatest Enemy* (Potomac Books, 2011) and *Muhammad: Islam's First Great General* (University of Oklahoma Press, 2011).

Barbara A. Gannon is an assistant professor of history at the University of Central Florida. She received her doctorate from Pennsylvania State University in 2005. Her areas of specialty are military history, the American Civil War and Reconstruction, veterans, and African American history. Her book *The Won Cause: Black and White Comradeship in the Grand Army of the Republic,* was published in 2011.

Bryan Garrett is a PhD student working in both environmental and transatlantic history, specializing in indigenous North African and North American cultures under French imperial rule, at the University of Texas at Arlington. He received an MA in modern and medieval Middle East and Europe at the University of North Texas. Garrett's dissertation focuses on Syrian migrants and issues of identity during the late 19th and early 20th centuries.

John A. Gentry teaches at the National Intelligence University in Washington, D.C., and is an adjunct professor at George Mason University. He is a retired U.S. Army Reserve officer, where his assignments mainly were in intelligence and special operations. For 12 years Gentry was an intelligence analyst at the Central Intelligence Agency and taught at the National Defense University. He received a PhD in political science from George Washington University. Gentry's most recent book is *How Wars Are Won and Lost: Vulnerability and Military Power* (Praeger Security International, 2012).

Jolyon P. Girard is professor emeritus at Cabrini College in Radnor, Pennsylvania. He received his BA in history from Washington and Lee University. After serving for 3 years as an officer in the U.S. Army, Dr. Girard earned his MA and PhD at the University of Maryland. He taught full-time at Cabrini for 37 years, served as chair of the History and Political Science Department for 17 years, and won a Lindbach Award for teaching excellence. In 2005, the Gilder Lehrman Institute of American History selected Dr. Girard as a scholar to attend a summer seminar in American foreign policy at Harvard University. When he retired from full-time teaching in 2008, Cabrini College established the Jolyon P. Girard Distinguished Scholar Program in his honor.

Peter Green was educated at Trinity College, Cambridge, where, after war service in Burma he took a First Class degree in classics (1950), going on to earn a PhD in 1954. He spent the 1950s as a London literary journalist and the 1960s as an expatriate writer and translator in Greece, where he was lured back into the academic world as a Greek historian. A visiting professorship at the University of Texas at Austin turned into a permanent appointment. Green is the author of many books, including a biography of Alexander the Great. Emeritus from 1997, Green now serves as an adjunct professor at the University of Iowa, where his wife is chair of the Classics Department.

Mary Hampton is the associate dean for academics at the Air Command and Staff College (ACSC) and has been a professor of national security at the ACSC since 2003. Prior to her work with the ACSC, Hampton was a professor of political science at the University of Utah for 15 years, where she went immediately after receiving her PhD from the University of California, Los Angeles (UCLA). Hampton's research focuses on international relations theory, European security, German security and foreign policy, transatlantic relations, Russian foreign policy, the media and foreign policy, and U.S. foreign and security policy. She has written extensively on NATO; European security; German foreign, domestic, and security policy; U.S. foreign and security policy; and identity politics in international relations. Hampton is the author of *A Thorn in Transatlantic Relations: American and European Perceptions of Threat and Security* (Palgrave Macmillan, 2013).

Eric Han is an assistant professor of history at the College of William and Mary and teaches courses on East Asian and Japanese history. He earned a PhD in Japanese history at Columbia University in 2009 and an MA in East Asian languages and cultures at the University of Illinois at Urbana-Champaign in 2001. Han's research examines modern Japanese history through local and transnational approaches and deals with the topics of nationalism, imperialism, migration, and Sino-Japanese relations. His dissertation "Narrating Community in Yokohama Chinatown, 1894–1972" analyzes the birth of a multiethnic community in a nominally monoethnic state and how local identities may empower Sino-Japanese reconciliation.

Alexis Herr received her doctorate in Holocaust and genocide studies from Clark University in 2014 and is the author of *The Holocaust and Compensated Compliance in Italy: Fossoli di Carpi, 1942–1952* (Palgrave Macmillan, 2016). From 2014 to 2016 she lectured at Keene State College and taught courses on the Holocaust, transitional justice after genocide, the Armenian Genocide, and Jewish history. Currently, Dr. Herr is conducting research on her next book project, titled *Italian Perpetrators on the Periphery of Genocide,* while serving as the Pearl Resnick postdoctoral fellow at the United States Holocaust Memorial Museum. Herr is also the founder of Assessing Atrocity (www.assessignatrocity.com), a website that provides a forum for scholars and human rights practitioners to discuss current events and educate readers on topics related to human rights and genocide.

Julie Holcomb is an assistant professor in museum studies at Baylor University in Waco, Texas. She is a past director and archivist of the Pearce Civil War and Western Art Collections at Navarro College in Corsicana, Texas. Dr. Holcomb earned a master's degree in library and information science in archives and records management and a PhD in transatlantic history. She specializes in museum and archival collections management and museum ethics. Additionally, Dr. Holcomb has written about women's reform work, abolitionism, and the American Civil War.

Gregory S. Hospodor earned his BA in history from the College of William and Mary, his MA in history from the University of Mississippi, and his PhD in history from Louisiana State University, where Charles Royster served as his adviser. Hospodor has presented scholarly papers and published on a wide range of topics related to the Mexican-American War, most recently a chapter on the home front in *Daily Lives of Civilians in Wartime Early America: From the Colonial Era to the Civil War* (2007). Presently, he serves as an associate professor of military history at the U.S. Army Command and General Staff College, Fort Leavenworth, Kansas.

Jonathan M. House received both his doctorate in military history and his commission in the U.S. Army from the University of Michigan in 1975. His military career included service in the Middle East branch, J2 (Intelligence) section, of the Joint Staff in the Pentagon during both the 1990–1991 and 2001–2003 periods, performing such roles as deputy commander, Iraq Intelligence Group (2002). House retired in 2006 as a colonel of military intelligence.

Dexter Hoyos studied Latin and Greek at the University of the West Indies, where she earned a BA, and McMaster University, Ontario, for his MA and then read Roman history for his DPhil at Worcester College, Oxford. From 1972 until 2007 he lectured at the University of Sydney, Australia, where from 1981 to 1990 he was head of its Latin Department. Retiring as associate professor, Hoyos has continued at Sydney as an honorary associate professor and research affiliate; he is also an honorary research affiliate in ancient history at Macquarie University, New South Wales. His research interests include Rome in the fourth and third centuries BCE, the Punic Wars, Roman political and constitutional history, and the history and culture of ancient Carthage. Hoyos is the author of several books as well as numerous papers and reviews in international scholarly journals.

Lance Janda is an associate professor in the Department of History at Cameron University in Lawton, Oklahoma. He received his PhD in U.S. history from the University of Oklahoma (1998) and his BA in history (1989) and MA in U.S. history (1990) from the University of Central Oklahoma. Janda is the author of *Stronger Than Custom: West Point and the Admission of Women* (Praeger, 2001) and has published numerous book chapters and articles in scholarly journals.

Kathryn Jasper is an assistant professor of history and an affiliate faculty member of European studies at Illinois State University. She earned her doctorate at the University of California, Berkeley, in history and medieval studies in 2012. Jasper was a Fulbright scholar to Italy in 2008 and has spent a number of years working in the archives of Florence and Rome. She has also participated in the excavation of an imperial Roman bath near Rome. In 2009, Jasper directed the archaeological survey of two monasteries in Tuscany. Recently she served as the medieval scholar in residence at Andrew College.

Jennifer Jefferis is an associate professor at the Near East and South Asia Center for Strategic Studies at the National Defense University in Washington, D.C. She specializes in religious extremism and political violence. Dr. Jefferis studied Arabic at the Arabic Language Institute at the American University in Cairo and has been awarded numerous teaching and research fellowships, including the Foundation for the Defense of Democracy's Counter-Terrorism Fellowship in 2009, a Schusterman fellowship from Brandeis University in 2010, and a grant to conduct research in Tunisia and Egypt from the Institute for National Security Studies in 2013. Her publications include *Hamas: Terrorism, Governance, and Its Future in the Region* (2016), *Armed for Life: Anti-Abortion Politics in the United States* (2011), and *Religion and Political Violence: Sacred Protest in the Modern World* (2009).

Brian Madison Jones, PhD, is an assistant professor of history at Johnson C. Smith University in North Carolina. His teaching interests include the presidency, Cold

War, and the influence of nuclear weaponry on American culture. Jones is a contributor to *The Encyclopedia of the Cold War: A Political, Social, and Military History* (ABC-CLIO, 2007) and received his PhD (2008) from Kansas State University, his MA (1999) from the University of North Carolina at Greensboro, and his BA (1997) from Appalachian State University in North Carolina.

George Kallander is assistant professor of history at the Maxwell School, Syracuse University, where he teaches courses on Korea, Mongolia, Japan, the Korean War, and socialism in East Asia. As associate editor for the journal *Asian Politics and Policy,* he works on articles and book reviews concerning the Koreas, Mongolia, and Japan. Dr. Kallander has held fellowships at the Academy of Korean Studies and the Weatherhead East Asian Institute (Columbia University) and was a dissertation research Fulbright scholar in Seoul, South Korea. He earned a PhD from Columbia University in 2006.

Robert B. Kane is the Air University director of history at the Air Force Historical Research Center, Maxwell Air Force Base, Alabama. He received his doctorate from the University of California, Los Angeles, in 1997. Dr. Kane spent 27 years on active duty with the U.S. Air Force from 1976 to 2001, retiring as a lieutenant colonel. From 2003 to 2005, he taught secondary school social studies in the Montgomery County, Alabama, school system. Beginning in July 2005, he served for several years as a historian for the Air Armament Center, Eglin Air Force Base, Florida. Dr. Kane published *Disobedience and Conspiracy in the German Army, 1918–45,* in 2002.

Mark D. Karau is a graduate of Florida State University. He is currently an associate professor of history at the University of Wisconsin–Sheboygan, where he teaches introductory courses in world history, Western civilization, and American history and advanced courses in World War I and World War II as well as the history of 20th-century Germany and Russia. Karau is a specialist in the history of Germany during World War I. He is the author of *Wielding the Dagger: The MarineKorps Flandern and the German War Effort, 1914–1918* (Praeger, 2003).

William Kashatus earned a doctorate in history at the University of Pennsylvania. He began his career as a historical interpreter at Independence National Historical Park in Philadelphia, where he also taught history and religion in the city's Quaker schools. Kashatus later served as assistant director of the Chester County Historical Society in Pennsylvania while teaching at West Chester University. A prolific writer, he has published more than a dozen books and is a regular contributor to *The Philadelphia Inquirer* and *Pennsylvania Heritage Magazine.* Kashatus currently teaches at Luzerne County Community College in Pennsylvania.

David M. Keithly is a professor at the American Military University. He earned his PhD from Claremont Graduate University and his MA from the University of Freiburg, Germany. Keithly served as an officer in the U.S. Navy Reserve for 16 years before transferring to the U.S. Air Force Reserve, where he currently holds the rank of lieutenant colonel. He is the author of several publications, including *The Collapse of East German Communism: The Year the Wall Came Down, 1989* (Praeger, 1992).

Ellis L. (Skip) Knox is an adjunct professor of history at Boise State University in Boise, Idaho. He earned his MA in medieval history at the University of Utah and his PhD in early modern European history at the University of Massachusetts. His areas of interest include the centuries from 1300 to 1700 and range from religious history—particularly pilgrimage and crusading—to urban social and economic history.

Conor Kostick is a research fellow in the Department of History at the University of Nottingham. His awards for his work as a historian include a British Academy Rising Star Engagement award, a Marie Curie fellowship, a Nottingham Advanced Research fellowship, an Irish Research Council fellowship, first place in the Dublinia Medieval Essay Competition, and a Gold Medal from Trinity College. Among Kostick's publications are *The Social Structure of the First Crusade* (Brill, 2008) and *The Siege of Jerusalem* (Continuum, 2009). He also served as editor of *The Crusades and the Near East: Cultural Histories* (Routledge, 2010).

Michael Ryan Kraig is an assistant professor of national security studies at the Air Command and Staff College, Maxwell Air Force Base, Alabama. He earned his PhD in political science from the State University of New York at Buffalo. Prior to joining the Air Command and Staff College, Kraig worked on U.S. foreign policy, international security, and the Middle East/South Asia at the Stanley Foundation, an operating foundation in Muscatine, Iowa, where he served as director of policy analysis and dialogue in 2005–2008 and as senior policy fellow in 2009.

Frederic Krome is an associate professor at the University of Cincinnati, where he teaches courses on the Holocaust, film and the history of World War II, and anti-Semitism. Krome received his PhD from the University of Cincinnati in 1992. He was the managing editor of the *American Jewish Archives Journal* at Hebrew Union College for nine years and a lecturer at Northern Kentucky University. Krome has contributed to various works, including the *Encyclopedia of American Jewish History* (ABC-CLIO, 2007).

John T. Kuehn is an associate professor of military history at the U.S. Army Command and General Staff College (CGSC), where he has served on the faculty since July 2000, retiring from the naval service in 2004. He earned a PhD in history from

Kansas State University in 2007 and holds master's degrees from the Naval Postgraduate School (1988, with distinction), CGSC (1997), and the School for Advanced Military Studies, Fort Leavenworth, Kansas (1998). Kuehn is the author of *Agents of Innovation: The Design of the Fleet That Defeated the Japanese Navy* (Naval Institute Press, 2008) and the coauthor of *Eyewitness Pacific Theater* (Sterling Books, 2008).

Tom Lansford is a professor of political science at the University of Southern Mississippi. From 2009 to 2014 he served as the academic dean of the University of Southern Mississippi, Gulf Coast. His areas of expertise include homeland security, international relations and security, U.S. foreign and security policy, and U.S. government and politics. Dr. Lansford is the author, coauthor, editor, or coeditor of 31 books and the author of more than 100 essays, book chapters, and reviews. His books include *9/11 and the Wars in Afghanistan and Iraq: A Chronology and Reference Guide* (ABC-CLIO, 2011), *A Bitter Harvest: U.S. Foreign Policy and Afghanistan* (Routledge, 2003), and the edited work the *Political Handbook of the World* (CQ Press, 2015).

Adam Lehman had a brief military career in the U.S. Navy before earning his BA in archaeology and classical civilizations from the University of North Carolina at Greensboro and his MA in maritime history from East Carolina University. Currently he is working as an assistant professor of history at Guilford Technical Community College in Jamestown, North Carolina. In 2015 the college presented Lehman with its President's Award for Outstanding Service and Innovation.

Xiaobing Li is a professor of history and the director of the Western Pacific Institute at the University of Central Oklahoma (UCO). From 2009 to 2014, he served as the chair of the Department of History and Geography at OCU. He first joined the faculty at OCU in 1993 after receiving his MA degree in 1985 and PhD degree in 1991, both from Carnegie Mellon University. His published works include Greenwood's *Civil Liberties in China; Voices from the Vietnam War: Stories from American, Asian, and Russian Veterans; A History of the Modern Chinese Army; Taiwan in the 21st Century; Voices from the Korean War: Personal Stories of American, Chinese, and Korean Soldiers;* and *Mao's Generals Remember Korea.*

Raymond D. Limbach is an independent historian. He has an MA in Land warfare (international perspective) with honors and a graduate certificate in German military studies from the American Military University. Limbach is an ongoing contributing member of the Pritzker Military Museum and Library (GLAM Project) and of the Society for Military History. He has contributed entries to *Russia at War: From the Mongol Conquest to Afghanistan, Chechnya, and Beyond* (ABC-CLIO, 2014) and *Germany at War: 400 Years of Military History* (ABC-CLIO, 2014) as well as the upcoming *Encyclopedia of Cyber Warfare* (ABC-CLIO, 2017). Other military history articles both published and pending are in *Encyclopedia Britannica.* Limbach has given various book reviews and lectures on different aspects of military history. He is a veteran of six years of active duty, with two tours in Vietnam.

Chris J. Magoc is a professor in and the chair of the Department of History at Mercyhurst University and also serves as the associate dean of the School of Social Sciences. Magoc teaches courses in American and environmental history and directs the Mercyhurst Public History program. He was the 2012 recipient of the Mercyhurst University Teaching Excellence Award and is also a Mercyhurst Research Fellow. Magoc is currently at work on *A Progressive History of the United States since 1945: American Dreams, Hard Realities* for Praeger. He has degrees in American studies from the University of New Mexico (PhD) and Penn State University–Harrisburg (MA). His published works include *Chronology of Americans and the Environment* (ABC-CLIO, 2011) and *Environmental Issues in American History* (Scholarly Resources, 2007).

Jeffery O. Mahan is an independent scholar who has contributed to such reference works as *Turning Points—Actual and Alternate Histories: A House Divided during the Civil War Era* (ABC-CLIO, 2007) and *The Encyclopedia of African American History* (ABC-CLIO, 2010) while he was a graduate teaching and research assistant at Texas A&M University.

Christoph T. Maier has taught for more than 20 years at the University of Zurich in Switzerland, where he is currently an associate professor of the history of the Middle Ages in the Department of History. He received his PhD from the University of London in 1990. Dr. Maier's published works include *Crusade Ideology and Propaganda: Model Sermons for the Preaching of the Cross* (Cambridge University Press, 2000) and *Preaching the Crusades:. Mendicant Friars and the Cross in the Thirteenth Century* (Cambridge University Press, 1994).

David F. Marley, an award-winning naval historian, attended Saint Andrew's College, Trinity College, at the University of Toronto and the University of Windsor, obtaining MAs in history and political science. A resident of Mexico City since early childhood, he authored the official catalog of the Serie Marina and various other colonial collections of the Archivo General de la Nación and also taught at the Instituto Nacional de Antropología e Historia, Colegio de México, and ConduMex. Marley's publications include *Mexico at War: From the Struggle for Independence to the 21st-Century Drug Wars* (ABC-CLIO, 2014), *Daily Life of Pirates* (Greenwood, 2012), *Pirates of the Americas* (ABC-CLIO, 2010), and *Wars of the Americas: A Chronology of Armed Conflict in the Western Hemisphere* (ABC-CLIO, 2008).

James I. Matray earned his doctorate at the University of Virginia. He taught for 22 years at New Mexico State University before he became Department of History chair at California State University, Chico, in 2002, where he now teaches as a faculty member. Matray received the Best Book Prize from Phi Alpha Theta in 1986, a Donald C. Roush Excellence in Teaching Award in 1988, and a Nicola D. Bautzer Advancement Award in 2003. He has written or edited 8 books and published more than 40 scholarly articles, essays, and book chapters. Among his published works are *Crisis in a Divided Korea: A Chronology and Reference Guide* (ABC-CLIO, 2016), *Northeast Asia and the Legacy of Harry S. Truman* (Truman State University Press, 2012), and *The Reluctant Crusade: American Foreign Policy in Korea, 1941–1950* (University of Hawaii Press, 1985).

Timothy May, PhD, is a professor in the Department of History, Anthropology and Philosophy at the University of North Georgia. He holds a PhD from Wisconsin and teaches classes on Islamic, Russian, and Central Asian history. May is the author of *The Mongol Art of War: Chinggis Khan and the Mongol Military System* (Westholme Publishing, 2007), *The Mongol Conquests in World History* (Reaktion Books, 2013), and *Culture and Customs of Mongolia* (Greenwood, 2009).

Sean J. McLaughlin received his PhD in 2010 from the University of Western Ontario, specializing in 20th-century American foreign policy, Franco-American relations, and the Vietnam War. He is currently an assistant professor of history at St. Mary's University in Halifax, Nova Scotia. McLaughlin's major ongoing research project is a monograph for the University Press of Kentucky on the failure of French attempts to dissuade the John F. Kennedy administration from escalating the American role in Vietnam from 1961 to 1963.

James Brian McNabb is an adjunct professor with Troy University's Master of Science in International Relations program. He has taught in the Middle East at the American University in Sulaimania, Iraq; in Central Asia at the Kazakhstan Institute of Management, Economics, and Strategic Research; and at California State University in San Bernardino's National Security Studies MA program. McNabb holds a master's degree in national security studies from California State University–San Bernardino and a doctorate in international politics from Claremont Graduate University.

Abraham O. Mendoza completed his BA in history at California Polytechnic State University in 2003 and his MA in history at San Francisco State University in 2005. He also undertook further graduate study in history at the University of California, Santa Barbara. His fields of specialized study include modern European history, modern German history, U.S. history, Holocaust and comparative genocide studies, world history, and war studies.

Kathryn Meyer earned her BA from the University of Vermont and her PhD at Temple University in Philadelphia. She is currently a professor in the Department of History at Wright State University, Dayton, Ohio. She is the author of *Webs of Smoke,* about the influence of international prohibition on the global opium market. Meyer has contributed numerous articles about espionage, drug trafficking, and vice in East Asia before and during World War II. She has received several grants, including a prestigious National Endowment for the Humanities research fellowship. Meyer has lived in both China and Japan, where she does much of her research.

Alexander Mikaberidze is the Sybil T. and J. Frederick Patten Professor of History at Louisiana State University in Shreveport. He holds a degree in international law from Tbilisi State University and a PhD in history from Florida State University. After diplomatic service at the Ministry of Foreign Affairs of Georgia, he taught European and Middle Eastern history at Florida State University and Mississippi State Universities and lectured on strategy and policy for the U.S. Naval War College. Dr. Mikaberidze is an award-winning author who has written extensively on the Napoleonic Wars and published several critically acclaimed references works with ABC-CLIO.

Thomas R. Mockaitis, PhD, is a professor of history at DePaul University, Chicago, Illinois. His published works include numerous books and articles on counterinsurgency and terrorism. Mockaitis team-teaches terrorism and counterterrorism courses internationally through the Center for Civil-Military Relations at the Naval Post-Graduate School. A frequent media commentator on terrorism and security matters, he has provided commentary on Public Television, National Public Radio, BBC World News, all major Chicago television stations, and various local radio programs. He appears regularly as a terrorism expert for WGN TV News. Mockaitis earned his bachelor's degree in European history from Allegheny College and his master's degree and doctorate in modern British and Irish history from the University of Wisconsin–Madison.

Michaela Hoenicke Moore, PhD, is an associate professor of history at the University of Iowa. Her primary field research is focused on political culture in the United States and European conceptualization of U.S. foreign policy between 1930 and 1950. Dr. Hoenicke Moore regularly teaches courses on U.S. foreign policy, transnational history, and international relations and, prior to her tenure at the University of Iowa, worked as a senior fellow in U.S. foreign policy at the German Council on Foreign Relations in Berlin. Hoenicke Moore is the author of *Know Your Enemy: The American Debate on Nazism, 1933–1945* (Cambridge University Press, 2010). She received her PhD from the University of North Carolina in 1998.

Jerry D. Morelock, PhD, retired from the U.S. Army as a colonel and since 2004 has been editor in chief of *Armchair General* magazine. A 1969 West Point graduate, Morelock is a decorated combat veteran of the Vietnam War who spent 36 years in uniform. From 1991 to 1994, Morelock was chief of the Russia Branch on the Joint Chiefs of Staff, coordinating U.S. government policy with Russia and the 15 republics of the former Soviet Union. His military assignments included service in Germany, Korea, Russia, China, the Republic of Georgia, Estonia, Romania, and Ukraine. Morelock's final active-duty tour was as the head of the History Department at the U.S. Army Command and General Staff College (CGSC). He earned a master's degree from Purdue University, a master of military art and science Degree from CGSC, and a PhD in history from the University of Kansas.

Nicholas Morton is a history lecturer at Nottingham Trent University specializing in the history of crusading and the medieval Mediterranean between the 10th and 13th centuries. He has published widely on the history of the Crusades and the military orders, including the monographs *The Teutonic Knights in the Holy Land, 1190–1291* (Boyden, 2009) and *The Medieval Military Orders, 1120–1314* (Routledge, 2012). Morton has also worked with Simon John to produce a book in honor of John France titled *Crusading and Warfare in the Middle Ages* (Ashgate, 2014).

Pavel Murdzhev earned his BA from the University of Veliko Turnovo, Bulgaria, in 1991. After receiving his MA in history from East Tennessee State University in May 2003, he earned a doctorate in European history at the University of Florida in December 2008. Since then, Murdzhev has served as a visiting instructor at the University of Central Florida and is currently teaching at Santa Fe College in Gainesville, Florida. His areas of specialization are medieval/early modern urban history and the archaeology and economic history of late Byzantium and its slavic neighbors, the Balkans, Eastern Europe, the Ottoman Empire, and the Mediterranean world.

Justin D. Murphy is the Brand Chair Professor of History at Howard Payne University, where he is also the dean of humanities and the director of the Academy of Freedom. He has taught courses on the French Revolution, the U.S. Constitution, modern political theory, and defense. Murphy is the author of *Military Aircraft, Origins—1918* (ABC-CLIO, 2004) and the coauthor of *Military Aircraft, 1919–1945* (ABC-CLIO, 2005). He holds an MA and a PhD from Texas Christian University.

Alan V. Murray is the editorial director of the International Medieval Bibliography, program director for the MA in medieval studies, and the senior lecturer in medieval studies at the Institute of Medieval Studies at the University of Leeds. His research interests include the Crusades to the Holy Land, medieval chronicles, chivalry, and tournaments. Murray has published widely on all of his research interests with such works as *Crusader Kingdom of Jerusalem: A Dynastic History, 1099–1125* (2000) and "Finance and Logistics of the Crusade of Frederick Barbarossa," which was featured in *In Laudem Hierosolymitani: Studies in Crusades and Medieval Culture in Honour of Benjamin Z. Kedar* (2007).

Jennifer M. Murray, PhD, is an assistant professor of history at the University of Virginia at Wise. Her research focuses on public and oral history, and she holds a special interest in American Civil War battlefield preservation. Murray is the author of *The Civil War Begins: Opening Clashes, 1861* (Center for Military History Publications, 2012) and *On a Great Battlefield: The Making, Management, and Memory of Gettysburg National Military Park, 1933–2012* (University of Tennessee Press, 2013). She received her PhD (2010) from Auburn University, her MA (2005) from James Madison University, and her BS (2003) from Frostburg State University.

Michael S. Neiberg is a professor of history in the Department of National Security and Strategy at the United States Army War College in Carlisle, Pennsylvania. From 2005 to 2010, he was a professor of history and the codirector of the Center for the Study of War and Society at the University of Southern Mississippi. Neiberg is the author of several books, including *Potsdam: The End of World War II and the Remaking of Europe* (Basic Books, 2015), *Dance of the Furies: Europe and the Outbreak of World War I* (Harvard University Press, 2011), and *The Blood of Free Men: The Liberation of Paris, 1944* (Basic Books, 2012). He received his PhD in history from Carnegie Mellon University in 1996.

Michael Nolte is a PhD student at the Strassler Center for Holocaust and Genocide Studies, Clark University, Worcester, Massachusetts. He worked as a research assistant for Dr. Gideon Greif at Yad Vashem, Givatayim, Israel, and edited the memoirs of Gertrud Müller, who was a member of the communist resistance against the Nazis and a survivor of the women's concentration camp Ravensbrueck. Nolte holds a degree from the University of Marburg, Germany, where he studied political science, philosophy, and sociology.

Meredith Oyen is an assistant professor of history at the University of Maryland, Baltimore County. She teaches courses in U.S. foreign relations and Asian studies and specializes in the history of Sino-American relations, transnational migration and transnational networks, and the international history of Asian migrations. Dr. Oyen received her PhD from Georgetown University in 2007 and taught for two years at the Johns Hopkins University–Nanjing University Center for Chinese and American Studies. She is the author of *The Diplomacy of Migration: Transnational Lives and the Making of U.S.-Chinese Relations in the Cold War* (Cornell University Press, 2015).

Phillip G. Pattee has been an associate professor of strategy and operations teaching at the U.S. Army Command and General Staff College since 2003. He is a retired U.S. Navy officer who previously served on the faculty of the U.S. Army War College, where he was awarded the Admiral William F. Halsey Chair of Naval Studies. Pattee earned a PhD in history from Temple University, a master's degree in strategic studies from the U.S. Army War College, and a master's degree in military art and science from the U.S. Army Command and General Staff College.

William Pencak was a professor emeritus of American history at Pennsylvania State University. He earned his PhD, MA, and BA at Columbia University. Pencak wrote several publications, including *War, Politics, and Revolution in Provincial Massachusetts* (Northeastern University Press, 1981), *Jews and Gentiles in Early America, 1654–1800* (University of Michigan Press, 2005), and *Historic Pennsylvania: An Illustrated History* (Historical Pub Network, 2008).

Allene Phy-Olsen, PhD, is a professor emerita of English at Austin Peay State University in Clarksville, Tennessee. She was named outstanding professor at George Peabody College in Nashville and received the Hawkins Award for outstanding publications at Austin Peay State University. Phy-Olsen is the author of four earlier books and hundreds of articles and reviews for both academic and popular journals. A world traveler, she has lectured widely on topics in literature and world religions in both the United States and Europe.

Jim Piecuch earned BA and MA degrees in history at the University of New Hampshire and a PhD at the College of William & Mary. He is an associate professor of history at Kennesaw State University in Georgia, where he won its Foundation Prize for scholarship in the humanities and social sciences. Piecuch specializes in the history of the American Revolution and has a related interest in Native American history. He is the author of several books, including *"The Blood Be upon Your Head": Tarleton and the Myth of Buford's Massacre* (2010) and *Three Peoples, One King: Loyalists, Indians and Slaves in the Revolutionary South* (2008).

Paul G. Pierpaoli Jr. is a fellow in military history at ABC-CLIO. A recipient of the Harry S. Truman Dissertation Fellowship, Pierpaoli received his MA and PhD degrees from Ohio State University. He has also served on the faculties of numerous schools, including Hampden-Sydney College and the University of Arizona. Dr. Pierpaoli has been the assistant editor for *Diplomatic History* as well as the *Journal of Military History* and has been the associate editor of numerous ABC-CLIO projects, including *American Civil War: The Definitive Encyclopedia and Document Collection* (2013) and *The Encyclopedia of the Korean War: A Political, Social, and Military History* (2010).

James Pruitt is currently finishing his dissertation, "Leonard Wood and the American Empire," at Texas A&M University. He received his MA at the University of Kentucky. From 2011 to 2014, Pruitt served as an adjunct faculty member in the Department of History at Texas A&M University–Corpus Christi. Prior to that, he taught history courses through the University of Maryland University College at various locations in Europe, Asia, and the United States.

Ethan S. Rafuse, PhD, is a professor of military history at the U.S. Army Command and General Staff College in Missouri. His research focuses primarily on the American Civil War, and he is the author of several books on the topic, including *Stonewall Jackson: A Biography* (ABC-CLIO, 2011) and *Robert E. Lee and the Fall of the Confederacy, 1863–1865* (Rowman and Littlefield, 2009). Rafuse holds a PhD in history and political science from the University of Missouri, Kansas City, and an MA and a BA from George Mason University in Virginia.

Jeanne Reames is an associate professor of history and the graduate program chair at the University of Nebraska at Omaha, where she is also the director of ancient Mediterranean studies. She served as Missouri Valley History Conference coordinator from 2012 to 2013 and as the University of Nebraska's Martin Professor of European History from 2009 to 2011. Dr. Reames earned her PhD in history from Pennsylvania State University. Her research interests include Argead Macedonia, Alexander the Great, Greek and Macedonian religions, and Greek gender studies. Dr. Reames coedited *Macedonian Legacies: Studies on Ancient Macedonian History and Culture in Honor of Eugene N. Borza* (Regina Books, 2009).

Priscilla M. Roberts studied as an undergraduate at King's College, Cambridge, where she also earned her PhD. She then spent four years in the United States on a variety of fellowships, including one year at Princeton University on a Rotary graduate studentship and a year as a visiting research fellow at the Smithsonian Institution, Washington, D.C. Dr. Roberts then moved to the University of Hong Kong as an associate professor of history. She spent 2003 at George Washington University as a Fulbright scholar. She is now associate professor of history at the City University of Macau. Dr. Roberts specializes in 20th-century diplomatic and international history. She is the author or editor of over 20 single-authored or coauthored books.

Andrew Robinson has taught politics at the University of Nottingham. His past teaching experience covers the history of ideas, Marxism, radical politics, and development studies. Robinson's work on the history of China includes a review of Giovanni Arrighi's *Adam Smith in Beijing* and a book section on the role of China in the world system. Robinson is the coauthor of *Power, Resistance and Conflict in the Contemporary World: Social Movements, Networks and Hierarchies* (Routledge, 2010).

William B. Robison earned his PhD in history at Louisiana State University (LSU) in 1983, where he held the T. Harry Williams Fellowship in History. Since then, Robison has been a faculty member in Southeastern Louisiana University's Department of History and Political Science, where he received the President's Award for Excellence in Teaching (1996), held the Fay Warren Reimers Distinguished Teaching Professorship in the Humanities (1996–1999), and serves as department head (1999–present). He has authored or edited several books and journal articles, including serving as coeditor of *Historical Dictionary of Late Medieval England, 1272–1485* (Greenwood, 2002).

Francisco J. Romero Salvadó is a reader of modern Spanish history at the University of Bristol. He is also a senior research fellow at the Cañada Blanch Research Centre (London School of Economics) and works with the Prince's Teaching Institute. Salvadó has written extensively on the transition from elite to mass politics, the post–World War I crisis, and the Spanish Civil War. He is the recent winner of a British Academy Award and the Leverhulme Trust Research Fellowship Award.

Rodney J. Ross is a senior professor of history and geography at Harrisburg Area Community College in Pennsylvania. He has contributed entries to several reference works, including *Encyclopedia of Media and Propaganda in Wartime America* (ABC-CLIO, 2010), *The Encyclopedia of the Spanish-American and Philippine-American Wars: A Political, Social, and Military History* (ABC-CLIO, 2009), and *The Encyclopedia of North American Colonial Conflicts to 1775: A Political, Social, and Military History* (ABC-CLIO, 2008). Ross received his EDD from Pennsylvania State University in 1973.

William D. Rubinstein, who was educated at Swarthmore College and Johns Hopkins University, has been a professor of social and economic history at Deakin University in Melbourne, Australia, and professor of history at the University of Wales–Aberystwyth and is currently an adjunct professor at Monash University in Melbourne, Australia. He is a fellow of the Australian Academy of the Humanities, the Australian Academy of the Social Sciences, and the Royal Historical Society. Rubinstein is the author of *The Myth of Rescue: Why the Democracies Could Not Have Saved More Jews from the Nazis* (Routledge, 1999).

John Ruddiman earned his BA degree summa cum laude from Princeton University and his MA and PhD from Yale University. He is an assistant professor in the History Department at Wake Forest University. His article "A Record in the Hands of Thousands: Power and Persuasion in the Orderly Books of the Continental Army" appeared in the October 2010 edition of the *William and Mary Quarterly*. Ruddiman is the author of *Becoming Men of Some Consequence: Youth and Military Service in the Revolutionary War* (University of Virginia Press, 2014).

Stanley Sandler retired after 14 years as a command historian with the U.S. Army's Special Operations Command at Fort Bragg, North Carolina. He has written or edited a number of books, including *Ground Warfare: An International Encyclopedia* (ABC-CLIO, 2002), *The Korean War: No Victors, No Vanquished* (University Press of Kentucky, 1999), and *Segregated Skies: All-Black Combat Squadrons of World War II* (Smithsonian Institution Press, 1992). Dr. Sandler received his PhD from the Department of War Studies at the University of London. He held the Conquest Chair in History at the Virginia Military Institute in 1999–2000.

Larry E. Schweikart is a professor of history at the University of Dayton and is also an American historian. He received his MA from Arizona State University and his PhD from the University of California at Santa Barbara. Schweikart is a prolific author whose publications include *Patriot's History of the Modern World: From the Cold War to the Age of Entitlement, 1945–2012* (Penguin Books, 2013), *What Would the Founders Say? A Patriot's Answers to America's Most Pressing Problems* (Sentinel, 2011), *7 Events That Made America America* (Sentinel, 2010), and *48 Liberal Lies about American History (That You Probably Learned in School)* (Sentinel, 2008).

Rebecca Seaman is a professor in the Department of Social and Behavioral Sciences (History) at Elizabeth City State University in North Carolina. She earned her MA (1989) and PhD (2001) in history from Auburn University. Dr. Seaman is the author/editor of *Conflict in the Early Americas: An Encyclopedia of the Spanish Empire's Aztec, Inca, and Mayan Conquests* (ABC-CLIO, 2013) and *Epidemics and War: The Impact of Disease on Major Conflicts in History* (ABC-CLIO, forthcoming 2017). She is also the managing editor of the *Journal of the North Carolina Association of Historians.*

Bevan Sewell is an assistant professor of American history at the University of Nottingham in England. He is also coeditor of the *Journal of American Studies,* which is published by Cambridge University Press. Sewell's main research focus is American political and diplomatic history in the 20th century. Sewell is the author of *The U.S. and Latin America: Eisenhower, Kennedy and Economic Diplomacy in the Cold War* (I. B. Tauris, 2016). In addition, he has published articles in *Diplomatic History,* the *English Historical Review,* the *International History Review,* and *Intelligence and National Security.*

Debra J. Sheffer, PhD, is a professor of history at Park University, Parkville, Missouri. She was a 2007 fellow at the West Point Summer Seminar in military history. Sheffr's published works include *The Buffalo Soldiers: Their Epic Story and Major Campaigns* (Praeger, 2015). She also made a contribution to *The Routledge Handbook of Military and Diplomatic History: The Colonial Period to 1877* (2014). Sheffer holds a doctorate from the University of Kansas in military history, U.S. history, and indigenous peoples.

Brooks D. Simpson received his BA degree from the University of Virginia (1979) and his MA and PhD degrees from the University of Wisconsin (1982, 1989). He taught at Wofford College for three years before joining the faculty at Arizona State University in 1990, where he is presently the ASU Foundation Professor of History. In 1995 Dr. Simpson was a Fulbright scholar at Leiden University in the Netherlands. His published works include *The Civil War in the East, 1861–1865* (Potomac Books, 2013), *Ulysses S. Grant: Triumph over Adversity, 1822–1865* (Houghton Mifflin, 2000), and *The Reconstruction Presidents* (University Press of Kansas, 1998).

George L. Simpson Jr. obtained his PhD in history from West Virginia University and was a Fulbright-Hays scholar in Kenya. His undergraduate degree was in economics, and his master's degree was in international relations. Simpson served in the U.S. Air Force Electronic Security Command and was a Middle East analyst during the 1970s and 1980s. He has taught for nearly 20 years at High Point University and has served as chair of the History Department there. Simpson's research and writing interests are in African and Middle Eastern history, but he also teaches Russian history. He is an editor of the *Journal of the Middle East and Africa* as well as a frequent contributor to ABC-CLIO.

Rosemarie Skaine is an author and sociologist whose published works include *Sexual Assault in the U.S. Military: The Battle within America's Armed Forces* (Praeger, 2015) and *Suicide Warfare: Culture, the Military, and the Individual as a Weapon* (Praeger 2013). In 2013, Skaine presented the keynote speech "Suicide Warfare and Violence against Women" for the interactive dialogue panel "Dying to Kill: The Allure of Female Suicide Bombers" at the United Nations Commission on the Status of Women 57: Elimination and Prevention of All Forms of Violence against Women and Girls. Skaine earned her master's degree in sociology at the University of Northern Iowa.

Brian G. Smith is an associate professor of political science at Georgia Southwestern State University in Americus, Georgia. He is currently the director of the Global Studies Program and the director of the European Union Studies Program at Georgia Southwestern. Smith was a Fulbright-Hays fellow, an assistant professor of political science at Middle Georgia College, a visiting professor at Colgate University, and a Joukowsky fellow at the Thomas J. Watson Jr. Institute for International Studies. He received both his MA and PhD in political science from Brown University.

Roger W. Smith is a professor emeritus of government at the College of William and Mary in Virginia, where he taught political philosophy and the comparative study of genocide. Educated at Harvard University and the University of California, Berkeley, he has written and lectured widely on the nature, history, and prevention of genocide and on the issue of denial. Smith is a cofounder and past president of the International Association of Genocide Scholars. In 2008 Armenia presented him with its highest civilian award, the Movses Khorenatsi Medal, for his contributions to international recognition of the 1915 Armenian Genocide. Smith has been coeditor of Genocide Studies International since its founding in 2013.

T. Jason Soderstrum is an independent scholar who has contributed to several reference works, including the *Encyclopedia of World War II: A Political, Social, and Military History* (ABC-CLIO, 2005), *The Home Front Encyclopedia: United States, Britain, and Canada in World Wars I and II* (ABC-CLIO, 2006), and *The American Economy: A Historical Encyclopedia* (ABC-CLIO, 2003).

Paul J. Springer is a full professor of comparative military studies and the chair of the Department of Research and Publications at the Air Command and Staff College, Maxwell Air Force Base, Alabama. His published works include *Outsourcing War to Machines: The Military Robotics Revolution* (Praeger, 2017), *9/11 and the War on Terror: A Documentary and Reference Guide* (ABC-CLIO, 2016), *Cyber Warfare: A Reference Handbook* (ABC-CLIO, 2015), and *America's Captives: Treatment of POWs from the Revolutionary War to the War on Terror* (University of Kansas Press, 2010). Springer holds a doctorate in military history from Texas A&M University and is a senior fellow of the Foreign Policy Research Institute in Philadelphia.

Scott L. Stabler received his BA from Baylor University, his master's degree from the University of Houston, and his PhD from Arizona State University, where he wrote a dissertation titled "Race, Reaction, Policy, and Perception: A Tri-Cultural Study of Postbellum America through the Life of General O. O. Howard." Stabler is currently an associate professor of history at Grand Valley State University in Grand Rapids, Michigan. In 2010, he received a Fulbright scholarship to teach in Ghana at the University of Cape Coast.

Nancy L. Stockdale is an associate professor of history at the University of North Texas, where she began teaching in 2006. She teaches a variety of courses on topics such as modern Middle Eastern history and gender, race, and class issues in Middle Eastern history. Stockdale received her PhD in history from the University of California, Santa Barbara. She is the author of *Colonial Encounters among English and Palestinian Women, 1800–1948* (University Press of Florida, 2007).

David Tal is a professor of history and the Kahanoff Chair in Israeli Studies at the University of Calgary and is a research fellow at the S. Daniel Abraham Center for

International and Regional Studies at Tel Aviv University. Professor Tal specializes in the history of the Middle East as well as nuclear disarmament. He is the winner of numerous grants and fellowships, including the Kennedy Library's Arthur Schlesinger Fellowship. Tal has published several books, including *The American Nuclear Disarmament Dilemma, 1945–1963* (Syracuse University Press, 2008) and *War in Palestine, 1948: Strategy and Diplomacy* (Routledge, 2004). He received his PhD degree in history from Tel-Aviv University in 1995.

Maxine Taylor received her BA in literature from the University of California, Santa Barbara, in 2005. She has worked in publishing and as a freelance writer/editor for almost 10 years, contributing to a variety of print and electronic products. Her areas of interest include cultural history, social anthropology, and the writings of minorities and other marginalized groups.

Frank W. Thackeray is a professor emeritus of history at Indiana University Southeast. He earned his BA at Dickinson College (1965) and his MA and PhD at Temple University (1977). A former Fulbright research scholar in Poland, Thackeray is the editor or coeditor of numerous books, including *Events That Changed Germany* (Greenwood, 2004) and the five-volume set *Events That Formed the Modern World: From the European Renaissance through the War on Terror* (Greenwood, 2012).

Donald E. Thomas Jr. is a professor emeritus at the Virginia Military Institute, where he taught modern European history with a concentration in modern Germany and offered courses in the Holocaust. Dr. Thomas contributed an article on that subject to Dr. Spencer C. Tucker's *The Encyclopedia of World War II: A Political, Social, and Military History* (ABC-CLIO, 2004).

David F. Trask is the former chief historian at the U.S. Army Center of Military History in Washington, D.C. A prolific writer, he is the author or editor of numerous books, including several on the Spanish-American War and World War I. Among his published works are *The War with Spain in 1898* (University of Nebraska Press, 1996) and *The AEF and Coalition Warmaking, 1917–1918* (University Press of Kansas, 1993).

Spencer C. Tucker graduated from the Virginia Military Institute and was a Fulbright scholar in France. He was a U.S. army captain and an intelligence analyst in the Pentagon during the Vietnam War, then taught for 30 years at Texas Christian University before returning to his alma mater for 6 years as the holder of the John Biggs Chair of Military History. Dr. Tucker retired from teaching in 2003. He is now the senior fellow of military history at ABC-CLIO. He has written or edited more than 50 books, including ABC-CLIO's award-winning *The Encyclopedia of the Cold War* and *The Encyclopedia of the Arab-Israeli Conflict.* Among honors he has received for his publications are three Society for Military History awards for best reference work in military history (2008, 2010, 2014) and five American Library Association RUSA Outstanding Reference Source Awards (2009, 2010, 2014, 2015, 2016).

Eleanor L. Turk is a professor of history emerita at Indiana University East in Richmond, Indiana. She completed her doctorate with Theodore S. Hamerow at the University of Wisconsin, then worked at the University of Kansas and Ithaca College before joining Indiana University. Her research and publications focus on imperial Germany and on German emigration. Turk's book *The History of Germany* (Greenwood, 1999) was named an Outstanding Academic Title by the American Library Association.

Mark E. Van Rhyn is a history instructor at the Louisiana School for Math, Science, and the Arts (LSMSA). He received his PhD in American History from the University of Nebraska, Lincoln, in 2003. Van Rhyn teaches courses on the American Civil War, American military history, and the American frontier at LSMSA. He contributed to *The Encyclopedia of World War II: A Political, Social, and Military History* (ABC-CLIO, 2004).

Marcos A. Vigil is an instructor in the Department of Joint Warfighting at the Air Command and Staff College, Air University, in Montgomery, Alabama. From 2011 to 2014 he worked as a joint operations planner for the U.S. Central Command. Vigil has a master's degree in space systems management/computer resources and information management from Webster University and a BA in anthropology/geography (remote sensing) from the California State Polytechnic University–Pomona.

James M. Volo is an affiliate faculty member of the physics program at Sacred Heart University and a historian. He received his bachelor's degree in American history from the City College of New York in 1969, his MA from the American Military University in 1997, and his doctorate from Berne University in 2000. He is the author of several reference works regarding U.S. military and social and cultural history and has served as a consultant for television and movie productions. Among his publications are several that he coauthored with his wife, Dr. Dorothy Denneen Volo, including *Daily Life in Civil War America* (Greenwood, 2009) and *Family Life in the 19th Century* (Greenwood, 2007).

John A. Wagner was educated at the University of Wisconsin–Oshkosh and at Arizona State University, earning his PhD in Tudor/Stuart British history at the latter institution in 1995. He has taught classes in European and U.S. history at Phoenix College in Phoenix, Arizona, and in early British and Tudor history at Arizona

State University in Tempe. Wagner is the author or editor of several books, including *Voices of the Reformation: Contemporary Accounts of Daily Life* (Greenwood, 2015) and *Encyclopedia of Tudor England* (ABC-CLIO, 2011).

J. Samuel Walker is the former historian of the U.S. Nuclear Regulatory Commission and an author whose research focuses on nuclear energy. He holds an MA and a PhD in history from the University of Maryland. Among his most recent works are *The Road to Yucca Mountain: The Development of Radioactive Waste Policy in the United States* (University of California Press, 2009), *Prompt and Utter Destruction: Truman and the Use of Atomic Bombs against Japan, Revised Edition* (University of North Carolina Press, 2005), and *Three Mile Island: A Nuclear Crisis in Historical Perspective* (2004).

Douglas B. Warner is an independent scholar who graduated with honors from the Virginia Military Institute in Lexington, Virginia, in 2003. He contributed to Dr. Spencer C. Tucker's *The Encyclopedia of World War II: A Political, Social, and Military History* (ABC-CLIO, 2004).

James H. Willbanks is the General of the Army George C. Marshall Chair of Military History at the U.S. Army Command and General Staff College (CGSC), Fort Leavenworth, Kansas. Prior to assuming the Marshall Chair, Willbanks served as director of the CGSC Department of Military History for 11 years. Dr. Willbanks holds a BA in history from Texas A&M University and an MA and a PhD in history from the University of Kansas. He is the author or editor of 14 books, including *A Raid Too Far* (Texas A&M Press, 2014), *Abandoning Vietnam* (University Press of Kansas, 2004), *The Battle of An Loc* (Indiana University Press, 2005), and *The Tet Offensive: A Concise History* (Columbia University Press, 2006).

Peter H. Wilson is Chichele Professor of the History of War at the University of Oxford. He studied at Liverpool, Stuttgart, and Cambridge before working at the Universities of Hull, Newcastle, and Sunderland. His research examines European political, military, social, and cultural history from 1500 to 1800, especially that of German-speaking Central Europe, as well as military history generally to 1914. Professor Wilson has published more than a dozen books, including *The Heart of Europe: A History of the Holy Roman Empire* (Harvard University Press, 2016) and *The Thirty Years' War: Europe's Tragedy* (Harvard University Press, 2009).

Bradford A. Wineman is currently a professor of military history at the United States Marine Corps Command & Staff College in Quantico, Virginia. He received his BA from the Virginia Military Institute (VMI) and his MA and PhD in history from Texas A&M University. Dr. Wineman has served on the faculties of VMI and the U.S. Army Command & General Staff College and currently teaches as an adjunct in Norwich University's Graduate Military History Program and Georgetown University's Security Studies Program. He has also served as an enlisted reservist in the U.S. Marine Corps Reserves with deployments to Iraq and Afghanistan. His academic research specializes in military history, military education, and civil military relations.

Gregory Wolf is a teacher at Buena High School in Ventura, California. He teaches advanced placement government and economics and also teaches economics, U.S. history, and geography. Wolf received an MA in history from the University of California in 2006. While in graduate school, he taught Western civilization courses and focused his research on European history, completing a master's thesis on Napoleon's Peninsular War in Spain. Following graduate school, Wolf went to work for ABC-CLIO as a writer/editor for world history for six years. In 2012 he decided to return to the classroom to teach and received his social science teaching credential and his master's degree in education from the University of California, Santa Barbara, in 2013.

Steven E. Woodworth, PhD, is a professor at Texas Christian University. He has also taught at Toccoa Falls College. Woodworth is the author of *This Great Struggle: America's Civil War* (Rowman and Littlefield, 2011), *Decision in the Heartland: The Civil War in the West* (Praeger, 2008), and *A Deep Steady Thunder: The Battle of Chickamauga* (Ryan Place Publishers, 1996) as well as the editor of *Cultures in Conflict: The American Civil War* (Greenwood, 2000) and *Grant's Lieutenants: From Cairo to Vicksburg* (University Press of Kansas, 2001). He received his PhD from Rice University in 1987.

Ian Worthington is a professor of Greek history and an adjunct professor of classics at the University of Missouri. He earned his BA from the University of Hull (UK), his MA from the University of Durham (UK), and his PhD from Monash University, Melbourne (Australia). He is the editor in chief of *Brill's New Jacoby,* a new edition of 856 fragmentary Greek historians involving a team of 120 scholars in 16 countries. Worthington has published 16 sole-authored and edited books and over 100 articles on Greek history, epigraphy, and oratory.

Clarence R. Wyatt has been the president of Monmouth College in Illinois since July 1, 2014. Prior to that he was the Pottinger Professor of History at Centre College in Danville, Kentucky. Dr. Wyatt received his BA in history and English from Centre and his MA and PhD from the University of Kentucky, where he studied under George C. Herring. Wyatt is the author of *Paper Soldiers: The American Press and the Vietnam War* (University of Chicago Press, 1993) and the coeditor of *Encyclopedia of Media and Propaganda in Wartime America* (ABC-CLIO, 2010).

Karl Yambert holds a PhD in anthropology from the University of California, Davis. He is the editor of *Security Issues in the Greater Middle East* (Praeger, 2016) and *The Contemporary Middle East: A Westview Reader*, 3rd ed. (Westview, 2012). In addition, he served as executive editor for anthropology, philosophy, and Latin American and Middle East studies for Westview Press in Boulder, Colorado. Dr. Yambert has provided content for both the *World at War: Understanding Conflict and Society* and *Modern Genocide: Understanding Causes and Consequences* databases at ABC-CLIO.

Hong Zhang is an associate professor of history at the University of Central Florida. She received her PhD from the University of Arizona in 1995. Her research interests range from U.S.-China relations and the social ramifications of economic reforms in rural China to interpretations of popular culture and modernity in urban China. She is the author of *America Perceived: The Making of Chinese Images of the United States, 1945–1953* (Greenwood, 2002).

Sherifa Zuhur has been a research professor of Islamic and regional studies at the Strategic Studies Institute of the U.S. Army War College. She has taught at the Massachusetts Institute of Technology; the University of California, Berkeley; UCLA; the American University in Cairo; and Ben-Gurion University. Dr. Zuhur's research includes Islamic movements, war and peace in the Middle East, modern Middle Eastern politics, and Islamic political and religious philosophy. She is a published author of 15 books and more than 140 articles and book chapters. Dr. Zuhur holds a BA in political science and Arabic language and literature, an MA in Islamic studies, and a PhD in Middle Eastern history from UCLA.

Index